Mental Retardation in America

The History of Disability

A series edited by Paul K. Longmore and Lauri Umansky

Mental Retardation in America

A Historical Reader

EDITED BY

Steven Noll and James W. Trent Jr.

NEW YORK UNIVERSITY PRESS

New York and London

NEW YORK UNIVERSITY PRESS
New York and London
www.nyupress.org

© 2004 by New York University
All rights reserved

Library of Congress Cataloging-in-Publication Data
Mental retardation in America : a historical reader /
edited by Steven Noll and James W. Trent, Jr.
p. cm. — (The history of disability series)
Includes bibliographical references and index.
ISBN 0-8147-8247-7 (cloth : alk. paper) —
ISBN 0-8147-8248-5 (pbk. : alk. paper)
1. Mental retardation—United States.
I. Noll, Steven.   II. Trent, James W.   III. Series.
HV3006.A4M435   2003
362.3'0973—dc22   2003018526

c 10 9 8 7 6 5 4 3 2 1
p 10 9 8 7 6 5 4 3 2 1

Contents

Contents

Mental Retardation in America

Introduction

Steven Noll and James W. Trent Jr.

When people call other people "idiot," they usually do so in the moment. Apart from time, "idiot" is not so much a label as it is an expression of a feeling, ordinarily an angry feeling. As such, human beings use "idiot" when they feel offended or feel their space or rights violated, even if the one named never hears the outrage. In these timeless moments of offense and violation, both strangers and close companions can receive the expression, can receive the insult. But the calling also solicits the history of a word. A word is a label when it has a history.

So the expressions "idiot," "you idiot," "you're an idiot," "don't be an idiot," and the like are more than momentary insults. They are also expressions that represent an old, if unstable, history. "Idiot" and other words that followed it—"imbecile," "feebleminded," "moron," "defective," "deficient," and "retard"—represent sets of cultural meanings over time. When North American authorities began to label human beings under their watch "idiots," they drew upon traditions that included, but also transcended, medical and rehabilitative philology. In doing so, they evoked St. Paul and St. Augustine, Luther and Calvin, Montaigne and Shakespeare, and Condillac and Locke.

In the 1840s, for reasons that even puzzled one of these authorities, Samuel Gridley Howe, this old history took a new direction. Several physicians in western Europe and in North America became interested in the essence and hierarchy of idiots. They did so, Howe supposed, because they believed that they could educate idiots.[1]

Even in the first decades of the nineteenth century, the claim that idiots could learn was never entertained. The French alienist Jean-Etienne Esquirol, following a tradition going back to John Locke, claimed that idiots had no minds. Philippe Pinel, his teacher, had dismissed Jean-Marc Itard's wild boy of Aveyron with the unwavering assertion, "C'est un idiot." It was

1

only after Edouard Séguin claimed that he could change idiots by educating them and, more fundamentally, that idiots could benefit from the effort that idiocy became something whose essence became important. To educate idiots was to lead them out of the absence of intelligence. Once idiots showed that they could learn, they became worth understanding, and they became worth changing.[2]

In nineteenth-century France, England, and North America, physicians of the mind made the first claims for the education of idiots. Edouard Séguin and Félix Voisin, in France, John Conolly, in England, and Samuel Gridley Howe and Hervey Wilbur, in the United States, were physicians. That physicians were the first professionals to claim the education of idiots is hardly unexpected. As either a discipline or a profession, education was only in its infancy. By the eighteenth century, mental medicine had found a place in both Europe and North America. In the case of idiocy, education appeared a component of medicine when it treated a flaw of nature. Education, like any other treatment, affected nature. Physicians treated idiots through a specialized method that Séguin called physiological education.

Although a part of a recognized profession, mental medicine enjoyed neither the public respect nor the state sanctions that it claims today. Well into the nineteenth century, mind doctors or alienists, as they called themselves, were hardly more respected than their colleagues in other areas of medicine. Drawing on eighteenth-century humanitarian rationalism, along with humoral medicine, these physicians of the mind began a new tradition of treating the diseases and wants of the mind. Idiocy represented the most prominent want.

What most notably separated these idiot doctors, like their alienist associates, from regular medicine was the asylum. Idiocy, like insanity, would be treated in institutions away from the routine distractions of community life. For Howe, Wilbur, and the other half-dozen American superintendents of the first idiot asylums, the institution represented an oasis of quiet, calm, and order away from the confusion of family and community life. In these settings, elementary-school youngsters would learn basic academic and social skills. The goal of this educational treatment was to return teenage idiots to their communities, where they could assume productive lives. Yet, by insisting on segregating their slow-minded pupils from the community, these early authorities set in motion a policy that would last for nearly 150 years: institutionalization.

Even before the Civil War, social changes brought on by the influx of immigrants were testing the educational focus of the idiot asylum. Why educate idiots for community jobs that immigrants could do more efficiently? After the war, with the triumph of free labor and the growth of industrialization, isolation shifted from the means to the end of education. By 1900, institutions that had once educated feeble minds to return to their communities were now increasingly segregating their pupils for lifelong care. As early as 1880, the feeble-minded adult began to replace the idiotic child in the professional and popular literature on "feeblemindedness," a term that came to replace idiocy. Rather than a child to be educated, feeble-minded adults became burdens to the social fabric. As burdens, they prevented families from participating in the nation's free-wage-labor market. In their sloth and ignorance, also, they were the easy prey of purveyors of vice. Petty thievery, vagrancy, prostitution, and illegitimacy—all were the outcomes of feeblemindedness left unattended. By the end of the century, medical superintendents like Pennsylvania's Martin Barr were calling for the total institutionalization of all feeble minds into what Barr called reservations.[3] Like the Indians of the New World, feeble-minded people would find in these settings protection from the duties and evils of the world.

Soon supplanting representations of adult social burdens were images of feeble-minded adults as social menaces. In the optimism of the pre-1917 new century, North Americans saw Mendelian heredity as a way to understand genetic transmission and to use that understanding to control social problems. Eugenics became the linkage between understanding and control, and feeblemindedness became its principal subject. In this context, diagnostic refinement became important. Added to the nineteenth century low-grade idiot and the higher-grade imbecile, in 1910 eugenicists created a new term for the highest level and most threatening feeble mind, the moron.

Accompanying eugenics in the shift to the "menace of the feebleminded" was a new tool in the identification of feeble minds—the intelligence test. The Binet-Simon test and others that followed it gave North American authorities the ability to make ordinal differentiations ("idiot," "imbecile," "moron," and the high and low grades of each) through the precise interval measurement of intelligence (the intelligence quotient). In this new science, "mental deficiency," a newly emerging term in the 1930s, began a three-decade shift from a psychiatric problem to a problem dominated by psychologists and educators.

But eugenics and testing had mixed blessings. Although they provided institutional superintendents the notoriety to alert the public to the threat of mental deficiency, they also drew attention to the limitations of the institution. By 1920, Barr's dream of total institutionalization looked unlikely. Testing, if it had done nothing else, had led authorities to claim the existence of large and multiplying numbers of feeble minds. Could state institutions, short of enormous public funding, house all feeble minds? Would taxpayers, even in economic good times, support such an undertaking?

Accompanying these questions was a shift in professional ideology. The Freudian-inspired ideas of adjustment and adaptation—both part of the movement to shift psychiatry from the asylum to the community—led medical superintendents to think about community services. Added to their claims for the "large numbers" of feeble minds, the superintendents advocated for a new community program: special education. In the community, these medical men could extend their authority beyond the institution. Thus, from the 1920s through the 1960s, custodialism expanded in both the institution and the community. In public facilities and in segregated classrooms, this expansion required segregation.

By the late 1940s, after nearly two decades of low public funding and ever greater demands to admit more inmates, institutions in the United States came under greater public scrutiny. Scandals in the postwar years, a greater public understanding of mental health, advocacy by President John F. Kennedy and his family, and a national awareness of civil rights led to public policy shifts in the late 1960s and 1970s. By the mid-1970s, the segregated public institutions and special classrooms lost favor with politicians, professionals, and the public. In this context, an odd alliance emerged. State officials eager to shift the funding of services from state to federal sources joined with parents ready to advocate for mainstream services for their disabled children. The alliance led to a radical policy shift from institutionalization to community services and from segregation to mainstreaming and community integration. For many people labeled mentally retarded, the change was a blessing. Free from old restrictions and old pity, these people began to thrive in schools and in workplaces across the United States. Others, however, found themselves in less fortunate circumstances. For these people, freedom from labels and restrictive programs meant only new labels and new restrictions. Today, in nominally integrated but still segregated classrooms and in workshops and nursing homes, these children and adults have become part of the new segregation. In neither a segregated special school nor a public asylum, they nevertheless experience their segregation in the community itself. Not quite away from able-bodied people, they are nonetheless not quite participants in community structures and mainstream institutions.

As these events occurred, North Americans wrote about the history of idiocy, what today we are likely to call developmental, intellectual, or learning disabilities. Edouard Séguin, who immigrated to the United States around 1850 (and anglicized his name to Edward Seguin), published an article in 1856 in which he compared the Idiot Asylum at Syracuse, in New York State, and the Barre Private School, in Massachusetts. The article represented the first history of North American services. In his influential 1866 book, *Idiocy,* Seguin also expanded this history to include a review of institutional services through the Civil War years. Nearly three decades later, Walter Fernald, the superintendent of the Massachusetts School for the Feeble-Minded, addressed the National Conference on Charities and Correction on the history of services for the feebleminded. A decade later, Martin Barr's 1904 book, *Mental Defectives: Their History, Treatment, and Training,* provided a perspective on the history of the threat of "mental defectives" to America's future. The first history to include a review of the influence of the adaptation and adjustment theme of the 1920s was Stanley P. Davies's 1923 book, *The Social Control of the Feeble-Minded,* published by the National Committee for Mental Hygiene. The first comprehensive history of developmental disabilities appeared in Albert Deutsch's 1937 volume, *The Mentally Ill in America: A History of Their Care and Treatment from Colonial Times.* In Chapters 16 and 17 of the book, Deutsch provided an overview of services in the United States from the 1840s to the 1930s. He was especially interested to show how the mental hygiene movement had made parole and community adjustment a new and progressive practice, but one nevertheless still dependent on the institution as the source of parole.[4]

In 1964 the psychiatrist Leo Kanner published a comprehensive history of mental retardation, and, in 1983 and 1987, Richard C. Schreenberger published a two-volume history of the subject. Both books were "achievement histories" in that they represented histories of the so-called progress of services. Their focus was on the work of great teachers, physicians, and psychologists. They told the stories of one achievement after another and of one great champion of service after another. Rarely did either author place his story in a changing economic, social, and political context. Finally, neither history included the voices of people affected by the services—people with disabilities, their caregivers, and their parents. Whiggish and hagiographic, both histories nevertheless provided chronological descriptions of events and people.[5]

The 1984 publication of Peter Tyor and Leland Bell's *Caring for the Retarded in America* marked a turn to critical studies of mental retardation. The book reviewed the intended ways that institutional authorities cared for their inmates, and it considered some unintended consequences of that care. In 1991, Philip Reilly's book *The Surgical Solution: A History of Involuntary Sterilization in the United States* traced the practice of sterilization in American institutions from the end of the nineteenth century to the 1970s. Reilly claimed that the rates of involuntary sterilization varied among the several states of the United States. He also showed that many Americans of differing political persuasions supported the procedure. Especially important were his portrayal of the extrainstitutional medical enthusiasm for sterilization and his interesting biography of Harry Laughlin, the most notorious North American proponent of involuntary sterilization. In 1994, James Trent and Philip Ferguson published histories of mental retardation in the United States. For Trent, this history showed a persistent, if ironic, linkage between care and control. Authorities survived economic changes and political and social forces by altering the demands of care. By keeping the focus of treatment on people labeled retarded, institutional authorities also kept the agenda of mental retardation away from the economic inequalities and the social and political injustices that have so consistently dominated the lives of the labeled. For Ferguson, what he called "chronicity," or the tendency to define certain people as hopeless and helpless, was not an essential definition but rather one shaped and reshaped by official custodians. These nineteenth- and early-twentieth-century experts assumed power over ability and disability, over trainability and untrainability, and over productivity and lack of productivity. To argue his case, Ferguson drew on the New York superintendencies of Hervey Wilbur and Charles Bernstein.[6]

In 1995, Edward Larson and Steven Noll published histories that dealt with mental retardation in the American South. Larson's subject was eugenics. Yet, eugenics in the South of the early twentieth century was linked, as Larson noted, with feeblemindedness. Indeed, in the South, state authorities justified building their first institutions in the name of eugenics. Unlike other institutions in the nation that were built at first as "schools," the institutions in the South had as their explicit purpose the incarceration and ster-

6

ilization of "the unfit." On the basis of legislative records and newspaper accounts, Larson argued that southern progressives had embraced eugenics; physicians and legislators who considered themselves part of the "new South" had supported eugenics and incarceration. Focusing on the same region, Noll argued that the care and control of intellectually disabled southerners were "two poles of a continuum." Noll claimed that care was reserved for severely disabled *incompetent* clientele, while control was reserved for higher-functioning *deviant* people. He traced the advent of this two-tiered institutional model in the South. Like Larson, Noll saw eugenics as the principal purpose for establishing institutions in the South.[7]

Martin Pernick's book *The Black Stork*, published in 1996, followed the public reaction to Harry J. Haiselden. A Chicago physician who allowed six "defective" babies to die, Haiselden publicized his actions to newspapers and starred as himself in the 1917 film *The Black Stork*. Shown in theaters throughout the nation, the movie, along with dozens of other popular films carrying a eugenics theme, showed the penetration of the eugenics movement in popular American culture between 1917 and 1930, a time when, Pernick argued, eugenics and euthanasia had wider support and practice than histories of eugenics have supposed. Also interested in eugenics, Nicole H. Rafter published *Creating Born Criminals* in 1997. The book traced the history of the so-called defective delinquent. Rafter used records of the Napanoch (N.Y.) Institution for Male Defective Delinquents to argue that anthropological and hereditary doctrines of the late nineteenth century led to the 1920s distinction between the "good" and the "bad" feebleminded.[8]

Since the mid-1980s, then, interest in the history of mental retardation in North America has burgeoned. Supplementing the volumes already noted are additional books, articles, and dissertations.[9] Like all good historical work, these writings have both addressed and raised difficult questions. Three of these questions have the potential for new historical explorations. First, unlike the historical literature on mental illness, the histories of particular institutions that housed mentally retarded people have not received the attention that they deserve. Second, histories that explore cultural representations of mental retardation need to be told. Finally, the literature on mental retardation could benefit from histories grounded in the perspectives of people labeled mentally retarded. The articles in this anthology go along way to address these questions.

This book represents an attempt to develop a history of retardation in America. As editors, we have endeavored to publish a work with a wide range of authors who approach the problems of retardation from many differing points of view. Some of the stories and topics will be familiar to students of the history of disabilities; others will not. Regardless, all the entries bring a fresh look at retardation in America. Up until the past fifteen years or so, this topic was terra incognita for mainstream American historians, relegated to historians of education and social work. The evolution of the disability rights movement and the passage of the Americans with Disabilities Act (ADA) in 1990 marked a milestone in the struggle for the basic civil rights of people with disabilities. Through that struggle has also come an understanding that disabilities have a history as well, that the social construction of disabilities has been shaped and changed by American history in general. Perhaps more important, the contours of American history itself have been affected by people with disabilities and by the changing notions of disability itself. Much good work is being done to integrate this new disability history into the broader vision of American history. Yet, even disability history tends to leave out the "feeble-minded."[10] The pieces in this work give voices to those we have not heard, by focusing on the interplay between "the retarded" and those who claim to speak for them, or guide them, or even control them. Many attempt to move past simply an examination of how "the retarded" were treated to an understanding of the meaning of retardation to America, and even to those individuals labeled as retarded themselves. They also examine the individuals labeled as retarded in a variety of settings, thus moving past the institution as the only place in which retarded people existed. This requires creative use of source material, as retarded people have been relatively invisible outside the confines of institutional supervision. These essays tie the history of retardation to broader themes of family history, women's history, legal history, and even labor history and military history. By doing that, they lay the groundwork for a new generation of researchers and writers to examine the historical dimensions of mental retardation in America.

This work is divided into five sections, each roughly following in chronological fashion major changes in the treatment of people labeled retarded in America. Each section is introduced by one or two primary-source documents, which provide an overview of the time period. Section I, entitled "Before the Asylum," looks at nineteenth-century America and the relationship among community care, the almshouse, and the beginnings of what the historian David Rothman calls "The Discovery of the Asylum."[11] A selection from Samuel Gridley Howe's 1848 Report to the Massachusetts Legislature and William Fish's medical thesis on idiocy begin this section. Howe, scion of a middle-class Boston family, dabbler in antebellum reformist causes, and committed antislavery activist, directed the New England Asylum for the Blind, opened in 1824.[12] With his expertise in the education and training of people with disabilities, Howe was the perfect person to lead a Massachusetts state commission "to inquire into the condition of Idiots of the Commonwealth [of Massachusetts], to ascertain their numbers, and whether any thing [sic] can be done in their behalf."[13] Making their report in February 1848, Howe and the other two commissioners set the stage for all future education and training of those individuals then labeled "idiots." Written nearly thirty years after Howe's report, Fish's medical thesis, completed in 1879, reflects the scientific findings and treatment methods of the period. Looking backward, Fish reviewed Seguin's ideas on educating "idiots"; looking forward, he anticipates pathological and hereditarian interests about "feeblemindedness." The two articles in this section build on Howe's and Fish's documents in a variety of ways. Philip Ferguson examines the notion of indoor poor relief in almshouses and its relation to the treatment of people later characterized as severely retarded. He ties the growth of these facilities to changes within the economic system of emerging capitalism within the United States. Howe recognized the problems with housing "idiots" in almshouses, where they could not receive specialized care and were simply warehoused. Ferguson shows that the custodial function of the almshouse continued even after the establishment of separate facilities, in spite of Howe's call for better care and specialized treatment. Penny Richards's piece starts where most studies of nineteenth-century retardation begin—with a quotation from Samuel Gridley Howe. Richards however, moves past the typical story of the development of institutions and breaks new ground by examining retardation and its relation to the nineteenth-century American family in a "normal" (and not institutional) setting. Using both family letters and prescriptive literature, she examines a world we have only begun to explore, one in which "the retarded" play an important role in defining the parameters of "normal" family life in the nineteenth century.

Section II examines the development of the category of mental retardation as an historical process. In 1800, people labeled as idiots and imbeciles were lumped with other groups of unfortunate and disadvantaged individuals into a mass known as the deserving poor—deserving of both God's blessings and human charity. By 1900, "the feebleminded" were classified as a discrete category, with scientific criteria for identification and specialized treatment modalities for care and control. The pieces in this section show that this transition was neither linear or predetermined. The movement toward a category of persons labeled as "retarded" reflected broader trends in both American intellectual and scientific thought and American popular culture. It mirrored the establishment of specialized professional organizations as America grappled with both industrial modernization and the breakdown of a religious worldview. The primary documents that open this section exemplify these changes. Both written in 1910, the pieces reflects the growing scientific basis for human classification, as well as the professionalization and specialization developing within that scientific community. The report and the editorial are from the pages of Volume 15 of the *Journal of Psycho-Asthenics,* the official journal of the American Association for the Study of the Feeble-Minded (AASFM). Founded in 1876, the AASFM (which survives today as the American Association on Mental Retardation) was the professional organization organized to discuss "all questions related to the causes, conditions, and statistics of idiocy, and to the management, training, and education of idiots and feebleminded persons; it will also lend its influence to the establishment and fostering of institutions for this purpose."[14] With these 1910 articles, the identification and labeling of individuals as mentally defective or feebleminded changed dramatically. The establishment of a psychological basis for the diagnosis of retardation—the standardized, normed intelligence test—gave the identification procedure the imprimatur of scientific validity. These pieces also mark the introduction of a new category of feeblemindedness—the moron, a coin termed by the influential psychologist Henry Goddard to categorize high-level mental defectives.

Following the lead of the *JPA* articles, the pieces in this section examine mental retardation as a condition to be observed, delineated, and classified. In this section, we see people labeled as mentally retarded viewed as objects—objects of pity, objects of scorn, objects of fear, objects of self-identification. The "other" was utilized to examine "normality," and the mentally retarded were used as stock literary devices to hold a mirror to American society. The chapters by David Wright and Daniel Kevles expressly address the scientific concerns involved in the classification of individuals as mentally retarded. Both authors examine the notions of racial hierarchies and atavistic retardation as they piece together the intellectual underpinnings of the establishment of the category of "Mongolian idiot" or "Mongoloid." Wright focuses on the English physician John Langdon Down and his joining of Darwinian theory and personal observation as he struggled to formulate a classification scheme for individuals he saw as having similar characteristics. Kevles focuses on the deracialization of the "mongoloid category," with the discovery in the late 1950s and early 1960s of the chromosomal abnormality (trisomy-21) that actually causes the syndrome known today as "Down Syndrome." Both authors show the importance of understanding retardation in a transnational setting; what passes for scientific knowledge does not stop at America's borders.

Janice Brockley takes an entirely different track in her piece. She examines how the notion of retardation and the "other" allowed ideas about the ideal American family to be shaped and changed throughout nineteenth- and twentieth-century America. By examining retardation in the light of the primary institution of socialization, the family, Brockley establishes a dialectical relationship between the two. In doing so, she sheds new light on not only how "the retarded" were viewed in community settings but also how this affected the structure and function of the American family over time. Leila Zenderland's work on Henry Goddard sheds new light on a seminal figure in the movement to categorize and classify individuals by their intelligence. Goddard was crucial as well in the transition in the way feeblemindedness was viewed—from a medical condition to a psychological construct. Goddard, a psychologist, brought the Binet intelligence test to America as a means of identifying the feebleminded and coined the term "moron" to describe a new category of mental deficiency. In 1912, he also wrote *The Kallikak Family*, possibly the most influential book in the history of mental retardation in America.[15] Zenderland examines Goddard's text not only for its scientific (or pseudoscientific) meaning but also for its symbolic meaning for Americans at a time when old faiths were being tested by new paradigms. It is precisely this combination of science and biblical truth that made Goddard's views so readily accepted in pre–World War I America and so naive (tragically so) for modern Americans. The two final pieces in this section not only fit in well with the idea of mentally retarded people as "the other" but also fit well together. American literature is filled with stories of dysfunctional figures who inform the reader of inherent truths hidden deep in the American psyche. Gerald Schmidt examines the work of John Steinbeck and William Faulkner, paying special attention to their major characters with mental disabilities. Schmidt sees these authors as reflecting the broader American culture's ambivalence about people with retardation—retarded people are to be both feared and held in reverence. Through their unique, unsullied perspectives, both Steinbeck and Faulkner allow readers to see what is truly meaningful in American life. Karen Keely builds on Schmidt's work by examining not only the fiction of Steinbeck and Faulkner but also shorter works by Jack London and Eudora Welty. Placing these works in the time frame of what she calls "The Age of Sterilization," Keely examines them in light of their mentally retarded narrators. Her nuanced understanding of the meanings these narrators bring to their stories gives us new perspectives on the interaction between American fiction and the realities of a society seemingly committed to eugenic sterilization.

Section III analyzes the nadir of the American experience with mental retardation, a time when persons labeled as retarded were feared for both their criminal instincts and their genes. Scientists, medical doctors, and psychologists railed about the "menace of the feeble-minded" and recommended segregation or surgery as the only solutions to this increasing problem. The boldest of the cries against this problem came from Harry Laughlin, a peripatetic crusader for eugenics and immigration restriction. Affiliated with Charles Davenport's Eugenics Record Office, Laughlin was a tireless crusader for the sterilization of those he considered a danger to society. His 1926 article in the *Journal of Psycho-Asthenics,* excerpted here, presages the 1927 United States Supreme Court decision in *Buck v. Bell,* in which Justice Oliver Wendell Holmes wrote the opinion that upheld eugenic sterilization. His words still stir strong emotions seventy-five years later:

> We have seen more than once that the public welfare may call upon the best citizens for their lives. It would be strange if it could not call upon those who already sap the strength of the State for these lesser sacrifices, often not felt to be such by those concerned, in order to prevent our being swamped with incompetence. It is better for all the world, if instead of waiting to execute degenerate offspring for crime, or to let them starve for their imbecility, society can prevent those who are manifestly unfit from continuing their kind. The principle that sustains compulsory vaccination is broad enough to cover cutting the Fallopian tubes. *Jacobson v. Massachusetts,* 197 U.S. 11 , 25 S. Ct. 358, 3 Ann. Cas. 765. Three generations of imbeciles are enough.[16]

The United States Supreme Court has never overturned *Buck v. Bell;* however, in May 2002, the State of Virginia honored, with a resolution and a historic highway marker, the memory of Carrie Buck, the young woman sterilized by the state in the test case that Holmes decided.[17]

The four chapters in this section build upon Laughlin's chilling introduction. Nicole Rafter analyzes the relationship between mental retardation and criminal behavior in the late nineteenth century. She examines this connection through the lens of gender as she tells the story of the operation of New York's Newark Custodial Asylum, an institution opened in 1883 and designed to house poor feeble-minded women. Ellen Dwyer's description of Craig Colony, a New York State institution for the "epileptic," tells of another scientific presumption that had dire consequences for those caught in its web. She analyzes the assumed linear relationship between epilepsy and mental retardation and the perceived necessity for institutionalizing persons who suffered from the seizure disorder. By focusing on Craig's patients and on their struggles to cross what she calls "multiple borders," Dwyer shows that institutionalization is never a simple, one-way street. Molly Ladd-Taylor builds on Dwyer's insights in her piece on eugenic sterilization in Minnesota during the 1920s and 1930s. Sterilization was contested ground, and Ladd-Taylor emphasizes that governmental penury, bureaucratic indifference, and even patient desires often played roles in the supposed scientific rationale for sterilization. By emphasizing the battles over sterilization rather than focusing on the overarching power of the state, Ladd-Taylor gives the reader a more nuanced view of how and why sterilizations occurred in the cultural context of the time.

In Section IV, the focus switches from institutions, sterilization, and the "menace of the feebleminded" to people with retardation within their family and in their communities. This section examines the hopes and promises, as well as the problems and pitfalls, as people with retardation began to come out of the shadows in mid-twentieth-century America. The primary source introduction to the section, a 1962 *Saturday Evening Post* article by Eunice Kennedy Shriver, sister to President John Kennedy and wife of the former Peace Corps director Sargent Shriver, is diametrically different in tone, outlook, and prognosis from Laughlin's call for eugenic sterilization. Shriver's article, positively titled "Hope for Retarded Children," embraces the postwar liberal consensus that saw government intervention and infusions of money as the cure for social problems. We now know the idealistic naivete of this solution. And Shriver's call to action seems hopelessly maternalistic (notice that the descriptor "children" is used throughout the article). Yet, there is much to praise in her demand that people with retardation be accorded the simple dignities of human existence, simply because of their common humanity. The Kennedy legacy with regard to retardation is a complex one, but

Eunice Kennedy Shriver's appeal to middle America marked a watershed in changing attitudes towards people with retardation.[18]

As with so many other aspects of American life, World War II provided an impetus for social change regarding the status of persons with mental retardation. In his article, Stephen Gelb examines this change in light of manpower needs during the war. World War II provided opportunities for many persons who had been labeled mentally retarded, especially those considered mildly retarded, to prove they could aid in the war effort. Would these changes remain after the war concluded, or were they simply expediency measures forced upon a society mobilizing for total war? The next four pieces analyze post–World War II America and find the basis for long-term change in how Americans viewed those labeled retarded. Kathleen Jones looks at the 1950s struggle of New Jersey parents to get better services for their retarded children. Placed within an analytical framework of "normal" family structure within the low-level (and sometime high-level) stresses of the cold war, Jones's work reveals how parents discovered a cause for group mobilization in their realization that they were not alone in facing the problems of raising a retarded child.[19] While Kathleen Jones sees the 1950s as a time of nascent parent activism, Katherine Castles is less sanguine about the pressures of normalization upon 1950s American families. She sees the concept of retardation changing in the postwar era. Retardation was not simply an individual problem on the one hand or a societal one on the other. It was a family problem and retardation and its consequences affected the family unit as a whole. Castles examines the tension between parents struggling to incorporate family members with retardation into the family and professionals, especially medical doctors, who used their expertise to convince parents that families could never be "normal" with retarded members. The final two pieces in this section move their gaze from the family to new methods of treating those labeled as mentally retarded. Wendy Nehring analyzes the development of the community clinic as an alternative to institutional care. Though backed by parent groups and increasingly supported by large federal infusions of cash, especially in the 1960s, these facilities rarely lived up to their billing as significant alternatives to the institution or to the risk of no care at all. Elizabeth Shores's piece investigates the search for a humane institutional model through her case study of the Arkansas Children's Colony. Established only in the late 1950s, this institution incorporated the latest designs and treatment plans for improving the lives of the individuals who lived there. David Ray, the dynamic superintendent of the facility, not only established the institution as a model but became a major figure in the nationwide struggle to provide more federal money to benefit people with retardation. The works by Nehring and Shores analyze the two parts of the push, in the 1960s, to make funding for the help of retarded persons a federal priority. Fueled by President Kennedy's personal commitment to this issue, retardation funding was a hot-button item in the heady days of the early 1960s. But Kennedy's death, the growth of military spending for the Vietnam conflict and the concomitant social turmoil fueled by that war, and the establishment of other domestic spending priorities left funding for retardation issues in the lurch. The failure of liberal assumptions about the efficacy of experts and about the value of large-scale, rather than community-based, initiatives also set the stage for a new era in the treatment of persons with retardation, one focused around rights, rather than public charity.

Atkins v. Virginia, decided by the United States Supreme Court in June 2002, may be the most important legal decision since the court ruled in *Wyatt v. Aderholt* (1974) that retarded persons have a right to appropriate treatment. The *Atkins* case ruled that persons classified as mentally retarded may not be put to death in capital cases. The decision is included as the introductory document in Section V. *Atkins* symbolizes the growing legal consensus that persons with mental retardation constitute a specific class worthy of protection (a concept that is evolving slowly under the Americans with Disabilities Act of 1990) while simultaneously being included in mainstream America.[20]

The four pieces in this section follow from the guidelines set out in *Atkins.* Deborah Metzel's work examines the spatial geography of mental retardation and finds important correlations between the success of community programs and the location of those programs within accepting communities. While that conclusion may seem intuitive, Metzel's nuanced approach places the discussion within a solid social science and historical framework. David Rothman and Sheila Rothman's piece is excerpted from *The Willowbrook Wars,* their classic description of the legal battles over the closing of Willowbrook State School in New York in the early to mid-1970s.[21] The Rothmans show how parents of and advocates for the individuals institutionalized at the hellish facility on New York's Staten Island used the legal system to provide the impetus not only for shutting it down but for furnishing appropriate community placement and support for former patients. Geoffrey Reaume's work on compensation in sheltered workshops shows how far the situation has changed since the 1960s and Eunice Shriver's call for more workshop jobs for persons with retardation. Reaume chronicles the rise of the movement for fair and equitable pay for workshop employees based on minimum-wage legislation. This movement marks the emergence of the retarded as a class of individuals organized around their entitled rights, rather than what is given to them out of a sense of societal obligation. Reaume leaves the reader with a sense of class empowerment, in which individuals with retardation can compete within the capitalist marketplace. Michael Bérubé's insightful think piece provides a suitable closing to the volume. How do "the retarded" fit into 2004 America's call for family values? How can individuals with retardation fit into the broad contours of American families? How is retardation determined by the society in which we live? By asking these questions, Bérubé forces us to look at America's past treatment of "the retarded" for clues to how these individuals will fit into our future.

Much still needs to be done to discover a full history of those persons labeled as mentally retarded in America. We need more histories of family life that include members who are retarded. The history of the most visible symbol of retardation in late-twentieth-century America, Special Olympics, has yet to be told. There is as yet little work on mentally retarded students in the public schools, both in separate facilities and classrooms and in more inclusive settings. More institutional studies focused on patients and staff rather than on administration and bureaucracy will add much to our knowledge of how these facilities actually operated. A legal history, tied to the rights revolution of the late twentieth century, of the development of the rights of those labeled as mentally retarded would show how legal struggles, rather than the medical ones of the previous 150 years, have shaped Americans and their relationship to retardation. Wider studies of advocacy groups, especially the Association for Retarded Children (ARC), will reveal how these organizations both shaped and were influenced by broader American attitudes. While the post–World War II period is usually (and generally rightfully) viewed as a time of hope in the story of retardation, we need to examination the horrific experiments with nuclear and germ warfare perpetrated upon retarded persons (usually institutionalized) in the name of cold-war research. Finally, the development of retardation self-advocacy groups in the past decade has opened new avenues for research on how persons with retardation view themselves and their society. Perhaps the next volume of the history of retardation in America will address these and other intriguing issues.

NOTES

1. Samuel Gridley Howe, "Letter to Dr. Gridley," *Correspondence Book, 1848–1858. Massachusetts School for Idiotic and Feeble-Minded Youth.* Samuel Gridley Howe Library Historical Collection. Walter E. Fernald State School.

2. James W. Trent Jr., *Inventing the Feeble Mind: A History of Mental Retardation in the United States* (Berkeley: University of California Press, 1994), 40–59.

3. Martin Barr, "The Imperative Call of Our Present to Our Future," *Journal of Psycho-Asthenics* 7 (1902): 5–8.

4. Edward Seguin, "Origin of the Treatment and Training of Idiots," *American Journal of Education* 2 (1856), 145–152, and *Idiocy and Its Treatment by the Physiological Method* (New York, W. Wood, 1866); Walter E. Fernald, "History of the Treatment of the Feebleminded," *Proceedings of the National Conference of Charities and Correction,* 1893, 450–457; Martin Barr, *Mental Defectives: Their History, Treatment, and Training* (Philadelphia: Blakiston, 1904); Stanley P. Davies, *Social Control of the Feebleminded: A Study of Social Programs and Attitudes in Relations to the Problem of Mental Deficiency* (New York: National Committee for Mental Hygiene, 1923); Albert Deutsch, *The Mentally Ill in America: A History of Their Care and Treatment from Colonial Times* (New York: Doubleday, 1937), 332–386.

5. Leo Kanner, *A History of the Care and Study of the Mentally Retarded* (Springfield, Ill.: Charles C. Thomas, 1964); Richard C. Schreenberger, *A History of Mental Retardation* (Baltimore: Brookes, 1983) and *A History of Mental Retardation: A Quarter Century of Promise* (Baltimore: Brookes, 1987).

6. Peter L. Tyor and Leland V. Bell, *Caring for the Retarded in America: A History* (Greenwich, Conn.: Greenwood Press, 1984); Philip R. Reilly, *The Surgical Solution: A History of Involuntary Sterilization in the United States* (Baltimore: Johns Hopkins University Press, 1991); Trent, *Inventing the Feeble Mind*; and Philip M. Ferguson, *Abandoned to Their Fate: Social Policy and Practice toward Severely Retarded People in America, 1820–1920* (Philadelphia: Temple University Press, 1994).

7. Edward J. Larson, *Sex, Race, and Science: Eugenics in the Deep South* (Baltimore: Johns Hopkins University Press, 1995); Steven Noll, *Feeble-Minded in Our Midst: Institutions for the Mentally Retarded in the South* (Chapel Hill: University of North Carolina Press, 1995).

8. Martin S. Pernick, *The Black Stork: Eugenics and the Death of "Defective" Babies in American Medicine and Motion Pictures* (New York: Oxford University Press, 1996); Nicole Hahn Rafter, *Creating Born Criminals* (Urbana: University of Illinois Press, 1997).

9. Janice Brockley reviews some of these works in her article "The History of Mental Retardation: An Essay Review," *History of Psychology* 2 (1999): 25–36.

10. Paul Longmore and Lauri Umansky's edited volume *The New Disability History American Perspectives* (New York: New York University Press, 2001) provides a useful

and comprehensive overview of the field. Of its fourteen chapters, one, Janice Brockley's "Martyred Mothers and Merciful Fathers: Exploring Disability and Motherhood in the Lives of Jerome Greenfield and Raymond Repouille," examines mental retardation.

11. David Rothman, *The Discovery of the Asylum: Social Order and Disorder in the New Republic* (Boston: Little, Brown, 1971).

12. Two new books discuss Howe's career as director of the New England Asylum. They also shed light on the relationship between antebellum reformism and the search to understand the origins of human language and intelligence. Howe's career in what would later be called "the helping professions" reflected his interests in both the compassionate and intellectual sides of these issues. See Ernest Freeburg, *The Education of Laura Bridgman: First Deaf and Blind Person to Learn Language* (Cambridge, Mass.: Harvard University Press, 2001), and Elisabeth Gitter, *The Imprisoned Guest: Samuel Howe and Laura Bridgman, The Original Deaf-Blind Girl* (New York: Farrar, Straus, and Giroux, 2001).

13. Samuel Gridley Howe, *On the causes of Idiocy, Being the Supplement to a Report by Dr. S. G. Howe and the Other Commissioners Appointed by the Governor of Massachusetts to Inquire into the Condition of the Idiots of the Commonwealth, Dated February 26, 1848* (repr. ed., New York: Arno Press, 1972; originally published 1858), v.

14. Article II, Constitution of the Association of Medical Officers of American Institutions of Idiotic and Feebleminded Children, passed June 7, 1876. (In 1900, the name of the organization was changed to the American Association for the Study of Feeble-Mindedness.) Constitution quoted in William Sloan and Harvey Stevens, *A Century of Concern: A History of the American Association on Mental Deficiency, 1876–1976* (Washington, D.C.: AAMD Press, 1976), 1–2.

15. Henry Goddard, *The Kallikak Family: A Study in the Heredity of Feeblemindedness* (New York: Macmillan, 1912). For more on Goddard and the writing of the Kallikak book, see Stephen Jay Gould, *The Mismeasure of Man* (New York: W. W. Norton, 1981), 158–174; John David Smith, *Minds Made Feeble: The Myth and Legacy of the Kallikaks* (Rockville, Md.: Aspen Systems Corp., 1985); and Leila Zenderland, *Measuring Minds: Henry Herbert Goddard and the Origins of American Intelligence Testing* (Cambridge: Cambridge University Press, 1998), 143–185.

16. *Buck v. Bell*, 274 U.S. 200 (1927). For a concise overview of Holmes's legal thought regarding the *Buck* decision, see William Leuchtenberg, *The Supreme Court Reborn: The Constitutional Revolution in the Age of Roosevelt* (New York: Oxford University Press, 1995), 3–25.

17. Carlos Santos, "Historic Test Case: Wrong Done to Carrie Buck Remembered," *Richmond Times-Dispatch*, February 17, 2002; Bob Gibson, "Carrie Buck Remembered," *Charlottesville Daily Progress*, May 7, 2002.

18. Edward Shorter, *The Kennedy Family and the Story of Mental Retardation* (Philadelphia: Temple University Press, 2000). The best description of the continuities and

changes in the post–World War II treatment of persons labeled as having mental retardation is a personal study, not a general overview. See Dave Bakke, *God Knows His Name: The True Story of John Doe No. 24* (Carbondale: Southern Illinois University Press, 2000).

19. Jones draws heavily on the literature of the family in cold-war America, much of which is very good but does not consider the relationship of a retarded family member to family structure. See Paul Boyer, *By the Bomb's Early Light: American Thought and Culture at the Dawn of the Atomic Age* (New York: Pantheon, 1985), and Elaine Tyler May, *Homeward Bound: American Families in the Cold War Era* (New York: Basic Books, 1988), for broad overviews of the relationship between family culture and the cold-war climate in post–World War II America.

20. *Wyatt v. Aderholt, Wyatt v. Stickney,* 325 F. Supp. 781 (M.D. Ala. 1971), 334 F. Supp. 1341 (M.D. Ala. 1971), 344 F. Supp. 373 (M.D. Ala. 1972), sub nom *Wyatt v. Aderholt,* 503 F. 2d 1305 (5th Cir. 1974). For more on the ADA and the struggle over the protection it provides for persons with disabilities, see the special volume of the *Annals of the American Academy of Political and Social Science* entitled "The Americans with Disabilities Act: Social Contract or Special Privilege?" Vol. 549 (January 1997), and Ruth O'Brien, *Crippled Justice: The History of Modern Disability Policy in the Workplace* (Chicago: University of Chicago Press, 2001), esp. 162–207.

21. David Rothman and Sheila Rothman, *The Willowbrook Wars: A Decade of Struggle for Social Justice* (New York: Harper & Row, 1984).

Part I

Before the Asylum

A Selection from Report Made to the Legislature of Massachusetts (1848)

Samuel G. Howe

The Report, . . . , was drawn up by the Commissioners appointed under the authority of an act of the Legislature of Massachusetts, dated the 11th of April 1846, "to inquire into the condition of the idiots of the Commonwealth, to ascertain their number, and whether anything can be done in their behalf. . . ."

The imperfect results of these inquiries were embodied in a report, made 15th March 1847, and printed by order of the legislature. . . . By diligent and careful inquiries in nearly one hundred towns in different parts of the state, we have ascertained the existence and examined the condition of five hundred and seventy-four human beings who are condemned to hopeless idiocy, who are considered as idiots by their neighbors, and left to their brutishness. They are also idiotic in a legal sense; that is, they are regarded as incapable of entering into contracts, and are irresponsible for their actions, although some of them would not be considered as idiots according to the definition of idiocy by medical writers. . . . These are found in 77 towns. But all these towns were not thoroughly examined. Take therefore only the 63 towns in which very minute inquiries were made. These contain an aggregate population of 185,942; among which were found 361 idiots, exclusive of insane persons. Now, if the other parts of the state contain the same proportion of idiots to their whole population, the total number in the commonwealth in between twelve and fifteen hundred!

It is recommended that measures be at once taken to rescue this most unfortunate class from the dreadful degradation in which they now grovel. The reasons for this are manifold, and hardly need to be repeated. In the first place, it would be an economical measure. This class of persons is always a burden upon the public. It is true, that the load is equally divided; it falls partly upon the treasury of the different towns, and partly upon the individuals; so that the weight is not sensibly felt; but still it is not a whit the less heavy for that. There are at least a thousand persons of this class who not only contribute nothing to the common stock, but who are ravenous consumers; who are idle and often mischievous, and who are dead weights upon the material prosperity of the state. But this is not all; they are even worse than useless; they generally require a good deal of watching to prevent their doing mischief, and they occupy considerable part of the time of more industrious and valuable persons. Now it is made certain, by what has been done in other countries, that almost every one of these men and women, if not beyond middle age, may be made to observe all the decencies of life; to be tidy in their dress, cleanly in their habits, industrious at work, and even familiar with the simple elements of knowledge. If they were all made to earn something instead of spending, wasting, and destroying, the difference would be considerable. It would be an economy to some towns to send a young idiot across the ocean if he could be trained to such habits of industry as to support himself, instead of dragging out a life of two or three score years in the almshouse, and becoming every year more stupid, degraded, and disgusting. Many a town is now paying an extra price for the support of a drivelling [*sic*] idiot, who, if he had been properly trained, would be earning his own livelihood, under the care of discreet persons who would gladly board and clothe him for the sake of the work he could do.

The moral evils resulting from the existence of a thousand and more of such persons in the community are still greater than the physical ones. The spectacle of human beings reduced to a state of brutishness, and given up to the indulgences of animal appetites and passions, is not only painful, but demoralizing in the last degree. Not only young children, but "children of an older growth" are most injuriously affected by it. What virtuous parent could endure the thought of a beloved child living within the influence of an idiotic man or woman who knows none of the laws of conscience and morality, and none of the requirements of decency? And yet, most of the idiots in our Commonwealth, unless absolutely caged up (as a few are), have, within their narrow range, some children who may mock them indeed, and tease them, but upon whom they in return inflict a more serious and lasting evil. Every such person is like a Upas tree, that poisons the whole moral atmosphere about him.

But the immediate adoption of proper means for training and teaching idiots, may be urged upon higher grounds than that of expediency, or even of charity; it may be urged upon the ground of imperative duty. It has been shown, that the number of this wretched class is fearfully great; that a large part of them are directly at the public charge; that the whole of them are at the charge of the community in one way or another, because they cannot help themselves. It has been shown, that they are not only neglected, but that through ignorance they are so often badly treated and cruelly wronged, that, for want of proper means of training, some of them sink from mere weakness of mind into entire idiocy; so that, though born with a spark of intellect which might be nurtured into a flame, it is gradually extinguished, and they go down darkling to the grave, like the beasts that perish. Other countries are beginning to save such persons from their dreadful fate; and it must not be, that here, in the home of the Pilgrims, human beings, born with some sense, be allowed to sink into hopeless idiocy, for want of a helping hand.

Massachusetts admits the right of all her citizens to a share in the blessings of education; she provides it liberally for all her more favored children; if some be blind or deaf, she still continues to furnish them with special instruction at great cost; and will she longer neglect the poor idiot— the most wretched of all who are born to her,— those who are usually abandoned by their fellows,— who can never, of themselves, step up upon the platform of humanity, will she leave them to their dreadful fate, to a life of brutishness, without an effort on their behalf?

It is true, that the plea of ignorance can be made in excuse for the neglect and ill treatment which they have hitherto received; but this plea can avail us no longer. Other countries have shown us that idiots may be trained to habits of industry, cleanliness, and self-respect; that the highest of them may be measurably restored to self-control; and that the very lowest of them may be raised up from the slough of animal pollution in which they wallow; and can the men of other countries do more than we? Shall we, who can transmute granite and ice into gold and silver— shall we shrink from the higher task of transforming brutish men back into human shape? Other countries are beginning to rescue their idiots from further deterioration, and even to elevate them; and shall our commonwealth continue to bury the humble talent of lowly children committed to her motherly care, and let it rot in the earth, or shall she do all that can be done, to render it back with usury to Him who lent it? There should be no doubt about the answer to these questions. The humanity and justice of the legislature will prompt them to take immediate measures for the formation of a school or schools for the instruction and training of idiots.

The benefits to be derived from the establishment of a school for this class of persons, upon humane and scientific principles, would be very great. Not only would all the idiots, who should be received into it, be improved in their bodily and mental condition, but all the others in the state and country would be indirectly benefited. The school, if conducted by persons of skill and ability, would be a model for others. Valuable information would be disseminated through the country; it would be demonstrated that no idiot need be confined or restrained by force; that the young can be trained to industry, order, and self-respect; that they can be redeemed from odious and filthy habits, and that there is not one of any age, who may not be made more of a man and less of a brute, by patience and kindness, directed by energy and skill.

It is not our duty to enter into any details of the plan of such a school, or schools; that must be left to abler hands. We close this part of our Report, therefore, by most earnestly recommending, that immediate measures be taken for the formation of such a school.

The Massachusetts legislature responded to Howe's report with the following resolutions:

Resolved, That there be paid out of the treasury of the Commonwealth, a sum, not exceeding twenty-five hundred annually, for the term of three years, for the purpose of training and teaching ten idiotic children, to be selected by the Governor and Council from those at public charge, or from the families of indigent persons in different parts of the Commonwealth, provided that an arrangement can be made by the Governor and Council with any suitable institution now patronized by the Commonwealth for charitable purposes; and provided that said appropriation shall not be made a charge upon the school fund.

Resolved, That the trustees of the institution undertaking the instruction and training of said idiots, shall, at the end of each and every year, render to the Government and Council an account of the actual expense incurred on account of said idiots; and if the amount expended shall be less than the sum received from the public treasury, the unexpended balance shall be deducted from the amount of the next annual appropriation.

Resolved, That the said trustees shall be authorized to require the authorities of any town which may send any idiot pauper to them for instruction, be required to keep them supplied with comfortable and decent clothing.

Approved by the Governor, 8th May 1848.

A Thesis on Idiocy

William B. Fish

Albany Medical College (1879)

Introduction

James W. Trent Jr.

William Fish was the second superintendent of the Illinois Asylum for Feeble-Minded Children at Lincoln. During its first half-century, the Illinois Asylum had seven superintendents. Lasting longer than his six successors, Charles Wilbur, who founded the institution in 1865, succumbed to a gubernatorial sack in 1883. During the same year, Fish arrived at Lincoln to take over Wilbur's duties. In 1893, when political change forced a turnover, Fish moved to Chicago, where he would leave the field of "feeblemindedness" to others. By that time, the asylum had become one of nation's largest residential facilities.

A member of one of New York State's most prominent political families, Fish had graduated from the Albany Medical College in 1879. For the three years (partly before and partly after his graduation), he practiced as an assistant to Henry M. Knight, the medical director of the Connecticut State School for Idiots and Imbeciles, at Lakeville.

Fish produced his handwritten "Thesis on Idiocy" at the Albany Medical College in 1879, only four years before he moved to the Illinois Asylum. The thesis reflected his experience at the Connecticut State School and his readings of contemporary writings from Great Britain and from the European continent.

Basing his thesis on both his experience and his readings, Fish introduced the document with a history of the education and treatment of idiots and imbeciles. After this review, he presented the prevailing claims for idiocy's etiology. These included "hereditary predisposition" and degenerative heredity; consanguine marriages (or the marriage of close relatives, usually cousins); scrofula; drunkenness; "impressions given to the child in uterine life"; and environmental conditions. Despite these hereditary factors, he noted that the most common form of idiocy, the "Mongolian type," was congenital.

Drawing on research more common at the time in Europe than in North America, Fish turned his thesis to the pathology of idiocy. He claimed that microscopic investigations of the brains of idiots often showed both structural and pathological abnormalities. Yet, he also noted that such examinations might just as likely reveal no irregularities.

Fish concluded his thesis with a brief discussion of the treatment of idiocy. Like most of his contemporaries, he indicated that the treatment of the idiot's mind was useless without concern for his or her body. Thus, proper nutrition, dietary caution, and hygiene became the first order of treatment.

There is nothing new in Fish's medical thesis. In it, he synthesizes his experiences and his readings, but he provides little analysis and no original research. What the thesis gives the twenty-first century reader is an excellent sense of the state of knowledge about intellectual disabilities at the end of the 1870s, a period in which authorities were convincing several legislatures to build and expand public facilities. Although education remained an interest, Fish's thesis reflects the movement of "idiocy" from a pedagogical concern to a problem of etiology, pathology, and treatment. Medicine had shaped thinking about intellectual disabilities from the beginning. Yet, by the 1880s, that thinking was becoming increasingly divorced from educational concerns. Fish's thesis reveals this change. By the end of the century, pathology would almost entirely replace pedagogy.

A Thesis on Idiocy

Idiocy like insanity has but recently received much attention at the hands of medical men, although like insanity, it has had an existence dating far back in the history of mankind.

The first attempt made to educate or improve the condition of this unfortunate class was as near as can be learned made in France during the seventeenth century by St. Vincent De Paul,[1] who gathered together a few idiots in the priory of St. Lazarus and attempted to teach them. The experiment, though continued for several years, did not prove successful. Subsequently

28

other attempts were made in France by different individuals but of these we have little record. In the year eighteen hundred a boy was found running wild in a forest in the center of France. He attracted considerable attention amongst scientific men, and was known as the "wild boy of the Aveyron," from the department in which he was captured.

He was taken to Paris and placed under the instruction of Itard,[2] a celebrated teacher of the deaf and dumb who thought him a savage, though it was afterwards ascertained that he was idiotic. Itard's attempt at his instruction though pursued for a period of six years with great diligence and care was unsuccessful.

It succeeded however in awakening an interest in the condition of the feeble minded and idiotic which afterwards bore fruit in the labor of Seguin and others. In the year 1818 the Asylum for Deaf and Dumb in Hartford, Conn. received a few idiotic and imbecile children, and an attempt was made to educate them. Though some improvement in their condition was made the experiment was after a few years discontinued.

Subsequently Guggenbuhl[3] of Switzerland, Saegert[4] of Berlin, and Seguin[5] of Paris opened schools for the training and instruction of idiots. To the latter (Dr. Seguin) is due perhaps more than to any other man the credit of bringing these unfortunates to the notice of the medical profession and the world, and of initiating a system of treatments which gave proof that much could be done to improve and elevate the hitherto friendless and neglected idiot.

In our own country the subjects of idiocy early claimed attention. Among those prominent in the early history of the work were George Sumner[6] of Boston, Dr. F. Backus[7] of Rochester, N.Y. and Doctors Howe[8] and H. B. Wilbur[9] of Massachusetts. Mr. Sumner (a brother of the late senator) while in Paris visited the training school of Dr. Seguin and became greatly interested in his work; this interest culminated in a series of letters which were published in an American magazine.

These letters attracted much attention and assisted by the efforts of Doctors Howe and Wilbur led to the establishment of training schools at Barre, and Boston, Mass. in the year eighteen forty-eight.

At the present time there are eleven institutions in this country devoted to the care and training of idiots and imbeciles having over fifteen hundred inmates.

The definition of idiocy by one of the latest writers on the subject is, "Mental deficiency or extreme stupidity [is a condition] depending upon malnutrition or disease of the nervous centres occurring either before birth, or before the evolution of the mental faculties in childhood."

Imbecility is generally understood to signify a milder form or idiocy, not necessarily congenital but supervening in infancy.

The distinction between these forms of mental deficiency and dementia should be clear and plainly marked, the latter differing in being a loss more or less complete through disease or injury of faculties once possessed. The classification of idiocy is as yet somewhat unsatisfactory. One of the latest is that of Dr. Ireland[10] of Scotland who bases his views upon the pathological conditions observed.

It is my purpose to discuss simply some of the forms of idiocy which came to my notice while under the preceptorship of Dr. H. M. Knight,[11] Superintendent of the Conn. State School for Idiots and Imbeciles in Lakeville.

The various causes of idiocy are of great importance and interest, not only as a study but also in view of their important bearing on the prevention of this condition.

Chief in importance is hereditary predisposition. Fortunately marriages between idiots and imbeciles are rare, for the offspring of such unions would invariably present some of the worst features of their parental taint and burden society with their support through life.

It is a work of great difficulty to obtain a correct family history from the parents of idiotic and imbecile children. Any tendency to mental deficiency or disease which may have existed either in themselves or their progenitors is acknowledged, if at all, with reluctance.

Dr. Grabham,[12] Superintendent of the Earlswood Asylum for Idiots, England reports that in eighteen percent of his cases hereditary taint was admitted, but he is convinced that it exists in a far greater proportion. In some cases where no mental deficiency was observed he found a great degree of eccentricity in one or both parents. The mother of one of his pupils from whom no history of mental disease could be obtained and who appeared to be intelligent and sane, was found to be frequently removing to new lodgings because, "Poison was put down the chimney in her food." Another lady having a child in the institution in a letter to him says, "My late husband used to think that there was no such place as hell but I hope now that he has found out his mistake." It is generally conceded by those conversant with nervous diseases that there is a neurotic diathesis, the manifestation of disease in the offspring of neurotic parents not being necessarily of the same character, but involving some part of their nervous organization.

Thus a woman suffering from epilepsy may give birth to an idiotic or imbecile child. The descendants of an insane father may be epileptic, insane or idiotic.

According to Ludvig Dahl,[13] a Danish writer on the subject, "A single pair free from any neurosis may give birth to healthy children, and yet some of their children, grand children, or great grand children may be insane or idiotic, while other members of the same family are healthy and intelligent." Why some members of a family should be deficient in intellect while others possess average, or more than average intelligence is a problem the solution of which is fraught with difficulty.

We observe in healthy intelligent families marked difference in the mental capacity of different individuals which cannot be explained by difference in education or training but which seem to have existed from infancy.

Consanguine marriages have been supposed to be a fruitful cause of idiocy. That they are factors to some extent in the causation of mental deficiency and disease cannot be denied. In the opinion of many who have carefully investigated the subject, their influence has been overestimated. Until recently no effort has been made to institute a fair comparison between the offspring of consanguine parents and those who were in no way related. The statistics given to the public have been with few exceptions remarkably one sided.

The number of idiotic and imbecile children whose parents were in any way related has been carefully ascertained and without any attempt to determine the numbers who were in no way deficient, yet whose parents were near relatives.

In this connection the statistics gathered by Auguste Voisin[14] and published in Paris 1865 are of interest. His observations were made in the commune of Batz, France.

He records forty six marriages between near relatives, five of cousins-german, thirty one of issue by issue of cousins-german, and ten by cousins of the fourth degree. To the five cousins-german, twenty three children were born, none of them being deformed or deficient. Of these, two died in infancy of acute disease. The result of the marriages of the thirty one cousins the issue of first cousins was one hundred and twenty children all of them being free from disease or deformity, of this number twenty four died of acute disease. To the ten cousins of the fourth degree twenty nine children were born all of average intelligence and free disease, three died in infancy.

But two couples of the forty six were unfruitful. The forty four remaining couples had one hundred and seventy four children of whom twenty nine died of acute diseases incident to childhood.

The most recent opinions on this subject are that in consanguine marriages the influence of a double heredity is transmitted, any tendency or predisposition to disease in the parents being increased proportionately in the children.

The scrofulous diathesis seems to favor or at least to accompany the production of idiocy, indeed it is almost exceptional to find an idiot who does not in some ways exhibit traces of this disease.

There is a difference of opinion in regard to drunkenness of parents as a cause of idiocy. Dr. Langdon Down[15] lays much stress upon the drunkenness of the fathers during coition. The following authentic case related to me by a medical superintendent, who however considered it exceptional would seem to substantiate this view of the subject.

A man who was in the habit of indulging in an occasional debauch, during one of these seasons came staggering home and meeting his wife laid hold of her and forced her to have intercourse with him. She became pregnant having no intercurrent accident during gestation, and at full term was delivered of a male child who was a complete idiot and when old enough to walk had the staggering gait and appearance of an intoxicated person.

Dr. Ireland in his valuable work on idiocy is not of the opinion that drunkenness of itself has much effect in the causation of idiocy or imbecility. He says, "Drunkenness brings other privations in its train which have their effect on the general health of a family. The parents of idiot children are often far from being intemperate or dissolute persons."

Much has been written of impressions given the child in uterine life by the mother, as a consequence of sudden fright, blows, falls, mental anxiety, and doubtless all these have more or less influence in the production of idiocy.

The conditions of our social life, the struggle for wealth, dissipations, mental strain and overwork on the part of one or both parents are among the predisposing causes of this sad condition, but squalor, deprivation, neglect and filth to a far greater degree, conspire to swell the list of inmates of our asylums and training schools.

The most common form of idiocy is that which is congenital. Idiots of this type and nearly all of a low grade of health and in physique as well as in mind show the effects of imperfect development and growth. As a rule their sensibility to pain is slight. Burns, cuts and bruises are in many cases endured with indifference; their circulation is feeble, and assimilation is imperfectly performed. They are apt to suffer from chillbluing upon slight exposure.

Glandular swelling ulcers and other symptoms of scrofula are commonly observed.

As their general health grows better their mental condition improves. A few months sojourn in an asylum where they are subjected to appropriate medical treatment often causes a marked change in their appearance for the better.

There is considerable difference in the mental and bodily condition of congenital idiots which has much to do with prognosis and treatment. There is observed occasionally amongst this class what has been called the Mongolian type. In the Conn. Training School there are three children, two boys and a girl in no way related who possess to a remarkable degree the expression of countenance, slanting eyes as of the Chinese.

Two cases selected from this class will illustrate some of the differences observed amongst congenital idiots.

G. F., male age eight is quick and active in his movements and very fond of gymnastic exercise in which he excels many of his comrades. He is good natured, fond of music, dances well and is a great mimic. When first received in the institution he feigned epilepsy so successfully as to deceive his attendant at first, but careful examination showed that it was an imitation of epileptic attacks observed by him since his admission to the school. He has improved under training but as yet cannot articulate perfectly or understand all that is said to him though his hearing is perfect.

The other case is less promising. T. Y., male age fourteen, is sluggish and apathetic, pays little attention to those about him, eats ravenously, cannot articulate, makes little or no improvement in school, is able however to attend to his wants and shows some advance in neatness of person.

There is much to interest the pathologist in this form of idiocy, though the results of pathological investigations are at present somewhat unsatisfactory. Cases have been noted where a post mortem showed a lack of the corpus callosum, but this same deficiency has been observed in persons who when living possessed average intelligence. A marked accompaniment of congenital idiocy is the vaulted or keel shaped palates resembling the impression of the keel of a ship. The teeth are subject to early decay and are irregular.

The researches of Dr. M. Jastrowitz[16] of Berlin in regard to the minute structure of the brain, which entails idiocy, are of great interest. He observes in the brain of the foetus fatty granular cells which he claims are of the same character as those found during the regeneration of a severed nerve. These cells, he asserts, normally develop into fully formed nervous tissue. In the congenital idiot he claims to have found these fatty granular cells, both in the brain and spinal cord after birth, hence his inference that the deficiency in congenital idiocy is due to the persistence of elements normal in the embryo, but which should have passed into another form in the mature human being.

These views however are not as yet accepted by many pathologists, and careful microscopic examination in some cases has shown nothing abnormal.

There is great need of a series of investigations embracing a wide range of cases, and it would seem that great advancement could be made if the superintendents of our asylums and training schools would combine and employ a competent pathologist, and contribute from time to time cases of interest coming under their notice. The fragile character of brain and nerve substance has heretofore been quite an obstacle to its successful microscopic study, but recent improvements in laboratory technology have overcome many obstacles which hitherto seemed insurmountable.

There is a type of idiocy characterized by very small head which is sometimes observed, though not very common. These microcephalics as they are called are fond of moving about, are sharp and quick in their movements but seem to be unable to pay continuous attention to any one object. The so called Aztec children exhibited in this country a few years ago were microcephalic idiots.

It is claimed that excluding hydrocephalics the average size of the heads of idiots is smaller than that of people of intelligence. August Voison[17] in an article published by him in Paris 1843 claims that the proper exercise of the intellectual faculties is impossible with a head from eleven to thirteen inches in circumference and a measurement of eight or nine inches from the root of the nose to the posterior borders of the occipital bone. This statement to the best of my knowledge has remained uncontradicted to the present time.

The following case observed at the Conn. Training School exhibits some of the peculiarities of this form of idiocy.

T. M., male age 15 is active, fond of notice, dances well, and safe when asleep, is constantly in motion, reminding one by his darting, quick movements of a humming bird, is a little disposed to be quarrelsome, is fond of gymnastic exercises, is not able to articulate but understands what is said of him, in attempting to whistle makes a noise like the peep of a chicken, imitates readily the actions of those about him but can't be induced to confine his attention to any one subject for a long time, makes little progress at school but his teacher thinks he has made some improvement in his attempts at articulation and hopes eventually that he will be able to talk. The causation of microcephalic idiocy is not well determined. It is claimed by some to be due to a premature closure of the sutures of the skull, but cases on record show that microcephalic children have been born with open sutures, hence it cannot be the cause in all cases. Microscopic examination has shown in some cases an undue amount of neuroglia in proportion to the numbers of nerve cells.

A large number of idiots suffer more or less from epilepsy. We observe in epileptic idiots the same differences in mental and bodily condition as in congenital idiots with the exception that they are generally better nourished. A considerable number are in a condition more nearly resembling dementia than true idiocy.

Opinions differ as to their capabilities for improvement, in some of our asylums they are regarded as incurable and are not received. Other institutions claim to have noticed marked improvement under treatment and regard the prognosis in their epileptic cases as favorable as that of any form of idiocy.

There is a form of idiocy common in Switzerland which though met with in other parts of the world is rare. Cretinism as it is termed is intimately associated with goitre. It would appear that the cause which produces goitre alone when not well marked, produces cretinism when acting with greater intensity.

It is generally conceded that cretinism is due to endemic influences, but the precise element or elements producing it have not as yet been determined.

It would be interesting to discuss some of the different views of writers on this subject but space will not permit.

There are other forms of idiocy which prevail to a greater or less degree as that characterized by a very large head (hydrocephalic). Idiocy caused by injuries to the brain by accidents (traumatic), and idiocy as a result of paralysis, but the consideration of them in detail would be far beyond the limits of this paper and their mere mention must suffice.

The treatment of idiocy should be both physical and mental and of course differs with the conditions of the individual case. Bearing in mind the old phrase, "mens sana in corpore sana," we should first direct our attention to the physical condition. Many of the cases received in our training schools and asylums have (previous to their admission) had the tendency to disease already existing increased by bad hygienic surroundings and improper or insufficient food. With these cases the prompt exhibition of tonics, and a supply of nourishing food will often in a short time cause marked improvement. As the general health improves, and from the first, habits of cleanliness should be taught, exercise in the open air and in the gymnasium encouraged and insisted on, and disposition to apathy or indifference should be combated. The importance of occupation of some kind cannot be overestimated. The simplest task calls for some exercise of the mind and assists in its development.

Many cases are deficient in muscular co-ordination and require careful training in this direction. Most asylums have connected with them work shops, and farms, which afford employment to the more advanced inmates. Gymnastic exercise and drill exerts a most salutary influence upon both body and mind. Music and dancing are heartily enjoyed by these unfortunates, even the most stolid and unpromising evince some pleasure when listening to music, while the more intelligent readily learn the changes of the dance. The mental training of idiots requires unwearied effort and patience. Some are unable to articulate plainly and others know but a few words, and invent words or sounds to express themselves. In these cases it becomes necessary often to place the lips and tongue in the position required to form the desired sounds. The kindergarten system of instruction is employed in most schools.

The more advanced pupils are taught the common English branches. But few are ever able to make much progress in arithmetic.

In the treatment of epileptic idiots the indications are to prevent the attacks or modify their character.

Experience shows that diet has an important bearing on this condition. Meat and nitrogenous food tend to increase the frequency of the epileptic seizures and should be given sparingly. In the way of medical treatment the zinc salts, nitrate of silver and atropia have been used, but in the majority of cases the bromides of potassium and sodium in full doses seem to be of the most service.

The necessity for training schools and asylums for the reception of the idiotic and imbecile is now unquestioned. Not only is it the duty of society to provide for these "feeble ones" but looking at the subject from an economic stand point it is found to be profitable to have institutions specially devoted to their care.

An idiot child in the family of a laboring man is a burden weighing heavily upon him, and may indirectly be the means of rendering the whole family dependent on the state for support.

Under proper training many cases improve to the extent of being able either partially or wholly to earn their living. These cases if left at home, or sent to the poor house, would be a constant expense to their parents or the state and remain through life burdens to society, outside of the circle of active human life and interest.

There is much in the work of training and education of this afflicted class to enlist our sympathy and interest. It is a grand thing to be able to throw even a feeble ray of light into the darkened mind and to develop capabilities for usefulness and enjoyment in those to whom life has heretofore been a dreary blank.

NOTES

1. Vincent de Paul (1581?–1660), French Roman Catholic cleric who founded hospitals and charitable organizations operated by priests and nuns known as Lazarists and Sisters of Charity. See *Webster's Biographical Dictionary* (Springfield, Mass.: Merriam, 1976), 1524.

2. Jean-Marc-Gaspard Itard (1774–1838), French physician who educated Victor, a "sauvage" found near Aveyron in 1799. See Harlan Lane, *The Wild Boy of Aveyron* (Cambridge, Mass.: Harvard University Press, 1976), and Roger Shattuck, *The Forbidden Experiment: The Story of the Wild Boy of Aveyron* (New York: Farrar, Straus, and Giroux, 1980).

3. Johann Jakob Guggenbuhl (1816–1863), Swiss physician whose Abendberg facility treated cretinism with mixed results. See R. C. Scheerenberger, *A History of Mental Retardation* (Baltimore: Brookes, 1983), 70–73.

4. Carl Wilhelm Saegert (?–1879), German teacher of the deaf and dumb who opened a school for idiots near Berlin around 1845. See R. C. Scheerenberger, *A History of Mental Retardation* (Baltimore: Brookes, 1983), 73.

5. Edward Seguin [né Edouard Séguin] (1812–1880), French educator and physician who immigrated to the United States and influenced methods for educating id-

iots. See James W. Trent Jr., *Inventing the Feeble Mind: A History of Mental Retardation in the United States* (Berkeley: University of California Press, 1994), 40–59, and Yves Pelicier and Guy Thullier, *Un pionnier de la psychiatrie de l'enfant: Edouard Séguin (1812–1880)* (Paris: Comité d'histoire de la Sécurité sociale, 1996).

6. George Sumner (1817–1863), American expatriate, lecturer to Americans on European affairs, and the brother of Senator Charles Sumner of Massachusetts. See Robert C. Waterson, "Memoir of George Sumner," *Massachusetts Historical Society Proceedings* 18 (September 1880): 189–223.

7. Frederick F. Backus (1794–1858), physician and New York State legislator who championed legislation for the first publicly supported school for idiots in the United States. See Bernard J. Graney, "Hervey Backus Wilbur and the Evolution of Policies and Practice toward Mentally Retarded People," Ph.D. diss., Syracuse University (1979), 49–53.

8. Samuel Gridley Howe (1801–1876), founding superintendent of the Perkins Institute for the Blind and of the first publicly funded school for idiots. See Harold Schwartz, *Samuel Gridley Howe: Social Reformer, 1801–1876* (Cambridge, Mass.: Harvard University Press, 1956).

9. Hervey Backus Wilbur (1820–1883), founding medical superintendent of the private idiot school at Barre, Massachusetts, and the first superintendent of the New York Asylum for Idiots. See Graney, "Hervey Backus Wilbur."

10. William W. Ireland (1832–1909), medical superintendent of the Scottish National Institution of Imbecile Children and, later, of private schools for such children; author of the first comprehensive book on feeblemindedness, *On Idiocy and Imbecility*, (London: J. & A. Churchill, 1877).

11. Henry M. Knight (1827–1880), superintendent and physician of the Connecticut State School for Idiots and Imbeciles at Lakeville. See "Henry Martyn Knight," in the *National Cyclopedia of American Biography*, vol. 15 (New York: White, 1915), 234–235.

12. George Wallington Grabham (1836–1912). Ireland, in *On Idiocy and Imbecility*, quotes Grabham, J. Langdon Down's successor at the Earlswood Asylum: "In many patients general sensation is very low in degree, the extraction of a tooth causing little or no pain. I have more than once or twice seen a comparatively intelligent boy sit quietly in a chair while his toe-nail was removed, requiring no one to hold him, and uttering no exclamation, but looking on as if interested, and stating that the operation did not hurt him" (256). On Grabham's fascinating career as a medical official in England and in New Zealand, see K. A. Simpson, "Grabham, George Wallington," in *A Dictionary of New Zealand Biography*, vol. 2 (1870–1900) (Auckland: Auckland University Press, 1994), 174–175.

13. Ludvig Vilhem Dahl (1826–1890), Danish-Norwegian physician at the asylum at Gaustad, interested in the inheritance of mental disability.

14. Félix Voisin (1794–1872), French alienist and associate of Edouard Séguin at

the Bicêtre asylum. A phrenologist, Voisin stressed the organic basis of intellectual disabilities. See René Semelaigne, *Les pionniers de la psychiatrice française avant et aprés Pinel* (Paris: J. B. Baillière, 1930), 180–184.

15. J. Langdon Down (1826–1896), medical superintendent at the Idiot Asylum at Earlswood (1858–1868) who identified the syndrome that bears his name. See O. Conor Ward, *John Langdon Down: A Caring Pioneer* (London: Royal Society of Medicine Press, 1998), and David Wright's article in this volume.

16. Moritz Jastrowitz (1839–1912), German neurologist whose 1871 studies of encephalitis and myelitis described spinal and brain tissue abnormalities in so-called congenital idiocy.

17. Auguste Félix Voisin (1829–1898), son of Félix Voisin (see note 14); French alienist known for his interest in hypnotism, heredity, and brain pathology. See "Auguste Voisin, Paris, 25 mai 1829–22 juin 1898; discours pronouncés sur la tombe de Auguste Voisin le 25 juin 1898" (Paris, 1898).

1

The Legacy of the Almshouse

Philip M. Ferguson

The nineteenth-century history of increasing government involvement in the lives of people judged mentally retarded begins with the rise of the almshouse. The role of the almshouses in the history of social policy toward severely retarded people (and all disabled people), however, tends to be overlooked in many accounts of the topic. For most of the nineteenth century, there were more so-called idiots living in these county and city institutions than in the large state asylums. For the most part, their treatment in these almshouses can only be described as abominable; a sort of passive neglect was the best they could hope for. Neglect was especially preferred as a treatment for those people judged to be both insane and violent (going by contemporary descriptions, some of these cases would today be labeled intellectually disabled or autistic). The notorious "crazy cellars" or dungeons held these poor souls: naked, chained, without heat or light.

However, beyond confining many people identified as idiots, the almshouse is important because it began in both policy and practice the approach to chronicity that later became the basis of asylum organization for severely retarded residents. The connection between the almshouse and the later asylums on this conceptual level has simply not been adequately examined. Making that connection allows one to see that the segmentation of idiot asylum history into eras of optimism followed by custodialism overlooks the thematic strands of medical incurability, economic uselessness, moral intractability, and aesthetic offensiveness that weave their way through the pattern of nineteenth-century practice. Those strands were first stitched together in the patchwork of county and municipal almshouses that arose throughout the Northeast in the first half of the nineteenth century.

It is certainly true that people had made the basic distinction between acute and chronic before the almshouses hit their stride in the antebellum years, even if all of the various dimensions of that distinction had not yet been elaborated. The Elizabethan Poor Laws, on which earliest colonial poor relief was based, made a crucial distinction between those sick, "impotent," and unable to work on the one hand and those sturdy but idle souls who were able but unwilling to work on the other. "Suitable" treatment followed. As early as 1751, the overseers of the poor in Boston contrasted the able-bodied paupers with the "distracted, helpless and infirm people" (cited in Jimenez, 1987, p. 55). Too many of the latter group, the overseers argued, kept the workhouse from being self-supporting. Furthermore, the American reformers knew their history well enough to identify the ancestry of such divisions of the poor as were "still presented to our notice" (New York State Board of Charities, 1869, Annual Report, p. 1).[1] What occurred in the early part of the nineteenth century was that this distinction became intensified and focused in the specific institutional form of the almshouse itself. Very quickly that distinction revealed the impossible dichotomy of purpose that masqueraded as a unified policy. "There should be one rule for every poor-house: Support for the infirm and helpless; hard work for the sturdy and strong" (NYSBC, 1869, p. lviii).

Unfortunately, even those reporting on the dismal results and the contradictory nature of the almshouses saw the solution in further specialization and intensification of service. The contradiction perpetuated itself. Dorothea Dix, an indefatigable investigator and spokeswoman on the evils of the almshouse for insane and idiotic people, made the people housed in the "crazy cellars" the focus of her numerous appeals for legislative action. In 1844, Dix visited New York to plead the institutional case even though the state had already established one such insane asylum in Utica. Her report on her visits to the counties of New York State is similar to many others she gave, yet affecting in its starkness. Dix's description of the accommodations for "a gibbering idiot, or a cowering imbecile, or perhaps a murmuring half demented creature" (Dix, 1844, p 110) is bluntly worded despite her constant "feminine" demurrals of embarrassment. The solution for Dix was not to return the sufferers to their families with ample "outdoor" support. She criticized family care of disabled relatives even more harshly than she did the almshouses. Instead, Dix became one of the earlier supporters of purely custodial state asylums for the incurably insane and idiotic (Dix, p. 67).

This chapter examines how in the short span of about twenty years the criticisms of a Dorothea Dix in 1844 came to replace the solicitations of a John Yates (secretary of state for New York) in 1824 to establish county almshouses to control and reform the idle poor. From this examination emerge three main points that form the basis for the interpretation of later developments in the specialized idiot asylums.

First, almshouses established the ultimately contradictory alms of deterring laziness, yet caring for the helpless in one and the same facility. The tension in this approach carried over into a clear, if unannounced, resistance among many poor people to the state's latest efforts to control their behavior. Poor families, including those with mentally retarded dependents, were not passive recipients of whatever poor relief the state and counties decided to give them. Some basic and sketchy demographics of those who lived in almshouses and of the changing composition of the inmates suggest that both state policy and the adaptability of the working poor affected the nature and function of the almshouse.

Second, the outcomes of chronicity were first institutionalized in the push of the almshouse movement for firmer distinctions between the able-bodied poor and the "truly needy," to borrow a phrase from a more recent era. The connection of chronic poverty with the officially proclaimed hopelessness of clinical prognoses began a line in the almshouse that one can follow down through the idiot asylums, perhaps even to policy debates of our own day. The spread of the wage labor system and commercial competitiveness in both urban and rural parts of the Northeast becomes a key to understanding the unavoidability of the connection.

Finally, the outcomes of remedial futility and economic poverty together bolstered a third outcome of chronicity (not new in itself), in the form of custodialism as not merely socially appropriate but also morally laudable. Custodialism, as a form of care, became the virtuous response of civic fathers to the reproachable sloth or burdensome incapacity of the chronic poor. The almshouse started an American tradition of formalized custodialism in its more vicious forms that tied economic failure and social deviance to moral categories and individual inadequacy.

These outcomes of chronicity functioned, then, as nonthreatening, reductionist explanations of systemic failure. The institutionalization of mentally retarded people in America began with the almshouses in the eighteenth and early nineteenth centuries, not with the first specialized idiot asylums of the 1850s and 1860s. The transition from the almshouse to the idiot asylum as the approved receptacle for poor idiots was, in fact, marked more by the continuities of the two models than by the disruptions. The almshouse system remains today largely in the form of nursing homes for elderly poor people. The legacy of its past, however, still influences the terms of debates on how best to serve disabled people. That legacy begins in the colonial era.

The Colonial Era

In colonial times, the connection between poverty and mental disability was overt and unquestioned. Disability was simply one of the many possible versions of dependency. Society did not become involved unless the economic stability of the family was threatened. Indeed, for practical purposes, the important distinction was one of dependency, not disability. The community concern was for those who, for whatever reason, could not make their own way in the world or be carried along by their families. Whether you could not walk or talk, or were old or orphaned, widowed or homeless, the etiology of your indigence was seldom an urgent question. What mattered to the community was, first, whether you were a resident; second, who would care for you; and third, how the provisions for care were to be handled.

In 1637, in what is probably the earliest surviving reference to idiocy among America's settlers, one Ambrose Harmor of the Jamestown settlement wrote a letter to England. He requested that the Crown provide him with an estate because of his extra burden of caring for "Benomie Buck, an idiot, the first in the plantation" (cited in Hecht and Hecht, 1973, pp. 174–75). In Massachusetts in 1680–81, extended court proceedings were conducted to determine whether the town of Taunton or Plymouth should bear the cost and responsibility of caring for John Harmon, a "decriped" pauper (Demos, 1970, p. 80). Even in these earliest days, the institutional solution to communal responsibility for feeble-minded citizens can be found. Perhaps the first retarded person to be institutionalized in North America was one Pierre Chevallier, admitted in 1694 to the Hospital General Charon in Ontario as a forty-four-year-old "innocent." He remained there until his death in 1735 (Griffin and Greenland, 1981).

Maintaining the Family

The first line of relief was certainly the family. However, disputes were fairly frequent over where responsibility rested when family support failed. The prevailing attitude does not seem to have been particularly sympathetic. One source reports that some communities forced the town paupers to wear brightly colored badges on their shirts, emblazoned with the letter "P" (Schneider and Deutsch, 1941, p. 4). While the basic procedure was common, at least in the Northeast, specific decisions over the nature and source of support became increasingly problematic throughout the colonial period and even into the 1800s (Yates, [1824] 1901).

Should the family falter, the normal community response was first to provide the support needed to keep the natural family intact. The town saw the stability of the family as usually the least expensive means of support, and thus maintenance of the family was viewed as fiscally prudent as well as Providentially ordained. "The catalyst for community involvement was the threatened disruption of the family unit; when insanity imperiled social stability, traditional criteria and means of relief were used. The needs of the insane and the needs of society were not in conflict and both were best served through supporting traditional roles for the family" (Rosenkrantz and Vinovskis, 1979, p. 191).

One common means of local support for disabled people, then, was direct support to the family involved, in the form of either straightforward cash payments or allocations of food and other supplies from the common stock kept by many communities for just such purposes. If such aid was not possible—because the person either had no family or was too disruptive to remain at home—then the person might be "bound out," or assigned to a designated guardian within another household in the community. In 1651, Roger Williams wrote a letter asking the Providence town council to make some such provisions for a woman who had become "distracted" (Rochefort, 1981, p. 113). By 1742, the Rhode Island colony had officially authorized town councils to assume full responsibility for the care of mentally disabled people and to name guardians of their estates as well as of their persons, when needed.

Sometimes the secular authorities came in conflict with the churches. Mary P. Ryan's account of life in and around Utica in the early nineteenth century (1981) shows how the various churches might step in with aid if they thought the town too hasty in breaking up a family through the binding-out process. Rural New York was still relying on the old colonial procedures in 1823, when the case of a Mrs. Startman is recorded in the minutes of the business meeting of Utica's First Presbyterian Church: "Mr. White reported that the town poor master would not extend relief to Mrs. Startman and family without the liberty of binding out her children" (cited in Ryan, 1981, p. 23). The church moved in with some direct support in an effort to keep the family together. Whether natural or assigned, then, the family unit was the centerpiece of local relief efforts.

> The actions of both the town and the church, in binding out children and the granting of relief, were supplementary to a basically household method of providing for the dependent population. . . . Neither required an independent agency or institution, be it an orphanage or a welfare bureau, to intercede in the relations of family, church, and town. Both relied on the household, either that of a subsidized widow or the one to which a dependent child might be bound out, as the basic location of this social service. The aged as well as widows and orphans could be accommodated within this system. (Ryan, 1981, pp. 23–24)

The Treatment of Strangers

Another feature of colonial poor relief, and one that became increasingly troublesome for municipalities to administer, was the method of determining the residency of a pauper and thereby the town responsibilities for his or her care. Settlement laws governing such town determinations became increasingly complex until, by the time of the Yates report on New York, in 1824, some 1,800 paupers—including 600 children—were moved from one town to another through legal warrants, at an expense "far exceeding $25,000." The cost of appeals by receiving towns added $13,500. According to Yates, the total expenditures in transportation and legal fees would have supported 1,283 paupers for a year (Yates, [1824] 1901, p. 946). Jimenez (1987, p. 54) reports that, in 1762, Boston officials even paid the entire cost of sending an insane pauper all the way back to Guernsey rather than assume responsibility for his care. Towns often accepted responsibility for their own citizens with some equanimity, if not generosity. Poverty was part of God's universe, an unavoidable element of the community. However, any possibility that the legal residency of the person might be assigned to another town was usually thoroughly explored. Responsibility to help extended to one's neighbor, not to strangers.

In their efforts to shave costs or avoid new ones, towns even devised methods to restrict the numbers of indigents further. Poor strangers were "warned out" of town before they could become legal residents. Some civic leaders apparently showed their fiscal responsibility by spiriting poor disabled residents into the next town at night. Klebaner (1976, p. 596) reports that Onondaga County, in upstate New York, commonly smuggled paupers into a neighboring county in a conspiracy between justices of the peace and overseers of the poor. "Many Massachusetts towns were alleged to engage in the happy practice of providing for the able-bodied state paupers (from whom labor could be gotten) while sending along the aged and infirm of this category to Boston" (Klebaner, p. 596).

Gradually, various direct or indirect subsidies of cash or supplies to families of the poor came to be known as outdoor relief. The term referred to any response that kept the poor person outside the almshouse. Technically, such remedies did not include binding out, which, together with apprenticeship, became increasingly impracticable in view of the growing reliance on wage labor. Outdoor relief became the target of reformist criticism as wasteful and indulgent of vagrancy. For the truly disabled person, outdoor relief was said to be simply inhumane. A new system, the almshouse, spread from the largest cities to dominate the secular systems of poor relief in the first years of the nineteenth century.

The picture we are left with of colonial treatment of insane and idiotic people is direct and uncomplicated, if not especially benevolent. The poor were seen mainly as an ordained part of the social structure. For the disabled population, poor or not, there was often little optimism about improving their condition. For the wealthy, though, this was simply a private trouble, not a public issue (Mills, 1959). If medical treatment was even available, it was usually harsh, ineffective, debilitating, or fatal. The disabled poor were surely visible in the community and were often maintained at home, as well. As with the poor in general, however, coercion, control, and cost containment could easily overrule even the reverence for family stability (Rosenkrantz and Vinovskis, 1979, p. 91). There was certainly a willingness to shun, segregate, and secure the most chronic, unproductive members of the colonies, especially if they were also disruptive in some way. Nonetheless, the public approach remained a local issue, with only the beginnings of larger governmental involvement through the occasional almshouse and hospital.

The Rise and Fall of the Almshouse: A Haven for the Dying and Disabled Poor

Only in such large population centers as New York City (1736), Boston (1664), and Philadelphia (1732) did the alternative of the almshouse become a major factor in poor relief in the colonial period. However, where it did arise, the almshouse from the beginning was the acknowledged last resort for the most troublesome or disabled cases. In most of these early almshouses, most of the inmates were seriously disabled or infirm.

Rothman (1971) analyzed the records of fifty admissions to the New York City almshouse from 1736 through 1746 (all that have survived out of probably 200 total admissions). "One-quarter of them were lame or blind, insane or idiotic; another quarter were not only very old but infirm, sickly, and weak" (p. 39). From this he concludes: "It is apparent that the institution held the exceptional case. The New York poor did not live in constant dread of the poorhouse" (p. 39). Even if the general, able-bodied poor had no such dread, however, one must wonder if the disabled pauper could have been free of such fear. This pattern continued for the other early almshouses, too. The "Book of Daily Occurrences" for the Philadelphia General Hospital (or Blockley, as it was better known) describes its youthful admissions in particular as cases of "feigned deafness, idiotic children, consumptive children" and other victims of disease or violence (Radbill, 1976, p. 752). Bellevue, in New York, and Kings County Hospital, in Brooklyn, also functioned, for most practical purposes, as free hospitals and orphanages for the poor (Klebaner, 1976, p. 207). Indeed, the poor were the only ones who would have used a hospital at all. Throughout the nineteenth century, for most Americans, "the word 'hospital' evoked emotions from fear to sheer terror. Hospitals were frequently associated with the poorest class and the makeshift pesthouses for victims of the much dreaded yellow fever and cholera epidemic" (Mottus, 1983, p. 1). By 1800, then, the almshouse of the large city was, both in fact and certainly in common perception, a home for hopeless causes. That status was to change fairly rapidly in the first fifty years of the new century.

The Jacksonian Reform Era

The big push for almshouses coincided with the rise in institutional solutions for all types of devalued, or simply nonproductive, groups of people. The period from roughly 1820 to 1850 saw a massive shift in the direction of both welfare and educational policy in the Northeast. The first school for the deaf, the first school for the blind, the first reformatory, the first large public insane asylum, the first idiot asylum, all got their start in this period in Massachusetts or New York.[2] Public education gained momentum and gradually became accepted by families of both the lower and the expanding middle classes (Katz, 1976). Elite boarding schools for children of the wealthy began in this period. The number of hospitals almost tripled between 1826 and 1850, from seventeen to forty-nine (Mottus, 1983). And, finally, there were the almshouses.

The almshouse went from an unpopular last resort in a few large cities and towns to the common practice of counties and cities across the Northeast and the Northwest. In 1824, three years after the famous Quincy report, there were some eighty-three almshouses in Massachusetts. By 1850, there were 204 (Klebaner, 1976, p. 74). When Secretary of State Yates surveyed poor relief in New York State in 1824, he found that 30 of the 130 cities and towns responding reported having an almshouse. Following Yates's suggestion to move to a county system, New York had almshouses in fifty-six of sixty counties by 1857, not counting the municipal almshouses that continued in some of the biggest cities (Report of Select Committee of New York Senate, [1857] 1976). In fact (though the law was repealed twenty-five years later), New York in 1824 mandated the establishment in each county of both an almshouse and a county superintendent of the poor (Schneider and Deutsch, 1941, p. 7). By the 1830s, a mill-town district in Pennsylvania would not show a trace of any disabled poor remaining in the town:

> Members of [the indigent poor] class of people were not visible in Rockdale, however, because, being unable to take care of themselves, they were for the most part housed in the "House of Employment" at Media, several miles away. This lowest group, physically extruded from the community and supported at public expense . . . included the insane, the mentally retarded, the chronically ill and handicapped, young orphans, some deserted

wives or widows with children too young to work, and no doubt one or two who simply could not seem to manage without constant supervision. (Wallace, 1978, pp. 44–45)

The official and unofficial calls for the installation of an almshouse system of poor relief almost always made two points. First, the care of lunatics, idiots, the aged, and the infirm was said to be much more humane with centralized and enlightened administration and housing. One of Yates's major criticisms was that "Idiots and lunatics do not receive sufficient care and attention in towns, where no suitable asylums for their reception are established" (Yates, [1824] 1901, p. 952). The second type of argument was the more negative one that outdoor relief was needlessly extravagant and unavoidably supportive of the very habits that produced the able-bodied pauper's indigence. Quincy concluded that "of all modes of providing for the poor, the most wasteful, the most expensive, and most injurious to their morals and destructive of their industrious habits is that of *supply* in their own families" (Quincy, [1821] 1971, p. 9).

The town of New Bedford, Massachusetts, reported that much the same reasoning lay behind its decision to open an almshouse in 1817, and the point again emerges that the two reasons were contradictory and antagonistic. On the one hand, custodial but kindly care was to be given to disabled people and the elderly. Yet, on the other hand, conditions were to be severe enough to deter the able-bodied poor from even applying for admission. Furthermore, the almshouses were also to be workhouses. Once inside, able-bodied poor were supposedly to work hard and long in facilities designed to house the chronically helpless and unproductive. The ultimate goal was to firmly separate the unproductive from the marketplace, leaving a working class "stripped for action" in the newly competitive society (Braverman, 1974; Katz, 1984; Katz, Doucet, and Stern, 1982).

Initially, the almshouses enjoyed at least partial success. There was little humanity or kindness in their custody of the helpless, but the poor tried hard to keep from being admitted. Even though outdoor relief was drastically curtailed from the 1820s through the 1840s, the almshouses continued to be populated largely by the chronically dependent classes of people. Yates termed them "permanent paupers" and found that almost two-thirds (65 percent) of the New York City inmates fit the description, including fifty-six idiots, thirty-five "palsey," and thirty-two "cripples" (Yates, [1824] 1901, p. 1011). The Massachusetts Pauper Abstracts from 1837 to 1860 list from one-third to one-half of inmates as "unable to perform any labor" (Report of the Special Joint Committee, [1859] 1976). In 1848, the main Philadelphia almshouse had a total of 1,588 inmates, but only 79 in male working wards. More than 700 resided in the hospital and lunatic asylum, and 540 in the wards for old men, old women, and the incurable (Klebaner, 1976, p. 21). Even the records of a rural county like Seneca, in the Finger Lakes region of New York, showed that, in the township of Seneca Falls, between 1842 and 1847, some 61 percent of the native-born men were classed as having some physical or mental disability (Altschuler and Saltzgaber, 1984, p. 582). From the other perspective, both newspaper accounts and observers' notes from the period make it clear that there continued to be a widely held aversion among the poor to going to the almshouse.

The Failure of Reform: Poverty and Chronicity

In a shift that began by the 1850s, most of the almshouses in New York State came to expend most of their relief on temporary shelter to able-bodied but unemployed people. Evidence suggests that in many locales, the working classes came to use the nearest poorhouse as a place of shelter in the winter or as temporary respite at other times when they traveled around the state looking for work. Lunatics and idiots still made up a sizable portion of the almshouse population, but they and the elderly were the only ones to stay for long stretches of time (Altschuler and Saltzgaber, 1984, p. 577).

Still, in an 1856 survey of "charitable institutions" around the state, a New York Senate committee commented on the continued disdain of the almshouse shown by most poor people. The tone of the remarks shows the humanitarian side of social welfare policy. In fact, the report in its entirety is a good example of the dichotomous instincts of reformers of this era that are so strikingly depicted in Rothman's *The Discovery of the Asylum* (1971) and that were at the contradictory core of the almshouse model. The reformers' optimistic belief in the curative powers of social engineering was matched by the darker fears that creeping chaos would ensue if the lower levels of society were left to their own devices. The poor were to be both comforted and controlled in the attitudes of those calling for more and more segregative facilities. If those attitudes were to accomplish their goal in practice, confinement had to be made more acceptable.

Poorhouses, properly conducted, might be what they were originally designed to be, comfortable asylums for worthy indigence. To suffer them to become unsuitable refuges for the virtuous poor, and mainly places of confinement for the degraded, is to pervert their main purpose; and the present management of them is such that decent poverty is virtually excluded until the last extremity of pauperism is reached, when the necessity of supporting mere existence compels it reluctantly to seek the scanty comforts of a poor house rather than to suffer the horrors of starvation outside. (Report of Select Committee, [1857] 1976, p. 6)

Most writings of this era were not nearly so beneficent in spirit; for most, the phrase "virtuous poverty" or "decent poverty" bordered on oxymoron. Even here, however, the antagonistic logic is conveyed. In colonial times, disability entailed poverty or dependence; either family or state had to step in to avert destitution. By 1850, the logic had reversed. *True* or *justifiable* poverty entailed disability, at least in the sense of explanation; the economic system would not allow capacity and effort to go unrewarded. This was the credo of the new commercial capitalists. Poverty, therefore, was either the avoidable result of individual laziness or intemperance or, if unavoidable, the empirical proof of chronic incapacity. The continued existence of gratuitous poverty in the new culture indicated natural, not social, deficiency. Most poverty was the justified result of evil or indolence, not virtue; what poverty remained was the residue of disease.

It was poverty that had to be explained now, not disability. The moral dimension augmented the economic and clinical dimensions. This moral augmentation is captured only two paragraphs below the passage just quoted. The ethical dichotomy of purposes was unnoticed by the writers, to be sure, and even more powerful because the contrast was unintentional: "Although pauperism is not in itself a crime, yet that kind of poverty which ends in a poor house, unless it is the result of disease, infirmity, or age, producing a positive inability to earn a livelihood, is not unusually the result of such self-indulgence, unthrift, excess, or idleness, as is next kin to criminality" (Report of Select Committee, [1857] 1976, p. 7).

In a survey of Connecticut towns in 1852, the General Assembly found only one town that attributed its increasing number of paupers to unemployment (another town rather tautologically found the cause of its increase in paupers to be a growth of poverty). Almost all of the 130 other towns that

51

replied attributed their pauperism to intemperance or immigration (Report of the Committee, [1852] 1976). Indeed, the very use of the noun "unemployment" to mean forced idleness was not to occur in print in America until 1887 (Keyssar, 1986, p. 4). Given the era's moral understanding of heredity, even lunacy and idiocy, if not the direct results of vile habits, were the legacy of intemperate parents. Pauperism was a moral choice, even a physical disease, as much as an economic outcome.

The Failure of Reform: A Description

The almshouse system in New York by 1860, then, embodied all of the ambivalence and contradiction inherent in the attitudes and practices of those in power toward the poor, disabled or not. The almshouse also shows the systemic effect of the rise of capitalism, with its boom-and-bust cycles and its need for a fluid but quiescent workforce (Scull, 1979, 1980). Most particularly, the almshouse shows that custodial incarceration of idiots did not begin in 1870 or so with the decline of the specialized asylums but rather was the continuing practice, and even policy, from the first almshouse institutions. As always, perhaps the most amazing numbers are those of the retarded people who remained in the community, living with family or friends.

Some Basic Numbers

Before interpreting these developments at more length, some simple numbers are needed to indicate where mentally retarded people were located in the middle of the nineteenth century. Table 1.1 is a compilation of the results from the New York Senate Survey of Charitable Institutions published in 1857. The survey covered all of the almshouses in the state, including the facilities in Kings County (Brooklyn) and New York City (Manhattan). The table shows numbers of inmates at almshouses in eight selected upstate counties, both urban (Albany, Erie, Monroe) and rural (Clinton, Schoharie, Seneca), as well as the two complexes in Brooklyn and New York City. The numbers for New York City are incomplete since the "average number of inmates" figure includes only the single building specifically designated as the almshouse, while all of the other numbers for the city apparently cover the entire welfare complex on several islands.

Table 1.1

Inmate Distribution in Selected City Almshouses of New York State in 1856

County	Inmates	Avg. No. Children under 16 Years	Total No. of Lunatics	Idiots	Deaths (%)	
Albany	350	80	7	34	71	(20%)
Broome	45	5	21	11	1	(2%)
Clinton	65	11	6	10	15	(23%)
Erie	300	75	71	11	83	(28%)
Monroe	360	75	28	8	46	(13%)
Oneida	222	42	3	13	–	(NA)
Schoharie	60	7	2	10	7	(12%)
Seneca	60	6	7	3	7	(12%)
Kings	1,365	424	20	59	342	(25%)
New York City	1,220	1,500	597	135	257	(21%)
State Totals	7,619	3,255	1,644	424	1,385	(18%)

Source: "Report of the Select Committee Appointed to Visit Charitable Institutions Supported by the State, and All City and County Poor and Work Houses and Jails," New York Senate Documents, 1857, no. 8 (Albany, 1859).

For the entire state, the average was 4.96 idiots in each of the fifty-five county almshouses (not including New York City and Kings County), compared with 15.2 lunatics. Overall, some 5.5 percent of almshouse residents were labeled idiots, and 16.8 percent were labeled lunatics. If New York City and Kings County are included, the percentage stays the same for idiots (probably because of an almost certain underreporting in Kings County) but climbs to 21.5 percent for lunatics. At the time of this survey, the Idiot Asylum at Syracuse had been open for about five years and had 104 children in residence. By comparison, there were 424 idiots reported in the almshouses, although most of those were more than sixteen years of age and technically ineligible for admission to Syracuse. The death rates probably speak for themselves. They confirm what the figures here do not show, that large numbers of elderly and infirm poor people continued to come—or be left—to die in the almshouses. For the entire state, some 18 percent of almshouse inmates died in 1856. However, even granting an enfeebled clientele, places where frequently more than one-fifth of the residents died each year were little more than segregated warehouses for the inconveniently old and ill.

The New York City charities commissioners bluntly stated the existing policy, one that almost flaunted a death rate as proof of a job well done. "Care has been taken not to diminish the terrors of this last resort of poverty because it has been deemed better that a few should test the minimum rate at which existence can be preserved, than that the many should find the poorhouse so comfortable a home that they would brave the shame of pauperism to gain admission to it" (New York City Board of Charities and Correction, 1876, pp. viii–ix).

The Range of Conditions

The death rate numbers fail to indicate the conditions (especially for lunatics and idiots) that contributed to so many deaths. The reformatory spirit of the Senate report in 1857 led to specific descriptions of the accommodations of every almshouse. In general, the committee found:

> The treatment of lunatics and idiots in these houses is frequently abusive. The cells and sheds where they are confined are wretched abodes, often wholly unprovided with bedding. In most cases, female lunatics had none but male attendants. Instances were testified to of the *whipping* of male and female idiots and lunatics, and of confining the latter in loathsome cells, and binding them with chains. . . . In some poor houses, the committee found lunatics, both male and female, in cells, in a state of nudity. The cells were intolerably offensive, littered with the long accumulated filth of the occupants, and with straw reduced to chaff by long use as bedding, portions of which, mingled with the Filth, adhered to the persons of the inmates and formed the only covering they had. (Report of Select Committee, [1857] 1976, p. 4; emphasis in original)

Of course, situations differed, and some almshouses were better than others. The Albany City and County Poor House was apparently one of the better ones. Its four buildings, including a pesthouse and a separate insane asylum, adjoined a 216-acre farm, and all able male inmates were apparently expected to work the farm. Among almshouses, farm work was seen as a way of cutting the costs of maintenance and also of teaching good habits of work to the able-bodied inmates; the farm colonies used on many of the large idiot asylums several decades later originated apparently in the almshouses. Such farms, however, failed in their cost-efficiency goal at both the almshouses and the asylums. Whether industrious habits were learned is unknown. The Albany house even had a school for the children, with a full-time teacher instructing them in speaking, reading, and writing English. A physician's daily visits were supplemented by visits from medical students at the local school.

And, although no treatment was given for the lunatics and idiots, seven cases of insanity were listed as cured.

At the other end of the spectrum were places like the Clinton County House, located outside Plattsburg. One "dilapidated" building housed an average of sixty-five inmates. There was no ventilation system, but there were so many cracks and crevices in the walls that in the winter "snow blowing through the crevices forms banks" (Report of Select Committee, [1857] 1976, p. 36). There was no attempt to separate inmates by age, disability, or sex. Indeed, men and women were allowed to "mingle promiscuously." There were no knives and forks, but perhaps there was little need. Until just prior to the inspection, the diet reportedly consisted of "pea and bran soup; Indian pudding and sweetened water" (p. 37).

There were six lunatics and ten idiots who apparently received especially gruesome treatment. Two lunatics never left their cells and were chained to the floor, with straw for a bed. Balls and chains on some were also used for restraint. Whipping was practiced. The committee summed up their feelings that "this house is a very poor one, indifferently kept, and a disgrace to the county in which it is located" (p. 38).

The New York City Almshouse

Special notice must be given to the Almshouse Department of New York City. In size and complexity, it was an entity unto itself. Prisons, workhouses, hospitals, orphanages, insane asylums, so-called colored houses, and even an almshouse proper were distributed throughout the city. Between 7,000 and 8,000 people were confined at any given time in the 1850s. Many of the specialized asylums were located on small islands in the East Fiver (Blackwell's and Randall's). Although it was not yet officially listed as a separate facility, there was separate housing for twenty-eight idiots on Randall's Island, near the nursery. When H. B. Wilbur was opening the state asylum for idiots in Albany (and later in Syracuse), he reported visiting Randall's Island to pick out some severely retarded children for his school. The committee was impressed, although there is no indication that anything other than separate facilities was given to these twenty-eight inmates. Certainly, the committee recognized the helplessness of the idiots that they saw at Randall's Island. "The committee were gratified to find that this unfortunate and generally neglected class here received that particular care and attention which their helpless condition requires, and that it is intended to secure for them all the benefit that they can receive from such special efforts for their improvements as are deemed practicable" (Report of Select Committee, [1857] 1976, p. 164). More than 100 other idiots, probably adults or multiply handicapped people of any age, did not receive these "special efforts."

The Legacy of the Almshouse Chronicity and Custodialism

By the end of the nineteenth century, almshouses were largely poorhouses for the elderly, the institutional precursors of today's network of nursing homes (Katz, 1984, 1986). By 1900, very few people labeled as insane were still living in county almshouses: 39 out of 5,602 total population in September 1901 (NYSBC, 1901, pp. 70, 74). Some 540 "feeble-minded or idiotic" people still lived in county almshouses, amounting to almost 10 percent of the total county almshouse population (NYSBC, 1901, pp. 75, 80). Certainly the early hopes and good intentions of the Jacksonian reformers in the 1820s had long since gone by the board. Almshouses were never really "workhouses"—self-supporting havens for the helpless and vocational training for the idle. In their failure to meet stated objectives, the almshouses contributed only the first of many disappointments to result from the institutional path taken in the antebellum years. The purpose of reviewing that failure is to establish the connection of the almshouse to the idiot asylum, which followed the very same path. There is one continuous line of concept and practice begun in the straw-covered cells of the almshouse and continuing through the back wards of the specialized prisons called asylums for the feeble-minded.

Three main points emerge from this examination of the role of almshouses in the nineteenth century. They outline a legacy for the idiot asylums that has been largely ignored by historians of mental retardation in the nineteenth century.

Contradictory Purposes

First, the almshouse failed because, as pointed out by Katz (1984), their contradictory purposes were never reconcilable. From their earliest colonial incarnations, almshouses were meant as homes for the helpless. With the reforms of the 1820s, following the Yates Report in New York, almshouses were also meant to serve the new function of imposing discipline and control upon the labor market. The able-bodied poor were meant to be deterred from even wanting to enter the almshouse but also, once inside, to be put to work. Certainly, the figures show that the number of disabled people supported by the almshouses as a percentage of the total inmate census did go down.

The story was the same or similar outside New York. The Pauper Abstracts in Massachusetts show that the number of idiots in that state's almshouses declined from 370 in 1837 to 306 in 1858 (reaching a low of 280 in 1856), while the total number of state paupers almost tripled (4,846 to 14,016) between 1837 and 1858 (Report of the Special Joint Committee, [1859] 1976, p. 131). Despite this increase in the number of the so-called able-bodied poor, the almshouses were never self-sufficient. Indeed, in Massachusetts, the value of inmate labor actually declined (Report of the Special Joint Committee, p. 131).

Some recent studies of almshouse history suggest that part of the reason for these numbers is that the working classes gradually came to use the almshouses for their own purposes in their struggle to survive in the new economy. One study of Seneca County in New York shows clearly that, while county officials were trying to use the almshouse as a kind of clearinghouse for redistributing paupers elsewhere, the poor were equally keen on using the almshouse as temporary shelter in moving as the seasons changed or as they moved from town to town (Altschuler and Saltzgaber, 1984). It was not just paupers who were using the almshouse but also temporarily unemployed members of the working class. Increasingly the almshouses became almost a network of hostels for temporary respite as the unemployed traveled the country looking for wage labor. On the basis of the results of his detailed analysis of the Erie County almshouse, Katz concludes:

> Its occupants, in general, were not passive, degraded paupers who drifted into poorhouses, where they lived out their lives in dependent torpor. On the contrary, most remained only for a short period. Whatever the official purposes of the poorhouse, the poor themselves put it to their own uses: in its early years as a short-term residence for native families in distress; and in later years, as a place to stay for a while during harsh seasons of the year, unemployment, or family crisis; as a hospital in which unmarried women could have their children; and, of course, as a place of last resort for the sick, helpless, and elderly. (Katz, 1983, p. 87)

From a narrower perspective, this change in the poorhouse population reveals a pattern that repeats throughout the history of the institutionalization of mentally retarded people—the rate of idiots left at large in the community remained much higher than the rate for the insane, with whom they were so often paired in statistics and conception. Whether or not the census data are reliable, the important point is that those who collected and those who reported cases of insanity and idiocy "saw" much more madness than imbecility about them. And the madness seemed to be spreading. As we saw, 21.5 percent of the inmates in New York in 1857 were classed as insane, compared with 5.5 percent for idiots (Report of Select Committee, [1857] 1976). The Pauper Abstracts for Massachusetts show a decrease in the number of idiots from 1837 to 1858, but the number of insane for the same period rose almost 60 percent. By 1857, in Massachusetts, the three state insane asylums housed an additional 400 insane paupers (Report of the Special Joint Committee, [1859] 1976, pp. 131-32). Perhaps most intriguing of all is what Edward Jarvis (a colleague of Howe's and an important statistician of insanity) found in Massachusetts in 1855: of 1,087 idiots identified, fully 60 percent were independent, compared with only 42 percent of the insane (Jarvis, [1855] 1971, p. 100). The reasons for the relatively low rates of institutionalization of idiots compared with lunatics are not entirely clear, but the pattern of admission clearly is one more source of continuity between the almshouse and the asylum.

Chronicity and Poverty

Perhaps the most important distinction in an entire century of increasingly specialized distinctions among segments of the poor was that between deserving and nondeserving paupers. It is here that the conceptual connection between chronicity and the economics of uselessness became institutionalized.

Several writers have detailed the changes in economic and social structure and their effects on welfare policy during the nineteenth century (Braverman, 1974; Katz, 1978, 1986; Piven and Cloward, 1972; Scull, 1979). For purposes of this study, the rise of commercial capitalism, not industrialization or urbanization—which came, for the most part, after the Civil War—best explains the need to rationalize and discipline a workforce new to the requirements of wage labor. As labor itself became a market in the new republic, more careful welfare policies that did not indiscriminately reward both the truly helpless and the merely lazy or intemperate were needed. Outdoor relief was seen as incompatible with a productive workforce. Centralized "indoor" relief models that were seen as more controllable and more rational ways to give out support replaced the distribution of "outdoor" payments. The point was to deter the pauper from ever entering the almshouse or, failing that, to make sure that those who should be working were separated from those legitimately excused. The latter were an inescapable burden, but the former were both a threat to be subdued and a challenge to be reformed. Both groups were defined by their relationship to productivity and "contribution." Jarvis was plain on the important elements of relief for the "truly needy":

> In whatever way we look at them, these lunatics [including idiots] are a burden upon the Commonwealth. The curable during their limited period of disease, and the incurable during the remainder of their lives, not only cease to produce, but they must eat the bread they do not earn, and consume the substance they do not create, receiving their sustenance from the treasury of the Commonwealth or of some of its towns, or from the income or capital of some of its members. (Jarvis, [1855] 1971, p. 104)

There was no obligation to feed without compensation those who were idiotic, insane, elderly, or orphaned. The new system demanded that "want" should serve as "the stimulus to the capable" (Scull, 1980, p. 41). The rigors of working for the county initially seemed both to promise instruction in the proper habits of industry for the pauper and to make it clear that custody did not imply comfort as well.

Simultaneous with the rise of the almshouse system, and continuing through the century, there was a spreading intensification and medicalization of relief to the poor in the form of institutions for specific categories of disease or disability, administered by medical doctors who specialized in mental disorders and controlled by the state, rather than by a city or county. Carried over from the almshouses, however, was the clear distinction between those who were potentially productive and those who were not.

Chronicity and Custodialism

The almshouse clearly established the connection between chronicity and custodialism, as well. The descriptions of inspectors, even allowing for some self-righteous hyperbole, paint a harsh and dismal picture even of relatively well-run facilities. Certainly, some of the almshouses were no worse than the best-run asylum, and they had the advantage of closer ties to inmates' communities. Nonetheless, the almshouses quickly devolved into a system notorious for the cruelty of its treatment of those least able to fend for themselves. For a victim unfortunate enough to combine the problems of idiocy or insanity with epilepsy, violent behavior, or severe physical disability, the prospects of life in an almshouse must have been nightmarish.

An adequate interpretation must go beyond pervasive sadism or moral obtuseness of poorhouse administrators. Rather, the contradictions of the almshouse purposes seem to ordain the ultimate triumph of deterrence and neglect as the mode of life in the almshouse. For those identified as helpless or chronic, the conclusion was that treatment regimens were pointless. Custody was all that was required if the condition was truly chronic. Benign maintenance and caregiving were hardly ever encountered in almshouse existence, where care was grudging, minimal, and often needlessly abusive. The purpose of the custody was to make it as unattractive as possible, to test the minimum required for survival.

At the heart of abusive custodialism was the individualistic ethic essential to the marketplace. The ideology of the new republic was the meritocratic one of social equality. If equality is guaranteed by the social system, then any inequality that persists must be part of the natural order or its violations. There must be an explanation for failure that faults the individual, not the system. Temporary failure must be explained as individual idleness or weakness of will. Chronic failure also must be individualized as nature's version of bankruptcy, with blame implicit at least for the parents, if not the afflicted themselves (Figlio, 1978). The moral element in the approach toward chronicity is social in origin, naturalistic (medical) in content, and individualistic in focus.

Custodialism was not the only legacy of the almshouse, but it was the one with the most practical consequences for the lives of those people left abandoned to it in the name of progress. The legacy of custodialism was carried over intact and uninterrupted into the "enlightened" era of the earliest specialized asylums.

NOTES

This is a slightly modified version of a chapter (pp. 21–43) published in the following book, now out of print: P. M. Ferguson (1994), *Abandoned to Their Fate: Social Policy and Practice toward Severely Retarded People in America, 1820–1920* (Philadelphia: Temple University Press).

1. For convenience, I will abbreviate the citations in the text for this information, other than some specific surveys and signed reports, as "NYSBC" followed by the year of the report being cited (e.g., NYSBC, 1867, p. xxv).

2. A facility designated as an insane asylum opened in Williamsburg, Virginia, in the eighteenth century. However, it remained small and uninfluential, was run by a single family, and was generally isolated from institutional developments even in other parts of the South. It is the kind of "first" that is more misleading than helpful in terms of the evolution of the institutions that followed. However, it is an interesting story in its own right. For more information, see Dain's institutional history of its first 100 years of operation, from 1766 to 1866 (Dain, 1971). There is a large and growing number of works of varying usefulness on the development of insane asylums during the eighteenth and nineteenth centuries, including Norman Dain (1964), the comprehensive accounts by Gerald Grob (1973, 1983, 1991, 1994), David Rothman's work (1971, 1978, 1980), and others (e.g., Jimenez, 1987; McGovern, 1985). However, to my taste, the most useful work in this area has been produced by Andrew Scull (1979, 1981, 1984, 1989, 1996 [coauthors C. MacKenzie and N. Hervey]).

REFERENCES

Altschuler, G. C., & J. M. Saltzgaber (1984). Clearinghouse for paupers: The poor farm of Seneca County, New York, 1830–1860. *Journal of Social History 17* (4): 573–600.

Braverman, Harry (1974). *Labor and monopoly capital: The degradation of work in the twentieth century.* New York: Monthly Review Press.

Dain, N. (1964). *Concepts of insanity in the United States, 1789–1865.* New Brunswick, NJ: Rutgers University Press.

Dain, N. (1971). *Disordered minds: The first century of Eastern State Hospital in Williamsburg, Virginia, 1766–1866.* Williamsburg, VA: Colonial Williamsburg Foundation.

Demos, John (1970). *A little commonwealth: Family life in Plymouth colony.* New York: Oxford University Press.

Dix, Dorothea L. (1844). Memorial to the legislature of the state of New York. *New York Assembly documents, no. 21.* Albany: State of New York.

Figlio, Karl (1978). Chlorosis and chronic disease in nineteenth-century Britain: The social constitution of somatic illness in a capitalist society. *Social history 3* (2): 167–97.

Griffin, J. D., & Greenland, Cyril (1981). Institutional care of the mentally disordered in Canada: A seventeenth-century record. *Canadian Journal of Psychiatry 26* (4): 274–78.

Grob, G. N. (1973). *Mental institutions in America: Social policy to 1875.* New York: Free Press.

Grob, G. N. (1983). *Mental illness and American society, 1875–1940.* Princeton, NJ: Princeton University Press.

Grob, G. N. (1991). *From asylum to community: Mental health policy in modern America.* Princeton, NJ: Princeton University Press.

Grob, G. N. (1994). *The mad among us: A history of the care of America's mentally ill.* New York: Free Press.

Hecht, Irene W. D., & Frederick Hecht (1973). Mara and Benomi Buck: Familial retardation in colonial Jamestown. *Journal of the History of Medicine 28*: 174–75.

Jarvis, Edward. (1855) 1971. *Insanity and idiocy in Massachusetts: Report of the Commission on Lunacy, 1855, by Edward Jarvis.* Cambridge, MA: Harvard University Press.

Jimenez, Mary A. (1987). *Changing faces of madness: Early American attitudes and treatment of the insane.* Hanover, NH: University Press of New England.

Katz, Michael B. (1976). The origins of public education: A reassessment. *History of Education Quarterly 16* (4): 381–407.

Katz, Michael B. (1978). Origins of the institutional state. *Marxist Perspectives 1* (4): 6–22.

Katz, Michael B. (1983). *Poverty and policy in American History.* New York: Academic Press.

Katz, Michael B. (1984). Poorhouse and the origins of the public old age home. *Milbank Memorial Fund Quarterly/Health and Society 62* (1): 110–40.

Katz, Michael B. (1986). *In the shadow of the poorhouse: A social history of welfare in America.* New York: Basic Books.

Katz, Michael B., Michael J. Doucet, and Mark J. Stern. (1982). *The social organization of early industrial capitalism.* Cambridge, MA: Harvard University Press.

Keyssar, Alexander (1986). *Out of work: The first century of unemployment in Massachusetts.* Cambridge: Cambridge University Press.

Klebaner, Benjamin J. (1976). *Public poor relief in America: 1790–1860.* New York: Arno Press.

McGovern, C. M. (1985). *Masters of madness: Social origins of the American psychiatric profession.* Hanover, NH: University Press of New England.

Mills, C. Wright (1959). *The sociological imagination.* New York: Cambridge University Press.

Mottus, Jane E. (1983). *New York nightingales: The emergence of the nursing profession at Bellevue and New York Hospital, 1850–1920.* Rochester, NY: UMI Research Press.

New York City Board of Charities and Correction (1876). Annual Report. New York, New York.

New York State Board of Charities (1896–1901). Annual Report. Albany, New York.

Piven, Frances F., & Richard A. Cloward (1972). *Regulating the poor: The functions of public welfare.* New York: Vintage Books.

Quincy, J. [1821] (1971). Report of the committee on the pauper laws of this commonwealth. In *The almshouse experience: Collected reports.* New York: Arno Press.

Radbill, Samuel X. (1976). Reared in adversity: Institutional care of children in the eighteenth century. *American Journal of Diseases of Children 130*: 751–61.

Report of the Select Committee Appointed to Visit Charitable Institutions Supported by the State, and All City and County Poor and Work Houses and Jails ([1857] 1976). In *The State and Public Welfare in Nineteenth-Century America: Five Investigations, 1833–1877.* New York: Arno Press.

Report of the Special Joint Committee Appointed to Investigate the Whole System of Public Charitable Institutions of the Commonwealth of Massachusetts during the Recess of the Legislature in 1858 ([1859] 1976). In *The State and Public Welfare in Nineteenth-Century America: Five Investigations, 1833–1877.* New York: Arno Press.

Rochefort, D. (1981). Three centuries of care of the mentally disabled in Rhode Island and the nation, 1650–1950. *Rhode Island History 40* (4): 111–32.

Rosenkrantz, Barbara G., & Maris A. Vinovskis (1979). Caring for the insane in antebellum Massachusetts: Family, community, and state participation. In Allan J. Lichtman & Joan R. Challinor, eds., *Kins and communities: Families in America* (pp. 187–218). Washington, DC: Smithsonian Institute.

Rothman, David J. (1971). *The discovery of the asylum: Social order and disorder in the New Republic.* Boston: Little, Brown.

Rothman, David J. (1978). The state as parent: Social policy in the Progressive era. In W. Gaylin, I. Glasser, S. Marcus, & D. J. Rothman, eds., *Doing good: The limits of benevolence* (pp. 68–95). New York: Pantheon Books.

Rothman, David J. (1980). *Conscience and convenience: The asylum and its alternatives in progressive America.* Boston: Little, Brown.

Ryan, Mary. P. (1981). *Cradle the middle class: The family in Oneida County, New York, 1790–1865.* New York: Cambridge University Press.

Schneider, David M., & Albert Deutsch (1941). *The history of public welfare in New York State, 1867–1940.* Chicago: University of Chicago Press.

Scull, A. T. (1979). *Museums of madness: The social organization of insanity in nineteenth-century England.* New York: St. Martin's Press.

Scull, A. T. (1980). A convenient place to get rid of inconvenient people: The Victorian lunatic asylum. In Anthony D. King, ed., *Buildings and society: Essays on the social development of the built environment* (pp. 37–60). London: Routledge and Kegan Paul.

Scull, A. T. (1981). "The Discovery of the Asylum" revisited: Lunacy reform in the new

American republic. In A. T. Scull, ed., *Madhouses, mad-doctors, and madmen: The social history of psychiatry in the Victorian era* (pp. 144-65). Philadelphia: University of Pennsylvania.

Scull, A. T. (1984). *Decarceration: Community treatment and the deviant—a radical view* (2nd ed.). Englewood Cliffs, NJ: Prentice-Hall.

Scull, A. T. (1989). *Social order/mental disorder: Anglo-American psychiatry in historical perspective.* Berkeley: University of California Press.

Scull, A. T., C. MacKenzie, & N. Hervey. (1996). *Masters of Bedlam: The transformation of the mad-doctoring trade.* Princeton, NJ: Princeton University Press.

Wallace, A. F. C. (1978). *Rockdale: The growth of an American village in the early industrial revolution.* New York: W. W. Norton.

Yates, J. ([1824] 1901). Report of the secretary of state in 1824 on the relief settlement of the poor. In New York State Board of Charities, *Thirty-fourth Annual Report* (pp. 937-1145). Albany: State of New York.

2

"Beside Her Sat Her Idiot Child"

Families and Developmental Disability in Mid-Nineteenth-Century America

Penny L. Richards

The moral to be drawn from the prevalent existence of idiocy in society is, that a very large class of persons ignore conditions upon which alone health and reason are given to men, and consequently they sin in various ways; they disregard the conditions which should be observed in intermarriage; they overlook the hereditary transmission of certain morbid tendencies, or they pervert the natural appetites of the body into lusts of diverse kinds,—the natural emotions of the mind into fearful passions,—and thus bring down the awful consequences of their own ignorance and sin upon the heads of their unoffending children.

—Samuel Gridley Howe, *Seventh Annual Report,* 2–3.[1]

In 1835, Thomas Cameron was a young postmaster in rural North Carolina; ten-year-old Lloyd Fuller was studying alongside his older brothers in their middle-class New England home. Thomas and Lloyd would today be considered developmentally disabled; in the 1830s, that difference alone did not disqualify them from work, education, social invitations, or travel. Popular fictional accounts in the 1840s depicted the families of such children as dedicated, loving, and spiritually improved by their challenges. By 1873, America had changed. In that year, Byron Woodhull's mother confessed to audiences about life with her teenaged son, "I am cursed with this living death." The federal census had begun to count people like him; the word "idiotic" occupied the same column in which convicts' crimes were noted.[2] In the 1860s and 1870s, fictional treatments highlighted the unbearable, maddening stress and guilt in families that included people with developmental disabilities.

What changed the experience and depiction of these families? Historians generally recognize that the midnineteenth century was a period of great public energy on the question of retardation: official counts appeared, state schools first emerged, and theories of heredity gained powerful scientific underpinning with the release of Darwin's works. But, while professional literature proclaimed improvement and optimism (at least initially), families experienced increasing shame and despair as the century passed its midpoint.[3] Parents and siblings, once admired for their devotion, became suspect in their neighbors' eyes. Fiction and essays in popular periodicals depicted them as desperate, crazed, and accursed and their children as disgusting horrors. Schools, now more standardized and bureaucratic, no longer served their children as once they had. Reports said that the new schools and medical ideas would open new worlds for their children; in practice, family life with retardation often became harsher and more isolated.

This last midcentury shift, like much in mental retardation historiography, has not been examined. An emphasis on the professional—on policies and theories, on institutions and their practices—has left the personal, the private, and the popular largely unexplored. Elizabeth Bredberg terms this missing work the "vernacular" history of disability.[4] Its sources and methods differ from those of the "expert" history, but its stories are necessary to complement and complicate the usual narrative. In this chapter, the vernacular and expert histories intersect: over the middle decades of the nineteenth century, family lives and fictional depictions reflected changes in the public discourse, though indirectly and with (perhaps) unintended consequences.

"It Is a Sacred Duty": Family and School in the Early Midnineteenth Century (c. 1830s–1850s)

Margaret Fuller (1810–1850), then a teacher and aspiring writer in New England, wrote home to her widowed mother in 1837: "Fit out the children for school, and let not Lloyd be forgotten." As the eldest child, Margaret took special interest in this brother, sixteen years her junior. Earlier in the 1830s, Margaret had tutored Lloyd herself, along with the brothers who fell between them in age. She knew Lloyd to be amusing, gentle, and strong, though a very poor scholar. His behavior had often been disruptive, but (she insisted to a doubting brother) he *"can* be influenced by kindness to do his duty." Later that year, she emphasized the importance of Lloyd's education to her own wellbeing, saying "I am so glad Lloyd is fairly at school, a weight is lifted from my consciousness."[5]

It is seldom noted that schooling was indeed possible for some children with mental retardation in the early nineteenth century. Thomas Cameron (1806–1874), a North Carolina teen, was sent to northern schools—including a military academy—in the 1820s, in the hope that colder winters would "brace" him and stimulate his mind.[6] Kemp Battle, another North Carolinian, remembered of his 1830s boyhood in Raleigh, "We had in school a half-witted boy who was not expected to learn anything but was sent to school to keep him out of mischief."[7] Lloyd Fuller was sent to an ordinary neighborhood school in 1837. Although many American children before 1840 attended little school, for a child of the educated classes, mental retardation (in the absence of serious physical or behavioral complications) was not automatic grounds for exclusion.

This de facto inclusion was possible in the first half of the nineteenth century for several reasons.[8] Schools were often autonomous, at most under the authority of a town or church. Admission, therefore, was at the discretion of the schoolmaster. At schools supported by tuition payments, no child could be turned away lightly. Age-grading was not yet practiced, allowing some children to progress more slowly without drawing unwelcome attention (or requiring special accommodation). The most widely employed pedagogies emphasized recitation, memorization, and routine, rather than abstract thought or independent written work. Finally, schools were expected to provide more than academic benefits. Boarding schools especially advertised the virtues of family-style nurture, protection, and character formation as their primary offerings. Said Margaret Fuller of Lloyd's placement at such a school: "If he does not learn much in lessons the influence on his character and manners is better."[9] The Camerons were similarly pleased that schooling had at least improved Thomas's social skills and personal habits.

Beyond the school years, an adult son or daughter with mental retardation provoked no shame in these families. In the 1830s, Thomas Cameron held a visible job, attended weddings and other social events, and voted regularly. He had responsibilities on the plantation and enjoyed riding his horse between the family properties without supervision, often carrying written messages back and forth. Family correspondence regularly mentioned his doings, his moods, and his affection for his nieces and nephews. "Thomas has given a good portion of his time to the children," wrote his brother in 1844, "they seem very much attached to him, as he unquestionably is to them."[10] As an adult with retardation, Thomas held a valued place in his family; his needs and interests were recognized but seldom patronized. While material fortune certainly made this arrangement easier to sustain, it was in no other way very remarkable. The middle-class Lloyd Fuller enjoyed a similar degree of family support and interest in his young adult years. Even after he was placed in a private asylum in 1848, Margaret Fuller wrote from Europe to another brother: "And poor Lloydie I hope much he is not unhappy; that his feelings are constantly consulted. It is a sacred duty. It is one I can truly say I never neglected for any other object."[11]

In the popular fiction of the 1840s, the family was regularly seen as both supportive of and enriched by a member with developmental disabilities. The "poor hardworking widow with her idiot son" was a well-established figure; in women's religious periodicals such as the *Ladies' Repository* and the *Southern Literary Messenger,* she was shown as an admirable character, wise and patient and loving, in no way to blame for her child's difficulties.[12] "Vagrant Thoughts and Sketches," an 1845 fable by a woman identified only as Mrs. Dumont, published in the *Ladies' Repository,* is a good example of the genre. It contrasts two girlhood friends, one of whom goes on to have an idiot son, the other a healthy son who becomes a criminal. Dumont recounts the first mother's early withdrawal from her accustomed social circles:

> Seldom even was she seen at the house of God. In the solitude of a sorrowful home, forgotten already by those whom she was wont to meet in the halls of pleasure, she watched over an *idiot* babe, from whose vacant eye even the maternal glance elicited no beam of light, And so her years wore on, devoted to the care of revolting idiocy, and utter hopeless helplessness.[13]

By the time these characters are encountered in the fable, however, the first girl has grown "full of peace, of piety, of heavenward trust, and perfect resignation," while the other is "inconsolable." "Beside her sat her idiot son, now grown to manhood," Dumont wrote, and, in contrast to her earlier hopeless description, "he was perfectly quiet, for habit seemed to have awakened in his mind some instinctive perception that it was *a holy place.*" The moral, that we "bestow our pity and our envy alike upon objects that are truly fit subjects of neither," emphasizes that the mother of the idiot child should not be pitied.

Margaret Fuller herself addressed the issue in "Caroline," an 1846 essay for the *New York Tribune*.[14] By this time, Fuller was an important voice in American Transcendentalism and the author of "Woman in the Nineteenth Century," an influential feminist tract.[15] She proposed that families with disabled members have a "purifying and softening influence" on those around them, serving as good examples. One paragraph might describe her own work with Lloyd (although in the third person):

> We have seen a similar instance in this country of voluntary care of an idiot, and the mental benefits that ensued. This idiot, like most that are called so, was not without a glimmer of mind. His teacher was able to give him some notions both spiritual and mental facts, at least she thought she had given him the idea of a God. . . . She had awakened in him a love of music, so that he could be soothed in his most violent moods by her gentle singing. It was a most touching sight to see him sitting opposite her at those times, his wondering and lack-lustre eyes filled with childish pleasure, while in hers gleamed the same pure joy that we may suppose to animate the looks of an angel appointed by Heaven to restore a ruined world.

There is no question that such constructions of developmental disability and family life are themselves fraught with uncomfortable stereotypes to our present-day eyes. The point, however, is that, in the 1840s, the stereotypes were at least generally benign, if rather maudlin, in their evocation of "angels" and a childlike pleasure in music, for example. (It should also be noted that the heavily sentimental tone of these stories and essays is not peculiar to the subject matter but a general feature of the magazine literature of the period.) A mother of a child with mental retardation, looking to her magazines for comfort, could have found herself reflected as an impossible ideal in the 1840s. But she would also have found recognition that her child was a teachable, spiritual being, capable of joy, and, further, that her work was hard but rewarding, worthy, and motivated by love.[16]

"There Must Have Been Sin": Midcentury Changes and the Question of Family Competence

The uplifting popular image of families of idiots contrasted profoundly with the expert opinions of midcentury America. Idiots, the learned reasoning went, were generally the offspring of diseased, sinful parents, who, in raising a child so marked by sin, were neglectful, overburdened, and driven to further sin. This construction corresponds to the notions held by Samuel Gridley Howe, a leading voice of reform in several fields, most notably the education of children with disabilities.[17] Dr. Howe undertook to study the issue of idiocy for the Commonwealth of Massachusetts; his landmark "Report Made to the Legislature of Massachusetts, upon Idiocy" (1848) resulted in the founding of the first state-sponsored school for idiots, the very next year. While Howe's study found no cases of intentional cruelty on the part of parents, he was still moved to "earnestly recommend that measures be at once taken to rescue this most unfortunate class from the dreadful degradation in which they now grovel."[18]

In the same report, Howe was more explicit about the religious feeling behind his belief about the parents of idiots:

It seemed impious to attribute to the creator any such glaring imperfection in his handiwork. It appeared to us certain that the existence of so many idiots in every generation *must* be the consequence of some violation of the *natural laws,*—that where there was so much suffering, there must have been sin.[19]

Not only did Howe and most of his colleagues assume that the biological parents of idiots were the cause of their troubles, but they further asked the state to become the metaphorical family of idiots (once they were rescued from their original homes). Howe's 1848 report was full of family language: he proclaimed that, with the advent of state-sponsored institutions, "at last the poor idiot is welcomed into the human family." He implored readers, "whenever the signal is given of a man in distress—no matter how deformed, how vicious, how loathsome, even, he may be—let it be regarded as a call to help a brother." He challenged the state: "shall our commonwealth continue to bury the humble talent of lowly children committed to her motherly care, and let it rot in the earth . . . ?"[20] By ignoring the existence of the real motherly care and brotherly help already extended to many idiots, Howe was able to make the state's entry into this work an obvious step, uncomplicated by an existing, often working system of support.

Coinciding with this rhetorical replacement of the natural family by the institution builders, the common school movement exerted its own pressures to exclude idiots from ordinary life. Horace Mann, "Father of the Common School movement," was Samuel Gridley Howe's closest friend and shared his taste for family metaphors. "When will society, like a mother, take care of *all* her children?" he asked in 1837.[21] Whereas boys like Thomas Cameron and Lloyd Fuller could, in earlier decades, have attended schools with their peers, they now encountered a more bureaucratized and standardized classroom. The schoolmaster lost much of his authority and flexibility when state boards of instruction were founded in the 1830s and 1840s. Lessons in textbooks such as the enormously popular McGuffey readers equated goodness and fast learning:

> Come, girls, let us play with our dolls. We will play school. Our dolls will be the children. Our dolls are as good as some children are. They have their books, and I think, they will learn very fast. Soon we shall see how well they can read. *This doll is not so good as the others.* She does not like to go to school very well. She must sit by me and look at her book. As soon as she can read well, she may go home and play. *She goes to school day after day, but she does not learn.* She can not write at all. She can not tell her name.[22] [emphasis added]

The function of common schools was neither to shelter privileged children nor to form agreeable habits but to educate the masses, with speed and efficiency. Mann said plainly that, "in a republic, ignorance is a crime," and compared an uneducated republic to a giant "whose brain has been developed only in the region of the appetites and passions, and not in the organs of reason and conscience.[23] The idiot, therefore, represented to Mann the gluttonous enemy of the state, the undisciplined opposite of the republican ideal.

One further midcentury shift requires notice. In the early nineteenth century, there was an active temperance movement, with accompanying literature. In that literature, an important message was that drunken parents harm their children. The mechanism of that harm was typically portrayed as physical, emotional, or financial: the child or the child's mother is physically harmed during an alcohol-induced rage, or the breadwinner's alcoholism severely reduces the family's income.[24] This is not to say that the idea of heredity was unknown in this period; in fact, there was a "vogue of social hereditarianism . . . well underway by the mid-nineteenth century."[25] In the 1840s, however, this vogue began to affect the way social activists, including temperance advocates, proceeded with their work. Soon, the temperance literature was full of warnings: "Instances are known where the first children of a family, who were born when their parents were temperate, have been healthy, intelligent, and active," noted the Reverend Dr. Edwards, in a typical tract, "while the last children, who were born after the parents had become intemperate, were dwarfish and idiotic."[26] Working backward from the evidence of an idiotic child, then, one might well discover an intemperate parent.

In short, in the midnineteenth century, expert opinions from various quarters shared a common dim view of the parents of children with mental retardation. For a multipurpose reformer like Howe, such parents had probably led lives in violation of nature and God's laws, since their children were themselves so clearly outside the natural order. For educational reformers like Mann, their children presented no less than a threat to the republic, because they would not easily fit into the scheme of common schools. For temperance advocates, the parents of idiots represented possible drinkers, carriers of a dread taint, whose moral weakness (more than their physical strength, as in previous constructions) had damaged their innocent children. All these perspectives were readily available to the general reading public: Howe's report, Mann's sermons, and temperance tales were all found repeated and discussed in the pages of the same women's periodicals that carried short stories like "Vagrant Thoughts and Sketches." As the century passed its midpoint, therefore, there was a perceptible change for the worse in how families were portrayed in popular fiction and, consequently, in how these families viewed themselves.

"I Am Cursed with This Living Death": Guilty and Distraught Parents in Life and Fiction, 1850s–1870s

It would be easy to assume that the advent of state institutions for the feebleminded had an obvious impact on families, simply by offering an alternative setting for their children's lives. But, by 1850, only a tiny handful of students had actually been admitted to state institutions.[27] There was no realistic possibility that most families could ever send their children to stay, even temporarily, at a state or private institution for the feebleminded. The effect of the midcentury institution boom (and its accompanying literature) was more subtle: families came to think of their members with developmental disabilities differently, as evidence of their parents' mistakes, or of a family taint. This could not help but set parent against parent, increase the resentment of caretakers, and isolate families from their friends and neighbors. Again, family stories and popular short fiction illustrate how the family dynamic changed in the wake of such guilt and fear. In these examples, parents, especially fathers, bear the blame for the problems of their defective children.

Victoria Woodhull and Her Son Byron

Perhaps the most visible parent of a child with a developmental disability in the 1870s was Victoria Woodhull. She and her sister Tennessee Claflin became the first female stockbrokers on Wall Street in 1870; that same year, the pair began a newspaper, *Woodhull and Claflin's Weekly,* which conveniently gave Victoria a public voice when she declared herself a candidate for president of the United States. Her family's history and living arrangements were a constant source of scandal; accusations of fraud, free love, prostitution, and dabblings in communism were not without basis. Woodhull herself provoked an enormous uproar by revealing the affair that the prominent clergyman Henry Ward Beecher was having with one of his parishioners.[28]

All this notoriety was far in the future for Victoria Woodhull when she became a mother in 1854. Just sixteen years old, she was married to Canning Woodhull, an unsuccessful doctor, and living in a cold Chicago tenement when the baby came on New Year's Eve. Named Byron (after the poet), he was "a half-idiot," a condition Victoria would soon come to attribute to her husband's drinking and abuse, among other causes. This belief—that her son was an idiot because his father drank—was to radicalize Victoria Woodhull. "It was that alone," she later explained, "that made me feel that I had nothing else to do but to ask from every platform on the face of the earth that woman should awaken to the responsibility of becoming mothers, by any possibility whatever never bearing a child that might be an imbecile or a criminal."[29]

Byron moved with his parents to San Francisco, then back to the Midwest (where his sister Zula was born), and later to New York City. There is no evidence that he ever attended school. When Victoria's campaign biography appeared, it described Byron (then a teenager) as

> endowed with just enough intelligence to exhibit the light of reason in dim eclipse: a sad and pitiful spectacle [roaming] from room to room, muttering noises more sepulchral than human; a daily agony to the woman who bore him . . . the uncommon sweetness of his temper [wins] everyone's love, [and] doubles everyone's pity.[30]

Byron was always cared for within his mother's home, first, by various relatives who lived with Victoria and, later in life, in England, by his younger, never-married sister. Photos of Byron Woodhull as an older man (he lived to age 77) show him to be well dressed and groomed.[31]

Victoria Woodhull eventually found the platforms she needed to deliver her message, inspired by Byron, to other mothers. Woodhull's political interests and acquaintances influenced the style and content of her argument. In 1871, her speech "On the Principles of Social Freedom" included this emphatic declaration: "I believe in *love with liberty*; in *protection without slavery*; in *the care and culture of offspring by new and better methods, and without the tragedy of self-immolation on the part of parents.*" Mothers, she proposed (on the basis of her own experiences and acquired free-love theory), could bear healthy children only by conceiving them in love and self-knowledge, rather than in obligation and ignorance, as she believed many wives did. Woodhull's conclusion, across many speeches of the early 1870s, was that marriage itself, as a structure, posed a danger to children by sexually enslaving their mothers and that the dismal state of sex education further endangered children by making their mothers ignorant as well as powerless. The offspring of such an arrangement would always risk serious debility, she argued, in a strange way echoing Howe's train of thinking, albeit from a radically different premise.

Nowhere was this theme more personalized than in Woodhull's 1873 speech, "Tried as by Fire." Presented on 150 nights in various cities, it was heard by an estimated 250,000 people.[32] Toward the end of her speech, she invited audiences into her personal life:

> Go home with me and see desolation and devastation in another form. The cold, iron bolt has entered my heart and left my life a blank, in ashes upon

my lips. Wherever I go I carry a living corpse in my breast, the vacant stare of whose living counterpart meets me at the door of my home. My boy, now nineteen years of age, who should have been my pride and my joy, has never been blessed by the dawning of reasoning. I was married at fourteen, ignorant of everything that related to my maternal functions. For this ignorance, and because I knew no better than to surrender my maternal functions to a drunken man, I am cursed with this living death.

Woodhull followed this immediately with a series of rhetorical questions:

Do you think my mother's heart does not yearn for the love of my boy? Do you think I do not realize the awful condition to which I have consigned him? Do you think I would not willingly give my life to make him what he has a right to be? Do you think his face is not ever before me pressing me on to declare these terrible social laws to the world? Do you think with this sorrow seated in my soul I can ever sit quietly down and permit women to go on ignorantly repeating my crime? . . . Do you think I can ever hesitate to warn the young maidens against my fate, or to advise them never to surrender the control of their maternal functions to any man?

"Ah!" she then gasped, no doubt to great dramatic effect. "If you do, you do not know the agony that rests here."[33] Of the quarter-million listeners who heard Woodhull those nights in 1873, some must indeed have known that "agony" from firsthand experience. Did they also consider themselves (or the fathers in question) cursed, and guilty of a crime? Victoria Woodhull might easily be dismissed as an unusual thinker on these and other matters. But mainstream short stories of the day also emphasized the theme of parental guilt and desolation.

Two Fictional Treatments of the Guilty, Distraught Father

Two short stories of the period, "The Squire's Son" and "Sanny," both authored by women, mirror Woodhull's concerns. In each story, the main characters and their affected children are male. While neither drinking nor sexual immorality precipitates either child's idiocy, both authors fault paternal behavior for unintentionally causing harm. In both stories, the fathers are devastated by their firstborn sons' idiocy. This appears in marked contrast to stories found in the same or similar periodicals just twenty years earlier, when authors did not trace idiocy to parental weakness and praised the experience of raising a child with retardation as spiritually enriching.

"The Squire's Son," by Miss T. Taylor, appeared in *The Ladies' Repository* in March 1867.[34] It begins as a folktale in form: the main characters are never named, nor is the setting made more specific than "in a pleasant country, on a high hill," on the estate of a "rich manufacturer, the wealthiest man of all the neighborhood." This man is, for all his wealth, miserable and cold-hearted. The reason soon becomes apparent: his wife and children have all died, except his eldest son, who was dropped by a nurse as a baby and is now "a poor, gibbering, crawling idiot boy." Although the origin of the boy's disability is mentioned (the head injury in infancy), the porter's wife explains matters further to her son Henry, an errand boy on the estate: "God is just. . . . He has give the rich man all his great possessions; and He has give me my children." The deaths and disabilities of his family, therefore, are also the result of God's judgment, a balance for the man's wealth.

Henry is eventually hired as the squire's son's caretaker and comes to admire the squire's devotion to his son, which he exercises to the complete exclusion of all other human connections:

> But while all called him cruel, hard-hearted, and many regarded him only with fear, Henry knew too well the tender chord in his soul that could be touched; for he had seen him clasp to his heart, with mingled love and anguish, the object that all willingly would have avoided . . . and he learned to know that all the love of humanity and kindness contained in the father's heart was centered upon his afflicted child.

At this point in the story, modernity appears. The squire "had heard of an institution where the afflicted had been greatly benefited; he even dared hope for the perfect restoration of mind and intelligence," and Henry joins in this optimism. Soon the son is placed in the institution, "under the care of a good man, who, under the guidance of Heaven, had conceived the plan of clearing the clouds that surrounded the darkened intellects of those under his direction." After more than a year, the son returns home, "cured" of his idiocy but fatally weakened physically. The boy's pious death transforms his father, whose "few remaining years" bear witness to the child's favorable impact on his father.

This ending would seem to fit with earlier treatments, in which the idiot's simple faith inspires those around him. But the father in this story is rendered utterly dysfunctional by the events in his life, including his son's disability; he is unable to treat others with kindness or even decency, and his very house is permeated with a forbidding air. He is not improved by the experience of parenting an idiot, only by the knowledge of his cured son's final peace. In its glowing depiction of schools for the feebleminded (and, indeed, this marks an early example of their appearance in fiction), and in its assumption that the parents of idiots suffer mentally and socially more than they benefit, "The Squire's Son" is a product of the post-midcentury spirit.

Another story, in which the father tells exactly how he destroyed his little son's mind, is "Sanny," by Mrs. James Neall, which appeared in the California-based *Overland Monthly* in September 1872.[35] In tone, "Sanny" is remarkably comic: the first-person narrator Edward, a first-time father enthralled by his new son and namesake, is prompted by every passing fad to try a new "system" of raising the boy. Colorful characters appear in the forms of an Irish nurse, a cousin, and an aunt, who (respectively) dose the child with odd folk cures, mock the father's strange plans, and preach about women's rights (the aunt is attending "the Women's Suffrage Convention," and "Sanny," the child's nickname, is a contraction of "Susan B. Anthony"). The child's mother is also involved, but, "patient as a saint," Nettie remains tolerant of the father's whims until late in the story. By then, little Sanny has endured his father's food preparations, movement cures, phrenological charts, air baths, sleep regimens, and oratorical training. Nettie is finally provoked to protest:

> You are taxing the child's nervous system beyond endurance, Edward. I will have no more of this. You shall not tamper with his strength and vitality. Let him play about as other children do. Cease to teach him what he cannot understand. . . . Give him intellectual culture when Nature demands it, and not when it is an unjustifiable stimulant.

The character Nettie is given dialogue that reflects the midnineteenth-century belief that too much education absorbed too early or too intensely could critically damage a child.[36]

Edward, Sanny's father, is eventually forced to concede that he has erred, and "suffering impels me to speak, as well as. . . to warn other parents of the consequences of a fatal forcing process." Sanny falls ill from the stress, and his death is feared; "[b]ut he lived; lived, to be oh, God! that I should speak the dreadful word—an idiot!" The doctor's explanation is in keeping with expert advice of the day: "You are paying the penalty of transgressed physical laws—a painful and sad one—but Nature demands the exaction, sooner or later. May God pity and help you." The narrative then jumps forward in time. Sanny has "bright and lovely" younger siblings now, and he is "gentle and harmless . . . ever seeking for something he has lost and cannot find. Poor child! It is the lost path. He is almost a man in years and stature; but I speak of him yet as MY BOY." Thus ends the otherwise comic story on a bittersweet note.

"Sanny" is curious in its tone but is clearly a product of its time. The father is horrified by his son's diagnosis and guilt-ridden with the belief that his own ambitions have doomed the prized son: "the compliments of my friends . . . and my own gratified vanity, blinded me," he confesses. The "transgression of physical laws" is seen as the sure path to ruin, just as men like Dr. Howe proposed. There is no intimation that raising Sanny after he is diagnosed has improved his parents, except in the sense that, when raising their subsequent children, "we have guarded them from precocity as we would have done from disease." Sanny's future is assured, not because he has been educated, nor necessarily because he has established himself as a valued member of his family, but because an aunt has provided for him in her will. While Sanny is not a candidate for the new state schools (which by 1872 had not yet reached as far west as the *Overland Monthly*), his story is told with knowledge of their rationales.

As the nineteenth century wound to a close, these assumptions about developmental disability and parental (especially paternal) guilt remained entrenched in popular culture. The Women's Christian Temperance Union, founded in 1874, produced a widely adopted hygiene curriculum that taught millions of children that intemperate parents would produce children bound for asylums.[37] Carry Nation, the temperance activist, was herself the mother of a disabled daughter and preached that the child's father's alcoholism was the cause of her problems: "Oh, the curse that comes through heredity, and this liquor evil, a disease, that entails more depravity on children unborn, than all else, unless it be tobacco," she wrote in her autobiography.[38] The stories of Lillie Chace Wyman, published in the 1880s, featured "half-witted" characters, but only as objects who needed rescue from their wretched homes.[39] The figure of the idiot's admirable mother, such a staple in early-nineteenth-century literature, would not reemerge for many years, and perhaps never again without the lurking question of blame and the glimmer of suspicion that her wellbeing is more threatened than improved by life with her child.

Philip Ferguson has commented that "mental retardation history is reflective, rather than formative, of the larger course of events in American society."[40] The history of retardation in America is dense with developments at the intellectual and professional level in the middle of the nineteenth century. All of these were part of broader trends toward state paternalism, toward the application of science to social policy, and toward the redefinition of many differences as pathological deviations from normality, to be studied and controlled. They reflect anxieties about an America that was becoming more diverse in many senses, about population pressures, about the obligations of prosperity. The nineteenth-century energy invested in building state asylums and special schools, and the flowering of professional organizations for their administrators, contributed to the sense of material busyness that eventually seemed, to the Progressivism of the early 1900s, more hollow than the likes of Howe and Mann had hoped.[41]

Private correspondence, speeches, sermons, and popular magazine fiction reveal how these broad trends swept not only the professionals but also families and individuals in their wake. It is not sufficient to know that families who wanted an education for their children with retardation faced increasing layers of official bureaucracy and theoretical discouragement as the nineteenth century progressed. We should also see that situation from the family's perspective, the teacher's perspective, and even the child's perspective (where possible), if we want to understand the full human impact of those policies and theories. The vernacular history also finds tensions that seldom reached the consciousness of the experts. The gender issues raised by short stories about child rearing and idiocy, for example, are more complex treatments of the care and control impulses within struggling families than Howe's reports could ever have indicated.

There is so much more to be learned about midcentury families and developmental disability. Though some family stories are told here, others should also be reconstructed. Though a few sentimental short stories, speeches, and essays are considered here as evidence of popular beliefs and as elements of the literate parent's environment, other examples and other literary forms should be similarly investigated. Current literature on parents and disability has pointed to recent technological changes (prenatal diagnoses, in utero and neonatal interventions) that are said to increase the sense of fault in the parents who nevertheless produce children with severe disabilities.[42] In the midnineteenth century, when American science began in earnest to claim the ability to predict (and prevent) the birth of children with defects, we can see the precursor of today's consequences: parents began to be held more responsible—by professionals, by popular culture, and in their own minds—when their children proved imperfect.

NOTES

1. S. G. Howe, *Seventh Annual Report on the Experimental School for Teaching and Training Idiotic Children* (Boston 1857).

2. The Woodhull quote is from her 1873 speech, "Tried as by Fire," published by Woodhull and Claflin in 1874 and reproduced in Madeleine B. Stern, ed., *The Victoria Woodhull Reader* (M&S Press: Weston MA 1974), on page 27 of the original pamphlet.

On the census, see, for example, the Sacramento City (CA) pages of the Federal Census, 1850, in which a prison "brig" full of convicts is enumerated, with their crimes listed in the column where "idiotic" would have been entered in other cases. Other California census pages in 1850 used the same column to list the number of horses a man owned or the average amount of gold he mined weekly. (Before 1850, the U.S. Census was less detailed and did not include specific information about disabilities.)

In midnineteenth century America, the term "idiot" was in general use for a person whose mental retardation was perceived to be significantly limiting, though the degree of limitation expected of an "idiot" was not well defined in popular culture. In this paper, "idiot" means a person understood by ordinary midnineteenth-century Americans to be so disabled, whether or not he or she would today be considered "a person with developmentally disabilities." While these categories certainly overlap, they are not identical; for that reason, the more precise term is used.

3. On this "Era of Hope," see Russell Hollander, "Mental Retardation and American Society: The Era of Hope," *Social Service Review* 60 (1986): 395–420; and James F. Gardner, "The Era of Optimism, 1850–1870: A Preliminary Reappraisal," *Mental Retardation* 31 (April 1993): 89–95.

4. Elizabeth Bredberg, "The History of Disability: Perspectives and Sources," *Disability Studies Quarterly* 17 (spring 1997): 110. See also Philip M. Ferguson, "Mental Retardation Historiography and the Culture of Knowledge," *Disability Studies Quarterly* 16 (summer 1996): 18–30; and Patrick McDonagh, "Literature and the Notion of Intellectual Disability," *Disability Studies Quarterly* 17(4) (fall 1997): 268–272.

5. "Fit out the children," S. Margaret Fuller to Margaret Crane Fuller, 5 September 1837; "*can* be influenced," S. Margaret Fuller to Richard Fuller, 3 June 1840; "I am so

glad," S. Margaret Fuller to Margaret Crane Fuller, 18 November 1837. All found in Robert N. Hudspeth, ed., *The Letters of Margaret Fuller,* vol. 1 (Cornell University Press: Ithaca 1983).

6. Penny L. Richards and George H. S. Singer, "'To Draw out the Effort of his Mind': Educating a Child with Mental Retardation in Early-Nineteenth-Century America," *Journal of Special Education* 31 (winter 1998): 443–466.

7. Kemp Plummer Battle, *Memories of an Old-Time Tarheel* (University of North Carolina Press: Chapel Hill 1945), 36.

8. These factors are discussed at greater length in Richards and Singer, *supra* note 7. On the issue of age-grading, see David L. Angus, Jeffrey L. Wollock, and Maris A. Vinovskis, "Historical Development of Age Stratification in Schooling," *Teachers College Record* 90 (winter 1988): 211–236; on the issue of recitation as dominant pedagogy, see William R. Johnson, "'Chanting Choristers': Simultaneous Recitation in Baltimore's Nineteenth-Century Primary Schools," *History of Education Quarterly* 34 (spring 1994): 1–23.

9. S. Margaret Fuller to Richard Fuller, 30 October 1838, in Hudspeth vol. 1, *supra* note 5.

10. Paul C. Cameron to the Misses Cameron, 8 February 1844, Cameron Family Papers, Southern Historical Collection, University of North Carolina at Chapel Hill. On Thomas Cameron's young adult years, see Penny L. Richards, "'He Well Deserves All Our Affection': Accepting and Accommodating Mental Retardation in a North Carolina Planter Family," paper presented at the Southern Historical Association meeting, November 1999, Fort Worth TX.

11. S. Margaret Fuller to Richard Fuller, 1 January 1848, in Robert N. Hudspeth, ed., *The Letters of Margaret Fuller,* vol. 5 (Cornell University Press: Ithaca 1988).

12. James Trent mentions this literary figure as appearing in Sunday School literature in 1840, in *Inventing the Feeble Mind: A History of Mental Retardation in the United States* (University of California Press: Berkeley 1994), 8. Other appearances in this period include: Susan Walker, "Worth vs. Beauty: A Tale, Chapters III–IV," *Southern Literary Messenger* 12 (April 1846): 219–231, in which an evil wealthy woman enfeebles her good servant's infant son with a blow of anger; Daniel Wise, *The Young Lady's Counsellor, or Outlines and Illustrations of the Sphere, the Duties, and the Dangers of Young Women* (Carlton and Phillips: New York, und. [1850s]), which includes—as an illustration of the power and sacrifice of maternal love—the story of a poor market-woman and her always-singing idiot son; S. H. Hammond and L. W. Mansfield, *Country Margins and Rambles of a Journalist* (J. C. Derby: New York 1855), in which a widowed servant woman and her son, "Silly Dick," are remembered as always together, Dick helping with the chores and talking to the birds, "a gentle, harmless creature, always obedient and affectionate, leaning upon his mother for protection with the perfect confidence of childhood, though in stature and strength almost a man" (196); and Sarah Josepha Hale, "Woodbine Cottage," *The Christian Keepsake and Missionary Annual*

for MDCCCXLIX (Brower, Hayes & Co.: Philadelphia 1849): 30–42 (though the poor widow character here, Mrs. Walton, does question whether her pride is to blame for the son's state). Most of the stories mentioned throughout this chapter may be found at the Making of America website maintained by the University of Michigan http://moa.umdl.umich.edu/moa/.

On the periodicals in question, see Geoffrey C. Orth, "Mary E. Lee, Martha Fenton Hunter, and the German Connection to Domestic Fiction in the *Southern Literary Messenger,*" *Southern Quarterly* 34(4) (1996): 5–13; Marian Adell, "Caroline Matilda Pilcher: The *Ladies' Repository*'s Ideal Christian Woman," *Methodist History* 34(4) (1997): 246–252; and Kathleen L. Endres, "A Voice for the Christian Family: The Methodist Episcopal *Ladies' Repository* in the Civil War," *Methodist History* 33(2) (1995): 84–97.

13. Mrs. Dumont, "Vagrant Thoughts and Sketches," *The Ladies' Repository* 5 (April 1845): 110–114.

14. Margaret Fuller, "Caroline," *New York Tribune,* 9 April 1846. On the various understandings of physical weakness among American Transcendentalists, see especially Cynthia J. Davis, "Margaret Fuller, Body and Soul," *American Literature* 71(1) (March 1999): 31–56. According to Davis, Fuller "sought to extend transcendence to even the weak in body," while Emerson and Thoreau scorned poor health as an utterly negative experience.

15. On Margaret Fuller, see Charles Capper, *Margaret Fuller: An American Romantic Life,* vol. I, *The Private Years* (Oxford University Press: New York 1992); Bell Gale Chevigny, *The Woman and the Myth: Margaret Fuller's Life and Writings* (Northeastern University Press: Boston 1994); Donna Dickenson, *Margaret Fuller: Writing a Woman's Life* (St. Martin's Press: New York 1994); and Joan vonMehren, *Minerva and the Muse: A Life of Margaret Fuller* (University of Massachusetts Press: Amherst 1994), among many other recent works.

16. On women's reading practices in antebellum America, see Mary Kelley, "Reading Women/Women Reading: The Making of Learned Women in Antebellum America," *Journal of American History* 183 (1996): 401–424. Although Kelley concentrates on book-reading, women can be assumed to have made similar "self-fashioning" uses of literary periodicals, especially those marketed as self-improving by the sponsoring denomination.

17. Harold Schwartz, *Samuel Gridley Howe: Social Reformer, 1801–1876* (Harvard University Press: Cambridge MA 1956) is the most recent full-length biography.

18. Quoted in Matilda Freeman Dana, "Idiocy in Massachusetts," *Southern Literary Messenger* 15 (June 1849): 367–370. Schwartz, *supra* note 17, 141, makes the statement that "the committee . . . found no instance of willfully unkind treatment of idiots."

19. Howe, from his "Report Made to the Legislature of Massachusetts, upon Idiocy," 1848, quoted in Schwartz, *supra* note 17, 140.

20. All three of these "family" quotes are found in Dana, "Idiocy in Massachusetts," *supra* note 18.

21. Mann's 1837 quote is found in Joel Spring, *The American School, 1642–1990* (Longman: New York 1990), 86. On Mann and Howe as best friends, see Schwartz, *supra* note 17, chapter 9. Howe also worked with Mann on the establishment of common schools: he was an inspector for Boston's first crop of grammar schools.

22. From the Project Gutenberg e-text, The New McGuffey First Reader, at http://sailor.gutenberg.org/etext98/1nmcg10.txt. While the Project Gutenberg version draws from several editions of the original text (and thus cannot be dated to a single year), there are many other passages like this one in the 1841 First Reader, for example.

23. Mann's quote is from his Twelfth Report to the Massachusetts Board of Education (1848), and is found in Spring, *supra* note 21, 52.

24. Jerome Nadelhaft, "Alcohol and Wife Abuse in Antebellum Male Temperance Literature," *Canadian Review of American Studies* 25(1) (1995): 15–43.

25. Charles E. Rosenberg, "The Bitter Fruit: Heredity, Disease, and Social Thought in Nineteenth-Century America," *Perspectives in American History* 8 (1974): 204.

26. Reverend Dr. Edwards, "On the Traffic in Ardent Spirits" (undated, mid-1800s), in *Selected Temperance Tracts* (American Tract Society: NY undated [mid-1800s]), 7.

27. Trent, *supra* note 12, 14, estimates that about a dozen students were being served by the two idiot schools in Massachusetts that year. Samuel B. Thielman, "Community Management of Mental Disorders in Antebellum America," *Journal of the History of Medicine* 44 (July 1989): 351–378, makes similar low estimates for the number of people with mental illnesses, most of whom "never saw an alienist, never visited an asylum, and were managed by a social network composed variously of family members, general physicians, clergymen, and governmental authorities."

28. On Victoria Woodhull, see Lois Beachy Underhill, *The Woman Who Ran for President: The Many Lives of Victoria Woodhull* (Bridge Works Publishing Co.: Bridgehampton NY 1995); Mary Gabriel, *Notorious Victoria: The Life of Victoria Woodhull, Uncensored* (Algonquin Books: Chapel Hill 1998); and Barbara Goldsmith, *Other Powers: The Age of Suffrage, Spiritualism, and the Scandalous Victoria Woodhull* (Knopf: New York 1998).

29. Quoted in Gabriel, *supra* note 28, 14, from a transcript related to Martin's suit against the British Museum, written by Victoria Woodhull (Martin) in 1894.

30. "Victoria C. Woodhull. A Biographical Sketch," by Theodore Tilton, published in 1871, quoted in Gabriel, *supra* note 28, 56.

31. There is an especially good photo in the Victoria Woodhull-Martin Papers at Southern Illinois University, reproduced in Gabriel, *supra* note 28, 294.

32. Underhill, *supra* note 28, 260.

33. Woodhull, "Tried as by Fire," *supra* note 2. This passage is found on page 27 of the original pamphlet (Stern does not independently number the pages of the reader). The present author is currently undertaking a study of this speech and its impact.

34. Miss T. Taylor, "The Squire's Son," *The Ladies' Repository* 27 (March 1867): 160–163.

35. Mrs. James Neall, "Sanny," *Overland Monthly* 9 (September 1872): 255–262.

36. On precocity/overeducation as a feared result of early schooling, see S. B. Woodward, "Treatment of Scholars," *North Carolina Journal of Education* 1 (July 1858): 214, excerpted in Edgar W. Knight, ed., *Documentary History of Education in the South before 1860* (University of North Carolina Press: Chapel Hill 1953); and George J. Makari, "Educated Insane: A Nineteenth-Century Psychiatric Paradigm," *Journal of the History of the Behavioral Sciences* 29 (1993): 8–12. While Douglas Baynton has proposed that the concept of "abnormality" as it emerged in the midnineteenth century never applied to those above the average, this may be a case of precisely that phenomenon; see Douglas C. Baynton, "Disability: A Useful Category of Historical Analysis," *Disability Studies Quarterly* 17 (spring 1997): 83, footnote 5.

37. S. A. Cook, "Educating for Temperance: The Women's Christian Temperance Union and Ontario Children, 1880–1916," *Historical Studies in Education* 5 (1993): 251–277. See also Carol Mattingly, *Well-Tempered Women: Nineteenth-Century Temperance Rhetoric* (Southern Illinois University Press: Carbondale 1998).

38. Carry A. Nation, *The Use and Need of the Life of Carry A. Nation* (F. M. Steres & Sons: Topeka 1905), 37.

39. E. C. Stevens, "'Was She Clothed with the Rents Paid for these Wretched Rooms?': Elizabeth Buffum Chace, Lillie Chace Wyman, and Upper-Class Advocacy for Women Factory Operatives in Gilded Age Rhode Island," *Rhode Island History* 52 (1994): 107–133.

40. Philip M. Ferguson, *Abandoned to Their Fate: Social Policy and Practice toward Severely Retarded People in America, 1820–1920* (Temple University Press: Philadelphia 1994), 83.

41. Richard Hofstadter, "Introduction: The Meaning of the Progressive Movement," in *The Progressive Movement 1901–1915* (Prentice Hall: New York 1963).

42. Gail H. Landsman, "Reconstructing Motherhood in the Age of 'Perfect' Babies: Mothers of Infants and Toddlers with Disabilities," *Signs: Journal of Women in Culture and Society* 24 (1998): 69–99.

Part II

Defining and Categorizing

Establishing "The Other"

Report of Committee on Classification of Feeble-Minded

Journal of Psycho-Asthenics 15 (1910)

At the meeting of the Association at Chippewa Falls in 1909, a committee on classification was appointed, consisting of Drs. Fernald, Goddard, Wylie, Bullard, and Murdoch.

At the Lincoln meeting, Dr. Goddard, the only member of the committee in attendance, presented the correspondence which had passed between the Chairman, Dr. Fernald, and the other members of the committee living outside of Boston, as abstract of which is given below.

The ideas of the individual members of the committee, as shown in the correspondence, were discussed at this meeting and the following classification agreed to, its adoption being considered as tentative. . . .

1. The term feeble-minded is used generically to include all degrees of mental defect due to arrested or imperfect development as a result of which the person so affected is incapable of competing on equal terms with his normal fellows or managing himself or his affairs with ordinary prudence.

2. The feeble-minded are divided into three classes, viz:

A. Idiots: Those so deeply defective that their mental development does not exceed that of a normal child of about two years.

B. Imbeciles: Those whose mental development is higher than that of an idiot but does not exceed that of a normal child of about seven years.

C. Morons: Those whose mental development is above that of an imbecile but does not exceed that of a child of about twelve years.

The descriptive terms heretofore accepted to express pathological and other definite characteristics, such as hydrocephalic, paralytic, mongolism, etc., may be used as prefixes or adjectives.

It was agreed that the Binet mental tests afforded the most reliable method at present in use for determining the mental status of feeble-minded children

It was agreed that there would be considerable advantage in sub-dividing the three classes into three groups each, and designating them by the pre-fixes, high grade, middle grade, and low grade, respectively.

The New Classification (Tentative) of the Feeble-Minded

Editorial

Journal of Psycho-Asthenics 15 (1910)

The action of the association on the report of the committee, illustrates the natural and logical blending of medical and psychological influences in the treatment of the subject of mental defect. In considering this classification, it is well to bear in mind the three phases which the subject presents, viz,: 1st, the nomenclature itself, 2nd, the adoption of psychological basis for grouping the cases and 3rd, the special psychological test used for determining the classification.

If it had been easy to advise a classification of general application it would have been done long ago, for there have been many students interested who were familiar with medical and pathological studies and who had plenty of material on which to work.

As to the nomenclature, the committee tried to retain the old terms so far as possible and still avoid confusion from the lack of uniformity and precision in former usage. In some respects, the English use of the term, mental deficiency, as applied generically, is preferable to our term, feeble-mindedness. The adoption of the English form in this country is not practicable, however, from the fact of the incorporation by statute of the term, feeble-minded, into the names of practically all of the institutions for this class in America, as stated in the correspondence. If it were not so the term could be retained for the highest grades and the other two terms, imbecile and idiotic, could still apply to the lower grades, as recommended by the committee, and thus avoid the necessity of any new term. However, applying the word feeble-minded generically, as the circumstances seemed to require, the committee were compelled to secure a new term for the high grade. The writer does not presume to pass upon the philological question involved in selecting, for instance, one Greek word in preference to another of similar meaning, nor to judge of the advantage of selecting from Greek, rather than Latin, but it is essential, however, that the word selected be simple in form. We are permitted to refer to Professor John C. Hutchinson, at the head of the Greek department of using the term, moron, recommended by the committee, and in treating it entirely as though it were an Anglo-Saxon word, that is, ignoring any attempt to follow Greek inflections. Either one of two or three other Greek words, as good as the one selected, might have been used, perhaps. However, this is immaterial so long as we can agree upon one definite term that is simple and presents no intrinsic objection to its use.

As to the matter of emphasizing a psychological basis for classification rather than a pathological one, we can see no serious objection to it, if thereby we secure a means of determining quickly even an approximate estimate of the child's mental ability by some system that is of general application and that presents to all, the physician, the teacher, the parent, and the student, alike, the same mental picture to be referred to a common mental standard. Who is there that does not have a mental picture always in view, of the activities and capacities of normal children at different ages? What more natural or rational than to compare the mind, backward in development, with a normal one? The only requirements for this are, 1st, a concise summary of the intellectual expressions of the mind of a child in groups corresponding to its different ages; and 2nd. some means of determining the group of expression that characterize the mentally deficient child under examination. It seems to us that the whole question of classifying upon a psychological basis, hinges upon whether these last requirements are met,— and this again hinges upon whether the Binet, or some other similar or equivalent system meets, or can meet, the requirements.

Dr. Goddard's examination of 400 children at Vineland seems to place them so accurately in the scale of intelligence already in use under Dr. Barr's classification and the other forms, as interpreted by Mr. Johnstone and his corps of teachers, that the results seem to them very satisfactory. We have experienced the same satisfaction in the results so far obtained by Dr. Kuhlmann in the examination of 150 children at Faribault during last September.

We have reason to congratulate the committee upon its work in laying so excellent a foundation and there remains only the careful testing out of a large number of cases and the securing of well-worked-out normal data from American school children, with the possible modifications and corrections that such experience may suggest, to give us a reliable and practicable standard for a psychological classification.

We must not be understood as belittling the pathological basis of the mental defect itself, for the recognition of the fact of a pathological basis is necessary for a more complete understanding of the case— both for scientific accuracy and for assisting in prognosis. The classification proposed provides a happy blending of the pathological and psychological descriptions.

We would, however, throw out a word of caution about the application of the mental tests. To do any scientific work properly, the operator must have had some training in scientific methods, and to secure reliable date concerning feeble-minded children, one must know from experience something of the nature of the class he is working with and must possess that peculiar, and not altogether common faculty of securing the absolute confidence of the child, and hence, the ability to obtain a full response in each case. The question of diagnosis of mental defect is often involved in court practice and it can readily be seen how easily unprincipled charlatans might exploit alleged laboratory tests in the interest of criminal offenses against feeble-minded women of the higher grades. It will be wrong to inculcate the idea that anybody without special training can diagnose and classify mental defect.

3

Mongols in Our Midst

John Langdon Down and the Ethnic Classification of Idiocy, 1858–1924

David Wright

I.

For the past two decades, historians of medicine have sought to construct narratives from below,[1] placing emphasis on the experiences of patients and their illnesses. This approach owes its origins to the American physician Henry Sigerist, who in the 1940s, called upon researchers to look beyond the "great men" of medical history and to locate our understanding of the history of health care in the social interactions between patient and doctor.[2] His clarion call arose from the realization, now much more widely acknowledged than during his own time, that the vast majority of sickness, and the interactions between healer and sufferer, occurred outside traditional realms of the medical profession and the clinic.[3] The advent of the "new" social history in academe in the 1960s and 1970s gave impetus to Sigerist's view of a medical history concerned with the cultural and social determinants of health, with lay and medical understandings of disease. It provided the intellectual groundwork for the creation of the social history of medicine as a discipline. A phalanx of historians and medical practitioners have now challenged the chimera of unfettered unilinear progress in the history of health, replacing an aging medical historiography with new investigations from an interdisciplinary perspective.[4]

Within the history of Anglo-American psychiatry, the social history of medicine approach has been pronounced in the publication of several excellent monographs on individual institutions.[5] In spite of, or perhaps because of, this unrelenting scrutiny, controversy over the rise of the asylum, and of professional psychiatry, persists. Indeed, it would not be an exaggeration to suggest that the history of psychiatry has been the most intensely debated area in the history of medicine during the past quarter century, presently boasting its own journal and several national and international societies.[6] Despite the acute attention paid to the social dimensions of incarceration and asylum treatment, the history of those whom the British now call the "learning disabled" and North Americans the "intellectually disabled" remains a relatively marginal topic. Roy Porter has recently suggested that part of the lack of interest in the "idiots" and "imbeciles" of yesteryear emanates from the attraction of the subject matter: "Madness continues to exercise its magic, but mindlessness holds no mystique."[7] Porter has something here. Western society places a premium on intelligence and creativity but tends to devalue historically those who could not, metaphorically or literally, make the grade. Intellectual disability, as a consequence, has languished in the periphery of the new historiography.[8]

Fortunately, this neglect is being redressed. The appearance in the past two decades of a handful of articles and monographs on the history of intellectual disability has revealed a subject area more contentious, challenging, and topical than some commentators previously have acknowledged. Researchers, for instance, have shown how discussions over the "danger of the feebleminded" during the first decades of the twentieth century intersected with the most important debates about national degeneration.[9] Those interested in race hygiene in the interwar period know only too well that the "mentally deficient" were among the first victims of the Nazi sterilization program, and that eugenic concerns about hereditarian transmission were realized in provincial and state legislation across the United States and Canada both before and after the Second World War.[10] A growing academic interest in disability studies,[11] particularly in North America, has given the history of "mental retardation" a wider audience.[12] The recent publication of Mathew Thomson's analysis of the "problem of mental deficiency" in interwar England and of Mark Jackson's analysis of the "fabrication of the feeble mind" during the Edwardian period offers the hope that the earlier American scholarship is now being replicated in Britain.[13] Unfortunately, too many excellent doctoral theses replete with original research have failed to find the light of publication as monographs.[14]

With the success of the social history of medicine, scholars who emphasize the great figures and discoveries of psychiatric history have come under attack, if not ridicule. It is true that much of what passed, in previous decades, as biographical work in the history of psychiatry was often Whiggish, descriptive, and hagiographical. But scholars have recently suggested that the pendulum has swung too far against biographical studies. Even historical sociologists, such as Andrew Scull, are arguing that social history needs to be rescued from mindless icon toppling. Both he and Edward Shorter have been at the forefront in forging new and sophisticated reinterpretations of important psychiatrists and their impact on society.[15] John Langdon Down is just such an individual who is deserving of reconsideration. Within traditional medical history, he is seen as a physician who was in advance of his time in the treatment, classification, and special accommodation for persons with intellectual disabilities.[16] Scheerenberger and Kanner classify him as one of the outstanding lights in the history of "mental retardation."[17] He is clearly seen, in the words of his most recent biographer, as a "pioneer," comparable in impact to Lister or Pasteur.[18] By contrast, Down has also proved extremely controversial, as the inventor of an overtly "racist" taxonomy of mental disability that stigmatized those with trisomy 21 for the next century. Stephen Jay Gould, for one, attacked Down's ethnic classification as typifying the racism of the Victorian era more widely, a theme recently taken up by disability scholars.[19]

This chapter seeks to reexamine the social history and intellectual legacy of John Langdon Down, charting his rise from near obscurity to the hallowed halls of the Royal College of Physicians, from a bright if unknown resident medical tutor to an acclaimed Victorian alienist whose atypical anthropological theories would forever associate his name with the archetype of intellectual disability. It locates Down's formulation of Mongolism within the context of the 1860s anthropological debates over racial genesis and evolution and contextualizes his ideas within the articulation of degeneration theory that was slowly gaining a foothold in intellectual circles in Europe, Britain and North America. Last, it reveals the alacrity with which Mongolism was accepted as a useful classification of idiocy, even when many contemporaries disputed or challenged the theoretical basis for Down's original ethnic classification. In the mid-Victorian period, there were no easily distinguishable national borders of professional discourse. Alienists traveled widely, consulted with colleagues on both sides of the Atlantic, and read other national professional periodicals. Down's ideas of Mongolism, published in British medical treaties and medical periodicals, quickly infiltrated the small but growing body of professional literature in North America and in the British colonies.

II.

In 1858, the British Parliament passed the Medical Registration Act, which established a General Medical Council empowered with overseeing a profession unified in theory, if not in practice.[20] Appearing on the first national medical register was the newly hired medical superintendent of the Earlswood Asylum, a recent graduate of London University Medical School named John Langdon Down. Down must have been fortunate in securing a position at a voluntary hospital at so young an age. Born in 1828 in Torpoint, Cornwall (southwest England), Down entered into a modest family of Irish lineage, the son of a West Country apothecary. As a young man, he worked under the supervision of his father before moving to London to apprentice to a surgeon in Whitechapel. Later, in 1847, he joined the Pharmaceutical Society. For the next three years, he was employed as a chemist, allegedly assisting Faraday in some of his now famous experiments, before traveling to Devon to recover from an undisclosed illness. In 1853, Down returned to London and enrolled as a medical student at the London Hospital.

As a student, Down had been fortuitously assigned to William J. Little, physician to the London Hospital. Clearly a very gifted student, Down passed the examination of the Royal College of Surgeons in April 1856 and his Licentiate of the Worshipful Society of Apothecaries in November of the same year.[21] At the London University examinations, he won three hospital gold medals and was voted best clinical student of his year.[22] Down's accumulation of academic prizes clearly impressed Little to the extent that the influential consultant offered him the opportunity to stay on at the London Hospital, acting as a tutor to other medical students, as a "resident accoucheur," and as a lecturer in comparative anatomy. With the rapid establishment of provincial infirmaries in the second half of the eighteenth century, the emergence of teaching schools in the early nineteenth century, and the development of more specialized medical knowledge during the first decades of the Victorian era, the medical profession became divided more and more along the lines of those who received elevated prestige and salaries within the voluntary hospitals and those who engaged in the more volatile and precarious field of community practice—the consultant–general practitioner divide that still dominates British medicine today. Sensing he might end up on the wrong side of the widening disparity in medical livelihoods, Down accepted Little's offer to remain on staff at the London. In addition to performing the onerous tasks of supervising attending medical students, tutoring, lecturing, and assisting hundreds of births, he completed his M.B., finishing second in his class, and began to work toward his M.D.[23] Like any young medical practitioner of his generation, he eagerly awaited the vacancy of a permanent hospital position.

His opportunity would arrive in the expanding asylum sector. English county pauper lunatic asylums were first established in the wake of the 1808 Asylums Act. In 1845, in the Lunatics Act, Parliament made the central provisions of the 1808 Act compulsory, in effect obliging all county magistrates to construct asylums for their poor insane. As has been shown elsewhere, most of the patients in these institutions were lunatics, rather than idiots.[24] Thus, in 1847, a small group of medical practitioners and nonconformist philanthropists led by the Congregationalist minister Andrew Reed established a charitable asylum designed specifically for idiots, first in a small home in London and in Colchester and later in a large purpose-built asylum in Redhill, Surrey, south of the metropolis. Constructed on Earlswood Common, the National Asylum for Idiots (later, Earlswood Asylum) had room for 500 patients in a training and vocational environment inspired by the Frenchman-turned-American Edouard Séguin. The National Asylum was copied by similar institutions for the eastern, western, and northern counties of England.[25]

In 1858, Dr. Maxwell, the resident medical superintendent at the Earlswood Asylum, resigned, leaving the position vacant. The patronage of William Little, a consulting physician to Earlswood, proved crucial for Down. Little lobbied John Conolly, former medical superintendent of the Middlesex County Pauper Lunatic Asylum (Hanwell), and Sir James Clark, Physician-in-Ordinary to the Royal Household, on Down's behalf, securing Down's appointment in the autumn of 1858. Both Little and Conolly had been associated with the Earlswood Asylum from its inception, acting as Honorary Visiting Physicians to the first homes and participating in the planning of the impressive new building on Earlswood Common. They shared professional interests in mental and physical disabilities in children. William Little is remembered for his research into spastic paralysis and credited as the "discoverer" of a form of cerebral palsy.[26] John Conolly was the most celebrated alienist of his generation, the champion of the nonrestraint movement. His brilliant, if somewhat inconsistent, life has been examined thoroughly elsewhere.[27] Less known are his ultimately unsuccessful attempts to establish an "idiot wing" at the giant Middlesex County Asylum

(Hanwell), in which he devised special educational approaches to idiot children during his tenure as visiting and resident physician in the 1840s. Along with Samuel Gaskell, former medical superintendent of the Lancaster Asylum and, from 1848, a national inspector of asylums with the Lunacy Commission,[28] Little and Conolly helped galvanize professional medical opinion behind the project to create a "National Asylum for Idiots." The appointment of medical men to asylum positions in the Victorian era was often mired in controversy, with critics contending that connections, rather than experience, usually won out.[29] Down still had to complete his M.D. during his first year of residency at Earlswood. He had no professional knowledge of the institutional treatment of the insane, let alone practical experience in treating and educating idiot children (though the fact that he was then a Dissenter may have helped with the Nonconformist board). In addition, he was entering into a position that was only modestly remunerated (150 pounds per annum), in an institution that was not completely finished, and under the authority of an asylum board that had fallen out with the Lunacy Commissioners. It was not the most auspicious way to begin a career, but it could have been much worse. He could have been scraping out a living in the overcrowded medical market of the mid-Victorian period or continuing to try to achieve middle-class respectability from the irregular earnings of a medical school lecturer. Instead, Down had something valuable and rare at the time—a guaranteed income, a degree of job security, and the potential to develop specialist skills. Although he would at first show signs of regret about his decision—having arrived at the asylum to experience life within a Victorian mental hospital for the first time—his accession to the position of resident medical superintendent would prove to be a turning point in his life.[30]

Under Conolly's mentorship, Down quickly familiarized himself with the practical aspects of asylum management. Reputedly a handsome and charming man, he revealed an ability to align himself strategically within the asylum community and among members of the Earlswood Board of Managers, a committee made up of lay as well as medical representatives. Within the first year of his superintendence, he persuaded the board to include for the first time a separate Report of the Medical Superintendent describing the medical and educational advances of the asylum as an appendix to the charity's annual report.[31] The thirty-year-old medical superintendent appreciated that the annual reports were sent to more than 10,000 subscribers, a certain way to elevate the medical profile of the institution and to spread his reputation to potential clientele of the southeast of England. Further, Down convinced the board to permit him to continue lecturing pupils and staff at the London Hospital, traveling north to the metropolis periodically to wax eloquently on "childhood diseases of the mind." Shortly thereafter, he was elected assistant visiting physician to the hospital, thereby maintaining important links to the medical elite of London.[32]

John Langdon Down's evident lack of asylum experience did not prevent him from converting to the cause of segregated treatment of the insane, soon proving a more effective proponent than even the elderly Andrew Reed, the asylum's founder. Through his annual reports and London Hospital lectures, Down used his position as a pulpit from which to preach the advantages of separate institutional care and education of idiot children. "In but few homes," he affirmed, "is it possible to have the appliances for physical and intellectual training adapted for the duration of the feeble in mind."[33] Down distanced the idiot asylums from the tide of criticism concerning the overcrowded conditions of county lunatic asylums and emphasized the lack of "scientific" education available to idiot children in those pauper institutions. In county asylums, Down contended, "the entire machinery is adapted for another class of patients, and the idiot residents forming but a small proportion, they are for the most part overlooked in the general routine of the establishment."[34] By advocating the creation of idiot institutions separate from lunatic asylums, Down contributed to a prominent tendency of the mid-Victorian medical profession: a desire to seek increasing specialization of knowledge and practice.[35] Larger and clearly differentiated hospitals afforded the opportunity, in the mindset of mid-Victorian proponents, for the benefit of classification and specialized treatment. Thus, Down welcomed, rather than lamented, the steady growth of the Earlswood Asylum from 306 patients to 455 patients under his stewardship. He sought not only to establish separate institutions for idiot children but to classify and separate idiot children by intellectual ability within idiot asylums:

> In small Institutions there must necessarily be commingling [sic] of the inmates, and the consequent danger of disadvantage resulting from the influence of the least intelligent upon those who are higher in scale. With our greatly increased family we have been enabled, by classification, to obviate this evil, and to supply them in their several rooms with the kinds of amusement and occupation suited to their various capacities.[36]

In the autumn of 1860, Down completed his informal asylum apprentice-ship. In a sojourn that had by then become a rite of passage, he secured leave from the board to travel to the birthplace of idiot asylums, Paris, to observe the practices of the successors of Jean-Etienne Esquirol and Edouard Séguin. He returned to England confident that Earlswood held a "prominent position of superiority" compared to its Continental counterparts.[37]

Although Down sought to shield his voluntary idiot asylum from unflattering associations with county pauper lunatic institutions, he faced many of the administrative burdens inherent in being an asylum superintendent in the mid-Victorian period. Under the English lunacy laws, he had to provide a history for all new admissions, complete with approximately forty separate findings. Discharge orders were completed upon the end of a stay, death notices pronounced upon the decease of a patient. The medical superintendent was required by law to visit all patients every day and to minister in particular to those who were infirm. Considering the number of patients who suffered through epileptic fits or who had contracted infectious diseases, this was no small burden. Abstracts of all deaths, discharges, and admissions were to be sent to the national inspectorate, the Lunacy Commission. Further, Down reported to the monthly meeting of the Earlswood board and wrote biannual reports to the Lunacy Commissioners and annual reports to the subscribers of the institution. He was also the administrative head of an institution of fifty attendants, nurses, and domestic staff and was responsible for attendants' moral behavior and their treatment of the inmates. Although being an asylum superintendent afforded some opportunity for research and public lectures and a modest degree of professional status, the drudgery of routine and repetitive administrative requirements burdened the overwhelming majority of the time of these alienists.[38]

Faced with considerable administrative responsibilities and an asylum of more than 400 patients, Down convinced the board to hire a young assistant medical officer, George Shuttleworth, who would later accept the position of medical superintendent of the Northern Counties (Royal Albert) Asylum for Idiots, near Lancaster, where he established a reputation in England second only to that of Down himself. Down elevated the medical dimensions of care and treatment within the quotidian experience of asylum life. His medical casebooks reveal that he relied on a multiplicity of chemical interventions for sedating excitable patients and for stimulating melancholic inmates. In a manner similar to the treatment conducted in lunatic asylums at the time,

Down regularly employed potassium bromide, chloral hydrate, and opium to "calm" patients. Cold showers were also used to quiet violent and "maniacal patients." In order to counter the outbreaks of scarlatina (scarlet fever) and cholera, he insisted on the construction of a detached infirmary, though it was not completed until after his departure. In most respects, the administration of daily medicines to patients and the strategies Down utilized to deal with the management of violent or aggressive behavior do not seem to have differed from those described by most asylum medical superintendents in the pages of the *Journal of Mental Science*[39] or those recommended by the Lunacy Commissioners in their annual reports.

III.

As would be natural for any person in his position, Down joined the Association of Medical Officers of Hospitals and Asylums for the Insane, the forerunner to the British Psychiatric Association. Founded in 1841, the association changed its cumbersome name in 1864 to the Medico-Psychological Association so as to impart a more medical and less administrative tone to the society. The society's members, who jovially referred to themselves as the "wandering lunatics," followed the predictable path of professionalization, establishing a journal, the *Asylum Journal* (from 1856, the *Journal of Mental Science*); soliciting original articles and case studies on the etiology, treatment, and pathology of insanity; and organizing meetings where a common sense of identity could be forged. Although the association self-consciously dropped any reference to "Asylum" both from its name and from the title of its journal, members were overwhelmingly drawn from purpose-built institutions for the insane. Consequently, the size of the association grew in proportion to the number of asylums in Great Britain. In 1827, there were nine lunatic and idiot asylums, with an average size of 116 inmates. By 1870, there were fifty-one such asylums, employing 250 medical practitioners, with an average size of 550 inmates. The psychiatric profession thus developed in response to the rising tide of the confinement of idiots and lunatics during the nineteenth century.[40]

Throughout the first half of the nineteenth century, medical thinking on idiocy and imbecility, as on insanity more generally, had been deeply influenced by phrenology. Franz Joseph Gall and his followers had advanced the idea that faculties of the mind could be localized cerebrally. Intelligence, affections, even religious observance could be measured through a careful examination of cranial size, structure, and topography. Although phrenology is now considered a pseudo-science, many aspects of its philosophy were embraced by alienists in the decades leading up to the Lunatics Act of 1845. Phrenology appealed to asylum medical superintendents in various ways. It offered a coherent "scientific" explanation for understanding mental disorder as a "disease of the mind" and thus legitimated medical hegemony over mental disorder and disability. By suggesting that innate faculties could be modified and improved, it also offered an optimistic impetus that appealed to reform-minded medical practitioners.[41] Although researchers have identified the mid-Victorian period as one in which the attractiveness of phrenology waned, because of both the death of the original prophets and the decline in the visible benefits of moral treatment,[42] the adherence to phrenological tenets persisted among the subgroup of asylum superintendents associated with the idiot asylums established in the 1850s and 1860s. Idiocy, it is important to emphasize, had been held in special regard by phrenologists, and treatises such as George Blackie's on cretinism in 1855 continued the fascination with cranial malformation and intellectual impairment.[43] Gall, as William Ireland, superintendent of the Scottish National Institute for the Training of Imbecile Children, would recall to his readers in his 1887 textbook, had identified idiot children as one clear proof that intellectual faculties were associated with cranial anomalies.[44] The continued association of John Conolly with the Earlswood Asylum (until his death in 1866) may have also influenced the young Langdon Down. Conolly took no measures to hide the influence of phrenology upon his own thinking, active as he was in the Warwick and Leamington Phrenological Association, as committee member of the [National] Phrenological Association in 1844, and as president of the Ethnology Society in 1855–56.[45] Shortly before his death, the famous alienist acknowledged that, "no person not altogether void of the power of observation can affect to overlook the general importance of the shape and even the size of the brain in relation to the development of the mental faculties."[46]

The influence of Conolly's ideas about cranial localization was not lost on Earlswood's new medical superintendent. In the early 1860s, Down began publishing articles in the *British Medical Journal* and the *Journal of Mental Science* on cerebral abnormalities, such as the imperfect formation of the corpus callosum, as well as describing the malformation of the mouth and tongue in idiot children.[47] Down's interest was also facilitated by the measurements required by the Lunatics Act of 1853. The first page of the medical casebook included lay information gleaned from the certificates of insanity and the reception orders, as well as a host of medical data that fell under the responsibility of the resident medical superintendent. Down thus not only was responsible for basic physical descriptions but also had to detail measurements of the skull's circumference, the width of the forehead, and the distance between the root of the nose and the occipital prominence at the back of the head.[48]

In the wake of Darwin's *Origins of the Species,* Down became drawn to the implications of evolutionary theory to ethnology, joining the Anthropological Society of London sometime in the early 1860s.[49] Several papers read before the Society in 1863–64 attest to its members' fascination with the relationship among racial development, intellectual ability, and cranial physiognomy.[50] Anthropological circles in 1860s London were gripped by contests between an older school of ethnology that believed in the essential "unity of mankind," the *monogenists,* and a new a radical group, led by Dr. James Hunt, who asserted the etiological separateness of racial "types," the *polygenists.*[51] In the midst of this debate, Down speculated about the racial implications of idiocy, proposing in one address that arrested racial development could result in idiocy. In a now famous paper delivered to the London Hospital, Down described the racial grouping of some of the patients he had encountered:

> I have been able to find among large number of idiots and imbeciles which came under my observation, both at Earlswood and the out-patient department of the [London H]ospital that a considerable portion can be fairly referred to one of the great divisions of the human family other than the class from which they have sprung. . . . The Great Mongolian family has numerous representatives, and it is to this division I wish . . . to call special attention. A very large number of congenital idiots are typical Mongols.

Down continued by describing the facial and cranial stigmata of a specific group of similarly looking idiot children:

> The hair is not black, as in the real Mongol, but of a brownish colour, straight and scanty. The face is flat and broad, and destitute of prominence. Cheeks are roundish, and extended laterally. The eyes are obliquely

placed, and the internal canthi more than normally distant from one another. The palpebral fissue is very narrow. . . . The lips are large and thick with transverse fissures. The tongue is long, thick, and much roughened. The nose is very small.[52]

Drawing on the flood of ideas in the 1860s about racial characteristics, he hypothesized that a possible explanation for the attributes was atavism, the spontaneous reversion of individuals to earlier "premodern" races of humans. Down postulated that certain types of mental disease could "break down" the racial barrier so as to "simulate features of the members of another [race]." Thus, the "great Mongolian family" represented, to him, the reversion of Caucasian children to an earlier, "less developed" race. "So marked is this [racial imprinting] that when placed side by side," Down affirmed, "it is difficult to believe that the specimens compared are not children of the same parents." He then proceeded to categorize the population of the Earlswood Asylum into "Mongolian," "Malay," "Ethiopian," "Aztec," and "Caucasian" idiots, attempting to incorporate each into his new anthropological hierarchy. But the Mongolian "family" was the most numerous—as many as 10 percent of his asylum could be grouped into this category, he conjectured. His paper, published the following year in the *Journal of Mental Science,* sought to advance his contention that idiocy occupied a place of central importance in the anthropological debates of the 1860s by illustrating that individuals could "revert" from one racial type to another. This, according to Down, disproved the polygenist belief that the races came from different sources.[53]

Down's "ethnic classification" of idiocy has been attacked historically by those who see it as an inherently "racist" ideology.[54] To do so is to decontextualize the anthropological debates of the mid-Victorian period. Anthropologists and ethnologists in the 1860s were attempting to come to grips with the impact of Darwin's revolutionary theory of evolution. Aligning himself with the more traditional and embattled school of humanitarian anthropology, Down asserted the ethnological relevance of his classification explicitly:

Apart from the practical bearing of this attempt at an ethnic classification, considerable philosophical interest attaches to it. The tendency today is to reject the opinion that the various races are merely variety of the human family having a common origin, and to insist that climatic or other influences are sufficient to account for the different types of man.

Here, however, we have examples of retrogression, or at all events, of departure from one type and the assumption of the characteristics of another. . . . These examples of the result of degeneracy among mankind appear to me to furnish some arguments in favour of the unity of the human species.[55]

To our ears, although Down's suggestion that Caucasians were more "developed" (in evolutionary terms) than "Mongols" is offensive, his views actually placed him in the "liberal" camp of thought, that is, with those who believed that all races stood on the same continuum and shared a common ancestry.[56] The alternate view, to which Down alluded, contended that other non-Caucasian and "inferior" races were derived from separate origins (and, by implication, Caucasians were of a superior racial type). This alternate school of ethnology had been used to assert the "natural state" of slavery, a question of some debate, especially considering that slavery was one of the central points of contention in the devastating American Civil War that had just ended.[57]

By the time his publication of an "ethnic" classification had appeared in the *Journal of Mental Science* in 1867, John Langdon Down had built up a devoted audience of students attending his lectures, titled "Medicine, Materia Medica and Comparative Anatomy," at the London Hospital.[58] The restrictions of an institutional post led to an incident that was all too common in public medical institutions and that reveals the fault lines that divide the ambitions of talented medical practitioners, the increasing specialization in Victorian medicine, the status of superintendents' wives within medical institutions, and an older tension of lay versus medical authority. Earlswood placed a limit on the number of private patients it would admit in any given year. It was, after all, a charitable asylum, built for the poorer classes, with only a few beds for private (paying) patients, not a large private (for-profit) licensed home. As a consequence, there were numbers of wealthy families who were willing to pay significant sums for an idiot son or daughter who had been refused for lack of space. By December 1867, there were fifty-one Payment Cases on the waiting list alone.[59] In that month, the Earlswood board was alerted to the fact that patients were being kept in the community and suspected that John Langdon Down was taking payments in addition to his contract.[60] At their monthly meeting, board members requested that the House Committee "inquire if any children other than their own are kept in the cottages of the attendants or servants of the institution."[61] The subsequent story of Down's sudden departure can only be gleaned from the minutes of the board, but several facts appeared uncontested. Sometime during 1867, or earlier, the wives of at least two attendants, Everett and Walker, had started to receive private patients in their cottages. Mrs. Everett had three patients, Mrs. Walker one. In return for their "services to the asylum," their husbands had received "increased" remuneration under the authority of Down. None of this, it appears, had been brought to the attention of the board. Summoned to explain his actions, Langdon Down was prickly and evasive, saying that there were indeed private patients being kept for a fee in attendants' cottages but that they were under the care of attendants' wives and that the whole arrangement was being supervised by Mary Langdon Down, his wife (who by his implication was not bound by his contract with the board). Further, Down admitted that there were "a few other [additional] patients" lodged similarly who were also under Mrs. Down's care and supervision. But "she alone" he insisted, "is responsible." He also argued that he was doing the board a favor by "preserving" excellent private candidates for future vacancies.

Mary Langdon Down, throughout her husband's tenure at the institution, played a central role in the smooth operation of the Earlswood Asylum. She was often seen counseling mothers of children who had recently been admitted, conferring with the matron of the institution regarding the behavior of the female attendants, and taking a leading role in the preparation of special events. Her activities appeared, thus, to conform to the accepted rituals of the wife of a superintendent without stepping outside the boundaries of the defined sex roles for middle-class women of her generation. Within the context of mid-Victorian conceptualization of marital contracts and the legal status of women more generally, the contract John Langdon Down had signed—that he must devote all his time to the patients at Earlswood and take no private patients—would have applied also to his wife by default. Down contended, however, that wives should be able to care for, and receive, private patients outside institutions, "as Mrs. Down would be to engage in literature, Mrs. Walker to keep a shop, or Mrs. Everett to take in dressmaking."[62] Down's retort was not as self-serving as it first appeared, inasmuch as there were several wives of asylum medical superintendents in England who were paid formally to serve as matrons to the same institution in which their husband worked.[63] However, John Langdon Down's case was not assisted by the fact that he had never formally requested remuneration for his wife and by the fact that all patients kept in private homes for a fee had to be legally registered with the Lunacy Commissioners, from whom neither he nor Mary had received approval. A man of Down's intelligence must have known that his actions were technically illegal. At the brink of what could have been a rather fascinating legal discussion, the dispute spun out of control. The board proposed to convene a "special Meeting" to be held on 14 February 1868. Before the board could meet, Down penned his resignation letter on 10 February, departing from the position he had held just shy of ten years, and for reasons which he described, in a pregnant way, as "cumulative." The board unanimously agreed to accept his resignation, assuring him "that he was quite in error in assuming that the Committee had come to foregone conclusions in relation to the questions contained in their letter to him."[64]

So what were the "cumulative" reasons that lay behind Down's apparently premature exit from the Earlswood Asylum? By 1868, Down had become the nationally respected leader of a movement for the care and treatment of idiot children. The demand from wealthy clients was so intense that he must have realized that his ten years at the Earlswood Asylum had served its purpose and that he could do better as the proprietor of a private institution of his own. Shortly after his resignation in 1868, he took up a Harley Street private practice[65] and received a license to found a private idiot establishment at White House, Hampton Wick, later renamed Normansfield Training Institution for Imbeciles. There he exploited the demand for asylum accommodation from the wealthier segments of the upper middle classes, charging £100 per annum to £200 per annum, with a license for 140 patients. Revealingly, the Lunacy Commissioners listed Normansfield as a Metropolitan Licensed House under the guidance of Dr. *and* Mrs. Down and stated that "Mrs. Down devotes her whole time to the management of the Institution."[66] Destined to be one of the largest private licensed homes in the country, Normansfield grew from 80 "students" in 1868 to its maximum of 140 in 1896, the year of Down's death. By this time, Down was a national and international expert on the mental diseases of childhood and youth and a prominent and respected member of the British medical establishment, having founded and presided over the Thames Valley branch of the British Medical Association and remaining a consulting physician to the London Hospital until his death. Down was also involved in local politics and administration, being appointed a justice of the peace for Westminster and Middlesex (1886), a county alderman in 1889, and remaining to his death a "pronounced" Liberal.[67] In 1885, he was invited to deliver the prestigious Lettsomian lectures, which formed the basis of his last major work. By then, this son of a West Country apothecary had crowned his career by having been elected a Fellow of the Royal College of Physicians. The continued prominence of his two surviving sons, Reginald and Perceval, who both read medicine at Cambridge and took over the operation of Normansfield upon the death of their father, maintained the Langdon Down name within the British medical establishment. Reginald, in particular, would be an important witness in the Royal Commission on Care and Control of the Feeble-minded. Langdon Down died in 1896 and received glowing tributes in the *Lancet* and in the *British Medical Journal.*[68] It had been a long journey from Torpoint, Devon.

IV.

It should be remembered that Down's novel classification of idiocy coincided with a flurry of publications on the taxonomy and education of idiot children, all published by the medical superintendents of the principal idiot asylums in Britain and North America. Until 1866, there were only a handful of books on the training and classification of idiot children. The first comprehensive set of articles appeared in French, penned by the famous Edouard Séguin. A physician at the Bicêtre Hospital in Paris, Séguin experimented with methods of training idiot children,[69] techniques that concentrated on the improvement of the mind through sensory experience and object association. Teaching began with discrimination, first of colors and numbers widely separated, and then, progressively, to finer discriminations. In the early 1840s, Séguin published several treatises in French on the treatment and education of idiots.[70] His works were reviewed widely in the British press and moved the French-speaking John Conolly to visit Séguin and study his techniques in 1846. Séguin had also inspired the first major American study of idiocy, that of Samuel Gridley Howe and his inquiry in the Commonwealth of Massachusetts, published under the title *On the Causes of Idiocy.*[71] In England, 1866 also witnessed the publication of *A Manual for the Classification, Training, and Education of the Feeble-Minded, Imbecile, & Idiotic* (1866), by William Millard, the lay superintendent of Park House, who had helped found the Eastern Counties Asylum for Idiots at Colchester, Essex, and the Eastern Counties Asylum's visiting physician P. Martin Duncan.[72] When Down's ethnic classification was published in the *Journal of Mental Science,* it was part of a torrent of new professional literature on idiocy, including his first major book, *A Treatise on Idiocy and Its Cognate Affections* (1867).[73]

The proliferation of ideas about idiocy had been encouraged by the expansion of asylums for idiots and by the eagerness of their medical superintendents to stake a claim in this new medical subdiscipline. In 1867, John Langdon Down, Fletcher Beach, William Ireland, and George Shuttleworth held the first ever medical conference on idiocy, in Belfast. The quartet represented the most influential idiocy alienists in Britain at the time. Fletcher Beach, the medical superintendent of the Metropolitan Asylums Board Darenth Colony for Idiot and Imbecile Children, was to have a long and successful career studying idiocy and epilepsy in children and represented the Royal College of Physicians before the Royal Commission on Care and Control of the Feeble-Minded in 1905.[74] William Wetherspoon Ireland graduated from medical school in 1858 and became the medical superintendent of the new Scottish National Institute for Imbecile Children at Larbert in 1869. His textbook appeared in 1877.[75] George Shuttleworth, briefly Down's assistant at the Earlswood Asylum in the late 1860s, enjoyed a reputation as medical superintendent of the Royal Albert Asylum, at Lancaster, and published widely in the 1880s on the etiology and training of idiot children, culminating in the publication of *Mentally Defective Children,* the standard textbook for the remainder of the century.[76] The establishment of idiot asylums had thus created a unique medical expertise that found its fruition in treatises on idiocy in the last third of the nineteenth century.

Shuttleworth had been initially the most supportive of Down's new formulation. After he left the Earlswood Asylum in 1870 to take up the superintendent's position at the Northern Counties (Royal Albert) Asylum, near Lancaster, he regularly employed the term "Mongolian" to describe patients fashioned after Down's new descriptive taxonomy, though, unlike Down, he believed that the etiology of Mongolism was related to intemperance in the parents, rather than, as Down hypothesized, to the degenerative influences of phthisis (tuberculosis). Like Down, however, he continued the interest in the cranial characteristics of idiocy, referring to the measurements of a "Mongolian idiot" in the *Journal of Mental Science,* in 1881.[77] Ireland, however, was more skeptical, having been present at the Medico-Psychological Association meeting in Scotland where Sir Arthur Mitchell and Robert Fraser had presented their paper "Kalmuc Idiocy," a formulation very similar to that of Down ten years earlier. Sir Arthur had spent several years as a Scottish Lunacy Commissioner, inspecting the insane in private care, and had made an observation stunningly similar to that of Langdon Down, namely that there was a group of similarly looking idiot children whom he believed bore facial stigmata reminiscent of the "Kalmuc" race. Also, like Down, Mitchell regarded the Kalmuc idiot as representing a state of incomplete physiological development.[78] That Mitchell and Fraser were unaware of Down's earlier paper is unlikely, though not impossible. Nevertheless, and perhaps in a fit of national pride, Ireland avoided Down's English appellation of Mongolism in his 1877 treatise, preferring instead to refer to "Scottish" Kalmuc idiocy. Even here, however, Ireland thought that the importance of this group, whatever the label, was being exaggerated, as he believed that only 3 percent of his own patients at the Scottish National Institution were thus affected.[79] Indeed, in *On Idiocy and Imbecility,* he advanced an entirely new system of classifying idiocy based on comorbidity and supposed etiology.[80] A recent biographer of Down suggests that the omission of Down's ethnic classification in Mitchell and Ireland's paper may explain the reprinting and reassertion of his famous "Ethnic Classification of Idiocy" London Hospital report, and other early papers, in his final treatise, *On Some of the Mental Affections of Childhood and Youth.*[81] Certainly, Down conspicuously placed his ethnic classification at the very beginning of his first Lettsomian lecture.[82]

The terms "Mongolism" and "Kalmuc" idiocy appeared almost immediately in American medical discourse in the late 1870s. The speed of acquisition may have been partly the result of the influence of Shuttleworth and Fletcher Beach, who attended the first meeting of the Association of Medical Officers of American Institutions for Idiotic and Feeble-minded Persons, in 1876. At the meeting, Hervey Wilbur, a colleague of Seguin, read a paper on "that modified form of cretinism quite common in this country [America] and Great Britain, which has been called the Mongolian or Kalmuc type of idiocy." Wilbur, while accepting the utility of the term "Mongolism," rejected Down's underlying theory and instead, like Seguin, placed the condition in the realm of cretinism. "I find little constant resemblance," he concluded, "to the Mongolian race in these degenerate human beings."[83] His contemporary, Albert Wilmarth, assistant physician at the Elwyn Training School, in Pennsylvania, was similarly skeptical of Down's anthropological theorizing. He nevertheless had been influenced by Dugdale's notorious study of the Jukes. J. L. Dugdale, in 1877, had published an account of the Juke family, because of which New York state had incurred "over a million and a quarter dollars of loss in 75 years, caused by a single family of 1,200 strong."[84] Over the course of the next two decades, similar stories of huge degenerate families appeared also in the English medical press, such as a case "in which an imbecile man and woman had over 200 descendants, all of whom were defective in some way or another."[85] Amid the incipient social Darwinism, Wilmarth, at the 1899 conference of the Association of Medical Officers of American Institutions for Idiotic and Feeble-Minded Persons, read a paper entitled "Mongolian Idiocy."[86] In keeping with hereditarian ideas at the time, he suggested that a hereditarian taint caused by arrested brain development, or brain damage, could be passed down to later generations, resulting in what was being called Mongolism.

The utility of the term "Mongolism" had thus taken hold, even though the underlying theoretical framework was challenged (the Kalmuc variation faded into obscurity). What had caused the greatest difficulty in the American acceptance of the underlying anthropological implications of Down's ethnic classification was, ironically, the question of race in postemancipation United States. For Down's theory to hold, it would be counterintuitive that black Americans could give birth to Mongoloid children since, in Down's theorizing, "Ethiopians" were less developed racially than even "Mongols." But American alienists began to observe the same "racial" features in children of African Americans. An American physician, Adrien Bleyer, for instance, found two "negro infants" whom he diagnosed as "negro mongoloid idiots." His publications suggested that Mongolism could occur in any race.[87] Notwithstanding the thorough discrediting of the evolutionary underpinnings of Down's 1866 paper, the term "Mongoloid idiot" continued to be used by American and European superintendents and researchers as a useful descriptive signifier.[88]

Even in the early twentieth century, the terms "Mongoloid idiocy" and, more popularly, "Mongolism" survived, even though the underlying theoretical premise had been attacked by most experts. However, Down's racial theorizing would undergo one last renaissance of sorts before it would be thoroughly discredited by Lionel Penrose in the 1930s. Dr. P. W. Hunter, who succeeded Shuttleworth at the Royal Albert Asylum in 1893, began to postulate that the reversion was not back to a primitive race but in fact to *primates*. "These morphological aspects of the condition," he opined, "suggested that the orang-utan possibly approached much nearer the lines of human ancestry than either the gorilla or the chimpanzee."[89] Francis Crookshank, a London physician who had had previous experience as an asylum medical officer, continued Hunter's argument with modification. Crookshank hypothesized that children with features of "primitive races" that were not fully developed in utero, rather than being "Mongoloid" in Langdon Down's sense, were in fact more like primates who preceded even the "inferior" Mongol race. In *The Mongol in Our Midst,* he brought these views to a popular audience.[90] In this manner, Mongoloid idiots were a unique remembrance, a missing link.

In a final ironic moment, Langdon Down's own son Reginald, who, with his brother Percival, had taken over the administration of the Normansfield training institution after their father's death in 1896, agreed. Reginald stated that "it would appear . . . that the characters which at first sight strikingly suggest Mongolian features are in no way characteristic of the race" and, if it were a reversion, "it must be a reversion to a type even further back than the Mongol stock."[91] Reginald is now best known as the individual who identified the peculiar hand prints of individuals with Down's Syndrome—the "presence of one, rather than two, transverse lines"—the so-called simian crease.[92] But here he was competing with his father in hypothesizing how far back "Mongoloid idiots" had regressed. While it is true that Crookshank's and the younger Down's work was highly criticized (even the eugenicist Alfred Tredgold rejected Crookshank's and, by implication, the senior Down's theories by stating that it was self-evident that the vast majority of individuals of Mongol ethnicity were not mentally deficient),[93] the appeal of the empirical observation of Mongoloid idiots would prove so useful that it would continue well after the World Health Organization voted overwhelmingly in 1966 to replace the name with Down's Syndrome.[94]

Conclusions

Mongolism thus occupied a highly significant place within the deluge of ideas unleashed by Darwin's revolutionary theories of the origins of humankind. Within this intellectual milieu stood Langdon Down, a medical practitioner whose intellect, powers of observation, and aptitude for self-promotion ensured him a place in the annals of medical history. His role, however, as both a champion of special institutional provision for the intellectually disabled and a promoter of "racialized" views of Caucasian superiority put him in an awkward category for present-day historians and biographers eager to appraise his reputation in medical history. As a medical professional, he followed a remarkable path upward through the medical hierarchy of his era, apprenticing as a young man, achieving the relevant

qualifications in apothecary, surgery, and, later, physic. He slowly insinu-
ated himself into the London elite, first as a lowly lecturer and later as a
member and fellow of the Royal College of Physicians, a career and upward
progression culminating in his Harley Street private practice. He rode the
wave of possibilities for the new medical specialization that occurred during his lifetime. His decision to leave Earlswood after ten years replicated
the path of many successful alienists of his generation. His mentor, John
Conolly, though he is famously associated with the Hanwell Asylum, resigned his position in order to establish his own private licensed homes in
the metropolis. Similarly, his Scottish colleague and competitor, William
Ireland, would retire from the Scottish National Institution to establish
three private residential schools of his own.[95] Whether Down had welcomed
his own departure, taking lucrative private patients with him from
Earlswood to his new institution, may remain forever unknown, though the
significant number of private patients who had previously appeared on
Earlswood registers and were then admitted to Normansfield does look
rather suspicious.

Down was thus a profoundly successful man in a dynamic and uncertain
medical market in the Victorian era, an example of the volatility and porosity
of the social structure of Victorian England. But what of his legacy in the
taxonomy of mental disability and his murky role in the minor scandal that
led to his own resignation? It does seem, in retrospect, that Down overre-
acted to the decision of the Earlswood board or management. Perhaps he
had grown tired of answering to the ministrations, or what he might have
seen as meddling, of lay members of the board. Perhaps the deaths of Andrew Reed, in 1862, and John Conolly, in 1866, had deprived him of powerful patrons who could mediate between the ambitions of the young alienist
and the interests of the lay philanthropists. By 1868, Down stood at the pin-
nacle of his career, so there seemed little reason to continue his association
with Earlswood indefinitely, though he must have regretted the embarrassment that surrounded his departure. Extraordinary for those familiar with
Victorian etiquette, the Earlswood board did not even mention, still less
thank, Langdon Down in the annual reports that followed his exit. Indeed,
the only correspondence remaining in the archives concerns accusations by
the board that Down had stolen medical case books of private patients from
the institution.

Down's novel ethnic classification was soon forgotten, but his designation of Mongoloid idiocy, adopted by other writers of textbooks on idiocy,

was used until well into the second half of the twentieth century, even after his racial theory was finally disproved by the ctyogenetic research of the 1950s. In a strange twist of fate, it was at the Royal Eastern Counties Institution (formerly Essex Hall), Colchester, the sister house to the original Asylum for Idiots, that, in the 1930s, Penrose would conduct his famous studies of the blood types of those suffering from "mongoloid idiocy." Debunking the "mongolian ancestry" of "Mongolian idiots," Penrose suggested that researchers adopt the phrase "Down's Syndrome" or "Down's Anomaly" to avoid Down's misleading appellation and theory.[96] French-speaking countries and jurisdictions, perhaps in a fit of cultural pique, never fully accepted Down's claim to fame and opted instead for *Trisomie-21,* perhaps in a nod to the French cytogeneticist Lejeune, who discovered the chromosomal abnormality in 1959.

Down's formulation of Mongolism must be seen in the context of mid-Victorian popular and professional debates about cerebral localization and evolutionary anthropology. As Roger Cooter has shown, phrenology proved attractive to asylum superintendents who sought to solve the complex nature of mental disorder by embedding psychological theory in the growing anatomical knowledge of the Victorian era. In his own way, Down was clearly trying to bridge phrenology and Darwinian evolutionary theory, attempting to find a science of the mind that was relevant to specialists in idiocy. Perhaps inadvertently, by theorizing "Mongoloid idiocy" as atavistic, as representing racial reversion, he and his colleagues in the other idiot asylums were also contributing to an emerging discourse on degenerationism. The last three decades of the nineteenth century were to witness the convergence of degeneration theory, fears over urban squalor and the declining (middle-class) birth rate, and the slow encroachment of the state, in the formulation of a murky social Darwinism that would ultimately give birth to the eugenics movement. If not in the midst of "Mongols," eugenicists felt surrounded by the danger of the feeble-minded. Rather than subjects of ethnological curiosity, the intellectually disabled soon became the objects of a darker campaign of forced segregation and sterilization.

NOTES

This chapter was first published in *Mental Disability in Victorian England: The Earlswood Asylum, 1847–1901,* by David Wright (Oxford Historical Monographs,

2001) and is reprinted here in a revised and abridged version by permission of Oxford University Press. © David Wright 2001.

1. R. Porter, "The Patient's View: Doing Medical History from Below," *Theory and Society* 14 (1985), 175–98.

2. H. Sigerist, *Civilization and Disease* (Ithaca, N.Y., 1943); Sigerist, *A History of Medicine* (New York, 1951).

3. J. Woodward and D. Richards, "Towards a Social History of Medicine," in Woodward and Richards (eds.), *Health Care and Popular Medicine in Nineteenth Century England* (London, 1975), 15–55; C. Webster, "The Historiography of Medicine," in P. Corsi and P. Weindling (eds.), *Information Services in the History of Science and Medicine* (London, 1983), 29–43.

4. R. Porter, "The Mission of Social History of Medicine: An Historical Overview," *Social History of Medicine* 8 (1995), 345–60.

5. The literature on the history of psychiatric institutions is immense. For notable case studies of asylums that examine the patient experience, see: N. Tomes, *A Generous Confidence: Thomas Story Kirkbride and the Art of Asylum Keeping, 1840–1883* (Cambridge, 1985); A. Digby, *Madness, Morality and Medicine: A Study of the York Retreat, 1796–1914* (Cambridge, 1985); S. E. D. Shortt, *Victorian Lunacy: Richard M. Bucke and the Practice of Late Nineteenth-century Psychiatry* (Cambridge, 1986); E. Dwyer, *Homes for the Mad: Life inside Two Nineteenth Century Asylums* (New Brunswick, 1987).

6. See the range of articles in the journal *History of Psychiatry* (est. 1991).

7. R. Porter, "Mother Says It Done Me Good," *London Review of Books,* 16 April 1997, 6.

8. A. Digby, "Contexts and Perspectives," in D. Wright and A. Digby (eds.), *From Idiocy to Mental Deficiency: Historical Perspectives on People with Learning Disabilities* (London, 1996), 1.

9. J. Trent, *Inventing the Feeble Mind: A History of Mental Retardation in the United States* (Berkeley, 1994); S. Noll, *Feeble-Minded in Our Midst: Institutions for the Mentally Retarded in the South, 1900–1940* (Chapel Hill, 1995); M. Jackson, *The Borderland of Imbecility: Medicine Society and the Fabrication of the Feeble Mind in Late Victorian and Edwardian England* (Manchester, 2000).

10. H. Simmons, *From Asylum to Welfare* (Downsview, Ont., 1982), Chapters 2, 3, 5; A. MacLaren, *Our Own Master Race: Eugenics in Canada, 1885–1945* (Toronto, 1990); I. Dowbiggin, *Keeping America Sane: Psychiatry and Eugenics in the United States and Canada* (Ithaca, N.Y., 1997).

11. For a recent publication on the history of disability in America, see Paul Longmore and Lauri Umansky (eds.), *The New Disability History: American Perspectives* (New York, 2001).

12. P. Tyor and L. Bell, *Caring for the Retarded in America* (London, 1984); P. M. Ferguson, *Abandoned to Their Fate: Social Policy and Practice toward Severely Retarded People in America, 1820–1920* (Philadelphia, 1994); and see note 9.

13. M. Thomson, *The Problem of Mental Deficiency: Eugenics, Democracy, and Social Policy in Britain, c. 1870–1959* (Oxford, 1998). See also Jackson, *The Borderland of Imbecility*.

14. For doctoral theses on the history of intellectual disability in Britain, see R. Neugebauer, "Social Class, Mental Illness and Government Policy in 16th and 17th Century England," unpublished Ph.D. thesis, Columbia University, 1976; H. Gelband, "Mental Retardation and Institutional Treatment in Nineteenth Century England, 1845-1886," unpublished Ph.D. thesis, University of Maryland, 1979; J. Saunders, "Institutionalized Offenders—A Study of the Victorian Institution and Its Inmates, with Special Reference to Late-Nineteenth-Century Warwickshire," unpublished Ph.D. thesis, University of Warwick, 1983; M. Barrett, "From Education to Segregation: An Inquiry into the Changing Character of Special Provision for the Retarded in England, c. 1846-1918," unpublished Ph.D. thesis, University of Lancaster, 1987; L. Zihni, "A History of the Relationship between the Concept and the Treatment of People with Down's Syndrome in Britain and America, 1867-1967," unpublished Ph.D. thesis, University of London, 1990.

15. A. Scull, C. MacKenzie, and N. Hervey, *Masters of Bedlam: The Transformation of the Mad-Doctoring Trade* (Princeton, N.J., esp. the Introduction; E. Shorter, *A History of Psychiatry; From the Era of the Asylum to the Age of Prozac* (New York, 1997).

16. C. A. Birch, "Down's Syndrome: John Langdon Haydon Down, 1828-1896," *The Practitioner* 210 (1973), 171.

17. L. Kanner, *A History of the Care and Study of the Mentally Retarded* (Springfield, Ill., 1964), 97-104; Richard C. Scheerenberger, *A History of Mental Retardation* (Baltimore, 1984).

18. O. C. Ward, *John Langdon Down: A Caring Pioneer* (London, 1998).

19. S. J. Gould, *The Panda's Thumb* (New York, 1980), 164-67; See, *inter alia*, C. Borthwick, "Racism, IQ and Down's Syndrome," *Disability and Society* 11 (1994), 403-10.

20. M. J. Peterson, *The Medical Profession in Mid-Victorian London* (Berkeley, 1978).

21. C. A. Birch, "Down's Syndrome," 171.

22. O. C. Ward, *John Langdon Down*, 24.

23. Obituary, John Langdon Haydon Down, *BMJ* [Oct. 17, 1896] (1896, ii), 1170-71; *The Lancet* [Oct. 17, 1896] (1896, ii), 1104-5.

24. D. Wright, "Learning Disability and the New Poor Law in England, 1834-1867," *Disability and Society* 15 (2000), 731-46.

25. D. Wright, *Mental Disability in Victorian England* (Oxford, 2001), Chapter 2.

26. R. Hunter and I. MacAlpine, *Three Hundred Years of Psychiatry, 1535–1860* (New York, 1983), 191; R. C. Scheerenberger, *A History of Mental Retardation*, 52-53.

27. A. Scull, "John Conolly: A Victorian Psychiatric Career," in Scull, *Social Order, Social Order/Mental Disorder: Anglo-American Psychiatry in Historical Perspective* (London, 1989), 162-212.

28. H. Freeman and D. Tantum, "Samuel Gaskell," in G. Berrios and H. Freeman (eds.), *150 Years of British Psychiatry, 1841–1991* (London, 1991), 448; K. Day and J. Jancar, "Mental Handicap and the Royal Medico-Psychological Association, 1841–1991," in Berrios and Freeman (eds.), *150 Years of British Psychiatry,* 268.

29. T. Turner, "Not Worth Powder or Shot," in Berrios and Freeman (eds.), *150 Years of British Psychiatry,* 7.

30. O. C. Ward, *John Langdon Down,* Chapter 5.

31. [Annual] Report, 1859, Archives of the Royal Earlswood Asylum (AREA), Surrey Record Office (SRO), 392/1/2/1, 154.

32. M. J. Peterson, *The Medical Profession in Mid-Victorian London* (Berkeley, Calif., 1978).

33. [Annual] Report, 1860, AREA, SRO, 392/1/2/1, 176.

34. Ibid.

35. R. Stevens, *Medical Practice in Modern England: The Impact of Specialisation on State Medicine* (New Haven, Conn., 1966).

36. [Annual] Report, 1859, AREA, SRO, 392/1/2/1, 157.

37. [Annual] Report, 1861, AREA, SRO, 392/1/2/1, 191.

38. T. Turner, "Not Worth Powder or Shot," 11.

39. The *Journal of Mental Science* was the official organ of the Medico-Psychological Association (MPA) of Great Britain. The *Journal* evolved into the *British Psychiatric Journal*; the MPA ultimately was renamed the British Psychiatric Association. See discussion later in this chapter.

40. A. Scull, *Museums of Madness: The Social Organisation of Insanity in Nineteenth-Century England* (London, 1979), 198.

41. R. Cooter, "Phrenology and the British Alienists circa 1825–1845," *Medical History* 20 (1976), 135–51.

42. Ibid.

43. G. Blackie, *Cretins and Cretinism* (Edinburgh, 1855), pp. 18–23, Tables I–III.

44. See reference in W. W. Ireland, *On Idiocy and Imbecility* (London, 1877), 28.

45. R. Cooter, *Phrenology in the British Isles: An Annotated Historical Bibliography and Index* (London, 1989), 81–82.

46. J. Conolly, Lecture on Mental Disease to the Royal Institution, as cited in J. Clark, *A Memoire of John Conolly* (London, 1869), 67.

47. J. L. Down, "Account of a Case in Which the Corpus Callosum and Fornix Were Imperfectly Formed and the Septum and Commission Were Absent," *Transactions of Royal Medical and Chirurgical Society,* 1861; "On the Condition of the Mouth in Idiocy," *Lancet,* vol. 1 [1862]; "An Account of a Second Case in Which the Corpus Callosum Was Defective," *Transactions of the Royal Medical and Chirurgical Society,* 1866. These articles are reprinted in J. L. Down, *A Treatise on Idiocy and Its Cognate Affectations* (London, 1867).

48. A special apparatus was used to measure the skulls of all new admissions and has survived in the Earlswood Asylum museum. O. C. Ward, *John Langdon Down,* 129.

49. *Lancet* obit., 1105.

50. See, *inter alia,* J. B. Davis, "The Neanderthal Skull: Its Peculiar Conformation Explained Anatomically," and J. Thurnam, "On the Two Principal Forms of Ancient British and Gaulish Skulls." *Memoirs Read before the Anthropological Society of London, 1863–4* (London, 1865).

51. G. W. Stocking, *Victorian Anthropology* (London, 1987), 245–48.

52. J. Down, "Observations on an Ethnic Classification of Idiots," *Journal of Mental Science* 13 (1867), 122.

53. Ibid., 121–23.

54. C. Borthwick, "Racism, IQ and Down's Syndrome," *Disability and Society* 11 (1994), 403–10.

55. J. L. Down, "Observations on an Ethnic Classification of Idiots," 123.

56. D. Kevles, *In the Name of Eugenics: Genetics and the Uses of Human Heredity* (New York, 1985), 160. See also Daniel Kevles, "'Mongolian Imbecility': Race and Its Rejection in the Understanding of a Mental Disease," in this book.

57. N. J. Stepan, *The Idea of Race in Science: Britain, 1800–1960* (London, 1982), 3, 33, 44–45. The degree to which Down's Nonconformist faith and Liberal politics made him a natural ally of monogenism requires further research.

58. J. L. Down, *On the Education and Training of the Feeble in Mind* (London, 1876), title page.

59. Agenda of the Board, AREA, SRO 392/2/3/3.

60. General and By-Laws for the Regulation of the Idiot Asylum (1857), AREA, SRO 392/14/2, 23, article no. 92.

61. Minutes of the Board, 15 January 1868, AREA, SRO 392/2/1/6, 124.

62. Letter from Down to the Board, 5 February 1868, as transcribed in the Minutes of the Board, ibid., 131–32.

63. E. Burrows, "Alienists' Wives: The Unusual Case of Mrs. John Conolly," *History of Psychiatry* 9 (1998), 291–92.

64. Minutes of the Board, AREA, SRO 392/2/1/6, 137–38.

65. C. A. Birch, "Down's Syndrome," 172.

66. Thirty-sixth report, Annual Report of the Commissioners in Lunacy (ARCL), Parliamentary Papers (PP), [1882] vol. 33, 134 (150).

67. Obituary, "John L. H. Langdon-Down, FRCP, JP," *BMJ* [Oct. 17, 1896] (1896, ii), 1170–71.

68. *BMJ* [Oct. 17, 1896] (1896, ii), 1170–71; *The Lancet* [Oct. 17, 1896] (1896, ii), 1104–5.

69. M. Simpson, "The Moral Government of Idiots: Moral Treatment in the Work of Seguin," *History of Psychiatry* 10 (1999), 228.

70. See, *inter alia,* E. Séguin, *Théorie et pratique de l'éducation des idiots* (Paris, 1841–42); *Hygiène et éducation des idiots* (Paris, 1843); *Traitement moral, hygiène et éducation des idiots et des autres enfants arriérés* (Paris, 1846); *Idiocy and Its Treatment by the Physiological Method* (New York, 1866).

71. S. G. Howe, *Report Made to the Legislature of Massachusetts on Idiocy* (Boston, 1848); Howe, *On the Causes of Idiocy* (Edinburgh, 1848).

72. M. Duncan and W. Millard, *A Manual for the Classification, Training, and Education of the Feeble-minded, Imbecile, & Idiotic* (London, 1866).

73. J. L. Down, *A Treatise on Idiocy and Its Cognate Affectations* (London, 1867).

74. Evidence, Royal Commission on Care and Control of the Feebleminded (RCFM), Parliamentary Papers (PP), 1908, vol. 8, 90.

75. W. W. Ireland, *On Idiocy and Imbecility.*

76. G. Shuttleworth, *Mentally Defective Children: Their Treatment* (London, 1895).

77. G. Shuttleworth, "Cranial Characteristics of Idiocy," *Journal of Mental Science* (1881), as reprinted in M. Rosen et al. (eds.), *The History of Mental Retardation* (Baltimore, 1976), 242; see also Shuttleworth, "Mongolian Imbecility," *British Medical Journal* (1909), 661–65.

78. A. Mitchell and R. Fraser, "Kalmuc Idiocy: Report of a Case of Autopsy with Notes on Sixty-two Cases," *Journal of Mental Science* 22 (1876), 169–79.

79. L. Zihni, "A History of . . . Down's Syndrome," 151–52.

80. W. W. Ireland, *On Idiocy and Imbecility.*

81. J. L. Down, *On Some of the Mental Affections of Childhood and Youth* (London, 1887).

82. J. L. Down, "The Lettsomian Lectures on Some of the Mental Affections of Youth," *BMJ* (1887, ii), 49.

83. H. B. Wilbur, "The Classification of Idiocy," Proceedings of the Association of Medical Officers of American Institutions for Idiotic and Feeble-Minded Persons (1876), Wellcome Trust Contemporary Medical Archives (WTCMA), 29–35.

84. J. L. Dugdale, *The Jukes: A Study in Crime, Pauperism, Disease and Heredity* (New York, 1877), 70. Dugdale's account of the Juke family was used to buttress many developing ideas about hereditary criminality and feeble-mindedness, including Francis Galton, *Inquiry into Human Faculty and Its Development* [1883] (London, 1911), 44. Later scare stories were recycled when H. H. Goddard followed with a similar study of the Kallikak family that purported to detail the creation of several generations of crime, pauperism, and physical and mental degeneration. H. Goddard, *The Kallikak Family,* 2nd ed. (London, 1912). See also Leila Zenderland, "The Parable of *The Kallikak Family*: Explaining the Meaning of Heredity in 1912," in this book.

85. Anon., "Imbecile and Epileptic Children in the Workhouses," *BMJ* [6 April 1895], (1895, ii), 773.

86. A. W. Wilmarth, "Mongolian Idiocy," Proceedings of the Association of Med-

ical Officers of American Institutions for Idiotic and Feeble-Minded Persons (1899), WTCMA, 57–61.

87. It is an interesting aside that Bleyer's interest in cytogenetics would contribute to the first articulation of a chromosomal abnormality long before its actual discovery in 1959. L. Zihni, "A History of . . . Down's Syndrome," Chapter 10.

88. See, *inter alia,* R. Jones, "The Mouth of Backward Children of the Mongol Type," *Journal of Mental Science* 36 (1890), 187; C. Oliver, "A Clinical Study of the Ocular Symptoms Found in the So-Called Mongolian Type of Idiocy," *Transactions of the American Ophthalmological Society* 6 (1891), 140–48; T. Smith, "A Peculiarity in the Shape of the Hands in Idiots of the Mongolian Type," *Pediatrics* (1896), 315; A. Garrod, "Cases Illustrating the Association of Congenital Heart Disease with Mongolian Form of Idiocy," *British Medical Journal* (1898), 1200, 1255.

89. As quoted in L. Zihini, "A History of . . . Down's Syndrome," 254.

90. F. G. Crookshank, *The Mongol in Our Midst* (London, 1924).

91. R. L. Langdon-Down, "Discussion," *Journal of Mental Science* 53 (1906), 187.

92. R. L. Langdon-Down, "Handprints," *British Medical Journal* 2 (1909), 665; See also F. G. Crookshank, "Hand-prints of Mongolian and Other Imbeciles," *Transactions of the Medical Society of London* 44 (1921), 155.

93. L. Zihni, "A History of . . . Down's Syndrome," 267.

94. F. Miller, "The Perseverance of 'Mongolism': The Old and the New in Medical Cytogenetics, c. 1950–1970," unpublished paper read before the annual conference of the American Association for the History of Medicine, 20/5/2000.

95. N. Anderson and A. Langa, "The Development of Institutional Care for 'Idiots and Imbeciles' in Scotland," *History of Psychiatry* 8 (1997), 255.

96. D. Kevles, *In the Name of Eugenics,* 161.

4

"Mongolian Imbecility"

Race and Its Rejection in the Understanding of a Mental Disease

Daniel J. Kevles

The first systematic identification of the disease that in the late nineteenth century came to be known as "mongolian imbecility" was made in 1866 by the British physician John Langdon Haydon Down. Down described a syndrome that, along with severe retardation, included an enlarged head and a prolonged, or epicanthic, fold to the eyelid. In Down's time, Western physicians had observed the syndrome only in Caucasians. Down supposed that the disease indicated a biological reversion in its victims to the Mongols of Asia, whom he thought they physically resembled and who he assumed were a surviving example of an earlier human type. Down interpreted the "fact" that Caucasians could produce mongols as evidence for "the unity of the human species"—a liberal idea that ran counter to contemporary theories that "inferior" human races had sprung from separate biological origins. Down believed the disease to be congenital rather than hereditary, and he speculated that the reversion might be caused by parental tuberculosis.[1]

The identification of the imbeciles with the Mongols of Asia—or, at least, with some general primitive type—persisted. In the 1920s, in the widely noted book *The Mongol in Our Midst*, the British physician F. G. Crookshank furthered this view by arguing that the syndrome might derive from a recessive "unit character," a vestige of man's evolutionary past, and that some Mongol blood no doubt flowed in the veins of many Europeans. "It is the 'Mongolism' rather than the idiocy that it is important to stress," Crookshank claimed, and he added that a portion of the native British population possessed "a kind of physical and psychical makeup that is coarsely and brutally displayed and accentuated in certain idiots and imbeciles."[2]

Lionel Penrose, a young student of mental disability, suspected that Crookshank's views were utter trash. A Quaker and a pacifist, he was skeptical of class and racial explanations of mental differences. He began investigating mongolian imbecility in 1931, when he was appointed to the staff of the Royal Eastern Counties Institution, a home for the mentally disabled in Colchester, England. His study was part of a larger investigation of the relative roles of heredity and environment in the generation of mental disease and disorder.

There were only forty-two mongol patients at Colchester; Penrose had to search out others from local and London hospitals and through mental health organizations, going so far as to track down an afflicted child whom he spotted on the street. He took special care to be certain that each patient he found was an actual victim of Down's Syndrome—a not inconsequential problem. Some cases were borderline; the severe retardation aside, one or more characteristics of the syndrome—besides the epicanthic fold and a high cephalic index, they included a fissured tongue and the so-called simian crease, a pronounced transverse palm line—could be found among normal people.[3] To test Crookshank's ideas, Penrose surveyed the blood types of 166 mongols and of a control group of 225 other mental patients. He found that the distribution of blood types in the mongol group was about the same as that in the control group. The results meant, he wrote to a fellow physician, that "mongolian imbeciles are no more racially Mongolian than other imbeciles."[4]

The outcome of the blood-type study gave Penrose special pleasure. He liked mongolian imbeciles. He liked them for their gentle, childlike quality, for what he called "their secret source of joy." He may have warmed to them, too, because their simple, trusting nature encouraged him to break through his normal reserve. Mongolian imbecility remained a major subject of Penrose's research to the end of his career. In later years, he set aside Saturdays for work with Down's-Syndrome children, observing and playing with them in the kindergarten swirl of his laboratory.[5] Yet, from the beginning he judged that Down's Syndrome merited special scientific attention, because it seemed so forcefully a product of action on the fetus by the intrauterine environment.

It was noticed early in the century that Down's-Syndrome births were related to the age of the mother, occurring much more frequently among women over thirty-five than among younger women. Nevertheless, there was considerable dispute about the role of maternal age in the origins of the syndrome. Some authorities claimed that what counted was not the mother's age but the father's. Others insisted that the critical factor was the place of the Down's offspring in the family birth order: the mongol was often the last in a long line of children, and it was therefore theorized that the syndrome resulted from the mother's "reproductive exhaustion." Then, too, a mother often produced a mongolian imbecile long after the birth of her last previous child, so length of time between births was also advanced as a cause.[6]

Beginning at Colchester, Penrose worked to extract the truth from the conflicting theories. To choose among the important factors in the birth of a Down's-Syndrome child, he adopted a simple statistical procedure: calculate the expected number of afflicted offspring on the hypothesis that one factor (for example, maternal age) made a difference while others (for example, birth order) did not; then compare the calculated expectation with the observed incidence. If the two figures matched closely enough, the hypothesis would be demonstrated. ("His statistics are definitely 'low brow,'" the great mathematical geneticist J. B. S. Haldane once remarked, "but I think effective for the purpose for which they are designed.")[7] The entire procedure demanded the gathering of complete and accurate family data. Penrose found that official case records of Down's-Syndrome patients were of little value. Richly rewarding were personal visits to the families (some of which rebuffed him) to gather data on the victims' parents, siblings, and other relatives; on numbers of miscarriages, stillbirths, and infant deaths; on the ages of children, parents, and grandparents. In due course, he had extensive information concerning some 150 families. Analysis of the data revealed that the birth of a Down's-Syndrome child did not depend upon paternal age. It did not depend upon birth order. It did not depend upon the length of time elapsed since the birth of the last previous child. In most cases, it depended only upon the age of the mother, with the probability of occurrence rising sharply for women over thirty-five.[8]

Just why advancing maternal age raised the probability of a Down's-Syndrome birth no one, including Penrose, could say. The prevailing medical speculation included degeneration of the ovum or an inadequate supply of nutrients to the fetus. Penrose himself wondered whether, at least in some cases, genetics might be at work. The evidence for a genetic role in Down's Syndrome was slight but real enough. It consisted mainly of the facts that some mongolian imbeciles were identical twins and that the syndrome sometimes manifested itself in more than one child in a family or occurred with higher than random incidence among the offspring of cousins. However, there was no way to distinguish between a genetic and an environmental hypothesis. Down's-Syndrome children born to the same mother gestated in the same intrauterine environment. Although Penrose was unable to clarify the causes of Down's Syndrome completely, his conclusions about its dependence on maternal age and its likely genetic origins in cases of familial incidence were definitive and rapidly came to be recognized as such.

The explanation for both random and familial occurrence came with the development of human chromosomal genetics in the late 1950s. Chromosomes are rod-shaped entities found in the nuclei of cells. They comprise DNA wrapped in a protein coat. They owe their name to the fact that, as scientists discovered in the nineteenth century, they turn color upon suitable staining. But, while they can thus be made evident under the microscope, cytological techniques available during the first half of the twentieth century could do no better than make them appear as something akin to the tangle of noodles in a soup. They were thus difficult to study or even to count accurately. Various determinations put the number of chromosomes in the normal human cell at forty-eight. However, in 1956, two cytologists collaborating in Sweden devised a combination of techniques that made the chromosomes sharply distinct and demonstrated that the human number is forty-six—the two sex chromosomes and forty-four autosomes (chromosomes independent of sex). Their achievement opened the field of human cytogenetics, including research into mental diseases and disorders in chromosomal terms.[9]

In France, the young geneticist Jérôme Lejeune had been thinking chromosomally about mongolian imbecility for several years. Lejeune's career in genetics started in 1952, when, as a recent graduate in medicine, he returned from military service to work with Raymond Turpin at the Hospital Saint-Louis, in Paris. Turpin, a professor of pediatrics at the University of Paris, was one of the very few people at the time in France who were interested in human genetics. His hospital practice included a group of Down's Syndrome patients, and he turned over responsibility for them to Lejeune.[10] Neither Turpin nor Lejeune believed John Langdon Down's original hypothesis that victims of the condition were throwbacks to some atavistic Mongolian "race." In his clinical work, Lejeune saw a Down's child from Indochina whose appearance differed sharply from that of normal children of the region; the syndrome stood out among Asians as well as among Caucasians.

Lejeune suspected that Down's Syndrome had something to do with hereditary mechanisms. Like a number of physicians elsewhere confronted with such inklings, he embarked on a postmedical course of study toward a doctorate in science with emphasis on biochemistry and genetics. Postwar French austerity made the task of research less straightforward: Lejeune had no laboratory, no microscope, only a single room without running water. Pondering what experimental research he might pursue under those conditions, he decided to concentrate on the palm prints of Down's victims.[11]

In 1953, Lejeune scrutinized the configurations of lines on the palms of 93 Down's patients, 246 members of their families, and 2 large control groups drawn at random—except that one group was evenly divided for sex—from the Parisian population. Lejeune assessed the configurations quantitatively and arrived at a numerical index of the degree to which, on a given palm, they occurred in association with each other. He found that the Down's patients had a strikingly higher associative frequency of abnormal palm lines than did the people in either of the control groups. To Lejeune, this signified that Down's Syndrome must involve some deep genetic change from the normal. One of the palm lines found in the syndrome was the so-called simian crease. Lejeune knew very little about primatology, but it occurred to him that a clue to the deep change might be found in the palm configurations of apes and monkeys—especially the lower-order monkeys from which the simian crease took its name.[12]

At the Natural History Museum, in Paris, he measured the configuration of palm lines on the skins of the apes and monkeys preserved there. The palm lines of normal human beings showed no resemblance to those of either the lower-order monkeys or the anthropoid apes—orangutans, gorillas, and chimpanzees. But there were extraordinary similarities between the Down's palms and those of the inferior monkeys—for example, mangabeys and macaques.[13] Lejeune supposed that the distinction between the palm lines of anthropoid apes and those of the lower-order monkeys must have resulted from the accumulation of numerous single-gene changes over evolutionary time. He speculated that the Down's palm lines, too, must arise from a polygenic difference between the Down's victims and normal human beings—occurring, obviously, not over evolutionary time but in one generation, from parent to child. Lejeune reasoned that the necessary change had to involve the only genetic material then known to be large enough to carry a polygenic message—a chromosome.[14]

124

At this point, Lejeune's mind turned to the haplo-four fruit fly. (Cytogeneticists designate as "haploid" those cells—for example, mammalian gametes—that contain only half the normal number of chromosomes. The haplo-four takes its name from the fact that it possesses only one member of the fourth chromosomal pair found in normal *Drosophila*.) The haplo-four fruit fly has various abnormal characteristics, including thinner bristles, a shortened body, and a prolonged larval stage. No one of these characteristics announces the haplo-four; they declare themselves as an ensemble—a syndrome. Lejeune thought of the haplo-four as a kind of "mongol fly." Just as the "mongol fly" was missing a chromosome, Lejeune came to think, in 1954, that the victims of Down's syndrome must lack a chromosome, too.[15]

Lejeune had by this time moved with Turpin's group to the Hospital Trousseau. He wanted to look at the chromosomes of his Down's patients, but he was not familiar with human cytogenetic techniques and was unable to find anyone in Paris who was. Besides, there was not much money for research and only limited laboratory facilities at the hospital. He therefore turned to various other subjects—mainly radiation genetics, for which Turpin, like many biologists, was able to raise funds in the mid-1950s. All the while, however, he had his chromosomal hypothesis in mind and kept hoping to test it, especially after the work of Tjio and Levan was published.

The opportunity arose in 1957, with the arrival in Turpin's clinic of Marthe Gauthier, a cardiologist who had recently learned the technique of tissue culture; Turpin authorized her to use it in collaboration with Lejeune.[16] Sometime about the spring of 1958, Gauthier cultured tissue taken from the fascia lata—the smooth connective tissue that covers muscle—of three Down's patients at the Hospital Trousseau. Lejeune, using the newly developed cytogenetic techniques, prepared karyotypes and examined them through a microscope discarded by the hospital's bacteriology laboratory; it was so worn that he had to stabilize its adjustment gears by inserting between them a piece of tin foil from a candy wrapper. He photographed the karyotypes with equipment borrowed from the pathology department, expecting them to show, like those of the "mongol fly," the absence of a chromosome. Instead, they showed that the Down's patients had forty-seven chromosomes, rather than forty-six.[17]

Lejeune wondered whether the extra chromosome was typical of Down's patients or an artifact of the tissue culturing. Aging cultures were known to produce chromosomal anomalies. But the cultures had been no more than a month old before he obtained the karyotypes—too short a time, Lejeune thought, for the aging phenomenon to occur. More troubling to him was a recent paper by Masuo Kodani, an American cytogeneticist then working with the Atomic Bomb Casualty Commission in Japan, which claimed that in some normal human beings the chromosome number might be forty-seven. If Kodani was correct, then the "extra" chromosome Lejeune had detected in his patients might not be extra at all and might have nothing to do with Down's Syndrome. In a lecture at McGill University, in September 1958, just after the Tenth International Congress of Genetics, in Montreal, Lejeune swallowed his doubts enough to show the photographs of the three Down's karyotypes and advance his belief that the cause of the syndrome was an extra chromosome. His audience seemed for the most part unconvinced.[18]

After he returned to Paris, Lejeune prepared karyotypes of cells from eight non-Down's patients at the Hospital Trousseau. Each of the karyotypes showed forty-six chromosomes. Though still somewhat anxious about putting his Down's results into print, he finally published the work in the *Comptes Rendus* of the French Academy of Sciences, in January 1959. In the same journal, in mid-March, he reported the results of an examination of nine Down's karyotypes and argued with greater confidence that the extra chromosome was the cause of the syndrome.[19]

Scientists in Britain soon provided Lejeune with solid reasons for confidence in his results. Working in ignorance of his efforts and approaching the problem in a much different way, several laboratories, including Penrose's, independently found the extra chromosome in Down's patients.[20] News of the Down's results moved the provost at University College London, where Penrose was now a professor, to send him a note: "It must be one of the most important things that has happened in genetical studies for a long time." And it was. Penrose remarked some months later that the events of the past year had amounted to "a major breakthrough in the science of human genetics," adding that he found "the photograph of the cell from the man with two extra chromosomes from which the intelligence level, the behavior and sexual characters can be confidently predicted, just about as astonishing as a photograph of the back of the moon."[21]

However, there was still doubt about the nature of the extra Down's chromosome. Penrose thought that it was a member of a trisomy—that is, the occurrence of one of the twenty-two autosomal chromosomes as a triplet rather than as a pair. Lejeune had not been certain—and neither had the other investigators—whether it was that or a supernumerary chromosomal piece of unknown origin. But within a year the abnormality was demonstrated to be indeed a trisomy—of the chromosome designated No. 21 by agreement at a genetics conference in Denver, Colorado, in April 1960. (The agreement assigned numbers to the chromosomes in order of descending size.)[22]

Also in 1960, investigators in Sweden, in addition to Penrose and others in England, concluded that a particular form of this trisomy accounted for the small number of cases of familial occurrence of Down's Syndrome. It arose from the presence in some people of what is called a translocation—in this case, the attachment of one of the 21-chromosomes to the 14-chromosome. If a gamete containing the 14-21 combination plus the other 21-chromosome was passed on to a fetus, the offspring would possess two regular 21-chromosomes plus the 21 on the No. 14. If a gamete transmitted the 21- and 14-chromosomes only in their hybrid form, the child would be normal. But because these chromosomes were attached to each other, the child would be a carrier, and his or her children would be at risk for trisomy-21.[23]

Lejeune, Penrose, and others publicly urged that the racially tinged nomenclature of mongolian imbecility be abandoned in favor of scientifically neutral terms, including "Down's Syndrome" or "trisomy-21."[24] The detection of its cause in chromosomal accidents finished off its vestigial association with racist atavism.

NOTES

1. J. Langdon Down, "Observations on an Ethnic Classification of Idiots," *London Hospital Reports,* 1866, reprinted in J. Langdon Down, *On Some of the Mental Affections of Childhood and Youth* (J. A. Churchill, 1887), pp. 210–17; Beth C. Kevles, "A History of Our Understanding of Down's Syndrome" (unpublished manuscript, 1981).

2. F. G. Crookshank, *The Mongol in Our Midst: A Study of Man and His Three Faces* (E. P. Dutton, 1924), pp. 5–6; Stephen Jay Gould, *The Mismeasure of Man* (Norton, 1981), pp. 134–35.

3. Penrose, "Report of the Research Department of the Royal Eastern Counties Institution," Sept. 1932; Frank Douglas Turner to Penrose, July 3, 1931, Jan. 5, 1932; Penrose to Turner, Jan. 4, 1932; and Essex Voluntary Association for Mental Welfare Materials, Lionel S. Penrose Papers, University College London Archives, file 130/7.

4. Penrose to Edmund O. Lewis, Feb. 8, 1932, Penrose to Peter K. McGowan, Feb. 13, 1932, Penrose Papers, file 147/3, file 149/3; L. S. Penrose, "The Blood Grouping of Mongolian Imbeciles," *The Lancet* 7 (Feb. 20, 1932), 394–95.

5. Author's interview with Harry Harris; Penrose, *Mental Defect* (Farrar & Rinehart, 1933), p. 102; author's interview with Shirley Penrose Hodgson.

6. Penrose, Draft note to *The Lancet,* March 14, 1938; Penrose Papers, file 61/1; Penrose, "The Relative Aetiological Importance of Birth Order and Maternal Age in Mongolism," *Proceedings of the Royal Society* 115 (1934), 431–32; Beth Kevles, "A History of Our Understanding of Down's Syndrome."

7. Haldane to Egon Pearson, March 27, 1944, Penrose Papers, file 49/1.

8. Penrose, "Report of the Research Department of the Royal Eastern Counties' Institution," Sept. 1932; Penrose to R. A. Fisher, Nov. 2, 1932; Penrose to Frank C. Shrubsall, Aug. 19, 1933; Penrose to R. L. Jenkins, Aug. 14, 1933, Penrose Papers, files 56/2, 61/2, 168/7, 142/5; Penrose, "The Relative Aetiological Importance of Birth Order and Maternal Age in Mongolism," *Proceedings of the Royal Society* 115 (1934), 431–50.

9. Malcolm Jay Kottler, "From 48 to 46: Cytological Technique, Preconception, and the Counting of Human Chromosomes," *Bulletin of the History of Medicine* 48 (1974), 467–93.

10. Author's interview with Jérôme Lejeune.

11. Ibid.

12. R. Turpin and J. Lejeune, "Étude dermatoglyphique des paumes des mongoliens et de leurs parents et germains," *La Semaine des Hôpitaux de Paris* 29 (Dec. 14, 1953), 3955–67; Lejeune interview.

13. Raymond Turpin and Jérôme Lejeune, "Analogies entre le type dermatoglyphique palmaire des singes inférieurs et celui des enfants atteints de mongolisme," *Comptes Rendus Académie de Paris,*" 238 (Jan. 18, 1954), 395–97.

14. Lejeune interview.

15. Ibid.

16. Ibid.

17. T. C. Hsu, *Human and Mammalian Cytogenetics: A Historical Perspective* (Springer-Verlag, 1979), pp. 39–40; Jérôme Lejeune interview; Jérôme Lejeune, Marthe Gauthier, and Raymond Turpin, "Les Chromosomes humains en culture de tissus," *Comptes Rendus de l'Académie des Sciences* 248 (Jan. 26, 1959), 602–3.

18. Lejeune interview; Masuo Kodani, "Three Diploid Chromosome Numbers of Man," *Proceedings of the National Academy of Sciences* 43 (1957), 285–92.

19. Lejeune, Gauthier, and Turpin, "Les Chromosomes humains en culture de tissus," pp. 602–3; Jérôme Lejeune interview; Jérôme Lejeune, Marthe Gauthier, and Raymond Turpin, "Études des chromosomes somatiques de neuf enfants mongoliens," *Comptes Rendus de l'Académie des Sciences* 248 (Mar. 16, 1959), 1721–22.

20. Letter from O. J. Miller to the author, Dec. 5, 1983; Penrose to Haldane, June 4, 1959, Lionel S. Penrose Papers, file 136; C. E. Ford, K. W. Jones, O. J. Miller, Ursula Mittwoch, L. S. Penrose, M. Ridler, and A. Shapiro, "The Chromosomes in a Patient Showing Both Mongolism and the Klinefelter Syndrome," *The Lancet* 1 (April 4,

1959), 709–10; Patricia A. Jacobs, W. M. Court Brown, et al., "The Somatic Chromosomes in Mongolism," *The Lancet* 1 (April 4, 1959), 710; author's interviews with Charles Ford and Patricia Jacobs.

21. Sir Ifor Evans to Penrose, May 22, 1959; Lionel Penrose, "Human Chromosomes," Oct. 22, 1959, Lionel S. Penrose Papers, files 175/5, 88/1.

22. Penrose, "Human Chromosomes"; Penrose, "Human Chromosomes for Beginners" [1962], Lionel S. Penrose Papers, file 88/5; Jérôme Lejeune interview; Jacobs, Brown, et al., "The Somatic Chromosomes in Mongolism," p. 710; Jérôme Lejeune, Marthe Gauthier, and Raymond Turpin, "The Chromosomes of Man," letter, *The Lancet* 1 (April 25, 1959), 885; "A Proposed Standard System of Nomenclature of Human Mitotic Chromosomes," *The Lancet* 1 (May 14, 1960), 1063–65.

23. M. Fraccaro, K. Kaijser, and J. Lindsten, "Chromosomal Abnormalities in Father and Mongol Child," *The Lancet* 2 (April 2, 1960), 724–27; P. E. Polani, J. H. Briggs, C. E. Ford, C. M. Clarke, and J. M. Berg, "A Mongol Girl with 46 Chromosomes," *The Lancet* 1 (April 2, 1960), 721–24; L. S. Penrose, J. R. Ellis, amd Joy Delhanty, "Chromosomal Translocations in Mongolism and in Normal Relatives," *The Lancet* 2 (Aug. 20, 1960), 409–10; C. O. Carter, J. L. Hamerton, P. E. Polani, A. Gunalp, and S. D. V. Weller, "Chromosome Translocation as a Cause of Familial Mongolism," *The Lancet* 2 (Sept. 24, 1960), 678–80; Lionel Penrose, "From Eugenics to Human Genetics," lecture, 1965, Lionel Penrose Papers, file 77/2.

24. Gordon Allen et al., "Mongolism," letter to the editor, *The Lancet* 1 (1961), 775.

5

Rearing the Child Who Never Grew

Ideologies of Parenting and Intellectual Disability in American History

Janice Brockley

American child-rearing advisers have historically urged parents to raise good citizens and upwardly mobile competitors for the workforce. By this standard, already established in the early nineteenth century, parents of intellectually disabled children were doomed to fail. "The parents of a normal child ... know ... that ultimately the child will become a self-sufficient adult," wrote Simon Olshansky, study director of the Children's Developmental Clinic, in Cambridge, Massachusetts, more than 150 years later, "By contrast, the parents of a mentally defective child will have little to look forward to; they will always be burdened by the child's unrelenting demands and unabated dependency."[1] The dilemma of rearing a dependent child in a society grounded in values of independence and competition has haunted American parents over the course of two centuries. This chapter examines how both popular and professional literature advised parents to cope with the intellectually disabled child. It is not a tale of increasing progress and acceptance. Twentieth-century writers of all kinds—popular and expert—were often less accepting of permanent disability within family homes than were their nineteenth-century predecessors. Throughout the nineteenth and twentieth centuries, discussions of intellectual disability contained a frequent tension between the consistent need for parental labor and devotion in caring for children with intellectual disabilities and public and professional criticism of parents' motives for and success in doing so.

In a supposedly meritocratic society, people with intellectual disabilities would never "merit" middle-class status. Their contributions to society would not earn the financial rewards required to achieve that position. "[S]ewage disposal, ditch digging, potato peeling, scrubbing of floors and other such occupations are as necessary and essential to our way of living as science, literature, and art," the prominent psychiatrist Leo Kanner cheerfully explained in 1949. "The more nearly the intellectually inadequate can be prepared for, and assigned to, jobs for which they are fitted, the more occasion is there for the intellectually more adequate to make corresponding use of their cognitive assets."[2] Under this plan, people with more severe disabilities would have to prepare for a life of complete dependency.

The vision of such a future was a blow to many middle-class parents, who wished to transfer their lifestyle and status to their children. "It is so hard to say that your child may grow up to be a dishwasher," wrote Richard H. Hungerford, father of an intellectually disabled child. "It is so hard to be without rancor to God or envy toward the more fortunate and yet train your son, who has been so 'sinned against,' to guard in drudgery the health of those who have so much."[3] Many middle-class parents feared that they could not permanently sustain, particularly after their deaths, a dependent child in a middle-class lifestyle within a society that provided limited social assistance. Fear that a vulnerable child would fall into poverty and abuse played a key role in some parents' embrace of institutionalization as a permanent solution for their children and remained a constant presence for many parents who kept their child in the community. The limited evidence suggests that nineteenth-century parents shared these fears, but their anxiety may have been slightly eased by greater social acceptance of extended family responsibility for the daily care of dependent family members.

Intellectually disabled children and their parents appeared in magazine fiction, novels, religious memoirs, autobiographies, and a rapidly expanding professional literature in the nineteenth and twentieth centuries. The changing character of American family life shaped the professional and popular discourse. In the early years of the republic, child-rearing guides and popular literature allocated to mothers new responsibility for their children's care and education, while fathers supported their families financially by working outside the home. Maternal domestic authority rested on the belief that women were fundamentally more moral, loving, and religious than men.[4] Despite the cultural transition that kept fathers physically removed from the home for many hours, recent historical research suggests that many fathers remained closely engaged with their children and involved in their care.[5] However, fathers' need to work outside the family home meant that they generally spent fewer hours with their children than did mothers.[6]

At the same time, formal education was becoming an increasingly important prerequisite for class status and social mobility. As early as the 1830s, middle-class urban fathers regarded providing their children with an education as an important component of their duties as a father. Increasingly, fathers sought to establish their children through formal schooling, not through ownership of land or apprenticeship.[7] When most "normal" children were expected to attend school, children who failed in school or were unable to attend because of their disabilities became both more visible and more problematic. New residential schools provided education for "idiots" or "mental defectives," but, by the 1880s, these rapidly expanding (both in number and in size) schools had become custodial institutions that provided long-term care instead of schooling.[8] The special education classes in the public schools, which came into existence in the late nineteenth and early twentieth century, focused on borderline or mildly feeble-minded children from the working class; children with severe intellectual disabilities and their parents found little community support.[9]

Beginning in the 1890s, rhetoric about families changed again. Professionals, physicians and the new social scientists, warned that the innate emotional and moral gifts for which women had previously been praised were not enough to raise children well. Instead, mothers needed expert scientific guidance.[10] Professionals argued that mothers of intellectually disabled children particularly needed help because they lacked the specialized treatment and training skills of professionals. Still, mothers were considered to be essential for child rearing. In fact, early-twentieth-century reformers tried to remove most children from residential facilities such as orphanages and to return them to their own homes or to alternative ones provided through foster care or adoption.[11] Children with intellectual disabilities remained a glaring exception to this practice. Public and private institutions continued to grow, and the majority of first admissions to public institutions up through the 1960s were less than twenty years old.[12] Residential institutions represented both a resource and a restriction to parents of intellectually disabled children, who had the choice of placing their child in an institution but who also faced the reality that there were few other supports besides institutions available to them.

Intellectually disabled children, therefore, were treated differently from other children. But the debates over their care exposed beliefs about "normal" family relationships and child rearing that were especially poignant for mothers of disabled children, who often lacked "normal" formal community supports. In the nineteenth century, mothers were praised for the natural devotion that allowed them to care for their disabled children. In the twentieth century, however, professional unease about mothers of disabled children revealed an underlying distrust of all mothers. Maternal devotion, psychologist, physicians, and other professionals suggested, was not genuine. Instead, it was often a cover for women's frustration at their confinement in the role of caregiver and in the home. Authorities as diverse as the psychologist John Watson, in the 1920s, the cultural commentator Philip Wylie, in the 1940s, and the feminist Betty Friedan, in the 1960s, warned that an unhappy mother might seek fulfillment by dominating the lives of her children under the guise of devotion, thus keeping them permanently dependent upon her. "[M]others who devoted *too* much of their lives to their children, mothers who had to keep their children babies or they themselves would have no lives at all, mothers who never themselves reached or were encouraged to reach maturity" threatened American's children, claimed Friedan.[13] A disabled child, under this model, would be the perfect target for an unfulfilled mother.

Fathers of intellectually disabled children also faced problems fulfilling their conventional role. Fathers were supposed to prepare their children, particularly sons, for success and independent adulthood. An intellectually disabled child confronted fathers with failure and the unpleasant reality that hard work might not always be rewarded with success. A disabled child also brought out the often hidden competition between father and child for the love of the mother that modern popular and professional literature implied underlay domestic life. Men needed emotional support and nurture from their wives—the same nurture and support that mothers gave their children. A disabled child's greater needs, professionals and fiction writers warned, might mean that the father's needs might not be fulfilled. In several ways, therefore, intellectual disability acted as a magnifying lens, revealing the cultural constructions of American family life, including hidden tensions and fears.

From the Moral to the Scientific Mother, 1850–1900

Popular fiction provides an intriguing picture of nineteenth-century ideas about intellectual disability and family life, one that is surprisingly similar to the ideas expressed in the professional literature of the time. In these vignettes, mothers often appeared as the savior of their "afflicted" children, while fathers were punished for their ambition and lack of love. Parents of an intellectually disabled son were especially vulnerable to criticism for failing to create an independent citizen and wage earner. A mother's moral duty to keep her sons free from sin might find consolation in a son's enforced innocence, but it was much harder to imagine a way that a mentally disabled son could fulfill the child-rearing goals of fathers. Consequently, while there were positive, sentimental portrayals in nineteenth-century fiction of mothers and feeble-minded sons, for fathers, a feeble-minded son almost always appeared as a punishment.

A good father, according to nineteenth-century fiction, wanted to establish his children in the world and to help them to rise in society, but he should not drive his children to fulfill his own ambitions and dreams. This was a particular danger for fathers, who, according to nineteenth-century popular writings, lacked women's spiritual gifts and nurturing abilities. In popular fiction, ambitious or unfit fathers might be punished by the lapse of a promising son into helpless idiocy. "[T]he compliments of my friends on his [son's] wonderful proficiency, and my own gratified vanity, blinded me," says a chastened father in one 1872 magazine story by a female author.[14] The father ignores the worried remonstrance of his wife and her female relations with a near-fatal result: driven into precocity by his father's ambition, the child collapses and almost dies. "Would that the white-winged angel had lifted my idolized boy in his arms, and so spared me the dreadful retribution I live to pay," concludes the father. "But he lived; lived, to be—oh, God! that I should speak the dreadful word—an idiot!"[15] Women might also be accused of encouraging precocity in their children in nineteenth-century fiction, but there was special venom to these stories and in the infliction of idiocy on a son as punishment for a father's ambition and lack of the female gift of child nurturance.

The ineptitude and unfitness of fathers comes out in other stories that use idiocy as punishment for male violence and immorality. In one story, a drunken father staggers while carrying his child and dashes his son's head against a doorpost, leaving him a "dumb idiot."[16] Another father, furious at his son's seeming disobedience, strikes his son with an iron whip handle on his head, his "child, my only son, dropt lifeless at my feet," only to later revive with an "idiot smile" on "his vacant countenance."[17] These were direct punishments for paternal misbehavior. Other fictional fathers are punished for their sins by their son's hapless bodies when they are born as idiots. Barnaby Rudge, in Charles Dickens's novel of that title, is an idiot in retribution for the murder his father committed before Barnaby's birth.[18] A dissolute father or an unloving marriage could also result in an idiot child.[19]

The focus on fathers and sons in these stories points to a distrust of fathers but also to a sense of sons as a special creation for men. The transformation of a promising son into an idiot constituted an emasculation of the child and, metaphorically, of the father, whose reproductive immortality was taken from him. The father who hit his son with a whip handle finds his boy has become strangely feminine. "All his manliness is gone," the father sadly notes, "he has become timid and feeble as a delicate girl."[20] His formerly masculine son no longer wishes to hunt and is scared of horses. The distraught father is able to bond with his son only in the feminine realm of the church, where they pray to their perfect "Heavenly Father."[21] To be an idiot was to not be a real man, and that failure seemed to nineteenth-century writers an especially apropos way to punish a failed fictional father.

Good mothers, according to nineteenth-century writers, lacked the ambition that plagued fathers. For them, an idiot son, and they were generally sons, had compensations. The historian Mary Ryan has described the fascination in sentimental fiction with the dead or dying son who returns to his mother's home and embrace.[22] Similarly, an idiot son remains forever childlike, innocent, and devoted to his mother. In Charles Dickens's *Barnaby Rudge*, Rudge's mother reflects: "the comfort springs that he is ever a relying, loving child to me —never growing old or cold at heart, but needing my care and duty in his manly strength as in his cradle-time."[23] An illustration in an early edition of the novel shows mother and son, happy together in their pastoral cottage garden. The mother's need to constantly give was best met by a permanently needy child. This son would never have to face the difficult transition to adult masculinity and leave the feminine sphere of the home. If he did so, he would need to be quickly retrieved.[24] If mothers played a role in civil society by educating and rearing their sons to be citizens, with the idiot son the system ceased to work, because, like Rudge, that son would not be a citizen.[25] Instead, Rudge and his mother remain comfortably isolated in their garden, happily cut off from the public sphere and liberal society. The greater importance of men as citizens who would enter the broader world, unlike women, who would remain in the domestic realm, probably explains why these were stories of sons, not daughters. A permanently dependent idiot son was an anomaly of note in American popular culture, while a permanently dependent daughter was simply routine.

There was no room in the garden for fathers. Significantly, Rudge's mother and most of the other mothers in these stories were widows without other sons.[26] The mother's devotion to her idiot child in these cases did not rob her husband or other potential male citizens of her services. According to the historians Peter L. Tyor and Leland V. Bell, institution authorities feared that caring "for a mentally defective child could exhaust a mother, forcing her to slight her responsibilities to other family members resulting in the disruption of the entire household. If family dislocation was severe enough, the family would be demoralized and soon pauperized."[27] The era's fiction agreed with the professional authorities: only a widow could safely care for an idiot son without threatening the rest of the family.[28]

The ideology of moral motherhood argued that all children needed the nurturing love of a devoted mother, and almost all mothers, according to popular culture, would automatically provide that devotion. The popular author Harriet Beecher Stowe suggested that if a mother had a disabled child, her love would become even more profound. "If a mother has among her children one whom sickness has made blind, deaf, or dumb, incapable of acquiring knowledge through the usual channels of communication," she asked, "does she not seek to reach its darkened mind by modes of communication tenderer and more intimate than those which she uses with the stronger and more favored ones?"[29] The tender love and attention of a mother could reach even the "darkened mind" of a child with intellectual disabilities. The benevolent mother acted as a heroine, using her innate maternal devotion to save her helpless child.[30]

The major American text on mental deficiency published in the nineteenth century built on this assumption. In it, Édouard Séguin, a French physician and an expert on the education of feeble-minded children, who had immigrated to the United States after the 1848 revolution in France and whose system of "physiological education" was used in almost all American and European institutions into the twentieth century, praised the careful labor of devoted mothers and their nurturing impact on disabled children.[31] In the professional literature, which drew on actual experience, female idiots appear much more often than in the popular literature. One young disabled woman's "gentle disposition, her affections and family feelings, testify of the angel spirit [her mother] which ministered to her and brought to her couch everything which could feed the body and the soul."[32] The mother's constant care of her child and her desire to expose her child to everything beneficial resulted in a gentle and affectionate young woman. A mother's "angel spirit" could create a loving child even out of a mental defective.

Seguin himself, writing in 1866, saw the mother as functioning under the influence of the physician, who would guide her and make her into the physician's tool in the home. She would apply the expert's techniques of child development to her child: "The arm of the mother becomes a swing or a supporter; her hand a monitor or a compressor; her eye a stimulant or a director of the distracted look."[33] Seguin and other professionals argued that mentally defective children, as both "ill" and "uneducated," demanded even more supervision than "normal" children from outside experts. Professionals would provide direction, and the mother would provide the "angel spirit." In this description, the father did not appear. In fact, the physician had seemingly taken over the father's role of wise, guiding patriarch against the mother's emotional devotion.

The absent father portrayed in popular fiction and in the professional literature may have been a distortion of reality. Historians suggest that nineteenth-century fathers were very involved with children who were seriously ill and in need of medical attention.[34] It seems clear that some fathers played a significant role in their disabled children's care. Seguin, for example, described a French couple that worked together to improve their daughter. Her mother "had never left her, had been deprived of sleep and of all distractions . . . in order to see her child sit, stand, walk, look, hear, speak, in one word, live," and her father "had left an honored grade in the army in order to relieve his wife in the pious incubation of their child."[35] Their efforts were rewarded when their daughter became able to care for herself, perform household tasks, and join social gatherings. Paternal devotion of this kind, however, rarely appeared in popular or professional discourse. Instead, moral mothers and dedicated physicians received almost all of the praise.

Balancing Love and Reason, 1900–1960

The nineteenth-century ideal of moral motherhood rewarded women with cultural authority through their irreplaceable emotional bond with their children. Idiocy fit comfortably into this pattern: the ever-devoted mother devoted herself to her eternal child. However, in the twentieth century, when emotion and intuition were superseded by science, mothers had no authority to defend their intimate knowledge of and experience with their children. Even the authenticity of that emotional connection came under professional and popular scrutiny. Like the fictional abusive fathers of the nineteenth century, twentieth-century mothers were accused of creating mental disabilities such as autism in their children by their inability to care for them properly. Finally, what had appeared as beautiful in nineteenth-century sentimental fiction—the tender relationship between a care-giving mother and her dependent son—struck at a nerve in later American culture: the fear that mothers would seek to prolong their cultural and social authority by essentially emasculating their sons, retaining them as permanent children and metaphorical idiots. Nineteenth-century popular literature still seemed comfortable with the idea that a few individuals, even a few male individuals, might never leave the domestic sphere; twentieth-century writers and experts were far less tolerant. What if mothers, the creators of new liberal citizens, were choosing to subvert the system by keeping their sons tied to the home? Sons with intellectual disabilities brought this fear out into the open because they were the perfect temptation—the eternal child.

There was an ambivalence in twentieth-century approaches to motherhood. In the eyes of society, an inability or unwillingness to provide good care for a child was the mother's fault, not the father's.[36] Parents of intellectually disabled children had a respectable alternative when they felt unable to care for their children: they could, at least in theory, place their child in an institution. However, the overwhelming emphasis on institutions as the best locus of care for feeble-minded people in the late nineteenth and twentieth centuries left many parents who did not wish to or were unable to institutionalize their child in an awkward position. Special education programs were not available to all children until 1975; for most of the century, such programs focused on children with mild mental disabilities. If parents chose to or, due to institutional overcrowding, were forced to keep their children at home, as most parents probably did, they were, with some limited exceptions, on their own. For some mothers this obligation to care was unbearable and unmanageable.

For the child at home, the mother was the obvious trainer. Slowly, in the 1920s and 1930s, advice books and other writings began to appear to advise her. The trickle of advice became a flood in the 1950s and 1960s. Despite this dependence on maternal labor, the professional literature was pervaded with a constant preoccupation that mothers were not properly training their children and would instead overprotect and spoil them or reject them and push them beyond their abilities.[37]

Mothers who elected to keep their children at home had difficulty finding support and guidance. They expressed their frustration in the stacks of letters they sent to the Children's Bureau, the federal agency in charge of programs for mothers and children, and to other child-rearing advisers from the 1920s on, asking for advice and guidance.[38] "I am told by a competent Child's Specialist that my little son age 7 months is backward + may always be a retarded child," one mother wrote, "I am determined to give him every advantage to develope [sic] mentally + feel sure that special training may at least help him."[39] She asked for literature to help her with this task. In 1932, Dr. Ella Oppenheimer, of the Children's Bureau, recommended the British physician John Thomson's 1924 book, *Opening Doors,* one of the few advice manuals available in the early twentieth century. Thompson gave responsibility for training to the mother. "This special training is to be *your work,* for no one else can do it as well as a mother," he explained.[40] Like Seguin earlier, Thomson drew on the well-established ideas of a mother's overwhelming love for her children and of the mother's specialized gifts for child rearing. His assumptions were still tenable in the early twentieth century, but as the decades went on mothers would be trusted less and less in the absence of expert guidance. In general, where a distrust of mothers grew quickly, alternatives to maternal care, such as support services, special education programs, or even expanded institutional care, grew much more slowly, leaving mothers with the responsibility for their children's training and care.

The perceived difficulty was that mothers could not be safely entrusted with the crucial work of training their children. Starting in the late nineteenth century, book after book, article after article, warned parents against overprotecting and spoiling a disabled child.[41] "In families where the mentally deficient child is the only problem we find that the child is usually so petted and spoiled that the mother is a mental and physical wreck through misguided attempts to make up to the child through physical means that which was lacking mentally," wrote Dr. Groves B. Smith, assistant superintendent at Beverly Farms, a private institution, in 1922.[42] "The withdrawal of the [mentally retarded] child from social contacts to protect him from hurt and the prolonged infantilization together serve to induce a suffocating atmosphere of self-pity and overprotection which in turn adds to the retardation," warned the psychiatric social worker Howard R. Kelman thirty years later.[43] Mothers' affection for their children caused them to care for their children so completely that the child's own abilities deteriorated or never developed. This "enervating affection" was gratifying for the mother but harmful for the child. In the words of a teacher, "[t]he mother in her misapprehended love for the child, being bent upon giving him (or herself) the gratification of the moment, loses sight of the future, which is being defeated by present indulgence."[44] In order to satisfy their own emotional needs, went the charge, mother kept their children dependent and incompetent.

Many parents took this threat very seriously and worked hard not to spoil their children. One way to do this was to control the mother's devotion to her child. The mother of a handicapped child must "have some outlet through which she can get away from her troubles . . . she must have some relief, and outside activities will help. She will be better for them, and at the same time she will make herself a better mother," warned Edward Dyer Anderson, a writer in *Hygeia,* the American Medial Association's health magazine for families, in 1934.[45] Practically, however, this could be hard to achieve. "My whole day is built around his [her mentally retarded son's] moods," one mother complained. "I used to leave him with a baby sitter once in awhile [*sic*], but he is getting so hard to handle lately when he is in a bad humor that I hate to and worry the whole time if I do."[46] Lack of support from the community and, sometimes, from fathers made it hard for mothers to find "an outlet." A mother, like the one who could not even find a babysitter, had little chance to develop other interests. The exclusion of many intellectually disabled children from public schools and other community activities put an even greater burden on mothers.

Many fathers provided only limited help with daily care and training. In general, fathers of disabled children may have been less involved in their care than fathers had been in the past. One 1950s study of parents of eventually institutionalized children found that

[i]t was inevitable for mothers to have a preponderant burden of care of the retarded child. A father's usual response to this problem was to work

harder, and thus spend more time away from home. It was not "natural" for most fathers to take over with the occasional care as they might have with a normal son or daughter.[47]

Caring for these children, then, was conceptualized as essentially a maternal, not a paternal, role.[48]

The specialized literature on disabled children reflects this gender division of parents' roles in child rearing. An advice manual published by the Federal Children's Bureau made the division plain. In figure 5.1, the father is a "companion" to his "fortunate" son. He provides entertainment and

Figure 5.1. Father and son as companions.
Source: Laura L. Dittman, *The Mentally Retarded Child at Home: A Manual for Parents* (Washington, DC: Children's Bureau, Social Security Administration, Department of Health, Education, and Welfare, 1959), 72.

guidance to his child. In figure 5.2, however, the mother takes on the hard work of daily care and training. Her child is not "fortunate" but merely receiving what every child could expect from his or her mother. *"Fathers, too, should take a part in teaching the mentally retarded child,"* urged the psychologists and educators Samuel A. Kirk, Merle B. Karnes, and Winnifred D. Kirk in a 1957 advice manual. That teaching, however, was limited to specifically masculine tasks and amusements. "It is true that the major responsibility for training the child is usually the mother's," the manual continued, "but there are many tasks about the house and yard for which fathers are responsible, such as mowing the grass, raking the leaves, washing the car, . . . and so forth."[49] Helping fathers with these masculine tasks offered a chance for boys to practice skills and to receive "recognition from their father."[50] A father's role was to offer emotional support and to be a companion and trainer in special masculine skills, not to be a caregiver and general trainer.

Many fathers took their responsibilities seriously and were intimately involved in the lives of their children. How many moved beyond companion to caregiver is hard to tell. The rigors of employment probably limited fathers' ability to participate in their children's daily care. In 1955, Frank Piccola, who refused to institutionalize his son Eddie, told *Coronet* magazine that he

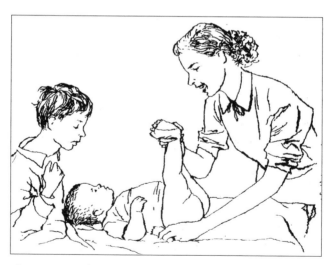

Figure 5.2. Mother as her infant's trainer and caregiver.
Source: Laura L. Dittman, *The Mentally Retarded Child at Home: A Manual for Parents* (Washington, DC: Children's Bureau, Social Security Administration, Department of Health, Education, and Welfare, 1959), 45.

looked forward to a time when "in six more years I'll get my pension and Eddie and I can spend more time together."[51] Most writers seemed to imply that a father's role was simply different. "One trouble with a father's writing this story," John Frank wrote in his memoir,

> is that he cannot properly account for a mother's point of view. . . . I was certainly deeply interested in John Peter. . . . I was deeply and emotionally concerned in everything that related to his welfare. But I had a good many other things to do. His place in the hierarchy of Lorraine's interests was inevitably far higher than in mine.[52]

Frank and many other fathers loved their children and were concerned about them, but their involvement in their children's lives was limited by time and social expectations. The level and the intimacy of care required by many children with significant disabilities, however, sometimes put them, even more than "normal" children, within their mother's domain.

Many mothers may have accepted this division of labor as appropriate.[53] In 1957, one mother wrote to *Children Limited,* the newsletter of the Association for Retarded Children, to defend fathers against the charge of disinterest. Men "are away all day at business," she explained. "They come home at night and spend a little while with the family before the kids have to go to bed."[54] However, she still found that her husband's emotional support and companionship was key to her care for her retarded son, Steve. "I could never get along without Steve's Dad to help," she claimed.[55] Specific negative comments about fathers did not often appear in the letters of mothers of intellectually disabled children, and mothers were often reticent in other forums, as well.[56] "Although several mothers complained about the husband's lack of understanding and help, an almost equal number denied this problem and felt, in a general and nebulous way, that the husband had been understanding and helpful," stated a 1961 study of group counseling program for mothers of retarded children.[57] "General and nebulous" was a less than ringing endorsement of the father's role, but mothers' overall reaction seems to have been resignation. "My husband has tried to be helpful," wrote one overwhelmed mother in 1963, "but he is 44 and is tired at the end of the day, commuting, etc., and he is no bundle of energy at night."[58]

Resources to assist mothers were limited. Siblings might help, either by caring for the child or by being independent and therefore requiring less care from mother.[59] For some siblings, this could be a heavy burden, as it was for the girl who was held out of school to care for her sister; others were less involved.[60] A prosperous family had more resources. It could hire additional caregivers to work in the home. Roy Rogers and Dale Evans even built a separate cottage next to the main house for Robin, their infant daughter with Down's Syndrome, and her nurse. That level of provision was out of reach for most parents. "I was disappointed in the story of Robin Rogers," wrote Lucille Stout, mother of a daughter with Down's Syndrome, after reading Dale Evans's memoir about her life with Robin. "It left me untouched and unhelped. Where I had not been able to provide even a separate room for my child, that family could build a separate house and staff it for their child. Their prestige was such that they did not have to worry about social stigma."[61]

Resources might be available to the affluent, but the lack of them could be highly frustrating to parents who had no option for help beyond public institutions. Residential placement in a school or institution, of course, was the final solution for some families at all income levels.

Practically speaking, the lack of alternatives, frequently including "normal" ones like day schools, left mothers responsible for the daily care of their intellectually disabled children. Mothers thus had many more opportunities to spoil their disabled children, and, according to professionals, the consequences were even more dangerous than with normal children.

For a mother to spoil her disabled child meant not only that she was deriving illegitimate emotional satisfaction from her child's dependence but also that she might neglect the rest of the family. Commentators implied that mothers' emotions and energies were the fuel for the family; without them, the family would cease to function. "It is easy for a mother to become a martyr to a mentally retarded child while neglecting the needs of the family as a whole," warned the educator Stella Stillson Slaughter in her 1960 advice manual. "The mother whose dedication to her mentally retarded child leaves little time for her to spend with other members of her family is placing great strain upon happy family relationships."[62] The disabled child would drain the mother for his or her own benefit, leaving the rest of the family neglected.[63] "Give your child his just share of your attention," warned Kirk and his coauthors, "but do not give him so much attention that you neglect other members of the family."[64] Sometimes writers focused on physical exhaustion. "The chief burden of care usually falls upon the mother," wrote Superintendent Johnstone, of the Training School at Vineland, in 1916;

"their other children are more or less neglected and often the husband finds the home a place of worry and irritability that tends to unfit him for his next day's work."[65] More often, in the following decades, concern focused on the disabled child as an emotional drain on the mother at the expense of the rest of the family. Having given all of her love to the one child, professional advisers claimed, the mother would have nothing left for the others.

Popular literature also warned that an intellectually disabled child could be a competitor or a threat to other family members. Time and love given such a child was stolen from the spouse and siblings. Some postwar confession magazine stories elaborated on this point.[66] Confession magazines were oriented toward a female working-class audience, but they often shared many of the assumptions of the professional literature about disabled children. In the evocatively titled 1955 story "Unfit Mother," a mother's passionate love for one child and her refusal to institutionalize him leads her to neglect the rest of her family and, ultimately, to the family's destruction.[67] In figure 5.3, her husband, or possibly his ghost, reproaches her for her neglect of himself and her teenage daughters in favor of her disabled son. The neg-

Figure 5.3. The anxious mother is accosted by her husband, or possibly his ghost, reminding her of her neglect of him and her daughters.
Source: "Unfit Mother," *Secrets* (March 1955): 14–15.

lected girls have been driven into delinquency and social isolation by the burden and stigma of their brother, but quickly returns to the family circle after the son is sent to an institution. In another story, a mother neglects her husband, Chuck, and her twin sons, Buster and Butch, in her devotion to her severely retarded daughter, Ellen, until a near-fatal accident realigns her thinking. "I realized more and more how much he'd [Butch] needed me—how much Buster and Chuck had needed me. They were starved for my love," she theatrically proclaims.[68] The implicit message of these stories is that the mother is squandering her emotional and physical resources on the disabled child, in the process destroying the rest of the family. In the less than subtle morality of confession literature, that destruction takes obvious forms, from car accidents to juvenile delinquency. Even worse, the disabled child fails to benefit from this overindulgence and is much happier when finally placed in an institution with specialized care.

Accusations that parents were spoiling a child, therefore, took many forms. A child could be spoiled by being given too many things, or by not receiving enough discipline, or even by being kept out of an institution where he or she could receive the training he or she required. The implicit boast was that a child who was not spoiled was helped to become independent. Independence for these children, however, was strictly limited, a matter of acquiring certain basic skills like dressing or self-feeding. Children with severe mental deficiencies would never attain the independent judgment that marked adulthood.[69] At the same time, their mothers were also locked in an equivocal position: they could not seek the same kind of self-development as men but should not find gratification in keeping their children in a dependent state. So mothers of intellectually disabled children were trapped—they needed to train their children for independence without ever letting them go. At the same time, enjoying their caregiving too much was a sign of an illegitimate desire to keep their child dependent.

The Search for a "Realistic Acceptance"

From the late nineteenth century through the 1950s, experts urged parents to be "realistic" about their disabled children. This dictum appeared in a number of forms over the decades. Early in the twentieth century, for example, institution superintendents like Johnstone criticized parents for "failing to admit that a child was feeble-minded even when so pronounced by experts" and for refusing to place their children in institutions.[70] After World War II, the attacks became more psychologically sophisticated. Social workers, physicians, and other professionals criticized parents for failing to achieve a realistic acceptance and an objective understanding of their child's condition. The term "acceptance" was frequently used to convey a complex of meanings about the appropriate emotional approach for a parent to take to his or her child. In 1954, Leonard Rosen, a special education researcher defined acceptance as "(1) [being] able to admit that her child was retarded, (2) no longer looking for a miraculous cure, (3) trying to act constructively for the child's present and future welfare."[71] A parent needed to be willing to work for his or her child but should do so from an objective understanding of the child and his or her problems. Members of the Association for Retarded Children (ARC), largely parents in these years, adopted this concept for themselves. "It is hard to look at a beloved child with eyes misted with father or mother love, and accept the fact of mental retardation," explained an editorial in a New Jersey ARC unit newsletter in 1953. "It is hard to love him with all your heart and yet see him objectively with all his limitations and possibilities. It is hard to plan wisely, and do the best you can for him and be satisfied with that best."[72] Both professionals and the parent advocacy movement urged parents to carefully balance emotional connection and objective assessment.

Professionals seldom explicitly discussed the role of fathers of intellectually disabled children. Implicitly, however, professionals sometimes divided the two roles—emotional connection and objective assessment—between the parents. The job of maintaining objectivity was often given to fathers, who supposedly had the skills, emotional detachment, and rational judgment that mothers lacked. Mothers were the caregivers, however flawed; fathers were the ultimate decision makers about major issues such as institutionalization. Despite the ideal of companionate marriage advocated by family guidance professionals and shared by many couples, fathers were often expected to take the burden of decision making from their wives in these cases. Fathers supposedly had the rationality to do so and were the producers of the financial resources that made many options, like private care and schooling, possible.

How this played out in actual families could vary widely. Two letters to Dr. Benjamin Spock in the early 1960s illustrate the diversity. One mother who desperately wanted to institutionalize her son complained that her husband was refusing to agree to place their son in the home that their physician had recommended. She complained that her husband did not have to share the labor and emotions of caring for their son, but, regardless of her complaints, her husband's veto seemed final.[73] Another family presented an alternative approach to the same problem of institutionalization. In this case, both parents were confused over what to do. "Now I am a fairly well educated woman and I always thought I could see a logical approach to our problems. But, this time Dr. Spock I am up against a stone wall," the mother wrote. "My husband is in as big a dilemma as I am."[74] In this family, the decision making was shared; even the older brother was consulted for his opinion.

There was a striking pattern among professionals, however, who sometimes assumed that fathers had the ability to make decisions with which mothers could not cope. For example, when the physician diagnosed John Peter Frank, John and Lorraine Frank's son, as physically and mentally disabled, the physician told John the full diagnosis and recommended institutionalization to him but told Lorraine only that John Peter was brain damaged.[75] The power to make decisions could be a lonely burden. During the long period he planned his son's institutionalization without his wife's knowledge, Frank suffered from hallucinations of a crying infant.[76] Some wives were sympathetic to their husbands' burden. The physician told Clarence Bogert Jr., or Bud, at his daughter Valory's birth that she was probably "mongoloid" but warned him not to tell his wife, Charlotte, until she noticed for herself. It took her eight months to realize her child's disability. "Poor Bud—what he went through in those months," recalled Charlotte to a magazine reporter, "leading a double life, talking to the doctor in private, visiting medical libraries for further study, always searching for any slight indication in Valory's behavior that would prove the doctor's suspicions wrong—and all the time unable to talk to me about what was on his mind."[77] Other wives may well have been less accepting of this forced ignorance, and undoubtedly some husbands refused to keep their knowledge secret.

In the postwar years, however, professional psychologists' assumptions about mothers made this emotional division even more complex. There had always been criticism of mothers who were too demanding and who were unable to accept that their children could not "live up to parental ideas of achievement."[78] In the years after World War II, however, professionals were fascinated by the idea that mothers of disabled children might be hiding rejection under the cover of apparent devotion.[79] "Parental rejection," wrote Gale Walker, superintendent of Polk State School, in 1950, "always exists to some degree even though unexpressed or camouflaged by over-concern and protectiveness."[80] Mentally retarded children were even more vulnerable than other children because they experienced so much rejection from people outside the family. "A mentally retarded child who does not experience acceptance and security in his house is, therefore, in greater danger of developing behavior difficulties than a normal child," wrote Anne Marie Grebler, a graduate student in education, in the *American Journal of Mental Deficiency*.[81] In these cases, loving and accepting parents, particularly mothers, needed to make up for the harsh criticism and prejudices of society.

Most professional articles that discussed the problem of acceptance considered both parents, and fathers, too, were sometimes criticized. Fathers' supposed detachment and ambition, in the eyes of some professionals, translated into rejection. However, the resulting damage was much less severe because fathers' acceptance was less important to their children's development. Thus, mothers were the real focus of most of the criticism. The natural love for a "crippled" child once praised by Stowe seems to have disappeared in these accounts. "[I]t becomes more difficult for the parent to give this affection [that the mentally retarded child requires,]" the educator Edward L. Rautman claimed, in 1949, "since for most parents a retarded child represents both a lost hope for the future and a continuous and ever-repeated disappointment in the present."[82] A mentally retarded child was such a profound disappointment that the parent, especially a middle-class parent, would have a very hard time maintaining the necessary love and affection. "[A] retarded youngster who comes from a family where the standards are so low as to make his own retardation inconspicuous . . . has a far more favorable educational and adjustmental prognosis," wrote Rautman, "than does a child who comes from a family setting in which his intellectual handicap places him below the level of the family aspirations."[83] In a time when middle-class children were supposed to earn their white-collar status through educational success, a mentally retarded child was permanently excluded from that competition. Whereas, in the nineteenth century, an idiotic child might offer emotional and religious consolations, many twentieth-century professionals implied that experts had to guide parents through education or counseling to perceive the value—which often remained vague in professional writings—of mentally retarded children, value that only experts could initially discern.[84]

Angels Unaware: Religious Discussions of Intellectual Disabilities

Despite professional criticisms of parents, there were some countercurrents in twentieth-century popular culture. Christian parent memoirs, for example, provided an alternative way to talk about children with disabilities and their parents.[85] Children with intellectual disabilities could be spiritually valuable in this discourse, and maternal sacrifice was often praiseworthy rather than suspect.

These memoirs were not isolated from the psychological assumptions of mainstream popular culture. One of the most popular books, Dale Evans Rogers's 1953 *Angel Unaware,* was a memoir of her life with her daughter Robin, who had Down's Syndrome. In a fairly common metaphor, Rogers argued that her daughter was an angel who had been sent down to bring the Rogers family closer to God. "I believe with all my heart that God sent her on a two-year mission to our household," she wrote, "to strengthen us spiritually and to draw us closer together in the knowledge and love and fellowship of God."[86] Despite her deep commitment to her daughter's spiritual dimension and her belief that God had sent Robin to educate the family spiritually, Rogers also described the dangers of being "too 'possessive'" about her daughter.[87] Rogers wrote her memoir from the perspective of her daughter, Robin, reporting to God in heaven after her death. "She was always praying for me, always hovering over me," "Robin" told God:

> Then she realized that giving me all her time and attention might be bad, too; there were other children in the house, and it wasn't fair to them. She tried to share her time and her love with Dusty and Cheryl and Linda [Robin's siblings] and Daddy, and to go on with her work.[88]

In fact, Rogers hired a full-time nurse to take care of Robin. The issue of rationing the mother's resources took on a new dimension in *Angel Unaware*: God and his mission for the Rogerses in show business were additional competitors for Dale Evans's time and attention.

Religious discourse might not always oppose psychiatric discourse, but it did allow some alternative themes to emerge. In Rogers's writing, Robin was an essential part of her family's life. Her disabilities served an important educational and religious purpose for her relatives. In some ways, *Angel Unaware* drew attention away from Robin as a person. The young child with Down's Syndrome who spoke little and had physical limitations and a fatal heart condition disappeared behind the recreated angelic Robin who narrated her story before going out to fly in heaven. The disabled individual was replaced by an "able," perceptive, articulate, idealized, and disembodied soul. The religious interpretation ran the danger of turning the individual into a moral lesson for others, rather than letting her be a human being. B. R.

Schmalzried Sr., a Catholic, wrote about his daughter with Down's Syndrome: "We must remember that Sunshine [Mary Margaret] and all the handicapped help the strong to become more charitable, more patient, and more Christian."[89] This attitude drew attention away from the disabled individual as human being with idiosyncratic wants and desires and turned him or her into one of the many lessons sent by God. At the same time, this sentimental and devout discourse allowed some religious parents to discuss their disabled children as valuable and contributing members of their families, justifying their presence in family life at a time when many professionals urged early institutionalization.[90]

Intellectual disabilities themselves, some religious writers argued, could be a spiritual gift. In 1951, Esther Vanamee Griffin, a Catholic and the mother of five children, described her severely disabled daughter, Sally, as an angel. "She can never offend God," Griffin recalled a friend explaining. "She is the only one [of Griffin's five children] who will never reach the age of reason, and she is completely doing the Lord's will now, without the freedom of choice between good and evil. And always *will*."[91] The permanent innocence Griffin praised showed an ideological continuity with nineteenth-century images of the natural innocence of idiots. Lack of intelligence translated into lack of temptation. This spiritual gift, however, also separated the "angel" from other people, including her family. Figure 5.4, from Griffin's article, shows Sally dancing alone, communing with nature. Her detachment from the world of "normal" humans was complete when her parents placed her, at the age of three, "in a little 'heaven on earth' [a private institution], surrounded by other little angels"—the other inmates.[92]

Spiritual and religious discussions also provided an alternative way to discuss motherhood. Charlotte D. Tucker, in her memoir, *Betty Lee* (1954) describes "a mother's love, your own child who needs you—the more helpless and afflicted, the greater your love and tolerance."[93] Tucker's assured description of her love for and devotion to her child lacked the mixture of guilt and unease found in most psychiatrically influenced discussions. In a religious memoir, sacrifice and caregiving had meaning and importance. Caring for an "angel unaware" was part of a spiritual calling. For some, this attitude was inadequate. "[I]t is impossible for me to find joy in the children's condition," sadly wrote J. Norman Heard, father of three intellectually disabled children and an ARC activist. "I have read letters from parents who have come to the realization that their children's retardation is a blessing in disguise. No doubt they are sincere in this belief, but it is one that God has not

151

yet given me the Grace to share."[94] Other parents reacted angrily to this approach and believed that the idea that a child's disability was a gift from God was an insult. However, for a mother who found herself dedicating her life to caregiving, it could be reassuring to believe that her work was important and served a larger purpose.

Miraculous Devotion: Parents Who Saved Their Children

An alternative secular strain of popular culture revered parents who refused to give up and who sacrificed everything to cure their child. Stories of

Figure 5.4. The "angel" dances alone, surrounded by nature.
Source: Esther Vanamee Griffin, "The Angel," *Catholic World* (April 1951): 35.

miracle cures suggested the existence of another popular ideal of parental self-sacrifice and devotion that coexisted with the psychological dictates of appropriate affection.

A reader of popular magazines in the twentieth century would find support for ideas of miraculous cures. "Brain Surgery Aids Retarded Children," claimed *Science Digest,* in 1951.[95] "[A] research team from the Brooklyn Jewish Hospital holds out hope that a cure for mongolism is just around the corner," promised the Catholic magazine *America.*[96] Medical discoveries could raise parents' hopes. The use of thyroid hormones to treat cretinism opened up possibilities to many parents in the 1920s. Later on, a test and treatment for phenylketonuria, or PKU, discovered in the late 1950s, gave new hope that doctors were "saving children from mental retardation."[97] Parents grasped at these expedients as possible salvations for their child: "I want to ask if there is such a treatment for dull children that are mentally weak and nervous [*sic*] I have heard that sometimes that such children had gland trouble thyroid or Pirenal gland trouble and that often could be corrected by having them treated is there such treatment if so how they treat it," wrote a mother, in 1928, to the Children's Bureau.[98] Thirty-five years later, a mother and her sister-in-law organized a careful search of the medical literature and began to work in "a local Retarded Children's Association in an effort to gain access to information which the latest in medical science and research can offer."[99] A letter to Spock was part of their effort to find

> any information about clinics or hospitals where research is being carried on in this field? Are any drugs or glandular extracts being administered to Mongoloids today? . . . Should these parents ask their pediatrician to get them an appointment to see a specialist in pediatric neurology . . . ? Is there a better clinic or hospital in the country to which you feel it would pay them to take this baby?[100]

Mental retardation professionals tried to discourage parents from searching for a cure. "It is best for parents to devote their time and energy to studying and planning ways and means of handling the problem," warned Kirk and his coauthors. "It is not wise for parents to spend excessive funds for the purpose of finding the basic causes and cures when in most instances these cannot be found."[101] Parents should accept the wisdom of professionals and care for their children as diagnosed.

Some parents, however, refused to accept a limited parental role. One proud mother wrote to the Children's Bureau to share her discovery that she had raised her son's IQ through psychiatric treatment, physical therapy, and vitamin supplements. She signed her letter with her name and the title "mother, teacher, student."[102] The image of parent as miracle worker spoke to a continued faith in the power and perceptions of parents and to a belief in the purity of their motives that was lacking from much of the professional literature. Nancy and David Melton, for example, violated every dictate of mental retardation professionals. Unable to accept their son Todd's diagnosis of mental retardation, they believed that "inside his thin, awkward frame there was a beautiful little boy longing to be freed."[103] Following the advice of Glenn Doman, of the Institutes of Human Potential, they reoriented their household around Todd's needs, ignoring the suggestions of the local physician and psychologist, even though Todd's constant therapy program occupied almost all of Nancy's time and left little for Todd's sister or David. The Meltons' memoir, published in 1968, was an early example of a genre of miracle cure stories written by parents of their children in the following decades. The stories presented an idealized view of parents' dedication and competence, but the standards of devotion advocated by parents like the Meltons were not standards that many parents were able or willing to achieve.

Activist Parents, 1940–1965

The postwar years put renewed emphasis on parents' dedication and work. Despite all the professional fears and criticisms, parents were crucial to the reform and expansion of services for intellectually disabled people in the 1950s and 1960s. "An intelligent parent of a retarded child must have a tremendous reservoir of courage, endless patients, staunch faith and enduring love if she (or he) is to help the child adjust to a world for which he is poorly equipped," claimed the journalist Evelyn Hart in a 1959 advice pamphlet, *How Retarded Children Can Be Helped.*[104] Social workers, physicians, psychologists, and other professionals often advocated therapy and guidance programs for parents, because parents were so important.[105] The programs would, it was hoped, excavate the appropriate emotions from parents and direct them into appropriate actions. Parents should pursue not supposedly hopeless cures, as had the Meltons, but community activism, preferably in cooperation with professionals. "Aside from the responsibilities accompanying direct home associations with his retarded child, the parent has the additional one of acquainting himself with opportunities afforded by school and community for the furtherance of his child's growth," wrote Stella Slaughter:

> If a parent finds his community lacking in opportunities for training and life adjustments for his mentally retarded offspring, he may feel compelled to instigate corrective measures. . . . The parent who is working to extend community opportunities for his mentally retarded child will ordinarily find the strength of his pleas multiplied by as many times as he finds parents to join him in his requests.[106]

As Slaughter acknowledged, parental labor was key to expanding social services.

A parent's realization of his or her need to participate in activism was a key component of acceptance of his or her child's disability. Dan Boyd, a parent and activist, described the "third stage" of acceptance in a frequently cited article. "Now, at last, I was able to look at life a little more objectively, to see more clearly, to think more rationally," Boyd recalled. "When we can do that, we are ready for the third stage in the growth of a parent of a mentally retarded child. We now begin to think more of what we can do for others, and less of what they can do for us."[107] The parent's loss would be transformed from an individual tragedy into the motivator of a social movement. Activism could also be therapeutic for parents, according to some professionals. "This sort of activity is therapeutic for the parents, who begin to turn their energies and hopes toward working in healthful, socialized channels with others, each drawing comfort and encouragement for the group," the psychiatric social worker Howard R. Kelman wrote, in 1953. "Eventually the child benefits, not only through the development of additional resources, but through the parents' developing a more realistic appraisal of the problem and of how it can best be solved."[108]

Parental activism also seemed to be a way for parents implicitly to make up for their children's wasted lives. If the child could not contribute to society, parents and experts suggested, the parent must transform the child's existence into a social contribution.[109] "I resolved that my child . . . was not to be wasted," wrote Pearl Buck about her daughter.

> If she could not make the contribution she should have made to her generation through her genius for music, if her healthy body was never to bear

fruit, if her strong energies were not to be creatively used, then the very facts of her condition, her existence as it was and is today, must be of use to human beings.[110]

Through writing or activism, parents could make their children useful to society by making them a stimulus for medical research, prevention efforts, and new social services. This drive to make the lives of their children count may explain why the newsletter of the National Association of Retarded Children boasted "that mentally retarded children were pioneers in the great experience that made the Salk polio vaccine possible . . . 63 patients at the Polk State School in Pennsylvania were given the vaccine with the consent and approval of their parents."[111] What would later be seen as an abuse of people unable to consent at the time seemed to Association of Retarded Children members to be a rare opportunity for the most excluded people to contribute to society.

In the 1960s, as professionals began to believe that children with intellectual disabilities, given remediation through early intervention and training, had greater potential than was generally assumed, parents' obligations grew even greater. What had earlier seemed a denial of reality—devotion to a child's care and training—became a virtue and an obligation. "You parents are the people who can do the most for your infirm child," wrote the Swiss psychologist Maria Egg in an advice book recommended by the executive director of the NARC:

> Therefore: don't look for miracle doctors or miracle drugs. You yourselves must do everything that can help improve your child's condition. . . . The kind of life your handicapped child will lead depends on you. For this, you need no specialized training, no degree or diploma: your patience, your understanding, your love, your burning desire to help your child—these are far more important.[112]

The provision of advice early on to help parents foster their children's development became more intense as the future possibilities became apparently greater.

As professionals like Egg praised parents' love and desire to help, they also imposed obligations on parents. Parents needed to use those feelings to help their children develop and live as productive lives as possible. Parents of intellectually disabled children needed to be trainers and caregivers at home and activists in the community. "You parents of retarded children have a mission that is greater than that of the care of your child," wrote Egg:

> You must get the best possible help for your child; you yourselves must seek the knowledge and skills that will enable you to offer your child the best. . . .
>
> In time your concern for your own child should grow into concern for all handicapped children. This means you should try to think more about what you can do for others and less about what others can do for your child.[113]

Whereas parents had been criticized earlier for doing too much, now they could be criticized for doing too little. The obligations went beyond simple child rearing to the incorporation of therapeutic skills into home care and to political advocacy in the community.

Conclusion

Discussions of intellectually disabled children and their parents are layered and mutable; the spiritually superior mothers of the nineteenth century were transformed into seductive captors of their children in the twentieth, while dangerously ambitious fathers in one century became rational and detached in the next. Professionals succeeded in acquiring huge cultural power, partially through their constant critiques of parents, but they were undercut to some degree by the continued respect for parents in certain segments of the popular culture. Popular and professional discourse struggled with a series of key questions: What was the value of an individual who would not become an independent worker and citizen? What were the legitimate rewards of caregiving? How should parents raise a child who was doomed to failure by contemporary social standards? There were never satisfactory answers to any of these questions. All of the criticisms of parents, however, failed to change the underlying reality that American society depended on individual parents to fulfill the difficult task of raising children who were socially stigmatized and rejected. The late-twentieth-century embrace of parents as crucial activists and caregivers also imposed burdens on parents who needed to make up, through their own labor and activism, for the limited social and community provision for people with intellectual disabilities.

NOTES

1. Simon Olshansky, "Chronic Sorrow: A Response to Having a Mentally Defective Child," *Social Casework* 43 (1962): 191.

2. Leo Kanner, *A Miniature Textbook of Feeblemindedness* (New York: Child Care Publications, 1949), 18.

3. Richard H. Hungerford, "On Locusts," *American Journal of Mental Deficiency* 54 (1949–50): 417.

4. There is a large literature on this subject. For a small sampling, see Ruth H. Bloch, "American Feminine Ideals in Transition: The Rise of the Moral Mother, 1785–1815," *Feminist Studies* 4 (1978): 101–126; Stephen M. Frank, *Life with Father: Parenthood and Masculinity in the Nineteenth-Century American North* (Baltimore: Johns Hopkins University Press, 1998), 38–39; Robert L. Griswold, *Fatherhood in America: A History* (New York: Basic Books, 1993), 30; Jan Lewis, "Motherhood and the Construction of the Male Citizen in the United States, 1750–1850," in *Constructions of the Self*, ed. George Levine (New Brunswick, NJ: Rutgers University Press, 1992), 143–163; Jan Lewis, "Mother's Love: The Construction of an Emotion in Nineteenth-Century America," in *Mothers and Motherhood: Readings in American History*, ed. Rima D. Apple and Janet Golden (Columbus: Ohio State University Press, 1997), 52–71; Rosemarie Zagarri, "Morals, Manners, and the Republican Mother," *American Quarterly* 44 (1992): 192–215.

5. Frank, 2–3, 31–35; Sally G. McMillen, "Antebellum Southern Fathers and the Health Care of Children," *Journal of Southern History* 60 (1994): 513–532.

6. Frank, 57–76, 82; Griswold, 2–4.

7. Frank, 153–158.

8. James W. Trent Jr., *Inventing the Feeble Mind: A History of Mental Retardation in the United States* (Berkeley: University of California, 1994), 38–39.

9. Robert L. Osgood, *For "Children Who Vary from the Normal Type": Special Education in Boston, 1838–1930* (Washington, DC: Gallaudet University Press, 2000), 67, 78–79, 82–83; Margaret A. Winzer, *The History of Special Education: From Isolation to Integration* (Washington, DC: Gallaudet University Press, 1993), 343.

10. Rima D. Apple, "Constructing Mothers: Scientific Motherhood in the Nineteenth and Twentieth Centuries," *Social History of Medicine* 8 (1995): 161–178.

11. At least in theory; as always, practice was more complicated. Intellectual disabilities, however, were noticeably different because residential institutions were the preferred solution for these children, rather than the last resort. Michael B. Katz, *In the Shadow of the Poorhouse* (New York: Basic Books, 1986), 118–121; Kriste Linden-

meyer, *A Right to Childhood: The U.S. Children's Bureau and Child Welfare, 1912–46* (Urbana: University of Illinois Press, 1997), 19–20.

12. Herbert Goldstein, "Population Trends in U.S. Public Institutions for the Mentally Deficient," *American Journal of Mental Deficiency* 63 (1958–59): 600; Trent, 265–266.

13. Betty Friedan, *The Feminine Mystique* (New York: Laurel Book, 1984), 192. See also Paul M. Dennis, "Between Watson and Spock: Eleanor Roosevelt's Advice on Child-Rearing from 1928 to 1962," *Journal of American Culture* 18 (1995): 46; Griswold, 94–97; Christina Hardyment, *Perfect Parents: Baby-Care Advice Past and Present* (New York: Oxford University Press, 1995), 173–175.

14. Mrs. James Neall, "Sanny," *Overland Monthly and Out West Magazine* 9 (Sept. 1872): 261. For a similar fictional incident, see Louisa May Alcott, *Little Men* (New York: Penguin Books, 1871; repr., 1994), 24.

15. Neall, 261.

16. "Highest House in Wathendale," *Harper's New Monthly Magazine* 3 (Sept. 1851): 526.

17. Ibid., 651, 652.

18. Charles Dickens, *Barnaby Rudge: A Tale of the Riots of 'Eighty* (New York: Oxford University Press, 1954), 564.

19. See "Unconvicted; or, Old Thorneley's Heirs, Chapters vii–viii," *Catholic World* 3 (Sept. 1866): 744. For a fictional mother who marries an unworthy man for money and is punished by the birth of an idiot son (she neglects him while avoiding home and husband), see Sarah Josepha Hale, "The Woodbine Cottage," in *Christian Keepsake and Missionary Annual for MDCCXLIX* (Electronic Text Center, University of Virginia Library, 1849), 39.

20. "The Son and Heir," *Living Age* 1 (27 July 1844): 653.

21. Ibid., 654.

22. I am here using and extending Mary P. Ryan's analysis of the appeal of dead children. Mary P. Ryan, *The Empire of the Mother: American Writing about Domesticity, 1830–1860* (New York: Harrington Park Press, 1985), 32, 69–70.

23. Dickens, 137.

24. If he did so, he would need to be quickly retrieved. For examples, see mothers' pursuit of their idiot sons gone astray in ibid.; William Wordsworth, "The Idiot Boy," in *The Poems,* ed. John O. Hayden (New York: Penguin, 1990), 281–295.

25. For discussions of women as creators of citizens in their sons, see Lewis, "Motherhood and the Construction of the Male Citizen in the United States, 1750–1850"; Linda K. Kerber, "The Republican Mother: Women and the Enlightenment—An American Perspective," in *Toward an Intellectual History of Women: Essays by Linda K. Kerber* (Chapel Hill: University of North Carolina Press, 1997), 41–62.

26. Some did have "normal" daughters. Apparently, nineteenth-century authors assumed that daughters required less attention or were less important.

27. Peter L. Tyor and Leland V. Bell, *Caring for the Retarded in America: A History* (Westport, CT: Greenwood Press, 1984), 87.

28. For two stories in which the care of an "imbecile" brother absorbs his sister's life and prevents her marriage, see ibid.; "Half a Lifetime Ago," *Harper's New Monthly Magazine* 12 (Jan. 1856): 185–202; J. T. Doyen, "Too Late," *Overland Monthly and Out West Magazine* 8 (March 1872): 253–259.

29. Quoted in Rosemarie Garland Thomson, *Extraordinary Bodies: Figuring Physical Disability in American Culture and Literature* (New York: Columbia University Press, 1997), 161.

30. Thomson suggests that disabled characters in nineteenth-century sentimental novels allow middle-class women to create a drama of benevolence where the liabilities of embodiment are displaced onto disabled characters. Benevolent women can then demonstrate their own empowerment by helping them (81–102). The relationship between a mother and her disabled child can be seen as a similar drama.

31. Edward Seguin, *Idiocy and Its Treatment by the Physiological Method* (New York: William Wood, 1866), 267; Tyor and Bell, 7–10.

32. Seguin, 312–314.

33. Ibid., 88. See also 87–89, 267, 280–287.

34. Frank, 76–80; McMillen, 514–531.

35. Seguin, 349.

36. For example, see Augusta Fink, *I-Mary: A Biography of Mary Austin* (Tucson: University of Arizona Press, 1983), 89, 109; Esther Lanigan Stineman, *Mary Austin: Song of a Maverick* (New Haven: Yale University Press, 1989), 68.

37. For growing suspicions of all mothers' abilities in this time period, see Apple.

38. Letters to the Children's Bureau and to the child-rearing advisers Angelo Patri and Benjamin Spock reveal parents' desire for information and advice on home training and care. (There are many letters scattered through the collections. For detailed references, please contact the author. See Children's Bureau, Record Group 102, National Archives, Washington, DC [CB]; Benjamin Spock Papers, Special Collections, Syracuse University Library, Syracuse University, Syracuse, NY; Angelo Patri Papers, Library of Congress, Washington, DC). For discussions of mothers' appeals for help with sick or disabled children, see Emily K. Abel, "Appealing for Children's Health Care: Conflicts between Mothers and Officials in the 1930s," *Social Service Review* 70 (1996): 282–304; Emily K. Abel, *Hearts of Wisdom: American Women Caring for Kin, 1850–1940* (Cambridge, MA: Harvard University Press, 2000); Molly Ladd-Taylor and U.S. Children's Bureau, *Raising a Baby the Government Way: Mothers' Letters to the Children's Bureau, 1915–1932* (New Brunswick, NJ: Rutgers University Press, 1986).

39. Mrs. GRS to CB, [February 1932], File 4-12-1-1, Central File [CF] 1929–32, CB.

40. John Thomson, *Opening Doors: A Little Book for the Mothers of Babies Who Are Long in Learning to Behave Like Other Children of Their Age*, 2nd ed. (London: Oliver & Boyd, 1924), 7.

41. For examples, see E. A. Farrington, *Mental Retardation in Children* (Haddonfield, NJ: 1933), 9–11; Ethel Horsefield, "Suggestions for Training the Mentally Retarded by Parents in the Home," *American Journal of Mental Deficiency* 46 (1941–42): 533; M. Arline Arbright, "Not So Fast, Please" (Milwaukee: Milwaukee County Association for Retarded Children, 1955), 13.

42. Groves B. Smith, "Practical Considerations of the Problems of Mental Deficiency as Seen in a Neuro-Psychiatric Dispensary," *Proceedings and Addresses of the American Association for the Study of the Feeble-Minded* (1922): 60.

43. Howard R. Kelman, "Parent Guidance in a Clinic for Mentally Retarded Children," *Social Casework* 34 (1953): 444.

44. Margaret Keiver Smith, "The Training of a Backward Boy," *Psychological Clinic* 2 (1908): 150.

45. Edward Dyer Anderson, "The Family and the Handicapped Child," *Hygeia* (April 1934): 309.

46. J. F. to Spock, 28 April 1960, File April 15–29, 1960, Box 6, Spock.

47. John N. Carver and Nellie Enders Carver, *The Family of the Retarded Child* (Syracuse: Syracuse University Press, 1972), 86.

48. Early-twentieth-century advice manuals consistently referred to the care of sick children as a mothers' role. See Ralph LaRossa, *The Modernization of Fatherhood: A Social and Political History* (Chicago: University of Chicago Press, 1997), 55, 60.

49. Samuel A. Kirk, Merle B. Karnes, and Winifred D. Kirk, *You and Your Retarded Child: A Manual for Parents of Retarded Children* (New York: Macmillan, 1957), 75. See also Benjamin McLane Spock and Marion Olive Lerrigo, *Caring for Your Disabled Child* (New York: Macmillan, 1965), 42.

50. Kirk, Karnes, and Kirk.

51. Frank Piccola and Ralph Bass, "We Kept Our Retarded Child at Home," *Coronet* (November 1955): 50.

52. John P. Frank, *My Son's Story* (New York: Knopf, 1952), 43.

53. Jessica Weiss, however, suggests that many mothers of "normal" children resented fathers' limited involvement in child rearing in the postwar years. See Jessica Weiss, "'A Drop-in Catering Job': Middle-Class Women and Fatherhood, 1950–1980," *Journal of Family History* 24 (1999): 374–390.

54. Mrs. Ralph T. Howe, "Why Fathers Don't Write," *Children Limited* (April 1957): 15.

55. Ibid.

56. For exceptions, see Harry V. Bice and Margaret G. Davitt Holden, "Group Counseling with Mothers of Children with Cerebral Palsy," *Journal of Social Casework* 30 (1949): 109; Regina Elkes, "Group-Casework Experiment with Mothers of Children with Cerebral Palsy," *Journal of Social Casework* 28 (1947): 97.

57. Robert M. Nadal, "A Counseling Program for Parents of Severely Retarded Preschool Children," *Social Casework* 42 (1961): 80.

58. Mrs.WBG to Spock, 20 August 1963, File Aug. 17–30, 1963, Box 14, Spock.

59. Carver and Carver, 61–65.

60. Agnes K. Hanna to HCR, 22 July 1940, file 7-6-1-2, CF 1937–1940, CB.

61. Lucille Stout, *I Reclaimed My Child: The Story of a Family into Which a Retarded Child Was Born* (Philadelphia: Chilton, 1959), 34.

62. Stella Stillson Slaughter, *The Mentally Retarded Child and His Parent* (New York: Harper & Brothers, 1960), 6–7.

63. For examples of these warnings, see Frank, *My Son's Story*, 94–96; K. S. Holt, "The Home Care of Severely Retarded Children," *Pediatrics* 22 (1958): 750; Dorothy Garst Murray, *This Is Stevie's Story*, 2nd ed. (New York: Abingdon Press, 1967), 88; Edith M. Stern and Elsa Castendyck, *The Handicapped Child: A Guide for Parents* (New York: A. A. Wynn, 1950), 136.

64. Kirk, Karnes, and Kirk, 69.

65. E. R. Johnstone, "Mental Defectives as a Home and School Problem," *Training School Bulletin* 13 (1916): 181.

66. See "Heartbreak Baby," *Secret Confessions* (April 1953): 33, 42–44; "This Is My Problem . . . Shall I Put My Daughter Away?" *True Confessions* (May 1944): 49, 69; "Unfit Mother," *Secrets* (March 1955): 14–15, 28–34; "We Sacrificed Our Children," *True Experience* (January 1963): 28–32, 71–75; "Why Doesn't My Baby Cry!" *Life Story Confessions* (January 1964): 22–25, 60–63.

67. "Unfit Mother."

68. "Why Doesn't My Baby Cry!" 63.

69. This was quite explicit, and the parent who had failed to accept this had failed to properly accept his or her child. For examples, see Elise H. Martens, "Parents' Problems with Exceptional Children," in *Office of Education Bulletin* (Washington, DC: Government Printing Office, 1932), 39–41; Hilda M. Stoddard, "The Relation of Parental Attitudes and Achievements of Severely Mentally Retarded Children," *American Journal of Mental Deficiency* 63 (1958–59): 587.

70. Johnstone, 180.

71. Leonard Rosen, "Selected Aspects in the Development of the Mother's Understanding of Her Mentally Retarded Child," *American Journal of Mental Deficiency* 59 (1954–55): 523.

72. "What Does Acceptance Mean?" *The Guardian* (September 1953), in file "Misc. Library Materials," Box 19, PARC.

73. JF to Spock, 28 April [1960], File Apr. 15–29, 1960, Box 6, Spock.

74. Mrs. WBG to Spock, 20 August 1963, File Aug. 17–30, 1963, Box 14, Spock.

75. For examples of this practice, see Howard R. Kelman, "The Effects of a Group of Non-Institutionalized Mongoloid Children upon Their Families as Perceived by Their Mothers," Ph.D. diss., New York University, 1958, 172.

76. Frank, *My Son's Story*, 88.

77. Joseph Shallit, "Hope and Help for America's Retarded Children," *Parents' Magazine* (July 1956): 64.

78. Esther Loring Richards, "Practical Aspects of Parental Love," *Mental Hygiene* 10 (1926): 230.

79. For examples, see Stanley C. Mahoney, "Observations Concerning Counseling with Parents of Mentally Retarded Children," *American Journal of Mental Deficiency* 63 (1958–59): 82; Winifred Wardell, "Case Work with Parents of Mentally Deficient Children," *American Journal of Mental Deficiency* 52 (1947): 93; G. H. Zuk, Ralph L. Miller, John H. Bartram, and Frederick Kling, "Maternal Acceptance of Retarded Children: A Questionnaire Study of Attitudes and Religious Backgrounds," *Child Development* 32 (1961): 538. For similar attacks in the confession magazine stories, see "Could I Love My Mongoloid Baby?" *True Secrets* (May 1959): 10–13, 32–34; "I Was an Unnatural Mother," *True Confessions* (December 1954): 33, 53–56; "My Monster Child," *Your Romance* (April 1954): 12–15, 64–66; "Retarded," *True Confessions* (July 1954): 21, 57–58.

80. Gale H. Walker, "Social and Emotional Problems of the Mentally Retarded Child," *American Journal of Mental Deficiency* 55 (1950–51): 132.

81. Anne Marie Grebler, "Parental Attitudes toward Mentally Retarded Children," *American Journal of Mental Deficiency* 56 (1951–52): 476.

82. Arthur L. Rautman, "Society's First Responsibility to the Mentally Retarded," *American Journal of Mental Deficiency* 54 (1949–50): 157.

83. Ibid.

84. For examples, see James C. Coleman, "Group Therapy with Parents of Mentally Deficient Children," *American Journal of Mental Deficiency* 57 (1952–53): 700–704; Cleo E. Popp, Vivien Ingram, and Paul H. Jordan, "Helping Parents Understand Their Mentally Handicapped Child," *American Journal of Mental Deficiency* 58 (1953–54): 530–534; Sylvia Schild, "Counseling with Parents of Retarded Children Living at Home," *Social Work* 9 (1964): 86–91.

85. All of the religious memoirs I have found from this time period are Christian. Frank was Jewish but not actively religious and deliberately chose to place his son in a Catholic institution because of the spiritual gifts of the nuns. Frank, *My Son's Story*, 92–93.

86. Daie Evans Rogers, *Angel Unaware* (Grand Rapids, MI: Fleming H. Revel, 1953), 7.

87. Ibid., 20.

88. Ibid., 21.

89. B. R. Schmalzried Sr., *Sunshine: A Slow Miracle* (Boston: Daughters of St. Paul, 1965), 79.

90. See also Sophia Gant, *"One of Those": The Progress of a Mongoloid Child* (New York: Pageant Press, 1957); Carvel Lee, *Tender Tyrant: The Story of a Mentally Retarded Child* (Minneapolis: Augsburg, 1961); Stout.

91. Esther Vanamee Griffin, "The Angel," *Catholic World* (April 1951): 35.

92. Ibid., 39.

93. Charlotte D. Tucker, *Betty Lee: Care of Handicapped Children* (New York: Macmillan, 1954), 19.

94. J. Norman Heard, *Hope through Doing* (New York: John Day, 1968), 149.

95. "Brain Surgery Aids Retarded Children," *Science Digest* (February 1951): 50.

96. "Mongoloids and Morality," *America* (September 29, 1956): 608.

97. Ruth Brecher and Edward Brecher, "Saving Children from Mental Retardation," *Saturday Evening Post* (November 21, 1959): 32, 39–40, 109–111.

98. Mrs. SJD to CB, 1 August 1928, File 4-13-3, CF 1925–28, CB.

99. Mrs. CB to Spock, 17 April 1963, File April 17–25, 1963, Box 13, Spock.

100. Mrs. CB to Spock, 17 April 1963, File April 17–25, 1963, Box 13, Spock.

101. Kirk, Karnes, and Kirk, 8.

102. IDL to CB, 27 September 1951, File 4-12-2-1, CF 1949–52, CB.

103. David Melton, *Todd* (Englewood Cliffs, NJ: Prentice-Hall, 1968), 22.

104. Evelyn Hart, *How Retarded Children Can Be Helped* (New York: Public Affairs Committee, 1959), 19.

105. For examples, see Anne C. French, M. Levbarg, and H. Michal-Smith, "Parent Counseling as a Means of Improving the Performance of a Mentally Retarded Boy: A Case Study Presentation," *American Journal of Mental Deficiency* 58 (1953–54): 13–20; Arthur Mandelbaum and Mary Ella Wheeler, "The Meaning of a Defective Child to Parents," *Social Casework* 41 (1960): 360–367; Marguerite M. Stone, "Parental Attitudes to Retardation," *American Journal of Mental Deficiency* 53 (1948): 363–372.

106. Slaughter, 131. For other examples, see "You Are Not Alone: Information Helpful to Parents of Retarded Children" (St. Paul: State of Minnesota, Department of Public Welfare, 1954), 18–19; Martens, 42.

107. Dan Boyd, "The Three Stages in the Growth of a Parent of a Mentally Retarded Child," *American Journal of Mental Deficiency* 55 (1950–51): 610.

108. Kelman, 447.

109. The feminist Barbara Hillyer argues that parents of disabled children are generally expected to make up for their children's lack of productivity "by providing educational and rehabilitative services, medical therapies, and so on in addition to their [the parents'] own normal work loads." Barbara Hillyer, *Feminism and Disability* (Norman: University of Oklahoma Press, 1993), 69, 68–70.

110. Pearl S. Buck, *The Child Who Never Grew*, 2nd ed. (Rockville, MD: Woodbine House, 1992), 26.

111. "Have You Had Polio Shots That Retardates Tested?" *Children Limited* (June 1959): 29.

112. Maria Egg, *When a Child Is Different: A Basic Guide for Parents and Friends of Mentally Retarded Children* (New York: John Day, 1964), 42.

113. Ibid., 135.

6

The Parable of
The Kallikak Family

Explaining the Meaning of Heredity in 1912

Leila Zenderland

Few works dealing with the subject of mental retardation have experienced as dramatic a rise and fall as *The Kallikak Family: A Study in the Heredity of Feeble-Mindedness,* a monograph by the psychologist Henry Herbert Goddard. First published in 1912, this short study chronicled the life of one institutionalized girl, pseudonymously named "Deborah Kallikak," and those of her relatives, both living and dead. To many of his contemporaries, Goddard's simple study seemed to suggest a scientific breakthrough in explaining the role played by heredity in causing the mental condition then called "feeblemindedness"; its publication quickly catapulted Goddard to the forefront of his field. Perhaps even more significant was this book's broad popular appeal. By 1939, *The Kallikak Family* had been printed twelve times in the United States alone and many more times overseas. Goddard's story was also told and retold countless times by others, for the saga of the Kallikaks found its way into scholarly journals and scientific texts, legislative debates and court cases, political speeches and popular magazines.[1]

Yet, if Goddard's reputation experienced a dramatic rise in 1912, largely as the result of this book, in later years it underwent an equally sharp fall. By the 1920s, *The Kallikak Family* had begun to be subjected to a series of scathing attacks that criticized both its methods and its findings. By 1940, the psychologist Knight Dunlap could pronounce this study scientifically dead. The "Kallikak phantasy," Dunlap wrote in *Scientific American,* had been "laughed out of psychology."[2]

In the decades since, Goddard's ideas about heredity have continued to attract attention—not because they merit support, but because they have been so resoundingly rejected. Later generations would find the methodological flaws and social biases that permeate this once-respected study increasingly obvious, and they have continued to expose its questionable data, specious arguments, and unsubstantiated conclusions. In recent decades, the Kallikak study has once again returned to psychology texts, but hardly in the way that Goddard envisioned. Goddard wrote his monograph to warn his contemporaries about the social dangers of "bad blood"; instead, his book has itself become an object lesson of a different sort, for it is now used largely to inform students about the far greater social dangers that emanate from "bad science."[3]

In many ways, the initial acceptance and later repudiation of *The Kallikak Family* in the years between 1912 and 1940 is not difficult to explain, for this book's history largely parallels the broader rise and decline of the American eugenics movement, with which it is closely associated. In explaining just what made both the Kallikak story and the early eugenics movement so convincing to a wide public, historians have usually stressed the political concerns of the day. These include the increasing virulence of American racist thought, as well as the rise in nativist sentiments fueled by massive immigration in the early decades of the twentieth century. Within this context, Goddard's Kallikak study is frequently discussed alongside other popular works promoted by prominent eugenicists, such as Madison Grant's 1916 anti-immigrant diatribe, *The Passing of the Great Race,* or Lothrop Stoddard's 1921 racist pronouncement, *The Rising Tide of Color.*[4]

Such interpretations, however, fail to fully capture the ways that this monograph embodied specific ideas about the causes and consequences of mental retardation in its own era. In fact, when viewed specifically within the context of ideas about "feeblemindedness," Goddard's monograph is particularly revealing, for it captured both scientific and popular beliefs about the larger meaning of heredity in a moment of transition. Despite its deceptively simple framework, *The Kallikak Family* actually contained a complex blend of new and old. Specifically, Goddard was able to graft contemporary biological theories—theories purportedly based on Mendel's newly rediscovered "laws of heredity"—onto an older and still-dominant set of medical beliefs that emphasized the interconnections between medical and moral "pathology." Equally significant, in recounting the history of the Kallikak family, Goddard introduced his new science to the public by presenting it in the form of a parable. To his contemporaries, such a blending proved both compelling and convincing; to today's audiences, it offers an intriguing portrait of a particular historical era, for it suggests the ways that medicine and morality, as well as science and religion, interacted in redefining the meanings of both "heredity" and "feeblemindedness" in 1912.

The fact that Henry Herbert Goddard became so involved in these debates is itself somewhat surprising, particularly considering his background. The son of a devout Quaker missionary from Maine, Goddard began his career as a Quaker schoolmaster. In this position, he became intrigued by the scientific studies of childhood then being promoted by the psychologist G. Stanley Hall. In 1899, Goddard earned his Ph.D. under Hall at Clark University, thus becoming an early practitioner of what was then called the "new psychology"—a research-oriented discipline that was trying to distinguish itself from philosophy. And, while his earliest research suggests no interest in studying either heredity or feeblemindedness, it does evidence a strong concern with exploring the relationship between religion and science, for Goddard's dissertation was entitled "The Effects of Mind on Body as Evidenced by Faith Cures." After graduating, Goddard was hired to teach psychology and pedagogy at the West Chester State Normal School, where he became president of his state's Child Study Association, an organization that encouraged psychologists and schoolteachers to collaborate on common educational problems.[5]

Among those particularly interested in child study, Goddard soon discovered, were teachers of what was already being called "special education," and particularly educators who worked in institutions. For these teachers, Hall's "new psychology" held particular promise, for it suggested new solutions to difficult pedagogical challenges. At a child-study meeting in 1900, Goddard met the educator Edward Johnstone, superintendent of the Training School for Feebleminded Girls and Boys in Vineland, New Jersey. Like Goddard, Johnstone believed that religious efforts at social reform ought to integrated with scientific understanding. "When the heart-broken parent asks why this affliction is placed upon him," Johnstone told parents of the Vineland children, "let him realize that God makes no mistakes, and these children may be the means of uplifting the world." In the years that followed, both Johnstone and Goddard became increasingly interested in promoting scientific work in this field. In 1906, Goddard accepted an offer from Johnstone to open a laboratory devoted to psychological research on the grounds of the Vineland institution.[6]

Goddard's earliest years as a researcher at Vineland show him experimenting in various ways—building new laboratory equipment, trying out new tests on children, and gathering ideas from doctors, teachers, and psychologists. Most promising of all, he reported after returning from a research trip to Europe in 1908, were the new "intelligence tests" developed by the French psychologist Alfred Binet and his assistant, Theodore Simon. By 1910, Goddard had become the first American psychologist to use Binet-Simon testing to diagnose feeblemindedness, first in his own institution and then in special classes in the New Jersey public schools. In the following years, he became an ardent promoter of the use of such testing as a diagnostic tool in classrooms, clinics, and courtrooms.[7]

It was in dealing with the question of causation, however, that Goddard found himself most frustrated. Despite his early optimism and enthusiasm about finding potential cures for the mental conditions that afflicted the children in his institution, nothing offered by his psychological laboratory proved particularly helpful, nor did his new equipment suggest any direction for research into the question of cause.[8]

In many ways, Goddard's frustration in finding answers to such questions mirrored that of the medical community of his day. Throughout most of the nineteenth century, doctors had been trying to find causes for a variety of baffling physical and mental conditions that afflicted children, many from birth. Most explained these conditions with the simple phrase "poor inheritance." Yet, just what doctors meant by this phrase, and what they believed these children had inherited from their parents, their families, or their society was vaguely expressed and loosely understood. Moreover, notwithstanding the biologist August Weismann's controversial proofs in the 1880s that acquired traits could not be inherited, most physicians still believed the contrary, for they found it difficult to accept the idea that environmental factors could not significantly affect pregnant women and their offspring.[9]

Many of these explanations, moreover, still reflected the profound influence upon medical practices of an older set of popular Christian beliefs. Among the most widely held of these was the idea that childhood infirmities were punishments for parental sins. After all, the Bible, many Americans believed, was explicit on this point. The sins of the fathers, it warned, would be visited "upon the children unto the third and fourth generation."[10]

By the mid-nineteenth century, most of Goddard's predecessors studying feeblemindedness had accepted scientific conceptualizations of a universe governed by natural laws and had rejected interpretations of this biblical passage that suggested direct divine intervention into human affairs. Even so, their very understanding of the "lawfulness" of natural phenomena still tended to reconcile newer scientific with older religious explanations. Most believed, for instance, that many human ailments, including those that afflicted children, could be alleviated if both parents and societies adhered to Christian codes of conduct.

Among the most prominent of the nineteenth-century reformers interested in this issue was Samuel Gridley Howe. If a child was born an idiot, Howe explained, this should not be seen as a special Providential dispensation; yet, at the same time, he cautioned, such a birth could not simply be excused as an "accident." Instead, Howe surmised, it was "merely the result of a violation of natural laws." Such medical "chastisements" had been "sent by a loving Father to bring back his children to obedience to his beneficent laws." Clues to these laws were "written upon every man's body," Howe argued, for man now knew that intermarriage among relatives, intemperance, attempts at abortion, and, above all, "self-abuse" could lead to tragic consequences. "Can there be so sad a sight on earth," Howe wondered, "as that of a parent looking upon a son deformed, or halt, or blind, or deaf" and knowing "that he himself is the author of the infirmity?" In obeying or defying God's laws, man made his world a heavenly home or a living hell. "Talk about the dread of a material hell in the far-off future!" Howe exclaimed. "The fear of that can be nothing to the fear of plunging one's own child in the hell of passion here." In all such cases, he added, "the fault lies with the progenitors."[11]

Similar arguments were expressed by many prominent nineteenth-century physicians. Among the most important of these was Edouard Séguin, a French doctor who became the first president of the Association of Medical Officers of American Institutions for Feeble-Minded and Idiotic Persons (the predecessor of the American Association for Mental Retardation). Séguin's ideas promoting new forms of physiological and sensory training would make him world famous as an educator. Yet, in discussing the question of causation, Séguin too linked medical theories with moral admonitions, for he too hoped that research on the "intimate, even secret, even criminal, causes of idiocy" might make young couples "aware of the dangers incurred in their posterity by any breach of the laws of moral health and society." Such an awareness would prove useful, Séguin told his fellow doctors, "particularly in spreading the dread of hereditary punishment set forth in the Bible."[12]

Moreover, according to both doctors and reformers, these connections between immoral causes and medical consequences affected more than young couples, for man was also married to society. "God has joined men together, and they cannot put themselves asunder," Howe warned.[13] In other words, private immorality had public consequences and required public responses. It was the rapidly changing nature of society, however, that was proving increasingly alarming to both reformers and physicians. As early as the 1840s, a wide range of European and American writers had begun to associate what they saw as the deteriorating conditions of urban, industrial life with a decline in private morality and a subsequent rise in defective births. Theories connecting these social, moral, and medical "pathologies" would dominate discussions about the causes of feeblemindedness for the next hundred years.

These theories owed their medical formulation largely to a religious French psychiatrist, Benedict Morel, who saw both physiological ailments and antisocial behavior as evidence of man's gradual "degeneration" from the perfect state of health that had been his "before the fall." In his influential 1857 tract, *Traité des dégénérescences physiques, intellectuelles et morales de l'espèce humaine*, Morel had insisted that a deteriorating environment could lead the species to degenerate—physically, intellectually, and morally. By the century's end, his writings had inspired a wide range of "degeneration" theories that connected feeblemindedness to other forms of medical or moral deviance, including insanity, alcoholism, pauperism, criminality, and promiscuity, and that linked all of these to contemporary social conditions. As one American medical authority on mental deficiency explained, in 1904, "Poverty, hard work, not infrequent intemperance, and many anxieties" might reduce an expectant mother to "quasi-imbecility." Such conditions might then lead to "direct transmission by her to offspring of weakness—mental, moral, or physical," as well as to a "lowering of moral tone," and these were "almost sure to develop idiocy or imbecility in offspring."[14]

By the early twentieth century, however, newer scientific theories had begun to challenge these medical views by drawing a sharper distinction between the meanings of "heredity" and "environment." Among those who hoped to separate hereditary from environmental influences, for instance, was the British scientist Francis Galton. For decades, Galton had been experimenting with new ways to measure the inheritance of specific traits; in 1883, Galton coined a new word, "eugenics," to refer to scientific efforts aimed at improving human breeding.[15] Even more crucial was the rediscovery of Gregor Mendel's experiments around 1900, for Mendel's work suggested a new set of natural "laws" that seemed to explain hereditary causation. In describing this new science to the public, scientists often tried to distinguish the newer biological meaning of inheritance from other meanings of this term. Man "stores knowledge as a bee stores honey or a squirrel stores nuts," the British biologist R. C. Punnett explained in *Mendelism,* a book written for popular audiences and published in 1909. Yet such hoarding had "nothing more to do with heredity in the biological sense," he added, "than has the handing on from parent to offspring of a picture or a title or a pair of boots."[16]

Among the earliest and most ardent of American Mendelians was the biologist Charles Davenport. Mendel's "laws of hereditary transmission," Davenport argued, applied not only to chickens and other animals he had been studying but also to man. The best way to study human heredity, he proposed, was to collect family "pedigrees" that would demonstrate the transmission of specific traits from one generation to the next. Seeking information on the transmission of damaging biological traits, Davenport wrote to persons who he believed might have access to such data. "Dear Sir," he wrote in a letter to the Vineland institution, in 1909, "Have you at your Institution heredity data concerning feeble mindedness?"[17]

Goddard's initial reply to Davenport's letter showed the meager state of his own research on heredity at the time. The data on heredity, he explained, were "so unreliable" that they were hardly worth tabulating.[18] This unreliability resulted largely from parents' genuine ignorance about the causes of their children's ailments; it was compounded, however, by a reluctance to divulge anything that might suggest what many parents and doctors often suspected was the real cause—secret sin. In fact, these problems had been hampering medical research for years. Getting family histories, Edward Johnstone had complained, was "often almost impossible." In one study, for instance, parents had attributed their children's mental handicaps not only to common diseases but also to snakebite, lightning, homesickness, and frozen feet, among other causes. On their children's applications to Vineland, many had listed other bizarre experiences. "Mother shocked by sight of woman with hare-lip," one parent reported as the cause of a child's condition. The "child swallowed a button," stated another. "Frightened by dull nippers of barber at first hair cut," another parent reported. Such results had led at least one doctor to distinguish "cause" from "*ascribed* cause" when dealing with patient records.[19]

Yet Goddard had in mind a means of circumventing some of these problems. The key, he told Davenport, was to contact "parties who know the family in question and are not too intimate to tell the truth about them."[20] Thus,
Goddard too apparently suspected that the real causes of mental deficiency
were being suppressed by families. The best way to discover them, Goddard
and Davenport agreed, was to hire a field worker who would independently
track down family histories.

Such a strategy fit well with Davenport's own plans for promoting large-
scale eugenic research in America. By 1910, using funds contributed by
wealthy benefactors, Davenport had opened a "Eugenics Record Office" at
Cold Spring Harbor, New York, to coordinate the collection of human "pedigrees." By 1911, he had instituted a summer program to train "field workers"
to gather this material. According to his plan, field workers would spend a
summer studying Mendelian science at Cold Spring Harbor; they would
then spend several weeks at institutions such as Vineland gaining experience
in recognizing human maladies. This combined training, both Davenport
and Goddard believed, would produce human "naturalists" capable of diagnosing and classifying traits like feeblemindedness when they encountered
them "in the field."[21]

In many ways, the field workers produced by this training program
greatly resembled their contemporary cousin, the social worker, whose professional role was also being defined in the same decade. Both positions involved information gathering through "friendly visiting"; both also depended upon "confidential relations" between worker and client. Perhaps
because of these qualifications, as well as their low pay, both jobs fell largely
to idealistic middle-class women.[22] Yet, despite these similarities, these two
groups of women had very different objectives, Davenport emphasized. Social workers were trained to gather information to help alleviate environmental hardships; by contrast, field workers, according to Davenport's plan,
would try to "unravel of the laws of inheritance." They could do this by
tracking down and recording all the information they could gather on "col-
laterals, descendants and consorts of all individuals the make-up of whose
germ plasm it is desired to understand."[23]

Among the field workers hired by the Vineland institution for this task
was Elizabeth Kite. Like Goddard and Johnstone, Kite approached her task
with a mixture of scientific and religious enthusiasm. A former school-
teacher, with a strong interest in social reform, Kite too had been raised by
Quaker missionaries. However, in 1906, she had experienced a religious con-

version; thereafter, she became an active member of the International Catholic Truth Society. And, notwithstanding her new training in Mendelian science, Kite's own views were apparent in the title she gave to an article describing her new work: "Unto the Third Generation."[24]

As a field worker, Kite spent several years tracking down the relatives of children in the Vineland school. In one case, she was able to supply Goddard with evidence tracing back six generations in the family of a young woman pseudonymously named "Deborah." Kite's data on this family, gathered from stories told by relatives, local historical documents, and her own observations and recorded in her own dramatic writing style, offered crucial evidence for Goddard's first book, *The Kallikak Family: A Study in the Heredity of Feeble-Mindedness.*[25]

Published in 1912, Goddard's book blended institutional observations provided by Deborah's teachers and doctors, psychological data gathered in his laboratory, discussions of Mendel's laws as explained by biologists, and evidence gathered by Kite "in the field." The history of this family, Goddard believed, offered a telling illustration of both the causes and consequences of feeblemindedness and of the larger meaning of heredity, both for the individual and for society.

Since this text was written for "lay readers" as well as for scientists, it opened in storybook form. "One bright October day, fourteen years ago," Goddard recounted, "there came to the Training School at Vineland, a little eight-year-old girl." He then told his readers how this child had been born in an almshouse to an unwed mother and how, because she "did not get along well at school and might possibly be feeble-minded," she had been sent to the Vineland Training School.[26]

Goddard then summarized this child's records. "Deborah" had arrived at this institution in 1897, nearly a decade before Goddard's psychological laboratory opened. On her application, institutional personnel had recorded a range of traits they found relevant to their diagnosis:

Average size and weight. No peculiarity in form or size of head. Staring expression. Jerking movement in walking. No bodily deformity. Understands commands. Not very obedient. Knows a few letters. Cannot read nor count. . . . Power of memory poor. . . . Can use a needle. Can carry wood and fill a kettle. Can throw a ball, but cannot catch. Excitable but not nervous. . . . Not affectionate and quite noisy. . . . Obstinate and destructive. Does not mind slapping and scolding. Deborah's mother somewhat deficient.

Grandfather periodical drunkard and mentally deficient. Been to school. No results.[27]

In the years that followed, Goddard reported, Deborah's Vineland teachers had traced her progress. Her temperament, "impudent and growing worse" by 1899, improved sporadically. By 1912, this twenty-three-year-old excelled in needlework, wood carving, basketry, gardening, and music and was helpful in handling children. Academically, however, she remained a poor reader, counted on her fingers, and had difficulty mastering abstractions. "She can put the right number of plates at the head of the table, if she knows the people who are to sit there," Goddard explained, "but at a table with precisely the same number of strangers, she fails in making the correct count."[28]

Goddard had tested Deborah on the Binet-Simon intelligence scale in 1910, when she was twenty-one years old. He found her to have "the mentality of a nine-year-old child with two points over," for she failed tests that involved repeating digits, counting coins, making rhymes, rearranging words in sentences, and defining abstract terms. And, despite the best efforts of her teachers, Goddard reported, Deborah had made little academic progress. Even more serious for society than her mentality, he added, was her sexuality, for, notwithstanding her weak mind, Deborah had grown into an attractive young woman. "To-day if this young woman were to leave the Institution," Goddard asserted, "she would at once become a prey to the designs of evil men or evil women and would lead a life that would be vicious, immoral, and criminal, though because of her mentality she herself would not be responsible. There is nothing that she might not be led into . . . ," he warned.[29] Thus, in discussing feeblemindedness, Goddard still closely linked this medical condition with its moral consequences, both for Deborah and for society.

Goddard then posed what he called "the ever insistent question": "How do we account for this kind of individual?" he asked. The answer, he told his readers, was now clear: "'Heredity'—bad stock." The human family, Goddard explained, contained stocks that "breed as true as anything in plant or animal life." And, whereas in the past such a statement would have been "a guess, an hypothesis," Goddard believed he had found "what seems to us conclusive evidence of its truth."[30]

This new evidence, he declared, had come from reports gathered by field workers. By diligently tracking down Deborah's relatives, Goddard reported,

Elizabeth Kite had made a deeply disturbing discovery. "The surprise and horror of it all," he recounted, "was that no matter where we traced them . . . an appalling amount of defectiveness was everywhere found." This defectiveness was evidenced not only by diminished mental capacity but also by social incapacity, for Deborah's relatives included numerous paupers, prostitutes, and petty criminals.[31]

Yet this story also contained a mystery, Kite had reported, for she had occasionally found herself amidst "a good family of the same name." Both of these families, she found, traced their ancestors back to eighteenth-century forebears named Martin Kallikak. The link between these two very different families was discovered, Goddard announced dramatically, when a relative "revealed in a burst of confidence the situation." She told Kite that "Martin had a half-brother" because, "'you see, his mother had him before she was married.'"[32]

Once this crucial bit of information had been revealed, Kite was able to solve the mystery of the good and bad branches of the Kallikak family. The situation could be traced, she reported, to Martin Kallikak Jr.'s illegitimate parentage. As Kite explained it, Martin Sr. was only fifteen when his own father died, "leaving him without parental care or oversight." After joining a Revolutionary War militia, this boy visited a tavern and met "a feeble-minded girl by whom he became the father of a feeble-minded son." Named Martin Kallikak Jr. by his mother, and abandoned by his father, this illegitimate child "handed down to posterity the father's name and the mother's mental capacity."[33]

The descendants generated by this secret sin, Goddard now reported, had left society with a long and dark legacy of medical and moral failure. Among 480 relatives, Goddard counted 36 illegitimate births, 33 sexually immoral persons, 24 alcoholics, 3 epileptics, 82 infant deaths, 3 criminals, and 8 keepers of houses of ill fame. These statistics were most striking when compared to those for the legitimate side of the same family, started a few years later when Martin "straightened up and married a respectable girl of good family." Whereas the illegitimate side had produced "paupers, criminals, prostitutes, drunkards, and examples of all forms of social pest with which modern society is burdened," the legitimate side had produced children with "a marked tendency toward professional careers." They had "married into the best families in their state, the descendants of colonial governors, signers of the Declaration of Independence, soldiers and even the founders of a great university." In short, this side of the Kallikak family had produced "nothing but good representative citizenship." (The "normal chart" for this side of the family was prepared by one of these descendents, who supplied Kite with a family genealogy. Apparently, Kite saw no problem in relying upon such a source to classify all 496 persons descended from this union as "normal people.")[34]

Kite's discovery of two such distinct family branches was particularly serendipitous, Goddard believed, for to him it suggested a natural control group. For Goddard, the good side of the family became "our norm, our standard, our demonstration of what the Kallikak blood is when kept pure, or mingled with blood as good as its own." It could be compared with "the blood of the same ancestor contaminated by that of the nameless feeble-minded girl." Goddard devised the family's pseudonym to account for this unusual situation, for he invented the name "Kallikak" by combining a Greek root meaning beauty (*Kallos*) with one meaning bad (*Kakos*).[35]

Goddard's next task was to use the facts he had gathered from his field worker to confirm Mendel's laws. In a chapter simply called "The Charts," he illustrated the presence or absence of the "trait" of feeblemindedness on two dozen heredity charts filled with black and white symbols—circles for females and squares for males, colored white for normal or black for feeble-minded. Such symbols allowed Goddard to dichotomize normal from feeble, fit from unfit, competent from incompetent, moral from degenerate. In years to come, such family charts would become a staple of the eugenics movement, for they offered the public a stark new sociobiology, vividly illustrated in black and white.[36]

Yet, charts alone, Goddard understood, would never appeal to the "lay reader," for facts and figures did not suggest "flesh and blood reality." To supplement such data, Goddard's text also included graphic accounts "written up by our field worker." "On one of the coldest days in winter," one such account began, "the field worker visited the street in a city slum." A "girl of twelve should have been at school," she reported, "but when one saw her face, one realized it made no difference. She was pretty," Kite reported, "but there was no mind there."[37]

Further visits disclosed many instances of "human degeneracy." Moreover, in case after case, Kite reported, serious medical ailments were clearly linked to shocking moral failures. One Kallikak relative had run off with gypsies. A father nicknamed "Old Horror" had lived with his daughters in a dwelling where "great scandals" had taken place. Another relative had had an illegitimate son by a man "high in the Nation's offices."[38]

By contrast, Kite also illustrated the "respectability and usefulness" found on the good side of this family. Such stories, she admitted, could never match "the bizarre experiences of the abnormal," but in her duties as a "naturalist" she recorded them as well. In fact, in Kite's telling, even the family furniture documented the benevolent influence of past generations, for their ancestral farm still contained "the same fireplace, the same high-backed chairs, the clock, desk, and china cupboard." Literally as well as figuratively, these descendents continued to enjoy the fruits of the family tree, for they returned each summer to consume "the luscious grapes and other fruit planted by their ancestor." These images contrasted starkly with tales told about the daily lives of Deborah's unfortunate cousins, who were photographed for Goddard's book in their ragged clothes in front of their ramshackle dwellings.[39]

Such stories, elaborated largely through anecdote, dialogue, and metaphor, offered the public a dramatic illustration of the differences between good and bad heredity. By linking the data recorded on Mendelian charts with incidents from actual lives, this book explained the new biological meaning of heredity in ways that contemporaries considered both logical and vivid. At the same time, it also suggested the broader meanings of this term by reminding parents of all that they might bequeath to a child—not only biologically, but also morally and materially.

Moreover, by closely linking moral and mental deficiencies, Kite's data and Goddard's interpretations suggested new biological explanations for a broad range of social problems that afflicted American society in the early twentieth century. Their conclusions proved particularly appealing to reformers frustrated by their inability to convince delinquents, paupers, or prostitutes to change their ways. "Why do we not *do* something about it?" Goddard's book asked. "What *can* we do?"[40] In posing such questions, Goddard's Kallikak study widened the social chasm that separated a hypothetical "them"—largely poor and problem-ridden families filled with "social pests" of all sorts—from an unspecified "us"—respectable citizens such as Goddard and his assumedly middle-class readers.

Yet, if the class biases that infuse this monograph are readily apparent, equally suggestive, especially in light of later historical attempts to explain its popularity, is what is left out. Despite its warnings about the dire social consequences emanating from low Binet scores and bad blood lines, Goddard's text was surprisingly free from both the racist and the nativist appeals that pervaded the writings of many of his eugenics contemporaries. This book mentioned no threats from racial miscegenation. It said not a word about white supremacy or Anglo-Saxon racial superiority. To the contrary, Goddard's most threatening biological and social troublemakers, the Kallikaks, were themselves white, Anglo-Saxon Protestants. Moreover, this family could hardly be considered immigrants, for according to the records that Goddard's field worker presented in great detail, Deborah Kallikak's ancestors had been living in America since at least the time of the Revolution.

Instead of the new social fears that alarmed his contemporary eugenicists, Goddard was still worried about the old ones: promiscuity, adultery, incest, crime, alcoholism, and idleness—in short, the perennial concerns of Christian middle-class moralists. Much of this book's broad appeal can be explained less by its promotion of eugenics (a word never actually used in this text) than by its fusion of a newer "Mendelism" onto an older and still highly potent Christian moralism. One can still discern, in Goddard's arguments linking Binet's tests with Mendel's laws, an older, subtle synthesis that implicitly linked children's ailments with their parent's secret sins. *The Kallikak Family* grafted the newer scientific concept of cause and effect onto an older and still potent biblical understanding of causes and their consequences. In fact, nowhere was Goddard's own missionary heritage more evident than in the way he explained the meaning of the Kallikak story to the public.

"We have here," Goddard wrote, "a family of good English blood of the middle class" that for four generations had maintained "a reputation for honor and respectability." Yet, when a "scion of this family, in an unguarded moment," stepped from "the paths of rectitude," he started a line of mental defectives. Martin Sr.'s career offered "a powerful sermon against sowing wild oats." He had done "what unfortunately many a young man like him has done before and since, and which still more unfortunately, society has too often winked at, as being merely a side step in accordance with a natural instinct, bearing no serious results." Martin may have believed his act "atoned for, as he never suffered from it any serious consequences." Even his contemporaries failed to appreciate the "evil that had been done." Its consequence, however, was "the real sin of peopling the world with a race of defective degenerates who would probably commit his sin a thousand times over."[41]

It had taken six generations to understand "the havoc that was wrought by that one thoughtless act," Goddard argued in his own homiletic voice. "Now that the facts are known," he intoned, "let the lesson be learned; let the sermons be preached; let it be impressed upon our young men of good family that they dare not step aside for even a moment. Let all possible use be made of these facts," he proclaimed, "and something will be accomplished." In trying to prove Mendelian laws, Goddard also produced a scientific sermon against promiscuity.[42]

The new biology, however, of course marked Goddard's sermon as different from those of his predecessors. Even had Martin Sr. stayed "in the paths of virtue," Goddard acknowledged, there still remained "the nameless feeble-minded girl." For her the question of virtue was irrelevant, for the feeble-minded, Goddard believed, were largely incapable of self-control. Society, Goddard now argued, would have to exercise both social and sexual control in other ways. Thus, he ended his monograph by introducing the public to the solutions then being discussed both by both medical superintendents and by eugenic enthusiasts: sexual sterilization (towards which Goddard remained skeptical) or lifelong institutional segregation (which he strongly advocated).[43]

To Davenport and his followers, the publication of *The Kallikak Family* was clearly welcome, for this book quickly became the most popular study associated with the American eugenics movement. In later decades, it would also prove useful to others promoting their own ideas about separating "good" from "bad" blood. In the 1920s, data concerning the Kallikak family were introduced as evidence in the case that reached the Supreme Court as *Buck v. Bell*—the case that, in 1927, legalized involuntary sterilization. In 1934, this book was republished in Nazi Germany at the time that the government was promoting the Nuremberg decrees. As late as 1961, the Kallikak story appeared in a textbook by the prominent psychologist Henry Garrett, a native Virginian who hoped to keep black and white blood separate and who believed that school integration was bound to "breed down" the white race.[44]

These later uses, however, had little to do with Goddard's own messages of 1912. Moreover, to those who read it at that time, these messages were clear, for contemporary reviewers immediately recognized and repeatedly commented upon this book's effective blending of science and sin. *The Kallikak Family*, a reviewer for *The Dial* concluded, was "a scientific study in human heredity, a convincing sociological essay, a contribution to the psychological bases of social structure, a tragedy of incompetence, and a sermon with a shocking example as a text." *The Independent* published a similar response. *The Kallikak Family*, its reviewer asserted, was "the most convincing of the sociological studies brought out by the eugenics movement." At the same time, one could hardly find "a more impressive lesson of the far-reaching and never-ending injury done to society by a single sin."[45]

Doctors of the day also found Goddard's analysis convincing, for it confirmed many of their own longstanding beliefs about the connections between medical and moral deviance. This study, reported a reviewer for the *Journal of Psycho-Asthenics,* the leading medical publication on mental deficiency, offered "one of the most enlightening and instructive contributions to heredity that has ever been made." The *Medical Record* also praised "this carefully worked out analysis and painstaking study of a concrete example of the workings of the laws of heredity as related to feeble-minded" and recommended it to "both the medical and the lay reader," for it was "as interesting as a romance" while also conveying "a moral and a great lesson."[46]

Goddard's most important audience, of course, was the "lay reader." Here his book evoked a strong response, for contained within it were many of the elements of a melodrama—colorful characters, tragic figures, a mystery, and a moral lesson. In February 1913, the popular poet Edwin Markham prepared an excerpted version of this story for a "Book of the Month" selection in *Hearst's Magazine.* "And a strange story it is," Markham exclaimed, "with every element of pity and terror, as we see ignorance and degeneracy stalking among men, leaving destruction and death in their wake." Goddard had recounted the "ghastly record of the descendants of Martin Kallikak, the reckless soldier, and the nameless, witless girl that followed the camp." And, while "poor Deborah's relations were smitten" with feeblemindedness, Martin "doubtless forgot the girl and her child but society for generations has been paying for the evil he set in motion."[47]

An even more unusual indicator of his book's popular appeal, and of its melodramatic potential, was an offer Goddard received from a prominent Broadway agent interested in securing the rights to his story for Joseph Medill Paterson, who hoped to adapt it for the stage. Patterson, a wealthy descendent of a famous publishing family, was then coeditor of the *Chicago Tribune;* years later, he would gain fame as the editor of the New York *Daily News* and the innovator of American tabloid journalism. And, while Patterson's Kallikak play was apparently never written, Goddard's response to his offer is still suggestive: he would be interested, Goddard replied, only if "assured that the play would carry the moral lessons which the book is intended to convey."[48]

Goddard did not specify which "moral lessons" he wanted to see dramatized. His short monograph, however, was filled with new lessons—lessons about the causes and consequences of feeblemindedness, about Binet's tests and Mendel's laws, about biological infirmities and social irresponsibility, about segregation and sterilization, about bad blood and bad behavior. Perhaps the book's most powerful lesson, however, was still its oldest. The deepest message of the Kallikak story was best illustrated not by tests or charts, or even by episodes of bizarre behavior. Instead, it was epitomized in another tale embedded in this text: the history of the Kallikak family Bible. Purchased in 1704, this Bible had been handed down from one generation to the next within the good side of the family. By 1912, it was in the possession of a minister and was "still in an excellent state of preservation." On its flyleaf, a father had inscribed a verse for his son: "So oft as in it he doth looke," he had "aye been guided by ye precepts in this booke." In words that still conveyed their own clear message to Goddard's contemporaries, this father had then enjoined his descendents to "walk in the same safe way."[49]

By combining such age-old messages with new Mendelian laws, Goddard's 1912 Kallikak study helped to introduce the public to both the new social meaning of feeblemindedness and the new scientific meaning of heredity. He had done so largely by telling a story that blurred together the many meanings of a "goodly inheritance"—biblical, medical, popular, and, now, biological. In recounting what had happened to the two branches of the Kallikak family, Goddard's narrative reaffirmed traditional beliefs about the interconnections between medicine and morality. At the same time, he mitigated the differences between older religious beliefs and newer scientific theories by producing what might be called a sermon of new science. Perhaps most important in explaining this book's immediate impact is the way that Goddard chose to present his version of science to the public. In using the saga of the good and the bad Kallikaks to explain the new meaning of Mendelian science, Goddard had in fact adapted one of the oldest and most effective of Christian strategies: teaching the people through parables.

NOTES

1. Henry Herbert Goddard, *The Kallikak Family: A Study in the Heredity of Feeble-Mindedness* (New York: Macmillan, 1912). On the production and reception of this book, see Leila Zenderland, *Measuring Minds: Henry Herbert Goddard and the Origins of American Intelligence Testing* (New York: Cambridge University Press, 1998), pp. 143–185, 321–333; and J. David Smith, *Minds Made Feeble: The Myth and Legacy of the Kallikaks* (Rockville, Md.: Aspen Systems Corporation, 1983).

2. Knight Dunlap, "Antidotes for Superstitions Concerning Human Heredity," *Scientific Monthly,* 51, no. 3 (September 1940): pp. 221–225.

3. See, for example, the discussion of Goddard's work in David Hothersall, *History of Psychology* (New York: Random House, 1984), or in Seymour Sarason and John Doris, *Psychological Problems in Mental Deficiency* (New York: Harper and Row, 1969).

4. For analyses of the broader rise and decline of the American eugenics movement, see Mark Haller, *Eugenics: Hereditarian Attitudes in American Thought* (New Brunswick: Rutgers University Press, 1963); Daniel Kevles, *In the Name of Eugenics: Genetics and the Uses of Human Heredity* (New York: Knopf, 1985); and Diane Paul, *Controlling Human Heredity: 1865 to the Present* (Atlantic Highlands, N.J.: Humanities Press, 1995).

5. Goddard, "The Effects of Mind on Body as Evidenced in Faith Cures," *American Journal of Psychology,* 10 (1899): pp. 431–502. On Goddard's early life, see Zenderland, *Measuring Minds.* On Hall, see Dorothy Ross, *G. Stanley Ross: The Psychologist as Prophet* (Chicago: University of Chicago Press, 1971).

6. E. R. Johnstone, "Report of the Superintendent," *Eighteenth Annual Report of the Vineland Training School,* 1906, p. 26. In 1902, the National Education Association's Department of Education for the Deaf and Dumb, the Blind, and the Feeble-Minded was renamed the Department of Special Education. On the relationship between psychology, child study, and special education, see Zenderland, *Measuring Minds,* pp. 44–70, 105–142.

7. Leila Zenderland, "The Debate over Diagnosis: Henry Herbert Goddard and the Medical Acceptance of Intelligence Testing," in Michael Sokal, ed., *Psychological Testing and American Society, 1890–1930* (New Brunswick: Rutgers University Press, 1987), pp. 46–74.

8. On Goddard's initial optimism about finding potential cures, see Zenderland, *Measuring Minds,* pp. 84–92.

9. On the persistence of such ideas, see Charles Rosenberg's chpater, "The Bitter Fruit: Heredity, Disease, and Social Thought," in his volume *No Other Gods: On Science and American Social Thought* (Baltimore: Johns Hopkins University Press, 1976).

10. This biblical phrase is found in Exodus 20:5 and Deuteronomy 5:9.

11. Samuel Gridley Howe, "On the Causes of Idiocy," in Marvin Rosen, Gerald R. Clark, and Marvin Kivitz, *The History of Mental Retardation: Collected Papers,* vol. 1 (Baltimore: University Park Press, 1976), pp. 31–60.

12. Edward Seguin, *New Facts and Remarks Concerning Idiocy.* Lecture before the New York Medical Journal Association, October 1869 (New York: Wood, 1870), p. 39. Seguin is best known as the author of *Idiocy and Its Treatment by the Physiological Method* (New York: Wood, 1866).

13. Howe, "On the Causes of Idiocy," p. 33.

14. On degeneration theories, see Daniel Pick, *Faces of Degeneration: A European Disorder, c. 1848–1918* (Cambridge: Cambridge University Press, 1989); Sander Gilman,

Degeneration: The Dark Side of Progress (New York: Columbia University Press, 1985); and Steven Gelb, "Degeneracy Theory, Eugenics and Family Studies," *Journal of the History of the Behavioral Sciences,* 26 (1990): 242-246. See also Martin Barr, *Mental Defectives: Their History, Treatment, and Training* (Philadelphia: Blakiston, 1904), pp. 95-97, 108.

15. Galton coined the word "eugenics" from a Greek root meaning "good in birth." On Galton's ideas about the meaning of inheritance, see Ruth Schwartz Cowan, *Sir Francis Galton and the Study of Heredity in the Nineteenth Century* (New York: Garland, 1985). On Galton's eugenics, see Haller, *Eugenics,* pp. 8-14; Kevles, *Name of Eugenics,* pp. 3-19; and Paul, *Controlling Heredity,* pp. 30-36.

16. R. C. Punnett, "Mendelism [*sic*] Inheritance in Man," *Vineland Training School Bulletin* 8 (September 1911): 78-80; this is an excerpt from Punnett, *Mendelism,* 3rd ed. (New York: Macmillan, 1911). The first American edition of Punnett's book was published in 1909.

17. Charles Benedict Davenport, "Fit and Unfit Matings," *Vineland Training School Bulletin* 7 (October 1910): 258-262. On Davenport's career, see E. Carleton MacDowell, "Charles Benedict Davenport, 1866-1944," *Bios* 17 (1946): 3-50; Charles Rosenberg, "Charles Benedict Davenport and the Irony of American Eugenics," in his book *No Other Gods,* pp. 89-97; and Kevles, *Name of Eugenics,* pp. 41-56. Charles Benedict Davenport to Edward Johnston [*sic*], March 9, 1909, Charles Benedict Davenport Papers, American Philosophical Society. Johnstone gave this letter to Goddard, who answered it.

18. Henry Herbert Goddard to Charles Benedict Davenport, March 15, 1908, Charles Benedict Davenport Papers.

19. E. R. Johnstone, "Some Reasons for Mental Deficiency," *Vineland Training School Bulletin,* Supplement, No. 1-46 (December 1907): 14. This list of "causes" as reported by parents was gathered for the census; see Frederick Howard Wines, "Report on the Defective, Dependent, and Delinquent Classes of the Population of the United States, as returned at the Tenth Census (June 1, 1880)," *House Miscellaneous Documents,* 47th Cong., 2d sess., 1882-1883, vol. 13, 240-241. On unusual causes cited by parents of Vineland children, see Henry Herbert Goddard, *Feeble-Mindedness: Its Causes and Consequences* (New York: Macmillan, 1914), pp. 55, 266, 436-437. A. C. Rogers, "On the *Ascribed* Causes of Idiocy, as Illustrated in Reports to the Iowa Institution for Feeble Minded Children," *Proceedings of the Association of Medical Officers of American Institutions for Idiotic and Feeble-Minded Persons* (1884): 296-301.

20. Goddard to Davenport, March 15, 1908, Charles Benedict Davenport Papers.

21. On field work, see Charles Benedict Davenport, Harry Laughlin, David Weeks, E. R. Johnstone, and Henry Herbert Goddard, *The Study of Human Heredity,* Eugenics Record Office (Cold Spring Harbor, N.Y.), Bulletin No. 2, 1911. See also Garland Allen, "The Eugenics Record Office, Cold Spring Harbor, 1910-1940," *Osiris,* 2nd Ser. 2 (1986): 225-264.

22. On the development of social work, see Roy Lubove, *The Professional Altruist: The Emergence of Social Work as a Career, 1880–1930* (New York: Atheneum, 1973); and Regina Kunzel, *Fallen Women, Problem Girls: Unmarried Mothers and the Professionalization of Social Work, 1890–1945* (New Haven: Yale University Press, 1993).

23. Davenport et al., *Study of Human Heredity*, p. 9.

24. On Elizabeth Kite's background, see Zenderland, *Measuring Minds*, pp. 159–161. Kite, "Method and Aim of Field Work at the Vineland Training School," *Vineland Training School Bulletin* 9 (1912): 81–87. Kite, "Unto the Third Generation," *Survey* (September 28, 1912): 789–791.

25. One of Kite's field reports, for example, is reprinted in Goddard, *Kallikak Family*, pp. 71–73.

26. Goddard, *Kallikak Family*, pp. 1–2.

27. Ibid., p. 2.

28. Ibid., pp. 2–12.

29. Ibid., pp. 10–12.

30. Ibid., p. 12.

31. Ibid., p. 16.

32. Ibid., pp. 16–17.

33. Ibid., p. 18.

34. Ibid., pp. 18–30.

35. Ibid., pp. 68–69.

36. Ibid., pp. 31–49.

37. Ibid., pp. 70–73.

38. Ibid., pp. 74–93.

39. Ibid., pp. 93–100. The photographs of the "bad" branch of the Kallikak family included in this book have generated a controversy of their own. In *The Mismeasure of Man* (New York: Norton, 1981), pp. 171–174, Stephen Jay Gould claims that Goddard, in an act of "conscious skullduggery," doctored these photographs to make his subjects look more menacing. This charge was later challenged, however, in several articles. For evidence that contradicts Gould's argument, see Raymond Fancher, "Henry Goddard and the Kallikak Family Photographs: 'Conscious Skulduggery' or 'Whig History'?" *American Psychologist* 42 (June 1987): 585–590; Michael Kral, "More on Goddard and the Kallikak Family Photographs," *American Psychologist* 43 (September 1988): 745–746; Sigrid S. Glenn and Janet Ellis, "Do the Kallikaks Look 'Menacing' or 'Retarded'?" *American Psychologist* 43 (September 1988): 742–743; and Leila Zenderland, "On Interpreting Photographs, Faces, and the Past," *American Psychologist* 43 (September 1988): 743–744.

40. Ibid., p. 101.

41. Ibid., pp 102–103.

42. Ibid., p. 103.

43. Ibid., pp. 103–109.

44. For later uses of *The Kallikak Family,* including testimony introduced into the case of *Buck v. Bell,* see Smith, *Minds Made Feeble,* pp. 135–172. The first German edition of *Die Familie Kallikak* was published in 1914, and the second in November 1933; it was also reprinted in Karl Wilker, trans., "Die Familie Kallikak," *Friedrich Mann's Pedagogisches Magazin* no. 1393 (1934). Henry Garrett and Hubert Bonner, *General Psychology,* 2nd rev. ed. (New York: American Book Company, 1961). Garrett's pamphlet, *Breeding Down,* is reprinted in Clarence Karier, ed., *Shaping the American Educational State: 1900 to the Present* (New York: Free Press), 1975), pp. 419–428.

45. These reviews are in *Dial* (October 1, 1912): 247 and *Independent* 73 (1912): 794.

46. A. C. Rogers, "Reviews and Notices: *The Kallikak Family. A Study in the Heredity of Feeble-Mindedness,*" *Journal of Psycho-Asthenics* 17 (December 1912): 83–84. Review of *The Kallikak Family, Medical Record* 83 (January 8, 1913): 126.

47. Edward Markham, "Book of the Month: The Kallikak Family," *Hearst's Magazine* 23 (February 1913): 329–331.

48. Alice Kauser [agent for Joseph Medill Patterson] to Henry Herbert Goddard, March 1, 1913; Goddard to Kauser, March 7, 1913, and March 11, 1913; Kauser to Goddard, March 12, 1913; Bleecker Van Wagenen to Goddard, March 26, 1913, and April 2, 1913; File 615, Henry Herbert Goddard Papers, Archives of the History of American Psychology, Akron, Ohio.

49. Goddard, *Kallikak Family,* p. 100.

7

Fictional Voices and Viewpoints for the Mentally Deficient, 1929–1939

Gerald Schmidt

American novelists writing on mental deficiency in the early twentieth century were faced with an artistic dilemma. The literary tradition of the holy fool, formerly the predominant model, could by no stretch of the imagination be reconciled with the "menace of the feeble-minded."[1] It was no longer possible to model fictional "mental defectives" on earlier "idiot" figures.[2] Instead, Steinbeck and Faulkner redefined the theme of mental deficiency within the framework of American fiction.

Naturalism as adopted by Norris and London provided a convenient point of departure.[3] The naturalistic emphasis on heredity and determinism corresponded to the interests of the American Association for the Study of the Feeble-Minded, soon to become the American Association on Mental Deficiency. It also allowed for the radical shift from Dickens's morally gifted fools to the amoral defectives found in twentieth-century American writing. This approach, however, presented the novelist with one important problem. In striking contrast to literary fools, degenerates in the naturalistic vein were lacking in emotional depth and, as such, unlikely to win the reader's sympathy. My contention is that Steinbeck and Faulkner sought to recapture the lost simplicity and sincerity of the holy fool in the voices and viewpoints of their mentally deficient characters.

The search for a purified idiom, an Edenic language devoid of undesired associations, had informed the development of American literature from the very beginning.[4] Within this tradition, the mentally deficient observer afforded an ingenious alternative to the popular child narrator. Intellectual disability was once more coupled with heightened powers of perception. An epistemological privilege replaced the ethical insight of the holy fool.

Innocent Offenders

The following section examines Steinbeck's use of mentally deficient viewpoints in relation to notions of "the imbecile with criminal instincts."[5] As I hope to show, the naive and childlike perspective of Tularecito and of Lennie Small is at odds with the implicit assumption that they pose a threat to their respective communities. It is this conflict that lends tragic stature to these characters.

Tularecito's story, which begins with his being discovered under mysterious circumstances and ends with his being committed to an "asylum for the criminal insane," is told in the fourth chapter of *The Pastures of Heaven* (1932).[6] Steinbeck offers an unambiguously naturalistic portrait of Tularecito:

> The baby had short, chubby arms, and long, loose-jointed legs. Its large head sat without interval of neck between deformedly broad shoulders. The baby's flat face, together with its peculiar body, caused it automatically to be named Tularecito, Little Frog. (36)

The name aptly conveys Tularecito's dual personality. It gives an impression of his animal physique, but it also strikes an imaginative note: the English translation, "Little Frog," fails to do justice to the original with its rich array of all five vowels. Throughout the chapter, Steinbeck modulates between two genres, the naturalistic short story and the fairy tale. Tularecito's "trogloditic [*sic*]" features are thus set off against an innate gift for "[carving] remarkably correct animals from sandstone" (36).

Although Tularecito's mental development stops before he reaches his sixth year, he is soon capable of doing "the work of a grown man":

> The long fingers of his hands were more dexterous and stronger than most men's fingers. On the ranch, they made use of the fingers of Tularecito. . . . He had planting hands, tender fingers that never injured a young plant nor bruised the surfaces of a grafting limb. His merciless fingers could wring the head from a turkey gobbler without effort. (36)

Steinbeck carefully balances admiration and precaution: Tularecito's hands are first of all able and powerful, even "tender," yet also, on occasion, "merciless." His manual skills are immediately put to use. As Franklin Gomez informs Miss Martin, "no one can make a garden as he can. No one can milk so swiftly nor so gently" (39). Tularecito's instinctive rapport with plants and animals allows Steinbeck to draw close to the vulnerable natural world of the Pastures of Heaven: young plants may suffer injuries, "the surfaces of a grafting limb" bruises. In a discussion of Emerson's "unconquered eye," Tony Tanner observed that "the naive eye—idiot, Indian, infant—seems to pay the most profitable kind of attention to things, to enjoy a lost intimacy with the world, to have the freshest, clearest perceptions."[7] Tularecito offers a clear instance of such a close "attention to things."

Tularecito's speeches, likewise, revolve around his immediate physical environment. One example occurs near the end of the story:

> "I am not like the others at the school or here. I know that. I have loneliness for my own people who live deep in the cool earth. When I pass a squirrel hole, I wish to crawl into it and hide myself. My own people are like me, and they have called me. I must go home to them, Pancho." (43)

In tone as well as in content, Tularecito's prose is plain and unassuming. The passage is free from naturalistic jargon ("trogloditic"). Steinbeck seems to have made a conscious effort to leave out recent loanwords from Greek, Latin, and the Romance languages. Earlier Latinate expressions such as "school" and "people" escape censure. The effect, in any case, is one of warmth and natural simplicity.[8] At this point, however, Tularecito parts company with vernacular narrators in the line of Huckleberry Finn. Even apart from the fact that he "[has] loneliness" for his relatives, his words lack fluency and colloquial ease. The passage is rooted in the first person singular: "I am," "I know," "I have," "I pass," "I wish," "I must." Sentences tend to fall into leaden trains of monosyllables. Steinbeck is at pains to give Tularecito a voice that befits his impaired mind.

The school episodes present the reader with a pessimistic counterpart to equivalent ones in nineteenth-century novels. Dickens had turned to the reform movement for a progressive paradigm that was re-enacted in the success stories of Smike, Maggy, and other grown-up children. Once they find a sufficiently patient teacher, these characters have little difficulty mastering abstract skills. Tularecito, however, "learned nothing at all" (37). Such tal-ents as he does possess are generally attributed to his alleged "supernatural origin," rather than to a learning process (36).

Steinbeck leaves little room for development. If Tularecito's artistic gift reveals itself at a young age, so does his violent temper. During the classroom fight, "Miss Martin's clothes were torn to streamers, and the big boys, on whom the burden of the battle fell, were bruised and battered cruelly" (38). On three previous occasions, Tularecito has been known to assault persons who "handled carelessly or broke one of the products of his hands" (37). Miss Martin promptly demands that he be punished, adding that "'he ought to be locked up'" to prevent further confrontations (39).

With the arrival of the second teacher, the narrative enters a new phase. Miss Morgan, one is told, "knew all about him [Tularecito], had read books and taken courses about him" (40). So far, there has been no indication of academic interest in Tularecito. The plural "books" and "courses" stretch the reader's credence. Miss Morgan's subsequent teaching methods, at any rate, betray no specialist's knowledge of his case. Tularecito is allowed to draw peacefully while the other children follow her lessons. He does not show the least interest in her words until she decides to read fairy tales to her class.

Having mentioned the fairy tale, Steinbeck promptly reminds the reader of its naturalistic counterpart. When, all of a sudden, Tularecito intercepts Miss Morgan on the way home, she feels "fear rising in her. The road was deserted—she had read stories of half-wits" (42). Steinbeck's chapter, one might argue, has more in common with these "stories of half-wits" than with fairy tales.

Encouraged by Miss Morgan, Tularecito proceeds to search for "'the little people who live in the earth'" (43). The final paragraphs focus on the clash between the innocent longing to find the gnomes and the ferocious attack on Munroe: "A savage growl spun him [Munroe] around. Tularecito came charging down upon him, leaping like a frog on his long legs, and swinging his shovel like a club" (45). Munroe is fortunate to survive the blow. In *The Grapes of Wrath* (1939), Tom Joad would kill a man with a shovel. It is hardly surprising that the chairman of the "medical board" refuses to acquit Tularecito. As he tells Gomez, "'you must see that we cannot let him go loose. Sooner or later he will succeed in killing someone'" (46). This is precisely what the narrative has led the reader to believe and accept.

"Johnny Bear," which was written in 1934 and first published in *Esquire* (September 1937) under the title "The Ears of Johnny Bear," can be read as an afterthought to the Tularecito chapter. Superficially, it is by far the least sympathetic depiction of a mentally deficient character in Steinbeck's work. Johnny in many respects resembles Tularecito, but he lacks the innate dignity of his predecessor. The narrator introduces him as follows:

> He looked like a great, stupid, smiling bear. His black matted head bobbed forward and his long arms hung out as though he should have been on all fours and was only standing upright as a trick. . . . He moved forward and for all his bulk and clumsiness, he seemed to creep. He didn't move like a man, but like some prowling night animal.[9]

Devolution is one available rationale. Johnny peers out from under the table "like an animal about to leave its den," and, in the course of the pub brawl near the end of the story, "his arms [enfold] Alex as the tentacles of an anemone enfold a crab" (98, 109). Johnny is poised on the threshold dividing human beings from animals, much as the Loma area, "with its fogs, with its great swamp like a hideous sin," is partly solid earth and partly water (102). The fact that he "seemed to creep" recalls Leviticus 11.41, in which "every creeping thing that creepeth on the earth" is declared an "abomination" not to be touched by humans.[10]

In his biography of Steinbeck, Jackson J. Benson quotes a helpful, previously unpublished note (14 June 1934), written as the story began to take shape under the working title "The Sisters": "I have thought of an objective point of view who might be valuable in a number of stories—the half-wit Indian boy who lives in Castroville."[11] A neutral, impersonal perspective takes the place of Tularecito's intuitive angle of vision.

Like Tularecito, Johnny is given a remarkable mimetic talent. He is able to echo any conversation he has overheard, regardless of whether he understands the words. As Alex Hartnell tells the narrator, "'he can photograph words and voices'" (97). Steinbeck pushes the theme of truthful representation—often an integral part of American fiction—to the extreme of mechanical reproduction.

Johnny habitually spies on the inhabitants of Loma and then offers to repeat what he has heard in exchange for glasses of whisky at the Buffalo Bar, the "'mind of Loma . . . our newspaper, our theatre and our club.'" His performances provide a uniquely democratic view of the village. He does not distinguish between Mrs. Ratz and the local "aristocrats," the Hawkins sisters (102).[12] If one recording pleases his audience, he will attempt to produce a comparable one.

The local community perceives Johnny's presence as a curse. Couples taking walks bring dogs to guard their privacy. The narrator refers to Johnny as "monstrous" and "horrible" (102, 105). When he asks why "'somebody hasn't shot him while he was peeking in windows,'" Alex replies that "'lots of people have tried, but you just don't see Johnny Bear'" (97). Later on, Alex seriously considers shooting him in the open and disposing of his body in the swamp. On these and several other occasions, the reader has good cause to question the judgment of both Alex and the narrator.[13]

Peter Lisca has read the story as, among other things, "an exploration of the artist's role in society."[14] Benson is more specific, drawing attention to "the 'half-wit' and his desire to communicate and to earn his drink, which becomes a marvelous metaphor for Steinbeck's own condition."[15] It soon becomes clear that the reader's sympathy should rest with Johnny, rather than with the patrons of the Buffalo Bar. Johnny's faithful imitations of other people's speeches are sharply set off against the unreliable testimony of the narrator.

One shortcoming of Steinbeck's narrative strategy is that it fails to make Johnny an engaging and rounded character. It does not, in other words, solve the principal problem posed by the naturalistic approach to mental deficiency. Steinbeck was not to return to Johnny's "objective point of view." On the contrary, he opted for an intensely subjective perspective, which he combined with a voice in the American vernacular tradition.

Significantly, "The Ears of Johnny Bear" was not accepted for publication until *Of Mice and Men* (1937) had made its full impact.[16] Lennie Small inherits Tularecito's instinctive love of nature. The following paragraph is taken from the opening scene:

> Lennie dabbled his big paw in the water and wiggled his fingers so the water arose in little splashes; rings widened across the pool to the other side and came back again. Lennie watched them go. "Look, George. Look what I done."[17]

Once more, Steinbeck tends to avoid Latinate loanwords of recent date. "Dabbled," "wiggled," and "splash" especially are firmly rooted in Dutch and German.[18] To a lesser extent, this tendency can be observed throughout the text: the "pendula" of Lennie's "heavy hands" form the most striking exception to the rule.[19] Lennie's fascination with the ripples on the pool is reminiscent of Thoreau: "It is a soothing employment . . . to sit on a stump on such a height as this, overlooking the pond, and study the dimpling circles which are incessantly inscribed on its otherwise invisible surface."[20] More than any other character discussed in this essay, Lennie exemplifies the "childlike wonder and directness" that R. W. B. Lewis detected in Thoreau's work.[21]

Benson has indicated that *Of Mice and Men* started out as a book for children.[22] All characters in the novel use an adolescent idiom, but, as might be expected, Lennie is given the most basic syntax and register. "'He won't do nothing like that. I know George. Me an' him travels together'" (874). Lennie's fluent, colloquial speeches at once place him in a specific literary tradition and reveal his childlike frame of mind. They bear no resemblance to the static prose of Tularecito. The characteristic contractions and double negatives impart life and momentum to his words.

Steinbeck's choice of register serves to conceal the naturalistic bias of the novel. Lennie longs to "pet," "stroke," and "tend" the "nice things" of which he is so fond, only to squash and break them within seconds (864). Early on in the story, George implores Lennie to "'do no bad things like you done in Weed'" (801). Having killed Curley's wife, Lennie "[whispers] in fright, 'I done a bad thing. I done another bad thing'" (865). The expression suggests a negligible offense. There is a marked disproportion between words and events. One might argue that it stems from a fundamental clash of genres, itself a development of the thematic and tonal ambiguity felt in the Tularecito chapter. The vocabulary, that is, belongs to children's literature, whereas the action unfolds according to naturalistic principles.

Even though, as Slim points out, Lennie "'ain't a bit mean,'" he is clearly a public danger (827). Allusions to the Weed incident are evenly spread across the narrative: "'So he reaches out to feel this red dress an' the girl lets out a squawk, and that gets Lennie all mixed up, and he holds on 'cause that's the only thing he can think to do'" (827). George is no less critical of the girl in the red dress than he is of Curley's wife. As it turns out, her fear is more than justified, but he dismisses her cries as "squawks," an expression that effectively conveys his opinion of her.

There are many such premonitions of the crisis. Yet, although the story gradually builds up to the death of Curley's wife, the reader has not been prepared for Lennie's unflinching egotism and mindless anger as he breaks her neck:

"Oh! Please don't do none of that," he begged. "George gonna say I done a bad thing. He ain't gonna let me tend no rabbits." He moved his hand a little and her hoarse cry came out. Then Lennie grew angry. "Now don't," he said. "I don't want you to yell." (865)

Lennie's simple, juvenile idiom stands in no relation to the suffering of Curley's wife. The "rabbits" in particular jar with the observation that "her eyes were wild with terror." Lennie thinks only of what will happen to him: "'George'll be mad'" (865). He forgets Curley's wife as quickly as he has forgotten the mouse and the puppy. When Lennie and George meet for the last time, Lennie simply admits to having done "'another bad thing.'" He expects George to "'give [him] hell,'" offers to "'go right off in the hills an' find a cave,'" and, without delay, moves on to their dream of owning a farm. Minutes later, he positively "[giggles] with happiness" (875–76). Curley's wife is not mentioned again.

The Tularecito chapter, "Johnny Bear," and *Of Mice and Men* all culminate in a violent confrontation that brings out the brute strength and irascible temperament of the respective characters. Written in the course of the 1930s, these texts drew on medical assumptions that dominated the history of mental deficiency in the opening decades of the century.[23] The appeal of Tularecito and Lennie as characters depends in equal measure on their fundamental innocence and a seemingly inevitable lapse into crime.

Degeneration and Descent

It is worth noting that Steinbeck's mentally deficient characters tend to be orphans: Tularecito is raised by Franklin Gomez, Johnny is fed and clothed by the Hawkins sisters, and Lennie is supported by Aunt Clara and George. The "little frog" Tularecito and Johnny Bear even seem to lack a shared human ancestry. Unlike Steinbeck, Faulkner paid close attention to the family background of figures such as Benjy Compson and Ike Snopes.

The family tree of the Compson clan invites a comparison with pedigree studies in the vein of Dugdale's *The Jukes* or Goddard's *Kallikak Family*. Table 7.1 depicts the Compson genealogy. Faulkner tells the story of an aristocratic family in decay, or, in his own words, "a story of blood gone bad."[24] Quentin MacLachan II is Governor of Mississippi. Jason Lycurgus II serves as a general in the Civil War. From this point on, the good fortune of the family begins to wane.

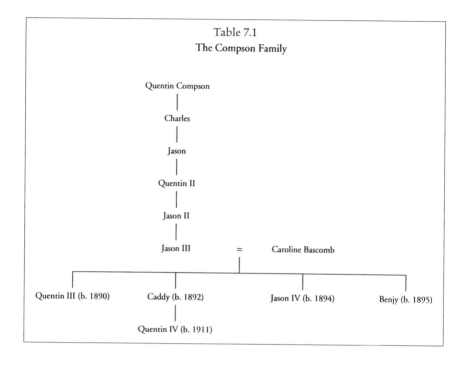

Table 7.1
The Compson Family

Quentin Compson

Charles

Jason

Quentin II

Jason II

Jason III = Caroline Bascomb

Quentin III (b. 1890)   Caddy (b. 1892)   Jason IV (b. 1894)   Benjy (b. 1895)

Quentin IV (b. 1911)

Jason III is an alcoholic. He dies in 1912, only twelve years after his father, the general. His oldest son, Quentin III, commits suicide on 2 June 1910. One year later, Caddy gives birth to an illegitimate daughter, whom she names after her late brother. Jason IV is given to choleric fits. He treats both Caddy and Quentin IV with brutal contempt. His malice is paralleled only by his greed. He robs Quentin IV of maintenance payments running to almost seven thousand dollars, which does not keep him from turning to the police for help when she breaks into his room and disappears with the money. Benjy, who is originally called Maury after his maternal uncle, has the mind of a baby.

The multiple Quentin Compsons (three male, one female) point to the theme of inbreeding associated with the Southern planter aristocracy. As John T. Irwin has put it, Benjy's condition "evokes the traditional biological punishment of that incest from which all doubling springs."[25] Quentin III's and Benjy's obsession with their sister, Caddy, strengthens the incest motif.

Mrs. Compson, as Cleanth Brooks emphasized, "feels the birth of an idiot son as a kind of personal affront."[26] Meditating on the suicide of her son, she tells Dilsey: "'I'm a lady. You might not believe that from my offspring, but I am.'"[27] It is worth noting that Mrs. Compson's claim to nobility is founded upon her Bascomb heritage: "'My people are every bit as well born as yours'" (27). Far from confirming her status, Faulkner refuses to develop a Bascomb genealogy. The previous Bascombs are not even given first names. Caroline and Maury's actions, at any rate, are no credit to their name. She is a hypochondriac who tyrannizes the entire household, and he is notable only for borrowing money from the Compsons and having an affair with the neighbor's wife.

In marked contrast to his mother, Jason IV cares little for lineage and nobility: "Blood, I says, governors and generals. It's a dam good thing we never had any kings and presidents; we'd all be down there at Jackson chasing butterflies" (138). His own hopes and aspirations rest not on the achievements of his famous Southern ancestors but on the New York stock exchange. *The Sound and the Fury* was published within weeks of the 1929 crash.

Writing to Malcolm Cowley (27 October 1945), Faulkner noted that Benjy "was gelded by process of law."[28] If the choice had been Jason IV's, Benjy would have been castrated long before reaching adolescence: "Having to wait to do it at all until he broke out and tried to run a little girl down on the street. . . . Well, like I say they never started soon enough with their cutting, and they quit too quick" (158). The Compson appendix leaves no doubt that Jason had "the creature castrated before the mother even knew it was out of the house." Once she has died, the reader is told, he does not hesitate to send Benjy to Jackson state asylum.[29]

A naturalistic reading of the novel could, justifiably, end here. What is more, there is a sense in which the principal literary model, Zola's *Rougon-Macquart* series of generation novels (1870–1893), does indeed conclude at this point. In both the "experimental novel" and the pedigree study, as Nicole Hahn Rafter has said of the latter, "the researchers began by assuming that which they then set out to prove."[30] Faulkner, however, enables characters such as Benjy and Ike to rise above the restrictions imposed by an essentially naturalistic plot. The most important means of doing so are the carefully crafted voices of these figures.

It was for good reason that Faulkner had Benjy narrate the opening section of *The Sound and the Fury*. If the Compsons, with the help of Dilsey and Roskus's family, keep Benjy under close supervision, he is also himself in a unique position to observe them. Jason IV and his parents speak without inhibition in his presence. Benjy is fifteen years old when he overhears the following conversation, the subject of which is his attack on the Burgess girl:[31]

> *How did he get out, Father said. Did you leave the gate unlatched when you came in, Jason.*
>
> *Of course not, Jason said. Dont you know I've got better sense than to do that. Do you think I wanted anything like this to happen. This family is bad enough, God knows. I could have told you, all the time. I reckon you'll send him to Jackson, now. If Mr Burgess dont shoot him first.* (32)

Benjy anticipates Johnny Bear in that he conveys other people's speeches oblivious of either content or possible implications. Dialogue provides a convenient means of characterization throughout Benjy's section. In young Jason IV, one can already recognize the self-righteous character who will drive his niece out of the house eighteen years later. His father sounds weak and hesitant in comparison. Jason III dwells on the past, whereas Jason IV calls for present action. Mr. Burgess emerges from the novel as a remarkably violent person. Jason IV later remembers that Mr. Burgess "knocked him [Benjy] out with the fence picket" (158), which is exactly what George Milton is forced to do when Lennie refuses to let go of the girl in the red dress.[32]

Caddy's glimpse through the upstairs window on the evening of Damuddy's funeral reveals very little: "'They're not doing anything in there.' Caddy said. 'Just sitting in chairs and looking'" (28). Benjy, however, registers both the symbolic "muddy bottom of her drawers" and the nervous comments of Versh, Jason, and Frony below:

> "Mr Jason said if you break that tree he whip you." Versh said.
> "I'm going to tell on her too." Jason said.
> The tree quit thrashing. We looked up into the still branches.
> "What you seeing." Frony whispered. (24)

Versh's warning suggests that this is not the first time Caddy has climbed the tree. Her daughter will regularly take advantage of the tree in front of her window. Jason IV lives up to his reputation of being a "'tattletale'" (72). As soon as Caddy is lost from sight, Benjy associates the "thrashing" of the leaves with the tree, rather than her. Faulkner carefully places his narrator so as to bring out the curious mixture of distrust and companionship among the children on the Compson estate.

André Bleikasten has argued that "Benjy is in a sense the most reliable narrator one can dream of: insofar as the recorded facts escape manipulation, his monologue achieves an objectivity in sharp contrast to the following sections."[33] In spite of a strong perceptive bias in favor of, for instance, Caddy or open fire, individual sensations are rendered with great accuracy and, within given passages, in strict chronological order:

> Versh's hand came with the spoon, into the bowl. The spoon came up to my mouth. The steam tickled into my mouth. Then we quit eating and we looked at each other and we were quiet, and then we heard it again and I began to cry. (16)

Causation is replaced by succession. Although it occurs only twice, all sentences could begin with the word "then." The movement of Versh's hand follows precise spatial prepositions: he dips the spoon "into the bowl" before lifting it "up to my mouth"; the hot "steam tickled into my mouth." Not one of the seven nouns in the first three sentences is granted an adjective. The long final sentence comprises five pairs of subject and predicate lined up in a single paratactic chain: "we quit eating," "we looked at each other," "we were quiet," "we heard it again," and "I began to cry." The comma following the third pair marks a caesura to coincide with the brief spell of silence. Benjy's sensory reportage reminds one of Ernest Hemingway's prose. Compare, for example, the following extract from *A Farewell to Arms,* also published in 1929:

> I lifted it [the mass of macaroni] to arm's length and the strands cleared. I lowered it into the mouth, sucked and snapped in the ends, and chewed, then took a bite of cheese, chewed, and then a drink of the wine.[34]

Frederic Henry's use of the conjunction "and," the adverb "then," prepositions, and punctuation matches Benjy's. As in the earlier example, there is a noticeable predominance of succession over causation. Tony Tanner's analysis of Hemingway's "unhurried sensations" also applies to Benjy's point of view: "The prose makes permanent the attentive wonder of the senses: it mimes out the whole process, impression by impression." Hemingway avoids "summary" and "a collapsing together of separate moments." Any "pause in reality must reappear in the prose."[35] These similarities are by no means accidental. Benjy's narrative voice reflects several central concerns of modernist

American fiction. One of the writers whose work needs to be taken into account here is Gertrude Stein.

In *Composition as Explanation,* a slender volume published by Leonard and Virginia Woolf's Hogarth Press, Stein considered the composition of *Three Lives.* Her starting point was a "prolonged present," out of which grew what she called a "continuous present": "In the first book there was a groping for a continuous present and for using everything by beginning again and again." Benjy offers a perfect example of a narrator locked in an infinitely "prolonged present."[36] His narrative falls into an associative pattern of new beginnings, just as the novel as a whole comprises four versions of one story.[37] Stein's characteristic repetitions with subtle variations find an analogue in the pervasive, ever-changing leitmotifs of Benjy's monologue.[38]

William Carlos Williams praised Stein for purging words of unwanted associations: "Stein has gone systematically to work smashing every connotation that words have ever had, in order to get them back clean."[39] As so often, William's literary criticism is relevant first and foremost to his own work. The underlying agenda is once more the search for a language that has not been spoilt by civilization. In this respect, also, the first section of *The Sound and the Fury* builds on the work of the early modernists. There is a literal sense of linguistic renovation. Faulkner invents a deceptively simple idiom, devoid of abstraction and figurative language. He conjures up a bewildering landscape using a surprisingly small number of reference points such as "the fence," "the grass," and "the trees." Each of these assumes a distinct physical identity. The words themselves may carry little connotative weight, but they quickly acquire significance within the text.

As far as etymology is concerned, Faulkner here shares Steinbeck's characteristic resistance to Greek and Latinate polysyllables. This tendency is brought into sharp focus whenever Benjy reports words spoken by his father, whose speech is saturated with scholarly loanwords: "'I admire Maury. He is invaluable to my own sense of racial superiority. . . . *Et ego in arcadia* I have forgotten the latin for hay'" (27). Since Quentin III strives to emulate his father, the reader experiences a similar etymological shift when Quentin takes over from Benjy at the beginning of the second section.

Irena Kaluza has discussed Benjy's idiolect in terms of "uniformity, inflexible rigidity and monotony."[40] Noel Polk, building on Kaluza's study, has urged a comparison with "the perspective of primitive painting."[41] One could argue, however, that Kaluza and Polk fail to give full recognition to the poetic subtlety and range of Benjy's narrative voice. The nearest equivalent in painting is primitive art as revalued by modernism.[42]

Faulkner never completely resigns himself to the elementary structures that seem to govern the text. Even the vocabulary is not as limited as Kaluza leads one to expect. Benjy's language could certainly be called basic, but not insensitive or crude. It is what sets him apart from the tainted branch of Zola's famous genealogical tree, on the one hand, and the mental defectives that mark the fall of respected families in the pedigree studies, on the other.

Ten years later, in *The Hamlet* (1940), Faulkner wove a point of view very similar to Benjy's into a third-person narrative.[43] Ike Snopes's abduction of the cow is for the most part rendered in free indirect style:

> As winter became spring and the spring itself advanced, he had less and less of darkness to flee through and from. Soon it was dark only when he left the barn, backed carefully, with one down-groping foot, from the harness-room where his quilt-and-straw bed was, and turned his back on the long rambling loom of the house.[44]

Although this passage opens the section, Ike is introduced simply as "he." His name is not mentioned until three pages later, by which time the reader has recognized him from Book I. In a similar way, the cow is first identified as such five paragraphs into the section. Ike's every movement is executed with trained precision: he descends from the harness-room with due care, testing the ground under his feet. The long second sentence slowly accumulates additional clauses. Ike's fear of darkness is developed later in the paragraph. At night, he is reduced to "the uncohered all-sentience of fluid and nerve-springing terror alone and terribly free in the primal sightless inimicality" (165). Solid physical objects, for example the "barn" or the "quilt-and-straw bed," are juxtaposed to verbose Latinate abstractions. The cow alone stands "solid amid the abstract earth" even in the dark (186).

Syntax and vocabulary alike are beyond Ike's grasp. Faulkner sidesteps the stylistic economy of Benjy's monologue: the continuous flow of associations is reflected in the syntax; Ike's bewilderment finds expression in Faulkner's own words.[45] The narrative perspective allows for a range of fine gradations. At times, introspection blends into detached observation. "The narrator," as François Pitavy has noted, "introduces into this magnificent pastoral a note of parody [*une distance parodique*] whereby the reader is constantly reminded that the story is indeed that of an idiot and a cow."[46] When

Ike first attempts to approach the cow, for instance, it "[scrambles] up the further bank, out of the water." He follows, "stepping gingerly down into the water," before "vanishing completely with one loud cry and rising again" (166). Soon afterward, Ike crosses the creek once more, stepping "onto" rather than "into" the water, "forgetting again that it will give under his weight" (175).

The narrative is interspersed with authorial metaphors and similes. Rain is falling "not in drops but in needles of fiery ice"; "each brief lance" is "already filled with the glittering promise of its imminent cessation like the brief bright saltless tears of a young girl over a lost flower" (184–85). Faulkner even incorporates a brief history of the woods and hills surrounding Frenchman's Bend, previously owned by the Chickasaw Indians, as well as elaborate allusions to Helen and Juno.

Ike inherits Benjy's strong sense of spatial order. Following his brief encounter with Jack Houston, the owner of the cow, he seeks out "the place where he had lain at each dawn for three months now, waiting for her [the cow]. It was the same spot; he would return as exactly to it each time as a piston to its cylinder-head" (177). Although he perceives "no distance in either space or geography, no prolongation of time for distance to exist in," he has explored his terrain with great patience and care (179). Restricted to the evidence of his senses, he gradually expands his subjective landscape, starting from the harness-room and reaching out towards the pasture, the creek, and the countryside beyond.

In an early review of *The Hamlet* for the *Cleveland Plain Dealer*, Ted Robinson wrote that Ike is "no mere halfwit, but a disgustful creature who cannot even speak intelligibly, and who is a prey to the most deplorable instincts."[47] Ike is, in fairness, the most conspicuously amoral character in the group. He is inconceivable in the nineteenth and unique in the twentieth century. Like Benjy, however, he is given a powerful voice and a highly sensitive point of view. In a chapter titled "Faulkner as Nature Poet," Brooks suggested that "perhaps the most elaborately lyrical of such passages in Faulkner" are found in Ike's section.[48] Pitavy speaks of "the almost awe-inspiring inflation of the rhetoric and the poetic diction, elevating the singular story to the level of a myth."[49] Ike's experience of rain may serve as an illustration:

> He watched it for some time and without alarm, wanton and random and indecisive before it finally developed, concentrated, drooping in narrow unperpendicular bands in two or three different places at one time, about

the horizon, like gauzy umbilical loops from the bellied cumulae, the sun-belled ewes of summer grazing up the wind from the southwest. (184)

Ike's narrowly confined mind seems only to add to Faulkner's freedom of expression. The exuberant play of phrases and images testifies to the fact that this is an invented, wholly artificial language. Whereas, in Benjy's monologue, Faulkner shuns Greek, Latinate, and French loanwords, he now delights in mixing etymological roots ("gauzy umbilical loops," "bellied cumulae"). All the same, it needs to be made clear that Ike's nature poetry is no more artificial than Benjy's observations and recollections. At first glance, the former could be mistaken for a caricature of Faulkner and the latter for one of Hemingway.

Still in the review of *The Hamlet* quoted earlier, Robinson asked his readers, "Is there anything for human amusement or instruction in the day-by-day activities of a completely mindless imbecile?"[50] It is precisely the lack of moral instruction that distinguishes characters such as Tularecito, Johnny Bear, Lennie, Lennie, Benjy, and Ike from their literary forebears. Their amoral, in some cases candidly sexual frames of mind and their "day-by-day activities" were in accord with and, to a certain extent, dictated by current or recent medical assumptions.

Faulkner did not break away from the naturalistic paradigm of "blood gone bad." What is more, he could be said to have followed it more painstakingly than Steinbeck. He did, however, endow Benjy and Ike with a depth of perception and expression that transcends their humble and often demeaning plot functions. Even though, in Steinbeck, the plot seems to prevail over the character, the fictional strategy is similar. The fact that Tularecito and Lennie are shown, in Tanner's words, "to enjoy a lost intimacy with the world" works against the naturalistic logic of their respective stories. Both Steinbeck and Faulkner succeed in turning an apparent disability into a privilege in literary terms.

NOTES

1. As intellectual disability in the novel is based on a mixture of literary conventions and contemporary perspectives, this essay examines characters labeled mentally deficient with regard to both their literary and their historical contexts.

2. Dickens's *Barnaby Rudge* (1841) and Dostoevsky's *The Idiot* (1868) may serve as

examples. In *The Secret Agent* (1907), Conrad strives to defend the literary fool against the encroachments of criminology.

3. It should be added that "there is no neat definition applicable to the movement in America," as Donald Pizer has made clear. *Twentieth-Century American Literary Naturalism: An Interpretation* (Carbondale: Southern Illinois University Press, 1982), xi.

4. The classic study of the subject is Tony Tanner, *The Reign of Wonder: Naivety and Reality in American Literature* (Cambridge: Cambridge University Press, 1965).

5. See Walter E. Fernald, "The Imbecile with Criminal Instincts," *Journal of Psycho-Asthenics* 14 (1909), 16–38.

6. *The Pastures of Heaven*, in *Novels and Stories, 1932–1937*, ed. Robert DeMott (New York: Library of America, 1994), 46. All subsequent quotations are from the edition cited.

7. Tanner, *The Reign of Wonder*, 34.

8. This is an extreme instance of a widespread stylistic preference among American writers of Steinbeck's generation. One thinks especially of William Carlos Williams's motto, "no ideas but in things," and of Steinbeck's insistence that he is a "writer" rather than an "author": "I don't know what an author does." "Conversation with Bo Beskow and Bo Holmström," Swedish Broadcasting Corporation (8 December 1962). Jackson J. Benson uses this line as an epigraph to *The True Adventures of John Steinbeck, Writer* (London: Heinemann, 1984).

9. *The Long Valley*, in *The Grapes of Wrath and Other Writings, 1936–1941*, ed. Robert DeMott (New York: Library of America, 1996), 95. All subsequent quotations are from the edition cited.

10. Patricia M. Mandia, too, has stressed that Johnny is a "beast-man," but her reading of the story is diametrically opposed to the present one. According to Mandia, Johnny is associated with "chaos and overt evil." "Chaos, Evil, and the Dredger Subplot in Steinbeck's 'Johnny Bear,'" in *Steinbeck's Short Stories in "The Long Valley": Essays in Criticism*, ed. Tetsumaro Hayashi (Muncie: Steinbeck Research Institute, 1991), 56.

11. Benson, *The True Adventures of John Steinbeck*, 244.

12. Names are indicative of social rank.

13. In this regard, it should be noted that Steinbeck was very fond of anemones, as books such as *Sea of Cortez* (1941), *Cannery Row* (1945), and *Sweet Thursday* (1954) show.

14. Peter Lisca, *The Wide World of John Steinbeck* (New Brunswick, NJ: Rutgers University Press, 1958), 96.

15. Benson, *The True Adventures of John Steinbeck*, 287.

16. Benson, *The True Adventures of John Steinbeck*, 360–61.

17. *Of Mice and Men*, in *Novels and Stories, 1932–1937*, 798. All subsequent quotations are from the edition cited.

18. The *Oxford English Dictionary* lists the Dutch "dabbelen" and the (Middle) Low German "wiggelen," "plasken," and "plaschen."

19. Mark Van Doren promptly found fault with the word: "It wouldn't have done

to write pendulums. That would have given the real sound and look of Lennie, and besides it is a real word." "Wrong Number," in *Nation* 114 (1937): 275. Steinbeck eventually decided to omit the metaphor ("Note on the texts," 903).

20. Henry D. Thoreau, *Walden,* ed. J. Lyndon Shanley (Princeton, NJ: Princeton University Press, 1971), 187–88.

21. R. W. B. Lewis, *The American Adam: Innocence, Tragedy, and Tradition in the Nineteenth Century* (Chicago: University of Chicago Press, 1955), 27.

22. Benson, *The True Adventures of John Steinbeck,* 325–26.

23. Gertie, the feeble-minded and naively promiscuous heroine of the early piece "Fingers of Cloud: A Satire on College Protervity," published in *The Stanford Speculator* (February 1924): 161–64, conforms to the corresponding female stereotype.

24. Taken from a 1955 interview with Cynthia Grenier. *Lion in the Garden: Interviews with William Faulkner, 1926–1962,* ed. James B. Meriwether and Michael Millgate (Lincoln: University of Nebraska Press, 1968), 222.

25. John T. Irwin, *Doubling and Incest/Repetition and Revenge: A Speculative Reading of Faulkner* (Baltimore: Johns Hopkins University Press, 1975), 156.

26. Cleanth Brooks, *William Faulkner: The Yoknapatawpha Country* (New Haven: Yale University Press, 1963), 334.

27. *The Sound and the Fury,* ed. David Minter (New York: Norton, 1987), 179. The Norton edition is preferable to the 1966 Chatto and Windus edition in that it offers the authoritative text established by Noel Polk. All subsequent quotations are from the edition cited.

28. *Selected Letters,* ed. Joseph Blotner (London: Scolar, 1977), 207.

29. "Appendix: The Compsons," in *The Portable Faulkner,* ed. Malcolm Cowley, rev. ed. (New York: Viking, 1967), 716–17. In *The Mansion* (1959), Faulkner was to bring Mrs. Compson back to life. She demands that Benjy return to his family. In due course, he sets fire to the house and dies in the flames.

30. Nicole Hahn Rafter, *White Trash: The Eugenic Family Studies, 1877–1919* (Boston: Northeastern University Press, 1988), 22. Zola's essay "Le Roman expérimental" was strongly influenced by Bernard's *Introduction à l'étude de la médecine expérimentale* (1865) and first published in 1879.

31. Faulkner specifies the age in a letter to Ben Wasson (early summer, 1929). *Selected Letters,* 44.

32. As George confides in Slim, "'I socked him [Lennie] over the head with a fence picket to make him let go.'" *Of Mice and Men,* 827.

33. André Bleikasten, *The Most Splendid Failure: Faulkner's "The Sound and the Fury"* (Bloomington: Indiana University Press, 1976), 86.

34. *A Farewell to Arms* (London: Jonathan Cape, 1929), 55.

35. Tanner, *The Reign of Wonder,* 247.

36. Gertrude Stein, *Composition as Explanation* (London: Hogarth Press, 1926), 16–18.

37. Faulkner claimed as much in one of the 1955 interviews at Nagano: "I wrote that same story four times." *Lion in the Garden,* 147.

38. See also Stein's comments on the uses of repetition in her *Lectures in America* (New York: Random House, 1935).

39. "A 1 Pound Stein," in *Selected Essays* (New York: Random House, 1954), 163.

40. Irena Kaluza, *The Functioning of Sentence Structure in the Stream-of-Consciousness Technique of William Faulkner's "The Sound and the Fury": A Study in Linguistic Stylistics* (Krakow: Nakladem Uniwersytetu Jagiellonskiego, 1967), 48.

41. Noel Polk, *Children of the Dark House: Text and Context in Faulkner* (Jackson: University Press of Mississippi, 1996), 101.

42. The conjunction of a quintessentially modernist voice and a mentally deficient speaker recalls Max Simon Nordau's influential *Degeneration,* according to which fin-de-siècle aesthetes, symbolists, and realists, among others, stood on the brink of clinical insanity. Near the end of the text, Nordau speaks of "the manifold embodiments of degeneration and hysteria in contemporary art, poetry, and philosophy," concluding that society suffers from "a serious mental malady, a kind of black death of degeneration and hysteria." *Entartung,* 2 vols. (Berlin: Carl Dunder, 1896), II, 521 (my translation).

43. Although the novel was not published until April 1940, it was written between November 1938 and October 1939.

44. *The Hamlet* (London: Chatto and Windus, 1965), 164. All subsequent quotations are from the edition cited.

45. In the original "Afternoon of a Cow" (1937), heavily revised for publication in *The Hamlet,* it is not Ike but a character called Mr. Faulkner who saves the cow from the fire. Near the end of the story, the first-person narrator informs Mr. Faulkner, "'I shall insist upon my prerogative and right to tell this one in my own diction and style, not yours.'" *Uncollected Stories of William Faulkner,* ed. Joseph Blotner (London: Chatto and Windus, 1980), 434.

46. François Pitavy, "Idiocy and Idealism: A Reflection on the Faulknerian Idiot," in *Faulkner and Idealism: Perspectives from Paris,* ed. Michel Gresset and Patrick Samway (Jackson: University Press of Mississippi, 1983), 106. See also the original article, "Idiot et idéalisme: Réflexion sur l'idiot Faulknérien," *Études Anglaises* 35 (1982): 416.

47. "The Hamlet," *Cleveland Plain Dealer,* 14 April 1940, 3.

48. Brooks, *The Yoknapatawpha Country,* 32.

49. Pitavy, "Idiocy and Idealism," 104.

50. "The Hamlet," 3. This was in many ways a typical response to the theme of mental deficiency in fiction. Steinbeck was not exempt from criticism along these lines. In a review of *The Long Valley,* for example, Ralph Thompson implored Steinbeck to "avoid cretins, fools, imbeciles, boobies, idiots, dolts and particular boneheads in the future." "Books of the Times," *New York Times,* 21 September 1938, 29.

BIBLIOGRAPHY

Benson, Jackson J. *The True Adventures of John Steinbeck, Writer.* London: Heinemann, 1984.

Bernard, Claude. *Introduction à l'étude de la médecine expérimentale.* Paris: Baillière, 1865.

Bleikasten, André. *The Most Splendid Failure: Faulkner's "The Sound and the Fury."* Bloomington: Indiana University Press, 1976.

Blotner, Joseph, ed. *Selected Letters of William Faulkner.* London: Scolar, 1977.

———, ed. *Uncollected Stories of William Faulkner.* London: Chatto and Windus, 1980.

Brooks, Cleanth. *William Faulkner: The Yoknapatawpha Country.* New Haven: Yale University Press, 1963.

Conrad, Joseph. *The Secret Agent: A Simple Tale.* Edited by Bruce Harkness and S. W. Reid. Cambridge: Cambridge University Press, 1990.

Dickens, Charles. *Barnaby Rudge: A Tale of the Riots of 'Eighty.* Oxford: Oxford University Press, 1954.

Dostoevsky, Fyodor. *The Idiot.* Trans. Constance Garnett. London: Heinemann, 1913.

Dugdale, Richard L. *"The Jukes": A Study in Crime, Pauperism, Disease and Heredity; also Further Studies of Criminals.* New York: Putnam, 1877.

Faulkner, William. *Absalom, Absalom!* London: Chatto and Windus, 1965.

———. "Appendix: The Compsons." In *The Portable Faulkner,* edited by Malcolm Cowley, rev. ed. New York: Viking, 1967, 704–21.

———. *The Hamlet.* London: Chatto and Windus, 1965.

———. *The Mansion.* London: Chatto and Windus, 1961.

———. *The Sound and the Fury.* Edited by David Minter. Text established by Noel Polk. New York: Norton, 1987.

Fernald, Walter E. "The Imbecile with Criminal Instincts." *Journal of Psycho-Asthenics* 14 (1909): 16–38.

Goddard, Henry Herbert. *The Kallikak Family: A Study in the Heredity of Feeble-Mindedness.* New York: Macmillan, 1912.

Hemingway, Ernest. *A Farewell to Arms.* London: Jonathan Cape, 1929.

Irwin, John T. *Doubling and Incest/Repetition and Revenge: A Speculative Reading of Faulkner.* Baltimore: Johns Hopkins University Press, 1975.

Kaluza, Irena. *The Functioning of Sentence Structure in the Stream-of-Consciousness Technique of William Faulkner's "The Sound and the Fury": A Study in Linguistic Stylistics.* Krakow: Nakladem Uniwersytetu Jagiellonskiego, 1967.

Lewis, R. W. B. *The American Adam: Innocence, Tragedy, and Tradition in the Nineteenth Century.* Chicago: University of Chicago Press, 1955.

Lisca, Peter. *The Wide World of John Steinbeck.* New Brunswick, NJ: Rutgers University Press, 1958.

Mandia, Patricia M. "Chaos, Evil, and the Dredger Subplot in Steinbeck's 'Johnny

Bear.'" In *Steinbeck's Short Stories in "The Long Valley": Essays in Criticism,* edited by Tetsumaro Hayashi. Muncie: Steinbeck Research Institute, 1991, 54–62.

Meriwether, James B., and Michael Millgate, eds. *Lion in the Garden: Interviews with William Faulkner, 1926–1962.* Lincoln: University of Nebraska Press, 1968.

Nordau, Max Simon. *Entartung.* 2 vols. Berlin: Carl Dunder, 1896.

Pitavy, François. "Idiocy and Realism: A Reflection on the Faulknerian Idiot." In *Faulkner and Idealism: Perspectives from Paris,* edited by Michel Gresset and Patrick Samway. Jackson: University Press of Mississippi, 1983, 97–111. Originally published as "Idiot et idéalisme: Réflexion sur l'idiot Faulknérien." *Études Anglaises* 35 (1982): 408–19.

Pizer, Donald. *Twentieth-Century American Literary Naturalism: An Interpretation.* Carbondale: Southern Illinois University Press, 1982.

Polk, Noel. *Children of the Dark House: Text and Context in Faulkner.* Jackson: University Press of Mississippi, 1996.

Rafter, Nicole Hahn. *White Trash: The Eugenic Family Studies, 1877–1919.* Boston: Northeastern University Press, 1988.

Robinson, Ted. "The Hamlet." *Cleveland Plain Dealer,* 14 April 1940, 3.

Stein, Gertrude. *Composition as Explanation.* London: Hogarth Press, 1926.

———. *Lectures in America.* New York: Random House, 1935.

Steinbeck, John. *Cannery Row.* New York: Viking, 1945.

———. "Fingers of Cloud: A Satire on College Protervity." *The Stanford Speculator* (February 1924): 161–64.

———. *The Grapes of Wrath and Other Writings, 1936–1941.* Edited by Robert DeMott. New York: Library of America, 1996.

———. *Novels and Stories, 1932–1937.* Edited by Robert DeMott. New York: Library of America, 1994.

———. *Sweet Thursday.* New York: Viking, 1954.

———, with Ed Ricketts. *Sea of Cortez.* New York: Viking, 1941.

Tanner, Tony. *The Reign of Wonder: Naivety and Reality in American Literature.* Cambridge: Cambridge University Press, 1965.

Thompson, Ralph. "Books of the Times." *New York Times,* 21 September 1938, 29.

Thoreau, Henry D. *Walden.* Edited by J. Lyndon Shanley. Princeton, NJ: Princeton University Press, 1971.

Van Doren, Mark. "Wrong Number." *Nation* 114 (1937): 275.

Williams, William Carlos. *Selected Essays of William Carlos Williams.* New York: Random House, 1954.

Zola, Émile. *Le Roman expérimental.* Paris: Charpentier, 1880.

———. *Les Rougon-Macquart: Histoire naturelle et sociale d'une famille sous le second Empire.* Edited by Henri Mitterand. 5 vols. Paris: Gallimard, 1960–1967.

8

Sexuality and Storytelling

Literary Representations of the "Feebleminded" in the Age of Sterilization

Karen Keely

In the first third of the twentieth century, the "menace of the moron" loomed as a perceived threat to the American way of life and ultimately, as I argue in this essay, challenged literary notions about telling stories. Americans worried that the so-called feebleminded, apparently unconstrained by reason and traditional mores, would succumb to lives of crime, indiscriminate sexual activity, and careless reproduction. Moreover, this last factor, given prevailing hereditarian beliefs, portended an ever-larger population of the mentally disabled who might terrorize "normal" America. Whereas James Fenimore Cooper, in his 1841 novel *The Deerslayer,* could portray the "simple" sister Hetty as sexually pure and her fiercely intelligent sister Judith as sexually fallen, mental disability had by the twentieth century become associated with rampant and uncontrollable sexuality. Indeed, urban reformers often feared developmentally disabled men as potential sexual predators and worried that a disproportionate number of women involved in prostitution were mentally impaired and unable to protect themselves sexually.[1]

This cultural anxiety about the unrestrained sexuality of the mentally impaired contributed to apprehension about narrative production both by and about the same population. The mentally disabled were considered inappropriately or even dangerously hypersexual, not only in their physical activity but also in their very language. If the "feebleminded" were sexually unrestrained in action, they might be similarly unbounded by social convention, and therefore shockingly explicit, in speech. Both their actions and their words—producing children and language—were potentially beyond the sexual pale. Not surprisingly, given the propensity of authors to use social phenomena as literary fodder, these fears of sexuality and sexual language became the stuff of fiction in the first forty years of the twentieth century, a period we might call the "Age of Sterilization." Literature itself saw a remarkable degree of innovation during this era, and the contemporaneity of literary modernism and the "menace of the moron" led surely and productively to experimentation in narrative form.

In this chapter, I examine four American authors who saw in the mentally impaired a unique opportunity to stretch the limits of storytelling. Jack London, William Faulkner, John Steinbeck, and Eudora Welty all problematize both mental hierarchies, which rank individuals according to their intelligence and discernment (as determined by social norms), and the traditionally corresponding narrative hierarchies, in which story-telling privilege resides exclusively with those of greater intelligence. When the noted eugenicist Henry H. Goddard argued that "Every feeble-minded person is a potential criminal . . . since the feeble-minded lacks one or the other of the factors essential to a moral life—an understanding of right and wrong, and the power of control,"[2] he could also have concluded that these same qualities are crucial to a narrating life as well, a life that by his definition the "feebleminded" were incapable of leading. Both judgment and control are necessary for conventional storytelling, and for London, Faulkner, Steinbeck, and Welty, stories of mental disability are thus the perfect laboratory for pushing the bounds and discovering the limits of narration in the modern work of fiction.

These threads came together during the years that I have termed the Age of Sterilization, stretching from 1907, when Indiana enacted the first compulsory sterilization statute, through the early 1940s, by which time most states' enforcement of such laws was declining. Sterilization of the eugenically "unfit" officially began in the United States when Indiana governor J. Frank Hanly approved a law requiring the state to sterilize all criminals and institutionalized "imbeciles." Over the next two decades, several other states followed suit with similar legislation. After several legal challenges on behalf of those threatened with such surgeries, involuntary sterilizations were declared constitutional by the Supreme Court in 1927 in the landmark case *Buck vs. Bell,* after which many states rushed to pass sterilization legislation. In 1937, Georgia became the last state to adopt such a law. Although psychiatric support for sterilization decreased as the 1930s progressed, public sentiment in favor of it grew during the decade, in part because Depression economics diminished social concern for "unproductive" members of society.

By 1941, the national total of forced sterilization cases had reached almost 36,000.[3]

The sterilization movement—which at its height targeted not only the mentally disabled but also the insane and some categories of criminals—suffered a permanently debilitating setback in 1942, when the U.S. Supreme Court, in *Skinner vs. State of Oklahoma,* unanimously struck down the Oklahoma law that mandated sterilization for criminals convicted of three felonies, an early version of the modern three-strikes rule. The law made exceptions for embezzlement, liquor law violations, and political offenses, thereby creating a class bias against people such as the litigant in the case, Jack T. Skinner, who had been convicted of stealing chickens, as well as of armed robbery. It was this uneven application of the law's penalties, rather than the impetus for the law itself, to which the Supreme Court objected, but the ruling had significant ramifications for many states' sterilization laws.[4] Moreover, as Americans grew increasingly aware during and after the war of the full extent of the Nazi eugenics programs, scientists and eugenicists became eager to separate themselves from such rhetoric, including the advocacy of forced sterilization. Although coerced sterilization continues to this day, after the atrocities of the Nazi Final Solution the rhetoric surrounding sterilization is no longer marked by such unabashed language of lives more and less worth living.[5] In the aftermath of the war, therefore, the Age of Sterilization gradually drew to a close.

Sexual expression and storytelling by the mentally disabled were inextricably linked from the onset of the era. As the Age of Sterilization was beginning, Jack London was creating the first "feeble-minded" narrator in fiction—one who is concerned with his own sexuality and story-telling power—in the 1914 short story "Told in the Drooling Ward."[6] London originally conceived of the story as the "Autobiography of an Idiot,"[7] and he makes an innovative move in offering narrative power to a mentally impaired character who recounts incidents from his life and comments vociferously on the state of the world around him. London approved of the social and legal movements that increasingly denied reproductive power to those people on the bottom rungs of the traditional mental hierarchy, but he questioned the accompanying denial of narrative authority to these same unfortunates. London argues through his mentally disabled and institutionalized narrator Tom that the correspondence between sexual reproduction and textual production is faulty and that all people, including those deemed "feeble-minded" by the rest of society, are entitled to the privilege of narrative.

The uniqueness of the narrator Tom is clear from the opening lines: "Me? I'm not a drooler. I'm the assistant. . . . I can walk, and talk, and do things. . . . That's going some for a feeb. Feeb? Oh, that's feeble-minded. I thought you knew. We're all feebs here. But I'm a high-grade feeb."[8] The "here" to which Tom refers is an institution based on the Sonoma State Home for the Feeble-Minded, which was located adjacent to London's ranch in northern California. The hierarchy of mental ability is especially important to Tom because he feels that his own classification impinges directly on his sexuality. He is very much concerned about and attuned to the arrivals and departures of members of the female nursing staff, not only because he works with them as an assistant but also because he is interested romantically in several of them, not surprising behavior in a twenty-eight-year-old man. Nothing ever comes of these attractions, however; he declares, "I've been acquainted with just thousands of nurses in my time. Some of them are nice. But they come and go" (1765). At one point Tom daydreams, "Some day, mebbe, I'm going to talk to Doctor Dalrymple and get him to give me a declaration that I ain't a feeb. Then I'll get him to make me a real assistant in the drooling ward, with forty dollars a month and my board. And then I'll marry Miss Jones and live right on here. And if she won't have me, I'll marry Miss Kelsey or some other nurse. There's lots of them that want to get married" (1766–67). Tom does investigate the possibility of marriage once but is officially rebuffed— not by the object of his affection, but by the doctors. He reminisces, "Sometimes I think I'd like to get married. I spoke to Dr. Whatcomb about it once, but he told me he was very sorry, because feebs ain't allowed to get married" (1765).

The fact that Tom is officially denied the opportunity for matrimony and, even more so, that he was once temporarily sent out of the institution to work on a local ranch indicates that he has been sterilized by order of the state of California. Two years into the Age of Sterilization, in 1909, California began sterilizing both the mentally impaired and the mentally ill; the statute was repealed in 1913 but amended and reinstated in 1917. Institutionalized people were often sterilized before they were sent out into the outside world where they could mingle with the opposite sex and where the opportunity for (or danger of) reproduction was greatly increased. California quickly took and retained the national lead in numbers of sterilizations, and a contemporary audience could not have read "Told in the Drooling Ward" without placing the story's narrator firmly within this context. Either through sterilization or simply through the sexual segregation of the institution, Tom's reproductive abilities have been eliminated for the comfort and ostensible protection of his fellow Californians.[9]

Tom nevertheless seizes control of his own narrative production despite the curtailment in his reproduction. Tom tells his listener,

> Miss Kelsey [a nurse] asked me once why I don't write a book about feebs. I was telling her what was the matter with little Albert. He's a drooler, you know, and I can always tell the way he twists his left eye what's the matter with him. So I was explaining it to Miss Kelsey, and, because she didn't know, it made her mad. But some day, mebbe, I'll write that book. Only it's so much trouble. Besides, I'd sooner talk. (1764)

The book that Miss Kelsey sarcastically suggests Tom write would apparently be intended for caretakers, nurses, and doctors, explaining the care and treatment of the mentally impaired, but the story that he actually tells is the history of his own adventures. Tom therefore insists on narrating his own subject matter in his own way, despite the societal and conventional impediments that stand in his path.

At the same time, however, it is important to note that Tom is telling not only his own story but also that of Albert, who can only twist his left eye and depends on Tom to translate that gesture into more traditional language. Although Tom identifies himself as a "feeb" in the story's opening lines, his insistence that he is not a "drooler" indicates that there is a clear hierarchy of mental ability in the Home; his role as an assistant places him firmly near the top of that hierarchy and therefore in a position of some power over other inmates—a power that is expressed through narrative authority. His story-telling confidence arises from his belief that he is actually of "normal" intelligence, or at least of far greater intelligence than the other inmates, a claim he makes regularly in the text. Among the Home's residents, weaker intelligences must apparently still rely on stronger minds to narrate their desires and their life stories to the outside world.

The story ultimately calls into question such mental hierarchies, however, for in Tom's role as mediator between the world of the Home, of the deviant, and the world of the outside, of the normal, he in many ways acts out the trope of the trickster figure, one who may be taking readers for a narrative ride. He admits to fooling people both within and outside the Home as to his mental ability and his intentions, explaining, "I could get out of here if I wanted to. I'm not so feeble as some might think. But I don't let on. I have too good a time" (1763-64). London finally argues that intelligence is indeterminable and that all we really know of each other is the stories that we tell about ourselves and others. If storytelling thus stands in for identity, then all people—whatever their determined mental rank—must have the right to narrate.

William Faulkner followed London's lead in 1929 with *The Sound and the Fury*, whose initial narrator is so mentally disabled as to challenge significantly received notions of narration. Benjy, perhaps the most famous "feeble-minded" narrator in literature, is sensual but not sexual, a distinction not recognized by his fellow townspeople, who have him castrated. Benjy is thirty-three years old but is considered a pre-articulate child mentally, and his importance to the novel, which begins and ends with him, is clear from the title, drawn from *Macbeth*: "a tale / Told by an idiot, full of sound and fury, / Signifying nothing." Benjy is too mentally impaired to recognize either chronology or causality, both of which could well be presumed necessary for conventional narration. His section of the novel is an internal and incoherent monologue, for he is incapable of actual speech. Throughout the novel, he is described by others as moaning and slobbering, and his family members (and his readers as well) are usually incapable of understanding his attempts at communication. His beloved older sister Caddy, whose absence (subsequent to her elopement) is the greatest tragedy of his life, continually tries to understand him, and her constant query "What is it. What are you trying to tell Caddy" is particularly ironic since it appears in the very section that Benjy is narrating.[10] That is, Benjy can echo Caddy's question internally without responding to or even understanding it.

Faulkner's Benjy suffers an even more drastic fate than Tom, for he is not only sterilized but also castrated when his sensuality is perceived as rampant sexuality and thus a threat to the community. Benjy spends most of every day at the gate, which is where his beloved sister Caddy used to meet him when she came home from school; because he has no sense of time, he does not realize that Caddy has been gone for years. The neighborhood girls who must walk past him on their way to and from school are afraid of him but are confident that he cannot get out; he merely runs along the fence, thinking that they are Caddy and trying to call to them but moaning incomprehensibly instead. One day, however, someone leaves the gate unlocked, and disaster follows:

They came on. I opened the gate and they stopped, turning. I was trying to say, and I caught her, trying to say, and she screamed and I was trying to say and trying and the bright shapes began to stop and I tried to get out. I tried to get it off my face, but the bright shapes were going again. They were going up the hill to where it fell away and I tried to cry. But when I breathed in, I couldn't breathe out again to cry, and I tried to keep from falling off the hill and I fell off the hill into the bright, whirling shapes. (34)

The link between sexuality and language is clear here, as Benjy's "trying to say" is interpreted by the community as a sexual attack. In the face of the town's moral outcry, the family has Benjy castrated, and at various points in the novel Benjy cries when he discovers, always anew, that his testicles are missing (47 and passim).

In the appendix that Faulkner wrote to the novel in 1946, he succinctly explains Benjy's fate: "Gelded 1913. Committed to the State Asylum, Jackson 1933" (213).[11] Once Benjy's family has dwindled away—through old age, suicide, and social banishment—so that his supporters are all gone, he is left to the mercies of his younger brother Jason, who had earlier suggested that the family "Rent him out to a sideshow; there must be folks somewhere that would pay a dime to see him" (123). Jason institutionalizes his brother, removing him from the only physical context he has ever known, a context that stands in for narration and temporality in his mind. Because Benjy has a sense of location and space in place of a sense of story, institutionalization ends his potential for narration just as castration eliminates his potential for sexuality.

In the last scene of the novel, before Benjy's institutionalization in the Appendix, the servant Luster is taking Benjy for his daily drive but absentmindedly turns left at the Confederate monument rather than their traditional right; at this rupture in Benjy's sense of geography, he screams loudly and repeatedly—the third-person narrator explains that "There was more than astonishment in it, it was horror; shock; agony eyeless, tongueless; just sound" (199)—until Luster and Jason can turn the horse around and circle the monument to the right. The narrator notes, "Ben wailed again, hopeless and prolonged. It was nothing. Just sound. It might have been all time and injustice and sorrow become vocal for an instant by a conjunction of planets" (179). Benjy's wail is perhaps the most articulate and compelling expression of such sorrow, more so than any traditional narrative attempts. This wordless expression of agony is central to the novel, and Faulkner's ultimate conclusion that such agony is endemic and inherently unspeakable makes an "idiot" no different from any other storyteller.

The "idiot" as storyteller is central as well to John Steinbeck's 1937 novel *Of Mice and Men*. The novel is built around Lennie, the character whose "slowness" has most filtered into the American popular consciousness.[12] The novel's title is drawn from Robert Burns's 1785 poem "To a Mouse"—"The best laid schemes o' mice an' men / Gang aft a-gley / An' lea'e us nought but grief an' pain / For promised joy"—and in Steinbeck's novel the "schemes" are plans for the land and household that the mentally impaired Lennie, his protector and friend George, and their fellow California migrant workers hope to share. The optimistic stories that the characters tell each other about this hoped-for future form the most consistent element of the text but ultimately "gang aft a-gley" when Lennie accidentally kills a woman and then dies himself at the hands of George, who is intent on protecting Lennie from the cruelties of a lynch mob. For Steinbeck, the sexuality of a "slow" mind such as Lennie's and the prevailing social fear of such sexuality together constitute the greatest threat to, and eventually the end of, storytelling within *Of Mice and Men*.

Alone of the mentally disabled characters I discuss here, Steinbeck's Lennie escapes the twin threats of sterilization and institutionalization, a fact that ironically contributes to his ultimate death. The exact nature of Lennie's mental disability is never explicitly defined; George's assessment is that "he's so God damn dumb" and "He ain't bright. Hell of a good worker, though. Hell of a nice fella, but he ain't bright."[13] The initial description of Lennie—"a huge man, shapeless of face, with large, pale eyes, with wide, sloping shoulders; and he walked heavily, dragging his feet a little, the way a bear drags his paws. His arms did not swing at his sides, but hung loosely" (4)—implies both his physical strength and his mental "slowness," which together bring about the climax of the novel. At one point, Crooks, the black field worker, tells Lennie that, without George's de facto guardianship, he would have no protection from the legal powers that control the lives of the mentally disabled: "They'll take ya to the booby hatch. They'll tie ya up with a collar, like a dog" (70). According to one estimate, a full quarter of California's itinerant farm workers in the 1920s were mentally impaired, and Lennie is thus in plentiful company as he makes his way up and down the state, following job availability with his protector George.[14]

Lennie and George have left a job in Weed because of this perceived danger of the sexuality of the mentally impaired. Lennie had been attracted to a girl's red dress and tried to feel it, but the girl misunderstood his inarticulate intentions and cried that she was being raped. George is certain that Lennie will not get a fair trial because of the strong association of the mentally impaired with sexual predation. The novel exonerates Lennie in the Weed incident but does ultimately argue that his sensuality, although expressed in aesthetic rather than explicitly sexual terms, is nonetheless threatening. After all, Lennie's love of stroking animals' soft fur leads to his accidentally killing a puppy and a mouse when he pets the animals too violently. Lennie's "slow" mind apparently causes his lack of physical moderation, and his sensual propensities are finally responsible for the death of Curley's wife (never named in the novel), who has been vamping all of the men on the ranch who work under her husband's direction. She and Lennie realize that they share an enjoyment in stroking soft material such as velvet, and she invites him to pat her hair to feel its softness. The scene quickly becomes sexual in tone if not in actual events:

> She took Lennie's hand and put it on her head. "Feel right aroun' there an' see how soft it is."
>
> Lennie's big fingers fell to stroking her hair.
>
> "Don't you mess it up," she said.
>
> Lennie said, "Oh! That's nice," and he stroked harder. "Oh, that's nice."
> (88)

As Lennie's excitement grows, the woman becomes afraid and tries to jerk away from him as she begins screaming. She has been telling him the story of her life, a narrative that hints at her sexuality, and she is afraid that Lennie's grip on her hair is a prelude to sexual attack. Lennie, still holding onto her hair, panics at her screams and shakes her to stop her crying. As she screams louder and his panic intensifies, he shakes her harder and harder until her neck breaks and she is finally quiet. Although one might argue that it is fear of "feeble-minded" sexuality rather than this sexuality itself that ultimately causes her death—Lennie had no sexual designs on her, and it is her screams that cause him to panic and clutch her hair more tightly—the earlier deaths of the mice and the puppy clearly indicate that Lennie's sensuality is in and of itself dangerous, whether or not the object of his desire fears him. The soft fur that excites Lennie is clearly associated with women's genitalia—a target of both fascination and repulsion in the novel, particularly given Curley's glove full of vaseline, designed for "keepin' that hand soft for his wife" (28), much to the disgust of the other men—and Lennie's killing of the small animals is thus a predecessor to the sexuality and violence in his killing of Curley's wife.

The friends dream of settling down in a small house on their own land where they could farm and raise chickens and rabbits, setting the conditions for and keeping all of the products of their own labor, a vision that proves equally alluring to their fellow laborers Crooks and Candy, who vow to join forces with the two men. Lennie is enthralled with this scheme, not for the economic independence that it offers but for his promised role in taking care of the rabbits, and he demands that George tell him the narrative about how they will "live on the fatta the lan'" over and over. Lennie knows the story well enough to prompt George during repeated retellings—"Tell about the house, George" (56) and "An I'd take care of [rabbits]. Tell how I'd do that, George" (57)—but feels unable to tell the entire story himself.

At the end of the novel, just before George kills Lennie to prevent his suffering at the hands of a lynch mob, Lennie finally takes a stab at narrating on his own when he hallucinates that first his Aunt Clara and then "a gigantic rabbit" both come "out of Lennie's head" (98) and speak in his voice. We could assume that he is remembering actual dialogue with his aunt—which would be remarkable enough, given his largely unoperational memory—but the rabbit is clearly an imaginative act, one based on George's repeated instructions about caring for the animals.[15] Even in this instance, however, Lennie remains in the position of auditor, listening to a story told in his own voice without identifying himself as the storyteller. Moreover, this narrative act is self-destructive for Lennie, for both his aunt and the rabbit mercilessly berate him for his stupidity and ineptness; the rabbit, for example, says to him, "You ain't worth a greased jack-pin to ram you into hell. Christ knows George done ever'thing he could to jack you outta the sewer, but it don't do no good. If you think George gonna let you tend rabbits, you're even crazier'n usual. He ain't. He's gonna beat hell outta you with a stick, that's what he's gonna do" (100). The accusations and insults are so vituperative that Lennie must block their voices—that is, his own voice in their personas—by covering his ears and yelling for George. Lennie has so completely absorbed the prevailing narrative about him that he does not have the freedom to create a new, positive narrative for and about himself. The imagined figures coming "out of Lennie's head" also recall Zeus's giving birth to Athena by splitting open his own head with an axe so that she can emerge fully formed, and this classical allusion strengthens the novel's connection between sexuality or reproduction and storytelling. Whereas the deity Zeus can survive this birthing, the mortal Lennie dies—with a bullet rather than an axe to the head—ultimately unable to live a sexual and narrative life.

The novel ends with not only Lennie's death but also the death of the story that has provided purpose and meaning to the other migrant workers' lives. Although there is nothing stopping George, Crooks, and Candy from fulfilling their dream of buying "a coupla acres," this scheme is no longer tenable without Lennie. Their "slow" companion had provided the manpower, but also the incentive and the audience, for this "scheme," but his sensuality, misunderstood as an uncontrollable sexual drive, leads to the inevitable end of story-telling potential for him, as well as for the wider community.

Finally, in 1941, as the Age of Sterilization neared its decline, Eudora Welty addressed the cultural anxiety that narration as well as sexuality by the mentally disabled was too illicit and shocking for social norms. In her short story "Lily Daw and the Three Ladies," the perceived danger of "feeble-minded" sexuality is in its excessively sexual storytelling, which becomes disruptive to the comfort of the community. The story is that of a young woman, Lily, threatened with institutionalization by the three ladies of the title because of her burgeoning sexuality. The women worry because Lily "has gotten so she is very mature for her age,"[16] and they fear that she will become sexually active. She has caused them concern by wearing petticoats as dresses, looking, as Mrs. Watts exclaims, "like a Fiji" (13). Although Lily's name denotes whiteness and purity, the ladies of the town clearly see the possibility for her to lose her "white" attitudes toward controlled reproduction and to adopt the "colored" practice of uncontrolled breeding apparently associated in their minds with tropical spots like the Pacific Islands. The three ladies have therefore decided that the proper place for Lily is the Ellisville Institute for the Feeble-Minded of Mississippi, where she will be segregated from men and therefore from the possibility of inappropriate sexual behavior and pregnancy. Lily, however, has a mind of her own (albeit a "slow" one) and announces that she would rather get married than go to Ellisville. A tent show has come through town the evening before, and Mrs. Watts, concerned about Lily's apparently growing sexuality, worries, "what did she do after the show?" (5). Mrs. Watts is perceptive in her question, for

Lily has in fact developed a tendre for one of the tent show musicians and announces that she is going to marry him. The women are horrified that she might have had sex with him, but when Mrs. Watts asks, "Did he—did he do anything to you?" Lily replies "Oh, yes'm" (11) with such calm unconcern that they cannot discern whether she understood either the question or whatever might have happened the previous night.

Although the question of Lily's chastity is never answered, the women assume the worst, that Lily is now impure as well as "feeble-minded." One of them screams, "We've really just got to get her there—now! . . . Suppose—! She can't stay here!" (14). If Lily is pregnant, the need for her institutionalization is even greater, at least according to the prevailing wisdom of the town. Indeed, out-of-wedlock pregnancy was often a justification used for diagnosing women as mentally disabled and thus committing them to institutions.[17] In order to convince Lily that Ellisville is the proper place for her, the women bribe her with gifts. Mrs. Watts's telling present is "a pink crêpe de Chine brassière with adjustable shoulder straps" (13), which seems to offer fun and frivolity and, potentially, seductiveness but actually provides socially sanctioned bodily repression and control, with only the pretence of freedom allowed by the "adjustable shoulder straps."

Lily never does reach Ellisville, for her musician shows up to marry her, contrary to the townswomen's expectations. By this time, she has decided that she wants to go to the institution, but the ladies once again override her desires and insist that she marry her suitor. The musician kisses her with a smack, "after which she hung her head" (19). Sexuality itself, despite the ladies' assumptions, apparently has no appeal and perhaps even has shame or repugnance for her. The ladies, however, are so blinded by their own prejudices about the sexual nature of the mentally disabled that they cannot see Lily as an individual woman with her own preferences; for them, she is merely and consistently a type, the sexually promiscuous "feeble-minded" girl who must be protected from her own lascivious nature through conventional means, through either institutionalization or marriage. Lily is not entirely vanquished, however, for later in the story her "[p]ink straps glowed through" the black dress that the women make her wear (15).

The sexuality of the mentally disabled not only is a source of horror for and threat to the "normal" members of the community but also provides titillation and vicarious thrill. Only one person in town, Estelle Mabers, is not excitedly provoked by the possibility of Lily's being married; Estelle, however, is depicted as not so bright herself—"she never understood anything"

(7)—as though not being shocked by a "feeble-minded" person's sexuality is tantamount to being "feeble" oneself. On the other hand, Aimee Slocum, the unmarried one of the titular three ladies, is beside herself at the thought of Lily's possible seduction. When Lily agrees that the "man last night" has done something to her, it is Aimee, presumably sexually inexperienced, who wants to know in detail, and yet is afraid to know, what that something is. She repeatedly screams "What?" at Lily but then runs out into the hall in fear of the answer. Mrs. Carson objects to the crudeness of this line of questioning and asks instead, "Tell me, Lily—just yes or no—are you the same as you were?" to which Lily replies, "He had a red coat. . . . He took little sticks and went *ping-pong! ding-dong!*" (11). At this, Aimee obviously imagines all sorts of incredible sexual goings-on and cries out, "Oh, I think I'm going to faint." She is apparently as excited as she is repulsed by the possibilities she envisions. It is Mrs. Watts who realizes that Lily is talking about the xylophone player, with whom Lily had been fascinated at the show the night before. It is his musical and not, one assumes, his sexual performance that has involved "little sticks" and strange noises. The sexuality of Lily's storytelling is thus only as illicit and licentious as her audience assumes it to be, but this fact is no protection for Lily's reputation when she has listeners such as Aimee. As the story ends, Lily and the musician are being hustled against her will to a preacher, who will through the marriage ceremony reinstate her into the community by legitimating her anticipated sexuality. Lily's future storytelling will thus be circumscribed; although she may have more stories to tell about little sticks and strange noises that will no doubt shock Aimee, the community has decided to make those stories "safe" by determining both her sexual experiences and its own potential interpretations of her stories.

Society's shaping and reception of stories by the mentally disabled is central to the four works I have addressed here, all of which point to the productive innovation that can arise when authors take advantage of a provocative cultural moment to push the perceived limitations of their art. Despite their various personal reactions to social control of the developmentally disabled—and London in particular was a eugenics proponent who argued publicly for involuntary sterilization[18]—these authors were as one in denouncing the presumed equation between the right to reproduce and the right to narrate. London, Faulkner, Steinbeck, and Welty all found that creating a mentally impaired storyteller allowed them effectively to explore received assumptions about narrative and to argue that all people, regardless of perceived mental ability, should be able to tell the stories of their own lives.

NOTES

1. Gregory S. Jackson, Rhoda Janzen, Maurice Lee, Michelle N. Mimlitsch, and Steven Noll read various drafts of this article, and I am grateful for their helpful suggestions. Henry Herbert Goddard, *Feeble-Mindedness: Its Causes and Consequences* (1914, rpt. New York: Macmillan, 1926), 13–15, 570; James W. Trent Jr., *Inventing the Feeble Mind: A History of Mental Retardation in the United States* (Berkeley: University of California Press, 1994), 141–43, 166–83; Daniel Kevles, *In the Name of Eugenics: Genetics and the Uses of Human Heredity* (1985, rev. Cambridge, MA: Harvard University Press, 1995), 108; Steven Noll, *Feeble-Minded in Our Midst: Institutions for the Mentally Retarded in the South, 1900–1940* (Chapel Hill: University of North Carolina Press, 1995), 19, 75–76, 112–16. In the 1910s there were at least seventeen studies on the mental abilities of prostitutes that concluded that between 30 and 98 percent of all prostitutes were mentally disabled; Mark Thomas Connelly, *The Response to Prostitution in the Progressive Era* (Chapel Hill: University of North Carolina Press, 1980), 41.

2. Goddard, *Feeble-Mindedness,* 514.

3. Philip R. Reilly, *The Surgical Solution: A History of Involuntary Sterilization in the United States* (Baltimore: Johns Hopkins University Press, 1991), 33; Kevles, *In the Name of Eugenics,* 114–18, 169; Ian Robert Dowbiggin, *Keeping America Sane: Psychiatry and Eugenics in the United States and Canada, 1880–1940* (Ithaca, NY: Cornell University Press, 1997), 123–24, 128–31. American eugenicists generally looked favorably upon the Nazi Eugenic Sterilization Law of 1933, which mandated sterilization for the mentally impaired and for others considered mental misfits, and in 1936, when the University of Heidelberg honored Harry Laughlin, head of the Eugenics Record Office, in Cold Spring Harbor, New York, and a sterilization advocate, with an honorary doctorate in medicine, he accepted the degree with pleasure as "evidence of a common understanding of German and American scientists of the nature of eugenics as research in and the practical application of those fundamental biological and social principles which determine the racial endowments and the racial health—physical, mental and spiritual—of future generations." Stefan Kühl, *The Nazi Connection: Eugenics, American Racism, and German National Socialism* (New York: Oxford University Press, 1994), 87–88.

4. Kevles, *In the Name of Eugenics,* 346–47.

5. Reilly, *The Surgical Solution,* 148–65; Kevles, *In the Name of Eugenics,* 275–76.

6. Don Graham argues that the "story seems to be a totally original creation" and is "a sui generis invention." "Madness and Comedy: A Neglected Jack London Vein," in *Critical Essays on Jack London,* ed. Jacqueline Tavernier-Courbin (Boston: G. K. Hall, 1983), 224, 227.

7. Jack London, "Autobiography of an Idiot" [notes for story], Huntington Library, Jack London Collection, JL 461/462.

8. Jack London, "Told in the Drooling Ward" (1914); rpt. in *The Complete Short Sto-*

ries of Jack London, vol. 3, ed. Earle Labor et al. (Stanford, CA: Stanford University Press, 1993), 1762. Future quotations from this text are cited parenthetically. In Tom's defining the neologism "feeb" for his audience, London is doing the same for his larger one, for the *Oxford English Dictionary* identifies this as the first usage of the shorthand term on record.

9. From the passage of the sterilization law in 1909 up to January 1, 1929, the Sonoma State Home for the Feeble-Minded sterilized 1,488 people, less than a quarter of the state's total sterilizations. Nazi eugenicists declared that they owed a great deal to their American counterparts, singling out the California sterilization program for special mention. Reilly, *The Surgical Solution,* 50; E. S. Gosney and Paul Popenoe, *Sterilization for Human Betterment: A Summary of Results of 6,000 Operations in California, 1909–1929* (New York: Macmillan, 1929), 159–60, 183; Kevles, *In the Name of Eugenics,* 118.

10. William Faulkner, *The Sound and the Fury* (1929; rpt. ed., David Mintner, ed., New York: Norton, 1994), 5 and *passim.* Future quotations from this text are cited parenthetically.

11. Benjy should actually have been institutionalized in the Ellisville State School for the Feeble-Minded—the same institution with which Lily Daw is threatened in Eudora Welty's "Lily Daw and the Three Ladies," also discussed, rather than in the State Insane Hospital at Jackson, where the Mississippi Code prohibited admittance of "mere idiots." Winthrop Tilley, "The Idiot Boy in Mississippi: Faulkner's *The Sound and the Fury,*" *American Journal of Mental Deficiency* 59, 3 (January 1955): 377.

12. For example, one Warner Brothers cartoon includes a monster who paraphrases dialogue from the novel as he attempts to hug and squeeze Bugs Bunny, to the latter's imminent danger, in a replay of Lennie's destructive fascination with rabbits.

13. John Steinbeck, *Of Mice and Men* (1937; rpt. New York: Penguin, 1994), 41, 34. Future quotations from this text are cited parenthetically.

14. Susan Shillinglaw, "Introduction" to Steinbeck, *Of Mice and Men,* xii. Another observer estimated that, on one California ranch, "fifty percent [of migrant children] are hopelessly retarded." Arthur Gleason, "Little Gypsies of the Fruit," *Hearst's International* 45 (February 1924): 160.

15. Margaret C. Roane takes a clinical approach to Lennie, arguing that his mental disability is due to "a bilateral lesion of the frontal hemisphere of the cerebrum" and that his hallucinations are a result "of the action of irritative phenomena on the temporal lobes of his brain," but this diagnosis seems to me less interesting and useful for understanding the novel than the possibility of Lennie's attempts at narration just before his death. "John Steinbeck as a Spokesman for the Mentally Retarded," *Wisconsin Studies in Contemporary Literature* 5 (summer 1964): 130.

16. Eudora Welty, "Lily Daw and the Three Ladies," in *A Curtain of Green and Other*

Stories (New York: Harcourt, Brace, 1941), 5. Future quotations from this text are cited parenthetically.

17. Noll, *Feeble-Minded in Our Midst*, 112–16. See also Goddard, *Feeble-Mindedness*, 499.

18. On September 5, 1913, for example, London wrote to Frederick H. Robinson, of the *Medical Review of Reviews*,

> In reply to your question: "Should criminals and defectives be sterilized?" I believe that it is much wiser to alter an individual before puberty than it is to execute him by hanging or electrocution, or to execute by hanging or electrocution the seed of his loins, because said seed has inherited the criminal and social destructiveness of said loins. I believe that the future human world belongs to eugenics, and will be determined by the practice of eugenics.

Letters of Jack London, vol. 3, ed. Earle Labor, Robert C. Leitz III, and I. Milo Shepard (Stanford, CA: Stanford University Press, 1988), 1226. Robinson had written to London on August 5, 1913, that the magazine was doing a symposium on the sterilization of the unfit and wanted his opinion. London's reply appeared in part in "A Symposium on the Sterilization of the Unfit," *Medical Review of Reviews* 20 (January 1914): 16.

Part III

The Age of Institutionalization and Sterilization

The Eugenical Sterilization of the Feeble-Minded

Harry Laughlin

The purpose of this paper is to discuss the part which eugenical sterilization may play in the attempt to reduce the number of feeble-minded persons in future generations.

A state has two major duties to perform in relation to the feeble-minded. First, it must care for those persons of defective mentality who are unable, adequately, to care for themselves, and who, consequently, are a menace to the state. Secondly, it should seek, so far as possible, to reduce to the minimum the production of feebleminded persons. The quality of the members of the population during the next future generation, in reference to inborn quality, reproduce most abundantly. The foundation principle of applied eugenics demands fit and fertile matings among the members of the present generation who are endowed with the finest physical, mental, and temperamental qualities, and it demands the prevention of reproduction by the present population who suffer from hereditary degeneracy.

Of the several kinds of social inadequacy with which the state must deal the most basic type is that of feeble-mindedness. It is not only a kind of inadequacy which shows primarily as such, but, also, it is interwoven as a considerable factor in nearly every other kind of inadequacy. It is axiomatic that crime, illegitimacy and pauperism are inextricably bound up with mental weakness. In order to cut off the supply of the feeble-minded at its sources it is necessary, first, to determine its cause. What part does hereditary [*sic*], on the one hand, and environment, on the other, play in the production of feeble-mindedness? The determination of these two factors in specific cases has made considerable progress in recent years. The method has been the careful analysis of case records and family pedigrees. In any given case, when a potential source of producing feeble-minded offspring is located, it is the duty, and it should be the purpose of the state to prevent reproduction.

There are no accurate data which show the relative numbers of feeble-minded persons who come from apparently normal and from patently feeble-minded parents. If the near kin, that is, the thirty or forty nearest blood-relatives of a pair of parents show no feeble-minded persons, the logical implication is that the stock is sound in reference to this specific defect. A feeble-minded child coming from such a pair would most likely have been produced by pathological causes, or at least by environmental as contrasted with hereditary factors. In such cases the primary responsibility for the care of the feeble-minded child, and for the prevention of more defective offspring from the same causes, rests with the parents themselves. Presumably, they are normal, intelligent, and social.

But the great mass of feeble-minded offspring come from family stocks which show not only low levels of intelligence but also a high frequency of other kinds of degeneracy. In such cases the parents are not often normal; they are unintelligent; they are socially inadequate, and therefore the responsibility for the care of their children and the prevention of further reproduction rests, of necessity, directly upon the state or organized society. In such strains the hereditary element runs exceedingly high, as contrasted with the environmental causes of degeneracy. For the social care and eugenical control of such families different methods have been proposed. Among these should be named segregation which proposes to institutionalize all feeble-minded persons of a definitely low degree, within the state. Another proposed remedy is sexual sterilization, while still others believe that the work of natural selection will in time eliminate the feeble-minded and prevent both the lowering of the general intelligence of the people and the development of special strains which are characterized by a high degree of feeble-mindedness. Segregation has the double advantage of taking care of the individual, eugenically, that is, in preventing his reproduction, and at the same time, in caring for him as a socially incompetent individual.

Modern segregation in state institutions is effective but it is exceedingly expensive. Care for part of the year in the almshouse is less expensive, but also less effective from every point of view. In an early study by Dr. C. B. Davenport, there is shown a pedigree in which a feebleminded girl is the central figure. The family history was called the "almshouse type of production of defectives," because the girl was a border line case and lived in the almshouse while bearing a child, then when able to work, left the almshouse, with her baby, in an asylum, and went out to work. Within the limits of her natural fecundity, she produced a series of illegitimate children. In this case the almshouse acted anti-eugenically, although in the case of emergency it charitably offered a home for the unfortunate girl. Modern state institutions provide for the permanent segregation [sic], and thus do not act anti-eugenically as some almshouses have done. Institutionalization, from the administrative point of view, has a great deal to learn from the practical side if it would segregate large numbers of the feeble-minded in a manner which is economically possible for the state. Perhaps the colonization of the border lines cases in a system which could produce wealth to one-half of the cost of maintenance and supervision is an ideal to work toward.

But there are limits to the possibilities of institutionalization. Eugenically, the lower level of desirable parenthood is much higher than the upper levels of possible institutionalization. It is this particular range between the upper levels of institutionalization and the lower levels of desirable parenthood which probably will be treated most successfully by the methods of eugenical sterilization. Segregation is doubtless a major factor in the solution of the problem of the feeble-minded. But the greatest menace comes from those feeble-minded persons who exist as border line individuals in free society; and who are physiologically capable of reproduction. They have proven to be reproducers of large numbers of offspring. Laws which refuse them marriage license [sic] are of no avail, because the feeble-minded, as one of the characteristics, cannot and do not obey the law in this respect. A large percentage of illegitimate children come from the border line cases of mentality. So long as a feeble-minded person is sexually capable of reproduction and is not protected by segregation in a modern institution, such an individual is a potential parent of more inadequates. Granting that segregation is a major factor is the solution of the problem, still it has been found eugenically necessary in many cases, when segregation ceases, to resort to sexual sterilization. If we state the general principle that the state must, at all hazards, prevent reproduction by the feeble-minded, especially by the moron or border line group, and if the state is making an effort to segregate the feeble-minded as completely as possible, still the provision might well be made that in case the feeble-minded individual of a definitely low level is sexually fertile and is found in the population at large, whether never having been institutionalized or about to be released from an institution, it seems sound to demand that such particular feeble-minded persons be subjected to sexual sterilization. In most such cases physiological sterility is the only safeguard against reproduction. Of course, the very lowest grades of the feeble-minded are not capable of reproduction. They receive social and medical bolstering up until natural selection eliminates them. But it is the border line group who, under a harsher civilization would be left to shift for themselves and who under the severe competition of many types of society, would be eliminated, are the greatest menace to modern society because, under the relatively easier life which modern economic and social organization affords, the border line cases are capable of existing and of reproducing their kind. A kindly social organization helps to create the menace of the feeble-minded; it should seek strenuously to remove this menace.

There is nothing inconsistent between the kindest and most effective care of the feeble-minded on the one hand, and their eugenical handling on the other. Welfare and charity demand that a person once born be given every opportunity and aid to live and to have a chance to develop and to enjoy the most that is in him. While eugenics agrees to this proposition, social welfare agencies must also agree to the eugenical principle that only those persons best endowed with superior mental, physical, and temperamental hereditary qualities should be permitted to reproduce, and thus to serve as seed-stock for the next generation.

Granted that it is necessary to supplement eugenical segregation with sexual sterilization, let us review the history of the movement and describe and evaluate its processes. Most of the cases of sexual sterilization under the present laws have been applied to the insane, although the remedy was originally and still is, most logically applicable to the feeble-minded. Twenty-three states have, up to the present time, largely through eugenical motives, created laws which provided for the sexual sterilization of certain degenerate individuals. In some of the earlier statutes there was a provision of punishment which was meant to be an especially poetic justice for certain types of sexual crimes. But experimental legislation and litigation have at last removed from the statutes all elements of punishment in the laws. Court decisions in several states have held that a sterilization statute, to benefit the individual and to improve the hereditary qualities of future generations, is a reasonable exercise of the police power of the state within the limitations of the state and federal constitutions. Thus, so far as constitutional limitations are concerned, a state may, if it desires, adopt for eugenical purposes the policy of sexual sterilization of certain natural classes of its population. I would refer particularly to two recent decisions; one by the Supreme Court of Michigan on June 18, 1925 and the second by the Supreme Court of Appeals of Virginia on November 12, 1925.

In the matter of legal procedure it seems to be the policy of the most successful laws and of the court demands that each particular case of sterilization must be ordered directly by a court of adequate jurisdiction, after due hearing which seeks to establish the facts in reference to a standard laid down by the state law, and which standard is applicable to all members of a definitely limited natural class, also described in the statutes. Eugenical sterilization is so serious a matter that it cannot be entrusted to purely administrative procedure to select and apply this particular remedy for degeneracy. The states have already had so much experience in developing laws in relation to such things as compulsory vaccination, which calls for the seizure of an individual and the application of a minor surgical operations, and in such other matters as compulsory commitment to hospitals for the insane and for the feeble-minded, that there are plenty of precedents in court procedure for use in guiding the selections of individuals for sexual sterilization. Such procedure can be rapid and effective, and it can duly protect the rights of an individual.

Surgically, the commonest form of sexual sterilization applied to the make is that of vasectomy. This is an operation which is about as serious as the extraction of a tooth. But on the other hand, the sexual sterilization of the female is much more serious. For women the simplest operation, so far as surgery has progressed up to the present time, calls for the opening of the abdominal cavity and the removal of a section of each of the fallopian tubes. To comply with surgical needs, considerable research in experimental surgery is needed. Specifically there is needed a much simpler operation for the certain sterilization of the female. The Committee on Maternal Health, of which Dr. Robert M. Dickinson is Chairman, has been conducting research along this line. The achievement of this particular development in surgical knowledge should be encouraged, and, if need be, subsidized by such societies as the present one which is devoted to the study of the feeble-minded.

There is a second study in physiology which is needed. Many of the individuals who are [sic] sexually sterilized ten or more years ago are still living. We have abstracts of their case histories up to the times of their sterilizations. These case histories should be brought down to date with the view to determining the physiological, mental, and temperamental effects upon each social type, sex, and age of persons sterilized, and classified, of course, by the type of operation. While some of the laws call for sexual sterilization for the benefit of the individual, such provisions are useless because the present laws which govern surgical practice in general permit any operation for the benefit of the individual, regardless of whether such operations may be made upon the reproductive organs, or may destroy the reproductive function. Sexual sterilization, for the benefit of the individual may or may not prove to be possible. The present indications are that it is possible, only in a few special cases, to justify the operation of sexual sterilization from the therapeutic motive. On the other hand, the indications seem to be that no physiological harm has come from the operations, although more exact data of benefit or harm must await the following up of the case histories.

The state which decides to adopt eugenical sterilization can, if it cares to, enter upon the policy very conservatively. After applying it legally and perfecting the administrative procedure and training its officers, it can widen the applicability more fully to meet the demands of protecting the state from reproduction by hereditary degenerates of all types, including the feeble-minded, especially by supplementing the custodial segregation of inadequates.

The fundamental soundness of the so-called Anglo-Saxon Bill of Rights in legal procedure is well illustrated in the matter of litigation which has followed experimental eugenical sterilization statutes. Eugenically, there is no object in sterilization for punishment. The courts were inclined to prevent sterilization as a punishment, on the grounds that it is cruel and unusual punishment. The later sterilization laws, therefore, quite consistently with the Bill of Rights, and, also, with eugenical demands, have eliminated the punitive element. Another important factor to be tried out by the law was the matter of class legislation. This fundamental principle of Anglo-Saxon law demands that the law apply with equal force to all members of the same natural class, and in defining a natural class, the law must take care not to name individuals, for such, if criminals were involved, would constitute a Bill of Attainder, nor to limit a class with boundaries artificial and unnatural. No more natural classes of the population than the feeble-minded, the criminalistic, and the insane can be found. Therefore the law in providing for the sexual sterilization of definite kinds of social inadequates, can easily locate a natural class fully within the demands of our constitutional prohibition against class legislation. But one manner in which some of the earliest sterilization laws violated the rule against class legislation was the provision for the sterilization of individuals in certain institutions. Eugenically, of course, in a modern institution, there is no object in sterilization. Only in the cacogenic individual at large is there an eugenical necessity for destroying the reproductive powers. The courts are inclined to hold it to be class legislation to require the sterilization of persons of a certain degree of degeneracy within a state institution, and not apply the same demands for the sexual sterilization of persons of the same degree of degeneracy who are found in the population at large. Thus, again, the Bill of Rights has worked hand in hand through judicial decision with the needs of eugenical progress in the application of eugenical sterilization. These decisions tend to give the American citizen more faith in the soundness of the basic principles of the common law under which he lives. . . . Supplementing these factors, eugenical sterilization is an agency which has proven to be feasible and effective from the legal, surgical, social, economic, and eugenical points of view. Practically it is beginning to fill an important place in social efforts to control hereditary degeneracy.

NOTE

This chapter is excerpted from "The Eugenical Sterilization of the Feeble-Minded," *Journal of Psycho-Asthenics* 31 (1926).

9

The Criminalization of Mental Retardation

Nicole Rafter

While people with mental retardation have been treated badly throughout history, their treatment reached a particularly low point in the late nineteenth century, when policy makers claimed that all mentally retarded people are by nature potential criminals.[1] It was no coincidence that this happened at the start of the U.S. eugenics movement, the widespread effort to improve American "stock" by encouraging socially useful people to reproduce and preventing the reproduction of those who seemed born to create social problems.[2] This chapter focuses on that pivotal point, about 1880, when the treatment of the "feebleminded" (as persons with mental retardation were then called) went from bad to worse. By necessity, it also focuses on the origins of the U.S. eugenics movement and the establishment of the first U.S. eugenic institution, for these phenomena are inseparable.

In what follows, I begin with biographical information on Josephine Shaw Lowell, the person who led the first U.S. eugenics campaign against the feebleminded, and then I trace the origins of Lowell's eugenic ideas. The next section follows the steps Lowell took to establish the Newark (New York) Custodial Asylum for Feeble-Minded Women; it is followed by a section that asks whether the institution realized Lowell's goals. In conclusion, I suggest why this first eugenic institution aimed at preventing reproduction by women, in particular, and also offer some answers to the question of why this institution and the early eugenics literature in the United States focused on the reproductive dangers of, not the immigrants and people of color whom later eugenicists identified as reproductive menaces, but native-born white people.

Leader of the Criminalization Campaign

Josephine Shaw Lowell, the standard-bearer of New York's campaign against the feebleminded, was one of the towering figures in nineteenth-century philanthropy. Lowell was still in her early thirties when, in 1876, New York's governor appointed her to the State Board of Charities (SBC), the agency responsible for coping with the state's welfare problems. Already well known in welfare work, Lowell now became the charity board's first female commissioner.

Lowell's personal history made her a heroic figure. During the Civil War, her brother, Robert Gould Shaw, had died in battle at Fort Wagner, commanding the Union army's first black regiment. Not long afterward, the war claimed Lowell's young husband, Colonel Charles Russell Lowell, leaving her pregnant with the daughter she bore a month later. Personal fortitude, a family tradition of social activism, and a comfortable income enabled Lowell to transcend these blows and become a pivotal figure in philanthropy, which she helped to transform from the unsystematic benevolence of the mid-nineteenth century into the professionalized charity of the early twentieth century. Lowell aimed at streamlining social welfare systems and tightening their control over deviants. Under her guidance, charity management began to incorporate the findings of the new social sciences, thus becoming more "scientific."[3] Lowell's first major accomplishment on the charity board was to define feebleminded women as a biological threat to society—what later generations would call "born" criminals.

Most of Lowell's biographers have minimized or entirely ignored her involvement with eugenics, perhaps because eugenics did not become an organized social movement until just before her death in 1905. Lowell nevertheless did help to validate eugenics reasoning by sowing fears of the promiscuous feeble-minded woman, a stereotype that became the propaganda centerpiece of subsequent eugenics campaigns.

The Roots of Lowell's Eugenical Ideas

Lowell's view of the feeble-minded woman as "depraved in body and mind"[4] built on the concept of degeneration, a set of beliefs that, although nearly forgotten today, nonetheless deeply influenced turn-of-the-century thinking about the nature of social problems.[5] (Indeed, if we do not understand what "degeneracy" meant to nineteenth- and early-twentieth-century writers, their commentaries on social problems will seem silly or incomprehensible. Once the concept is grasped, however, the meaning of those observations becomes clear and logical.) Roughly synonymous with "bad heredity" and conceived as an invisible attribute of the "germ plasm" or "blood," degeneration was pictured as a tendency to devolve to a lower, simpler, less civilized state. Nineteenth-century theorists taught that the downward spiral into degeneration could be brought on by immorality (drinking, gluttony, or sexual excess) and that, if sustained, it could damage the germ plasm. Thus, future generations could inherit the degenerative tendency. However, whereas bad living could induce degeneration, clean living might reverse the process: in a few generations, a family that carefully avoided vice might restore itself to normality.

This nineteenth-century view of degeneration as protean and mutable, heritable but nonetheless susceptible to environmental influences, encouraged theorists to conceive of social problems such as insanity, poverty, intemperance, and criminality as interrelated and interchangeable, mere symptoms of the underlying degeneration. For example, one of Lowell's contemporaries wrote that intemperance and poor heredity were "so inextricably mixed, so interdependent," that intemperance could lead to "vice, crime, insanity, idiocy, pauperism, not confined to the one intemperate generation, but handed down to children and children's children, perhaps in an inverse order, pauperism, idiocy, insanity, crime, intemperance."[6] Conceiving social problems to be heritable and interchangeable, Lowell and other degenerationists naturally looked for connections among the feebleminded and other problem groups such as criminals and paupers.

Nineteenth-century thinking about evolution reinforced the degenerationist association of socially problematic behaviors with reversion to a lower form of life. Charles Darwin's *Origin of Species* (1859) seemed to depict a titanic, ubiquitous struggle between primitive and complex organisms. In *The Descent of Man* (1871), Darwin explained that evolution creates hierarchies of intelligence, morality, and other human characteristics. "The several mental and moral faculties of man have been gradually evolved," he wrote, so that "we may trace a perfect gradation from the mind of an utter idiot, lower than that of an animal low in the scale, to the mind of a Newton."[7] Herbert Spencer and other so-called social Darwinists advised that socially problematic groups should be left to die out, like inferior species. "Under the natural order of things," Spencer wrote, "society is constantly excreting its un-healthy, imbecile, slow, vacillating, faithless members"; to aid the unfit would merely thwart this "purifying process" of extinction.[8] Lowell did not go so far as to suggest abandoning the unfit to die, but her view of feeble-minded women as social refuse certainly echoes the teachings of Spencer and other prominent evolutionists.

Lowell's eugenicism also drew on a reputable scientific tradition. As early as 1621, in *The Anatomy of Melancholy,* the English scholar Robert Burton wrote that parents could cause insanity "by Propagation." Citing biblical and classical sources for the idea that "like begets like," Burton stated that melancholy "is an hereditary disease," a madness passed from parent to child. Anticipating nineteenth-century degenerationists, Burton held that environmental influences can affect heredity and that bad heredity can man-ifest itself in a variety of weaknesses. "If a drunken man get a childe, it will never likely have a good braine," Burton explained, also predicting that "foolish, drunken, or haire-braine women, most part bring forth children like unto themselves." Burton concluded this passage of his famous treatise on a eugenical note, remarking that "it were happy for humane kinde, if only such parents as are sound of body and minde, should be suffered to marry."[9] Darwin gave similar eugenic advice in *The Descent of Man,* recom-mending that "both sexes ought to refrain from marriage if they are in any marked degree inferior in body or mind."[10] Lowell was one of the first Amer-icans openly to support involuntary eugenic measures, but she was not alone. At a meeting where she advocated reproductive controls on feeble-minded women, an Iowa physician argued that "the state should prohibit the marriage of all persons who had, at any time after arriving at the age of eighteen years, been supported in any penal or charitable institution, or who are suffering from any incurable bodily infirmity or deformity."[11] Degenera-tionists had reached the sobering conclusion that society was a kind of body, a network in which a diseased member could infect the whole. Eugenics—what Lowell called "extinction of the line"[12]—seemed to be the best way to deal with those who were biologically, morally, and socially diseased.

By far the most influential American degenerationist was Richard L. Dug-dale, author of *"The Jukes": A Study in Crime, Pauperism, Disease and Heredity* (1877). A New York City businessman, Dugdale was keenly interested in so-cial welfare problems, a concern that led him to become one of the nation's first social scientists. He published the initial version of his "Jukes" master-piece just before Lowell joined New York's charity board.[13] This horrific study of a rural clan that (Dugdale estimated) had over seven generations produced 1,200 bastards, beggars, murderers, prostitutes, thieves, and syphilitics became an immediate best-seller, and "Jukes" became a synonym for degeneration on both sides of the Atlantic.

"*The Jukes*" gave the nascent eugenics movement a central, confirmational image, that of the inbreeding, rural family dwelling in "log huts and hovels, . . . hot beds where human maggots are spawned."[14] Dugdale's tract became famous partly because its complex charts and statistics seemed scientific and partly because its language is evocative and vaguely titillating. Above all, however, it succeeded because it provided reformers like Lowell with genealogical proof of what they had come to suspect about bad heredity.[15]

Although Dugdale cautioned against hasty conclusions, his book was widely read as proof of heredity's dominance over environment. This interpretation was fostered by Dugdale's use of hereditarian terminology ("criminal stock," "Juke blood," "reversion"). Nor was it entirely a misinterpretation, for Dugdale's genealogical method *assumed* that the various Juke sins might be at least partially hereditary, symptoms of the more fundamental malaise of "degeneration." Conceptualizing criminality, idiocy, and so on as signs of a shared, underlying affliction, he considered them to be interchangeable; thus "disease in the parent will produce idiocy in the child"; thus "prostitution in the women is the analogue of crime and pauperism in the males"; thus "the crime of one generation may lay the foundation for the pauperism of the next." Dugdale's methodology—the questions he asked about the Jukes—drew on degeneration theory ("Does this person represent a family or near kinsfolk who have been accused of the same or similar offenses? . . . Is epilepsy . . . or any mark of hereditary insanity, known to exist . . . in . . . the father, mother, sister, brother, uncles, aunts, grandfather, or grandmother?"). Predictably, his methodology also confirmed degeneration theory, providing apparent proof that, for example, a feeble-minded woman could produce criminals and paupers.[16]

"*The Jukes*" profoundly impressed Lowell and her fellow commissioners. When it appeared, the SBC was in the midst of a poverty crisis. In retrospect, one can see that social factors such as the demobilization of Civil War soldiers and a severe financial depression were escalating poverty in the 1870s. Policy makers who had to cope with the spread of poverty tended to blame the poor themselves, however, as their term "pauperism" suggests. Unlike "poverty," "pauperism" refers to an ingrained condition, that of being impoverished. It connotes blameworthiness and something close to somatic inferiority. Midcentury hopes of restoring deviants to normalcy had withered; "heredity" was becoming a way to explain both the ailments of the poor and policy makers' failures to cure them. Better record-keeping and the centralization of deviant populations, moreover, now made it easier to investigate family backgrounds, increasing the probability of detecting deviant ancestors.

In a massive study, "The Causes of Pauperism," released just as Lowell joined the SBC, board secretary Charles S. Hoyt concluded that "the number of persons in our poor-houses who have been reduced to poverty by causes outside of their own acts is . . . surprisingly small." Like Dugdale, Hoyt began with hereditarian assumptions and reached hereditarian conclusions: "The element of heredity enters so largely in the problem of pauperism that it should receive special attention. . . . There is a large number of families throughout the State . . . the sole end of whose existence seems to be the rearing of children like themselves." Hoyt, too, assumed that the various forms of degeneration were interrelated; paupers, for example, were "feeble minded."[17]

Lowell thus joined an agency deeply troubled by pauperism and primed to accept the proposition that feeble-minded women could be one of its sources.

The Criminalization Campaign

Receptive though other charity board members seem to have been, the legislature and the general public were unlikely to embrace a proposal for something as radical and untried as a eugenic institution. Moreover, even though Lowell's SBC associates worried about the apparent fecundity of feeble-minded women, these men originally planned to provide noncoercive custodial care for mentally retarded adults of both sexes, with no age limit.[18] Lowell had to persuade them to focus more narrowly on fertile women and to establish for this group an asylum combining the noncoercive models of sheltering home and hospital with that of the prison.

Defining the Problem

For decades, inspectors had been complaining that some poorhouse inmates were weak-minded women with numerous children. They depicted these women as doubly deviant: defective (mentally retarded) and dependent (unable to support themselves). Adding a third measure of deviance, Lowell further defined feeble-minded women as "depraved" or criminalistic, a step she accomplished in a series of talks she gave in 1878 and 1879. She called for two new women's institutions, a reformatory prison for those who might be salvageable and a custodial asylum for the feebleminded, who by definition were not. But she did not in fact clearly distinguish among the forms of degeneration:

> Reformatories are needed for women who are now almost constantly inmates of public institutions, whether jails, penitentiaries or poor-houses, and who perpetuate the classes of criminals and paupers, themselves belonging alternatively to both. . . . They are constantly sinking deeper and deeper into the abyss of vice and crime . . . and are, moreover, . . . producing children who are almost sure to inherit their evil tendencies. These women are the same individuals whether they be committed to jails and penitentiaries as criminals or to poor-houses as vagrants and paupers.[19]

Criminality, pauperism, and "evil" heredity could not be separated.

To launch her campaign, Lowell recited horror stories that would galvanize her audience. Drawing from Hoyt's pauperism report, she quoted passages that seemed to prove that "one of the most important and most dangerous causes of the increase of crime, pauperism, and insanity, is the unrestrained liberty allowed to vagrant and degraded women":[20]

> "In the Albany County poorhouse, a single woman, forty years old, . . . the mother of seven illegitimate children; the woman degraded and debased, and soon again to become a mother. . . .
>
> "In the Essex County poorhouse, a . . . widowed woman, twenty-four years old, and two children aged respectively four and five years, both illegitimate and feeble-minded and born in the poorhouse, the latter being a mulatto."[21]

For another horror story, Lowell turned to *"The Jukes"*: "Mr. Dugdale has computed that in seventy-five years the descendants of five vicious pauper sisters amounted to twelve hundred persons, and had cost the State of New York more than one million and a quarter dollars."[22] In Dugdale's version, the Juke family tree is headed by a sire, Max Juke; in Lowell's version, degeneration flows from Max's five daughters.

To make her institutional solution to the problem seem to be inevitable, Lowell employed strategies that the sociologist Joel Best calls the "rhetoric of rectitude" and the "rhetoric of "rationality.""[23] She simultaneously argued that helpless women must be protected against wickedness (her appeal to rectitude) and that society must protect itself against such wicked women (her appeal to rationality). This double-pronged appeal enabled Lowell's audience to rationalize eugenic institutionalization as an act of kindness, and it led directly to Lowell's conclusion that an asylum was absolutely necessary:

> What right have we to-day to allow men and women who are diseased and vicious to reproduce their kind, and bring into the world beings whose existence must be one long misery to themselves and others?[24]

> Shall the State of New York suffer a moral leprosy to spread and taint her future generations, because she lacks the courage to set apart those [feebleminded women] who have inherited the deadly poison and who will hand it down to their children, even to the third and fourth generations?[25]

Linking dependency, defectiveness, delinquency, and degenerate heredity, Lowell fashioned the image of the weak-minded mother of criminals.

Establishing the Institution

To establish the asylum, Lowell needed the support of four groups: the SBC; officials of New York's older asylum for the retarded, the Syracuse Asylum for Idiots; New York's legislature; and leaders in the village of Newark, where the new institution was to be located. The first group, the charities board, apparently gave her no trouble at all, for just four days after Lowell made her initial presentation on the problem, Charles S. Hoyt, the SBC secretary, was arranging for her to meet with officials of the Syracuse Asylum for Idiots to work out details for the new institution.[26] In all likelihood, Lowell had spoken with her fellow commissioners informally before starting her public campaign, assuring herself of their backing.

Lowell's next alliance, with Dr. Hervey B. Wilbur, superintendent of the Syracuse Asylum, was potentially much more difficult. Wilbur, since the mid-nineteenth century a national champion for persons with retardation, had long argued that special education within institutional settings might cure, or at least considerably alleviate, the problem of mental disability. However, when Lowell turned to Wilbur for help, he, his Syracuse Asylum, and the national's entire system of institutions for the mentally retarded were at a point of a painful transition, for they were having to shift their mission from cure to custody. As Wilbur was well aware, a decade earlier, New York State had opened a second institution for the insane, a custodial asylum for chronic cases to supplement the more treatment-oriented insane asylum at Utica. Now Wilbur had to admit that the mental retardation system, too, needed a second, custodial asylum, this one to shelter Syracuse's "graduates" and other homeless adults with retardation. Thus, he agreed to support Lowell's plan.[27]

However, Wilbur and his trustees—the second group whose support Lowell needed to proceed—disputed every aspect of her proposal aside from its custodial thrust. They projected plans for a noncoercive institution combining the models of hospital and home where relatively able feeble-minded people could care for invalids. Moreover, they wanted the new institution to receive both men and women, and they opposed Lowell's eugenic motives. As a result, when an SBC delegation led by Lowell met with Wilbur and his trustees to formulate plans, both parties had to compromise. They jointly decided that the new asylum should open only on an experimental basis and under the supervision of the Syracuse institution.[28]

Lowell dealt next with the legislature, from which she needed funding. Making the best of the Syracuse officials' resistance, she found a way to avoid confrontation with this third group: an experimental institution could be established without legislation and therefore without discussion of its eugenic purpose. Lowell arranged for an appropriation of $18,000 to be inserted in the state's 1878 supply bill.[29] The Newark Custodial Asylum was founded in one sentence as a line item.[30] The Syracuse subcommittee members maintained silence about the institution's eugenic goal, tersely noting only that "the motives which prompted the conference [with Lowell's delegation] need not here be mentioned."[31] Resisting pressure from the charity board, they refused to make the asylum permanent immediately because they were not convinced that it would defeat "the evil [feeblemindedness] it was designed to meet" and because "the public" (like themselves) did not yet "appreciate" its necessity.[32]

Property owners in the village of Newark, fifty miles west of Syracuse, contacted Wilbur with an attractive offer: he could locate the new asylum in their uninhabited religious academy, rent-free, if the state would refurbish the building. In haste to lease what he thought would be temporary quarters, Wilbur disregarded the site's small size and inadequate water supply. A former poorhouse superintendent was hired to manage daily operations, and thus opened, in 1878, the Custodial Asylum for Feeble-Minded Women.

Wilbur and his board continued to resist Lowell's "partial and narrow" definition of the feeble-minded woman as a eugenic menace.[33] Describing himself as "not very zealous" about the new asylum, Wilbur argued that idiots (as he preferred to term persons with mental retardation) seldom reproduce, that there were in fact "few imbecile and idiotic females in the county poor-houses," and that the asylum "offer[ed] a sort of premium upon the mismanagement of county poor-houses" that permitted sexual contact among residents.[34] His trustees, unenthusiastic about managing an institution located two counties away on an unsuitable site, refused opportunities to buy the property cheaply. After Wilbur's death in 1883, they decided to terminate the trial program by transferring Newark's inmates to a new Syracuse dormitory built specially for them.[35]

The eugenic experiment would have collapsed at that point had New York's state legislature not suddenly made Newark an independent, permanent institution with its own board. Although the local residents who ensured the institution's survival repeated Lowell's eugenical claims, there is no evidence that this fourth group of supporters had much interest in eugenics. It is clear, however, that they profited from the institution's presence in their town and from its expansion, which they actively promoted.[36]

Learning of the plan to close Newark, two local state assemblymen, Silas S. Pierson (or Peirson, as his name is also spelled in the records) and Edwin K. Burnham, led Wayne County (pro-Newark) in a legislative battle with Onondaga County (pro-Syracuse) over the institution's location.[37] After calling for Lowell's help in lobbying the state senate, Wayne County's forces triumphed. Ties with the Syracuse Asylum were severed, and for the next eight years Newark was run as a fiefdom by Pierson, as president of its board; Burnham, as its secretary; and Eliza C. Perkins, the wife of Pierson's banking partner, as treasurer.[38]

Pierson and the Perkinses sold land to the institutions; the deeds were authorized by Burnham, Wayne County's notary public.[39] Treasurer Perkins disbursed funds to the firm of Pierson and Perkins[40] and to her husband, whom she hired to landscape the asylum. Other town residents also sold property to the expanding institution, worked at it, and received contracts to provision it; they would have been indebted to the officials who had secured the asylum for their village and who were closely involved in its management. Indeed, the asylum may have been the small town's most profitable venture. Pierson and Perkins resigned when investigations in 1893 and 1894 uncovered their financial misdoings and other officials' cruelty to inmates.[41] Burnham stayed on, however, replacing Perkins as treasurer and, as the institution's receipts show, continuing to write checks to Pierson's relatives.[42]

The Custodial Asylum in Operation

To drum up business for "the Custodial" (as the asylum was locally known), trustees attended the annual conventions of poorhouse superintendents, warning of the dangers of feeble-minded women and soliciting transfers. Pierson, for example, assured the poorhouse managers that each had the "right to a certain amount of room" at the Custodial, which, having expanded to forty acres, could accommodate another 1,000 to 1,200 women.[43] These public relation efforts produced a steady flow of inmates, stimulating growth.

During the few years of life that remained to him after Newark opened, Dr. Wilbur, too, dutifully funneled inmates into it. Cognizant as he always was of his responsibilities, no matter how unpleasant, he sent every poorhouse superintendent a brochure outlining the new institution's twofold purpose: Newark would provide custodial care for "unteachable idiots" and Syracuse graduates (his own aim), and it would prevent "imbecile and idiotic females" from giving "birth to illegitimate children" by providing protection "from the dangers to which their want of intelligence exposes them" (Lowell's goal). "Young and healthy" women, the brochure announced, would receive preference.[44] Lowell joined the search for women who could be committed to the institution. Making sure her SBC colleagues had copies of Wilbur's circular, she asked that each, "when he visits poorhouses . . . [,] enquire especially if there are any young girls or women

242

who should go to the Asylum and if he finds any, . . . have them transferred." She herself wrote numerous letters to ensure action on potential commitments.[45]

What sorts of women were committed to the Custodial? As of September 30, 1900, the asylum held 414 inmates, nearly all of whom had been delivered directly from poorhouses; thus, they were indeed the paupers whose reproduction Lowell hoped to staunch. Most were also, as the rules required, "of a child-bearing age,"[46] usually defined as years fifteen to forty-five, although this was often stretched at both ends of the scale. Some suffered from severe mental defects, but the majority seem to have been only mildly retarded. Many worked within the institution, some operating sewing machines on which they produced clothing and other institutional supplies. A few were probably not retarded at all by today's standards but considered so at the time because of the almost automatic equation of female sexuality with mental subnormality.[47] Other inmates were the insane or otherwise difficult women whom poorhouse superintendents sometimes managed to dump at Newark.[48]

Even by the loose criteria of the time, few Custodial inmates lived up to their reputation as fountainheads of vice and illegitimacy. According to the highest estimate given in an annual report, no more than half had ever borne children, in or out of wedlock; other reports set the figure at 25 percent. Judging from an 1898 study of 500 evidently consecutive commitments, the actual rate may have been under 5 percent. The author of this study, the physical anthropologist Aleš Hrdlička, was not without his biases (he wrote that "the adult female imbecile is almost as a rule, more or less of a sexual libertine"), yet he found that only 18 of the 500 "had children, 5 as married and 13 as unmarried." Of these children, only 4 were reported feebleminded. But Hrdlicka felt that his data sorely underreported the problem and concluded that "society . . . should make most strenuous efforts to hinder similar untoward production."[49] His report reinforced the feeble-minded woman's sluttish image.

Reports on the Custodial regularly included a paragraph or two of official language on the dangers of feeble-minded women. For example, one claimed that "most" of the inmates were "of depraved origin . . . with a hereditary bias to go astray."[50] Other asylum records stressed the inmates' "monster evil" and "abnormal animal passion." The institution's trustees boasted that by 1890 it "had already prevented the illegitimate birth of from one to two thousand feeble-minded children."[51]

Because the Custodial's bylaws did not provide for involuntary commitments, one might ask why inmates did not simply leave. Probably many remained because they had no alternative place to live and no one on the outside to rescue them. Mentally disabled to some degree, the majority lacked the personal resources to make other arrangements and perhaps mistrusted their own ability to cope in the outside world. In addition, officials made departure difficult. The Custodial was fenced, and, until the turn of the century, inmates were seldom allowed to leave their buildings even under supervision. Thus, for some, commitment was unquestionably involuntary.[52] For others, Newark may have provided a relatively good home.

That the asylum provided a much-needed service for some inmates is suggested by a letter of 1894 from Mrs. Elizabeth Goodings to SBC secretary Charles Hoyt begging him not to discharge her daughter. Mrs. Goodings dictated this letter to explain that Emily, placed at Newark many years earlier by Dr. Wilbur, was now about to be released "as she had passed the child-bearing age."

> The facts of the case are these: I am totally without income (77 years of age) and dependent upon my soninlaw [sic]. . . . He will not be willing to receive Emily into his home. . . . It would break my heart if my oldest child should be obliged to go to a county house or insane asylum. . . . Does it not seem cruel to throw these children back into the condition from which you have taken them . . . [?] With the exception that they cannot propogate [sic] their kind, will not their last condition be as sad as their first[?][53]

This letter shows that relatives were aware of the Custodial's eugenic purpose, that Emily was mentally disabled in her family's estimation, and that Newark provided help to impoverished but caring parents who simply could not cope with feeble-minded offspring. Studies of other nineteenth-century institutions have similarly found that impoverished families committed relatives because they had no alternatives.[54] For the destitute and the desperate, even repressive institutions might provide havens.

The Custodial's eugenical purpose shaped admission and discharge policies in at least three ways. The asylum apparently received a few women who were normal (or nearly so) because they were sexually active. At the same time, it resisted the commitment of "unteachable" cases—the most obvious candidates for custodial care—perhaps because they appeared to be infertile. In addition, the asylum often discharged those who, like Emily, had "passed the child-bearing age," ejecting older women who no longer posed a eugenic threat.

We do in fact have a "control" group to help us further gauge the impact of Lowell's eugenic mission. As noted previously, in the early 1880s the Syracuse asylum's trustees erected a building for inmates of the Custodial, which they hoped to shut. When Newark gained independence, the Syracuse building became a residence for young female graduates of the training school, comparable to Newark's commitments. Although Syracuse became more custodial at this time, it never operated as cheaply as Newark, and its inmates received a higher level of care. They were not abruptly discharged at menopause, nor is there any evidence that they experienced the punitive treatment to which Custodial inmates were sometimes subjected. And they were not closely confined. In a letter of 1885, Wilbur's successor as superintendent at Syracuse described his strenuous efforts to find a new home for a woman of twenty, committed "7 or 8 years ago as a private pupil" but now deserted by her family.[55] Syracuse was attempting to discharge a member of the very group that Newark wanted to lock up for eugenic reasons.

Conditions at the Custodial were worse than those at some poorhouses. Impure water and inadequate sewage were constant problems and, according to the institution's physician, a cause of illness. Inmates sickened and died from typhoid, cholera, and malaria. Lacking a separate hospital, the asylum could not isolate ill patients or others stricken by epidemics of flu or measles. C. C. Warner, the first overseer, performed some minor surgery himself.[56] The local resident who succeeded him, Langdon Willett, was eventually fired for cruelty to inmates. The state's miserliness toward these women, and the managers' determination to hold operating costs to poorhouse levels, meant that overcrowding and fire hazards were addressed at a dangerously slow pace. Until 1894 there were no pictures on the walls and no opportunities whatsoever for outdoor exercise. Existence must have been monotonous and bleak at this institution, where already unfortunate women were denied liberty so that they could not bear children.

Some improvements occurred after 1893, when Custodial mismanagement prompted two SBC investigations. The first inquiry "fully and clearly showed that the superintendent, matron and first assistant matron had each of them repeatedly inflicted corporal punishment upon the defenseless inmates under their care, and that such punishments had frequently been of grossly cruel and inhuman character."[57] Two inmates so punished "were patients in the hospital with acute diseases, both of whom died soon thereafter, and . . . a number thus punished were insane." The superintendent, it came out, "practices a unique form of punishment upon the patients, by tripping them from behind and letting them fall on their backs."[58] On one occasion, the matron and her assistant, before beating a Mary Moore "with a ferule, had put the inmate in a straitjacket, tied her feet together, and stuffed her mouth with a towel."[59] The three principals in this scandal were dismissed. The doctor was retained, however, even though she, too, came under a cloud for having punished sick inmates.

The second investigation, triggered late in 1893 by "some charges made to the Governor against the . . . Custodial Asylum,"[60] led to the shakeup of the board mentioned earlier. Insane women were shipped elsewhere, as were "a number of helpless bed-ridden cases and cases of advanced age, no longer needing its [the asylum's] protecting care"; the new superintendent reported that he "rarely" needed to resort to restraints.[61] By the century's end, the water was drinkable, although it was still inadequate to quell a fire. Inmates were occasionally taken on outings. For better or worse, they were now encouraged to celebrate Children's Day.

Why Women?

The Newark Custodial Asylum criminalized a condition, that of carrying bad heredity. This was evidently the first time in U.S. history that the body itself was criminalized. Previously only prohibited acts could be punished; now the category of punishable phenomena expanded to include a condition, the state of degeneration. A new concept of dangerousness was emerging in which the thing to be feared was not harms but individuals.[62]

Why was the first stage of eugenic criminology marked by new iconography of the Bad Woman, rather than the Bad Man (or both), and by the establishment of an institution to prevent female but not male reproduction? Answers to this question lie in the social context in which the asylum at Newark was founded and in Lowell's personal situation.[63]

The Social Context

Women's roles underwent dramatic shifts in the late nineteenth century. Middle-class women like Lowell entered the public sphere to work for reforms in the treatment of disenfranchised groups such as other women, children, and the feebleminded. Simultaneously, working-class women moved into the paid labor force and grew socially independent.[64] These transformations set off a punitive reaction to female independence and sexuality, much as they precipitated slightly later clampdowns on prostitution.

New York's charity board commissioners and other middle-class reformers struggled against the erosion of traditional standards of propriety. The nineteenth-century trend toward sexual repression accelerated about 1870, moving from what the historian Charles Rosenberg calls "the level of individual exhortation to that of organized efforts to enforce chastity upon the unwilling."[65] Although the purity crusades against abortion, illegitimacy, masturbation, prostitution, and so on did not ignore men, they stressed control of women's sexuality.[66] Moreover, women who did not fit the mold of the True Woman were now castigated as sexually and morally unnatural.[67] Middle-class women who undertook charity work did not escape such charges, but working-class women were at even greater risk. And women who ended up in poorhouses, especially if they had children of indeterminate origin, were particularly likely to become lightening rods for turn-of-the-century sexual and gender anxieties.[68]

Lowell's campaign, conducted in this context of role disturbances, reaffirmed traditional biological beliefs about gender. Her call for an institution that would protect infirm women against "degrading influences"[69] flowed from the tenet that women are naturally weaker than men. Feeble-minded women, according to this line of reasoning, are especially weak, an extreme version of the biologically helpless female. Lowell's call for the protection of society against feeble-minded women followed from the conviction that women are more responsible than men for the health of their progeny. This conviction was partly an artifact of hereditarian methodologies: genealogists of degeneration found it easier to identify their subjects' mothers than fathers—thus, women headed most branches of the Juke family tree.[70] In addition, the belief that women determine future generations' biological well-being was deeply rooted in nineteenth-century culture and reiterated in many contexts other than that in which Lowell worked.[71] Eugenic imagery of degenerate women was congruent with and actually close to familiar beliefs about the nature of all women. The stereotype of the feeble-minded woman came into focus before that of the feeble-minded man in part because the former was nearer to hand.

Lowell's campaign paralleled other social crusades of its day. Middle-class women participated heavily in these crusades, which often also aimed at sexual purity. Moreover, interest in eugenics was widespread among late-nineteenth-century feminists, who drew on the doctrine to exalt women and justify female control of conception.[72] Whereas other feminists used eugenics arguments to emancipate "worthy" women, however, Lowell used them to incapacitate the unfit.

In a period when poor women were gaining some economic and sexual autonomy, Lowell's campaign extended state control over such women on the ground that their bodies posed a moral, medical, and social danger. The possibility that poor women might use their bodies unconventionally threatened the biological understanding of gender as fixed and immutable. Newark's creation signified a new stage in governmental management of bodies that, if independent, appeared likely to become problematic and "chaotic."[73] It affirmed the view of the unregulated female body as immoral, diseased, irrational, or mindless.[74]

In addition, Lowell's campaign quasi-legally confirmed the double standard of sexual morality. The double standard, as analyzed by the law professor Frances Olsen, consists of two ideas: the notion that "non-marital sex . . . separated from emotional commitment . . . is . . . desirable for men but devaluing for women" and the categorization of women as "moral or immoral, good girls or bad girls, virgins or whores."[75] The Custodial Asylum, founded amid challenges to the double standard, punished (only) women for extra-marital sex and reinforced the virgin/whore dichotomy. It also legitimated a correlate of the double standard, the belief that women need special protection, by picturing these particular bad women as incapable of informed sexual consent, driven to fornication by degenerate biology or tricked into it by predatory men. Out-of-wedlock pregnancy in poor women (or even its possibility) became synonymous with feeblemindedness.

Lowell's Personal Situation

Lowell's own circumstances probably contributed to the gender specificity of her campaign. Her charity board colleagues would have assumed that, like other middle-class women engaged in philanthropic endeavors, Lowell would concentrate on the problems of women, children, and other groups associated with the female "sphere." To be an effective commissioner, however, Lowell would have had not only to confirm this assumption but also to establish herself as her male colleagues' equal in other areas. Furthermore, Lowell herself was something of a deviant. Like the feeble-minded woman whom she sought to bring under control, Lowell was a single mother. Moreover, instead of withdrawing into widowhood, she entered the male world of social reform. Her power did not derive from a man, and she was neither subservient nor accommodating. (Indeed, her correspondence as an SBC commissioner shows that she issued orders with regal authority.)[76] A public figure, she risked the charges of "unnaturalness" to which independent women were exposed.

Lowell's campaign—one of her first acts as a commissioner—accomplished several ends. Designating feeble-minded women as unfit, it confirmed her own membership among the fit and thus among "true" women. There could be no doubt that, despite her unorthodox personal circumstances, she was normal and good. The campaign established her authority on women's issues while at the same time it showed the other commissioners a hard-headed way to cope with their most pressing problem, hereditary pauperism.

The White Other

Late-nineteenth-century diatribes against the feebleminded introduced a discourse on the dangers of what the sociologist Ruth Frankenberg, in a different context, calls the "white Other."[77] Lowell's degenerate was neither black nor foreign-born; she was native-born, rural, impoverished, and white. This is not what the secondary literature on the U.S. eugenics movement, which emphasizes campaigns against native blacks and swarthy Europeans, would lead us to expect.[78] Nonetheless, in the criminological context, what eugenicists spoke of with greatest alarm was the degeneration of poor whites.

These particular eugenicists focused on the culture of rural poverty, defining it as marginal, inferior to their own. In so doing, they established themselves as a group entitled to scrutinize others, evaluate them, and, if necessary, imprison them.[79] Much as the white authors of racial and colonial discourses were what Frankenberg calls "the nondefined definers," so too those who produced eugenic criminology assumed and demonstrated their own normalcy by portraying the white Other as different.

The distinction between good and bad whites formed one of the main binaries of eugenic criminology. From one perspective, eugenics was primarily a way of organizing social control around a set of opposites. "Intelligence," for example, became a caste mark, with "good" intelligence signifying the law-abiding middle class and weak-mindedness indicating the degenerate. Previously, the cultural field had not been so deeply split by dualisms. After the 1880s, however, criminological tracts devoted themselves to establishing polarities. In this cosmography, the polar opposite of all that was civic-minded and socially valuable was the feeble-minded woman. The Newark Custodial Asylum, in both its founding and its operation, confirmed this opposition.

NOTES

1. Earlier versions of this chapter appeared as Chap. 2 in Rafter 1997 and as Rafter 1992a.

2. Similar developments occurred at about the same time in England and, with more variation, in other countries as well.

3. On Lowell's role in the development of state welfare, see Beatty 1986; de Forest et al. 1905; Lane 1973; Saveth 1980; Stewart 1911; and Taylor 1963.

4. Lowell 1879a: 193.

5. European versions of degeneration theory have attracted more attention than have those of the United States. On the concept, see Chamberlin and Gilman 1985; Dowbiggin; 1991; Nye 1984; Pick 1989; Rafter 1988; Rafter 1992b; Sarason and Doris 1969; and Walter 1956.

6. Reynolds 1879: 211. For other examples, see Henderson 1893; U.S. Dept. of the Interior 1883; and Wines 1888.

7. Darwin [1871] 1986: 495.

8. Spencer, *Social Statistics* (1851), 323–324, as quoted and cited in Sarason and Doris 1969: 225.

9. Burton [1621] 1989: 207, 209.

10. Darwin [1871] 1986: 918. On the next page Darwin approvingly refers to the view of his cousin, the eugenicist Francis Galton, that "if the prudent avoid marriage, whilst the reckless marry, the inferior members tend to supplant the better members of society."

11. Reynolds 1879: 214 Reynolds presented this paper at the same conference where Lowell's paper "One Means of Preventing Pauperism" (1879a) was read.

12. Lowell 1879a: 199.

13. Dugdale 1874.

14. Dugdale 1877: 54.

15. For a more detailed account of the appeal and impact of "The Jukes," see Rafter 1988: introduction. As Dugdale himself explains, "The Jukes" consisted of many families with many different names. His genealogical methodology may have been inspired by *Heredity Genius,* in which Galton ([1869] 1952: v) devised a family-tree type of notation to trace the offspring of "four hundred illustrious men." Dugdale's genius lay in applying this method to bad families. The charting of bad families became one of the major techniques of eugenics research.

16. Dugdale 1877: 50, 24, 45. Dugdale's schedule of "Points of Inquiry" appears in Dugdale 1874: 127–128.

17. Hoyt 1876: 288, 289; for his "Schedule of Inquiries, see pp. 294–295.

18. New York State Board of Charities, *Annual Report, 1876,* p. 15.

19. Lowell 1879b: 173.

20. Lowell 1879a: 189.

21. Lowell 1879a: 189–190.

22. Ibid., 196–197.

23. Best 1987: 116.

24. Lowell 1879a: 193.

25. Ibid., 199–200.

26. New York State Archives, State Board of Charities, correspondence 1867–1902: vol. 8, pp. 14, 21. The sequence of steps in Lowell's campaign can be pieced together from information in Stewart 1911 and Devine 1905.

27. New York State Asylum for Idiots, *Annual Report, 1878,* pp. 2–3, 6. For an overview of the development of the mental retardation system in the nineteenth century, see Trent 1994.

28. Ibid., 7.

29. New York State Board of Charities, *Annual Report, 1878,* p. 283; New York State Board of Charities, *Annual Report, 1879,* p. 122. Correspondence makes it clear that Lowell arranged the appropriation; see New York State Archives, State Board of Charities, correspondence 1867–1902: vol. 8, pp. 120, 121, 137.

30. The hint of sneakiness indicates a lack of public support for eugenic measures at this point in time.

31. New York State Board of Charities, *Annual Report, 1878,* p. 283.

32. New York State Asylum for Idiots, *Annual Report, 1879,* p. 13.

33. Wilbur, in Association of Medical Officers of American Institutions for Idiotic and Feeble-Minded Persons [1878] 1964: 100.

34. Wilbur, in Association of Medical Officers of American Institutions for Idiotic and Feeble-Minded Persons [1879] 1964: 165; also see Wilbur 1880.

35. New York Asylum for Idiots, *Annual Report, 1884,* pp. 7–8.

36. New York County Superintendents of Poor, *Proceedings, 1888,* pp. 29–31; New York County Superintendents of Poor, *Proceedings, 1890,* p. 78.

37. New York State Custodial Asylum for Feeble-Minded Women 1893: 13–16.

38. Mrs. Perkins is invariably listed as "Mrs. E. C. Perkins" in the institution's reports. I was finally able to confirm her relationship to Pierson's partner through New York State Office of General Services, n.d.: deed 70, which lists "Charles H. Perkins and Eliza C. his wife."

39. New York State Office of General Services, nd: deeds 66 and 70.

40. New York State Custodial Asylum for Feeble-Minded Women, *Annual Report, 1890*, p. 11.

41. New York State Custodial Asylum for Feeble-Minded Women, *Annual Report, 1893*, p. 6; New York State Custodial Asylum for Feeble-Minded Women, *Annual Report, 1894*, p. 9; New York State Board of Charities, *Annual Report, 1893*, pp. xli–xliv, 142–144.

42. In the late 1970s, when I saw these receipts, they were in the Historical Museum of the Newark Developmental Center, Newark, New York.

43. New York County Superintendents of Poor, *Proceedings, 1890*, p. 79. Pierson anticipates 1,000 or more inmates; New York State Custodial Asylum for Feeble-Minded Women, *Annual Report, 1893*, pp. 18–19.

44. A copy of the original circular can be found in New York State Archives, State Board of Charities, correspondence 1867–1902: vol. 18, p. 53, on the reverse of a letter from J. S. Lowell to James O. Fanning, assistant secretary of the SBC, Nov. 1, 1881. Wilbur quotes the circular in New York Asylum for Idiots, *Annual Report, 1880*, p. 16, and he reports mailing it to every poorhouse superintendent in the state in a letter of Nov. 10, 1878, to James O. Fanning (New York State Archives, State Board of Charities, correspondence 1867–1902: vol. 9, p. 226).

45. New York State Archives, State Board of Charities, correspondence 1867–1902: vol. 9, p. 238, Lowell to James O. Fanning, Nov. 14, 1878 (quoted letter), vol. 11, p. 12; vol. 14, pp. 30, 39; vol. 18, pp. 16, 53.

46. New York State Custodial Asylum for Feeble-Minded Women, *Annual Report, 1887*, p. 6 ("rules and regulations" state that Newark is for "feeble-minded women of a child-bearing age").

47. See, e.g., New York Asylum for Idiots, *Annual Report, 1882*, p. 14 ("a few of the cases sent, were committed because they were wanton in their habits rather than lacking in intelligence"). Also see Bragar 1977; Noll 1995a; Rafter 1992a; Simmons 1978; and Tyor 1977.

48. E.g., New York State Custodial Asylum for Feeble-Minded Women, *Annual Report, 1896*, p. 13.

49. Hrdlicka 1898: 74–75.

50. New York Asylum for Idiots, *Annual Report, 1880*, p. 9. Curiously, in the same paragraph, this report states that "only two or three of them were of wanton propensities": one had been impregnated by a poorhouse superintendent, another by a member of her employer's family (10). Bragar (1977) finds the same sort of contradic-

tion in the Syracuse Asylum's records for 1890–1920. She distinguishes between two contrasting strands of commentary about adult feeble-minded females. The "official perspective," voiced by the superintendent to the outside world, repeated the usual clichés about the eugenic dangers of feeble-minded women. But line staff portrayed the women as relatively normal. Thus, there were "not one but two institutional perspectives" (Bragar 1977: 66).

51. New York Asylum for Idiots, *Annual Report, 1896,* p. 13; New York State Custodial Asylum for Feeble-Minded Women, *Annual Report, 1890,* p. 5, citing an unnamed authority, perhaps a member of the SCB or perhaps nonexistent.

52. In a letter of Feb. 8, 1884, Newark's new superintendent, C. C. Warner, wrote Charles Hoyt, of the SBC, about a poorhouse inmate delivered clandestinely by "two strong men." "She was violent and one of the most Profane Persons that was ever in any Institution that I ever had charge of—More than one attendant carries marks where she has scratched or bit them and many are afrid [*sic*] of her" (New York State Archives, State Board of Charities, correspondence 1867–1902: vol. 23, p. 79).

53. New York State Archives, State Board of Charities, correspondence 1867–1902: vol. 42, p. 199 (letter dated June 19, 1894). I have changed the names of both mother and daughter.

54. Brenzel 1983; Dwyer 1987, 1992.

55. James C. Carson to Charles C. Hoyt, August 1, 1885 (New York State Archives, State Board of Charities, correspondence 1867–1902: vol. 26, p. 85).

56. C. C. Warner to Charles Hoyt, Feb. 1, 1884 (New York State Archives, State Board of Charities, correspondence 1867–1902: vol. 23, p. 62), reports that a Newark inmate could now take some nourishment since he had "removed three badly decayed teeth."

57. New York State Board of Charities, *Annual Report, 1893,* p. xlii.

58. Ibid., 143.

59. Ibid., 142.

60. Charles McLouth (a Newark board member) to Charles Hoyt, December 26, 1893 (New York State Archives, State Board of Charities, correspondence 1867–1902: vol. 40, p. 129).

61. New York State Board of Charities, *Annual Report, 1893,* pp. xliii, xliv.

62. On the emergence of "the dangerous individual," see Foucault 1988.

63. A third answer, an apparent tendency to test social control innovations on women, children, and other groups that are vulnerable to infantilization and unable to resist, is discussed in Rafter 1992a: 26.

64. Peiss 1986.

65. Rosenberg 1976: 73.

66. D'Emilio and Freedman 1988; Pivar 1973.

67. Gallagher and Laqueur 1987; Haller and Haller 1974. On the True Woman, see Welter 1966.

68. Also see Groneman 1994 on nineteenth-century attributions of nymphomania, another female somatic disorder.

69. Lowell 1879a: 197.

70. Also see Neff, Laughlin, and Cornell 1910; Hahn 1980.

71. See, e.g., Rosenberg 1976: chaps. 2 and 3.

72. Gordon 1977: 112.

73. Smart 1989: 103.

74. Much has been made of nineteenth-century male physicians' leadership in the diseasing of women's bodies (see, e.g., Mitchinson 1991). In Newark's case, however, the key physician, Hervey Backus Wilbur, *fought* efforts to biologize deviance. It was Lowell, the feminist, who rejected Wilbur's expertise and who defined feeble-minded women as triply deviant degenerates.

75. Olsen 1984: 402, n. 70.

76. New York State Archives, State Board of Charities, correspondence 1867–1902.

77. In her study of "the social construction of whiteness," Frankenberg (1993: 196) speaks of "Western colonial discourses on the white self, the non-white Other, and the white Other too."

78. But see Larson 1991, according to which "reactionary racism did not underlie passage of Georgia's sterilization law" (63), and Noll 1995b, arguing that white racist and elitist attitudes caused eugenicists to exclude African Americans with mental retardation from institutions.

79. Rafter 1984.

REFERENCES

Association of Medical Officers of American Institutions for Idiotic and Feeble-Minded Persons, *Proceedings.*

Beatty, Barbara R. 1986. "Lowell, Josephine Shaw." Pp. 511–515 in Walter L. Trattner, ed., *Biographical Dictionary of Social Welfare in America.* New York: Greenwood Press.

Best, Joel. 1987. "Rhetoric in Claims-Making: Constructing the Missing Children Problem." *Social Problems* 34: 101–121.

Bragar, Madeline C. 1977. "The Feebleminded Female: An Historical Analysis of Mental Retardation as a Social Definition, 1890–1920." Ph.D diss., Syracuse University.

Brenzel, Barbara M. 1983. *Daughters of the State: A Social Portrait of the First Reform School for Girls in North America, 1856–1905.* Cambridge, Mass.: MIT Press.

Burton, Robert. 1621/1989. *The Anatomy of Melancholy.* Repr. Oxford: Clarendon Press.

Chamberlin, J. Edward, and Sander L. Gilman, eds. 1985. *Degeneration: The Dark Side of Progress.* New York: Columbia University Press.

Darwin, Charles. 1859. *On the Origin of the Species by Means of Natural Selection or, The Preservation of Favored Races in the Struggle for Life.* London: J. Murray.

———. 1871/1986. *The Descent of Man and Selection in Relation to Sex.* Repr. n.p.: Telegraph Books.

de Forest, Robert W., Joseph H. Choate, William R. Stewart . . . and Many Others. 1905. "In Memorium: Josephine Shaw Lowell." *Charities and the Commons* 15: 309–335.

D'Emilio, John, and Estelle B. Freedman. 1988. *Intimate Matters: A History of Sexuality in America.* New York: Harper & Row.

Devine, Edward T. 1905. "Mrs. Lowell's Services to the State." *Charities and the Commons* 15: 319–322.

Dowbiggin, Ian. 1991. *Inheriting Madness: Professionalization and Psychiatric Knowledge in Nineteenth-Century France.* Berkeley: University of California Press.

Dugdale, Richard L. 1874. "A Report of Special Visits to County Jails for 1874." Prison Association of New York, *Annual Report, 1874,* pp. 129–192. New York Sen. Doc. No. 78, 1875.

———. 1877. *"The Jukes": A Study in Crime, Pauperism, Disease and Heredity; also Further Studies of Criminals.* New York: G. P. Putnam's Sons.

Dwyer, Ellen. 1987. *Homes for the Mad: Life inside Two Nineteenth-Century Insane Asylums.* New Brunswick, N.J.: Rutgers University Press.

———. 1992. "Stories of Epilepsy, 1880–1930." Ch. 12 (pp. 248–272) in Charles E. Rosenberg and Janet Golden, eds., *Framing Disease: Studies in Cultural History.* New Brunswick, N.J.: Rutgers University Press.

Foucault, Michel. 1988. "The Dangerous Individual." Pp. 125–151 in Lawrence D. Kritzman, ed., *Michel Foucault: Politics, Philosophy, Culture—Interviews and Other Writings, 1977–1984.* New York: Routledge.

Frankenberg, Ruth. 1993. *White Women, Race Matters: The Social Construction of Whiteness.* Minneapolis: University of Minnesota Press.

Gallagher, Catherine, and Thomas Laqueur. 1987. *The Making of the Modern Body: Sexuality and Society in the Nineteenth Century.* Berkeley: University of California Press.

Galton, Francis. 1869/1952. *Hereditary Genius: An Inquiry into Its Laws and Consequences.* Repr. New York: Horizon Press.

Gordon, Linda. 1977. *Women's Body, Women's Right: Birth Control in America.* New York: Penguin.

Groneman, Carol. 1994. "Nymphomania: The Historical Construction of Female Sexuality." *Signs* 19: 337–367.

Hahn, Nicolas F. [Nicole F. Rafter]. 1980. "Too Dumb to Know Better: Cacogenic Family Studies and the Criminology of Women." *Criminology* 18: 3–25.

Haller, John S., Jr., and Robin M. Haller. 1974. *The Physician and Sexuality in Victorian America.* Urbana: University of Illinois Press.

Henderson, Charles R. 1893. *An Introduction to the Study of the Dependent, Defective and Delinquent Classes.* Boston: D. C. Heath and Company.

Hoyt, Charles S. 1876. "The Causes of Pauperism." In New York State Board of Charities, *Annual Report, 1876,* pp. 95–331.

Hrdlička, Aleš. 1898. "Anthropological Studies." *Journal of Psycho-Asthenics* 3: 47–75.

Lane, James B. 1973. "Jacob A. Riis and Scientific Philanthropy during the Progressive Era." *Social Service Review* 47: 32–48.

Larson, Edward J. 1991. "Belated Progress: The Enactment of Eugenic Legislation in Georgia." *Journal of the History of Medicine and Allied Sciences* 46: 44–64.

Lowell, Josephine Shaw. 1879a. "One Means of Preventing Pauperism." National Conference of Charities and Correction, *Proceedings 1879,* pp. 189–200.

———. 1879b. "Reformatories for Women." New York State Board of Charities, *Annual Report, 1879,* pp. 173–180.

Mitchinson, Wendy. 1991. *The Nature of their Bodies: Women and Their Doctors in Victorian Canada.* Toronto: University of Toronto Press.

Neff, Joseph S., Samuel Laughlin, and Walter S. Cornell. 1910. *The Degenerate Children of Feeble-Minded Women.* Philadelphia: Department of Public Health and Charities.

New York County Superintendents of Poor, *Proceedings.*

New York State Archives, Albany. New York State Board of Charities. Series A1977, *Correspondence 1867–1902.*

New York State Asylum for Idiots (Syracuse), *Annual Reports.*

New York State Board of Charities, *Annual Reports.*

New York State Custodial Asylum for Feeble-Minded Women (Newark Custodial Asylum), *Annual Reports.*

New York State Office of General Services, Bureau of Land Management, Albany. *Deeds to Newark Custodial Asylum.*

Noll, Steven. 1995a. *Feeble-Minded in Our Midst: Institutions for the Mentally Retarded in the South, 1900–1940.* Chapel Hill: University of North Carolina Press.

———. 1995b. "Under a Double Burden: Florida's Black Feeble-Minded, 1920–1957." Ch. 11 (pp. 275–297) in David R. Colburn and Jane L. Landers, eds., *The African American Heritage of Florida.* Gainesville: University of Florida Press.

Nye, Robert A. 1984. *Crime, Madness, & Politics in Modern France: The Medical Concept of National Decline.* Princeton, N.J.: Princeton University Press.

Olsen, Frances. 1984. "Statutory Rape: A Feminist Critique of Rights Analysis." *Texas Law Review* 63: 387–432.

Peiss, Kathy. 1986. *Cheap Amusements: Working Women and Leisure in Turn-of-the-Century New York.* Philadelphia: Temple University Press.

Pick, Daniel. 1989. *Faces of Degeneration: A European Disorder, c. 1848–c. 1918.* Cambridge: Cambridge University Press.

Pivar, David J. 1973. *Purity Crusade: Sexual Morality and Social Control, 1868–1900.* Westport, Conn.: Greenwood Press.

Rafter, Nicole Hahn. 1988. *White Trash: The Eugenic Family Studies, 1877–1919*. Boston: Northeastern University Press.

———. 1992a. "Claims-Making and Socio-Cultural Context in the First U.S. Eugenics Campaign." *Social Problems* 39: 17–34.

———. 1992b. "Criminal Anthropology in the United States." *Criminology* 30: 525–545.

———. 1994. "Eugenics, Class, and the Professionalization of Social Control." Ch. 13 in George Bridges and Martha Myers, eds., *Inequality, Crime, and Social Control*. Boulder: Westview Press.

———. 1997. *Creating Born Criminals*. Chicago: University of Illinois Press.

Reynolds, Amos. 1879. "The Prevention of Pauperism." National Conference of Charities and Correction, *Proceedings 1879*, pp. 210–216.

Rosenberg, Charles E. 1976. *No Other Gods: On Science and American Social Thought*. Baltimore: Johns Hopkins University Press.

Sarason, Seymour B., and John Doris. 1969. *Psychological Problems in Mental Deficiency*, 4th ed. New York: Harper & Row.

Saveth, Edward N. 1980. "Patrician Philanthropy in America: The Late Nineteenth and Early Twentieth Centuries." *Social Service Review* 54: 76–91.

Simmons, Harvey G. 1978. "Explaining Social Policy: The English Mental Deficiency Act of 1913." *Journal of Social History* 11: 387–403.

Smart, Carol. 1989. *Feminism and the Power of Law*. New York: Routledge.

Stewart, William Rhinelander. 1911. *The Philanthropic Work of Josephine Shaw Lowell*. New York: Macmillan.

Taylor, Lloyd C., Jr. 1963. "Josephine Shaw Lowell and American Philanthropy." *New York History* 44: 336–364.

Trent, James W., Jr. 1994. *Inventing the Feeble Mind: A History of Mental Retardation in the United States*. Berkeley: University of California Press.

Tyor, Peter. 1977. "'Denied the Power to Choose the Good': Sexuality and Mental Defect in American Medical Practice, 1850–1920." *Journal of Social History* 10: 472–489.

United States Department of the Interior, Census Office. 1883. *Statistics of the Population of the United States at the Tenth Census (June 1, 1880)*. Washington, D.C.: Government Printing Office.

Walter, Richard D. 1956. "What Became of the Degenerate? A Brief History of a Concept." *Journal of the History of Medicine and Allied Sciences* 11: 422–429.

Welter, Barbara. 1966. "The Cult of True Womanhood: 1820–1860." *American Quarterly* 18: 151–174.

Wilbur, Hervey B. 1880. "Instinct not Predominant in Idiocy." In Association of Medical Officers of American Institutions for Idiotic and Feeble-Minded Persons. *Proceedings, 1880*, pp. 135–144.

Wines, Frederick Howard. 1888. *Report on the Defective, Dependent, and Delinquent Classes of the Population of the United States as returned at the Tenth Census (June 1, 1880)*. Washington, D.C.: Government Printing Office.

10

The State and the Multiply Disadvantaged
The Case of Epilepsy

Ellen Dwyer

Introduction

For many years, an economics of compassion has shaped public policy, with the earliest and most generous social assistance programs targeting those with the greatest economic potential. The last (and often least) help has gone to those expected to improve slowly, if at all. This calculus first manifested itself in nineteenth-century America, when states began to build specialized social welfare institutions. First helped were the poor, orphans, and the insane, then the deaf and the blind, and finally those with multiple disabilities.[1] In part, this governmental preference for compassionate investments most likely to produce future social dividends reflects taxpayers' fiscal priorities. It is less obvious why academic scholarship has so often replicated this value system, what amounts to a grim political triage. Yet, just as legislators and taxpayers often have relegated "defective dependents" to the back wards of state institutions, scholars have relegated them to the back wards of history. Particularly neglected (by both politicians and academics) have been the most disadvantaged, those with both physical and mental impairments.

Not until the late twentieth century did such individuals finally began to achieve equal access to a range of institutions and social programs. Equal attention from historians began about the same time. In the past four decades, an important body of scholarship has begun to emerge that recreates the history of those with mental and physical handicaps and of public policies directed at them. Peter Tyor and Leland Bell's *Caring for the Retarded in America* (1984) offered a useful overview. In the two decades that followed, scholars such as James Trent, Nicole Rafter, Philip Ferguson, and Steven Noll filled in and expanded its basic narrative.[2] However, much remains to be done. This essay builds on such work and uses the history of a specialized institution for epileptics, New York State's Craig Colony, to extend our historical understanding of those designated intellectually defective and their families.

While not an obvious source for the neglected history of mental retardation, Craig Colony has several advantages for historians of that subject. Craig Colony's rich and detailed patient case files are perhaps the most complete source on the categorization and care of epileptics with learning disabilities. These files contain a wide range of items, including commitment papers, family and medical histories, Colony treatment plans (when they existed), families' letters inquiring about the health and wellbeing of institutionalized members, notes from colonists to the superintendent, and members' work histories.[3] When used in conjunction with the Colony's annual reports and the published writings of its doctors, they suggest the extraordinary historical diversity of responses to even the most severely impaired. They remind us that in the past, as in the present, families and communities looked to a variety of institutions for help with mentally handicapped members, not just to schools for the so-called feebleminded. Thus, the Colony, with its large proportion (sometimes as high as 80 percent) of "intellectually defective" patients with seizures, provides a useful point of comparison with state-run schools. Its history also suggests the expansive quality of labels of defectiveness, as the alleged intellectual deficits of many of its patients were not noticed until their commitment to the Colony. (The frequency with which epileptics were assumed to be feeble-minded and the feebleminded particularly prone to seizures is shown as well by the many institutions that held both, such as the Florida Farm Colony for Epileptics and the Feeble-Minded, whose story has been told by Steven Noll. In addition, the early-twentieth-century National Conference of Charities and Correction had a single Standing Committee on the Feeble-Minded and Epileptics.) In particular, records of patients whose histories at admission mention school and work experiences suggest the ease and frequency with which the assignment of one stigmatizing label (epileptic) prompted others (such as "feeble-minded" and "insane"). Their subsequent experiences within the institution, as well as the Colony's long and usually unsuccessful struggle for

259

adequate funding, also make clear that the harsh calculus that shaped state-level fiscal policies influenced the Colony's internal workings for its entire history, from 1896 to 1967.

A Brief History of Craig Colony

When New York State legislators approved funding for the Craig Colony for Epileptics, in 1894, their intent was to establish an institution that would protect "dependent epileptics" from a hostile society and the society from them. Initially, the State Board of Charities and the early Colony managers also hoped that it would become "the seat of clinico-pathological investigations of a high order,"[4] and they attempted to restrict admission to those patients most likely to benefit from Colony life. Yet, even at this early and relatively optimistic point in the Colony's history, the vision of those who ran it was circumscribed. They saw their purpose not as curing and releasing patients but as keeping them isolated in this remote institution in southeastern New York. Southeast of Rochester in Sonyea, New York, the institution was built on the site of a former Shaker community. There, it was hoped, epileptics would be returned, as far as possible, "to a primitive condition of life," isolated permanently from the stresses of modern civilization. As early as their second report, alongside positive rhetoric about their hope of building a self-sufficient community, a literal colony, the managers prominently featured statistics on patients' "stigmata of degeneration": asymmetries and deformations of the ears, palate, face, and cranium. The conclusion they drew from these was grim. While the Colony had the potential to ennoble and elevate those who lived there, many of the colonists were "defective human beings, too often representing a perverted and unfinished product of the human race." Because of the epileptic's mental limitations, they proclaimed, "We shall not attempt to supply him with what Nature has denied. . . . We shall endeavor to educate him simply."[5] While such negative and highly charged language was typical of turn-of-the-century medical writing about a range of dependent defectives, the Craig Colony managers and their superintendents found it particularly appropriate for their epileptic charges.

The Colony grew quickly. From a population of little more than 100 in 1897, by the end of the first decade of the early twentieth century it had some 840 beds. One hundred of these were in two sex-segregated infirmaries that had been built to hold the many "bedridden and crippled" (hardly promising colonists) sent from county almshouses. Those who ran the Colony were unhappy about the increasing pressure to take the weakest of New York's citizens. Doctor William Spratling, the Colony's first superintendent, complained bitterly in his sixth annual report about the ever larger numbers of "idiots, imbeciles, and the feeble-minded" for whom he had responsibility, claiming that they threatened to subvert the Colony's goal of financial and social independence. His solution to this local problem was visionary, albeit dystopic: he called for laws that would forbid the marriage of epileptics, so as to keep them from reproducing and handing on their defective germ plasm.[6] Such an argument was not new. Indeed, even before the Colony opened in 1896, the editor of a leading medical journal had suggested that New York also needed mandatory sterilization laws for all chronic epileptics so that "the tribe of these degenerate State wards may not be increased under the fostering care of the commonwealth."[7] However, first Spratling and then his successor, William Shanahan, devoted substantially more energy to campaigning for eugenics legislation than to enlarging the medical understanding of seizure disorders.[8] Their efforts did not flag until the 1930s, when eugenic solutions generally began to lose favor in the United States. Even then it is not clear that Shanahan's views changed. Although he stopped mentioning eugenics laws in his annual reports and writing about them in state and national medical journals, by that point he and his fellow physicians at the Colony had become isolated from the medical mainstream, especially in neurology and psychiatry. For the most part, they seemed to have given up attending specialized national conferences and publishing in medical journals. The superintendent's once lengthy annual reports on the Colony dwindled to a formulaic recounting of institutional statistics and news. Thus, it is hard to celebrate Shanahan's retreat from the political fights for eugenics marriage and sterilization laws, accompanied as it was by a larger retreat from the public sphere (professional as well as political) of all of the Craig Colony doctors in the 1930s and 1940s. During this period, they also largely stopped complaining about inadequate research funding and became more reluctant than ever to release Colony "defectives" to their families.[9]

While Craig Colony was underfunded and hence understaffed for its entire history, its situation worsened substantially during World War II and after. At times during the 1940s, it was unable to keep or replace many of those doctors and attendants for whom it had funding, let alone add to their numbers. While the improved job opportunities during and after the war were partly responsible for this situation, it was but an aggravated version of the Colony's long-standing difficulties, the product of its isolated location, difficult working conditions, and low salaries. The shortage of attendants was a particularly acute problem because, at institutions like Craig Colony, as the historian James Trent has noted, "the attendant, not the educator or the physician, was . . . the most crucial actor in the lives of inmates."[10] At the same time as staff-patient ratios worsened, the character of the new admissions to Craig Colony changed. New antiseizure medications and a stronger job market made institutional care increasingly unappealing to high-functioning individuals with epilepsy and their families. The Colony beds did not remain empty but were increasingly filled by the multiply disabled until, in 1967, Craig Colony was converted formally from a treatment center for those with seizures to a residential institution for the severely retarded.[11]

Categories of Intellectual Ability—and of Patient Care

As the preceding brief history makes clear, a constant subtext in the Colony's annual reports was the unwelcome burden of patients perceived to have learning disabilities as well as seizures. During the Colony's first decades, many such men and women were described as "feeble-minded," a catchall phrase used for adults dulled by large doses of bromides, children excluded from public schools because of their seizures, and babies so brain-damaged at birth that they could not hold up their heads as they grew older. Beginning in 1910, however, the Craig Colony doctors began to assess new patients in more precise ways with the help of the Binet-Simon intelligence test, which had been presented by the psychologist Henry Goddard to the American Association for the Study of the Feeble-Minded (hereafter referred to as the AASFM). Using data collected from the large-scale administration of the Binet-Simon test, Goddard had challenged nineteenth-century notions about the improvability of "backward" students. Their abnormality was permanent, he claimed, and he gave the roughly 2 percent of children who previously had been thought of as slow or dull but who still were able to function at school and in their communities the new label of "moron."[12] In 1910, the AASFM incorporated this new category into its categories of mental defect. "Idiots" were those with Binet-Simon scores of 25 or lower, "imbeciles" had scores from 25 to 55, and "morons" had scores from 55 to 75.[13] The admitting doctors at Craig Colony did the same, although in 1917 they

262

replaced Binet-Simon with the Yerkes-Bridges scale. The latter, they argued, used a point-scale that measured mental abilities more accurately than did the Binet age-scale, with its "all or nothing" system of giving credit.[14] For the most part, patient case records offer few insights into how these various intelligence tests were administered at Craig Colony. In 1917, however, Arthur Shaw, a particularly energetic third assistant physician at Craig Colony, described his procedures for examining new male patients. He used an impressively complex system, which did not rely exclusively on "thumbnail tests" but involved a thorough review of each patient's clinical history, as well as lengthy conversations with interested patients.[15] Although there is no evidence that other doctors took such care, beginning in 1910, every Craig Colony patient at admission had his or her intelligence assessed. The resulting labels were most powerful for the "imbeciles" (especially lower-level imbeciles) and "idiots," as such patients were assigned to one of the infirmaries or to closed cottages located away from the administrative center of the colony. Despite the significant medical and custodial needs of the feeblest patients, the staffing ratios were lowest in their buildings. They also had to share space with the colony's troublemakers, who (especially if aggressive adolescents) were transferred for periods of time to the Loomis and the Schuyler Infirmaries. There they were unable to cause problems for the medical staff, but they frequently preyed upon long-term residents, by and large the weakest and least competent members of the Colony.[16]

Luckier were those designated "morons," if under the age of seventeen and reasonably well behaved, or "imbeciles" with IQs of 50 or higher. These young patients were sent to the Colony school, which educated from 90 to 200 students a year. Early on, the Craig school, like institutions for the feebleminded, focused primarily on what was called "habit training," rather than on academics, stressing the "skills useful for institutionalization--socialization, punctuality, obedience to authority, patience, teamwork and respect for the rights of others."[17] In 1908, Superintendent Spratling, noting that most epileptics were barred from attending public schools because of their affliction, argued that they needed "muscular . . . not mental education."[18] Nonetheless, until the 1940s, there were almost always a few studying for New York State Regents examinations or taking standard high school subjects. And there remained a small number of severely handicapped children in the classrooms, perhaps in response to parental pressure on the institution. In 1908, for example, Spratling told the story of the girl who took ninety days to lay three sticks in the form of the letter A. Older adolescents were trained as well in specific industries, including brick making, dairy farming, and sewing, as part of the effort to make Craig "a Colony of production as well as a Colony of consumption."[19]

In 1920, the Colony School became an extension teacher training site for Geneseo State Normal School. Although there clearly were students of normal intelligence at the school, the focus was on training teachers for what later would be known as special education classes, and its first director, a Doctor Bucke, was especially interested in applying the principles of abnormal psychology to education.[20] Among other things, the school offered educators the opportunity to study the deterioration of intellect among those with epilepsy through the repeated administration of intelligence tests.[21] For a time in the 1930s, in addition to continued habit training (needed because the average epileptic, before institutionalization, most often was allowed to lead an "aimless, idle existence," doctors charged), the School had Girl Scout and Boy Scout troops, as well as musical training for the children, which culminated in an operetta called *The Magic Bean Stalk,* and physical training for the younger ones, which, doctors noted, often produced a reduction in their seizures. In asking for funds to continue these activities, the Craig superintendents repeatedly told legislators of the enormous importance of school attendance to children whose lives in other ways were so different from those of their friends and siblings outside the institution.[22]

In the early 1940s, the School's census, never large, dropped drastically as (or so the doctors said) the intelligence of the new young patients declined. Although, for many years, only students with IQs of 50 or above (and who were physically mobile) had been allowed to attend, in the mid-1940s the admission requirement was lowered to an IQ of 40. Finally, in 1951, when an energetic new superintendent, Henry Brill, was made superintendent, all potential students were taken to school, regardless of their recorded IQs, because, Brill argued, initial tests might reveal more about patients' past intellectual deprivation than about their capacity and potential.[23] Once there, however, they received only minimal training from teachers constrained by poorly furnished classrooms and inadequate supplies. By this point, the Colony had almost 2,300 patients, most of whom got only the most basic custodial care.

Categories of Patients: Idiots

Whatever the decade, the saddest and most difficult cases at Craig Colony comprised patients with such severe neurological problems and learning disabilities that they were designated "idiots." These tended to be children, a large percentage of whom died within a decade of their admission, most often from pneumonia or tuberculosis. Until the late 1940s, when their relative numbers began to increase dramatically, "idiots" constituted between 4 and 12 percent of the new admissions each year. Like families in the institutions studied by the historians Mark Friedberger and David Wright, most parents sent even severely handicapped children to Craig Colony with great reluctance, acting out of exhaustion—financial, physical, and emotional.[24] In looking at nineteenth-century England, Wright found that families often affected the length of stay of their children, taking them home when they felt capable again of caring for them. A similar situation existed at Craig Colony, where arguments between parents or doctors over whether children, even the most handicapped, should be released appear often in the institution's patient records. Unfortunately for the families, if their children had been sent to Craig Colony certified as "mental incompetents," only a court order could get them released. Most frequently, the parents of children who needed constant care sent them to Craig Colony at a relatively early age, but some were able to delay institutionalization for many years. An extreme but poignant example involves a woman admitted in 1946, at the age of forty-three, whose seizures had started when she was four. Although the Craig doctors found her unable to respond to stimuli, "completely disoriented," and capable of making only "a few animal-like sounds," her mother had waited until enfeebled by old age to institutionalize her daughter.[25]

In addition to noting the reluctance families often felt about institutionalization, patient records, even those of the most handicapped children, are filled with evidence of conflicts between parents and doctors over the children's abilities and treatments. For example, one fourteen-year-old girl was described by her parents as having good common sense and as being active "in work and play" and "at ease with friends," whereas the admitting doctors characterized her simply as "an idiot in fair general health." In response to repeated pleas from the girl's mother and a Public Welfare home investigation, Shanahan finally allowed her to go home for a time. Doctors frequently dismissed or ignored families' evaluations as overly optimistic, even though parents protested (for example, one mother said about her mute child,

"When he was home he knew lots of things but didn't talk"). When one "deeply retarded" adolescent died after less than two years at Craig, her parents (who had tried unsuccessfully to bring her home) wrote angrily that they would never recommend the Colony to anyone.[26]

The case histories of idiot epileptics are grim, filled with terms like "defective," "degenerate," and "pathological," and they describe children who refuse to eat and who withdraw from their surroundings.[27] Thirteen-year-old John, for example, was described as "a wet and soil case and mentally an idiot of low grade." His hearing was poor, and he spoke only Yiddish. In response to the doctors' letters, his mother wrote sadly, "Your letters regarding my son have almost taken away from me that great comforter of the unfortunate, Hope. Is it really true, doctor, that I must regard my poor boy as lost both to me and the world forever? Will life have no meaning for him anymore?" Two years later, John died of pneumonia.[28]

In many instances, even when parents and doctors disagreed about the extent of a particular patient's disability, "idiot" patients clearly were severely handicapped. At the same time, the parents were right to suspect that, dumped into cribs in the Schuyler or Loomis Infirmaries, these children received minimal care at best. Those ambulatory, particularly if male, were highly vulnerable to physical and sexual abuse by less handicapped patients who had been sent to the Infirmaries as punishment for misbehavior. It is only fair to add that Craig Colony often complained that its facilities and staff for "the helpless" were inadequate, but records where babies are referred to as "it" (as in the case of two-year-old Betty: "It takes its bottle of milk with avidity") remain difficult to read.[29]

"Idiot" patients sorely taxed the Colony's resources with their multiple needs. They had to be fed, washed, changed, medicated, and, in some cases, kept from mutilating themselves. Even when not in a convulsive state, they were likely to injure themselves or others if not watched carefully (and they seldom were). In 1897, the New York State Board of Charities characterized idiots as "continuing only an animal existence, with no mental relations to their surroundings."[30] While later doctors and social welfare workers avoided such shockingly harsh language, they did not abandon the attitudes that underlay it and shaped the allocation of scarce resources. As a result, for the duration of the Colony's existence, idiot patients lived out their often short lives in large, poorly staffed infirmaries that were often rife with infectious diseases.[31]

Categories of Patients: Imbeciles

With IQs generally measuring between 30 and 70, imbeciles, Superintendent Shanahan noted, sometimes made good colonists and sometimes did not. Ranging from twenty-two to thirty-two of the new admissions each year, "imbeciles" included both individuals who had "deteriorated" from a higher level of functioning as a result of their seizures and children just above the category of "idiot" who often needed a great deal of attention, even when able to take some care of themselves. For example, an eleven-year-old boy with an IQ of 30 was described as having the "appearance, manners, and facies typical of a primary dement." He could control his bowels and feed himself but, "like all of his grade," had poor habits of personal hygiene. Nine-year-old Edward had similar problems. Born with Bell's palsy and injured by obstetrical instruments during delivery, he was cared for by his parents until 1919, when they sent him to Craig Colony. After Edward's father complained repeatedly but to no effect about the lack of supervision in the children's ward (after one visit, he claimed to have found forty children locked into a room with one nurse), he took his son home again. Five years later, however, he was forced to recommit the boy. Shanahan was reluctant to accept him because the father had been so critical and because the institution still could not provide the level of care demanded by the parents. Edward's case history reveals that parents sometimes spent years providing intensive care but then found themselves unable to continue. Although he claimed to have spent thousands of dollars caring for Edward, in 1926, the father wrote sadly that his son's condition was so poor that the family could no longer care for him at home. Three years after his readmission, Edward died of pneumonia and was buried in the Colony cemetery.[32]

Patients labeled imbeciles varied more than those considered idiots and often were described as having deteriorated from a higher level of functioning. At one end of the spectrum were the thirty-six-year-old man who, after he died, was described as having spent two and a half years at the Colony living "an uneventful vegetative existence" and the young male patient with Jacksonian epilepsy, perhaps related to his cerebral palsy, who was considered a typical imbecile.[33]

Laughs without cause. Makes purposeless movements. Silly and inattentive. Comprehension and judgment are very low. He is in constant motion and hyperactive. Will not obey simple commands. . . . Speech is defective and will not answer questions.

At the other end of the spectrum were foreign-born patients, most often from Eastern Europe and Russia, whose poor performance on intelligence tests reflected at least in part their lack of knowledge of English, and a difficult category of patients, prone to disruptive and antisocial behavior, who were labeled "moral imbeciles." Typical was the adolescent Tom, who was criticized for fighting with other patients and occasionally stealing from them. During his six years at Craig, Tom wrote endless letters of complaint both to the Colony superintendent and to his parents, asking to be allowed to return home so that he could either attend high school or join the army. "I just can't stand it up here any longer," he wrote to his mother in January 1940. "The nurses are kicking me around . . . please take me home by next week." In response to Tom's repeated efforts to elope, the Craig Colony doctors characterized him as manipulative and lacking "insight." Eventually, in August 1945, Tom successfully ran away. His subsequent history was not detailed beyond the last note in his file, written by a woman for whom he subsequently went to work. Now twenty-three, Tom "does not know the value of the dollar as he spends his money as fast as he gets it and has gone after the girls."[34]

Much more often than those of "idiots," the case histories of "imbecile" patients suggest the high levels of interpersonal violence within the Colony. As one father observed in amazement, "Why the kids up there are a bunch of rough necks they wear (sic) fighting each other and everything. I seen boys take fits (sic) every five minutes and no one to look over them they just leave them lay there." For example, a sixteen-year-old male imbecile with an IQ of 43 was admitted in 1934 but stayed less than seven months. Although deaf and partially paralyzed, Frank fought constantly with other patients and was beaten by attendants. After his father took the boy home for Christmas vacation, he did not return. A seven-year-old boy sent to Craig Colony in 1925 complained to his parents that the other boys hit and bit him. When the parents in turn complained to Shanahan, the superintendent denied the charges, claiming that the boy "is so retarded mentally that he does not quarrel to any appreciable extent with other children." Eventually, the child was paroled home, but his parents had trouble dealing with his frequent and intense seizures and returned him to the Colony. There he remained until his death in 1947, growing duller and more crotchety each year.[35]

In these and similar cases, Craig Colony consistently denied allegations of abuse and neglect, even while it conceded severe understaffing. Because of its remote location, heavy work loads, and low pay, it had difficulty attracting and keeping staff. As a result, many patients were barely supervised. Among the adolescent males, in particular, this permitted the development of a number of gangs, the most violent of which were notorious for their sexual exploitation of weaker patients, as well as for endless fighting. In the 1930s, a group calling itself the "G-Men" even made plans to kill an unpopular attendant. While violence among female patients was reported less often, it too appeared in individual accident reports, several of which describe suspicious deaths in the course of patient conflicts. Most often, the aggressors were patients labeled imbeciles or morons or they were attendants; the victims came from across the patient population, but idiots were the most vulnerable and the least able to protect themselves from sexual predation. Seemingly, the institution did little to stop such attacks, beyond making notes in patient records about suspected assaults "causing perineal lacerations" and referring to particularly notorious offenders as "old perverts" or "sodomites."[36]

The case records of imbeciles, like those of idiots, are filled with heartbreaking stories of parents giving up beloved children reluctantly and, in some cases, taking them home again after relatively short periods of institutionalization. Thus, for its entire history, the Colony (often unwillingly) offered respite care as well as long-term custody. For example, in 1946, one mother committed her four-year-old child to Craig Colony because she had become "rundown taking care of her child and . . . fearful that she would have a nervous breakdown." A few days after her child's admission, the mother wrote the first of many letters to the superintendent. "I am sure you understand how a mother's heart is breaking and how she worries," she said. Three years later, the father requested the patient's transfer to Letchworth Village because it was closer to the family's home. Once the family agreed to pay the traveling expenses for an exchange of patients with Craig Colony, the trade was made.[37]

By the 1930s, Craig Colony often demanded a home inspection by a social welfare agency, along with a state Supreme Court order, before releasing a patient committed as incompetent. Its concerns were multiple and, in the case of young women, clearly dictated by fear of pregnancies. However, it could do little to stop patients from running away and parents from taking them out for rides or home for vacations and not returning them (although at times the doctors did threaten to take legal action against such parents). A substantial number of higher-functioning imbecile males thus escaped the confines of the Colony. For the most part, their subsequent histories are not told in their case records, although there are occasional references to requests from other state institutions, most often for the insane, asking for information about their time at Craig Colony. Much rarer are the inquiries from employers or prospective employers about former patients' seizure histories.

Categories of Patients: Morons

Patients in the category of "moron" were among the most promising members of the "defective classes." Their IQs tended to hover between 65 and 85, and, through the 1940s, they constituted 30 to 40 percent of new admissions every year. Included in this group by Colony doctors were "borderline" cases, but not "dull normals." If young, so-called morons attended the Colony school; if older, they were assigned to occupational and recreational therapy programs. As the twentieth century progressed, "morons" stayed at the Colony for increasingly short periods of time. The clinical assessments of their intelligence were markedly less consistent than those of idiots and somewhat less than those of imbeciles (many of whom had "deteriorated" in the institution from their admission status as "morons").[38] For example, an adolescent girl admitted to the Colony in 1927 initially was characterized as a "moron" but later was described as having "average intelligence." A month after having been admitted, she went home on vacation and, unhappy about the Colony's overcrowding, did not return.[39]

Occasionally, especially in the first three decades of the twentieth century, the Colony attempted to prevent even voluntarily committed morons from leaving after a short period of treatment. For example, when the parents of twelve-year-old Jesse wanted him returned home because they could not afford the trip from New York City to visit him, Shanahan refused and referred in a threatening letter to laws that made it illegal to "entice inmates from public institutions." Because Samuel had not been declared legally incompetent, however, Shanahan eventually had to concede and let the boy return to his parents. While Colony doctors had a general antipathy toward releasing patients, they were particularly concerned about those designated "morons" because this group (among "mental defectives") was most likely to marry and hence reproduce. They also were the most useful at the Colony, able to perform well a number of tasks, from cleaning and farming to nursing sick patients and caring for severely handicapped small children. By the late 1930s, the Colony's usual practice was to encourage courts to declare applicants for voluntary admission incompetent, as this gave the Colony much more control over their eventual disposition.[40] When patients labeled morons were able to obtain a release, many subsequently found employment; during World War II, some of the men joined the military.

Until the mid-1920s, patients considered "morons" often were described as having typical "epileptoid" personalities or mental status; subsequently, similar patients were described as psychopaths. The language of numerous journal articles describing "epileptoids" was replicated almost verbatim in casebook entries, where epileptoid patients were described as self-centered, overly supersensitive, quarrelsome, manipulative, and often deceitful. Among other uses, this characterization of difficult or unhappy patients as "epileptoids" allowed Craig doctors to dismiss their complaints without investigation. Families were less easily persuaded to dismiss patient discontent. Adolescents, in particular, often expressed anger and even suicidal despair at being confined in a large institution far from home. A number threatened suicide (a sixteen-year-old girl was finally removed by her family after she wrote a letter saying, "if you make me stay here for good, I'll only kill myself"); they also complained about the poor quality of the Colony's educational programs (to which the doctors fairly consistently responded that such patients lacked "insight" into the reasons for their commitment and the larger needs of the institution). Bored teenage boys frequently got into trouble, manipulating younger boys, stealing, or running away. Ward notes capture the doctors' frustration with such patients; one was variously described as "bright," a "low grade moron," "trustworthy," and a "moral degenerate."[41]

By the onset of World War II, Craig Colony was receiving substantially fewer patients in the "moron" category, and those coming for treatment, especially the adults, were using the Colony as a therapeutic retreat, a place where their medications might be adjusted or they could get a break from the stresses of their daily lives. For example, twenty-four-year-old Elizabeth first spent a year at Craig in 1939 and was discharged unimproved. She then married, but not happily. A craniotomy at Strong Hospital in Rochester did not eliminate her monthly petit mal seizures. After returning to Craig in May 1946, she stayed only a month. On leaving, she thanked the doctors "for

271

letting her try it again" but said her place should go to someone in greater need. That same year, thirty-one-year-old Arthur, who also had had unsuccessful surgery for his seizures (leaving him with two horseshoe-shaped scars on the top of his head), came to Craig Colony in the hope of finding an anti-seizure medication with fewer side effects than the ones he had already tried (which included phenobarbital, dilantin, and tridione). Unhappy at the Colony, he left after four months. The doctors worried about his future, for his seizures were too frequent, they feared, for him to find regular employment. Arthur's records contain three months' worth of aftercare notes taken by a social worker in his home town. Because he could not find a job, he had to rely on his mother's factory wages for support; eventually, he got twenty-seven dollars a month from public welfare, which he allegedly spent betting on horses. His manner was "paranoid," noted his disapproving social worker, and he had "extremely grandiose ideas about himself." She discontinued Arthur's office visits after he made inappropriate personal remarks to her, and the last note in Arthur's file noted his reinstitutionalization—this time at Middletown State Homeopathic Hospital.[42]

Both the Colony and local social workers had difficulty achieving long-term reintegration of patients with seizures like Arthur's, even when their mental retardation was slight. Female patients were even more likely to be shy and socially maladroit. Twenty-five-year-old Sylvia had an endocrine imbalance that had produced weight gain, as well as seizures and limited intelligence. After two years of high school and four years of art weaving, she was sent to Craig for treatment of her seemingly uncontrollable "nerve attacks." Her mother hoped she would get psychiatric care, along with antiseizure medications. But Sylvia was unhappy at the Colony; she abused other patients, threatened suicide, and found herself shunned by her colleagues, who refused to include her in events like dances and movies. In a letter to her mother, Sylvia complained, "The way I'm dressed here I feel like a slobby slob and frozen turnip. At least I like to look clean and presentable all the time. Not only when company comes." A year later, Sylvia went home on parole. Although her mother continued to complain of Sylvia's "rather childish ways" and excessive dependence, the social worker was pleased by her neat appearance and enthusiastic work. She tried to encourage the mother to let Sylvia "think a little more for herself." Whether the strategy worked in the short run is not clear; the social worker's notes ended abruptly in October 1946, and the next item in Sylvia's record is dated eleven years later: a request for her records from Creedmoor State Hospital, where she had become a patient.[43] Thus, in even larger numbers than epileptics designated imbeciles, those labeled morons often left Craig Colony after several months or even years, a period long enough to provide a respite for families or to get their medications adjusted. Like Sylvia, after a period of years some ended up back in state institutions, most often those closer to their homes. Because the Craig Colony records typically end with those recommitments, their subsequent medical careers cannot be traced. The records are even blanker on what happened to those who managed to escape further state attention.

Conclusion

This history of Craig Colony begins with a story of fiscal policies and institution building. It ends with the story of a patient, one of those especially ill served by those policies and the institution they produced. In 1940, an adolescent boy arrived at Craig Colony. He was described by the admitting staff doctor as a partially paralyzed, mute child with an IQ of 20 or less. The Colony did little for such patients. Like most of the seriously impaired patients, he was assigned to a remote building, far from administrative and medical offices. There he quickly lost weight and animation, for the staff had neither the time nor the patience to care for children, despite their need of a wide range of help. John, however, was not entirely without resources. His mother, who had institutionalized him reluctantly, barraged the Colony's superintendent with letters of complaint. Although she had sent her son to the Colony for treatment, on each visit she found him weaker. "Since he is so difficult to care for, would you [tell us how] to take him out of Craig Colony," she finally asked in mid-January 1941. She then made plans to take her son home, less than four months after his admission. Sadly, he died hours before his discharge, the cause of death being given as "inanition of idiocy." Angrily, his mother wrote to the Colony's medical staff:

> Why do you people take children when you can't give them proper care, let alone feed them? You can't deny that the main reason he died was due to starvation. . . . You probably through [thought] at first [I] weren't interested in the boy. The only reason we sent him there was because we were told he could be cared for and given treatments which we couldn't give him and not because we wanted to get rid of him. . . . Institutions of that sort are for animals, not those poor unfortunates there and if there is any

place that needs investigating yours is it, and not the homes you send them too [sic].[44]

As John's mother suspected, his story was not unique. Overburdened and underfunded for its entire history, Craig Colony offered particularly poor care to its weakest, most handicapped patients. Initially, the Colony's board of managers and superintendent had tried to restrict admissions so as to exclude the sick, infirm, and severely impaired. However, their protests were ignored by state legislators, local boards of charity, and desperate families. The results were dreadful. Small children with multiple handicaps spent their lives in cribs set in rows in large, bleak rooms; adolescents became both initiators and victims of sexual aggression; the elderly, as well as the young, died when they could no longer feed themselves. In part because of the relative inaccessibility of the Colony, located as it was in a remote part of New York State, it received relatively few visitors and even less state-level oversight. Despite a number of parental complaints like that lodged by John's mother, only once, in 1943, late in its history, did Craig Colony receive the sort of legislative attention that periodically exposed to public view the flaws of other, more centrally located state institutions.

Scholars and families familiar with the problems of large state institutions will not be surprised by the sad stories of so many Craig Colony patients and their families. Because its funding levels were even more inadequate than those of other state institutions, such as mental hospitals, however, its history is particularly grim. This relative disadvantage was not lost on the Craig Colony superintendents, who complained repeatedly but to no effect that mental hospitals, under the jurisdiction of the same state agency, got substantially more money per capita. Yet, the differentials in internal therapeutics and programming make clear that Colony administrators replicated locally the state-level economics of compassion. Consistently, from 1896 until 1967, they spent more time and money on "normal" epileptics than on those with learning problems, on morons (the most promising of the so-called feebleminded) than on imbeciles and idiots, on teenagers and young adults than on the aged and multiply handicapped babies.[45] Thus, Craig Colony's history supports the argument of the historian James Trent that "the economic vulnerability of these people [the mentally retarded] and their families, more than the claims made for their intellectual or social limitations, has shaped the kinds of treatment offered them."[46]

When, in 1965, the New York State legislature converted Craig Colony into a state school for the mentally retarded, it brought to an official close its long history as a specialized institution for epileptics. In some ways, the institution now named the Craig School looked very different from the institution described in the preceding pages. The almost 2,000 patients, most of "subnormal intelligence," nonetheless were offered a wide range of services, ranging from physiotherapy and speech therapy to bowling alleys and a golf driving range. (As in earlier days, however, the number who benefited from these was not specified.) Yet, in many ways, it was the same. The infirmary continued to grow and the educational program to contract. On an annual basis, the Craig Colony superintendent (now called its director) continued to complain about inadequate funding and the difficulties of attracting and keeping competent staff. Typical was the 1967 report that described an innovative and successful intensive treatment program for severely retarded children. The program greatly reduced its destructive and aggressive behavior while teaching good habits, but funding constraints limited it to only twelve of the many children who would have benefited from participation.[47]

There remains much to be learned about the experiences of those designated "mentally retarded" and their families. The Craig Colony records make clear that their history is far from static or predictable. Some parents, for example, managed their children's institutional experiences, whenever possible, in ways that have been underexplored, thus confirming David Wright's observation that the history of the family deserves "center stage in the transnational drama of institutionalization."[48] Labels, too, were more complex than historians often appreciate. Patients labeled "imbeciles" at admission might be described as "fairly intelligent" in a later case note; caught in dull routines and heavily drugged, those "bright" and "alert" when they first arrived at the Colony sometimes deteriorated into "hopeless dements" after years of institutional care. These observations, however, serve to romanticize the Colony story. More often than not, despite families' best efforts, institutionalized members died in the overcrowded Craig Colony back wards, some because their weakened immune systems were particularly vulnerable to the infectious diseases, such as tuberculosis and pneumonia, that periodically swept through, others simply of old age. At best, family power often was limited to the ability to get a patient transferred from Craig Colony to a state hospital or school closer to home. This last phenomenon merits further study. While it is widely known that even specialized social welfare institutions held a wide range of patients, the frequency with which patients moved in and out of different ones has not been studied adequately. Neither have the implications for patient care and family satisfaction of commitment to different institutions. We do not know what happened when Craig Colony patients were released or eloped and then later were recommitted to a state lunatic asylum or mental hospital, often located closer to their families. Did their situations worsen, improve, or remain more or less the same? What of the "feeble-minded" patient moved from the Rome State School to Craig Colony? Thus, stories remain to be told and histories (especially of transinstitutionalization) to be written. It is to be hoped that, despite the continuing influence of the economics of compassion on public policy, its grip on scholarship is being not just loosened but interrogated, analyzed, and even challenged.

NOTES

1. Ellen Dwyer, *Homes for the Mad: Life Inside Two Nineteenth-Century Asylums* (New Brunswick: Rutgers University Press, 1987), pp. 29–54. A similar comment on the relative neglect of epileptics appeared in an 1889 essay by Frederick Peterson, the leading proponent of colonization. He noted that "for every other defective class provision has been made in greater or less degree, for the insane, for idiots, for the deaf and dumb and blind, for the sick and the crippled, for the aged and infirm, for young malefactors in reformatories, for the negro, and for the Indian" but that the sufferer from epilepsy had been left "to shift for himself" when not locked up in an insane asylum. In contrast to the Craig Colony superintendents, Peterson was very optimistic about the potential of epileptics, arguing that most were intelligent and able to learn trades and become self-sufficient. Frederick Peterson, "The Colonization of Epileptics," *Journal of Nervous and Mental Disease*, Vol. 15 (December 1889), pp. 753–763; see also Peterson, "Outline of a Plan for an Epileptic Colony," *New York Medical Journal*, Vol. 56 (1892), pp. 96–98, and Peterson, "Presidential Address on the Care of Epileptics," *The Medical News*, Vol. 83, no. 3 (July 18, 1903), pp. 97–99.

2. Peter L. Tyor and Leland V. Bell, *Caring for the Retarded in America; A History* (Westport, CT: Greenwood Press, 1984); James W. Trent Jr., *Inventing the Feeble Mind: A History of Mental Retardation in the United States* (Berkeley: University of California Press, 1994); Steven Noll, *Feeble-Minded in Our Midst: Institutions for the Mentally Retarded in the South, 1900–1940* (Chapel Hill: University of North Carolina Press, 1995); Nicole Hahn Rafter, ed., *White Trash: The Eugenic Family Studies, 1877–1919* (Boston: Northeastern University Press, 1988); Rafter, *Creating Born Criminals* (Urbana: University of Illinois Press, 1997). For a collection of historical essays on mental retardation in Great Britain, with many parallels to the American experience, see David Wright

and Anne Digby, eds., *From Idiocy to Mental Deficiency: Historical Perspectives on People with Learning Disabilities* (London: Routledge, 1996), and Mark Jackson, *The Borderland of Imbecility: Medicine, Society and the Fabrication of the Feeble Mind in Late Victorian and Edwardian England* (Manchester: Manchester University Press, 2000).

3. The patient case histories for Craig Colony have been deposited in the New York State Archives in Albany. In this essay, patient names and other identifying characteristics have been disguised so as to protect the confidentiality of these medical records.

4. W. A. Hunt, "The Relation of the State to the Epileptic," *Northwestern Lancet,* Vol. 17 (1897), pp. 1–5. An early optimistic assessment of Craig Colony can be found in Sydney Brooks, "A New York 'Colony of Mercy,'" *The American Monthly Review of Reviews* (1900), pp. 313–318. Its author stresses the Colony's determination to admit only those "who stand a reasonable chance of profiting by the life to be provided them" (p. 314), a determination quickly undermined by pressure from individuals, families, and politicians to admit the most desperately ill. As a result, the ideal of a self-sufficient community, one that could support itself as an independent "colony," quickly disappeared.

5. "Second Annual Report of the Board of Managers of Craig Colony," printed in *The Thirtieth Annual Report of the State Board of Charities,* pp. 199, 210–211; *Third Annual Report of the Board of Managers of Craig Colony to the State Board of Charities, for the Fiscal Year Ending September 30, 1896* (Buffalo, NY: Matthews-Northrup, 1896), p. 35. (Hereafter annual reports will be referred to by the abbreviation AR.)

6. *The Seventh AR of the Board of Managers of the Craig Colony for Epileptics at Sonyea, Livingston, Co., N.Y., Adopted by the Board of the Colony at a Meeting Held at the Colony, October 9, 1906* (no place or date of publication), pp. 9, 28.

7. "Craig Colony for Epileptics," *Alienist and Neurologist,* Vol. 15, no. 3 (July 1894), pp. 388–389.

8. For examples of Spratling's similar views, see his description of the 1905 campaign to get a state law prohibiting the marriage and intermarriage of defectives, which passed the Senate but not the House in New York (*The Thirteenth AR of the Craig Colony for Epileptics to the State Board of Charities, Adopted by the Managers at a Meeting in Sonyea Hall at the Colony, October 9, 1906,* p. 27; see also William P. Spratling, "The Principles of Colony Building for the Defective Classes," *American Journal of Insanity,* Vol. 61 (July 1904), pp. 77–80. Relevant articles by William Shanahan include the following (listed chronologically): "The Care and Treatment of Epileptics," *New York State Journal of Medicine,* Vol. 11, no. 11 (November 1911), pp. 18–24; "History of the Establishment and Development of the Craig Colony for Epileptics Located in Sonyea, New York," *Epilepsia,* Vol. 3 (1911/1912); "Why the Marriage of Defectives Should Be Prevented When Possible," *Epilepsia,* Vol. 5 (1914–1915), pp. 94–100, 153–161; "The Problem of Epilepsy in New York State," *Psychiatric Quarterly,* Vol. 1, no. 2 (1927), pp. 160–183; "History of the Development of Special Institutions for Epileptics in the

United States," *Psychiatric Quarterly*, Vol. 2, no. 4 (1928), pp. 422–434. While the Colony did perform some ovariotomies in its first four decades, it never sterilized patients in large numbers. More often, records note that patients had been sterilized before being sent to the institution. According to Spratling, the Colony's policy on gynecological surgery was one of "abundant caution" as, in some cases, such surgery had negative effects (The Craig Colony for Epileptics, *The Fourteenth AR to the State Board of Charities* [1907], p. 72). For the larger literature on the American eugenics movement, see, among others, Daniel J. Kevles, *In the Name of Eugenics: Genetics and the Use of Human Heredity* (Berkeley: University of Califonia Press, 1985); Edward J. Larson, *Sex, Race, and Science: Eugenics in the Deep South* (Baltimore: Johns Hopkins University Press, 1995); and Angus McLaren, *Our Own Master Race: Eugenics in Canada, 1885–1945* (Toronto: McClelland and Stewart, 1990).

9. For examples of inertia, therapeutic nihilism, and lack of a sense of mission at Craig Colony in the 1930s and 1940s, see the following, often starkly brief reports: *Forty-Third AR of the Craig Colony at Sonyea, N.Y., to the Commissioner of Mental Hygiene, for the Fiscal Year Ending June 30, 1936* (Craig Colony Press, 1936); *Forty-Fifth AR . . . for the Fiscal Year Ending June 30, 1938* (Craig Colony Press, 1938), in which is noted the death of long-time (1894–1938) member of the board of managers, Frederick Peterson; *Fiftieth AR . . . for the Fiscal Year Ending March 31, 1943*, in which the superintendent (still Shanahan) comments that drugs were being dispensed "so far as funds permitted" (p. 14); and the *Fifty-Fifth AR . . . for the Fiscal Year Ended March 31, 1948* (Craig Colony Press, 1949), which again presented as new the old complaint that the institution was increasingly receiving epileptics "of low mental and physical capacity" (p. 5).

10. Trent, p. 129.

11. See the Colony's annual reports for the years between 1945 and 1967.

12. For a discussion of Goddard's work, see Trent, pp. 158–161, as well as Michael M. Sokal (ed.), *Psychological Testing and American Society, 1890–1930* (New Brunswick: Rutgers University Press, 1987); Leila Zenderland, *Measuring Minds: Henry Herbert Goddard and the Origins of American Intelligence Testing* (New York: Cambridge University Press, 1998).

13. Noll, p. 30.

14. *The Twenty-Fourth AR of the Managers and Officers of the Craig Colony for Epileptics, Sonyea, Livingston County, N.Y., Transmitted to the Legislature January 9, 1918* (Albany: J. B. Lyon Co., 1918), p. 89.

15. Ibid.

16. For examples of patients in the Loomis and Schuyler Infirmaries being mistreated or abused by other patients, see the following cases: 02784, 06981, 06994, 07229, 12238, and 12839.

17. Trent, p. 109.

18. The Craig Colony for Epileptics, *The Fifteenth AR of the Managers and Officers,*

Adopted by the Board of Managers at a meeting in Sonyea Hall at the Colony, October 13, 1908, p. 44.

19. Ibid., Caption to Plate 13, p. 60; p. 31.

20. State of New York, *The Twenty-Ninth AR of the Managers and Officers of the Craig Colony, Sonyea, Livingston County, New York, Transmitted to the Legislature, Jan. 1, 1923* (Craig Colony Press, 1922), pp. 9–11.

21. State of New York, *The Twenty-Fifth AR of the Managers and Officers of the Craig Colony for Epileptics, Sonyea, Livingston County, N.Y., Transmitted to the Legislature January 9, 1918* (Albany: J. B. Lyon, 1919), p. 39.

22. State of New York, *The Twenty-Sixth AR of the Managers and Officers of the Craig Colony for Epileptics, Sonyea, Livingston, N.Y.* (Albany: J. B. Lyon, 1920), p. 31; State of New York, *Fortieth Annual Report of the Board of Visitors and Officers of Craig Colony, Sonyea, N.Y., to the Commissioner of Mental Hygiene, for the Fiscal Year Ending June 30, 1933* (Craig Colony Press, 1933), pp. 21–22.

23. State of New York, *Fifty-Eighth Annual Report of the Board of Visitors of Craig Colony, Sonyea, N.Y., to the Department of Mental Hygiene for the Fiscal Year Ended March 31, 1951* (Utica: State Hospitals Press, 1951), pp. 15–17.

24. Mark Friedberger, "The Decision to Institutionalize: Families with Exceptional Children in 1910," *Journal of Family History,* Vol. 6 (1981), pp. 396–409; David Wright, "Family Strategies and the Institutional Confinement of 'Idiot' Children in Victorian England," *Journal of Family History,* Vol. 23, no. 2 (April 1998), pp. 190–208.

25. Patient case number 13107.

26. Patient case numbers 09708, 01281.

27. For example, see patient case numbers 03142, 03156, 04945, 06051, 06911, and 06945.

28. Patient case number 03142.

29. Patient case number 06945.

30. State of New York. No. 29, Senate, *Thirtieth AR of the State Board of Charities* (February 25, 1897), p. 60.

31. Patient case number 04848.

32. Patient case numbers 04878 and 05224.

33. Craig Colony, *Twenty-Second AR,* p. 111; patient case number 06351.

34. Patient case number 12301.

35. Patient case numbers 10923, 09390, 09762.

36. For examples of sodomizing or seduction, see patient case numbers 00087, 03122, 03522, 05952, 10919, 10922, 12093, 12239, 12255. For the "G-men" story, see patient case number 12093. For bullies, see patient case numbers 02784, 06982, 06994, 07339, 12238, 12239. For specific patient case reference, see case number 05984.

37. Patient case number 13052.

38. This was hardly surprising, of course. There is a large literature on the negative impact of institutionalization on intelligence and social skills.

39. Patient case number 07011.

40. See Trent, p. 229, for a general discussion of how this happened in institutions around the country.

41. Perhaps the best-known articulations of the notion that epileptics could have a particular mental orientation that constituted an "epileptoid" personality were offered by L. Pierce Clark, a New York City neurologist who started his career at Craig Colony and who served as a consultant to the institution for many years. Typical essays by Clark include "Conscious Epilepsy," *Proceedings of the American Medico-Psychological Association,* Vol. 16 (1903), pp. 245-250; "Is Essential Epilepsy a Life Reaction Disorder?" *American Journal of Medical Sciences,* Vol. 158 (1919), pp. 703-711; "A Psychogenic Study of Epilepsy in a Child," *Archives of Neurology and Psychiatry,* Vol. 6, no. 5 (November 1921), pp. 587-588; "The Epileptic Psyche," *State Hospital Quarterly,* Vol. 11, no. 3 (May 1926), pp. 33-36. For patient records that contain reference to typical epileptoid personalities, see (among others) case numbers 06956, 04442, and 01587.

42. Patient case numbers 12915 and 12929.

43. Patient case number 12794.

44. Patient case number 11688.

45. Typical of the Colony's problems from early in its history and its response to them (which changed little over time) was the following comment, made in 1900: "The doctrine of fitness for colony life needs to be reiterated time and again for the benefit of those who would pervert the main purpose of the Colony by making it a common receptacle for the vase army of unsuitable, incurable and helpless cases who might be given admittance." *The Seventh AR,* p. 28. State of New York, *Seventy-Third AR of Craig Colony School and Hospital, Sonyea, N.Y., to the Department of Mental Hygiene, for the Fiscal Year Ended March 31, 1966* (Utica: State Hospitals Press, 1966), p. 8.

46. Trent, p. 50.

47. State of New York, *Seventy-Fourth AR of Craig Colony School and Hospital, Sonyea, N.Y., to the Department of Mental Hygiene, for the Fiscal Year Ended March 31, 1967* (Utica: State Hospitals Press, 1967), pp. 6-9; State of New York, *Sixty-Eighth AR . . . for the Fiscal Year Ended March 31, 1961* (Craig Colony Press, 1963), p. 8; State of New York, *Sixty-Seventh AR of the Board of Visitors of Craig Colony . . . for the Fiscal Year Ended March 31, 1960* (Craig Colony Press, 1962), p. 19.

48. Wright, p. 198; see also Trent, pp. 225-250.

11

The "Sociological Advantages" of Sterilization

Fiscal Policies and Feeble-Minded Women in Interwar Minnesota

Molly Ladd-Taylor

In the past twenty years, eugenic sterilization has made its way into our nation's historical memory, and the disturbing stories of eugenics victims like Carrie Buck have been told in dozens of books and films. While attention to this repugnant part of the American past is long overdue, it is disquieting that almost all journalistic (and many scholarly) accounts of sterilization follow the same basic narrative: experts infatuated with the pseudoscience of eugenics and even Nazism abused state power to sterilize people allegedly, but not really, mentally retarded. Surgical sterilization is deplored, but the overall lesson is in keeping with the conservatism of our times: beware of "experts," and beware of government power.[1]

Depicting compulsory sterilization as a Nazi-like scandal in America's past elicits powerful emotions, but it is more useful as catharsis than as history. Although it feels good to contrast an enlightened us of today with a prejudiced them of the past, doing so neither helps us to comprehend the tragedy of eugenics nor prevents it from happening again. In truth, as many historians have pointed out, eugenic sterilization programs were established not simply because Nazi-inspired doctors manipulated the state and tried to rid society of those they considered unfit but because of a melange of factors that are much more mundane: professional self-interest, fiscal politics, political expediency, and deep-felt cultural beliefs about economic dependency, disability, and gender.[2]

This essay examines eugenic sterilization as it operated within the health and welfare bureaucracy of one midwestern state. Minnesota is a useful site for a case study because its liberal reputation and relatively homogeneous population require us to rethink the conventional paradigms of sterilization history. Despite the loathsome rhetoric of Charles Dight, secretary of the Minnesota Eugenics Society, whose fan letter to Hitler is preserved at the state historical society, Minnesota's eugenic sterilization program was characterized more by ordinariness than by extremism. While eugenics and publicity about the "menace of the feebleminded" played an important role in obtaining public support, Minnesota's sterilization law would not have passed without the sponsorship of politicians and mental health professionals concerned as much with fiscal politics—containing welfare costs and reducing the budget of state institutions—as with the prevention of hereditary defects. When historians turn our attention from the intellectual arguments of the bill's most vocal supporters to the actual implementation of policy, the routine and bureaucratic nature of the state's sterilization program becomes clear.[3]

A case study of sterilization in Minnesota also serves as a reminder of the eugenics movement's appeal in the American midwest. Prior to 1946, more "feeble-minded" persons were sterilized in Minnesota and Michigan than in all the southern states combined.[4] Although the numbers are small when compared to Nazi Germany or the state of California, at least 1,843 Minnesotans (79 percent of them women) were legally sterilized by June 1946. The greatest numbers were sterilized in the late 1930s, when relief rolls expanded because of the Depression. The number of operations dropped off during World War II, not because of revelations of Nazi eugenic excesses but because of a shortage of medical and nursing personnel. Despite a 1946 election-year scandal over sterilizations performed at the state institution, the operations continued, although in vastly reduced numbers, until the law was changed in 1975.[5]

Minnesota's sterilization program existed alongside a liberal child welfare system and an "outstanding" program of legal guardianship for people with mental disabilities that won national praise. In 1962, President Kennedy's Panel on Mental Retardation cited Minnesota's guardianship program as a model that should be studied by other states.[6] The state's School for the Feebleminded, established at Faribault in 1879 and led from 1885 to 1917 by A. C. Rogers, its medical superintendent and the influential editor of the *Journal of Psycho-Asthenics,* was among the nation's foremost custodial institutions for the feebleminded. Although Rogers died in 1917, his vision of the institution, enthusiasm for research, and advocacy of guardianship with supervision for those who could return to the community framed Minnesota's mental deficiency policy for decades. By the 1930s, Minnesota was considered the most "feebleminded-conscious" state in America, lauded for its comprehensive program for people with mental disabilities.[7]

Minnesota's eugenic sterilization law, passed in 1925, was a vital part of the state's mental deficiency program. Unlike most state sterilization statutes, the law in Minnesota was "permissive"—meaning that it was not limited to institutionalized persons—and it was "voluntary." An operation could be performed only on a feeble-minded (or insane) person committed to state guardianship, and only after careful investigation; consultation with three experts (a "reputable" physician, a psychologist, and the superintendent of the School for the Feebleminded); and the written consent of the spouse or nearest kin. If no relative could be located, the State Board of Control as legal guardian could give consent. The officials who ran Minnesota's sterilization program saw it as a humane and progressive policy, consistent with the enlightened social welfare measures for which their state was known. They did not sterilize very young children and rarely authorized operations over the objections of family members. The fact that the legal foundation for sterilization was created by the state's Commission on Child Welfare indicates its roots in progressive social reform.[8]

Ironically, surgical sterilization was established as part of Minnesota's child welfare system just as the system as a whole was becoming more liberal. In Minnesota as elsewhere in the United States, the 1910s and 1920s saw the repudiation of the nineteenth-century strategy of "saving" children by breaking up impoverished families and a growing emphasis on keeping poor children out of institutions and at home with their mothers. The new consensus on child welfare—that institutions were bad, and that government bore some responsibility for children's wellbeing—was articulated at the 1909 White House Conference on the Care of Dependent Children. "Home life is the highest and finest product of civilization," delegates resolved. "Except in unusual circumstances, the home should not be broken up for reasons of poverty, but only for considerations of inefficiency or immorality." The vagueness of the terms "inefficiency" and "immorality" suggests the power that individual caseworkers could wield over parents who were poor.[9]

Following the White House Conference, a number of states, including Minnesota, reorganized their child welfare systems. In 1917, the Minnesota legislature passed its Children's Code, a package of thirty-five laws that strengthened and streamlined the state's authority over child welfare, and established the legal framework for eugenic sterilization. The Code strengthened guardianship laws for neglected, dependent, and delinquent children (and defective adults); established a children's bureau within the State Board of Control; set up a licensing system for maternity hospitals and child care institutions; and revised Minnesota's state's juvenile court and mothers' pensions systems. Mothers' pensions, which became the cornerstone of the new child welfare policy, were modest stipends intended to enable impoverished widows and other "deserving" mothers to keep their children at home (and out of institutions). Minnesota passed its mothers' pensions law in 1913. In 1935, the Social Security Act made the program, then called Aid to Dependent Children, national in scope.[10] Although mothers' pensions redefined most impoverished mothers and children as worthy of aid, the older and more punitive approach to child welfare persisted for parents perceived as unfit. There were, in effect, two strands of child welfare policy in the early twentieth-century United States: one for the children of (newly) deserving "normal" mothers and another for those still considered undeserving: the inefficient or immoral—and the "defective." The two strands were closely connected; indeed, mothers' pensions might not have been instituted for widows and "deserving" mothers had not more punitive programs continued for the rest.

The inadequacies and injustices in the mothers' pensions program have received a great deal of scholarly attention, but surprisingly little has been written about what happened to parents deemed too immoral or inefficient to be eligible for aid.[11] In Minnesota at least, many of these families were classed as mentally deficient, or feeble-minded. For them, child welfare programs differed little from the punitive child-saving methods of the nineteenth century. Although in the abstract the policy of family preservation still applied, many "defective" families were broken up, at least temporarily. Social workers worked closely with law enforcement officials to ferret out neglectful parents (and feeble-minded parents were virtually presumed to be neglectful). Wives and children were often placed in the state institution. Long after social workers rejected institutions for "normal" children on the grounds that they destroyed individuality, stunted intellectual and social growth, and prevented the development of independence and self-control, institutionalization remained the strategy of choice for feebleminded youth and their mothers.[12]

Thus, while the Progressive-era changes to child welfare expanded the number of mothers and children considered deserving of aid, they also widened the gulf between the "normal" poor and those considered feeble-minded. As social workers began to view family dysfunction as the result of inadequate surroundings or emotional difficulties, they envisioned improving the parenting skills of "normal" people through education, therapy, or a change in environment. By contrast, mothers who were mentally deficient seemed hopeless cases. And, in a circle especially vicious to the mothers so labeled, hopeless cases seemed mentally deficient.[13] To policy makers and social workers living in a culture that preached the infallibility of science, eugenics provided a compelling explanation for the persistence of poverty and family dysfunction in the wake of liberal social welfare reform. By the 1910s, the hereditary nature of most mental retardation was assumed. Eugenicist family studies, such as Henry H. Goddard's sensational *The Kallikak Family* (1915) and *Dwellers in the Vale of Siddem* (1919), by Minnesota's A. C. Rogers and Maud Merrill, scientifically "proved" that feeblemindedness was inherited, that mentally deficient families reproduced faster than the general population, and that mental defectives were responsible for a host of social problems, including pauperism, illegitimacy, and crime.[14]

Intelligence tests gained acceptance as a diagnostic tool in the same years. In 1910, A. C. Rogers hired the psychologist Frederick Kuhlmann to direct the Bureau of Research at the Faribault School. Kuhlmann, a student of G. Stanley Hall, was one of the first Americans to refine and use the Binet-Simon intelligence test, and he worked tirelessly to promote the test in Minnesota; his goal was to eventually test every child in a statewide "census" of the feebleminded. The intelligence test made it possible for the first time to identify "high-grade" mental defectives—people of borderline intelligence who lived outside the institution and were not immediately recognizable as retarded—and it led to an enormous increase in the numbers of people diagnosed as feeble-minded. Convinced of the urgency of the mental deficiency problem but well aware that it was impossible to institutionalize every feeble-minded Minnesotan, reformers set their sights on surgical sterilization. Although a bill introduced into the Minnesota legislature in 1913 died in committee, by 1917 the state's Commission on Child Welfare, building on Rogers's support for a revised sterilization law, registered general approval of the policy. Minnesota became the seventeenth state to legalize eugenic sterilization in 1925. Two years later, the U.S. Supreme Court ruled compulsory sterilization constitutional in *Buck v. Bell*.[15]

285

Minnesota's sterilization law was administered as part of its child protection system. The 1917 Children's Code gave the State Board of Control broad powers of legal guardianship over illegitimate, dependent, and neglected children and over "defective" individuals regardless of age. It empowered county or probate judges to commit feeble-minded individuals to state guardianship, even without the consent of a parent or guardian. (The guardianship was for life, unless the person was specifically discharged from state supervision.) To assist the courts in determining who was feeble-minded, the law required the Board of Control to provide mental examiners to give IQ tests to people who came before the court on a variety of charges, including delinquency, illegitimacy, child neglect, and poor schoolwork. Once committed as feeble-minded, an individual became a ward "protected" by the state. He or she had no civil or political rights: a ward could not vote, own property, manage his or her financial affairs, or marry without the state's permission. The Board of Control, as legal guardian, decided whether the feeble-minded ward should be placed in an institution or remain in the community under a social worker's supervision. As the state's central welfare agency, the Board also had authority over public institutions (including the state prison and insane asylum), the state children's bureau, hospitals and programs for people with physical disabilities, and (especially during the Depression) general relief. County child welfare boards served as local agents of the Board and carried out its work at the county level.[16]

During the 1920s, the expansion of intelligence testing and the enlarged authority of the courts to commit people as feeble-minded led to a dramatic increase in the number of Minnesotans determined to be mentally deficient and committed to state guardianship. Most of the increase—and most of the people sterilized—were "high-grade" feebleminded, or morons, and many of them would not be considered to have a mental disability today. Since the statutory definition of a "feeble-minded person" as someone "who is so mentally defective as to be incapable of managing himself and his affairs, and to require supervision, control and care for his own or the public welfare" was vague (and did not even mention IQ), county judges had wide latitude in making commitment decisions. To ascertain who was feeble-minded, judges looked first at the results of an intelligence test, conducted by a mental examiner at the Board of Control. In recent years, scholars have questioned the objectivity of the IQ test, pointing out that it tests literacy more than native intelligence and probing its class and cultural bias. The fact that the tests in Minnesota were often conducted under appalling conditions—

such as in "a crowded room, in a home with a child often pounding on the door, in the yard or in the car"—no doubt contributed to the large numbers of people (and especially poor people) found to be feeble-minded in the state.[17]

Despite Kuhlmann's insistence that IQ alone was sufficient to determine mental deficiency, in practice a diagnosis of feeblemindedness had as much to do with lower-class status and behavior as with the results of a mental examination. This was especially true because county judges who had the authority to commit someone as feeble-minded encountered mainly people already in trouble with welfare agencies or the law. Unmarried mothers, for example, were often determined to be feeble-minded and brought under state guardianship simply because they had a child outside of marriage and could not provide support. Similarly, in Minneapolis's Hennepin County, more than half of the 120 morons committed in 1927 had been "grossly delinquent," while another 20 percent had been charged with incorrigibility. To make a commitment decision, county judges took into account a range of factors beyond IQ, including an individual's health, family background, home environment, school or work record, and general deportment. No doubt many concurred with the characterization, probably written by Kuhlmann, of mentally deficient adults as those who "lack common sense, foresight, are unable to resist ordinary temptations, act on impulse, and have little or no initiative. They have about the same desires as normals, including sexual, but lack ability to control them. They usually have poor homes." Although still used to describe the alleged behavior of an urban underclass, these traits are now more likely to be attributed to a "culture of poverty" than to mental retardation or genetic defect.[18]

The large increase in the number of people found to be feeble-minded and committed to state guardianship precipitated a crisis in the overcrowded state institution. In his 1922 biennial report, Faribault superintendent Guy Hanna reported that the school had exceeded its capacity, largely because of the institutionalization of morons. Quoting Walter Fernald, the respected superintendent of the Massachusetts School for the Feebleminded, Hanna distinguished those "high-grade" feeble-minded women and men from the "ordinary defective, . . . [the] innocent feeble minded children" who were institutionalized because they could not be cared for at home. "Many of this class have been immoral and have committed criminal acts," he wrote; "[they] are defiant, abusive, profane, disobedient, destructive and incorrigible generally." Their presence in the institution not only had a "very bad influence" on the other patients, it also contributed to the problem of overcrowding. By 1925, the year the sterilization bill was passed, 2,341 inmates, about half of them women, crowded into an institution intended for 1,900, and there was a long waiting list.[19]

One way state officials attempted to deal with the overcrowding at the Faribault School—and to save money—was by releasing, or "paroling," inmates to local communities. "It will never be possible to herd all defectives into institutions," explained the Board of Control, "and their useful labor under supervision will be an economic gain to the community." The parole policy in Minnesota was based on the colony idea of Rome (N.Y.) State School superintendent Charles Bernstein, but Minnesota's program was geared almost exclusively to women, and—perhaps because it began without the support of Superintendent Hanna—it was largely independent of the School for the Feebleminded. In 1924 the Board of Control and the Women's Welfare League of Minneapolis established the Harmon Club, a home for feeble-minded wards working in the community; within a few years, the policy of parole was well established, and two more clubhouses had opened in the state. The vast majority of parolees were women who worked in domestic service, laundries, restaurants, or small factories while living in state-run clubhouses like the Harmon Club or, less often, with local families as live-in maids. There were few paroled men, partly because of local opposition to their living outside the institution and partly because the jobs available in cities were mostly "women's" jobs, such as domestic service. (The few male parolees were farmhands.) Parole benefited feeble-minded girls, explained the Board of Control, because they were "much happier than they could be inside the institution," and the steady supply of low-wage workers was good for the community. Although some parolees were discharged from guardianship, most remained wards of the state and were supervised by the Board of Control or the county child welfare boards. Despite the fact that the state's main goal was to save money by making the clubhouses self-supporting, one social worker, Mildred Thomson, recalled that the clubhouse program was, in the context of the 1920s, a "great advance" for the mentally retarded.[20]

According to Thomson, who headed Minnesota's Bureau for the Feebleminded from 1924 to 1959, the 1925 sterilization law—or at least, professionals' support for it—was in large measure the product of those plans for community living. To be sure, the bill would not have passed without the vigorous lobbying of eugenicists, especially Dight, who encouraged and exploited popular fears about the menace of the feebleminded. Yet the men and women with a professional stake in the care and supervision of the feebleminded considered the principal benefit of the sterilization law to be that it made "possible many paroles which could not otherwise have been planned for" by eliminating the possibility that feeble-minded women living outside the institution would get pregnant.[21]

Although convinced that most feeblemindedness was inherited, Minnesota officials consistently stressed the "sociological advantages" over the "eugenic benefits" of sterilization. "The genetic argument for sterilization is plausible," one explained, "yet the stronger reason is that they [morons] are unfit for parenthood." The Board of Control repeatedly rebuffed the efforts of Dight and his fellow eugenicists to emulate California and sterilize greater numbers of the "unfit"; Thomson recalled ducking out a side door so that she would be "not in" whenever Dight visited her office. Instead of the sweeping sterilization program favored by eugenicists, the state chose to take a more cautious approach based on the social work principles of individual casework. (Of course, the emphasis on casework and supervision was in state employees' professional self-interest.) A memo titled "History of the Sterilization of the Feeble-Minded," distributed by the Board of Control, criticized the "over zealous" claim that sterilization was "wholly justified by the eugenic factors" and rejected "wholesale sterilization" as impractical and inadvisable. Instead, it endorsed "selective sterilization" in individual cases. For state officials, the "socio-economic justification of sterilization, that the feeble-minded parent cannot provide a stable and secure family life for his children," was paramount. Sterilization policy was as much about preventing child *rearing* by the so-called feebleminded as it was about preventing child *bearing*.[22]

The "sociological advantages" of sterilization—and the centrality of commitments of the feebleminded to the state's welfare and juvenile justice systems—are abundantly clear in the state archives. Although the wide range of cases warns against overgeneralization, the admissions and medical records of the Faribault School for the Feebleminded, where the operations were performed, show the connection experts perceived among economic dependency, sexual impropriety, and mental deficiency. Most women sterilized in Minnesota during the interwar years were either young sex "delinquents," often unmarried mothers, who were committed as feeble-minded through the court system, or slightly older women with a number of children on public assistance. Immoral or inefficient mothers (or both), they were ineligible for mother's pensions but needed some kind of government aid. These desperately poor women were labeled feebleminded and committed to state guardianship largely because they had no family that could or would support them, and guardianship shifted some of the economic burden of caring for them from the county to the state.

The largest portion of sterilized women were sex "delinquents," unmarried but sexually active women who either had children or might have children they could not support. Most historians who have noted the association between "feeblemindedness" and female delinquency have emphasized the efforts of experts and parents to control young women's sexuality, and indeed this was a factor in Minnesota's sterilization program.[23] Faribault admissions records regularly reported patients' sexual histories. Yet a closer look at the case histories of feeble-minded "sex delinquents" complicates the picture often drawn by historians—and proponents of sterilization—which highlights these women's sexual rebelliousness and agency. Some feebleminded women undoubtedly were resisting the norms of a repressive society, but others were victims of incest or sexual abuse; had untreated (and often undiagnosed) mental, physical, or learning disabilities; or came from families unable or unwilling to support them during economic hard times. Take the case of Lola, who was sterilized in 1938, two months after her twenty-first birthday. Lola's father had committed suicide, and social workers described her mother, a polio survivor, as a "very incompetent person." Lola herself had been sent to a correctional institution when she was just sixteen years old for "excessive indulgence" with middle-aged men. Although never actually delinquent, Lola was described as "very stubborn, even refusing to go to a doctor when necessary." She was "a girl who needs a family," Thomson observed; she got sterilized instead.[24]

An even sadder case was that of Lucille, a "feeble-minded" mother of two illegitimate children, who was said to have "cohabited" with her father and brother. (The father served time in the state prison for incest.) Lucille, whose first child died at the age of one week, was admitted to the Faribault School for the Feebleminded at the age of nineteen, when her second child was one year old. The Superintendent thought Lucille overly inclined to worry about her surviving child but wrote that she was "quiet, well-mannered, and responds to kind treatment. Her delinquencies seem to have been beyond her control, and she has none of the tendencies towards prostitution." Still, he attributed Lucille's unhappiness and "delinquencies" to mental retardation, rather than to sexual abuse or grief over the loss of her children.[25]

Extramarital sexual behavior was considered a leading indicator of feeble-mindedness, but it was certainly not the only one. On a list of five women between the ages of eighteen and twenty-five considered for sterilization and release into the community in May 1933, not one is described in terms of sexual immorality or delinquency. Instead, four of the five—all of whom had IQs in the 60s—are considered to have "feeble-minded" mothers. This fact seems to support the eugenic belief that mental retardation is hereditary, so it is worth noting that the case histories contain no reference to eugenicist concepts of family pedigree, or even to other "defective" family members. Instead, they are written in the language of social work, emphasizing the negative impact of poverty and inadequate home conditions on children. According to the report, two sisters, whose father was deceased and whose mother was in an institution, came from a family with "no delinquent tendencies . . . just extreme poverty and mental backwardness." As evidence for the feeble-mindedness of the mothers of two other girls, the report notes that one had an illegitimate child and the other was receiving county aid.[26]

Supposedly incompetent mothering, often reflected in poor home conditions, was another rationale for sterilization. Take the case of Elizabeth, a farmer's wife and mother of two. In 1926, at the age of twenty-four, Elizabeth was declared feeble-minded and made a ward of the state on the grounds that she was unable to keep a clean home or properly care for her children. Admitted to the Faribault School for sterilization and education in "some habits of cleanliness and good housekeeping," Elizabeth was returned to her husband after the surgery. Yet she did not get along with her husband or his parents. She accused them of being cruel to her and ran away to Minneapolis with one of her children. In 1930, just three years after being sterilized and released from the Faribault School, Elizabeth was sent back to the institution because she was homeless and could not support her child. Desperate to get out, she finally agreed to go back to her husband and was discharged to him in 1932. No doubt Elizabeth's "feeblemindedness" was related to the fact that she was not a compliant wife, yet had no job skills or family of her own to fall back on.[27]

If Elizabeth was too rebellious and stubborn, most feeble-minded women were considered too passive for motherhood. Ada, an unmarried mother who left school after flunking eighth grade, was typical. The medical staff at Faribault described Ada as attractive, agreeable, and cooperative, but overly susceptible to influence and unable to make decisions. (This was despite her refusal to take a job that required supervision—after her employer got her pregnant!) Similarly, Mary, a thirty-six-year-old mother of ten children, was determined to be "inadequate" in the home and unable to care for her children. Although her conduct was deemed appropriate and she did not use alcohol or drugs, she was described as "dull and rather slovenly." Convinced that improvement was unlikely (twenty years earlier, her schoolwork had been poor), the medical staff considered sterilization.[28]

The feeble-minded mothers and potential mothers portrayed in the records of Minnesota welfare agencies and the Faribault School carried to an extreme the image of the dangerous mother that emerged in the psychiatric and child guidance literature of the interwar period. Prior to the First World War, child psychologists attributed juvenile misbehavior to a range of causes, including ignorance, a bad environment, and heredity. By the 1920s, however, they saw flawed mothering as the explanation for virtually all behavioral problems. Middle-class housewives might smother their children; working-class mothers rejected them by going out to work.[29] But the most ruinous condemnation was saved for allegedly feeble-minded mothers, who were neglectful almost by definition. Too much aggression and too little initiative were both considered evidence of feeblemindedness in women; as well, they were signs of a pathological or rejecting mother—signs of a mother who posed a danger to her child. This is why, in spite of a general policy of family preservation, Minnesota social workers frequently tried to remove children from feeble-minded mothers. By expressing special concern for the normal children of mentally deficient parents, social workers revealed both their bias against the feebleminded and their rejection of the eugenicist assumption that mental deficiency was invariably transmitted to the next generation. As an officer of the Children's Protective Society complained, "Mental defectives have undiminished powers of procreation, but often have not the power to support children and generally have little or no ability either to guide or to discipline them. Often the children of a feebleminded mother by the time they are 10 years old have more intelligence than their mother and consequently dominate her."[30]

The damage a feeble-minded mother could do to a normal child is illustrated in the case of Martin X, an illegitimate and allegedly neglected child of a feeble-minded woman whose case history was "fairly typical." The fifth of seven children, Martin had no respect for his mother because he was smarter than she was—and knew it. School officials considered him neglected; he was dirty, often absent, and uninterested in his studies. A visiting nurse described Martin's mother Katie as "simply impossible" and worried what would become of the boy if he continued to live with "this woman in this environment." In the spring of 1933, when Martin was ten, the nurse's fears were realized. Martin joined a gang, looted automobiles and broke windows, and stole money from his mother's purse. When a social worker advised Katie to hide her money, the boy sneered, "I am smarter than her, she can't hide her money where I can't find it." The case worker concluded that the boy's delinquency was "a natural result of his mother's inadequacy."[31]

Martin's case was written up to illustrate the point that social workers were powerless to *prevent* Martin's delinquency. Since his mother had not been committed to state guardianship, it was only after Martin got in trouble with the law and had to go before the Juvenile Court that the state was empowered to remove him from his mother's custody. For the social worker who wrote up his case, the system had failed Martin; social workers needed more power to intervene. Committing more feeble-minded parents to state guardianship and removing children from their homes might help, but the most effective way to "protect the child handicapped by being born to mentally deficient parents," she maintained, was to prevent the feebleminded from having children at all.[32]

As the timing of Martin X's story suggests, concern that the poor parenting skills of feeble-minded women would lead to juvenile delinquency escalated during the economic crisis of the 1930s, when the system of parole and family support networks both broke down. With factories and restaurants going out of business, middle-class families no longer able to afford domestic help, and "normal" people competing with the feebleminded for the few remaining jobs, most feeble-minded wards found themselves out of work. The Harmon Club closed in 1933, not only because of cost, Thomson recalled, but because unemployed girls kept getting into trouble. For social workers charged with caring for feeble-minded wards, the difficulties of supervision were compounded by the pressures of other administrative responsibilities, especially the distribution of emergency relief. Frustrated by high case loads, disjointed relief policies, and limited resources, a significant number of Minnesota welfare workers concluded that "eugenic" sterilization was a viable and indeed humane solution to the seemingly endless cycle of family poverty, dysfunction, and delinquency. "The number of children, their doings, the whole thing piles up so terribly that one cannot face it," a social worker from St. Paul despaired. "We don't know what the answer is. I think it is not so much a matter . . . of getting the feebleminded committed, but of . . . catching the feebleminded girls and boys before they can marry and establish homes."[33]

Given the strong association between feeblemindedness and economic dependency, it is not surprising that the Depression brought a substantial increase in the number of commitments, institutionalizations, and sterilizations (although still only a fraction of supposedly feeble-minded Minnesotans were under state guardianship). In 1935, a law backed by Kuhlmann provided for, but did not fund, a statewide census of the feeble-minded with the aim of identifying all mentally deficient Minnesotans in order to begin supervision and control at an earlier age. Yet, for the most part, the rise in commitments, and even the debate over the need for a census of the feebleminded, took place within the state bureaucracy. There was little public discussion of the "menace of the feebleminded"—or of mental retardation at all—outside professional circles. Popular concern for and about Minnesota's most vulnerable residents was drowned out by the magnitude of the economic crisis.[34]

The public's indifference nothwithstanding, the state greatly extended its control over "feeble-minded" Minnesotans during the Depression, and it did so mainly because of fiscal politics; county officials wanted to limit the number of families who had to go on relief. County welfare boards ordered IQ tests for parents and children living in "deplorable" conditions, and "in many instances whole families were then committed to guardianship as feebleminded." Perhaps, as Thomson suggested, placing entire families under state guardianship made harried judges and county welfare workers feel "satisfied that they had taken some kind of action" in a crisis. More likely, county judges and welfare boards committed so many people to state guardianship because doing so obliged the state to share the cost of supporting them, not only if the ward were institutionalized but also if he or she remained in the county. In any case, many of those committed as feebleminded during the Depression were not really retarded, and, as Thomson conceded with grand understatement, "their frustrating experiences made them resentful." Court action was required to reverse the commitment; however, not even the State Board of Control had that power.[35]

The history of sterilization in Minnesota is not simply a tale of victimization, however, for many families resisted the state's intrusions. Some petitioned the state to have their loved ones "restored to capacity" and discharged from state guardianship, in spite of the expense. Others simply ran away, becoming lost from the authorities (and the historical record). A few even tried to turn the system to their own advantage. Thus, a social worker who thought that sterilization was a "questionable remedy" for most problems of feeblemindedness observed that it "has worked out well in families where there were already enough children and the mother and father were convinced that there should not be any more." Unfortunately, the records are silent on how often "eugenic" sterilization was really contraceptive in purpose. But there are tantalizing hints. Faribault admissions records reveal the existence of a small number of women, like Annie, the wife of a farm laborer on public assistance and mother of ten living children, who entered the institution expressly "for sterilization" and expected to return home upon recovery. But state-funded contraceptive sterilization required an extraordinary sacrifice on the part of the woman, for the operation could legally be done only on individuals who had been committed as feebleminded (or insane) wards of the state—and who had thereby relinquished their political and civil rights. Tragically, some Minnesota women were so desperate for health and contraceptive care that they permitted—and in some cases even asked—social workers to find them feeble-minded and hence "unfit" mothers so they could be sterilized under a eugenics law.[36]

Eugenic sterilization became routine in interwar Minnesota because it served many functions within the state's welfare system. For eugenicists, it served as a stepping stone to more sweeping laws that would curb the fertility of all the unfit. For county welfare officials and the voting public, it was a way to reduce public expenditures, or at least to shift the costs of "child" welfare to another level of government. For front-line social workers with high case loads and limited resources, it was a way to reduce the numbers of feebleminded and maybe make their jobs more manageable and secure. For a few family members, eugenic sterilization was a form of birth control at a time when other types of contraception were unavailable.

Although Minnesota's sterilization program wound down during the Second World War, dependency, disability, and poverty persisted, and state and county authorities continued to exercise enormous power over the people they "protected." In 1965, a University of Minnesota law professor, Robert J. Levy, issued a sharp rebuke to probate judges and welfare boards for abusing Minnesota's celebrated guardianship program. Noting the disparity between the "law on the books" and the "law in action," Levy contended that judges often committed people for economic reasons and that county welfare departments manipulated the guardianship program to solve vexing social problems. They institutionalized troubled youth who were not really retarded, for instance, and pressured state wards to give up their children or consent to sterilization.[37]

Such misuse of power in liberal Minnesota, decades after "eugenics" was discredited and sterilizations slowed, shows the need to rethink the conventional "lessons" of eugenic sterilization. The suffering of most sterilization survivors was hardly limited to the surgery, and the two-dimensional tale of Nazi-like state versus victims of sterilization does not do justice to the complexity, and real tragedy, of their lives. In our current climate of frenzied tax cuts, resentment of social welfare spending, and hostility to "big" government, it is crucial to remember that the history of eugenic sterilization is not a simple story about the dangers of pseudoscience and an intrusive state. It is a sad and disturbing tale of political expediency and taxpayer stinginess that reveals the heavy price that individuals—and, indeed, the entire society—pay when the most vulnerable members of a community do not have access to the services and resources they need.

NOTES

This chapter is a revised version of "'Fixing Mothers': Child and Compulsory Sterilisation in the American Midwest, 1925–1945," which appeared in Jon Lawrence and Pat Starkey, eds., *Child Welfare and Social Action in the Nineteenth and Twentieth Century: International Perspectives*. It is reprinted here by permission of Liverpool University Press.

1. See, for example, "Against Her Will: The Carrie Buck Story" (Wilmington Film and Video Production Studios, 1994); "The Lynchburg Story: Eugenic Sterilization in America" (Audio Visual Services, 1993); "The Sterilization of Leilani Muir" (National Film Board of Canada, 1996); Allan Chase, *The Legacy of Malthus: The Social Costs of the New Scientific Racism* (New York: Knopf, 1976); J. David Smith and K. Ray Nelson, *The Sterilization of Carrie Buck* (Far Hills, N.J.: New Horizon Press, 1989).

2. These "mundane" factors are explored in James W. Trent Jr., *Inventing the Feeble Mind: A History of Mental Retardation in the United States* (Berkeley: University of California Press, 1994); Steven Noll, *Feeble-Minded in Our Midst: Institutions for the Mentally Retarded in the South, 1900–1940* (Chapel Hill: University of North Carolina Press, 1995); Philip R. Reilly, *The Surgical Solution: A History of Involuntary Sterilization in the United States* (Baltimore: Johns Hopkins University Press, 1991); Molly Ladd-Taylor, "Saving Babies and Sterilizing Mothers: Eugenics and Welfare Politics in the Interwar United States," *Social Politics* 4 (spring 1997): 136–153.

3. Charles Dight to Adolf Hitler, August 1, 1933, Scrapbook, Eugenics Files, Charles Fremont Dight Papers, Minnesota Historical Society, St. Paul, Minnesota

(hereafter cited as MHS); Mildred Thomson, *Prologue: A Minnesota Story of Mental Retardation* (Minneapolis: Gilbert Publishing Company, 1963). Also see Gary Phelps, "The Eugenics Crusade of Charles Fremont Dight," *Minnesota History* 49 (fall 1984): 99–108.

4. In this essay, I use terms such as "feebleminded," "mentally defective," and "mentally deficient" freely, usually without quotation marks. Although offensive today, these words capture with precision the perceptions of their time. As well, they are more inclusive than the current terminology because they refer to people whose behavior would now be viewed through a cultural or psychological lens. The statistical comparison is from Birthright, Inc., "Sterilizations Officially Reported from States Having a Sterilization Law up to January 1, 1946," pamphlet, Sterilization Statistics folder, Association for Voluntary Sterilization Supplement Records, Social Welfare History Archives, University of Minnesota, Minneapolis, Minnesota.

5. E. J. Engberg to Carl Swanson, June 22, 1946, Superintendent's Correspondence, Faribault State School and Hospital Records, MHS (hereafter cited as FSSH); Reilly, *Surgical Solution*, 140–143. According to slightly different figures from the sterilization advocacy group Birthright, Minnesota had performed 2,204 sterilizations by January 1946, 65 percent on feeble-minded women. Eighteen percent of sterilizations were performed on women and men classified as insane. Birthright, "Sterilizations Officially Reported."

6. Stanley Powell Davies, *The Mentally Retarded in Society* (New York: Columbia University Press, 1959), 159; President's Panel on Mental Retardation, *A Proposed Program for National Action to Combat Mental Retardation* (Washington, D.C.: Government Printing Office, 1962), 152.

7. Thomson, *Prologue,* 29–30; Mildred Thomson, "Social Aspects of Minnesota's Program for the Feebleminded," *Proceedings from the American Association on Mental Deficiency* 44 (1939–1940): 238–243.

8. Insane (but not feeble-minded) persons had to be institutionalized for six months prior to sterilization. The law is reprinted in Charles Dight, *History of the Early Stages of the Organized Eugenics Movement* (Minneapolis: Minnesota Eugenics Society, 1935), 9–10. See also Minnesota Child Welfare Commission, *Report of the Minnesota Child Welfare Commission* (St. Paul, 1917). Both are available in MHS.

9. Quoted in Molly Ladd-Taylor, *Mother-Work: Women, Child Welfare and the State, 1890–1930* (Urbana: University of Illinois Press, 1994), 137. See also Michael B. Katz, *In the Shadow of the Poorhouse: A Social History of Welfare in America* (New York: Basic Books, 1986), 113–129.

10. Edward MacGaffey, "A Pattern for Progress: The Minnesota Children's Code," *Minnesota History* (spring 1969): 229–236; Esther Benson, "Organization of Public Welfare Activities in Minnesota," unpublished M.A. thesis (University of Minnesota, 1941), 80–85. On the spread of mothers' pensions, see Theda Skocpol,

Protecting Soldiers and Mothers: The Politics of Social Provision in the United States, 1870s–1920s (Cambridge, Mass.: Harvard University Press, 1992).

11. Joanne Goodwin, *Gender and the Politics of Welfare Reform: Mothers' Pensions in Chicago, 1911–1929* (Chicago: University of Chicago Press, 1997); Gwendolyn Mink, *The Wages of Motherhood: Inequality in the Welfare State, 1917–1942* (Ithaca: Cornell University Press, 1995), 27–52; Ladd-Taylor, *Mother-Work*, 135–166.

12. U.S. Children's Bureau, *Public Child-Caring Work in Certain Counties of Minnesota, North Carolina, and New York* (Washington, D.C.: Government Printing Office, 1927), 14; Galen A. Merrill, "State Care of Dependent Children in Minnesota," *Quarterly Representing the Minnesota Educational, Philanthropic, Correctional and Penal Institutions* 23 (August 1923): 6–23; Charles Hall to Oscar Hallam, November 27, 1926, Department Of Public Welfare Library, MHS.

13. See, for example, Florence Goodenough, "Education of the Feebleminded in the Home," typescript, n.d., Department of Public Welfare Library, MHS.

14. A. C. Rogers and Maud A. Merrill, *Dwellers in the Vale of Siddem* (Boston: Richard Badger, 1919). See also Nicole Hahn Rafter, ed., *White Trash: The Eugenic Family Studies, 1877–1919* (Boston: Northeastern University Press, 1988), and Leila Zenderland, *Measuring Minds: Henry Herbert Goddard and the Origins of American Intelligence Testing* (Cambridge: Cambridge University Press, 1998).

15. Thomson, *Prologue*, 56–61; Daniel J. Kevles, *In the Name of Eugenics: Genetics and the Uses of Human Heredity*, rev. ed (New York: Knopf, 1995).

16. Benson, "Organization of Public Welfare Activities," 75–90; Robert J. Levy, "Protecting the Mentally Retarded: An Empirical Survey and Evaluation of the Establishment of Guardianship in Minnesota," *Minnesota Law Review* 49 (1965): 821–887.

17. Levy, "Protecting the Mentally Retarded," 826; Mildred Thomson, "My Thirty-Five Years of Work with the Mentally Retarded in Minnesota," typescript, 1961–62, 133, MHS; Stephen Jay Gould, *The Mismeasure of Man*, rev. ed. (New York: Norton, 1996).

18. Board of Control, *Biennial Report of the Division of Research for the Period Ended June 30, 1926*, 9; Hennepin County Child Welfare Board, *Annual Report for 1927*, 14; "Report on Census of the Feeble-Minded," typescript, n.d. [1936], Department of Public Welfare Library, MHS.

19. Minnesota State School for the Feebleminded, *Biennial Report for the Year Ending 1922*, 5–6; *Biennial Report for the Year Ending 1926*, 11, FSSH.

20. Board of Control, *Biennial Report for 1924*, 18; Board of Control, *Biennial Report for 1932*, 22–23; Thomson, *Prologue*, 53–55.

21. Thomson, *Prologue*, 55; Board of Control, *Biennial Report for 1928*, 19.

22. Goodenough, "Education of the Feebleminded"; Caroline Perkins, "Summary of the Following Papers," n.d. [1934], Department of Public Welfare Library; Thomson, *Prologue*, 55; Dight, *History*, esp. 9–21; "History of the Sterilization of the Feeble-Minded," typescript, n.d., Superintendent's Correspondence, FSSH.

23. Mary Odem, *Delinquent Daughters: Protecting and Policing Adolescent Female Sexuality in the United States, 1885–1920* (Chapel Hill: University of North Carolina Press, 1995); Regina Kunzel, *Fallen Women, Problem Girls: Unmarried Mothers and the Professionalization of Social Work, 1890–1945* (New Haven: Yale University Press, 1993); Peter Tyor, "'Denied the Power to Choose the Good': Sexuality and Mental Defect in American Medical Practice, 1850–1920," *Journal of Social History* 10 (1976–77): 472–482; "Report of Club-House for Feeble-Minded Girls from November 1924 to January 1926," Superintendent's Correspondence, FSSH.

24. Mildred Thomson, "Supervision of the Feeble-Minded by County Welfare Boards," Paper given to the American Association of Mental Deficiency, May 1940, Department of Public Welfare Library, MHS.

25. "Possibilities for Clubhouse (Sterilized 9/29/28)," enclosed in J. M. Murdoch to Mildred Thomson, November 13, 1928; "Parole Cases #II," typescript, 1934, Superintendent's Correspondence, FSSH. All of the names are pseudonyms.

26. "Girls Who Could Be Considered for Sterilization," typescript, May 10, 1933, Superintendent's Correspondence, FSSH.

27. "Parole Cases IV," typescript, 1934, Superintendent's Correspondence, FSSH.

28. Medical Staff Minutes, December 7, 1937, and September 28, 1936, FSSH.

29. Kathleen Jones, "'Mother Made Me Do It': Mother-Blaming and the Women of Child Guidance," in *"Bad" Mothers: The Politics of Blame in Twentieth-Century America,* ed. Molly Ladd-Taylor and Lauri Umansky (New York: New York University Press, 1998), 99–144.

30. Charles E. Dow, "The Problem of the Feeble-Minded III," typescript, August 9, 1934, Department of Public Welfare Library, MHS.

31. Florence Davis, "The Neglect of Children as Related to Feeble-Mindedness," typescript, September 21, 1934, Department of Public Welfare Library, MHS.

32. Ibid.

33. "Minutes of the Fourth Meeting of the Committee for the Discussion of Problems of the Feebleminded," May 2, 1934, Department of Public Welfare Library, MHS.

34. Thomson, *Prologue,* 90–99; Board of Control, *Biennial Report of the Division of Research for 1936,* 17–20.

35. Thomson, *Prologue,* 79–80.

36. Dow, "The Problems of the Feeble-Minded III"; Medical Staff Minutes, May 10, 1937, FSSH. On the contraceptive uses of eugenic sterilization, see Ladd-Taylor, "Saving Babies and Sterilizing Mothers," 147–149, and Johanna Schoen, "Between Choice and Coercion: Women and the Politics of Sterilization in North Carolina, 1929–1975," *Journal of Women's History* 13 (spring 2001), 132–156.

37. Levy, "Protecting the Mentally Retarded."

Part IV

From Top and Bottom

Parents and the State
in the Mid-Twentieth Century

Hope for Retarded Children

Eunice Kennedy Shriver

Forty-three years ago this month, in Brookline, Massachusetts, my mother and father were looking forward with great anticipation an joy to the birth of their third child. . . . Rosemary was born September 13 at home—a normal delivery. She was a beautiful child, resembling my mother in physical appearance. But early in life Rosemary was different. She was slower to crawl, slower to walk and speak than her two bright brothers. My mother was told she would catch up later, but she never did. Rosemary was mentally retarded. For a long time my family believed that all of us working together could provide my sister with a happy life in our midst. My parents, strong believers in family loyalty, rejected suggestions that Rosemary be sent away to an institution. . . . Yes, keeping a retarded child at home is difficult. . . . When my father became ambassador to England, Rose came to London with us and was presented to the king and queen at Buckingham Palace with Mother, dad, and my sister Kathleen.

In 1941, when we returned to the U.S.A., Rosemary was not making progress but seemed instead to be going backward. At twenty-two, she became increasingly irritable and difficult. She became somber and talked less. Her memory and concentration and her judgment were declining. My mother took Rosemary to psychologists and to dozens of doctors. All of them said her condition would not get better and that she would be far happier in an institution, where competition was far less and where our numerous activities would not endanger her health. It fills me with sadness to think that this change might not have been necessary if we knew then what we know now.

My mother found an excellent Catholic institution that specialized in the care of retarded children and adults. Rosemary is there now, living with others of her capacity. . . .

Like diabetes, deafness, polio, or any other misfortune, mental retardation can happen in any family. It has happened in the families of the poor and the rich, of governors, senators, Nobel prize winners, doctors, lawyers, writers, men of genius, presidents of corporations—the President of the United States. . . .

There are, in fact, 126,000 babies born in this country every year who for one reason or another will not achieve an intelligence equal to that of a child of twelve. There are approximately 5,400,000 retarded children in the United States—about 3 percent of our population. By 1970, because of the increase in population and the decrease in infant mortality, there will be over 1,000,000 more. Even now, mental retardation afflicts ten times as many people as diabetes, twenty times as many as tuberculosis, and more than six hundred times as many as polio. . . .

In this era of atom-splitting and wonder drugs and technological advance, it is still widely assumed—even among some medical people—that the future for the mentally retarded is hopeless. The truth is that 75 to 85 percent of the retarded are capable of becoming useful citizens with the help of special education and rehabilitation. Another 10 to 20 percent can learn to make small contributions, not involving book learning, such as mowing a lawn or washing dishes. Only about 5 percent—the most severely retarded cases—must remain completely dependent all their lives, requiring constant supervision.

Furthermore, science is making great strides towards unlocking the causes of retardation. There are more than 200 known diseases or conditions which can result in some degree of mental retardation. Today scientists know how to prevent retardation in many of these cases, and there is every reason to believe we are on the horizon of more exciting new discoveries. . . .

I remember well one state institution we visited several years ago. There was an overpowering smell of urine from clothes and from the floors. I remember the retarded patients with nothing to do, standing, staring, grotesque—like misshapen statues. I recall other institutions where several thousand adults and children were housed in bleak, overcrowded wards of 100 or more, living out their lives on a dead-end street, unloved, unwanted, some of them strapped in chairs like criminals. . . .

One sun-drenched morning this summer my husband and I visited a completely different sort of center—the Southbury Training School near Waterbury, Connecticut. . . . Southbury is a community for the retarded, rather than an institution. Its 1,540 acres contain many of the elements of everyday life—a farm, a bakery, a shoe-repair shop, beauty shops, barbershops, a clothing store, and a cafeteria . . . for the most part they are manned by the retarded. . . . These are 2,000 "residents" of the picturesque cottages, which is one of the five or six best state institutions we have ever toured. . . .

Unless a person has had intimate contact with the mentally retarded or has seen them under such conditions as those at Southbury, the mind's-eye impressions are likely to be deeply prejudiced. We discovered that anew this summer when we decided to use our Maryland farm, "Timberlawn," as a day camp for retarded children in the Washington, D.C., area. Thirty four children were referred to us by special schools and clinics in the area. At the same time, we recruited twenty-six high school and college students—most of them with no prior experience along this line—to work as volunteer counselors during the three weeks of the camp. What struck us immediately was that the counselors came to us with all the average prejudice and misunderstanding still current among the general public. They had heard, for example, that retarded children were "difficult," "unteachable," "helpless," "belligerent."

Who or what was there to fear? Should anyone be afraid of Wendell, a nine-year-old boy with the mental ability of a boy of four? . . . Two things at the camp especially impressed the counselors. First, the retarded children were manageable, with the right approach. . . . Second, the counselors discovered that the retarded child may be capable of demonstrating unsuspected skills: that Veronica, for instance, could paint an appealing likeness of the President and his family standing in front of the White House, that a boy who couldn't read or write was the best natural athlete in the camp.

The same assets of stability and unsuspected talent have made possible important breakthroughs in the employment of retarded persons. There is no excuse for these people having to live neglected lives in the dark garrets and medieval institutions which are hangovers from yesteryear. . . .

Today, on New York's suburban Long Island, mentally retarded workers are using their skills in the highly competitive electronics industry. This started earlier this year after Mr. Hank Viscardi, head of Long Island's renowned Abilities, Incorporated, attended a meeting of the President's

Panel on Mental Retardation. Mr. Viscardi, who was legless at birth, employs 400 physically handicapped workers. . . . Last spring about twenty retarded people started training at company headquarters on Long Island. . . .

Despite such successes, employment for the retarded is still in its infancy. One difficulty is ingrained public prejudice which is so damaging to these people. . . . The vast majority of the mentally retarded are not emotionally disturbed. They do not "go berserk." They simply lag behind in their intellectual and physical skills, usually from birth. They often strike people as odd in their behavior because the mind of a small child inhabits the body of a much older person.

To our surprise and consternation we found out that most doctors and scientists, like the general public, considered mental retardation a hopeless field for research. Established research scientists saw little connection between their studies and mental retardation. Young researchers wanted to do cancer or heart research and get dramatic results. . . . Until recently most medical school had no instruction in mental retardation. But Doctor [Robert] Cooke has instituted at Johns Hopkins the first formal course on this subject at a U.S. medical school, with the help of five outstanding young scientists who have recently decided to concentrate in this field. This year 150 students, interns, and residents took this advanced Johns Hopkins instruction before fanning out over the country to put it to use. . . .

The public and the governments they support are slowly awakening to the needs of the retarded. Yet, even today, less is being done at the community level than for any other afflicted group. Those of us whose families are touched by this tragic condition can help, but broad support is essential to meet retardation squarely and eventually lick it. Interested citizens in any community could take on projects such as these:

- Women's clubs or service-club auxiliaries could help expectant mothers make full use of the local prenatal clinics—or establish them if they do not now exist. . . .
- Sports and civic clubs—or even private citizens—can start recreation programs for the retarded. As we discovered at our summer day camp, the children can swim, play ball, paint, ride, and use many other skills. It is startling that there are no special recreation programs for the retarded in 99 percent of American communities.
- Junior Chambers of Commerce or other business groups could start sheltered workshops for the retarded. Some 2,500 retarded persons were

helped by vocational training, but this does not even meet the needs of the State of Wisconsin.

Twenty years ago, when my sister entered an institution, it was most unusual for anyone to discuss this problem in terms of hope. But the weary fatalism of those days in no longer justified. The years of indifference and neglect are drawing to a close, and the years of research and experiment, faithful study, and sustained advance are upon us. To transform promise to reality, the mentally retarded must have champions of their cause, the more so because they are unable to provide their own.

12

"Mental Deficients" Fighting Facism

The Unplanned Normalization of World War II

Steven A. Gelb

1.

In the late 1930s, American workers in the field of mental deficiency disputed the nature of the condition they treated. The consensus of the 1910s that the IQ score, in itself, was a reliable indicator of mental capacity and that persons with mental retardation were a homogeneous group were breaking down.[1] Follow-up studies of persons diagnosed as feeble-minded showed that many of them had made better social adjustments than their prognosis would have indicated possible.[2] A controversy arose over the related issues of the constancy of IQ scores and whether or not environmental influences could induce changes in IQ.[3]

This uncertainty developed even as enrollments in both public school special education classes and institutions for the "feebleminded" grew significantly.[4] During the Depression, waiting lists for institutional admittance lengthened and overcrowding within facilities increased, even as institution superintendents were forced to work under tighter budgets.[5] Perhaps partly as a result of these pressures, parole programs for the release of persons diagnosed with mild retardation became commonplace.

At the outbreak of the war, leaders in the field, responding to these points in question, attempted to formulate precise and comprehensive definitions of mental retardation that would clarify clinical practice.[6] Their reformulations, however, were still grounded on earlier assumptions of what constituted deficiency. As Doll put it, the *concept* of mental deficiency today is clear enough; the difficulty lies rather in the inadequate employment of means by which the accepted definitions are satisfied. There is little dispute on the essentials of an inclusive concept of mental deficiency, but there is an evident reluctance to assemble the evidence necessary to meet these requirements in a given case.[7]

Those essentials consisted in the beliefs that the "mentally deficient" mind was qualitatively different from a normal one, that the difference was biological in origin, that it was manifested in a premature arrest of mental development, that it caused social incompetence, and that it was incurable.[8] As Kuhlmann summarized the argument, the "mentally deficient" child was "inferior, not in degree, but in kind."[9] And, for Doll, "mental deficiency" was a "psychological atavism," a throwback to an earlier stage of physical and cultural development that could be compared to that of man's evolutionary ancestors. In this light, those afflicted with the condition might almost be considered another species.[10]

The prevailing belief in the difference and inferiority of those labeled "mentally deficient" was reflected in the objectives of the American Association on Mental Deficiency (AAMD), published during the war years, that placed a strong emphasis on social control. These goals included "extra-institutional supervision of all defectives in the community," "the segregation of mentally deficient persons in institutional care and training, with a permanent segregation of those who cannot make satisfactory social adjustments in the community," and "parole for all suitable institutionally trained mentally defective persons."[11] In concert with these goals, a subcommittee on "Social Control" was active in the organization during the early 1940s.

It should not be surprising, then, that experts forecast a limited role for persons with mental retardation when a national emergency burst upon the country after the bombing of Pearl Harbor in 1941. As mobilization began, superintendents became aware that many parolees and runaways from their institutions were succeeding in enlisting in the armed services. In some cases, selective service boards requested information from institutions about enlistees who were former inmates. After some discussion, mental deficiency experts decided that selected cases should be permitted to enlist, although their overall prognosis for the "deficient" soldier was not a positive one.[12] They argued that modern war required a great deal more than courage, that the soldier of the forties, "as a rule, must be able to read and take down directions from printed diagrams and maps, as well as service and assemble complicated mechanized units, such as tanks, anti-aircraft guns, planes, and precision instruments."[13] They saw the "mentally deficient" as unlikely to master such highly techincal tasks.

A proposal for the use of "mental deficients" during the crisis, published by the AAMD in 1942, stated that most did not have what it takes to adjust to warfare or even to modified military duties. Although a few might serve their country well, the cost of sorting through the mass of defectives to find those who could succeed appeared prohibitive.[14]

Eugenicists of the period also argued that if local draft boards sent only normal minds to the front while they left men with defective minds behind in safety, casualties of war would lower the general intelligence of the American male population. Thus, the perceived deficits of the "mentally deficient," which made them less valuable than supposed normals, also made them more expendable and potentially useful as cannon fodder. One superintendent noted that Hitler, already engaged in fighting on two fronts, "would like to have a million or two men like our stable morons to throw against the Russian lines."[15]

This eugenic view notwithstanding, the official position put forth by the AAMD's Committee on the Social Control of Mental Deficiency in 1942 did not advocate a direct military role for the "mentally deficient." Instead, the Committee called for training them to hold menial jobs that would release more capable persons for military service and complicated work in defense industries. There was also a paternalistic rationale for this proposal. Some felt that employed "mental defectives" were less likely to feel badly about their necessary exclusion from playing a direct part in the war.[16]

2.

Social conditions, however, created a different and more important role than that foreseen by the experts. At the beginning of U.S. involvement in the war, conscription centers operated under constraints that made careful selection impossible. As many as ten thousand men a day were inducted at the beginning of the war. By year's end, the army was accepting men who were able to understand only simple orders given in English, whether or not they were able to read and write.[17] Standards were adjusted later, and accounts written by several psychologists attached to the armed services indicate that the sorting of soldiers and standards of acceptable mental proficiency varied at different induction centers.[18]

What is clear by all accounts is that the services were much more reluctant to make a diagnosis of mental deficiency, and lose a potential soldier, than school personnel and institutions of mental deficiency had been when conducting assessments for other purposes and under different circumstances. The overall rate of rejection for mental deficiency was only seven per 1,000 for whites and ten per 1,000 for blacks. (To put such a figure in perspective, one may recall that, when compared with figures from the 1978–1979 school year, it indicates that, statistically, blacks were almost 100 times less likely to be identified as mentally deficient by the services in World War II than they would have been by schools in some southern states more than thirty years later.)[19]

Military psychologists, becoming far more critical than civilian psychologists working in peacetime at schools, announced that IQ tests were inadequate as a measure of recruits' ability. Staff members attached to the Adjutant General's office, which was responsible for research on the classification of soldiers, stated flatly that "the MA [mental age] and I.Q. are not meaningful in the Army situations in terms of the evidence available."[20] They and others charged the test with insensitivity to relevant social factors in soldiers' backgrounds. Experience convinced them that failures on mental tests were much more likely due to causes other than mental deficiency. Chief among these was inadequate education. But psychologists were also aware of the score-depressing effects of membership in ethnic and/or linguistic minority groups, emotional problems, organic pathology, fatigue (tests were sometimes administered as late as 3 A.M.), and extreme shyness ("bucoliphrenia") in recruits from isolated rural settings.[21] Furthermore, the tests were seen as largely unreliable when administered to blacks, especially so for those from the South.[22]

Under the rationale that the military situation justified shortcuts, military psychologists devised a host of new, shorter tests for screening recruits.[23] Some of these were informal; for example, at one center a single question was used to distinguish between those men who needed to be studied further and those who did not.[24] Although these measures were not computed as intelligence quotients, military authorities claimed that the army accepted men with mental ages of eight years, while the navy's standard was ten and one-half years.[25]

But even potential soldiers who failed such coarse screenings were not immediately disqualified from service. Instead, the army instituted training courses intended to remedy deficits wherever possible. Such a program for "retarded" soldiers was put into effect in July 1943, at the Engineer Replacement Center in Fort Belvou, Virginia. The initial recruits included feeble-minded individuals, psychopaths, psychotics, drug addicts, and the physically handicapped. Remediation included a course in elementary education and military engineering subjects that had been designed for illiterates and non-English speakers (including a mental therapy class for those who needed it), a physical coordination and elementary military subjects class "for soldiers of low grade mentality who [were] particularly deficient in the ability to coordinate their muscular movements," and an individual attention and observation course for soldiers whose military potential seemed most questionable, intended to determine whether there might be some way to help the weakest individuals become useful to the armed services.[26] Instructors recommended each referred soldier, following special training, for either discharge from the army, return to regular training, or transfer to another special course for additional training. This model was replicated at several other centers.[27]

Thus, the armed services were more interested in making marginal recruits useful than in labeling them. Given their purpose, it is not surprising that so many previously institutionalized mental defectives were accepted into the services, despite the pessimism among the mental deficiency establishment over their ability to make a contribution in combat. The labeled, like the nonlabeled, wanted to do their part for their country, and, as Doll put it, they "entered the armed services by one route or another, some with the approval of some of us, and some over the protest of others."[28]

As war progressed, institutional superintendents were surprised by, impressed by, and frequently proud of the war contributions made by "their boys." The Newark State School released the story of a diagnosed "imbecile" with an IQ of 48 who had been paroled in 1941 for employment and then "escaped" and entered the army. By 1945, he had been promoted to private first class, served in four Pacific campaigns, and received a presidential citation. Three other Newark State parolees had been promoted to the rank of sergeant, several more were corporals, and another had become a seaman, first class.[29] Of 114 institutional parolees, Bassett estimated that 83 percent were doing well, 10 percent were having questionable success, and only 7 percent had failed.[30]

Similar results were reported by Michigan's Wayne County Training School. Eighty-eight percent of the group had adapted successfully to life in the military, and 31 percent of these had received promotions. The authors of this study divided their subjects into "moron" and "dull normal" groups to see whether IQ affected adaptiveness. They concluded that it did not.[31]

And when the private institution in Elwyn, Pennsylvania, queried a group of military-age parolees, it found that the number of respondents who had been deferred from service for any cause was negligible. The mean IQ of this group was 69, the range of IQ was 46–91.[32] Their success led the study's authors to conclude that "apparently it is neither the mental nor scholastic level of the individual which determines his usefulness to the Armed Forces, but, instead, the personal traits and characteristics which have developed in him during his period of growth."[33]

Not all reports were so positive, however. Doll, pessimistic at the outbreak of the war, admitted later that the odd "high grade moron" might have been successful, but he still maintained that 90 percent were military liabilities. This conclusion was not supported, however, by empirical data.[34] Some studies, however, did find mixed success for men who had previously been institutionalized, although none supported Doll's degree of pessimism.

For example, the superintendent of the Sonoma State School, in California, made a data-based estimate that, of 147 previously institutionalized men, more than two-thirds had made unsatisfactory adjustment to the military. Most of the reported problems, however, were due to unsatisfactory conduct, not incompetence, and the tally included soldiers who had gone AWOL or committed assaults, car thefts, or forgeries. A smaller group was diagnosed as having psychopathic personalities.[35]

Perhaps the most trustworthy findings are those of a large-scale survey of approximately 8,000 soldiers, the majority of whom had IQ's below 75. Of this group, 56 percent of male soldiers made satisfactory adjustment to military life, while the other 44 percent were discharged for various reasons. Again, although some were released due to incompetence, more frequently the cause was some kind of behavioral problem.[36] The study's author concluded that "personality factors far overshadowed the factor of intelligence" in determining how successful any individual might adjust to the military.[37]

The war also created work opportunities for persons who had been identified as mentally deficient and thus marginally employable. Most of the residents of the Wayne County Institution who were paroled during the first year of the war were either gainfully employed or in the armed forces. These men were not a selected group of higher functioning mental deficients but a representative cross-section of that institution's population. Most had obtained their jobs independently, and a large proportion of these were above the unskilled level.[38] The author of the study concluded that a large proportion of previously institutionalized mental deficients "are actually capable of handling substantial jobs."[39]

Similar findings were reported in California. Parolees from the Sonoma State facility were employed during the war years in several occupations. The vast majority were performing good work and were receiving good salaries. Most also demonstrated that they were able to manage their own money successfully.[40] The superintendent of the facility stated that the men "should receive commendation for their good work, which is on a comparable basis with normal individuals who usually get most of the praise."[41]

And in New Jersey, institution workers expressed surprise at the aptitudes that persons identified as mentally deficient demonstrated in war-related activities. Those who remained in the state's five facilities were given tasks with real responsibility, such as serving as night attendents. And those both inside and outside institutional walls donated blood, assisted blood banks, knitted sweaters for the Red Cross, donated to war-bond drives and funds for the support of Chinese children, made surgical dressings, worked voluntarily over lunch hours and on Sundays, participated in drives to save rationed materials, and performed air raid duty.[42]

3.

Expanded wartime needs for military and industrial labor rapidly transformed the social status of the "mentally deficient." From a marginalized and stigmatized position, they achieved substantial normalization under social conditions that required their full participation in the war effort. The degree of their integration and success in this altered social setting was energizing for the field of mental deficiency. At war's end, though, when the American political economy reverted to "normal" and the status of the newly integrated reverted to prewar conditions, the field had to contend with the discrepancy between what had been predicted for the labeled and what they had actually done. But, while the conflict and its labor needs ensued, mental-deficiency authorities, buoyed by strong feelings of patriotism, valued their clients in a new way. In 1943, the editor of the *American Journal on Men-*

tal Deficiency forgot the tone of prewar writing and even the published "objectives" of the AAMD—which continued to advocate segregation and sterilization for the mentally handicapped—that were located elsewhere in the journal. At the height of American involvement in the war, the editor claimed that

> each individual, the basic unit of society, must be advantageously related to the total social structure. Not one should be neglected—either in a state school, in a factory, in a university or elsewhere. Each human being has an unalterable fundamental value in the total biocultural economy man—no matter what the intelligence quotient or the "property quotient" may be. . . . We are now seeking all possible sources of manpower for the war effort and we shall also have to do so in the effort to reconstruct society. ...[43]

As the nation united against a common enemy, some workers suggested that mental ability was not as important as society had earlier assumed it to be. Persons identified as stupid had been segregated from society for years, but the greatest problems of humanity, like the war itself, were caused by those of normal intelligence. As Kanner put it, "all the feebleminded of the world from the dawn of mankind to this day have 'cost' a negligible fraction of the life and substance destroyed by the machinations of one Adolf Hitler and his gang."[44]

Nor could earlier, more pessimistic descriptions of mental retardates compete with appeals to unity and patriotism in shaping mental-deficiency workers' responses to the accomplishments of their clients during the war years. Pride is evident in one worker's statement that mentally deficient individuals "have not been deficient in physical health, moral courage, stamina, loyalty, patriotism, marksmanship or family devotion or willingness to die for a cause."[45] Another noted that the mental deficient was

> serving his country well in the theatres of war, in the factories, on the farms, and on the home front. Many institutions proudly display service flags with blue and gold stars upon them—they also hang in the special schools—but more important they hang in the windows of many homes across this nation.[46]

There was a general consensus that mentally deficient persons had earned a better place for themselves in the postwar world.[47] Even their purported

315

differences from "normals" were now described as virtues. They were said to be willing to work steadily at monotonous jobs as long as their need for approval and reassurance was met.[48] With proper guidance, it was argued, the mentally deficient would be able to handle many more jobs than had been previously thought possible. Only Doll sounded a note of dissension by arguing that "the mentally deficient who may be occupationally and socially successful today as a result of the critical shortage of civilian manpower will presumably quickly be shuffled back to poverty and dependency when the war is over."[49]

In short, the tone of writing about the mentally deficient, Doll's excepted, changed from a prewar concern over social control and a focus on deficients' differences from "normals" to an appreciation of their common humanity, and even to the view that both science and society had oversold the importance of intelligence.

Yet Doll's comments were prescient. At the conclusion of the war, normalization for many of the labeled deficients disappeared along with the labor shortage caused by the conflict. Within the more restricted opportunity of "normal" economic conditions, the retarded were again seen as marginal members of the work force and their purported differences from "normals" once more assumed their prewar salience.[50] Now the field of mental deficiency moved to reconcile the conflict between prewar conceptions of the retarded and the unexpected experience of the war by retroactively relabeling those who had been normalized during the was as "pseudo-feebleminded," that is, as persons of normal intelligence who had been misdiagnosed. This was justified by the rationale that mental deficients, by definition, are not able to succeed in society.[51] Similarly, reservations about the limitations of intelligence tests were somewhat muted in comparison to those expressed during the war years, and the essential "unity" of all members of society was forgotten as the field of mental deficiency refocused itself upon the attributes thought to distinguish "defectives" from normals.[52]

4.

These rapid changes are instructive regarding the issue of mainstreaming, the role of mild intellectual deficiency in society, and that of psychologists as gatekeepers to that condition. During the mass unemployment of the Great Depression in the 1930s, that diagnostic gate opened widely; waiting lists for admittance to institutions for the feebleminded lengthened as overcrowding within facilities intensified.[53] As has been shown here, however, diagnosticians in the armed services narrowed that opening considerably and, in wartime, normality was discovered where pathology had been previously inferred. The differences between diagnostic procedures and operational definitions of mental deficiency in the Depression and during the war that followed were related not only to different purposes for diagnosis but also to differences in existing opportunity structures available to potential retardates. The result was that mental deficits that had earlier been seen as responsible for the low social status of labeled individuals were rendered invisible when the services of the same individuals became vital to national purposes.

The speed and apparent unanimity with which diagnosticians in the armed services put aside intelligence tests because of their alleged insensitivity to social factors stand in sharp contradistinction to the well-documented postwar overrepresentation of minority students in classes for the mildly retarded and to the existence, as well as the entire tenor, of the debate over IQ bias that was conducted in the late 1960s and in the 1970s. It appears that the existence of economically surplus populations provides the unacknowledged, yet normative, context within which psychology constructs its mildly mentally retarded subject.

NOTES

Earlier versions of this work were presented at the meeting of the History of Education Society, November 1988, Toronto, Canada, and at the meeting of the Cheiron Society, Kingston, Ontario, June 1989.

1. Meta L. Anderson, "Education for Social Maturity," *Training School Bulletin* 33 (1937): 185–192; Edgar A. Doll and B. Elizabeth McKay, *Journal of Educational Research* 31 (1937): 90–106; and S. W. Bijou, "The Problem of Pseudo-Feeblemindedness," *Journal of Educational Psychology* 30 (1939): 519–526.

2. Warren R. Baller, "A Study of the Present Social Status of a Group of Adults, Who, When They Were in Elementary Schools, Were Classified as Mentally Deficient," *Genetic Psychology Monographs* 18 (1936): 165–244; Anderson, "Education for Social Maturity," 185–192; Doll and McKay, "Social Competence," 90–106; and Cutts, "Mentally Handicapped," 269.

3. See Harold M. Skeels and Harold B. Dye, "A Study of the Effect of Differential Stimulation on Mentally Retarded Children," *Proceedings of the American Association on*

Mental Deficiency 44 (1939): 114–136; Guy Montrose Whipple, ed., *The Thirty-Ninth Yearbook of the National Society for the Study of Education-Intelligence: Its Nature and Nurture*, parts 1 and 2 (Bloomington, IL: Public School Publishing, 1940); and Henry L. Minton, "The Iowa Child Welfare Research Station and the 1940 Debate on Intelligence: Carrying on the Legacy of a Concerned Mother," *Journal of the History of the Behavioral Sciences* 20 (1984): 160–176.

4. William Sloan and Harvey A. Stevens, *A Century of Concern: A History of the American Association on Mental Deficiency, 1876–1976* (Washington, DC, 1976); and R. C. Scheerenberger, *History of Mental Retardation* (Baltimore, 1983).

5. Norma E. Cutts, "The Mentally Handicapped," *Review of Educational Research* 11 (1941): 261–276.

6. Edgar A. Doll, "The Essentials of an Inclusive Concept of Mental Deficiency," *American Journal of Mental Deficiency* 46 (1941): 214–219; Frederick Kuhlmann, "Definition of Mental Deficiency," *American Journal of Mental Deficiency* 46 (1941): 206–213; and Lloyd N. Yepsen, "Defining Mental Deficiency," *American Journal of Mental Deficiency* 46 (1941): 200–205.

7. Doll, "Essentials of an Inclusive Concept," 214.

8. Ibid., 216–218.

9. Kuhlmann, "Definition," 212.

10. Edgar A. Doll, "Notes on the Concept of Mental Deficiency," *American Journal of Psychology* 54 (1941): 116–124.

11. "Objectives of the Association," *American Journal of Mental Deficiency* 49 (1944): 1.

12. H. H. Ramsey, "How the High Grade Mentally Defective May Help in the Prosecution of the War," *American Journal of Mental Deficiency* 47 (1942): 77–78; "Selective Service and the Mentally Retarded," *American Journal of Mental Deficiency* 48 (1943): 120–121; Edgar A. Doll, "Mental Defectives and the War," *American Journal of Mental Deficiency* 49 (1944): 64–67; and Fred Otis Butler, "Mental Defectives in Military Service and Wartime Industries," *American Journal of Mental Deficiency* 50 (1945): 296.

13. "Selective Service," 120.

14. "Report of a 'Proposal to Use the Services in the War and Post-War Effort of Persons New (*sic*) Unplaceable in Competitive Work,'" *American Journal of Mental Deficiency* 47 (1942): 77–78.

15. Ramsey, "High Grade Mentally Defective," 77–78.

16. "A Proposal to Use the Services in War and Post-War Effort of Certain Person Now Unplaceable in Competitive Work," *American Journal of Mental Deficiency* 47 (1942): 148–152.

17. William C. Menninger, "The Problem of the Mentally Retarded and the Army," *American Journal of Mental Deficiency* 48 (1943): 55; and Emil Frankel, "Incidence of Previous Institutional Care among Selective Service Registrants—The New Jersey Experience of 100,000 Men," *American Journal of Mental Deficiency* 49 (1944): 72.

18. Donald E. Baier, "The Marginally Useful Soldier," *American Journal of Mental*

Deficiency 48 (1943): 62–66; Louis L. McQuitty, "A Program for the Classification and Training of Retarded Soldiers," *Psychological Bulletin* 40 (1943): 770–779; W. A. Hunt, C. L. Wittson, and M. M. Jackson, "Selection of Naval Personnel with Special Reference to Mental Deficiency," *American Journal of Mental Deficiency* 48 (1944): 245–252; Staff, Personnel Research Section, Classification and Replacement Branch, the Adjutant General's Office, "The New Army Individual Test of General Ability," *Psychological Bulletin* 41 (1944): 532–538; H. C. Eaton, Margaret Wilson Gallico, and Catherine A. Campion, "Care in the Diagnosis of Mental Deficiency," *American Journal of Mental Deficiency* 49 (1945): 450–452; William A. Hunt and Iris Stevenson, "Psychological Testing in Military Clinical Psychology: I. Intelligence Testing," *Psychological Review* 53 (1946): 25–35; and Thomas R. Weaver, "The Incident of Maladjustment among Mental Defectives in Military Environment," *American Journal of Mental Deficiency* 51 (1946): 238–246.

19. Leonard G. Rowntree, Kenneth H. McGill, and Thomas I. Edwards, "Causes of Rejection and the Incidence of Defects among 18 and 19 Year Old Selective Service Registrants," *Journal of the American Medical Association* 123 (September 1943), 183; and Steven A. Gelb and Donald T. Mizokawa, "Special Education and Social Structure: The Commonality of 'Exceptionality,'" *American Educational Research Journal* 23 (winter, 1986): 543–557.

20. Staff, "New Army Individual Test," 532.

21. Hunt, Whittson, and Jackson, "Selection of Naval Personnel," 246; and Hunt and Stevenson, "Psychological Testing," 30.

22. Hunt and Stevenson, "Psychological Testing," 30.

23. J. G. Colman, "A Rapid Determination of Intellectual Adequacy for the Naval Service," *Naval Medical Bulletin* 42 (1944): 1093–1095; R. J. Lewinski, "Notes on the Original and Revised Kent Scales in the Exam of Navy Recruits," *Journal of Educational Psychology* 35 (1944): 554–558; and Staff, "The New Army Individual Test," 532.

24. Hunt and Stevenson, "Psychological Testing," 27. The question was, "If your shadow points to the northeast, where is the sun?"

25. Menninger, "The Problem of the Mentally Retarded," 61; Hunt, Wittson, and Jackson, "Selection of Naval Personnel," 249; and Scheerenberger, *History of Mental Retardation*, 214.

26. McQuitty, "A Program for Classification," 771–772.

27. Ibid., 772; A similar "special training unit" is described in Menninger, "The Problem of the Mentally Retarded," 58–60.

28. Doll, "Mental Defectives and the War," 66.

29. Hiram G. Hubbel, "Mental Defectives in the Armed Services," *American Journal of Mental Deficiency* 50 (1945): 136–137.

30. Dorothy M. Bassett, "New Jersey Institutions for Mentally Deficient: Their Contribution and Place in the War Effort," *American Journal of Mental Deficiency* 49 (1944): 75–59.

31. Robert H. Haskell and Alfred A. Strauss, "One Hundred Institutionalized Mental Defectives in the Armed Froces," *American Journal of Mental Deficiency* 48 (1943): 67–71.

32. E. Arthur Whitney and E. M. MacIntyre, "War Record of Elwyn Boys," *American Journal of Mental Deficiency* 49 (1944): 80–85.

33. Ibid., 83.

34. Doll, "Mental Defectives and the War," 66.

35. Butler, "Mental Defectives in Military Service," 296–297.

36. Weaver, "The Incident of Maladjustment," 238–240.

37. Ibid., 243.

38. Thorleif G. Hegge, "The Occupational Status of Higher-Grade Mental Defectives in the Present Emergency. A Study of Parolees from the Wayne County Training School at Northville, Michigan." *American Journal of Mental Deficiency* 49 (1944): 86–98.

39. Ibid., 97.

40. Butler, "Mental Defectives in Military Service," 298–299.

41. Ibid., 299.

42. Bassett, "New Jersey Institutions," 75–79.

43. "Editorial," *American Journal of Mental Deficiency* 47 (1943): 255–256.

44. Leo Kanner, "Pseudo-Feeblemindedness," *The Nervous Child* 7 (1948): 369. In a similar vein, Horace G. Miller, "The Place of the Feeble-Minded in the Post-War World," *American Journal of Mental Deficiency* 49 (1944): 99–101, argued that the cult of intelligence had led to humanity's current crisis and that what was now needed was not more training of the intellect but less repression and an end to division between emotions and cognition.

45. Ray Graham, "The Illinois Program of Special Education in Public Schools for the Educable Mentally Handicapped Children," *American Journal of Mental Deficiency* 51 (1947): 461.

46. Lloyd Yepsen, "Post-War Problems in Guidance of the Mentally Subnormal," *American Journal of Mental Deficiency* 50 (1945): 292.

47. Butler, "Mental Defectives in Military Service," 300; Yepsen, "Post-War Problems," 292; and Willam H. Dunn, "The Readjustment of the Mentally Deficient Soldier in the Community," *American Journal of Mental Deficiency* 51 (1946): 48–51.

48. Dunn, "Readjustment of the Mentally Deficient," 48; and Yepsen, "Post-War Problems," 292.

49. Doll, "Mental Defectives and the War," 67.

50. Scheerenberger, *History of Mental Retardation,* 50.

51. Hunt, Wittson, and Jackson, "Selection of Naval Personnel," 250; Edgar A. Doll, "Is Mental Deficiency Curable?" *American Journal of Mental Deficiency* 51 (1947): 420–428.

52. By focusing its attention on the construct of "pseudo-feeblemindedness" the

field was able to buttress the prewar belief that the "feebleminded" were genuinely different from "normals." See, for example, Edgar A. Doll, "Feeble-Mindedness versus Intellectual Retardation," *American Journal of Mental Deficiency* 51 (1947): 456–459; Grace Arthur, "Pseudo-Feeblemindedness," *American Journal of Mental Deficiency* 52 (1947): 137–142; Kanner, "Pseudo-Feeblemindedness," 365–397; Renatus Hartogs, "The Pseudo-Feebleminded Child and Adolescent in Court," *The Nervous Child* 7 (1948): 425–431; Debra Safian and Ernest Harms, "Social and Educational Impairment Wrongly Diagnosed as Feeblemindedness," *The Nervous Child* 7 (1948): 416–420; Charlotte H. Waskowitz, "The Psychologist's Contribution to the Understanding of Pseudo-Feeblemindedness," *The Nervous Child* 7 (1948): 398–406; R. H. Cassell, "Notes on Pseudo-Feeblemindedness," *Training School Bulletin* 46 (1949): 119–127; and Wilson H. Guertin, "Mental Growth in Pseudo-Feeble-Mindedness," *Journal of Clinical Psychology* 5 (1949): 414–418.

53. Sloan and Stevens, *A Century of Concern,* 152; and Scheerenberger, *History of Mental Retardation,* 193.

13

Education for Children with Mental Retardation

Parent Activism, Public Policy, and Family Ideology in the 1950s

Kathleen W. Jones

In the early summer of 1954, legislators in New Jersey renewed the state's commitment to providing special education at public expense for children with mental retardation, a responsibility first undertaken during the early-twentieth-century flurry of educational reforms associated with the Progressive movement. Known as the Beadleston Act, after its sponsor, Republican assemblyman Alfred N. Beadleston, the legislation directed local school boards to "provide suitable facilities and programs of education or training for all the [state's] children . . . classified as educable or trainable."[1] The law charged school districts with the task of identifying children left out of the existing educational structure and then furnishing them with local classes or with access to schooling in neighboring districts. When the Beadleston Act was written, the terms "educable" and "trainable" referred to degrees of mental retardation. Experts assumed that educable children were capable of minimal academic work, while trainable students would need to be schooled in personal care and social adjustment, in hopes of enabling them to develop some occupational skills not dependent on academic training.[2] Beadleston's legislation covered all but those with the most severe forms of mental retardation. New Jersey schools were directed to provide educational services to those children who required more care than "normal" youth but who were living at home with families, rather than being institutionalized in one of the state's four training schools.

During the Progressive years, New Jersey had been in the forefront of states that mandated special education classes, but since then its leadership had lapsed. What explains the timing of this new educational policy? To be sure, the decision to provide for special classes in the public schools fits into a broader pattern of post–World War II educational expansion. The promise of college opportunities for veterans, fallout from the decision in *Brown v. Board of Education,* the educational competition aroused by the Soviets' launching of Sputnik, and the critical need for new schools to accommodate children of the baby boom—all these factors drew legislators in the 1950s to acknowledge and accept the expense of new educational initiatives. The Beadleston Act came in the wake of other measures to finance more schools for New Jersey's growing youth population. The legislation might also be seen as a consequence of midcentury professional specialization in the field of "mental deficiency," to use one of the contemporaries' terms. The historian James W. Trent Jr. has argued that, after the war, psychologists and educators extended their control over research into mental retardation. Expansion of special education classes in local communities may have represented a strong claim to professional dominance.[3]

Though part of the postwar trend in schooling and certainly a prize fought for by the experts, the passage of New Jersey's special education legislation can tell another story, separate and distinct from the histories of education policy or professional boundary disputes. When looked at from this vantage point, the protagonists in the story were not the specialists but the families who banded together in community support groups and in 1948 incorporated as local "units" of the New Jersey Parents Group for Retarded Children. In this story, the special education advocated in 1954 was an affirmation of postwar middle-class domesticity.

More than a decade ago, both Edward Berkowitz and Gerald Grob called on historians to ask new questions about the history of mental retardation. According to Berkowitz, the histories of disabilities were written from two perspectives. These studies either presented the issues facing professionals and social service agencies or they discussed the disabled themselves.[4] Mental retardation, however, has always been more than an issue for the experts or a problem for the individual. It has also posed a unique dilemma for the families of children diagnosed with developmental disabilities, and it is from this context of family life that I want to assess the meaning of special education and the rise of parent activism in the 1950s. During the postwar years, the representations of family that found such prominence in the popular culture moved the New Jersey parent groups to political activity on behalf of their own and all children with mental retardation. This activism, while ostensibly aimed at making "imperfect" families more "normal," initiated a radical reshaping of the meaning of family normality.

Domesticity and Mental Retardation

A recent rash of histories has made clear that family life during the 1940s and 1950s was never as idyllic as TV sitcoms once might have led us to believe. Nonetheless, it is also obvious that, however far from the ideal, the behavior of white, middle-class, suburbanites in their Levittown-like homes was attuned to the canons of domesticity. To quote the historian Elaine Tyler May, middle-class Americans experienced a "reaffirmation" of domesticity in the middle decades of the twentieth century, after years of challenges from demands of depression and war. Sharply differentiated gender roles were central to postwar domestic ideology; husbands and wives were expected to spend much of their time in different spaces, with vastly different responsibilities. The glue in these marriages was to be a spirit of companionship and affection that women's magazines termed "togetherness." Although postwar men and women may have found fulfillment through lives very different from this prescription, "family" was, as May's white middle-class subjects confirmed, central to individual happiness, and "togetherness" was to be the essence of the family experience.[5]

Postwar domestic ideology put children at the core of the togetherness and happiness that domesticity was to foster. Child-rearing experts, family sociologists, mental health workers, and individual parents all concurred; children were a source of pride and satisfaction in an otherwise hostile and uncontrollable universe. Ernest Groves and Gladys Hoaglund Groves, sociologists whose text on the family was popular college reading material during the 1950s, counted children among the factors that contributed to a successful marriage.[6] May's historical research shows that middle-class parents internalized such advice. For the mothers and fathers May studied, "family togetherness, focused on children, was the mark of a successful and wholesome personal life." The baby-boom birth rates attested to their commitment to this ideal. As described by a psychologist years later, the postwar era was a time in which the men and women were comfortable and secure in their separate spheres where "together they would raise perfect children."[7]

Nowhere in this picture of familial bliss was there space for a child who failed to measure up, who was not "perfect," not, in the 1950s discourse of mental retardation, "normal." Yet, in these same years, experts estimated that from 1 to 3 percent of the babies born to these parents would be developmentally disabled.[8] How, then, was the child with mental retardation to be fitted into the midcentury ideal American family? And how did the family ideology of the postwar years shape parental responses to the "imperfect" child? When early-twentieth-century eugenists such as Henry Goddard connected class status, ethnicity, and moral degeneracy with "mental deficiency," guilt and shame seemed to dominate the emotions of middle-class parents raising a child with mental retardation.[9] The connections to family failings may have led to secrecy. Families who could afford the costs resorted to private institutionalization.

After World War II, physicians and psychologists continued to recommend the institutionalization of children with mental retardation. In light of the teachings of child psychiatrists and child guidance advocates, experts of the 1950s believed that family togetherness would be irredeemably disrupted by the heavy demands on a mother's emotions and the time required to care for such a child. Marriages would be weakened, and siblings would suffer from lack of attention. By removing the "imperfect" child from the family portrait, families could preserve the trappings of domesticity and return to "normal." The prominent child psychoanalyst Erik Erikson and his wife, Joan, followed this advice in 1944 when their son was born a "Mongolian idiot" (a child with Down Syndrome). In an effort to preserve family harmony, the Eriksons kept his existence secret from their other children, telling them that the infant had died at birth.[10]

At the same time, these same experts, as purveyors of the canons of domesticity, offered contrasting advice to mothers of "normal" children. Postwar child-rearing literature chastised the woman who emotionally and physically "rejected" her child and condemned the mother who worked outside the home or gave more time to volunteer activities that to parenting.[11] In light of such prescriptions, the decision to institutionalize one child, even for the sake of another, must have been heartrending for parents of this generation, and not all chose to follow the advice of the experts. Perhaps best known were the movie actor Dale Evans and her cowboy husband, Roy

Rogers. Their daughter Robin, born with Down Syndrome, remained with the family until her death at age two. Evans, who during the girl's lifetime had hidden the condition from the press, grieved over the death by writing a book to memorialize Robin's short life. *Angel Unaware* was a best-seller in the 1950s, and as letters to Dale Evans attested, her decision to keep Robin in the family was one that resonated with many parents who faced the same choice.[12] For other parents, keeping a child at home was not always such a deliberate choice; lack of suitable institutions and long waiting lists ensured that, for some families, togetherness would have to include the presence of a child with mental retardation.

Whether institutionalized or at home, children with mental retardation represented a dissonant presence in a culture permeated with togetherness and domestic perfectionism. Notions of the public "menace of the feeble-minded," popular in the early years of the century, had largely dissipated by the postwar years, only to be replaced by fears of mental retardation as the destroyer of family harmony. John P. Frank, law professor and father of a son with severe mental retardation, published the story of his family's decision to institutionalize Petey at a very young age. Petey was diagnosed with "brain atrophy"; the Franks sought expert advice, and in the book Frank revealed his fears. "How could one remain a normal human being when living with a much-loved mentally defective person?" At first the Franks believed it could be done, but, after much agonizing, Lorraine Frank became convinced that to refuse to do so would be "ruining John's career" and "sacrificing the chance for a normal life for our expected [second] child." Throughout the book, both husband and wife used the word "normal" when referring to what was lost with Petey's presence and what would be gained by Petey's institutionalization.[13]

Families such as the Eriksons and the Franks reformulated the meaning of family togetherness to exclude a child, while Evans and Rogers used secrecy to include and maintain a semblance of normality. The activities and goals of the men and women who founded the New Jersey parent organizations were equally shaped by the demands of postwar domesticity. These parents, however, were determined to make their children a public and a private presence, a part of "family."

In March 1951, Lee Marino, the father of a mentally retarded child and a founding member of the New Jersey Parents Group for Retarded Children, lectured a New York audience of "mental deficiency" experts on the purpose of his organization. Parents in this era invested heavily in their children,

Marino told the assembled experts, but, for him and others like him, that investment did not pay the same dividends. Their families carried a special burden, one that seemed to put normal family relations out of reach, and they wanted to do something about it. It was time the public recognize, Marino argued, that "having retarded children is not a disgrace and that they can be assisted and that they are entitled to aid."[14] The New Jersey Parent Group intended to pursue both recognition and entitlements. The parent activists Marino represented flaunted family imperfections as they undertook to construct for themselves and demand from the government services that would enable them to capture a modicum of "normal" childhood for their "exceptional" children and an image of family togetherness for their "exceptional" families.

The New Jersey Parent Groups

The instigator of the New Jersey parents movement was Laura Blossfeld, a Bergen county housewife and mother of a nine-year-old son with mental retardation. Blossfeld knew well the isolation brought about by the stigma attached to mental retardation and by the sheer physical effort required to care for such a child. But she also knew she was not the only mother in her county who was facing this burden. "When I took Ricky for a walk," she recalled, "I would see them [others like her who were coping alone with the problems of mental retardation]." On October 12, 1946, Blossfeld placed a notice in a local paper, asking others to join her in forming a group for all parents of children with mental retardation. "Each parent can ultimately help his own child by doing something to help all children similarly affected. . . . Therefore, I suggest an organization for all parents of mentally retarded children[, one that] may well prove to be the first chapter in a nationwide organization." A Bergen county judge and the wife of a psychology professor replied to Blossfeld's notice, and the three met in 1947 to form the first New Jersey Parents Group for Retarded Children.[15]

By 1950, the solitary group (then representing parents from Bergen and Passaic Counties) had expanded to seven chapters, or "units," with a state organization to coordinate activities. To trace the activism of the parents movement, I have concentrated on the members and the records of three of these first units, the original Bergen-Passaic group (B-PU), a spinoff in nearby Essex County, which included the city of Newark (EU), and a smaller chapter, the Raritan Valley Unit (RVU), composed of parents in and around the university town of New Brunswick.[16]

Northern New Jersey parents were not the only ones to organize in the years immediately after World War II. In nearby New York City, a newspaper appeal similar to Blossfeld's led, in 1949, to the founding of the Association for the Help of Retarded Children. The Parents Council for Retarded Children organized in Rhode Island in 1951, shortly after the September 1950 meeting at which New Jersey parents joined delegates from twenty-three groups representing fourteen states to establish the National Association of Parents and Friends of Mentally Retarded Children. The group changed its name in 1952 to the National Association for Retarded Children (NARC). At present the group is known as The Arc of the United States.[17]

It comes as no surprise that the originator of the New Jersey parent groups was a mother. Mothers' organizations in the United States have a history extending back at least to the 1830s, when church-affiliated mothers' clubs formed for both self-edification and to help the children of the poor. In the early twentieth century, child study clubs and the National Congress of Mothers (which became the PTA) continued this dual tradition. Before midcentury, however, few parent organizations addressed directly the problems of their own children with physical or mental handicaps. A Council for the Retarded Children of Cuyahoga County was founded in Cleveland in 1932, and, in Washington state, parents of children in a state institution for retardation created a support group in 1936. Both groups were isolated expressions of need, and neither expanded beyond the local area. Parents of children disabled by polio united in New York City in the early 1940s, and similar groups gained momentum after a polio epidemic in 1946. Polio survivors were educated at home or placed in separate classes, and the parents in this organization sought school integration. The United Cerebral Palsy Association also emerged during these years. But, unlike the polio and mental retardation organizations, the Cerebral Palsey Association was never a parent-led group.[18]

Parent activism on behalf of physically and mentally handicapped children appeared during the 1940s and 1950s in part because of the interest of psychologists and educators. Certainly the grass-roots NARC groups received considerable support from professionals organized as the American Association of Mental Deficiency, and, in the case of New Jersey, from state officials responsible for New Jersey institutions. Each expected the parents to be strong allies, adding popular legitimacy to professional knowledge.

Laura Blossfeld remembered that the parents in her Bergen county group took their idea for a state organization to Lloyd Yepsen, then director of New Jersey's Division of Classification and Education, which was responsible for training programs in the state's institutions, and after 1953 director of the state's new Division of Mental Deficiency. Although Blossfeld found him "leery" and at first reluctant to share with the group the names of parents raising their children at home, this state official soon became one of the group's most active professional supporters. For Yepsen, eager to expand his unit's budget, working with a group of committed parents promised benefits, and he participated in the meeting in 1949 that created the statewide umbrella organization. Other psychologists and educators were willing speakers at the monthly meetings of the local groups. Anna Starr, the psychologist who directed the Rutgers Psychological Clinic, was an adviser to the state organization and frequently spoke to the parent groups, as did education specialists from the local school districts.[19]

Despite the interest of the retardation specialists, the New Jersey members were proud of the parent leadership of their units, and, even as professionals benefited from the efforts of these groups, professionalism should not be seen as the driving force behind the parent activism of the 1940s and 1950s. More important was a postwar culture horrified by Nazi atrocities and eager to validate a new belief in "human rights." Added to this general climate was a local culture of town boosterism and volunteerism. In the towns represented by the three units, joiners could participate in Junior Leagues, Lions Clubs, Knights of Columbus, and Jewish women's organizations, and these groups are singled out only because their members merited mention by the parents for sponsoring events for their children.

Most important, however, was the intense middle-class familialism of the postwar years. The claims of domesticity brought these particular families together and structured the activities of the NARC units. In their published literature and news releases, the units pressed the traditional goals of mothers' groups—mutual support and public awareness. In addition, the groups voiced a spirit of entitlement that was decidedly new and grounded in the family ideology of togetherness. Their children were a part of the family and deserved the same degree of care, concern, and, ultimately, services that the family (and the community) offered its "normal" children. Their definition of family and children also went beyond biological boundaries. The publicity from the New Jersey units spoke of the inclusion in their projects of all children with mental retardation.[20]

Local People and Local Projects

Participants in the three New Jersey units covered the broad range of occupations and incomes that constituted the "middle class" during the postwar years. A list of early members from the Raritan Valley Unit included a minister, a research assistant at a local chemical plant, the owner of a real estate agency, a university professor, an author, a secretary, and many housewives.[21] To outsiders, the unit might have looked like any suburban volunteer or women's civic organization, but the New Jersey groups were never exclusively women's clubs. While many of the officers (especially the secretaries and the newsletter editors) and the committee heads were women, the presidents of the units were usually men. The nominal membership fee enrolled the entire family and brought affiliation with the state and national organizations and the right to participate in the programs of the local unit. The groups were structured to include all members of the family in unit activities.

The simple act of joining an organization was for many parents the first step toward acquiring domestic normality. Even though participation in civic organizations was a characteristic of postwar middle-class domesticity, the extra work required to raise a child with mental retardation or the shame and guilt many parents professed may have prevented these parents from becoming joiners. A national study of groups for parents of children with handicaps found that often the unit was the only community club to which a family with mental retardation owed allegiance.[22] Once a member, parents were entitled to one night out each month at the regular unit meeting, which included dinner and a speaker. When both parents attended, unit meetings could foster the spirit of companionship between husband and wife that experts worried about in couples rearing children with mental retardation.

Women were often brought into the group through work on one of the units' many committees. Judith Feist, of the Raritan Valley Unit, described the isolation she felt as the mother of a severely retarded child. Even her mother-in-law was horrified that Feist talked openly about her son; the elder Mrs. Feist let Judith know that this boy would "ruin the chances" of his sibling. At Feist's first meeting, in 1953, Bernice Carlson, an experienced RVU member, extended a welcome, set Feist to work on the newsletter; in a few years, both Feist and her husband were leaders in the local chapter. Nearly forty years later, the emotional release this woman had experienced in a room where her "problem" was shared by others was still very real. The parent group could not make Feist's son "normal," but it did offer her a setting in which her family's experiences were not exceptional.[23]

From the first, the New Jersey parent groups enrolled families with children in institutions and also those with children living at home. For parents in both situations, group participation offered ways to reaffirm difficult decisions about care and placement, decisions that forced families to face the extent of their distance from the domestic norm. As noted, experts in family relationships were telling these families that siblings would suffer and that the husband-wife relationship would deteriorate as more and more of a mother's time was committed to the care of a youngster with developmental disabilities. For parents such as John and Lorraine Frank, the threatened psychological ramifications helped to rationalize their decision to sever the physical bond between parent and child, and they were ready to publicize the experience in order to justify the choice.

Locally, Bernice Carlson, the corresponding secretary and newsletter editor of the RVU, used her position in the group to advance the cause of institutionalization and to urge greater support, both public and private, for the state's system of institutions. Her daughter, she told a reporter in 1952, was still a valuable part of her family, and her two children at home had not forgotten their sister.[24] But the decision to institutionalize Marta had been taken to preserve the family unit. For the Carlsons, as for many of the first NARC members, middle-class domesticity required that their "exceptional" children be cared for in nonfamilial settings where they would not disturb or be disturbed by the emotional content of the postwar family. Membership in the parent group made possible mutual support and public acknowledgement of their choice. As the RVU's first president told a local radio audience, if he had had a support group when his family was facing the decision to institutionalize, the choice would have been much easier.[25]

The activities of the parent groups were structured in ways that enabled families to include institutionalized children in the scripts of togetherness. The B-PU and the EU sponsored monthly family bus trips to the state institutions. All three chapters developed maintenance programs for all children in institutions. Bergen-Passaic parents with very young children at the North Jersey Training School organized in 1950 to "see that the babies got good care." Mothers in the organization took turns doing things for the children (such as giving hair cuts), while the fathers organized a building and grounds committee to install a play yard. Indeed, benevolence committees were among the most active of the units' divisions. For holidays especially, the parents wanted to acknowledge that children in institutions, not just their own but all the children, were part of family life. Christmas gifts and birthday cards sent by the members enabled some parents to include an absent and imperfect child in the ritual events of childhood, either directly or as surrogate parents for the many children in state institutions.[26]

During the postwar decade, New Jersey funded four institutions for people with mental retardation, two for boys and men (the New Lisbon State Colony and the Woodbine State Colony) and two for girls and women (the North Jersey Training School at Totowa and the Vineland State School). Both types of institutions were divided according to degree of retardation, with one serving "low-grade cases" and the other the "higher-grade cases." In addition, the state operated a separate institution at Skillman for people with epilepsy. The Training School at Vineland was the state's best-known private institution. Responsibility for administering all the state's institutions fell to the New Jersey Department of Institutions and Agencies. New Jersey, according to the psychologist and mental deficiency expert J. E. Wallace Wallin, had one of nation's "most ramified systems of institutions," making it easier than in many states to meet the needs of people with a range of mental retardation handicaps.[27] Broad coverage did not mean that the institutions were without flaws. Programs did not cover all ages; at Totowa, for example, only girls ages six to eighteen years were admitted. Parents seeking admission for their children were often met with waiting lists. Moreover, state funding did not allow for extra frills. As one of the first projects, the RVU's benevolent committee sent 1,000 "badly needed" mittens to boys at New Lisbon.[28]

Awareness of the inadequacies of institutions, both in quantity and in quality, first drew these postwar parents into political activity. On behalf of her parent group, Bernice Carlson directed a letter to the editor of the New Brunswick paper supporting a proposed bond issue on the ballot in 1949. A significant part of the money was earmarked for the state training facilities; Carlson wrote to appeal to the family instincts of the voters. Care in the state institutions was good, but Carlson drew attention to he paucity of spaces. Private care was available, but, Carlson asked, "Could you afford $2,700 a year if your child should need this training year after year? Would you want to go to the bottom of a long waiting list? Or will you vote 'yes' on the bond issue for $25,000,000 for state institutions?"[29] Another bond issue in 1952 also mobilized the parent groups. The EU newsletter, *The Guardian,* called the bond issue an "absolute necessity" and urged members to "tell the story" of the lengthy waiting lists to friends, to "speak publicly" to church and service groups, and to "distribute flyers" to shoppers and commuters. When the bond issue passed, the newsletter editor praised the work of unit members who distributed "13,000 leaflets" and published "at least twelve letters" to local papers.[30]

Unit leaders prodded members to make sure local legislators knew the group's position on any state legislation affecting families with mental retardation. One way to accomplish this end was to forge ties with interested state administrators, and the groups often consulted with Lloyd Yepsen. Parents in charge of the New Jersey ARC appointed Yepsen to the group's education committee, which was coordinating the creation of private schools for children excluded from the public school system. The appointment helped to ensure that the parents had a committed voice in the state's bureaucracy.[31] Another path was through testimony before state officials, and in 1952 the EU's president urged "all our members who can possibly arrange to do so" to attend a local public hearing of the state's Commission to Study the Problems of the Mentally Deficient.[32]

Institutionalization was not always an alternative for parents of children with mental retardation. Total numbers were hard to come by, but an informal survey of EU members reported 310 children with mental retardation, 221 of whom were "at home." As Carlson's letter to the editor suggested, private institutions were costly, and state institutions had too few spaces. In 1952, *The Guardian* noted that there was a nine-year wait for admission to New Lisbon. Some parents had no choice but to integrate a child with mental retardation into the family unit. Other parents neither sought nor desired institutionalization. For both groups of parents, membership in one of the local units of NARC legitimated their family's difference and at the same time validated its normality.[33]

The essence of postwar togetherness was leisure time devoted to family activities; for families with a member with mental retardation, participation in community recreational projects often posed logistical problems even if their "exceptional" children had been included in the invitations. Usually, however, no accommodations were made for these children, and units filled the void, creating spaces in which families coping with mental retardation could emulate the recreational togetherness of their "normal" neighbors. Unit-sponsored parties for parents and children provided members with some of this family fun; the annual Christmas parties were reported on in

the newsletters with pleasure as "all" children, those with mental retardation and their "normal" siblings, enjoyed the rituals of the season. Unit-
led canteens for young people taught the social skills needed by adolescents to enjoy restaurants with their families. For several years in the early
1950s EU parents could enroll their children in "learn-to-swim" programs.
As the editor of *The Guardian* wrote, "This is your program. It's for the
whole family."[34]

Nothing was more emblematic of postwar family togetherness than the
summer vacation. In 1955, the Essex Unit confronted this problem directly
and offered parents the opportunity for a vacation at the beach, in a setting
willing to accommodate all members of the family, regardless of disability.
"A real break is in store for some retarded children, their brothers and sisters
and mothers!" *The Guardian* announced. "The Ruth Kohn Summer Home, a
delightful residence in Long Branch, is opening its doors for two 2-week periods to families with retarded children, as it has in the past to normal families. For the first time families (mothers and children) for whom a vacation
at the shore has seemed impossible because the retarded child would not be
acceptable in a commercial lodging, or because of the expense, will be able to
enjoy the rest and relaxation of two weeks amid the sea breezes."[35]

By providing opportunities for public displays of togetherness, the family
parties, family meals, family swimming, and family vacation helped to nor-
malize the lives of parents and their children with mental retardation. According to James W. Trent Jr., the parents of NARC constructed themselves
and their children as "victims" in order to claim special services, but there
was no sense of victimization in these New Jersey units.[36] Instead, these parents deified a particular vision of family life and set out with determination
to incorporate their less-than-perfect families into that realm.

The New Jersey parent groups expressed that determination in part by de-
signing ways to give their youngsters access to the rituals of a 1950s childhood. By "rituals" I mean the rights of passage through which middle-class
children passed when growing up in the postwar years. Summer camp was
one of those rituals, an experience not readily available to children with
mental retardation. Each of the units opened a summer camp during the
1950s. Happy Day Camp, the Raritan Valley's operation, began in 1951 as a
two-week program "to promote socialization, to help the youngsters improve their coordination and increase their attention span, and to give them
as much sound healthy fun as possible." In 1956, a reporter for the Bound
Brook newspaper described the Happy Day Camp as a "real camp" with

hikes, sports, swimming, and crafts.[37] In 1950, EU parents began to send their children to the Bergen-Passaic Unit's Camp Rainbow, and six years later, with the help of the Junior Leagues of Montclair, Newark, and the Oranges, Essex parents opened their own Camp Shady Nook. Fifty-five children enrolled for the first six-week program. Said *The Guardian*, "A number of reports have come through from the parents that the camp program is filling what would otherwise be a real gap in the summer program for the children."[38] To be sure, camp provided a respite for mothers, the primary caretakers of these children. This function, however, does not negate the primary intent of using the "camp" format for summer activities; for children with mental retardation, the camps paralleled the experiences of "normal" middle-class boys and girls.

Units designed many of their recreational activities with younger children in mind, and the parent groups were slower to recognize the separate needs of adolescents with mental retardation. Perhaps the parents' delay represented the strength of numbers; by the teen years, many of their youngsters had gained admission to one of the state institutions. Nonetheless, in 1956, David Ginglend, director of the RVU's Happy Day Camp, told local papers he hoped the counties' many retarded teenagers would enroll in camp activities that summer. A desire to structure the leisure-time activities of their adolescents also motivated parents to open the teen canteens during the winter months. The RVU's "Happytimers" program offered adolescents and young adults a chance to dance, to eat, and to develop social skills, a recreational program not unlike those sponsored through high schools for the siblings of these "exceptional" teens.[39]

Through camps, swimming programs, and canteens, parents enabled their children to engage in the recreational rituals of childhood, but attendance at school remained the most important marker of the "normal" rites of passage. Laura Blossfeld, in recalling the strong emphasis on education among the early parent groups, termed it a "magic wand" for some parents who thought acceptance in public schools would "make their children normal." Despite her own skepticism about inclusion, Blossfeld's comment suggests the degree to which many parents saw the right to public education as a fundamental part of childhood and of family life.[40] Along with the benevolence committees, units gave education committees prominent places in the administrative apparatus of the groups. Efforts to realize the right to schooling at public expense involved the New Jersey parent groups in their most active campaigns.

In New Jersey, the parent groups of the 1950s were building on a history of state interest and action in the field of mental retardation. During the early twentieth century, the state had been in the forefront of educational reform and mental retardation research. In 1911, New Jersey became the first state to mandate special education programs for children with handicaps, although the program proved more inclusive on paper than in reality.[41] Despite the early and strong interest, separate classes were among the first programs to suffer during the Depression years, and many local programs were closed because of financial constraints.[42]

Technically, the state remained committed in the postwar years to "special education." However, a belief that the law required classes only for children termed "educable" (and excluded those labeled "trainable"), the stinginess of local school districts, and a dearth of trained teachers drastically limited the availability of such classes, even as the need, defined by numbers, was becoming more acute. A state census, undertaken in 1953 and one of the first legislative measures endorsed by the parents groups, identified 12,306 children in need of special education; only 3,602 "educable" students were receiving it.[43] This was the social setting in which the Board of Directors of NARC proposed an "Educational Bill of Rights for the Retarded Child," a statement of public responsibility to provide "every American child" with a school program "suited to his particular needs and carried forward in the environment most favorable for him."[44]

To meet their particular needs, New Jersey parent groups at first created a separate educational structure, a stopgap measure until they could convince the state to make the necessary provisions for both their "educable" and "trainable" children. In Ridgewood, Kay Gould established the Village School after her son with Down Syndrome was dismissed from a public school class. Bergen-Passaic Unit members acted as volunteers.[45] The Nancy-Luzon Training School opened in Roselle (Union County), in 1950, and in the first six months thirty students participated in its programs. "Although our school leaves a lot to be desired," the directors reported in the B-PU's newsletter, "we are content and encourages [sic] to work further for the retarded child. The emotional block which most of our children have built up because of their retardation is slowly being overcome by the fact that they are doing something worthwhile and they feel they are more like normal children."[46]

The Essex Unit's education committee, headed by Elizabeth M. Boggs, was one of the most active. EU organized a psychological testing and evaluation service through which the educational needs of local children could be evaluated. By May 1951, the EU had also opened six private classes, operating out of churches and a local settlement house. Lloyd Yepsen offered assistance from the Department of Institutions and Agencies, but the Essex parents rejected the offer, fearing the funds would weaken their claim to a public education for their children.[47]

In addition to sponsoring separate classrooms, parent groups also began to pressure local boards of education to create special classes in the public schools. Groups across the state cheered the Tri-County Unit's successful drive to establish a trainable class in the Camden public school system, in 1951—the first district in the state to open a class at the instigation of a parent group. Jersey City started a class for "mongoloids" in the same, and, between 1951 and 1952, Nutley, Passaic, and Elizabeth also acceded to the parents' pressure for special classes. "We are *happy* to announce the closing of our North Essex class because of the decision of the Nutley Board of Education to open a class for trainable retarded children," *The Guardian* editor wrote, in September 1951. A report eight months later noted the "improved manners and willingness to cooperate" of the ten children enrolled in the Nutley class.[48]

Operating separate schools and conducting campaigns in individual school districts proved both costly and inefficient for the parent groups. Separate parent-run schools functioned "on a shoestring . . . [dependent on] the good will of whatever church, community house, or veterans' organization will give them space . . . [and on] the devotion of teachers who value pioneering above pay." The words came from Elizabeth Boggs, of the Essex County Unit, as she stated the case for government assistance to special education. Parents of children with mental retardation only wanted "something of the same opportunity afforded parents of normal youngsters to receive skilled assistance from trained teachers in the rearing of their children." Urban centers sometimes had classes for the "educable" students, and institutions cared for the most severely retarded. The children in between—those psychologists called "trainable"—fell into a broad gap in the state's educational programs. "We parents know," Boggs concluded, "that we cannot fill this gap alone [because these programs] must be publicly supported in order to reach all the children who need it."[49]

After the birth of their son, in 1945, Elizabeth Boggs and her husband, Fitzhugh, moved to Montclair, in Essex County, in search of good public schools. David never attended the Montclair schools; an illness in infancy left him both physically and mentally disabled. At the time Boggs was a research chemist with a Ph.D. from Cambridge University. After David's illness, she changed her career from science to advocacy. Both parents were founding members of the Essex County Unit; both were driving forces in both the state and national associations, with Elizabeth serving as NARC president from 1958 to 1960 and Fitzhugh as president of the EU and as delegate to the national conventions. Elizabeth Boggs would go on to become a member of President Kennedy's Panel on Mental Retardation and play an instrumental role in expanding the federal definition of disabilities to include people with physical handicaps.[50]

A self-described "nonprofessional mover and shaker," Boggs worked actively in the early 1950s for the expansion of public education for all children with mental retardation. Officially, however, the impetus for state legislation came from the New Jersey Commission to Study the Problems and Needs of Mentally Deficient Persons, appointed by the governor in 1950. In March 1953, an interim report from the Commission concerning the education of children "not accommodated in residential schools" recommended that the State Department of Education assume responsibility for all of these students and that state aid be provided to offset the additional expense to school districts. John Shannon, an assemblyman from Newark (in Essex County) and a high school teacher, was one of seven Commission members. With the recommendations in hand, Shannon returned to the state assembly to sponsor the first attempt to legislate new special education provisions for New Jersey.[51]

Acting both up front and behind the scenes to formulate Shannon's legislation, however, were the parents of the New Jersey units of NARC. Lee Marino, a past president of the New Jersey Association for Retarded Children and an affiliate of the EU, was also a Commission member. Elizabeth Boggs helped to write Shannon's bill and directed the parents' campaign on behalf of the legislation. As Boggs remembered the events, Shannon was in a rush—his term was expiring, he wanted to leave the education bill as his legislative legacy, and he had a competitor. Assemblyman Alfred Beadleston had begun to express an interest in special education reform. To speed up the process, Shannon turned to the parents, requesting that Boggs, as chairperson of the state council's education committee, draft a new special education policy. In 1953, Shannon's proposal, hastily written by Elizabeth Boggs, was introduced in the State Assembly.[52]

Boggs recalled with pride the NJ-ARC's first lobbying effort—the "crash program"—put together by the parent groups to gain passage of the Shannon bill. "For every child a fair chance" served as the rallying cry.[53] The General Assembly passed the Shannon bill, but, in the Senate, opposition developed. Educators, urged on by the state Commissioner for Education, argued that there were too few students to make such a law practical. They also claimed that experience had proved that children with an IQ under 50 (those who fell in the "trainable" category) could not be educated in an academic sense. Local boards of education opposed the bill for fiscal reasons, fearing that, as written, the legislation would make them responsible for children who belonged in institutions. Although the Senate eventually approved the measure, Governor Alfred Driscoll vetoed it, asking the legislators to resubmit a more acceptable proposal for special education classes. Shannon did not return to the state legislature in 1954, leaving Beadleston to sponsor the revised "Act Concerning the Education and Training of Mentally Retarded Children."[54]

This time, the parent groups mobilized all their forces to ensure passage. The state council of the New Jersey units distributed 25,000 summaries of the new bill, local units held special forums to acquaint school officials with the bill's provisions, individual members flooded their representatives with letters of support, and representatives of the parent groups rallied in Trenton.[55] The Beadleston Act passed without opposition and was signed into law by a new governor, in July 1954. After signing, Robert Meyner gave his pen to John J. Mitchell, the legislative chairman of the New Jersey Association for Retarded Children—a gesture acknowledging the role parent groups had played in this particular bit of special education history.[56]

The Beadleston Act enabled many more New Jersey families to participate in the rituals that mark the passages of childhood. In 1953, just before the Beadleston legislation, New Jersey schools offered 276 classes for children termed educable. Five years later, for the 1958–1959 school year, 686 classes accepted these students. Figures for trainable classes were more significant. From a mere five public school classes before Beadleston, the number jumped to 155 at the end of the decade.[57] Compliance remained slow, however, despite the assistance of state funding, and there was a loophole. Those children labeled severely and profoundly retarded were specifically excluded from the act's benefits. After 1954, as parent groups closed their classes for "trainable" children, they began to supply day-care activities for home-based children with severe mental retardation, in preparation for new campaigns for publicly funded education.[58] Local units also developed preschool programs to socialize children for entry into the newly available public school classes.

Services neglected by the new legislation should not detract from the significance of the parents' political activism. Nor should the uses to which "special education" classes would be put in the ensuing decades diminish their importance in the mid-1950s. For the families who built the New Jersey ARC, the potential abuses of "special education"—the segregationist structure that enabled school districts to isolate troublesome youngsters and minority students—were not apparent. Viewing the world as they did, from within a framework of middle-class domesticity, the parent groups forged beyond the patterns of the past, the shame and guilt associated with mental retardation because of ties to individual and family failings. Middle-class parents of children who had been excluded from the educational process, to whom special education classes had not been directed, integrated special education into a vision of family life and turned to state government to guarantee the participation of their children in one of the key rituals of childhood—going to school.

Mental retardation was a social issue and a professional problem in post–World War II America, but, above all, it was a family matter. At a time when raising "perfect" children was one of a family's primary functions, a small but relatively privileged class of American parents found that the mental retardation of their offspring belied the promise of domesticity. In contrast to histories that find the construct of middle-class domesticity a tool of only limited use when exploring the behavior of ordinary men and women of the 1940s and 1950s, the story of the parent groups is a testimony to the power of middle-class family values. As they united in local chapters to gain mutual support and political leverage, these parents designed programs and services to replicate the cultural model of domestic togetherness. They believed in the value of education, in healthy play, in togetherness, and in the obligation of parents to promote the happiness of their daughters and sons. Middle-class parents of "normal" youngsters shared these goals. At the same time, the insistence of NARC parents that the child with mental retardation was a "child" first and "retarded" second did not mask the special qualities of their lives and the different paths they had to take to fulfill the 1950s canons of domesticity.

During the 1950s, that path led parent activists to look to the state to promote the trappings of domesticity. The relationship between family and state grew increasingly complex in the twentieth century. Historians often easily assume that adherence to traditional domestic values was imposed on unwilling or, at the least, unaware families from without, through expert advice or through government programs.[59] The parent movement of the 1950s suggests, instead, that some postwar families found that only through government programs were they able to provide all their children with the trappings of a middle-class childhood.

Seen in this light and from the vantage point of a feminist critique of domesticity, the parent movement of the 1950s was a conservative influence reaffirming a stifling set of values: nuclear families, domesticity, and togetherness. Moreover, the classes created by special education legislation were damaging for many youngsters without mental retardation who were willfully misidentified and segregated in inappropriate classrooms. I argue, however, that by changing the direction from which we look at these local people, the parent activism of the postwar years can be seen to have had radical import.[60] Parent organizations demanded that local, the state, and, ultimately, the federal government live up to the liberal ideal of providing equally for the welfare of all citizens. The support needed to make these families less exceptional expanded the government's range of social responsibilities. Furthermore, by emphasizing the role of the state in achieving domestic perfection, these activists began to require policy makers to reconceptualize middle-class domesticity to include one form of "imperfect" family.

The meaning of "family" remains a contested terrain in the United States. In some areas, families with members of different races are still looked at askance, and gay and lesbian couples face legal restrictions in nearly all states. The New Jersey parents who belonged to the Association for Retarded Children during the 1950s represented an opening wedge, a small part of late-twentieth-century efforts to expand the boundaries of family to include members of many shades, varieties, and even "imperfections."

NOTES

1. "An Act Concerning the Education and Training of Mentally Retarded Children in the Public School Systems of the State, and Supplementing Title 18 of the Revised Statutes," *The Acts of the One Hundred and Seventy-Eighth Legislature of the State of*

New Jersey and Seventh under the New Constitution (Trenton, 1954), p. 688. There were a total of four "Beadleston Acts," one directed towards the physically handicapped, one for the mentally retarded, one outlining financial responsibilities, and one establishing diagnostic procedures.

2. In 1954, "educable" referred to children "capable of achieving a limited to a moderate degree of proficiency in the basic learning skills." "Trainable" pupils fell "below the limitations" of the educable group; these children would "never achieve a useful knowledge of academic skills," but with proper education they could be expected to learn social skills and become "economically or occupationally useful," in their own homes or in a "sheltered" environment. Separate classes for educable students were far more widely available in the postwar years than were classes for children deemed "trainable." The particular reference for these quotes is Arthur S. Hill, *The Forward Look: The Severely Retarded Child Goes to School,* Federal Security Agency, Office of Education Bulletin 1952, No. 11 (Washington, D.C.: Government Printing Office, 1952), p. 4. These definitions were, however, widely used in the decade after World War II. See also J. E. Wallace Wallin, *Children with Mental and Physical Handicaps* (New York: Prentice-Hall, 1949), pp. 10–42. Wallin, a psychologist and the leading proponent of special education, discussed the situational determination of the definition and the variable meanings of mental retardation. Here, I am using the "educational definition," but Wallin pointed to equally important social and occupational definitions, as well as to anatomical and psychological definitions; although situational, all Wallin's definitions were based on deviation from a presumed norm.

3. James T. Patterson, *Brown v. Board of Education: A Civil Rights Milestone and Its Troubled Legacy* (New York: Oxford University Press, 2001); Daniel A. Clark, "'The Two Joes Meet—Joe College, Joe Veteran': The G.I. Bill, College Education, and Postwar American Culture," *History of Education Quarterly* 38 (1998): 164–189; James W. Trent Jr., *Inventing the Feeble Mind: A History of Mental Retardation in the United States* (Berkeley: University of California Press, 1994), pp. 244–245. Postwar baby-boom children began to reach public-school age in the early 1950s, but the increased numbers of students was matched by a commitment to the education of all students. See Lawrence Cremin, *The Transformation of the School: Progressivism in American Education, 1876–1957* (New York: Vintage Books, 1964), pp. 328–332. On the growth of special education classes throughout the decade, see Romaine P. Mackie, *Special Education in the United States: Statistics, 1948–1968* (New York: Teachers College Press, 1969).

4. Edward Berkowitz, "Historical Aspects of Disability," *Disability Studies Quarterly* 8 (summer 1988): 42. Gerald Grob also challenged historians to ask new questions about mental retardation. See his comments in the review of *Caring for the Retarded in America: A History,* by Peter L. Tyor and Leland V. Bell, *History of Education Quarterly* 26 (1986): 306–313. More recently, Paul K. Longmore and Lauri Umansky have made the same point in their "Introduction: Disability History: From the Margins to the Mainstream," in *The New Disability History; American Perspectives* (New York: New York

University Press, 2001), pp. 1–29. Histories of mental retardation have most often taken the institution as the focus. See Peter L. Tyor and Leland V. Bell, *Caring for the Retarded in America: A History* (Westport, Conn.: Greenwood Press, 1984); Steven Noll, *The Feeble-Minded in Our Midst: Institutions for the Mentally Retarded in the South, 1900–1940* (Chapel Hill: University of North Carolina Press, 1995); and Trent, *Inventing the Feeble Mind.* Philip M. Ferguson, in *Abandoned to Their Fate; Social Policy and Practice toward Severely Retarded People in America, 1820–1920* (Philadelphia: Temple University Press, 1994), specifically calls on historians to begin to look at the families (pp. 167–168). Janice Brockley, "History of Mental Retardation; An Essay Review," *History of Psychology* 2 (1999): 25–36, provides a review of recent literature.

5. Elaine Tyler May, *Homeward Bound: American Families in the Cold War Era* (New York: Basic Books, 1988). Others who make similar arguments include Stephanie Coontz, *The Way We Never Were: American Families and the Nostalgia Trap* (New York: Basic Books, 1992); Joanne Meyerowitz, ed., *Not June Cleaver: Women and Gender in Postwar America, 1945–1960* (Philadelphia: Temple University Press, 1994); and Jessica Weiss, *To Have and to Hold: Marriage, the Baby Boom, and Social Change* (Chicago: University of Chicago Press, 2000). To the contrary, Glenna Matthews, *"Just a Housewife": The Rise and Fall of Domesticity in America* (New York: 1987), argues that domesticity was devalued in twentieth century because of the intrusion of homemaking experts. On "togetherness," see Otis Stiese, "Live the Life of *McCall's,*" *McCall's* (May 1954): 27, cited and discussed in Weiss, *To Have and to Hold,* pp. 114–139.

6. According to the text, men and women who were "willing to develop the values of parenthood" could expect to "find happiness and enrichment in having children." Ernest R. Groves and Gladys Hoagland Groves, *The Contemporary American Family* (Philadelphia: Lippincott, 1947), p. 752.

7. May, *Homeward Bound,* p. 137. The emotional value of children in twentieth-century families has been described also by Viviana Zelizer in *Pricing the Priceless Child* (New York: Basic Books, 1985). The psychologist was Joseph Adelson, quoted in May, *Homeward Bound,* p. 58.

8. Wallin, *Children with Mental and Physical Handicaps,* p. 29.

9. On Goddard and his views on the "feebleminded," see Leila Zenderland, *Measuring Minds: Henry Herbert Goddard and the Origins of American Intelligence Testing* (New York: Cambridge University Press, 1998). Trent, *Inventing the Feeble Mind,* pp. 130–183, explains the "menace of the feebleminded."

10. On advice to institutionalize see Trent, *Inventing the Feeble Mind,* pp. 230–237. Erikson's story is told in Lawrence J. Friedman, *Identity's Architect: A Biography of Erik H. Erikson* (New York: Scribner, 1999), pp. 208–215. See also the stories of Pearl Buck, *The Child Who Never Grew* (New York: J. Day Co., 1950), and John P. Frank, *My Son's Story* (New York: Alfred A. Knopf, 1951).

11. Nearly any child-rearing manual from the postwar years contained these messages; Benjamin Spock's *Baby and Child Care* (1946) would become infamous for the

pediatrician's hostility toward working mothers. See the discussions of maternal rejection in Ruth Feldstein, *Motherhood in Black and White: Race and Sex in American Liberalism, 1930–1965* (Ithaca: Cornell University Press, 2000).

12. Dale Evans Rogers, *Angel Unaware* (Westwood, N.J.: Revell, 1953); samples of the letters are reprinted in Maxine Garrison, *The Angel Spreads Her Wings* (Westwood, N.J.: Revell, 1956).

13. Frank, *My Son's Story*, pp. 119, 161.

14. "Children's Census Is Advocated Here," *New York Times*, 21 March 1951. This article and the reports of the conference published in local New Jersey newspapers were saved in scrapbooks by the Raritan Valley Unit of the Association for Retarded Citizens/New Jersey. The scrapbooks remain with the unit. Hereafter cited as RVU Scrapbooks.

15. Laura Blossfeld, interview by author, tape recording, Teaneck, New Jersey, 19 May 1990. Hereafter cited as Blossfeld Interview. Also see "The Association for Retarded Citizens, Bergen-Passaic Counties" (typescript, 1985), in the possession of the Association for Retarded Citizens/Bergen-Passaic Chapter. The Chapter also supplied a copy of Blossfeld's "Letter to the Editor."

16. A spinoff group formed in nearby Essex County in 1948, and five more chapters organized after the Essex and Bergen-Passaic groups sponsored a statewide meeting at Rutgers University in March 1949. In 1950, the seven units were incorporated as the New Jersey Parents Group for Retarded Children. The story—the legend—of the formation of the New Jersey Parents Group is reported in Mrs. John R. Clark, "A Study in Progress" (New Brunswick, N.J.: New Jersey Association for Retarded Children, 1969). A copy is located in the files of the Association for Retarded Citizens/New Jersey, New Brunswick, New Jersey. My thanks to Karl Greiner, of ARC-NJ, for making it available. The Rutgers meeting was well covered by the local press. These articles were collected by unit members and preserved in scrapbooks. In researching the New Jersey parent groups, I have relied on newsletters and scrapbooks from the three units, as well as interviews with individuals active during the early years of each chapter. Each of the units published a newsletter, printed monthly and mailed to all members. Copies of the newsletters of the B-PU (*The Parents Voice*) and the EU (*The Guardian*) are maintained in the local offices of the ARC units. A nearly complete run of the RVU newsletter (no title; printed as a letter to members) is housed with the Bernice Carlson Papers, de Grummond Children's Literature Research Collection, McCain Library and Archives, University of Southern Mississippi, Hattiesburg, Mississippi. Both the RVU and the EU also made available scrapbooks (hereafter cited as RVU Scrapbooks and EU Scrapbooks) of news clippings about the local unit and state and national events. Minutes of group meetings and group correspondence files were not available.

17. On the earlier groups see Robert M. Segal, *Mental Retardation and Social Action: A Study of the Associations for Retarded Children as a Force for Social Change* (Springfield,

Ill.: Thomas, 1970), pp. 25-26. For the Rhode Island unit see Barbara Bair, "The Parents Council for Retarded Children and Social Change in Rhode Island, 1951-1970," *Rhode Island History* 40 (1981): 144-159. Based on interviews with participants, Bair's study points to the significance of personal political connections for the group's ability to achieve its goals. The EU newsletter, *The Guardian*, described the founding of NARC and made regular reports on national developments. See also Dorothy H. Moss (Secretary of NARC), "Parents on the March," *Journal of the American Public Welfare Association* 2 (January 1953): 28-33, for a succinct account from an insider. Trent, *Inventing the Feeble Mind*, pp. 240-242, discusses the work of the national organization in the 1950s. Information on the current organization can be found at the group's website, http://www.thearc.org/.

18. On nineteenth-century mothers' clubs, see Richard Meckel, *Save the Babies: American Public Health Reform and the Prevention of Infant Mortality, 1850–1929* (Baltimore: Johns Hopkins University Press, 1990); and Mary P. Ryan, *Cradle of the Middle Class: The Family in Oneida County, New York, 1790–1865* (New York: Cambridge University Press, 1981). On mothers' activism (and the use of maternal imagery in women's activism) in the early twentieth century see Molly Ladd-Taylor, *Mother-Work: Women, Child Welfare, and the State, 1890–1930* (Urbana: University of Illinois Press, 1994); and Robyn Muncy, *Creating a Female Dominion in American Reform, 1890–1935* (New York: Oxford University Press, 1991).

Other parent organizations of the 1950s are discussed in Alfred H. Katz, *Parents of the Handicapped: Self-Organized Parents' and Relatives' Groups for Treatment of Ill and Handicapped Children* (Springfield, Ill.: Thomas, 1961); Joseph Levy, *Parent Groups and Social Agencies: The Activities of Health and Welfare Agencies with Groups of Parents of Handicapped Children in Chicago* (Chicago: University of Chicago Press, 1951); and Phyllis Rubenfeld, "Education in Public Schools for Cerebral Palsy and Mentally Retarded Children: The Parent Movement in New York City, 1946-1975" (Ed.D. diss., Columbia University Teachers College, 1984).

The local nature of the first parent groups for children with mental retardation is noted in Segal, *Mental Retardation and Social Action*, p. 24.

19. Blossfeld Interview. Yepsen's participation in the organizational meeting for the state council was reported in *The Parents Voice* (December 1949). Biographical information on Yepsen can be found in "The Yepsen Story—Career Man," *The Shield* 2 (June 1953); and on Starr in "Dr. Starr Receives Rutgers Award for Work with Clinic," *New Brunswick Sunday Times*, 24 October 1954. Both clippings were saved in the EU Scrapbooks. On Anna Spiesman Starr see also her file in the Rutgers Faculty Biographies Collection, Rutgers University Library, New Brunswick, N.J.; and Anne Spiesman Starr, *The Rutgers Psychological Clinic, 1929-1956: A Chronicle and an Interpretation* (New Brunswick, N.J.: n.p., 1971). Newsletters of each of the units announced monthly speakers and frequently gave brief summaries of the talks.

20. Trent, too, attributes the timing of the parent organizations to changes in the

family and notes the middle-class and upper-class composition of the groups (*Inventing the Feeble Mind,* pp. 239–240). There is little evidence in the records I have looked at that parent groups made any deliberate commitments to serving the needs of the poor or of minorities. Members spoke of their work as benefiting *all* children with mental retardation (which may have been code words for children whose families were not of the same economic status as the group members). The units offered sliding payment scales for their educational and recreational services. The $1.00 fee (raised to $3.00 in 1952) was not designed to exclude many from membership; however, inclusiveness did not seem to extend to group activities. In published pictures of group programs—camp and school—all the children appear to be Caucasian.

21. Segal discusses the white-collar bias of NARC (*Mental Retardation and Social Action,* pp. 47–69). Information on the families in the Raritan Valley Unit was pulled from the unit's scrapbooks and from stories in the group's newsletter. A news report on the first convention of the state organization noted that with mental retardation found "on all social and economic levels," the state organization included "holders of Ph.D. degrees, lawyers, pediatricians, bankers, business executives, teachers, clerks and laborers . . . all drawn together by the common bond of their retarded children." "Parents Plan Drive to Better Schools for Mentally Deficient," *New Brunswick Sunday Times,* 22 April 1951. RVU Scrapbooks.

22. Katz, *Parents of the Handicapped,* p. 60.

23. Judith Feist, Interview with the author, tape recording, New Brunswick, New Jersey, November 3, 1989.

24. "Family Album: The Carlson Family of Middlebush," *New Brunswick Sunday Times,* 20 April 1952. RVU Scrapbooks. Carlson was both secretary and publicity director of the RVU. She was also the author (with the RVU's camp director, David Ginglend) of *Play Activities for the Retarded Child: How to Help Him Grow and Learn through Music, Games, Handicraft, and Other Play Activities* (New York: Abingdon Press, 1961). Another story of parental commitment to institutionalization came from B-PU's Virginia Kane. Her article, "My Daughter Is at the Vineland State School," was printed in *The Parents Voice* (August–September 1954). Kane compared Vineland to a "good boarding school" and concluded, "We went through long hard months of deliberation before making application, and longer harder months of tiring effort to have her admitted once her name was on the waiting list. Since she has been at the institution we have never once regretted our decision." The article is a description of the home-like atmosphere of the institution and a list of the activities that tied this institutionalized two-year-old to her family.

25. Alfred Dorn, Interview for WCTC Radio, 5 May 1950. RVU Scrapbooks.

26. "Nursery Group Organizes," *The Parents Voice* (December 1950). Every year the groups filled Christmas bags for children and adults in the state institutions. Benevolence committees were particularly concerned about the "forgotten" children, those whose families could not or would not remember them. Members made sure these

children received cards on their birthdays. Projects directed by the benevolence committees were reported regularly in the newsletters of all three units. "Bus Trip News" was a regular column in *The Parents Voice,* while *The Guardian* printed bus sign-up forms in each issue.

27. J. E. Wallace Wallin, *Education of Mentally Handicapped Children* (New York: Harper and Brothers, 1955), pp. 12–13.

28. A report in the EU newsletter on the 1952 state bond issue noted that there were 742 individuals on waiting lists for the state's four institutions. "The $25,000,000 Bond Issue, A Must," *The Guardian* (November 1952), p. 1. The need for mittens was described by RVU president Alfred Dorn, Interview for WCTC.

29. Bernice Carlson, "Letter to the Editor," *New Brunswick Evening News,* 30 October 1949. RVU Scrapbooks.

30. "The $25,000,000 Bond Issue, A Must," *The Guardian* (November 1952); "Institutions Bond Issue Passes," *The Guardian* (December 1952).

31. Yepsen's statements of support can be found in the *Welfare Reporter,* the state agency's monthly journal. Notes on his participation in parent group activities are in the local newspaper articles clipped for the RVU Scrapbooks.

32. "Your Attendance Will Count," *The Guardian* (February 1952).

33. "Report on Questionnaire to Parents," *The Guardian* (September 1951).

34. The scrapbooks and newsletters contain many accounts of family parties and picnics. On the RVU's Happytimers canteen, "Understanding Youngsters Make 'Happy Timers' Times Real Happy," *New Brunswick Sunday Home News,* 23 October 1960. RVU Scrapbooks. On EU's teen project, issues of *The Guardian,* beginning in January 1952, reported on the activities of the group. The swim program was described in "Swimming Program Open to All Retarded Children and Escorts," *The Guardian* (September 1953).

35. "Vacation at the Shore for All Your Children—And Mama Too!" *The Guardian* (April 1955).

36. Trent, *Inventing the Feeble Mind,* p. 241.

37. "Summer School Set for Retarded," *Newark Evening News,* 26 May 1955. "Happy Day Camp Aids Mentally Retarded Youth," Bound Book, 19 July 1956. RVU Scrapbooks.

38. "A Look at Shady Nook," *The Guardian* (July–August 1956).

39. "Understanding Youngsters Make 'Happy Timers' Real Happy." RVU Scrapbooks. The Essex Teen Canteen (for teens ages fifteen to nineteen) opened one night a week beginning in February 1952.

40. More than forty years later, Blossfeld remained skeptical of the early emphasis on education and the later goals of deinstitutionalization and mainstreaming; some youngsters, like her son, were unmanageable at home and required institutional support. Blossfeld Interview.

May notes that "success" for middle-class parents of "normal" children was defined as the "ability to keep children in school through high school." *Homeward Bound,* p. 108. See also Carl C. Zimmerman and Lucius F. Cervantes, *Successful American Families* (New York: Pageant Press, 1960).

41. As elsewhere, special education in New Jersey developed in the context of early-twentieth-century urban class and ethnic tensions. The programs functioned as one means to control, in a public institution, poor, immigrant children whose personalities, intellectual accomplishments, and language did not fit them for integration into the classrooms of the average and the middle class. Special education was not directed toward families with social standing; education reformers and mental retardation experts agreed that these families would have little need for services for the "feebleminded." At the time, mental retardation was presumed to be a class-based phenomenon, usually the product of degenerate living and poor heredity. Marvin Lazerson argues that special education was clearly a class phenomenon and that it did not touch disabled children from the middle class (p. 33). Marvin Lazerson, "The Origins of Special Education," in Jay G. Chambers and William T. Hartman, eds., *Special Education Policies: Their History, Implementation, and Finance* (Philadelphia: Temple University Press, 1983), pp. 15–47, represents this perspective.

To date, no one has studied the actual composition of the early special-education classes. Special education experts were relying in part on the work of Henry H. Goddard who created genealogies of the "feeble-minded" inmates of the New Jersey Training School for the Feeble-Minded, in Vineland. Goddard was research director at Vineland and a figure with national stature in the field of mental retardation. Goddard's equation of mental retardation with antisocial behavior (both criminal and sexual) contributed to the widespread fear of the "feebleminded" as a public menace and to plans for sterilization of inmates in state training facilities. On the other hand, Vineland also offered summer courses for public school teachers that provided instruction in the most up-to-date methods for handling special education classes. On Goddard and the Vineland Training School, see Tyor and Bell, *Caring for the Retarded in America,* pp. 106–112, and Zenderland, *Measuring Minds.*

42. On the development of special education classes throughout the United States, in addition to Lazerson, "The Origins of Special Education," see Margaret A. Winzer, *The History of Special Education: From Isolation to Integration* (Washington, D.C.: Gallaudet University Press, 1993), pp. 366–385; Joseph L. Tropea, "Bureaucratic Order and Special Children: Urban Schools, 1890s–1940s," *History of Education Quarterly* 27 (1987): 29–53; Joseph L. Tropea, "Bureaucratic Order and Special Children: Urban Schools, 1950s–1960s," *History of Education Quarterly* 27 (1987): 339–361. For a historical overview of the educational philosophy behind special education see Philip L. Safford and Elizabeth J. Safford, *A History of Childhood Disabilities* (New York: Teachers College Press, 1996), pp. 153–187. Specific to New Jersey history, see Patricia A. Holliday, "The Development of Education for the Severely and Profoundly Retarded Child in the State of New Jersey: 1950–1983" (Ph.D. diss., Rutgers University, 1984),

pp. 30–61; Shirley Staub, "Developments in Special Education in New Jersey since 1900" (Ed.D. diss., Lehigh University, 1978); and Interagency Committee for Education of the Handicapped, "Opportunities for Handicapped Children in the Public Schools of New Jersey," (Montclair, N.J., 1967), pp. 1–3.

43. Census figures reported in Holliday, "Development of Education," p. 28.

44. "An Educational Bill of Rights for the Retarded Child," reprinted in *The Guardian* (May 1954).

45. Although this project was kept separate from the Bergen-Passaic Unit to which Gould belonged, that group's newsletter reported school news in each issue, and unit members acted as school volunteers. Letter from Laura Blossfeld to author, May 22, 1990.

46. "Union School," *The Parents Voice* (January 1950); "Report from the Nancy-Luzon School," *The Parents Voice* (July 1950).

47. On the opening of the psychological clinic, Elizabeth M. Boggs, Interview with Author, tape recording, Hampton, N.J., May 17, 1990; hereafter cited as Boggs Interview. See also announcements of the clinic's work in individual issues of *The Guardian*; students who planned to attend EU-sponsored schools were required to undergo a clinic evaluation. The formation of clinics was on the agenda of other units in the in the 1950s, but the provision in the Beadleston Act for school diagnosis seemed to dampen enthusiasm for this particular project. Rejection of state aid, see Boggs Interview; and Bertha Clark, *A Study in Progress; The History of the New Jersey Association for Retarded Children* (New Brunswick, N.J.: New Jersey Association for Retarded Children, 1969), p. 22.

48. "Camden Opens Special Class," *The Parents Voice* (February 1951). "School Offers Aid to Retarded Child," *New York Times,* 1 June 1952. RVU Scrapbooks. "Nutley to Start Special Class," *The Parents Voice* (August 1951); "School Projects," *The Guardian* (September 1951); "Nutley School District Trainable Class," *The Guardian* (April 1952).

49. Elizabeth M. Boggs, "The Case for Special Schools," *Welfare Reporter* 5 (March 1951): 5–6, 15–16.

50. In addition to the Boggs Interview, biographical information on Elizabeth Boggs can be found in "Elizabeth M. Boggs Receives J. E. Wallace Wallin Award," *Exceptional Children* 54 (September 1987): 85–88; and Wolfgang Saxon, "Obituary: Dr. Elizabeth Monroe Boggs, 82, Founder of Group for Retarded Children," *New York Times,* 30 January 1996, B16.

51. Clark, *A Study in Progress,* p. 28. Commission to Study the Problems and Needs of Mentally Deficient Persons, *Mental Deficiency in New Jersey: A Report to Governor Robert B. Meyner and the Members of the Senate and General Assembly* (Trenton, 1954), pp. 73–83.

52. Boggs Interview. According to Laura Blossfeld, Beadleston became involved in the plans of the parent group, when, at a state council meeting on strategies to

obtain legislation, a Monmouth county member piped up, "I know Al Beadleston" and offered to contact him. Blossfeld Interview. Boggs remembers, however, that Beadleston had a cook whose child had cerebral palsy, prompting Beadleston to announce his intention to pursue special education issues in the legislature.

53. Boggs Interview. Unit members inundated state legislators with letters in support of the Shannon bill. The campaign of the Bergen Passaic unit was reported in "Bill A-414 Still in Senate!" *The Parents Voice* (May 1953). The campaign slogan was a phrase from the 1950 White House Conference on Children.

54. Elizabeth Boggs, in interview with the author, reported the objections of the Department of Education. See "Who Shall Train the Retarded?" *Irvington Herald*, 16 July 1953, EU Scrapbooks, for an incident of Board of Education opposition. Driscoll's veto included his account of the opposition united against the bill. *Veto Messages of Hon. Alfred E. Driscoll, Governor of New Jersey* (Trenton, 1953), pp. 85–87.

55. Clark, *A Study in Progress*, p. 28.

56. "Bills Signed by Gov. Meyner," *The Parents Voice* (August–September 1954).

57. New Jersey Commissioner of Education's Commission on the Education of the Handicapped, *The Education of Handicapped Children in New Jersey, 1954–1964* (Trenton, 1964), p. 16.

58. Of one such program, the Raritan Valley Unit's "Saturday Class," its parent-director observed that this was "the only schooling these children would ever know." "Mentally Retarded Children Aided by Saturday School," *New Brunswick Sunday Times*, 21 November 1954. RVU Scrapbooks.

59. See, for example, Barbara Ehrenreich and Deirdre English, *For Her Own Good: 100 Years of the Experts' Advice to Women* (New York: Anchor Books, 1989; 1978).

60. Similar arguments have been made about other organizations. See Lynn Weiner, "Reconstructing Motherhood: The La Leche League in Postwar America," *Journal of American History* 80 (1994): 1357–1381; and Weiss, *To Have and to Hold*. Other deliberate uses of motherhood and familialism for subversive activities during the postwar years are described by Deborah A. Gerson, "'Is Family Devotion Now Subversive?' Familialism against McCarthyism," in Meyerowitz, ed., *Not June Cleaver*, pp. 151–176; and Amy Swerdlow, "Ladies' Day at the Capitol: Women Strike for Peace versus HUAC," *Feminist Studies* 8 (1982): 493–520.

14

"Nice, Average Americans"

Postwar Parents' Groups and the Defense of the Normal Family

Katherine Castles

In 1949, a mother of a five-year-old boy with mental retardation placed an advertisement in a New York city newspaper, searching for other parents in similar situations. She wrote, "Surely there must be other children like him, other parents like myself. Where are you? Let's band together and *do something* for our children!"[1] This mother's search succeeded spectacularly; after several meetings, a parents' association was organized, and within a year the Association for the Help of Retarded Children (AHRC) had around a thousand members. Parents raised money, organized a diagnostic clinic and social activities for their children, provided mutual support, and soon became involved in state politics. Traditional social service agencies and mental health professionals looked on with a mixture of admiration and alarm, speaking of these parents' "terrific sense of missionary purpose" and "wild zeal."[2]

In the years after World War II, variations on AHRC's story were repeated all over the United States. Numerous parents of children with mental retardation independently chose, all at the same time, to organize, to go public with their children's problems, and to push for better facilities and more sympathetic public attitudes toward mental retardation. A 1950 survey found eighty-eight local parents' groups, with 19,300 members, spread over nineteen states. Of those groups, seventy-seven had been formed between 1946 and 1950.[3] In 1950, representatives of AHRC and other local groups organized the National Association for Retarded Children (NARC), the predecessor of what is now The Arc. By 1960, NARC had 681 local affiliates and a membership of 62,000.[4] While the national organization remained relatively weak and underfunded during these early years, parents at the local level possessed enormous enthusiasm and organizational vigor.

Parents' groups during these years achieved only modest changes in social policy regarding mental retardation. More dramatic, at least initially, was the rapid transformation in how mental retardation was portrayed in the media and other public forums. Historians of disability have frequently observed that our understanding of disability—who is considered disabled, how disability is defined, what cultural meanings are ascribed to a particular disability—is shaped largely by the social context and the historical moment in which the disability occurs.[5] Mental retardation, like other disabilities, is a complex social category whose boundaries and meanings are shaped in different ways by different historical actors, acting within different cultural and social frameworks. In the years after World War II, parents of children with mental retardation both benefited from and contributed to a radical change in public discourse about who the mentally retarded were and what it meant to be mentally retarded. The rise of postwar parents' groups, and both the scope and the limits of their effectiveness in this era, must be understood in the context of this broader change in mental retardation's cultural significance.

Disability is most often viewed through the lens of whatever social issues and cultural anxieties seem central to society at a given time. Before World War II, public discussions of mental retardation were dominated by the eugenics movement, which sought to defend the white middle class against the supposed threat posed by individuals seen as genetically inferior—most often immigrants, poor whites, or black Americans. Low intellectual functioning was seen as linked not only to genetic "degeneracy" but also to low social class, sexual misbehavior, criminal tendencies, and a variety of other social ills.[6]

This understanding of mental retardation did not disappear with the decline of the eugenics movement after World War II. However, it became less prominent, and new concerns came to the fore. Increasingly, discussions of disability in general, and mental retardation in particular, revolved around the more general issues of how to create and maintain well-adjusted, "normal" families; how to integrate those families into a harmonious community; and how to deal with those children who would never be normal or (by postwar definitions) well adjusted. Under the influence of the eugenics movement, mental retardation had been imagined as a problem of lower-class, sexually aggressive juvenile delinquents. After World War II, on the other hand, the American preoccupation with the idealized middle-class family, with a mother at home raising psychologically healthy children, led to a rising concern for mental retardation as a problem of young children and their families.[7]

Retarded children born into white, middle-class families became the center of public attention, and solutions to the problems of mental retardation were increasingly aimed at helping the rest of the family as much as the disabled child. Parents' groups made good use of this development and were instrumental in furthering it. Yet, the new rhetoric of the retarded child could be deployed in different ways, not all of them particularly progressive or beneficial to individuals with mental retardation. To many people, including much of the medical profession, raising a retarded child at home seemed increasingly dangerous to the family as a whole. There was a fine line between emphasizing the family in order to advocate for retarded children and invoking perceived threats to the family to justify fearful and punitive attitudes toward those children.

The postwar rise of organizations for parents with retarded children was very much a generational phenomenon. Parents who founded and joined these groups were primarily young mothers and, to a lesser extent, fathers whose children were just reaching school age. Many of these children were moderately or severely retarded and thus were excluded from the public school system, since those schools that had special education programs generally accepted only children with mild retardation. A primary goal of NARC and its affiliates was to expand school facilities for children with IQs below 50. Many local NARC chapters founded their own private schools, nurseries, or other day programs for members' children.[8] Although many parents of institutionalized children were active participants in NARC, they tended to organize in separate local affiliates, and there were tensions between parents of institutionalized and home-raised children.[9]

In many ways, the formation of local organizations for parents of retarded children was a natural outgrowth of the more general expansion of civic and community organizations during the postwar years. Postwar Americans were a generation of joiners: they joined churches, PTAs, Kiwanis, the Rotary Club, and other organizations in huge numbers. The increased mobility of American families, the growing isolation of the nuclear family from extended family ties, and the formation of new communities in the suburbs all encouraged this trend. Young families moving into new neighborhoods were quick to form new ties to their neighbors, both formally and informally, and to join together to solve community problems.[10] Parents' groups were both a variation on this type of organization and a response to the heightened sense of isolation that families with retarded children felt when excluded from core community institutions such as public schools and PTAs.

Medical charities and health organizations dedicated to particular illnesses or disabling conditions also grew spectacularly during this period. The most well-known example of this type of organization is the March of Dimes, which was founded in the 1930s to combat polio and became a model of successful fundraising and charity for health causes. The number of national voluntary health organizations in the United States grew from around 15 in 1940 (including such older groups as the Red Cross) to more than 100 in 1961.[11] Some of the new organizations, such as United Cerebral Palsy and the League for Muscular Dystrophy, were founded by parents, and parents were often very active in local units of national agencies such as the March of Dimes.[12] NARC borrowed many of its fundraising and publicity tactics, and parts of its agenda, from these medical charities.

However, none of the other medical charities was really comparable to NARC in its determination to maintain parent dominance at all levels, its strong resistance to professionalization of the group's leadership, and its mistrust of both the medical profession and the more established social welfare agencies. The differences between NARC and other health organizations with parent involvement stemmed largely from the enormous stigma attached to mental retardation, even in comparison with other types of disability. For respectable mothers and fathers to discuss openly a child's retardation in front of strangers, or to identify themselves publicly with other parents of retarded children, was a dramatic step in 1945. Parents who wrote about their children in these early years often did so anonymously.[13] In the aftermath of the eugenics movement, mental retardation was still often viewed as part of a more general, genetically based social deviance that might reveal the "bad stock" of the entire family. Describing her decision to join a parent group, one mother wrote,

> I silently shuddered as I thought that we were joining the ranks of freaks in the eyes of our community. What we found was, for me, an amazing sight. There was a group of nice, average, Americans talking in that animated

manner which characterizes any meeting of a P.T.A., service club, or church gathering.[14]

Another mother explained, "I wasn't exactly expecting to see the abnormal kind of people you see at a side show, but I wasn't sure."[15] While an organization like the March of Dimes could take for granted that its chosen cause was socially acceptable, parents of children with mental retardation had to constantly argue that they and their families were normal and respectable. NARC publications invariably highlighted the fact that mental retardation could be found in any family, "regardless of economic status, race, color or religion." Parents reminded the public that the high and mighty as well as the humble, those from "fashionable Park Avenue" as well as from rural farm houses, participated in NARC activities.[16]

To some extent, parent activists were radicalized by their strong awareness of their own stigmatized position. They were relatively mistrustful of outsiders, taking steps to maintain their independence both from mental health professionals and from other community agencies.[17] They could be angry and combative, although less radical NARC members tended to view too much anger as immature.[18] One early NARC activist who was not a parent later described an early organizational meeting in these terms:

> The collection of parents who were not resigned to the fact that a retarded child could belong to them were there with fire in their eyes. . . . The parents took the meeting over screaming and shouting their cause. And not willing to accept the program as planned.[19]

Parents were militant enough that social service professionals worried that these new parents' groups were "pressure groups" that might "cause difficulties for the established agencies."[20]

At the same time, though, NARC's desire to identify itself as an organization of "nice, average Americans" comparable to other mainstream civic groups shaped not only its rhetoric but also its reform agenda. Parents' insistence on their own respectability not only protected them from some of the stigma attached to mental retardation as a problem of the deviant lower classes but also helped them shape an alternative definition of mental retardation as a social problem faced by ordinary Americans—which, for the most part, meant middle class and white. In their rhetoric and their politics, parents' groups were firmly middle class, even while the individuals served by public mental retardation facilities and special education classes remained disproportionately poor, African American, and Hispanic.[21] Parents' groups showed little interest in addressing the problems faced by impoverished people labeled as mentally retarded. Their focus was on gaining services and public sympathy for the moderately retarded children of respectable American families. During these early years, they avoided public conflict with institutions, state agencies, and professionals, preferring instead to develop political ties and lobbying power as interested insiders.[22] The actual class background of NARC members at the local level could be quite diverse, especially when local groups could offer direct services such as school programs; an informal survey of the occupations of NARC members in Pittsburgh in 1960 found a wide range of blue-collar and white-collar workers.[23] Nonetheless, mental retardation as portrayed by these parents was emphatically *not* a problem of poverty, class, or race.

When parent activists explained their situation to the public, they focused on the problems faced by the entire family. As parents told the story, perfectly normal and blameless families that had the misfortune to produce children with mental retardation found themselves stigmatized, isolated from neighbors and community, forced to maintain a veil of protective secrecy around these children, and subjected to psychological stress that could tear apart marriages and permanently traumatize the other children in the family. In her account of mothering a daughter with mental retardation, Pearl Buck explained that

> Neighbors whisper that so-and-so's child is "not right." The family is taught to pretend that poor Harry or Susie is only slow. The shame of the parents infects all the children and sorrow spreads its blight.[24]

A 1955 NARC pamphlet asked, "what price can we place on the suffering endured by the family of each child when their neglected needs provoke mental illness, marriage breakdown and disrupted lives for other children."[25] The reform agenda of NARC in its early years aimed to ease the social isolation of retarded children and their families, while also providing badly needed concrete services. As Gunnar Dybwad, then executive director of NARC, explained in 1963, in the past the mentally retarded, as soon as he was recognized as such, was a "displaced person," displaced from the community literally whenever possible [by institutionalization], and figuratively otherwise—there were no services for him or his family, and no end to the rejection he suffered.[26]

Inclusion of children with moderate retardation in public special education was often discussed in the context of the broader need for community inclusion of people with mental retardation and their families.[27] Early parents' groups also fought for inclusion of their children in other mainstream community institutions such as churches and synagogues, as well as the establishment of "normal" social activities such as scouting troops and summer camps for retarded children.[28] In a generation of Americans intent on building healthy families and developing new community ties, parents with retarded children did not fit in. In a society where deviation from conventional family ideals was seen as potentially devastating, parents' groups sought to restore some degree of normality to their family lives.

The idea that children with mental retardation might disrupt their families and communities was not, in itself, a new development. The eugenics movement had encouraged fears that individuals with mental retardation would behave in dangerous ways, becoming criminals or sexual deviants as they reached adolescence. Furthermore, both professionals and the general public had long been concerned that children with mental retardation would pose too great a burden to their families, placing mothers in particular in a dangerous position. In the 1930s, however, concerns about the family focused largely on the more practical aspects of the problem: the time and energy a mother required to care for a disabled child and the financial burden of either home care or institutionalization. Doctors also worried about the impact of a retarded child in the home on the family's social status, especially if the parents were wealthy or otherwise of high status, and questioned whether adolescent daughters could attract potential husbands if a retarded sibling was present. These were serious concerns, serious enough to justify institutionalization, but they were not the same concerns that preoccupied postwar parents' groups.[29]

During the 1940s and 1950s, across many different areas of American life and culture, potential threats to the family were increasingly conceptualized in psychological terms. There was increased public concern for the psychological environment in which children were raised and the possibility of psychological harm if children were raised improperly. Expanding on the work of the child guidance movement of the 1920s and 1930s, doctors and other professionals elaborated a broad spectrum of illnesses and negative personality traits that could be attributed to problems in parenting—which, for the most part, meant problems in mothering. Mothers were often seen as dangerous influences, with enormous power to scar their children in any number of ways. Mothers might become too emotionally attached and over-involved with their children, or they might stay too distant and reject their children, with profound psychological damage likely in either case. This new emphasis on the psychological merged with the broader postwar emphasis on the idealized family and permeated popular culture. All sorts of spokespersons, from the child-rearing expert Dr. Spock to civil rights activists, incorporated the psychology of the family into their thinking.[30]

Not surprisingly, then, when parents' groups explained the problems facing families with retarded children, they framed those problems in terms of mental illness and psychological trauma. They argued that the stress and secrecy surrounding the child's retardation, the isolation from the outside world, and the experience of social rejection would lead to mental breakdown in the parents and, equally important, in the child's brothers and sisters. Parents' groups could play a crucial role, not only in gaining new services and new legislation for people with mental retardation but also in overcoming the shame and isolation that psychologically crippled the family. Thus, describing the first meeting of what would become AHRC, a father wrote,

> They were reticent, brooding, tragedy-haunted parents. . . . They were diffident and cautious at first—even with each other. Then slowly they began to thaw out. The old habits of distrust and cold withdrawal gave way before the warmth and excitement of this common experience which had drawn them together.. . . . One by one they rose and cast aside the usual feelings of guilt and shame to tell a familiar story of bafflement and despair.

Without this type of therapeutic experience, this father explained, both parents and siblings "become a social island, isolated by despair and misunderstanding, often so emotionally upset by the problem that they need psychological help."[31] One 1950 magazine article about the new parents' groups and other developments in the field of mental retardation described a twelve-year-old girl who suffered a "nervous breakdown" and was placed in a mental hospital after being forced to go out in public with her retarded sibling.[32] Postwar Americans took the experience of stigma very seriously indeed, and in this context parents' groups were doubly important as arenas for psychological self-help as well as instruments of social change.[33]

The constellation of social problems that parent activists evoked in their rhetoric and publicity campaigns proved highly effective in gaining public attention and in shaping a new public discourse about mental retardation. Although NARC could not compete with the established health organizations that served more socially accepted constituencies, such as the March of Dimes, parents' groups were quite successful in gaining media coverage and in setting the terms of that coverage. According to NARC activists, in the early years of parents' groups most magazines refused to print articles about mental retardation, perhaps on the grounds that the subject was too depressing.[34] Gradually, though, parents wrote articles themselves or worked with journalists to publish optimistic human-interest pieces declaring an era of "new hope" for retarded children. These articles, like NARC's own literature, stressed that mental retardation could appear in any family, regardless of class or race. They depicted appealing young retarded children, virtually ignoring the existence of adolescents and adults with mental retardation, and often profiled the children's parents, as well. They stressed the mental anguish and social isolation of these families but spoke encouragingly of increasing public understanding and sympathy towards mental retardation, as well as the psychological benefits offered by parents' groups.[35]

After decades during which mental retardation was associated with genetic degeneracy and antisocial behavior, individuals with mental retardation were tentatively included in the broader social category of unfortunate handicapped children, innocent and sympathetic. Suddenly, mental retardation was a problem that could affect any family, rather than a sign of the entire family's innate inferiority. Parents' groups encouraged the identification of mental retardation with physical disabilities such as polio. As one AHRC advertisement put it, "you see no braces on his legs, no supporting crutch. . . . Yet his affliction is all the more tragic. . . . Because, you see, it is his little brain that is crippled."[36] They emulated the public relations campaigns of other child-focused disability groups, turning appealing young boys and girls into national poster children and recruiting celebrities to participate in the yearly Retarded Children's Week.

In keeping with this strategy, parents' groups encouraged the old idea that individuals with mental retardation were eternal children, possessing childlike qualities of innocence, simplicity, and emotional dependence regardless of their chronological age. They described their sons and daughters as children "who never grew," less capable than other children but equally "loving and affectionate."[37] This model of mental retardation not only fit perfectly with the prevailing poster-child style of disability advocacy but also strengthened parents' own positions as spokespersons for their children. As long as individuals with mental retardation could still be viewed as helpless children, parents' roles in representing their children's interests and speaking for their children remained intact. At the same time, mental retardation could still be understood as a problem threatening the family as a whole, even when the child with mental retardation was actually an adult.

In this new climate, mental retardation could attract public support from journalists and politicians as a worthy charitable cause, even in the absence of concrete political power on the part of parents' groups. In several cases, state governors agreed to speak at the very first conventions of associations for retarded children, endorsing these groups before they were even formally organized.[38] However, public displays of benevolence did not necessarily translate into any dramatic increase in government funding or services for mental retardation during the early years of NARC. Furthermore, in many ways, the new model of mental retardation reflected the interests of middle-class parents far better than the interests of individuals with mental retardation.

As later activists recognized, the idea that adults with mental retardation were the mental equivalents of children was both inaccurate and extremely paternalistic.[39] In addition, the exclusive focus on retarded children from "normal" middle-class families prevented parents' groups from addressing the issues faced by isolated adults with mental retardation or by families that did not fit this model. The real irony of the early parents' groups, though, was the extent to which their understanding of mental retardation could seriously harm exactly those young retarded children from middle-class families that NARC was most vocal in representing. The postwar concern for the mental health of the retarded child's family could easily shade into a conviction that the family needed to be rescued from the child's presence. It was only a short step from imagining the family's imminent disintegration to demonizing the young child as an unacceptable threat to his brothers, sisters, and parents. Although parent activists, sharply aware of their children's public image, rarely took this step themselves, others were not so careful.

New developments in the 1940s and 1950s in the medical profession's response to young children with mental retardation provide the clearest evidence of how the heightened fear of family problems could affect these children. Increasingly, doctors and mental health professionals argued that the only way to protect the family, especially the nondisabled siblings, was to institutionalize the retarded child at a very young age. Many pediatricians and family physicians advocated separating infants from their mothers permanently, at the hospital if possible, when the infant had an identifiable condition linked to mental retardation, such as Down Syndrome. These doctors felt that early separation was both easier on the family and more easily accomplished, since the mother might not be willing to give up the child at a later date.[40]

In most cases, early institutionalization had no conceivable benefit for the children themselves. In fact, many infants were simply placed away from their birth families in foster care, since institutional space was scarce. The primary focus was on rescuing the marriage, the mother, whose problems were "in many respects, more serious than those faced by the child," and the siblings, who would otherwise be deprived of normal lives and "obsessed with a feeling of family shame."[41] This willingness to sacrifice a child with mental retardation in order to preserve the family was not in itself surprising, given prevailing assumptions about the worthlessness of these children's lives.[42] What was new, though, was the attempt to send young retarded children away automatically and universally and the insistence that all families everywhere, without exception, were incapable of raising a retarded child.

This new pessimism was closely linked to the medical profession's increasing interest in psychological theorizing. As doctors redefined the threat posed by the child as primarily psychological in nature, they came to see that threat as intrinsic to the very presence of the child in the home, rather than flowing from any of the numerous concrete demands of raising a disabled child. Doctors often assumed that mothers and, to a lesser extent, fathers would reject the child:

The parent is repelled by the unfortunate child's mental inadequacies, by his grotesque physical appearance, by awareness of the social stigma which he has brought on the family.[43]

Or, conversely, the mother might become overattached to the child and neglect the rest of the family. Such overattachment might itself be a sign of guilt and perhaps even inward rejection of the child. Other sons and daughters raised in this environment would undoubtedly be traumatized, both by the mother's failure in parenting and by the social rejection they would experience outside the family. Even doctors who rejected the extreme solution of infant institutionalization agreed that these family problems were to be expected as a matter of course.[44]

For children under six, the rate of new admissions to public institutions for mental retardation doubled between 1945 and 1955, even taking population growth into account. The total institutionalization rate stayed essentially level during this period, after accounting for population growth, while children under six went from 9 percent to 19 percent of new admissions.[45] These figures probably understate the trend toward removing young children from the home, since they do not include infants placed in foster care or in children's wards of general hospitals. According to one study, in comparison with older admissions and those with milder retardation, young children admitted to institutions were more likely to come from middle-class, educated families with white-collar occupations.[46]

In part, the increasing numbers of young children in public institutions was simply a function of new admissions policies in some states that allowed the admission of children under six for the first time and of the construction of new nursery facilities. Rising institutionalization rates were driven by an increase in available space for infants as much as by any increase in demand for that space. Institutional officials, however, made it clear that the increase in residential facilities for younger children was itself a result of increasing community pressure to accommodate those children.[47] As one state mental health official explained,

Mental hygiene education has been sufficiently widespread to create a greater demand for the removal of young idiot children from the home. Social workers recognizing them are prone to advise institutionalization. . . . Physicians, who now receive more psychiatric training, are also alert to the social implications of an idiot child in the home.[48]

Mental health professionals thus attributed the shift in the institutional population to an increased desire to give the rest of the family a normal, healthy life.

In the late 1950s, surveys of parents at mental retardation clinics and in parents' groups found that roughly half of all parents had been instructed by their doctors to immediately institutionalize their retarded child, with the proportion much higher when the child was diagnosed with Down Syndrome.[49] Parents also reported pressure from their ministers, friends, and even other family members to place their children in institutions.[50] One mother reported,

> When Janie first came home to stay I developed an irrational, but nevertheless horrifying, fear of arrest each time I took Janie beyond the boundaries of our property. Coupled with this was the fear that she would be snatched away from me and hustled off to an institution.[51]

Some parents came to accept the idea that institutionalization was necessary for the sake of the rest of the family.[52] Others, of course, disregarded their doctors' advice and valued their children's presence at home, either permanently or until lack of community services made it impractical. Few parents were aware of that the extent to which the looming disapproval of their choice to keep young retarded children at home was a recent development, rather than just a remnant of outdated prejudices.

NARC and the local parents' groups thus operated within a larger context of heightened postwar anxiety about the possible breakdown of the family, expressed most frequently in psychological terms. They invoked this anxiety in order to draw public attention to the problems faced by themselves and their children. In doing so, they helped to recategorize mental retardation as a respectable social problem worthy of interest and sympathy. At the same time, though, NARC rhetoric echoed and reinforced the fear that these children were dangerous, not by virtue of poor genetics or antisocial behavior but simply as disruptive presences in otherwise stable families.

Of course, parents' groups did not believe that institutionalization was the only solution to this threat. In fact, parents' groups strongly objected to the medical overemphasis on institutionalization, especially criticizing the pessimism and scare tactics adopted by the family doctors who had first informed them of their children's disabilities.[53] Although parent activists shared with the most pessimistic doctors a common understanding of the dangerous consequences of mental retardation, they differed sharply in their understanding of the situation as a whole. This difference went beyond a simple disagreement about the necessity of institutionalization. NARC activists sought to deflect blame from the children themselves to the larger society, arguing that better public understanding of mental retardation and greater community acceptance of their children were key factors in preventing the problems associated with mental retardation. They located the problem not in the presence of the retarded child but in the community's failure to accept and accommodate that presence. In fighting the stigmatization of mental retardation, parent activists found themselves challenging not only the old eugenic understanding of mental retardation as lower-class social deviance but also the more basic assumptions that underlay the medical model of disability. They called into question the idea that both problems and solutions could be found in the disabled individual alone.

This broadened understanding of disability could have quite radical implications. Today, disability rights activists emphasize the distinction between the traditional medical model of disability, which focuses on the individual's physical or mental condition as the primary problem, and their own model of disability as a social phenomenon. They argue that the adverse consequences of physical or mental disability result primarily from society's negative reactions to disability and the lack of accommodations for disabled individuals. Even the most severely disabled people cannot be dismissed as incapable of leading fulfilling lives, since there is nothing inherent or inevitable about this incapacity.[54] NARC in its early years was conservative by the standards of later disability advocacy, and generally unwilling to challenge social convention. Yet, early NARC activists articulated a clear critique of the medical model and fought to make the public understand that, even in the absence of new medical cures for mental retardation, there could still be new hope for their children. As an AHRC leader put it, after describing several cases of unhappy parents taught by their doctors to fear their Down Syndrome children,

> The problems . . . had their roots in the orientation given to the parents and the misinformation that the community believed in. The frustration, guilt, and hostility created in the family tends to isolate them from everyone, and the child is isolated along with them. . . . These problems are imposed on the mongoloid child from without. . . . If we do not handicap the mongoloid child by giving him a prejudiced family overwhelmed with guilt, fear, and ignorance, in most cases his chances of adjustment in a family care program are good.[55]

364

While professionals focused on parents' failure to accept their children fully, parents complained in response, "we have accepted our children, but how can we get the neighbors and the general public to accept them?"[56] Parents activists were very much aware, as professionals often were not, that the key to improving life for their children was not individual but social change, encompassing improvements in both public attitudes and community social services.

Parent activists in the postwar years were clearly limited by the social concerns and assumptions of their time, as well as by their own tendency to represent just one segment of the diverse population with mental retardation. Yet, in articulating their understanding of mental retardation, parents challenged their society's assumptions about what it meant to be healthy or normal. They argued for the possibility of a happy, psychologically well-adjusted family in which disabled family members were neither cured, hidden away, nor capable of overcoming their disability enough to approximate normality. In spite of their anxiety about the mental health of the family, they refused to equate mental health with the ability to function normally or to accept the idea that healthy children could grow up only in completely normal households. They portrayed family disorder as a result of the community's inability to accept difference as much as the family's own intrinsic abnormality.

Parents argued for their own inclusion in an imagined community of ordinary, middle-class American families. In some ways, this was a limited goal. Yet, to include individuals with mental retardation in such a community required substantial social change, given both the traditional stigma attached to mental retardation and the new fears of retarded children as threats to the family. By insisting on their own identity as ordinary American parents, parents faced with severe but manageable problems, NARC activists offered a broader and more flexible model of a normal American family. In stressing the need for social acceptance and accommodation of retarded children, parents offered a deeper understanding of disability, what it meant, and how it might be addressed.

NOTES

1. Quoted in Eugene Gramm, "New Hope for the Different Child," *Parents Magazine* 26 (September 1951): 48.

2. Quoted in Alfred H. Katz, *Parents of the Handicapped: Self-Organized Parents' and Relatives' Groups for Treatment of Ill and Handicapped Children* (Springfield, IL: Charles C. Thomas, 1961), 144–46. For a detailed history of AHRC and other New York parents' groups, see Herbert Lerner, *State Association for Retardation Children and New York State Government, 1948–1968* (New York: New York State Association for Retarded Children, Inc., 1972). I use the terms "mental retardation" and "retarded children" in this paper to indicate the terminology used by 1950s parents' groups. More recently, advocates and self-advocates have come to believe that these terms are too stigmatizing and have searched for alternatives.

3. Woodhull Hay, "Associations of Parents for the Mentally Retarded: Summary of a Survey, June–July 1950," Folder 11, Container 2, Salomea Novak Schmidt Papers (Western Reserve Historical Society, Clevelend, OH).

4. National Association for Retarded Children, *Annual Report* (New York: NARC, 1964).

5. James W. Trent Jr., *Inventing the Feeble Mind: A History of Mental Retardation in the United States* (Berkeley: University of California, 1994); Paul K. Longmore and Lauri Umansky, eds., *The New Disability History: American Perspectives* (New York: New York University Press, 2001). See also Douglas Baynton, *Forbidden Signs: American Culture and the Campaign against Sign Language* (Chicago: University of Chicago Press, 1996).

6. Steven Noll, *Feeble-Minded in Our Midst: Institutions for the Mentally Retarded in the South, 1900–1940* (Chapel Hill: University of North Carolina Press, 1995); Trent, *Inventing the Feeble Mind.*

7. On postwar family ideals, see Elaine Tyler May, *Homeward Bound: American Families in the Cold War Era* (New York: Basic Books, 1988); Arlene Skolnick, *Embattled Paradise: The American Family in an Age of Uncertainty* (New York: Basic Books, 1991).

8. Lerner, *State Association for Retarded Children*; Hay, "Associations of Parents for the Mentally Retarded"; Joseph H. Levy, *Parent Groups and Social Agencies: The Activities of Health and Welfare Agencies with Groups of Parents of Handicapped Children in Chicago* (Chicago: University of Chicago, 1951); Barbara Bair, "The Parents' Council and Social Change in Rhode Island, 1951–1970," *Rhode Island History* 40 (November 1981): 144–59.

9. For example, Dorothy G. Murray, *This Is Stevie's Story* (Elgin, IL: Brethren Publishing House, 1956), 78–79; "Proceedings of the Fourth Annual Convention of the Ohio Association for Retarded Children, Dayton, Ohio, April 27–29, 1956," Folder 19, Container 2, Schmidt Papers.

10. William H. Chafe, *The Unfinished Journey: America since World War II,* 3rd ed. (New York: Oxford University Press, 1995), 117–22; Alan Ehrenhalt, *The Lost City: Discovering the Forgotten Virtues of Community in the Chicago of the 1950s* (New York: Basic Books, 1995); Kenneth Jackson, *The Crabgrass Frontier: The Suburbanization of the United States* (New York: Oxford University Press, 1985).

11. Ad Hoc Committee on Voluntary Health and Welfare Agencies in the United

States, *Voluntary Health and Welfare Agencies in the United States* (New York: Schoolmaster's Press, 1961), 9.

12. David L. Sills, *The Volunteers: Means and Ends in a National Organization* (Glencoe, IL: Free Press, 1957); Katz, *Parents of the Handicapped.*

13. "School for a Different Child," *Parents' Magazine* 16 (March 1941): 30, 79–81; "Not Like Other Children," *Parents' Magazine* 18 (October 1943): 34, 98–102; "We Committed Our Child," *Rotarian* 67 (August 1945): 19–20. On the difficult decision to make a retarded daughter's story public, see Pearl S. Buck, *The Child Who Never Grew* (New York: John Day, 1950), 5–9.

14. Violet Ebb Lundquist, "I'm Glad We Kept Janie at Home," *The Iowan* 6 (June–July 1958): 28–31.

15. Letha L. Patterson, "Growing into Leadership," *Adult Leadership* 3 (September 1954): 8–9.

16. National Association for Retarded Children, *The Child Nobody Knows* (New York: NARC, 1955); "New National Organization Formed to Help the Mentally Retarded," Folder 11, Container 2, Schmidt Papers. See also Buck, *The Child Who Never Grew,* 12; Murray, *This is Stevie's Story,* 136.

17. Folder 8, Container 2, Schmidt Papers; Box 7 and Box 19, Pennsylvania Association for Retarded Children, Allegheny County, Chapter Records (Archives of Industrial Society, University of Pittsburgh, Pittsburgh, PA).

18. Murray, *This is Stevie's Story,* 110–12; Patterson, "Growing into Leadership."

19. "Under Oath," Folder 5, Container 4, Schmidt Papers.

20. Levy, *Parent Groups and Social Agencies,* 53; Katz, *Parents of the Handicapped.*

21. Georges Sabagh, Harvey F. Dingman, George Tarjan, and Stanley W. Wright, "Social Class and Ethnic Status of Patients Admitted to a State Hospital for the Retarded," *Pacific Sociological Review* 2 (fall 1959): 76–80; Lloyd M. Dunn, "Special Education for the Mildly Retarded: Is Much of It Justifiable?" *Exceptional Children* 35 (September 1968): 5–22; Jane R. Mercer, "Sociological Perspectives on Mild Mental Retardation," in *Social-cultural Aspects of Mental Retardation,* ed. H. Carl Haywood (New York: Appleton-Century-Crofts, 1970), 378–94.

22. Lerner, *State Association for Retardation Children.*

23. Box 10, Pennsylvania Association for Retarded Children, Allegheny County Records. See also Bair, "The Parents' Council and Social Change in Rhode Island." A 1970 study of several local NARC affiliates found that the membership was disproportionately middle and upper class but that a substantial minority of the parents were low income. There was very little racial diversity. Robert M. Segal, *Mental Retardation and Social Action: A Study of the Associations for Retarded Children as a Force for Social Change* (Springfield, IL: Charles C. Thomas, 1970), 47–60.

24. Buck, *The Child Who Never Grew,* 8.

25. NARC, *The Child Nobody Knows.*

26. Gunnar Dybwad, "The Role of Public and Voluntary Services in Prevention

and Treatment," Folder on President's Panel on Mental Retardation, Box 8, Pennsylvania Association for Retarded Children, Allegheny County Records.

27. Samuel R. Laycock, "Community Understanding of the Exceptional Child," *Exceptional Children* 21 (November 1954): 47–49.

28. Hay, "Associations of Parents for the Mentally Retarded"; Reinhold A. Marquardt, "The Ideal Climate for Growth," in *The Exceptional Child and the Christian Community*, ed. Hilmar A. Sieving (River Forest, IL: Lutheran Education Association, 1956), 49–92; Dorothy G. Murray, "A Parent Speaks to Pastors on Mental Retardation," *Pastoral Psychology* 13 (September 1962): 23–30; Daniel J. Silver, "The Retarded Child and Religious Education: A Case Study," *Religious Education* 52 (September–October 1957): 361–64.

29. Janice A. Brockley, "Martyred Mothers and Merciful Fathers: Exploring Disability and Motherhood in the Lives of Jerome Greenfield and Raymond Repouille," in *The New Disability History: American Perspectives,* ed. Paul K. Longmore and Lauri Umansky (New York: New York University Press, 2001), 293–312; R. L. Jenkins, "Management of the Retarded Child," *American Journal of Diseases of Children* 52 (September 1936): 599–607; Herman Yannet, "An Evaluation of the Problem of the Care of the Mentally Defective in Connecticut," *Connecticut Medical Journal* 6 (April 1942): 261–64.

30. Brockley, "Martyred Mothers and Merciful Fathers"; Kathleen W. Jones, *Taming the Troublesome Child: American Families, Child Guidance, and the Limits of Psychiatric Authority* (Cambridge, MA: Harvard University Press, 1999); Molly Ladd-Taylor and Lauri Umansky, eds., *"Bad" Mothers: The Politics of Blame in Twentieth-Century America* (New York: New York University Press, 1998); Ruth Feldstein, *Motherhood in Black and White: Race and Sex in American Liberalism, 1930–1965* (Ithaca: Cornell University Press, 2000).

31. Gramm, "New Hope for the Different Child."

32. Judith Crist, "Not Quite Bright!" *Better Homes and Gardens* 28 (April 1950): 148–56.

33. On the social functions of organizations of people with shared stigma, see Erving Goffman, *Stigma: Notes on the Management of Spoiled Identity* (Englewood Cliffs, NJ: Prentice-Hall, 1963).

34. "Fiction, TV, Radio Drop MR Taboo," *Children Limited* 3 (June–July 1954): 4; speech by Edith Stern, c. 1950, Folder 11, Container 2, Schmidt Papers.

35. Gramm, "New Hope for the Different Child"; Crist, "Not Quite Bright!"; Howard A. Rusk and Eugene J. Taylor, "Mentally Retarded Children," *American Mercury* 69 (December 1949): 698–703; Steven M. Spencer, "Retarded Children Can Be Helped," *Saturday Evening Post* 225 (October 11, 1952): 26–27, 107–11; "Retarded Children," *Life* 37 (October 18, 1954): 119–27; "Magazine Articles on Mental Retardation," *American Journal of Mental Deficiency* 60 (October 1955): 410–11.

36. Reproduced in *Our Children's Voice* 3 (January–February 1951): 4.

37. Buck, *The Child Who Never Grew*, 55.

38. "An Address on The Retarded Child by Governor Luther W. Youngdahl at the First National Convention of Parents and Friends of the Retarded," Minneapolis, Minnesota, 1950, Folder 11, Container 2, Schmidt Papers; Taylor R. Kennerly, *History of the North Carolina Association for Retarded Children, Inc.: The First Fifteen Years* (Greensboro, NC: NCARC, 1968), 8.

39. "The Older Retardate: What Can We Do for the Child Who Is No Longer a Child?" *Children Limited* 9 (June–July 1960): 24; "Convention to Stress Adult Needs," *Children Limited* 10 (January–February 1961): 1.

40. C. Anderson Aldrich, "Preventive Medicine and Mongolism," *American Journal of Mental Deficiency* 52 (October 1947): 127–29; Alastair Beddie and Humphry Osmond, "Mothers, Mongols and Mores," *Canadian Medical Association Journal* 73 (August 1, 1955): 167–70; Simon Olshansky, Gertrude C. Johnson and Leon Sternfield, "Attitudes of Some GPs toward Institutionalizing Mentally Retarded Children," *Mental Retardation* 1 (February 1963): 18–20.

41. Aldrich, "Preventive Medicine and Mongolism," 128.

42. Brockley, "Martyred Mothers and Merciful Fathers."

43. Harry Bakwin, "Informing the Parents of the Mentally Retarded Child," *Journal of Pediatrics* 49 (October 1956): 486–98.

44. Bakwin, "Informing the Parents"; Henry C. Schumacher, "A Program for Dealing with Mental Deficiency in Children up to Six Years of Age," *American Journal of Mental Deficiency* 51 (July 1946): 52–56; John J. Waterman, "Psychogenic Factors in Parental Acceptance of Feebleminded Children," *Diseases of the Nervous System* 9 (June 1948): 184–87; Donald H. Jolly, "When Should the Seriously Retarded Infant Be Institutionalized?" *American Journal of Mental Deficiency* 57 (April 1953): 632–36; Reynold A. Jensen, "The Clinical Management of the Mentally Retarded Child and the Parents," *American Journal of Psychiatry* 106 (May 1950): 830–33.

45. U.S. Bureau of the Census, *Patients in Mental Institutions,* 1945–1946 (Washington, DC: Government Printing Office, 1948); U.S. National Institute of Mental Health, *Patients in Mental Institutions,* 1947–1955 (Washington, DC: Government Printing Office, 1949–1957); U.S. Bureau of the Census, *Estimates of the Population of the United States, By Single Years of Age, Color, and Sex, 1900–1959,* No. 311 in *Current Population Reports;* P-25 *Population Estimates and Projection* (Washington, DC: Government Printing Office, 1965).

46. George Tarjan, Stanley W. Wright, Harvey F. Dingman, and Georges Sabagh, "National History of Mental Deficiency in a State Hospital II. Mentally Deficient Children Admitted to a State Hospital Prior to Their Sixth Birthday," *American Journal of Diseases of Children* 98 (September 1959): 370–78.

47. William W. Fox and Earl H. Reed, "A Modern Unit for Infant Mental Patients," *Hospitals* 24 (December 1950): 40–44; Hans Meyer, "Problems Relative to the Acceptance and Reacceptance of the Institutionalized Child," *Archives of Pediatrics* 73 (August 1956): 271–75.

48. Quoted in Lerner, *State Association for Retarded Children,* 29.

49. Charlotte Waskowitz, "The Parents of Retarded Children Speak for Themselves," *Journal of Pediatrics* 54 (February 1959): 319-29; Richard Koch , Betty V. Graliker, Russell Sands, and Arthur H. Parmelee, "Attitude Study of Parents with Mentally Retarded Children: I. Evaluation of Parental Satisfaction with the Medical Care of a Retarded Child," *Pediatrics* 23 (March 1959): 583-84; Rudolf P. Hormuth, "Home Problems and Family Care of the Mongoloid Child," *Quarterly Review of Pediatrics* 8 (November 1953): 271-80.

50. Murray, "A Parent Speaks to Pastors on Mental Retardation"; Lucille Stout, *I Reclaimed My Child: The Story of a Family into Which a Retarded Child Was Born* (Philadelphia: Chilton Co., 1959), 50.

51. Lundquist, "I'm Glad We Kept Janie At Home."

52. Stout, *I Reclaimed My Child*; John P. Frank, *My Son's Story* (New York: Alfred A. Knopf, 1952).

53. Waskowitz, "The Parents of Retarded Children Speak for Themselves"; Joseph T. Weingold, "Panel on Rehabilitation of the Mongoloid Child: Introductory Remarks," *Quarterly Review of Pediatrics* 8 (November 1953): 253-54; "More about 'Self-Determination,'" *Children Limited* 3 (June-July 1954): 10.

54. Michelle Fine and Adrienne Asch, "Disability beyond Stigma: Social Interaction, Discrimination, and Activism," *Journal of Social Issues* 44 (spring 1988): 3-21; Harlan Hahn, "The Politics of Physical Differences: Disability and Discrimination," *Journal of Social Issues* 44 (spring 1988): 39-47; Irving Kenneth Zola, "Toward the Necessary Universalizing of a Disability Policy," *Milbank Quarterly* 67, Supp. 2, Pt. 2 (1989): 401-28; Tom Shakespeare, ed., *The Disability Reader: Social Science Perspectives* (New York: Cassell, 1998).

55. Hormuth, "Home Problems and Family Care," 274-80.

56. Laycock, "Community Understanding of the Exceptional Child."

15

Formal Health Care
at the Community Level

The Child Development Clinics
of the 1950s and 1960s

Wendy M. Nehring

During the height of the eugenics movement before World War I, child guidance clinics provided mental health care to children at risk for delinquency. Using psychoanalytic techniques and a staff consisting of a psychologist, a psychiatrist, and a social worker, these clinics served many children; the exact number is not known. Most notable among the initial child guidance clinics was Lightner Witmer's psychological clinic at the University of Pennsylvania, which opened in 1896, and William Healy's juvenile-court clinic in Chicago, which was established in 1909.

After the war, in 1921, the National Committee for Mental Hygiene of New Jersey conducted a survey to identify the number of children in New Jersey presumed to be in need of the services provided by child guidance clinics; it found that of the children who appeared in juvenile court, 66 percent were mentally retarded and 19 percent needed mental health and behavioral services. The total number of children surveyed was not given. With the growth of the mental hygiene movement after World War I, services for children with mental retardation were scant as child guidance clinic personnel concentrated on children with behaviorial and emotional problems. This discrepancy in services is profound given the significant difference in numbers shown in this one survey (Levine & Levine, 1970). In fact, enrollments of children with mental retardation in institutions away from the family were increasing rapidly at this time.

In 1949, nearly forty years after the founding of child guidance clinics, parents in New York began to advocate for diagnostic and health clinics for their children with mental retardation. They reasoned that their children had as much right to receive comprehensive care and support as did children with mental illness. They also knew that clinics already existed for children with cerebral palsy, vision and hearing problems, and cleft lip and cleft palate (Birch, 1953). They pushed for child development clinics that would provide accurate evaluation and diagnosis, casefinding, treatment plans that included health, physical, social, and medical recommendations, and lifetime follow-up. In short, parents wanted an explanation for their children's mental retardation, a prognosis, and community resources that would offer services to meet their children's needs (Rubinstein, 1962). A few clinics did exist at that time for children with mental retardation across the country, but their main focus was to label and sort people for commitment to institutions or special education classes (Hormuth, 1957).

The Early Child Development Clinics

Along with this movement to develop specialized clinics for children with mental retardation came the establishment of the National Association for Retarded Children (NARC), a national parent organization. By 1955, NARC and its local parent groups had advocated for and established thirty-three clinics. Hospitals, private foundations, and other parent groups founded other clinics (Hormuth, 1957; Rubinstein, 1962).

Several issues needed to be resolved as these clinics came into being: diagnostic definitions, treatment approaches, organizational mission and structure, and methods of follow-up. Even though authorities had written about the classification of mental retardation for more than eighty years, the staff of these early clinics continued to discuss definitions of mental retardation so that they could place parameters around who could and who could not attend the clinic. As a result, the early clinics were organized in many different ways, often based on the professional perspectives of their directors. Hospital-based clinics with physicians or nurses in charge were medically oriented, and psychiatrists often used psychoanalytic methods. Some clinics were staffed by members of only one discipline, whereas other clinics used a multidisciplinary approach. The staffing also influenced the casefinding and treatment approaches, including the number of visits needed for an accurate diagnosis (Hormuth, 1957; Rubinstein, 1962). This diagnostic process could last from one day to a few years (Koch & Gilien, 1965). Only Hormuth (1957) discussed the goals of his clinic for children of different ages: prevention, diagnosis, and health supervision for the infant; educational preparation and programming, diagnostic etiology, and play groups for the one- to five-year-olds; and health supervision, vocational appraisal, and planning for the future for adolescents and young adults. It is interesting to note that out of the efforts of these first clinics with preschool and school-age children emerged the term "schologenic" to describe the child who "tests" in the range of mental retardation only in the school setting (Lesser, 1958), years before Mercer (1973) made the term "six-hour child" famous. Last, follow-up procedures such as home visits by public health nurses and approaches for dealing with waiting lists also varied. A clinic's objectives, finances, and staff size often predicted the extent of its follow-up services (Hormuth, 1957; Rubinstein, 1962).

Wortis (1954) believed that such clinics needed a budget of $5,000: $4,000 for the annual salary of a social worker and $1,000 for the secretary's salary. He charged clients on a sliding scale from nothing to $40 for a complete diagnostic evaluation. Wortis then suggested ways for extending the services and budget of the clinic over time, with an advisory board that included a representative of area parent groups, such as the local NARC chapter.

Clinic Staff

The staffs of the early child development clinics for children with mental retardation varied from unidisciplinary to multidisciplinary. Yet, most authors who wrote about clinic staffs for these clinics during the 1950s and 1960s spoke of multidisciplinary staffs drawn from several disciplines: a physician (usually a pediatrician), a nurse, a psychologist, a social worker, a school teacher or nursery school teacher, a child development specialist, a nutritionist, a genetic counselor, an occupational therapist, a play therapist, a physical therapist, a speech therapist, and a hearing specialist (Faber, 1968; Koch & Dobson, 1971; Lesser, 1958; Levinson, 1952; Rubinstein, 1962; Wellin et al., 1960). From their experiences, the different disciplines developed many diagnostic and evaluative techniques (Baerwald & Rock, 1971; Haar, 1966; Hormuth, 1963).

The physician was responsible for the diagnosis, after a comprehensive history and physical examination, appropriate lab work, x-rays, and encephalography. The physician then informed the parents of the diagnosis (Faber, 1968; Koch & Dobson, 1971; Lesser, 1958; Levinson, 1952; Rubinstein, 1962; Wellin et al., 1960).

The psychologist performed a number of intelligence and personality tests to determine the child's level of retardation and educational needs. The typical tests used were the Binet-Simon (for children under five years of age), the Wechsler Intelligence Scale for Children (children five years and older), and the Vineland Social Maturity Scale for Adaptive Living (Faber, 1968; Koch & Dobson, 1971; Lesser, 1958; Levinson, 1952; Rubinstein, 1962; Wellin et al., 1960).

The nurse often worked with the child and family during the clinic visit and later in a home visit to provide parental teaching and counseling and to help parents with their child's care plan. Some clinics had a clinic nurse and contracted out with the local public health department to have public health nurses make the home visits. During these visits, the public health nurse assisted the parents with health practices, habit training, and discipline. The public health nurse also provided needed psychoemotional support to the parents (Holtgrewe, 1961; Koch & Gilien, 1965; Leckner, 1964; McDermott, 1960; Owens, 1964) and evaluated the home environment (Haar, 1966). These public health nurses were also instrumental in casefinding, prevention efforts (e.g., neonatal screening), and referrals to the local child development clinics (Faber, 1968; Koch & Dobson, 1971; Lesser, 1958; Levinson, 1952; Rubinstein, 1962; Wellin et al., 1960).

The social worker was also responsible for counseling parents and for providing information about community resources. Staff members from additional disciplines, such as the school or nursery school teacher, the child development specialist, the nutritionist, the genetic counselor, the speech therapist, the occupational therapist, the play therapist, the physical therapist, or the hearing specialist, were used when the child's condition warranted their expertise (Faber, 1968; Koch & Dobson, 1971; Lesser, 1958; Levinson, 1952; Rubinstein, 1962; Wellin et al., 1960). Finally, clinic staff helped parents to form parent groups that offered education and support to the families (Birenbaum, 1969).

Three Child Development Clinics

Traveling Clinic Project, Children's Hospital of Los Angeles

The Traveling Clinic Project with the Children's Hospital of Los Angeles opened in 1959. Its goals were to:

(1) Demonstrate the multidisciplinary approach to the problem of the young mentally retarded child,

(2) Interest and inform professional personnel in the field of mental retardation, and

(3) Stimulate communities to develop resources and facilities for the care of the retarded and their families. (Baerwald & Rock, 1971, pp. 445–446)

The staff members of this clinic believed that it was imperative that they operate within a city with a population of at least 100,000 in order to attract enough clients to keep the clinic solvent. On the other hand, the staff worked and consulted with people from less populated areas in southern California to develop their own clinics; they used a "train-the-trainer" approach that provided instruction in the organization of the clinic, diagnostic evaluation, parental and family counseling, postconference discussions among the professionals, and follow-up services. Requests for this assistance usually came from county health departments; often, the local coordinator was a public health nurse. In order to "sell" the clinic to the local leaders and politicians, members of the Traveling Clinic Project provided lectures and often a "staffing" of a local child. This staffing consisted of an evaluation of the child from each discipline's perspective; for example, the physician assessed the child's medical status, the psychologist assessed the child's psychological and emotional status, and the nurse assessed the child's home environment, safety issues, nutritional needs, and the family's health practices and educational needs regarding the child. This provided southern California with a model of coordinated community care for a specific population (Baerwald & Rock, 1971).

Clinic for Child Study, the University of Washington, Seattle

Deisher and Justice (1960) discuss the function of the multidisciplinary group in the diagnostic evaluation of a child with mental retardation as part of their description of the Clinic for Child Study. At this clinic, the staff were joined by professionals from the community who were interested in the specific child to discuss the findings and the recommendations for care. After this meeting, the parents discussed the results with the clinic pediatrician. Finally, a comprehensive summary of the meetings held at the clinic was sent to the person who referred the child, to the family, and to the local health department. Interestingly, when the referring professional was a physician, the pediatrician at the Clinic for Child Study called that physician to discuss the results, rather than sending a summary.

Institute for Neurological Organization, New York

A major force at the Institute for Neurological Organization was Dr. Glenn Doman, who developed the "patterning" technique. This method was used to place the child's body in prescribed positions so that "information could be supplied to the brain which would make it possible for the child to develop the necessary sensory pathways" (Faber, 1968, p. 255). Doman claimed that the method would allow the child to move toward normalcy in each domain of development. Faber (1968) noted that the staff at the institute classified three different types of children as retarded:

> Some children are born with undersized heads, the microcephalics. These we cannot help. A second type is a psychotic brain, which appears to be normal, but which we do not know enough about to help. The third type is the child whose brain developed normally but sustained damage either before, during, or after birth. The first two types we cannot help. The third we have answers for. Those we can help. (p. 259)

The diagnostic procedures at this institute differed from those at other child development clinics, although the time required for the process—three days—was the same as at other clinics. On the first day, the child underwent twelve hours of diagnostic evaluation. On the second day, the parent spend another twelve hours attending lectures on brain functioning and on the patterning method. On the third day, the parents were taught how to perform the patterning schedule for their child. A follow-up was done every two to three months for further reevaluation and "reprogramming." Faber (1968) stressed that the staff instructed the parents that "if they do not do what they are supposed to do, the Institute will drop them" (p. 259).

Parental Satisfaction with the Child Development Clinics

Parents often heard the words "mental retardation" for the first time when the physician reported the results of their child's diagnostic evaluation. Koch and Dobson (1971) wrote:

> Unfortunately, however, this first contact is often unsatisfying and frustrating for parents. Too frequently, the physician is unable to diagnose a positive cause for the mental retardation, and even if the etiology is ascertainable, he may have no adequate therapy to recommend. He may also lack the techniques which will help him predict the child's future intellectual potential. Consequently, it is not uncommon for such parents to "shop" for additional medical opinions; they are dissatisfied with their physician's initial appraisal and they hope for miracle solutions. (p. 151)

For the first time, techniques for giving parents the diagnosis of mental retardation and supporting them in their initial reaction became a focus of discussion. Parents wrote about what professionals could do to help them (Patterson, 1956), and professionals spoke about how to counsel parents of children with mental retardation (Barnard, 1968; Beck, 1959; Oberman, 1963). Both sides based their descriptions on personal experiences. Supporting the proliferation of publications about the child development clinics and the professional and parental roles were federal agencies, principally the Children's Bureau.

The Federal Influence

As early as 1955, NARC lobbied Congress for federal funding for child development clinics. This funding provided for early diagnosis and comprehensive evaluation, information and counseling for the parents, and lifelong, age-appropriate services. Joining NARC were interested clinic personnel and other professionals who supported coordinated services from the federal to the local level (Stevenson, 1952; U.S. Department of Health, Education, and Welfare, 1962). In 1957, Congress allocated $16 million for maternal and child health grants. A small portion of this funding, $1 million, was set aside for projects specific to children with mental retardation. NARC hoped that

377

an additional $1 million would be added to this sum. As noted earlier, NARC had assisted in the development of child development clinics in the years prior to this funding. Demonstration clinics were already operating in four states (the Los Angeles clinic was one of these early funded child development clinics). By 1957, an additional thirty-one clinics received maternal and child funding.

In 1961, President Kennedy called for a national plan to support persons with mental retardation. He emphasized the need to improve diagnostic and evaluation procedures, standards of care across the lifespan, family support and teaching, professional education and training, public understanding, and available clinics and agencies. He appointed the President's Panel on Mental Retardation (later the President's Committee on Mental Retardation) to address these needs (President's Panel on Mental Retardation, 1962).

President's Panel on Mental Retardation

Over the next few years, the newly appointed President's Panel on Mental Retardation published several reports. Of note were *A Proposed Program for National Action to Combat Mental Retardation* (1962) and *Report of the Task Force on Coordination* (1963).

The first report was written as an answer to the president's request for a national plan. In this publication, the members of the panel outlined the following critical areas: creation of a continuum of care, lifelong health supervision, neonatal screening, identification of high-risk populations, comprehensive diagnostic evaluation by knowledgeable professionals, access to such services among rural and underserved populations, professional education and training, access to public education for children with mental retardation, research, and "a fixed point of referral and information" (President's Panel on Mental Retardation, 1962, p. 92). As one member of the panel wrote, in a separate article, "The various services that should be available in this array must be marshaled in different ways and in different combinations for different people in accordance with their needs at different times" (Hormuth, 1963, p. 30). Hormuth (1963) also stressed the importance of professionals becoming knowledgeable in the field of mental retardation and being able to apply their knowledge in various settings.

The President's Panel on Mental Retardation (1962) also recommended that the U.S. Children's Bureau, the U.S. Public Health Service, and state departments of health and education collaborate in the delivery of health, educational, and social services. Finally, leaders in the field called for the establishment of one lead agency in each community to provide a "life consultation service" for persons with mental retardation and their families (President's Panel on Mental Retardation, 1962, p. 92).

In 1963, the President's Panel on Mental Retardation specifically addressed the need for the coordination of services and for the establishment of a fixed referral point. The panel suggested a statewide advisory board that would consist of professional and lay members who would routinely review the state plan. This recommendation was implemented with the initiation of state planning councils to conduct this review, discuss current needs of this population, and recommend plans to correct problems. The panel also described the need for a specific community agency to coordinate information and referral.

The Children's Bureau

The Children's Bureau had provided programs for children of all backgrounds since its inception in 1912. In providing direction and funding to the demonstration clinics, the Children's Bureau identified the following goals:

(1) To investigate and report on the effect of mental retardation on family life and on the impact of environmental conditions on mental and social growth,
(2) To identify and interpret the role of social agencies in services to the retarded and to stimulate these agencies to assume their responsibilities,
(3) To extend and strengthen basic child welfare services and to establish specialized resources and facilities as appropriate, and
(4) To increas the knowledge and skill of child welfare and other social work personnel through inservice training and professional education opportunities. (U.S. Department of Health, Education and Welfare, 1962, p. 49)

The Children's Bureau reported that by 1960, the demonstration child development clinics in forty states had served approximately 12,000 children with mental retardation and their families. Of this number, 75 percent of the children were under ten years of age. The staff of the Children's Bureau claimed that their efforts had increased the numbers of families who kept their children at home rather than institutionalize them and had even increased the number of families who had withdrawn their children from institutions. Furthermore, the Children's Bureau had persuaded administrators of well-child clinics to include casefinding, referral, and follow-up health supervision of the children seen in the clinics. It also encouraged higher standards of care and increased licensing requirements for child care agencies and nursery schools that cared for children with mental retardation. The Children's Bureau also recognized the adolescent with mental retardation in the community and developed early specialized programs for this age group (U.S. Department of Health, Education, and Welfare, 1962). For many consecutive years in the 1960s, Hormuth (e.g., 1963) distributed across the country a listing of clinical programs for children with mental retardation.

The Children's Bureau, moreover, supported the training and education of professionals in the field of mental retardation. By 1962, it reported that 4,500 medical students, interns, and residents had received some degree of professional education; 1,200 nursing students had received some training or had had experience working with children with mental retardation; more than 25,000 public health nurses had obtained in-service training in the care of children with mental retardation; and more than 300 other professionals had been trained for leadership positions in the field of mental retardation. In-services and workshops for professionals in the community were provided when requested (U.S. Department of Health, Education, and Welfare, 1962).

As part of the Children's Bureau funding for education, monies were available for the development of educational materials, including pamphlets, books, and films. Public health nurses received education in the care of children with mental retardation and in techniques for teaching and counseling parents (Children's Bureau, 1964; Dittman, 1965; Holtgrewe, 1961; Wolff, 1964). The film "The Public Health Nurse and the Retarded Child" won third place in a national contest organized by a film producers' association (U.S. Department of Health, Education, and Welfare, 1962). Agencies that received funding from the Children's Bureau were required to have a public health nurse as part of the clinic team. Since many directors of the clinics did not know how to use a public health nurse, the public health nurses had to carve out their own role, and this resulted in the development of new educational materials (Marion Holtgrewe, personal communication, July 22, 1992).

The final area funded by the Children's Bureau was research. Studies on the characteristics and problems of adolescents with mental retardation living at home (Hammar & Barnard, 1966) and on the effectiveness of a child development clinic (Deisher & Justice, 1960) were among the research undertaken by child development clinics.

Directions at the Close of the 1960s

In 1965, Congress implemented the Mental Retardation Facilities and Community Mental Health Centers Construction Act of 1963 (P.L. 88-164), which provided funding for the establishment of the first university-affiliated facilities (UAF) and programs (UAP). These university-based facilities and programs were developed and funded to provide education, service, and research to individuals with mental retardation and their families. By the late 1960s, many child development clinics of the 1950s and early 1960s had become part of the newly formed UAFs and UAPs, although independent and privately funded clinics, especially in rural areas, continued to operate. The 1960s and 1970s ushered in an era of federal support, professional development, better services, and increased public understanding to enhance the lives of persons, especially children, with mental retardation.

In 1970, a document entitled *Report to the President: White House Conference on Children* was published. The authors noted that health care services for all children were inadequate and that only a coordinated, integrated, and multidisciplinary system would be appropriate. Could the authors have learned something from the efforts in behalf of children with mental retardation? The authors also recommended preventive measures to decrease the incidence of mental retardation and other handicapping conditions; they recommended, among other practices, developmental screening at different points throughout childhood. The authors also called for the use of paraprofessionals, provision of family stipends, inclusion of the retarded in the broader society, widespread accessibility of facilities, national health insurance, and community resource directories, all of which remain important issues today.

The child development clinics for children with mental retardation and their families were instrumental in the development of the diagnostic and evaluation techniques that are currently in place. The coordination and continuum of care for this population has moved more slowly. If we consider all the topics that were discussed in the 1970 report to the president and that were addressed throughout the discussion of child development clinics in the 1950s and 1960s, we must ask whether we have persisted in taking small steps across time or whether we have fallen asleep and recently awakened to the recommendations made to the president thirty years ago.

REFERENCES

Baerwald, A., & Rock, H. L. (1971). A teaching and community organization demonstration. In R. Koch & J. C. Dobson (Eds.). *The mentally retarded child and his family: A multidisciplinary handbook* (pp. 445–455). New York: Bruner/Mazel.

Barnard, K. E. (1968). How families react to the crisis of mental retardation. Unpublished document. University of Washington-Seattle.

Beck, H. L. (1959). Counseling parents of retarded children. *Children, 6,* 225–230.

Birch, J. W.(1953). Patterns of clinical services for exceptional children. *Exceptional Children, 19,* 214–222.

Birenbaum, A. (1969). Helping mothers of mentally retarded children use specialized facilities. *Family Coordinator, 18,* 379–385.

Children's Bureau. (1964). *Feeding mentally retarded children: A guide for nurses working with families who have mentally retarded children.* Washington, DC: Author.

Deisher, R. W., & Justice, R. S. (1960). Effectiveness of community resources in helping mentally retarded children. *American Journal of Public Health, 50,* 43–49.

Dittman, L. (1965). *The nurse in home training programs for the retarded child.* Washington, DC: Children's Bureau, U.S. Department of Health, Education, and Welfare.

Faber, N. W. (1968). *The retarded child.* New York: Crown.

Haar, D. (1966). Nurse is important in diagnostic clinic. *Children Limited, 15* (2), 7–9.

Hammar, S. L., & Barnard, K. E. (1966). A review of the characteristics and problems of 44 non-institutionalized adolescent retardates. *Pediatrics, 38,* 845–857.

Holtgrewe, M. M. (1961). *The role of the public health nurse in mental retardation.* Washington, DC: Children's Bureau, U.S. Department of Health, Education, and Welfare.

Hormuth, R. P. (1963). A proposed program to combat mental retardation. *Children, 10* (1), 29–31.

Hormuth, R. P. (1963). *Clinical programs for mentally retarded children: A listing.* Washington, DC: Children's Bureau, U.S. Department of Health, Education, and Welfare.

Hormuth, R. P. (1957). Community clinics for the mentally retarded. *Children, 4,* 181–185.

Koch, R., & Dobson, J. C. (1971). The multidisciplinary team: A comprehensive program for diagnosis and treatment of the retarded. In R. Koch & J. C. Dobson (Eds.). *The mentally retarded child and his family: A multidisciplinary handbook* (pp. 151–155). New York: Bruner/Mazel.

Koch, R., & Gilien, N. R. (1965). Diagnostic experience in a clinic for retarded children. *Nursing Outlook, 13* (3), 26–33.

Leckner, E. J. (1964). The public health nurse in a program for the mentally retarded. *Children, 11,* 70–74.

Lesser, A. J. (1958). New programs for mentally retarded children. *American Journal of Public Health, 48,* 9–14.

Levine, M, & Levine, A. (1970). The more things change: A case history of child guidance clinics. *Journal of Social Issues, 26* (3), 19–34.

Levinson, A. (1952). *The mentally retarded child: A guide for parents.* New York: John Day.

McDermott, I. K. (1960). *Public health nursing in a mental retardation program.* New York: National League for Nursing.

Mercer, J. A. (1973). *Labeling the mentally retarded: Clinical and social system perspectives on mental retardation.* Berkeley: University of California Press.

Oberman, J. W. (1963). The physician and parents of the retarded child. *Children, 10* (3), 109–113.

Owens, C. (1964). Parents' reactions to defective babies. *American Journal of Nursing, 64,* 83–86.

Patterson, L. L. (1956). Some pointers for professionals. *Children, 3* (1), 13–17.

President's Panel on Mental Retardation. (1962). *A proposed program for national action to combat mental retardation.* Washington, DC: Author.

President's Panel on Mental Retardation. (1963). *Report of the task force on coordination.* Washington, DC: Author.

Report to the President: White House Conference on Children. (1970). Washington, DC: U.S. Government Documents.

Rubinstein, J. H. (1962). Role of the diagnostic clinic in the care of the mentally retarded child. *American Journal of Mental Deficiency, 66,* 544–550.

Stevenson, G. S. (1952). A community program for the mentally retarded. *American Journal of Mental Deficiency, 56,* 719–726.

U.S. Department of Health, Education, and Welfare. (1962). *Mental retardation: Activities of the U.S. Department of Health, Education, and Welfare.* Washington, DC: Author.

Wellin, E., Scott, A. B., Johnson, G. C., Marks, J., Bliss, M., & Goldstein, S. (1960). Community aspects of mental subnormality—a local health department program for retarded children. *American Journal of Public Health, 50,* 36–42.

Wolff, I. S. (1964). *Nursing role in counseling parents of mentally retarded children.* Washington, DC: Children's Bureau, U.S. Department of Health, Education, and Welfare.

Wortis, J. (1954). Towards the establishment of special clinics for retarded children: Experiences and suggestions. *American Journal of Mental Deficiency, 57,* 472–480.

16

A Pivotal Place
in Special Education Policy
The First Arkansas Children's Colony

Elizabeth F. Shores

Parents of children with mental retardation began a movement across the nation after World War II to improve conditions at state-sponsored residential schools for children with disabilities and to provide local day classes for children with mild to moderate mental retardation. Advocacy in Arkansas for special education proceeded along twin tracks, with some citizens concentration on a residential "colony," others working for less restrictive services that would allow children with special needs to remain with their families, and still others working for both approaches. Arkansas had been slower than other southern states to provide any services to children with mental retardation. Since 1888, Arkansas's only state-sponsored service for children with disabilities had been minimal custodial care at the mental hospital in Little Rock, the state's capital. The hospital's administrators had consistently protested the placement of "feeble-minded" children and adults there, arguing that they were not equipped or staffed to handle such cases. Progress in Arkansas toward special education remained slow until Governor Orval E. Faubus took office, in January 1955.

During his first weeks in office, Governor Faubus supported establishment of a pilot residential school that quickly became a model for special education services, even attracting the interest of President John F. Kennedy's administration. Hailed as a "noninstitutional institution," the Arkansas Children's Colony catapulted its first superintendent, David B. Ray, into the leadership of the national movement to deinstitutionalize children with mental retardation. At the same time that Governor Faubus received world-wide opprobrium for resisting federally ordered racial desegregation of schools, Ray promoted integration of children with disabilities into the mainstream of local public school life.[1]

In the South and around the nation, states and private agencies had for decades sponsored large institutions specifically for the care of retarded persons. Though the South had lagged behind the nation in providing custodial care or institutional education, Kentucky founded the State Institution for the Feeble-Minded in 1860, and nine other southern states followed suit by 1923. Some superintendents of southern residential institutions began advocating local special education classes and other services as early as 1929 but received only limited political support.[2]

In the following decades, there was little support nationwide for community-based services such as assessment and evaluation, early intervention, child care, public school special education classes, family counseling, psychiatric care, protective services, recreational programs, vocational training, job placement, and geriatric care for persons with mental retardation. The national lobby for mental health care by the 1940s supported the shifting of mentally ill patients from large institutions to community centers but did not propose the same for Americans with mental retardation. When advocates of deinstitutionalization for persons with mental illness even addressed mental retardation, they usually advocated improvement and expansion of large state-sponsored institutions. A survey in 1955 did find that at least twenty-three states had permissive legislation allowing special education classes in public schools and that many of those provided some degree of incentive for the establishment of such classes. Yet, even in states that required school districts to provide special education, not every child received appropriate educational services. Stanley Powell Davies reported, in 1959, after surveying the status of special education, that "it is not unusual, especially in rural and semirural districts, to find children who have been excluded by action of a local board, without legal sanction." Davies found that financial aid varied considerably, with some states paying the full costs of transportation and education of children with special needs. "Even in progressive states nothing like a complete program of special classes has as yet been organized, yet no other agency can begin to make so effective a contribution to the welfare of the retarded," he wrote.[3]

By the time Ray, the executive director of the Arizona Society for Crippled Children and Adults, moved to Arkansas in January 1957 to plan the new Arkansas Children's Colony, critics of institutional care were beginning to argue in favor of public-school special education and other community-based services. A writer in the journal *Exceptional Children* argued, in 1953, that mentally retarded persons should not be segregated from other school-age children. The *American Journal of Mental Deficiency* carried an essay in 1954 that declared the individual's right to live in a more normal environment:

> [C]hildren have certain special and inalienable rights, because they are children, to live in homes and communities which approach as nearly as possible the desirable standards of normal homes and communities. Society does not possess the moral right to confine these children during this formative period of their lives to institutional plants in conditions so foreign to the normal needs and interests of childhood as to stunt and warp permanently their growth and development and thereby handicap them still further in taking their rightful place in society. There is no excuse, in our opinion, and this includes the item of cost, for perpetuating in new institutional plants for children or in major additions to old ones the traditional forbidding, unhomelike, large, more or less congregate type of unit which has earned for itself in the aggregate the term "institutional" with its unfortunate implications.

In the first significant federal action related to special education, the U.S. Congress appropriated $675,000 for research in special education in 1957, with Senator Lister Hill, of Alabama, an important sponsor. The Council of State Governments recommended in 1958 that states mandate education for children with retardation, subsidize local special education classes, and "complement" those classes with residential care and schooling for children with severe disabilities. When Christine Ingram updated her classic work, *Education of the Slow-Learning Child*, in 1960, she observed that recognition of "the exceptional child's right to an education" was growing rapidly. And Ray's earliest public remarks indicated an awareness of the current thinking about deinstitutionalization for persons with mental retardation.[4]

Yet, custodial care remained the only service available to Arkansas children with mental retardation, either at Arkansas State Hospital, where, since its founding, thousands of Arkansans with mental retardation had been inmates alongside persons with mental illness, or at the state's four reform schools, where some children with mental retardation, white and black, were incarcerated. Superintendents of all four schools protested that those children needed a different kind of service. The dean of Arkansas Boys' Training School, the school for white youth, said, in 1962, that "these boys are being done an injustice by being committed to an institution that is not set up to deal with their problems." Few school districts in the state offered special education classes, and parents in several communities started tiny private programs out of desperation. For example, the Pulaski County Exceptional Children's Association employed a teacher for a class in donated space at the Izard Street Church of Christ in Little Rock but struggled to meet the expenses of the fledgling program. An insurance executive in Little Rock, Nils Florentz, whose daughter was mentally retarded, began a crusade in 1946 to establish more special education classes in local schools and to establish a publicly funded "colony" for mentally retarded children in Arkansas. The concept of a colony where persons with mental deficiency could live for a time before returning to the community was not new. Numerous institutions around the country, notably Rome State School, in New York, had experimented (though with limited success) with training "morons" to hold jobs and return to the colonies in the evenings. Florentz was a persistent, even irritating, advocate for a colony, lobbying legislators constantly between 1946 and 1954. William Maxwell Howell, a sympathetic senator in the Arkansas General Assembly whose district included most of Pulaski County, characterized Florentz as "a burr under my saddle blanket." With state revenues limited, however, Florentz found few supporters in the legislature.[5]

The turning point for Florentz and other parent crusaders came in 1954. In the gubernatorial campaign that year, Florentz met the Democratic nominee, Orval E. Faubus. Faubus was not particularly aware of the plight of children with mental retardation at Arkansas State Hospital. However, he had long been concerned about conditions at the hospital. As a young man, he observed a newly released mental patient who wolfed down an enormous breakfast after returning to his family home in Huntsville, Arkansas. The scene made an indelible impression. Faubus later recalled that the man "had lice. He was dirty beyond description and starving. . . . [T]his was just too much for me to ignore if I had any opportunity to do something about it." Faubus developed an additional resolve to help children with special needs and their families after a long private meeting in 1954 with his campaign supporter and friend in the newspaper business, Keith Tudor, of Arkadelphia, and Tudor's wife. The Tudors described their struggles to care for a child with mental retardation. Governor Faubus was struck by the expense the Tudors incurred to enroll their child in a residential school in another state, recalling later that "it cost at that time $200 a month for tuition . . . that was a big amount then, almost more, well more than most people could bear." Florentz reinforced the Tudors' lobbying by providing Faubus with rent-free accommodations during the transition between the Democratic primary and the gubernatorial inauguration in January 1955.[6]

Already aware of the poor conditions at Arkansas State Hospital and newly attuned to the needs of children with mental retardation, Faubus agreed to support authorization of a pilot colony, despite a limited state budget. His backing moved the legislature to overwhelmingly support the bill during the first weeks of the 1955 legislative session. Act 6 of 1955 authorized the governor to appoint a board of directors, answerable to the governor, for the prospective Arkansas Children's Colony. A modest appropriation allowed the board to begin researching colony designs and to search for an executive director. Governor Faubus appointed Florentz chairman of the new board and made Tudor a board member.[7]

The board consulted J. Thomas McIntire, the superintendent of the Arizona Children's Colony and the former director of the Vineland Training School, a prestigious private school for retarded children, at Vineland, New Jersey. McIntire had helped establish and operate the first cottage-type school in the United States at Southbury, Connecticut, a state recognized for its progressive services to children with mental retardation. A respected leader in the field, he also was a consultant to institutions in Florida, North Carolina, Texas, Nevada, and Oklahoma. McIntire recognized Governor Faubus's support for the prospective colony as a powerful springboard for advancing progressive policies toward children with special needs. He urged his friend and adherent David Ray to apply for the position of superintendent. Ray had risen from janitor to assistant director of the New Iowa Hospital School for Handicapped Children, the site of important innovations in special education, and, after coming to Arizona, he looked to McIntire as a mentor. McIntire told Ray that he believed that the political support in Arkansas for the colony made the state a land of tremendous opportunity for creating new services to children with disabilities. Ray recalled later, "McIntire thought that it was going to be one of the best opportunities in the United States to develop something . . . but even more importantly, was the fact that this facility would have a board and direct access to the governor and seemed to have the making of solid support from the legislature." Ray accepted the position of superintendent in January 1957. During the same period, Governor Faubus won legislative approval for a tax program to support education. Part of the new revenue, $1.6 million, was earmarked for construction and operation of the colony.[8]

Ray's first task was to plan and build the colony. He and Florentz contacted administrators of sixty-seven institutions to solicit ideas. They visited fourteen residential facilities in twelve other states, sometimes with other colony board members. Ray later described the custodial model they found in some states: "Massive buildings; boys and girls regimented into enormous dining rooms and sleeping areas; grounds enclosed by high fences; untrained people serving as houseparents, attendants and teachers; and limitations on visits by parents." He and Florentz wanted to build a facility that would be quite different from the depressing large institutions built in the past. The board agreed to create a facility that would be more educational and home-like than traditional custodial, hospital-like institutions. Working with the architectural firm Ginocchio Cromwell & Associates, in Little Rock, and using McIntire's Arizona Children's Colony as a model, they designed the "compact cottage plan," with the new institution designed like a small village. Children would occupy eight small one-story dormitories, each with two bedrooms and sixteen beds in each bedroom. There would be space for 256 children in all. As an alternative to large hospital-like buildings, the cottage design was not original, nor were the cottages as small as some reformers recommended, but other innovations, particularly the lack of vehicular traffic between the buildings, made the Arkansas colony distinctive.[9]

Although the colony's layout was the facility's most innovative aspect, Ray and the colony board also promoted an up-to-date program of care and education for residents. The program ranged from preschool experiences to academic instruction, vocational training, and social development, with the goal that each child "become an active, participating member of his society." They emphasized that the new colony was an educational institution, not a custodial one, and that cottage and classroom experiences would complement and bolster each other. Ray added, "Happiness has to come first with these children." As the colony program took form, children were able to participate in Scouting, intramural softball, bicycling, fishing, bus rides, religious activities, and games. Teachers emphasized "learning by doing," believing that "each child must be taken where he is and [allowed to] proceed at his own rate until he has reached his fullest development." In part because of the potential for collaborating with Arkansas State Teachers College, in Conway, to teach the colony residents and to provide a practicum site for special education students from the college, Ray, the colony board, and Governor Faubus chose Conway as the location of the colony after considering seventy possible sites in twelve counties.[10]

Along with design and location of the colony, Ray and the board had to establish priorities for selecting applicants to the colony. Ray and the board decided to first admit children with mild mental retardation, despite his belief that such children should receive local public education, in order to demonstrate to the Arkansas Department of Education and local school districts that special education was feasible and practical. Ray told members of the Rotary Club in Conway that first preference for admission would be school-age and educable children and that custodial care of children and adults with severe retardation was a later goal. He envisioned that most of the original colony residents eventually would enter schools in their hometowns. Ray and board members continually encouraged local communities to develop classes for "trainable" and "educable" children, sheltered workshops, and diagnostic services, offering the staff of the colony as consultants to local communities. Gerard J. Bensburg Jr., a psychologist at the Arkansas Child Development Center, in Little Rock, who helped screen applicants to the new colony, also advocated public school classes for children with mental retardation and greater integration of services at the local level. Even as plans for the colony were under way, Bensburg commented, in 1958, that "one of our primary purposes is to help keep the retarded child with his parents in his own community." As for clients at the other end of the continuum of special needs, the ones who truly needed residential placement at the colony, Ray's director of cottage life, Richard Mason, hoped the colony could eventually provide private or semiprivate bedrooms and opportunities to work in the local community.[11]

But parents in Arkansas who were desperate for immediate help did not always appreciate the policy distinction between degrees of mental retardation. From the beginning, the colony maintained a long waiting list of applicants. Ray and the colony board selected the original group of 256 residents from a list of 1,400 applicants. The board eventually tried to guarantee each Arkansas county a number of spaces in the colony on the basis of county population.

Race was another factor in admissions policy. The original group of students did not include black children, but, in subsequent biennia, as the legislature increased funding, the colony board built additional cottages and service buildings, quietly admitting the colony's first black students by 1965 (that year 11 percent of the colony's 519 residents were black). Ray avoided confrontations over racial integration of the colony but pointed out that mental retardation also afflicted children of color in a 1958 fact sheet about the planned colony.[12]

The colony (known today as the Conway Human Development Center) formally opened in Conway on October 4, 1959, in the same month that the United Nations General Assembly adopted the Third Declaration of the Rights of the Child, for the first time specifically addressing the child's right to a free public education and to "grow up in the care and under the responsibility of his parents"—provisions that implied a right to local public special education. Three thousand persons attended the opening ceremony at the colony. The positive reaction to the new institution was immediate. One visitor wrote that "the first impression one has upon entering the Arkansas Children's Colony is one of cheer and happiness." McIntire told Arkansans at the dedication ceremony, "Right now, your state is in advance of many states that have had institutions for years." Within a year, the Canadian Association for Retarded Children ranked the Arkansas Children's Colony as the best facility for children with retardation in the United States on the basis of physical plant, philosophy of operation, and curriculum. Developmental disabilities service agencies in South Carolina and Oklahoma adopted the Arkansas colony as a model for new facilities in their states. The state of South Carolina looked to the colony for inspiration as it planned a new institution in Charleston. Legislators in that state consulted Ray and sent their own consultant to Conway to inspect the colony. Governor Henry Bellmon, of Oklahoma, consulted Ray in 1963 in connection with a new residential program for children with mental retardation in Tulsa and subsequently wrote to him, "Oklahoma is anxious to take the lead in the field of Mental Retardation [and I] assure you of our full intention to work with you." The *Tulsa Tribune* referred to the Arkansas program as "pioneering." The American Institute of Architects published a photograph of a colony cottage play yard on the cover of its journal in February 1962.[13]

But the colony's national impact came less with its modest innovations in design and curriculum than in allowing its director a platform from which to advocate the offering of a whole spectrum of services to the mentally retarded in the least restrictive environments. In his contacts with Arkansas parents, service providers, state policy makers, and Governor Faubus, Ray persistently emphasized the need for comprehensive services extending far beyond the Children's Colony. He told the colony board, in June 1958:

A practical state program includes mental hygiene clinics for identification and guidance, a program for instructing families in the nature of mental deficiency and proper methods of care and training, special education in the public school, institutional care and training for those children that cannot be adequately provided for in their homes or community, and research to develop ways of preventing mental deficiency and to improve present or establish new methods of care and training.[14]

His argument that a state-sponsored residential school should exist to serve children whose needs could not be met by local schools predated the theoretical work on continuum models by Stanley Deno (1970) and Maynard Reynolds (1976). The underlying premise of the continuum model was that children with mental retardation and other disabilities were entitled to an education the least restrictive environment, a position that became federal law in 1975 with passage of Public Law 94-142.[15]

During the same months that Governor Faubus drew world attention for defying the federal government over racial desegregation of Central High School, in Little Rock, Ray and his board chairman, Nils Florentz, laid the political groundwork in Arkansas for comprehensive educational services to children with mental retardation. Ray traveled frequently to speak to local civic and parent groups, sometimes with Florentz or with Jake Sklar, of the new Arkansas Association for Retarded Children (AARC), making an estimated seventy-two presentations between January 1957 and July 1958. Their first objective was to build public support for more construction funds for the colony, but Ray repeatedly stressed the need for a continuum of services. For example, he told the Pilot Club, a women's organization in Conway, in 1957, that "the Children's Colony is not an answer to all the retarded child's problems." He complimented parents in West Memphis for starting the private Happi-Time School for children with mental retardation and said the colony would work toward "an enriched curriculum in Arkansas' public schools, special classes and even special schools in larger cities, home training and vocational training." To the West Memphis Rotary Club, he said "the colony at Conway is only a spoke in a wheel—and a very long overdue one." He added that local communities should take responsibility for the other 18,000 children with special needs in Arkansas, pointing out that local special education classes would be far more economical than residential care and education at the colony. Ray often recruited support among the socially and politically prominent. Jeannette

Rockefeller, a former social worker and the wife of Winthrop Rockefeller, a wealthy Republican newcomer to Arkansas, joined his cause, saying, in a speech to the Northeast AARC, that local communities should provide health, psychological, and social work services to children with mental retardation and their families. Ray twice arranged for Gunnar Dybwad, executive director of the National Association for Retarded Children (NARC), to come to Arkansas to challenge the state to do much more for children with mental retardation. When Dybwad came, in April 1958, to speak at the organizational meeting of the AARC, he bluntly told his audience that most children with mental retardation did not need institutional care and that parents should work for public special education classes. Dybwad spoke to the AARC again in June 1960, praising Arkansas's colony but saying that the state should create "classes for less seriously retarded children in the public schools" and "training and facilities for retarded adults to earn part of their own way."[16]

Ray established ties with existing social service organizations in the state, becoming president-elect of the Arkansas Conference of Social Work. He also significantly strengthened and expanded the network of citizen advocates for comprehensive, community-based services by helping parents around Arkansas form state and local chapters of NARC and by using the groups as a network for spreading the message that the colony should only be one program in a continuum of local and state services. He arranged for Governor Faubus to speak at the organizational meeting of AARC in the Hotel Marion, in Little Rock, which attracted 361 parents, and at at least one other AARC meeting, stirring the political synergy between a popular governor and parents who were passionate about their cause. Ray summarized these networking and advocacy efforts in the 1963 edition of the colony's manual for parents:

> The Colony Board and staff have encouraged communities throughout the State to develop local programs for the retarded. Such local services as trainable classes, public school special classes, sheltered workshops, and diagnostic services have been developed. The psychological and educational staff at the Colony, where time has permitted, has given consultation in the local communities to many public school administrators and teachers in the screening of students and in the mechanics of setting up classes for the retarded. In addition, the educational staff at the Colony has developed a complete curriculum for the education and training of all

types of retarded children. This has been made available to public schools throughout Arkansas.[17]

Governor Faubus supported Ray's attempts to promote comprehensive, community-based services, appointing an advisory committee on comprehensive services and involving Ray in its deliberations. Persuading local school administrators to open their doors to children with special needs was not easy, however. Sklar, the vice president of AARC, commented, in July 1959, that school officials "aren't too keen about starting special education classes." Three years later, the state's education commissioner, Arch Ford, said that state funding for local classes was severely inadequate.[18]

During the same time that he promoted a continuum of services within Arkansas, Ray found a place among policy makers at the national level. Two months after taking the job in Conway, he attended a meeting of the American Association on Mental Deficiency, and that summer he participated in a two-week workshop at Columbia University, in New York. Once the new colony opened, Ray emphasized its modest innovations to attract national attention to Conway and then worked to refocus that attention onto the importance of community-based services. In 1960, Ray participated in a conference on needs for special education and rehabilitation in the South. Eunice Kennedy Shriver, the vice president of the Joseph P. Kennedy Foundation and President Kennedy's sister, heard Ray testify and told him that she would like to visit the colony in Conway. The same year the American Association on Mental Deficiency (AAMD) elected Ray a regional officer, and Ray hosted a regional meeting of the AAMD in Conway. At that meeting he chaired a panel discussion, "Changing Concepts in the Development of State Institutions for the Retarded." He subsequently chaired the AAMD's planning board in 1963.[19]

President Kennedy appointed twenty-seven persons to the President's Panel on Mental Retardation in 1961, with Eunice Shriver as a consultant, and charged it with developing a national plan "to combat mental retardation." The panel invited Ray to comment on the needs in the field, and Ray responded, in 1962, with a nine-page letter, arguing for a continuum of services: "For a problem that is so vast, there is no one answer that will solve it all. . . . I would like for you to understand that even though my major responsibility falls in the residential program area, I am most interested in seeing that . . . our nation develop adequate programs and services . . . on a local and state and national level." Ray also made twenty-two broad recommendations in the areas of early intervention, clear delineation of mental health and mental retardation services, expanded teacher training, vocational training and employment, and the design of residential facilities, emphasizing the need for services at the local level. The President's Panel subsequently made ninety-five recommendations, including deinstitutionalization and a continuum of services from home-based to residential, that echoed many of Ray's suggestions and became the foundation for modern federal policy on developmental disabilities services.[20]

Ray took advantage of the Arkansas news media's interest in his recommendations to the President's Panel to again promote comprehensive services in the state. He commented, in 1968, "[W]hen I went to Georgia, they played up the fact that I was going down to testify before President Kennedy's panel. Well, this . . . wasn't publicity for me, but it was publicity for the field of mental retardation. And the papers played this up, and when I got back, they wanted interviews on what took place there and what recommendations, and this gave us something to build on in Arkansas."[21]

Continuing to seek attention from national policy makers, Ray invited other leaders in the mental retardation movement to visit the colony. Their reactions were positive. "I can say quite candidly that your plant and program is the best that I have ever seen in any public institution," said Dr. Edward L. Johnstone, president of the Woods Schools and Residential Treatment Center in Langhorne, Pennsylvania, and a member of a group of consultants that toured Arkansas in 1962 to study the state's mental health problems. John J. Noone Jr., of the National Institute on Mental Health, called the colony "an outstanding institution and one of the best" after visiting it the same year. Noone commented, "It seems to me that the Colony represents some fine new thinking. . . . [Y]ou have blazed new trails with the result that it is a 'non-institutional institution.'"[22]

Ray's strategy of combining public relations and policy advocacy climaxed when Eunice Shriver finally came to Conway, in May 1963, to speak to the AARC. It was a dramatic occasion, with the news media making much of the fact that Shriver and Governor Faubus shared the stage when he presented an Arkansas Traveler certificate to her. After touring the colony, Shriver praised its "home-like" cottages. She said she was impressed by research on special education that was under way at the colony and predicted that Arkansas could be the leading state in research on mental retardation.[23]

While Eunice Shriver's on-stage meeting with Orval Faubus seemed like the highlight of her visit to Arkansas at the time, the greater significance became apparent a few weeks later, when she and Sargent Shriver asked Ray to lend a hand in the Kennedy administration's attempt to pass federal legislation regarding mental retardation. The Shrivers wanted Ray's expertise as well as his connections to powerful members of Congress, including Arkansans Wilbur Mills, chairman of the House Ways and Means Committee, and Representative Oren Harris, a member of the Interstate and Foreign Commerce Committee, who had introduced legislation written by the President's Panel on Mental Retardation to fund research on mental retardation; and Senator Lister Hill, a leading liberal in the Senate with a particular interest in developmental disabilities services. They asked Governor Faubus to give Ray a leave of absence. With the Arkansas governor's approval, Ray was in Washington within a week. He later described Faubus's role in the Washington assignment:

> When Sarge called me—and I had never met him—I was out in Portland for a meeting of the American Association on Mental Deficiency. And that was after Eunice had come to Arkansas. He asked me to stop by Washington. I had breakfast at their house. Mike Feldman was there, and [Shriver] said, "This is what we want you to do." That was on a Saturday morning, and he said, "Can you start Monday?" I said, "Goodness, I'm running an institution in Arkansas." And so Sarge said, "What would it take to get you released?" And I said, "Well, the Governor would have to do it." And he picked up the phone and called Governor Faubus right while I was there. I wasn't in Washington on Monday, but I was there on Wednesday. That's how fast it worked.[24]

Ray was appointed a special adviser to Anthony J. Celebrezze, secretary of the federal Department of Health, Education, and Welfare. His responsibilities included congressional lobbying and technical assistance to Stafford Warren, President Kennedy's special assistant on mental retardation. Ray worked to educate members of Congress about the need for a range of services for the mentally retarded and to rally constituents to lobby their representatives. Noting the lack of wide support in Congress for new mental retardation services, Ray and Sargent Shriver met with many members individually to request their support. Ray's years of networking with parent and professional organizations proved invaluable, as he was able to generate support among representatives' constituents for the legislative proposals. Ray described his work in a 1968 interview: "Any time I wasn't on the Hill, I was on the telephone or meeting with groups . . . we had a groundswell that started that was most impressive to Congress . . . I just know it because I saw areas that changed and I saw congressmen that changed." One of Ray's de facto responsibilities was to regularly report to Eunice Shriver, who often called him on Friday evenings for updates before joining the president at the Kennedy family residence at Hyannis Port. His close working relationship with Mrs. Shriver, who frequently prodded her brother to support special education, put Ray just one person away from the president himself. President Kennedy encouraged Ray and Shriver to keep working. Ray recalled, in a 1968 interview, that his encouragement "certainly gave me the feeling of wanting to do a little more."[25]

Governor Faubus continued to provide help and support to Ray. When two of Arkansas's representatives in Congress, Senator John L. McClellan and Representative Ezekial C. Gathings, were reluctant to support the presidential panel's proposals, Ray prevailed upon Governor Faubus to lobby them. "After I alerted him to what the problem was, on his personal visits to the people on the Hill, [Faubus] brought out to both of these congressmen his desire to see mental retardation legislation passed." Governor Faubus, chairman of the Southern Governors Conference that year, also agreed at Ray's request to endorse the administration's proposals and to make room on the conference agenda for Warren. "Even though at that time Faubus had a name for fighting the federal government . . . he gave a glowing introduction to Dr. Warren and also plugged that Arkansas was doing a great job for the retarded through the new Arkansas Children's Colony," Ray recalled, in 1968. The centerpiece of the administration's legislation was the proposal by Wilbur J. Cohen, assistant secretary of the Department of Health, Education, and Welfare, to provide grants to states to develop comprehensive plans for developmental disabilities services. Wilbur Mills sponsored the legislation, which passed on a unanimous voice vote after heavy lobbying by Sargent Shriver, Ray, and Mills, as the Maternal and Child Health and Mental Retardation Planning Amendments, or Public Law 88-156. The Senate also supported the bill overwhelmingly. Ray attended the ceremony in the Oval Office when President Kennedy signed the bill into law.[26]

Shortly after Ray returned to Arkansas, Eunice Shriver wrote to thank him for his help: "To be an important influence as you were in getting national legislation passed, which will affect the lives of the mentally retarded in the years to come, should give you great pride. . . . [A]s I told Governor Faubus, Arkansas is fortunate in having you. . . . Hope you will keep in close contact with us in the weeks to come, and we will certainly call on you for advice and suggestions."[27] President Kennedy was assassinated six weeks later.

Ray returned to the colony eager to expand the state's developmental disabilities services beyond residential care. Recognizing political reality and particularly the influence of parents like Florentz, he told his board, in January 1964, "It was most important in the early years of development of the Colony that we highlight the five percent of the retarded who needed the institution. . . . But . . . we urgently need to do something for the ninety-five percent. I am convinced that the problem of mental retardation is so complex that many agencies and many individuals are needed to solve it." Ray urged the board to expand its role beyond directing activities at the small colony in Conway to collaborate with numerous state agencies in planning comprehensive services.[28]

Eunice Shriver called on Ray again, in February 1964. Worried that her brother's assassination would slow the momentum of the movement for special education, she asked Ray to work full-time in Washington promoting the Kennedy special education agenda, offering him a position on the payroll of the Joseph P. Kennedy Foundation. Ray accepted and wasted no time alerting his allies on Capitol Hill that he was coming back. Representative Mills congratulated Ray, while expressing regret that Arkansas was losing him to Washington. Senator Hill replied, "My dear Dave, congratulations to you on your new position. You have my very best wishes for continued success in your career in behalf of the mentally retarded." He promised to meet with Ray soon and said he looked forward to "close cooperation."[29]

The Kennedy Foundation awarded grants to universities and other institutions as seed money for research on mental retardation. Ray reviewed grant proposals and usually accompanied one of the Kennedys on visits to grant recipients. He also handled congressional relations for the Foundation. The Congress passed President Lyndon Johnson's Elementary and Secondary Education Act (ESEA) during that period and then amended the new law, in November 1965, to provide federal assistance to state-supported programs for children with special needs. Sargent Shriver wrote to Ray, in December 1965, that "during your tenure [with the Foundation] the cause of [mental retardation] has certainly advanced nationally—and a large part of that progress was brought about by your assiduous attention to all the details of our cause." Ray worked for the Foundation for eighteen months, until President Johnson appointed him director of the new President's Committee on Mental Retardation, which included the secretary of health, education, and welfare as chairman, the secretary of labor, the director of the Office of Economic Opportunity, and others. The committee provided advice and assistance, evaluating the "adequacy of the national effort to combat mental retardation," coordinating activities of federal agencies, providing a liaison between federal activities and state and local governments, foundations and private organizations, and mobilizing support for mental retardation activities among professional organizations. Vice President Hubert Humphrey called Ray's appointment "excellent." In his new position, Ray advised the president, helping steer federal policy on mental retardation over the next five years and promoting deinstitutionalization for most persons with mental retardation, community-based services, and interagency collaboration.[30]

As the White House's leading spokesman for the cause of special education, Ray delicately framed his vision when speaking to old-guard institution administrators. For example, he told an audience in South Carolina, in 1966, that alternatives to institutions were imperative for most clients but added:

> I do want to point out something. I used to be superintendent of an institution. I still feel this is important. Institutions of the future will become more important and not less important but it will be a different type of institution than that you have known. It will be community and regional oriented. . . . So as we talk about community services, I do not want to downgrade the role of the institution. It has a need, and as far as I am concerned will continue to have a need. But it will be a different type of role.

He was less diplomatic in a speech back at the Arkansas Children's Colony, stating flatly that "for all the progress, we haven't touched the needs of seventy-five percent of the retarded because ninety-five percent of the money spent so far has served the middle class." He also said public schools were not doing enough for retarded children.[31]

The President's Committee's recommendations over the next few years also reflected the policies Ray had supported for a decade. In 1967, the committee echoed the plea that Ray made to the President's Panel on Mental Retardation in 1962, as well as his statements to the colony board in 1963. The committee listed ten "urgent" needs:

- Accessibility of services to more people, including the poor
- More recruitment of professionals and support staff for mental retardation services
- "Fuller use of existing resources" through service coordination
- "More public-private partnerships in program development, services and research"
- A national mental retardation information and resource center
- Better application of research findings
- Early identification and treatment of the mentally retarded before they enter school through screening and special preschool classes
- Long-range state and local planning to meet the needs of mentally retarded children and adults, including "renewed attention . . . to public facilities and programs for the five percent of the mentally retarded who require full- or part-time residential care"
- Clarification of the legal status and rights of the individual with mental retardation
- "Bold, original thinking" on questions such as employment, assisted living, service in rural areas, and the "moral and ethical implications of technological findings in the genetics and management of mental retardation"

That year, Congress funded regional resource centers to provide screening and to strengthen recruitment of special education teachers. During its second year in operation, the President's Committee focused on three issues: residential care, professional and volunteer development, and the relationship of poverty to mental retardation. The committee had twenty-four members, including Eunice Shriver and Jeanette Rockefeller, whose husband had succeeded Faubus as governor of Arkansas. It recommended regulation of residential facilities to improve quality, greater service integration to help persons with mental retardation and emotional problems, grants and other programs for professional development, and, most significant, comprehensive health care and education for children from birth. The committee declared that poverty caused and nurtured mental retardation and urged "all speed in the war on poverty." Congress enacted the Handicapped Children's Early Education Assistance Act in 1968 to sponsor experimental early childhood education programs for children with disabilities.[32]

In its 1969 report, the committee reiterated the need for early intervention in the lives of children in low-income, disadvantaged neighborhoods. It praised President Richard Nixon for creating the federal Office of Child Development to foster new services to children under six years of age and to integrate existing services. The committee also recommended better connections between programs for school-age children, adolescents, and adults with mental retardation. It again emphasized the need for in-service training for professional and support staff. It was harsh in its judgment of local school districts, which it said "have not, in the main, accepted responsibility to educate all children." Arguing that persons with mental retardation had the same rights as other Americans, the committee reproduced, in its 1969 report, the 1968 Declaration of General and Special Rights of the Mentally Retarded by the International League of Societies for the Mentally Handicapped. That declaration specifically mentioned the right to special education and the child's right "to live with his own family or with foster parents [and] to participate in all aspects of community life" or, if necessary, to live in institutions that were as home-like as possible.[33]

Propelled by the momentum the Kennedy administration had established, by Mills's legislation of 1963, and by the policy recommendations of the President's Committee, which Ray directed, the federal government rapidly expanded its role in developmental disabilities services. New legislation provided funds to help states implement the comprehensive plans drafted under Public Law 88-156. The 1965 ESEA (Public Law 89-10) funded new special education programs for children with various disabilities. PL 89-313 provided additional federal support for state-sponsored schools for the handicapped. Congress also authorized financial aid to retarded children and spouses of members of the armed forces and expanded the special education provisions of ESEA the following year. Congress passed Public Law 89-750, the Education of the Handicapped Act, in 1966, providing new federal grants for states to initiate, expand, and improve special education and establishing the National Advisory Committee on Handicapped Children as part of the Office of Education. In 1967, Congress provided new funding for research in mental retardation, which Ray had recommended in 1962, along with physical education and recreation programs for persons with handicaps. In 1968, it funded new research into preschool education for children with handicaps and better professional development for personnel. Congress passed additional legislation in 1969, Public Law 91-230, the Elementary, Secondary, and Other Educational Amendments of 1969, to further stimulate states to develop special education programs.[34]

Federal funds stimulated the establishment of many new services during the 1960s, allowing Arkansas, for instance, found residential facilities at Arkadelphia, Jonesboro, Warren, and Alexander during the Faubus administration. Many local school districts across America continued to exclude children with disabilities, however, and advocacy for equal access to schools mounted. The Pennsylvania chapter of NARC finally sued the Commonwealth of Pennsylvania in 1971, demanding appropriate educational opportunities for school-age children with mental retardation. The United Nations declared, the same year, that the person with mental retardation had the same rights as any other individual, including the right to education that allows him to "develop his ability and maximum potential." The U.S. Supreme Court ruled in favor of the Pennsylvania parents in 1972, finding that children with mental retardation were entitled to a free and appropriate education. The U.S. Congress finally enacted a guarantee of free public education to children with disabilities in 1975 with the Education for All Handicapped Children Act (Public Law 94-142).[35]

During his years as the first superintendent of the Arkansas Children's Colony at Conway, Ray struck a balance between satisfying Arkansas parents desperate for immediate assistance and advocating the long view in policy formation—his actions in keeping with the remarks of Elizabeth M. Boggs, another leader in developmental disabilities services. Boggs observed, in 1958, that "so much in the years to come will depend on what we fashion with the money we have now—the buildings we design, the precedents we establish, the administrative structures, the built-in devices for evaluation, what we teach about mental deficiency in universities.. ... Along with money we need intelligence, courage, imagination, determination, cooperative effort, and a sense of direction." Ray possessed that sense of direction. Even as he helped select a site and worked with architects to build the original Arkansas Children's Colony, Ray worked toward the creation of a full spectrum of services to children with special needs. He persistently warned parents, school administrators, legislators, and Governor Faubus that the new colony should be but one "spoke in the wheel" of disabilities services. Through shrewd advocacy and public relations, Ray helped persuade the Kennedy and Johnson administrations and Congress to begin providing educational opportunities to children with mental retardation and other disabilities.[36]

The culture shock of racial desegregation of schools during the same period overshadowed Arkansas's and the nation's gradual accommodation of children with special needs, but the policy changes of the 1960s concerning special education were no less momentous, no easier to adopt, nor any easier to implement. Children with disabilities were, after all, victims of discrimination, too. As the Carnegie Council on Children put it, "Their oppression takes many forms: outright prejudice against handicapped people of all ages, job discrimination against disabled adults, and well-meaning but destructive misconceptions that exaggerate the true limitations of many handicaps."[37]

Along with Ray, other Arkansans—Florentz, Mills, Harris, and Faubus—contributed in various ways to the emerging national policy that all Americans, including children with mental retardation, were entitled to live and learn in the least restrictive situations possible. Throughout his administration, Governor Faubus closely monitored the colony board's activities. He advised members of AARC on lobbying legislators for funding for more cottages and other facilities at the colony and promoted private fundraisers for the colony. He took the time to approve the Conway location for the colony in August 1957, even as segregationists were pressing him to stop the scheduled racial desegregation of Central High School, in Little Rock. Perhaps Faubus was truly empathetic toward children deprived of an education because of disabilities, or perhaps his initial support of the Arkansas Children's Colony was simply political reimbursement to Florentz and Tudor for campaign favors. The governor apparently used the colony to repay other political debts, instructing the board to appoint his allies to the colony's staff and reserving final approval of most staff appointments. Governor Faubus may have hoped that the Arkansas Children's Colony would enhance his image, possibly as a counterbalance to the international condemnation he received for resisting racial desegregation of schools. At the dedication of the colony in October 1959, two years after the September 1957 Central High crisis in Little Rock, he alluded to deinstitutionalization and better conditions "for all people, regardless of station in life, race, or creed" as goals of his administration. He boasted to the members of the Southern Governors Conference, in 1963, that the colony was a model for the nation. He touted the innovations of the colony as he campaigned for reelection. A campaign brochure in 1964 declared, "The Children's Colony, established under the administration of Governor Faubus, is one of the most modern in the nation. Hundreds of children now receive care and training never before provided by the State of Arkansas. Ask the parents of these children what Governor Faubus has done for their children. . . . Governor Faubus is pledged to continue the expansion of these facilities in order to provide needed care for others who cannot yet be admitted." Ray helped boost Governor Faubus's image, calling the governor "very wise" in a 1958 statement and using the governor's growing popularity in the state to stimulate parallel public support for the colony at Conway. By supporting legislation to create the Arkansas Children's Colony as one of his first gubernatorial acts, Governor Faubus advanced the state in terms of segregated residential education for children with mental retardation, if not in terms of universal integrated public education. Yet, Faubus also lent his considerable political support to the cause of comprehensive community-based services for children with special needs at several critical points: when he approved the choice of David B. Ray as the first superintendent of the colony; when he supported Ray's networking and advocacy for local public special education; and when he lobbied on behalf of the Kennedy administration's proposals in 1963.[38]

Governor Faubus provided overt as well as tacit support for Ray's activities in the policy arena, as Ray quickly achieved one of the most influential federal positions in developmental disabilities services. Their collaboration was mutually beneficial. Despite his association with a residential school, Ray consistently supported deinstitutionalization and comprehensive community-based services for children with mental retardation. He shrewdly cooperated with the goals of parents in Arkansas, legislators, and Governor Faubus to build the colony according to the most current thinking on residential school design. He then used the institution's modest innovations to attract new attention to his accomplishments and thus to the cause of deinstitutionalization. He so impressed high-ranking members of the Kennedy administration, including the president's sister Eunice Kennedy Shriver and brother-in-law Sargent Shriver, that they recruited him to take part in their campaign for special education and a broader federal role in developmental disabilities services.

The story of the establishment of the first Arkansas Children's Colony is an interesting example of the intersection of politics and special education policy and a counterpoint to the conventional understanding of Orval Faubus as merely a segregationist and reactionary. Arkansas's public schools gradually provided special education in local communities; later, as broader community-based services to families became available, the original colony and similar centers around the state became homes for an aging population of persons with severe or multiple disabilities. As a residential program for children with mild to moderate mental retardation, then, the colony at Conway was an anachronism when it opened and yet a springboard for active federal policy—a pivotal place in special education history.

NOTES

Research for this article was supported in part by the Arkansas Humanities Council and the National Endowment for the Humanities; the Arkansas Historic Preservation Program, an agency of the Department of Arkansas Heritage; and the Center for Arkansas Studies at the University of Arkansas at Little Rock.

1. Elizabeth F. Shores, "'Idiots and Imbeciles': Children with Mental Retardation at Arkansas State Hospital, 1883–1958," *Pulaski County Historical Review* 44 (spring 1996): 2–20.

2. Steven Noll, *Feeble-Minded in Our Midst: Institutions for the Mentally Retarded in the South, 1900–1940* (Chapel Hill: University of North Carolina Press, 1995), 12.

3. H. L. Beck, *Social Services to the Mentally Retarded* (Springfield, IL: Charles C. Thomas, 1969), 70–82; Stanley Powell Davies, *The Mentally Retarded in Society* (New York: Columbia University Press, 1959), 173–179.

4. David B. Ray, interview by author, Little Rock, February 2, 1995; Christine P. Ingram, *Education of the Slow-Learning Child*, 3rd ed. (New York: Ronald Press, 1960), 376; Albert Deutsch, *The Shame of the States* (New York: Harcourt, Brace, 1948), 123; E. Rosell, "Some Principles and Philosophy in the Planning and Development of Institutional Plants with Particular Reference to Visitation for the Mentally Retarded," *American Journal of Mental Deficiency* 58 (1954): 597; Daniel A. Felicetti, *Mental Health and Retardation Politics; The Mind Lobbies in Congress* (New York: Praeger, 1975), 28; "Report of the Conference on the Problems of the Mentally Retarded in Arkansas" (Little Rock, June 18–20, 1962), 17, 37–41, Historical Research Center, University of Arkansas for Medical Sciences, Little Rock, cited hereafter as UAMS Archive.

5. Shores, "'Idiots and Imbeciles'"; "Report of the Conference on the Problems of the Mentally Retarded in Arkansas," UAMS Archive; Benton Courier, February 18, 1960; "Worthy Aid Program Falters," September 1956, scrapbooks, Archive, Conway Human Development Center (CHDC), Conway, Arkansas, cited hereafter as CHDC scrapbooks; Arkansas Democrat, April 1958, CHDC scrapbooks; Fay Williams, "His Mission: To Help Retarded Children," *Arkansas Democrat* magazine, February 1955, CHDC scrapbooks; Noll, *Feeble-Minded in Our Midst*, 145; William Maxwell Howell, interview by author, Little Rock, October 4, 1994.

6. Orval E. Faubus, interview by author, Little Rock, October 4, 1994 (source of all quotations in this paragraph); anonymous interview by author.

7. "Child Colony Plan Suggested," January 1955, CHDC scrapbooks; "Children's Colony Becomes a Law," Memphis *Commercial Appeal*, January 1955, CHDC scrapbooks; "Quick Approval Given to Children's Colony," Memphis *Commercial Appeal*,

January 1955, CHDC scrapbooks; "Clark May Give Bill to Exempt Industry 10 Years," CHDC scrapbooks; Conway *Log Cabin Democrat,* October 2, 1959.

8. Ray, interview, February 2, 1995; Conway *Log Cabin Democrat,* October 2, 1959; Beck, *Social Services to the Mentally Retarded,* 85; "Little Rock District, AFWC to Meet at Hotel Marion," *Arkansas Gazette,* March 1958, CHDC scrapbooks.

9. Arkansas Children's Colony, "A Complete Community for the Mentally Retarded Built on the 'Compact Cottage Plan,'" Conway, 1961, in the possession of David B. Ray, Atlanta, Georgia; "The Arkansas Children's Colony," *Blue Cross Blue Shield Scribe,* November–December 1959, 3-14; *Arkansas Gazette,* January 27, 1958; Gunnar Dybwad, *Challenges in Mental Retardation* (New York: Columbia University Press, 1964), 94; John J. Truemper, *A Century of Service, 1885–1985: At the Firm of Cromwell Truemper Levy Parker & Woodsmall* (Little Rock: August House, 1985), 47, 70-71.

10. "Colony Begins Evaluation of Children," May 1959, CHDC scrapbooks; "Psychologist Hired by Children's Colony," *Arkansas Democrat,* July 1959, CHDC scrapbooks; Dick Mason, "The Mentally Retarded," in the possession of David B. Ray; David B. Ray, interviews by author, Little Rock, February 2, 1995; April 18, 1996; *Arkansas Gazette,* August 8, 1957; Conway *Log Cabin Democrat,* October, 2, 1959; "Report of the Conferences on Problems of the Mentally Retarded in Arkansas," UAMS Archive; David B. Ray Jr., "Wanted: A Site to Build a State Institution for the Mentally Retarded," *American Journal of Mental Deficiency* 63 (May 1959): 1098-1103; Arkansas Children's Colony, "Parent's Manual," 2nd ed. (Conway, 1963), 23-24, in the possession of David B. Ray; B. R. Teague, "The Site Decision for the Arkansas Children's Colony (1957)," *Faulkner (County) Facts and Fiddlings* 37 (spring 1995): 1-2.

11. Arkansas Department of Health Mental Retardation Planning Project, "Comprehensive Mental Retardation Plan for Arkansas," 13, and "Mental Retardation in Arkansas: Studies of Selected Services, 1964 through 1966," ix (Little Rock, 1966), File 2, Box H17, Mental Retardation Planning Project Collection, UAMS Archive; Jack Blalock, "Retarded Children's Center Uses Normal Surroundings," *Arkansas Gazette,* April 1958, CHDC scrapbooks; Sara Murphy, "Finding the Right Place for the Retarded Child," November 1958, CHDC scrapbooks; Ray, interview, February 2, 1995; "Colony's Dedication Is Set," Conway *Log Cabin Democrat,* August 1958, CHDC scrapbooks; Dick Mason, "Planning for the Educable and Trainable Adult Retarded," in the possession of David B. Ray.

12. *Arkansas Democrat,* May 22, 1959; Ruth Malone, "Arkansas Children's Colony at Conway Swamped with Applications," *Arkansas Gazette,* May 1959, CHDC scrapbooks; Mental Retardation Planning Project, "Mental Retardation in Arkansas"; Arkansas Children's Colony, "Progress Report of the Arkansas Children's Colony, Jan. 1, 1957–June 30, 1958," in the possession of David B. Ray.

13. E. Chanlett and G. M. Morier, "Declaration of the Rights of the Child: A Historical Review," *International Child Welfare Review* 22 (1968): 4-8; Crosse Colony Board

of Directors, Minutes, May 10, October 14, 1962, Archive, Division of Developmental Disabilities, Arkansas Department of Human Services, Little Rock, cited hereafter as DDS Archive; Arkansas Children's Colony, "Parent's Manual," 23–24; *Tulsa Tribune,* July 26, 1963; *Arkansas Gazette,* October 5, 1969; *Arkansas Democrat,* September 4, 1960; "South Carolina May Duplicate Colony Program," December 13, 1960, CHDC scrapbooks; Governor Henry Bellmon, of Oklahoma, to David B. Ray Jr., June 26, 1963, in the possession of David B. Ray; *Journal of the American Institute of Architects* 37 (2), cover.

14. "Social Work Conference Elects," *Arkansas Democrat,* March 1958, CHDC scrapbooks; "Mrs. J. W. Graney on Committee for Mental Retardation," CHDC scrapbooks; "Parents of Retarded to Organize," March 1958, CHDC scrapbooks; Conway *Log Cabin Democrat,* August 1, 1957; "Report of the Conference on the Problems of the Mentally Retarded in Arkansas," 27–28, UAMS Archive; Mental Retardation Planning Project, "Comprehensive Mental Retardation Plan for Arkansas," 56; Acts of Arkansas, 1947, pp. 815–816.

15. Arkansas Children's Colony, "Progress Report of the Arkansas Children's Colony, January 1, 1957 to June 30, 1958," in the possession of David B. Ray; H. Rutherford Turnbull III et al., "A Policy Analysis of 'Least Restrictive' Education of Handicapped Children," *Rutgers Law Journal* 14 (1983): 520–521; Ray, interview, February 2, 1995.

16. Harry S. Ashmore, *Civil Rights and Wrongs: A Memoir of Race and Politics, 1944–1994* (New York: Pantheon, 1994), 124–133; "Founder of School to Attend Meeting," April 1958, CHDC scrapbooks, Conway *Log Cabin Democrat,* August 1, 1957; "Mrs. Rockefeller Lauds Local 'Cottage of Hope,'" April 2, 1960, CHDC scrapbooks; "Need for Training Retarded Children Told Rotarians," *Crittenden County Times,* February 1959, CHDC scrapbooks.

17. *Arkansas Gazette,* April 28, 1958; June 19, 1960; Arkansas Children's Colony, "Parent's Manual," 23–24.

18. Arkansas Children's Colony Board of Directors, Minutes, May 10, October 14, 1962, DDS Archive; Mental Retardation Planning Project, "Comprehensive Mental Retardation Plan for Arkansas," 13; "Educational Needs for Retarded Students Told," July 1959, CHDC scrapbooks; *Arkansas Democrat,* April 16, 1962.

19. Arkansas Children's Colony Board of Directors, Minutes, March 20, 1957; April 2, 1958, DDS Archive; Conway *Log Cabin Democrat,* January 28, 1960; "Mental Health Group Elects Officers," October 17, 1960, CHDC scrapbooks; "250 Expected at Regional AAMD Meeting," November 3, 1960, CHDC scrapbooks; *Arkansas Gazette,* November 4, 1960.

20. President's Panel on Mental Retardation, "Mental Retardation: A National Plan for a National Problem, Chart Book" (Washington, DC: GPO, 1963); David B. Ray to Leonard W. Mayo, May 22, 1962, 2–8, in the possession of David B. Ray; S. Ellen Finch, "Deinstitutionalization in Mental Health and Mental Retardation

Services," *Psychosocial Rehabilitation Journal* 8 (January 1985): 36–47; David B. Ray, interview by John F. Stewart, March 5, 1968, 6, John F. Kennedy Library Oral History Program, Boston; David Braddock, *Federal Policy toward Mental Retardation and Developmental Disabilities* (Baltimore: P. H. Brookes, 1987), 19.

21. Ray, interview, March 5, 1968, 7.

22. Arkansas Children' Colony, "Parent's Manual."

23. Conway *Log Cabin Democrat,* May 6, 1963; Memphis *Commercial Appeal,* May 6, 1963.

24. W. W. Rogers et al., *Alabama: The History of a Deep South State* (Tuscaloosa: University of Alabama Press, 1994), 578–579; Memphis *Commercial Appeal,* May 6, 1963; Ray, interview, March 5, 1968, 10, 32.

25. Little Rock *Arkansas Statesman,* June 7, 1963; *Arkansas Gazette,* May 31, 1963; Conway *Log Cabin Democrat,* May 30, 1963; Ray, interview, March 5, 1968 (second quotation), 31.

26. Ray, interview, March 5, 1968, 21–22; U.S. Department of Health, Education, and Welfare Children's Bureau, "Legislative Developments: Maternal and Child Health and Mental Retardation Planning Amendments of 1963" (Washington, DC, 1963), Mental Retardation Planning Project Collection, File 20, Box 3, H-34, UAMS Archive; 88th Congress, House of Representatives, Report No. 637, August 5, 1963, 8–9, File 20, Box 3, H-34, UAMS Archive; Edward D. Berkowitz, "The Politics of Mental Retardation during the Kennedy Administration," *Social Science Quarterly* 61 (June 1980): 128–143; Arkansas Children's Colony Board of Directors, Minutes, October 31, 1963, DDS Archive.

27. Eunice K. Shriver to David B. Ray, October 7, 1963, in the possession of David B. Ray.

28. David B. Ray Jr., Memorandum to Board of Directors, Arkansas Children's Colony, January 10, 1964, in the possession of David B. Ray.

29. Wilbur D. Mills to David B. Ray, February 24, 1964, in the possession of David B. Ray; Senator Lister Hill to David B. Ray, March 6, 1964, in the possession of David B. Ray; Conway *Log Cabin Democrat,* April 1, 1964.

30. Sargent Shriver to David B. Ray, December 5, 1965, in the possession of David B. Ray; Vice President Hubert H. Humphrey to Wilbur Cohen, August 31, 1965, in the possession of David B. Ray; Mental Retardation Facilities and Community Mental Health Centers Construction Act (PL 88-164, 1963); Ray interview, April 18, 1996; Braddock, *Federal Policy,* 172; David B. Ray, "Who Are the Mentally Retarded?" transcript of speech at conference in South Carolina, March 2, 1966, in the possession of David B. Ray; F. J. Weintraub et al., *Public Policy and the Education of Exceptional Children* (Reston, VA: Council for Exceptional Children, 1976), 100–108.

31. Ray, "Who Are the Mentally Retarded?"; Conway *Log Cabin Democrat,* December 1, 1967.

32. President's Committee on Mental Retardation, "MR 67: A First Report to the

President on the Nation's Progress and Remaining Great Needs in the Campaign to Combat Mental Retardation" (Washington, DC: GPO, 1967), 19–30; Weintraub et al., *Public Policy*, 101–102; President's Committee on Mental Retardation, "MR 68: The Edge of Change" (Washington, DC: GPO, 1968).

33. President's Committee on Mental Retardation, "MR 69: Toward Progress: The Story of a Decade" (Washington, DC: GPO, 1969), 9–30.

34. President's Committee on Mental Retardation, "MR 67"; Edwin W. Martin Jr., "Breakthrough for the Handicapped: Legislative History," *Exceptional Children* 34 (1968): 494, 497; Truemper, *A Century of Service*, 47, 70–71; A. P. Turnbull and H. R. Turnbull III, *Families, Professionals, and Exceptionality: A Special Partnership* (Columbus, OH: Merrill, 1986), 169; B. R. Gearhart and F. W. Litton, *The Trainable Retarded: A Foundations Approach* (St. Louis: C. V. Mosby, 1975), 11–12.

35. Gearhart and Litton, *Trainable Retarded*, 15–16; John Gliedman and William Roth, *The Unexpected Minority: Handicapped Children in America* (New York: Harcourt Brace Jovanovich, 1980), 173–178; The Education for All Handicapped Children Act (PL 94-142, 1975); Jane Knitzer, *Unclaimed Children: The Failure of Public Responsibility to Children and Adolescents in Need of Mental Health Services* (Washington, DC: Children's Defense Fund, 1982); Finch, "Deinstitutionalization," 36–47.

36. Elizabeth M. Boggs, "State Programming for the Mentally Deficient," *Community Organization, 1958* (New York: Columbia University Press, 1958), 138–139; H. Rutherford Turnbull III et al., "A Policy Analysis of 'Least Restrictive' Education of Handicapped Children," *Rutgers Law Journal* 14 (1983): 489–540.

37. Gliedman and Roth, *Unexpected Minority*, 3–4.

38. "Citizens Called on to Back Annual Horse Show," April 1958, CHDC scrapbooks; *Arkansas Gazette*, August 1, 1957; Charles E. Acuff, memorandum, April 15, 1965, in the possession of Charles E. Acuff; Orval E. Faubus, *Down from the Hills* (Little Rock: Pioneer, 1980), 187; Arkansas Association for Retarded Children Board of Directors, Minutes, July 28, 1960, in the possession of Sam Sanders, Little Rock; Arkansas Children's Colony, "Progress Report"; Arkansas Children's Colony Board of Directors, Minutes, August 10, 1965; April 22, 1967, DDS Archive; *Arkansas Democrat*, October 5, 1959; Ray, interview, March 5, 1968; "Keep Arkansas' Program of Proven Progress: Vote for Governor Orval E. Faubus," campaign leaflet, 1964, Arkansas History Commission, Little Rock.

Part V

The Promise and Problems of Community Placement

Back to a Beginning?

U.S. Supreme Court Decision on Capital Punishment and Mental Retardation (2002)

U.S. Supreme Court,
Atkins v. Virginia 122 S. Ct. 2242,
Decided 6/20/2002 6-3 for reversal,
Justices Stevens, O'Connor, Kennedy, Souter,
Ginsburg, and Breyer in the majority,
Justices Rehnquist, Scalia, and Thomas dissenting.

Justice John Paul Stevens delivered the opinion of the court.

Those mentally retarded persons who meet the law's requirements for criminal responsibility should be tried and punished when they commit crimes. Because of their disabilities in areas of reasoning, judgment, and control of their impulses, however, they do not act with the level of moral culpability that characterizes the most serious adult criminal conduct. Moreover, their impairments can jeopardize the reliability and fairness of capital proceedings against mentally retarded defendants. Presumably for these reasons, in the 13 years since we decided *Penry v. Lynaugh* 492 U.S. 302 (1989), the American public, legislators, scholars, and judges have deliberated over the question whether the death penalty should ever be imposed on a mentally retarded criminal. The consensus reflected in those deliberations informs our answer to the question presented by this case: whether such executions are "cruel and unusual punishments" prohibited by the Eighth Amendment to the Federal Constitution.

I

Petitioner, Daryl Renard Atkins, was convicted of abduction, armed robbery, and capital murder, and sentenced to death. At approximately midnight on

413

August 16, 1996, Atkins and William Jones, armed with a semiautomatic handgun, abducted Eric Nesbitt, robbed him of the money on his person, drove him to an automated teller machine in his pickup truck where cameras recorded their withdrawal of additional cash, then took him to an isolated location where he was shot eight times and killed. . . . At the penalty phase of the trial, the State introduced victim impact evidence and proved two aggravating circumstances: future dangerousness and "vileness of the offense." . . . In the penalty phase, the defense relied on one witness, Dr. Evan Nelson, a forensic psychologist who had evaluated Atkins before the trail and concluded that he was "mildly mentally retarded." His conclusion was based on interviews with people who knew Atkins, a review of school and court records, and the administration of a standard intelligence test which indicated that Atkins had a full-scale IQ of 59. The jury sentenced Atkins to death, but the Virginia Supreme court ordered a second sentencing hearing because the trial court had used a misleading verdict form. . . . At the resentencing, Dr. Nelson again testified. The State presented an expert rebuttal witness, Dr. Stanton Samenow, who expressed the opinion that Atkins was not mentally retarded, but rather was of "average intelligence, at least," and diagnosable as having antisocial personality disorder. The jury again sentenced Atkins to death. The Supreme Court of Virginia affirmed the imposition of the death penalty. Atkins did not argue before the Virginia Supreme Court that his sentence was disproportionate to penalties imposed for similar crimes in Virginia, but he did contend "that he is mentally retarded and thus cannot be sentenced to death." The majority of the state court rejected this contention, relying on our holding in *Penry*. The Court was "not willing to commute Atkins' sentence of death to life imprisonment merely because of his IQ score. . . ." Because of the gravity of the concerns expressed by the dissenters and in light of the dramatic shift in the state legislative landscape that has occurred in the past 13 years, we granted certiorari to revisit the issue that we first addressed in the *Penry* case.

II

The Eighth Amendment succinctly prohibits "excessive" sanctions. It provides: "Excessive bail shall not be required, nor excessive fines imposed, nor cruel and unusual punishments inflicted." In *Weems v. United States*, 217 U.S. 349 (1910) we held that a punishment of 12 years jailed in irons at hard and painful labor for the crime of falsifying records was excessive. . . . As Justice Stewart explained in *Robinson* [*Robinson v. California*, 370 U.S. 667 (1962)]: "Even one day in prison would be a cruel and unusual punishment for the 'crime' of having a common cold." . . .

Guided by our approach in these cases, we shall first review the judgment of legislatures that have addressed the suitability of imposing the death penalty on the mentally retarded and then consider reasons for agreeing or disagreeing with their judgment.

III

The parties have not called our attention to any state legislative consideration of the suitability of imposing the death penalty on mentally retarded offenders prior to 1986. In that year, the public reaction to the execution of a mentally retarded murderer in Georgia apparently led to the enactment of the first state statute prohibiting such executions. In 1988, when Congress enacted legislation reinstating the federal death penalty, it expressly provided that a "sentence of death shall not be carried out upon a person who is mentally retarded." In 1989, Maryland enacted a similar prohibition. It was in that year that we decided *Penry*, and concluded that those two state enactments, "even when added to the 14 States that have rejected capital punishment completely, do not provide sufficient evidence at present of a national consensus." 492 U.S., at 334.

Much has changed since then. Responding to the national attention received by the Bowden execution [Jerome Bowden, a convicted felon with mental retardation, was executed in Georgia in 1986] and our decision in *Penry*, state legislatures across the country began to address the issue. In 1990 Kentucky and Tennessee enacted statutes similar to those in Georgia and Maryland, as did New Mexico in 1991, and Arkansas, Colorado, Washington, Indiana, and Kansas in 1993 and 1994. In 1995, when New York reinstated its death penalty, it emulated the Federal Government by expressly exempting the mentally retarded. Nebraska followed suit in 1998. There appear to have been no similar enactments during the next two years, but in 2000 and 2001 six more States—South Dakota, Arizona, Connecticut, Florida, Missouri, and North Carolina—joined the procession. The Texas Legislature unanimously adopted a similar bill and bills have passed at least one house in other states, including Virginia and Nevada.

It is not so much the number of these States that is significant, but the consistency of the direction of change. Given the well-known fact that anti-crime legislation is far more popular than legislation providing protection for persons guilty of violent crime, the large number of States prohibiting the execution of mentally retarded persons (and the complete absence of States passing legislation reinstating the power to conduct such executions) provides powerful evidence that today our society views mentally retarded offenders as categorically less culpable than the average criminal. The evidence carries even greater force when it is noted that the legislatures that have addressed the issue have voted overwhelmingly in favor of the prohibition. Moreover, even in those States that allow the execution of mentally retarded offenders, the practice is uncommon. Some States, for example New Hampshire and New Jersey, continue to authorize executions, but none has been carried out in decades. And it appears that even among those States that regularly execute offenders and that have no prohibition with regard to the mentally retarded, only five have executed offenders possessing a known IQ less than 70 since we decided *Penry*. The practice, therefore, has become truly unusual, and it is fair to say that a national consensus has developed against it.

To the extent there is serious disagreement about the execution of mentally retarded offenders, it is in determining which offenders are in fact retarded. In this case, for instance, the Commonwealth of Virginia disputes that Atkins suffers from mental retardation. Not all people who claim to be mentally retarded will be so impaired as to fall within the range of mentally retarded offenders about whom there is a national consensus. As was our approach in *Ford v. Wainwright*, with regard to insanity, "we leave to the States the task of developing appropriate ways to enforce the constitutional restriction upon its execution of sentences." 477 U.S. 399.

IV

This consensus unquestionably reflects widespread judgment about the relative culpability of mentally retarded offenders, and the relationship between mental retardation and penological purposes served by the death penalty. Additionally, it suggests that some characteristics of mental retardation undermine the strength of the procedural protections that our capital jurisprudence steadfastly guards.

As discussed above, clinical definitions of mental retardation require not only subaverage intellectual functioning, but also significant limitations in adaptive skills such as communication, self-care, and self-direction that became manifest before age 18. Mentally retarded persons frequently know the difference between right and wrong and are competent to stand trial. Because of their impairments, however, by definition they have diminished capacities to understand and process information, to communicate, to abstract from mistakes and learn from experience, to engage in logical reasoning, to control impulses, and to understand the reactions of others. There is no evidence that they are more likely to engage in criminal activities than others, but there is abundant evidence that they often act on impulse rather than pursuant to a premeditated plan, and that in group settings they are followers rather than leaders. Their deficiencies do not warrant an exemption from criminal sanctions, but they do diminish their personal culpability.

In light of these deficiencies, our death penalty jurisprudence provides two reasons consistent with the legislative consensus that the mentally retarded should be categorically excluded from execution. First, there is a serious question as to whether either justification that we have recognized as a basis for the death penalty applies to mentally retarded offenders. *Gregg v. Georgia*, 428 U.S. 153 (1976) identified "retribution and deterrence of capital crimes by prospective offenders" as the social purposes served by the death penalty. Unless the imposition of the death penalty on a mentally retarded person "measurably contributes to one or both of these goals, it 'is nothing more than the purposeless and needless imposition of pain and suffering,' and hence an unconstitutional punishment." *Enmund*, 458 U.S., at 798.

With respect to retribution—the interest in seeing that the offender gets his "just deserts"—the severity of the appropriate punishment necessarily depends on the culpability of the offender. Since *Gregg*, our jurisprudence has consistently confined the imposition of the death penalty to a narrow category of the most serious crimes. For example, in *Godfrey v. Georgia*, 446 U.S. 420 (1980), we set aside a death sentence because the petitioner's crimes did not reflect "a consciousness materially more 'depraved' than that of any person guilty of murder." Id, at 433. If the culpability of the average murderer is insufficient to justify the most extreme sanction available to the State, the lesser culpability of the mentally retarded offender surely does not merit that form of retribution. Thus, pursuant to our narrowing jurisprudence, which seeks to ensure that only the most deserving of execution are put to death, an exclusion for the mentally retarded is appropriate.

With respect to deterrence—the interest in preventing capital crimes by prospective offenders—"it seems likely that 'capital punishment can serve as a deterrent only when the murder is a result of premeditation and deliberation,'" *Enmund*, 458 U.S. at 799. Exempting the mentally retarded from that punishment will not affect the "cold calculus that precedes the decision" of other potential murderers. *Gregg*, 428 U.S. at 186. Indeed, that sort of calculus is at the opposite end of the spectrum from the behavior of mentally retarded offenders. The theory of deterrence in capital sentencing is predicated upon the notion that the increased severity of the punishment will inhibit criminal actors from carrying out murderous conduct. Yet it is the same cognitive and behavioral impairments that make these defendants less morally culpable—for example, the diminished ability to understand and process information, to learn from experience, to engage in logical reasoning, or to control impulses—that also make it less likely that they can process the information of the possibility of execution as a penalty and, as a result, control their conduct based upon that information. Nor will exempting the mentally retarded from execution lessen the deterrent effect of the death penalty with respect to offenders who are not mentally retarded. Such individuals are unprotected by the exemption and will continue to face the threat of execution. Thus, executing the mentally retarded will not measurably further the goal of deterrence.

The reduced capacity of mentally retarded offenders provides a second justification for a categorical rule making such offenders ineligible for the death penalty. The risk "that the death penalty will be imposed in spite of factors which may call for a less severe penalty," *Lockett v. Ohio*, 438 U.S. 586 (1978), is enhanced, not only by the possibility of false confessions, but also by the lesser ability of mentally retarded defendants to make a persuasive showing of mitigation in the face of prosecutorial evidence of one or more aggravating factors. Mentally retarded defendants may be less able to give meaningful assistance to their counsel and are typically poor witnesses, and their demeanor may create an unwarranted impression of lack of remorse for their crimes. As *Penry* demonstrated, moreover, reliance on mental retardation as a mitigating factor can be a two-edged sword that may enhance the likelihood that the aggravating factor of future dangerousness will be found by the jury. 492 U.S., at 323–325. Mentally retarded defendants in the aggregate face a special risk of wrongful execution.

Our independent evaluation of the issue reveals no reason to disagree with the judgment of "the legislatures that have recently addressed the matter" and concluded that death is not a suitable punishment for a mentally retarded criminal. We are not persuaded that the execution of mentally retarded criminals will measurably advance the deterrent or the retributive purpose of the death penalty. Construing and applying the Eighth Amendment in light of our "evolving standards of decency," we therefore conclude that such punishment is excessive and that the Constitution "places a substantial restriction on the State's power to take the life" of a mentally retarded offender. *Ford,* 477 U.S., at 405.

The judgment of the Virginia Supreme Court is reversed and the case is remanded for further proceedings not inconsistent with this opinion.

It is so ordered.

17

Historical Social Geography

Deborah S. Metzel

"Scale," in historical social geography, is not constant but instead suggests that social relations are both absolute and relative. The locations of both institutions and group homes for mentally retarded people have signaled different degrees of exclusion as social policy and societal perceptions have changed.

This chapter aims to present an analysis of the social geography that can be seen in the locations of service sites for people with mental retardation. For the most part, we focus on the formal services provided by institutions and formal community services. Informal services in the communities, provided by what are now called "natural supports" and generic community services, remain a mystery, since there is little record of them in the historical landscape. By examining the spatial outcomes of social policies for people with mental retardation, we can establish a historical social geography that helps us to understand present-day social geographies and leads us to consider the significance of where people are placed in relation to one another.

The Social Policies and Spatial Outcomes for People with Mental Retardation

The link between formal social policies for people with mental retardation and the spatial outcomes of particular locations can be tracked through a variety of historical documents on the two formal service systems: state institutions and local community services. Education, custodial care and socioeconomic class are entangled constants that have played major roles in both service systems. The social geography based on the differentiation of

420

the degrees and types of mental retardation is also important but is not addressed in this chapter.

Formal services developed as mental retardation began to be differentiated as a particular type of social "problem" that could and should be treated. Usually physicians, early professionals in the field, created the mental retardation services landscape, both figuratively and literally, through the professional societies, the publications, and, of course, the physical institutions that expressed different social policies throughout time. Except for public special education, formal community services developed as extensions of institutions and were intended to help prevent more admissions into those already crowded facilities. Meanwhile, provided by families, other relatives, neighbors and others, informal and unrecorded services helped those people whose retardation was not considered an extraordinary problem or whose families could not afford formal services. (See Figure 17.1.)

Figure 17.1. Period, policy, and place

Period	Policy	Place
Colonial period–1850s	Indoor or outdoor relief	Communities
1850s–1870s	Education in schools	Communities, then rural locations
1870s–1880s	Education and protection in asylums	Rural locations
1890s–1920s	Protection in institutions	Rural locations
	Public school education and community supervision	Communities
1930s–1950s	Custodial care in institutions	Rural locations
	Nascent, parent-organized, community-based services	Communities
1950s–1970s	Custodial care continues	Rural locations
	Expansion of community-based services	Communities
1970s–1990s	Deinstitutionalization	Communities
	Rapid growth of community-based services	Communities

The Colonial Period–1850s: Outdoor and Indoor Relief

There is little to indicate that, prior to the mid-1800s, people with mental retardation were treated differently than other dependent people in America. Poverty, caused by any number of conditions, was usually the root cause of dependency, and it was remedied by either "outdoor" or "indoor" relief.

"Outdoor relief" meant that families, relatives, neighbors, and the general community financially supported dependent people in local households (Scheerenberger 1983, 99), keeping them in their midst "without disrupting their lives" (Rothman 1971, 30). For example, in 1661, "Iddiot" John Deanne was "boarded out" to a Mr. Richard House (Deutsch 1937, 48). In contrast, dependent people who used "indoor relief" were likely to be placed in an almshouse, house of correction, or hospital, which was often located in the midst of the community. In Boston, in the late 1660s, the poorhouse was at the head of the Commons.

The 1850s–1870s:
Education for Feeble-Minded Children

After success in educating feeble-minded children was impressively demonstrated in Europe in the 1800s, private and states schools were opened in the United States to educate and train children, who, it was believed, would then return to their families as productive family members. Usually families paid for their child's education, though sometimes the state provided the funding. Private schools were located in the homes of the physicians or teachers who operated them, making their location a direct consequence of the physicians' or teachers' own choice of where to live. This was feasible since the schools usually did not have more than twenty students, but eventually the schools accepted more students, often making relocation necessary.

In addition to private schools, many states opened their own training schools as the success of and the growing need for such schools became evident. Their early locations reflected common sense, the optimistic social policy of providing education for feeble-minded children, and politicians' self-serving humanitarianism. Some town and urban locations were selected purposely, perhaps on the advice of Edward Seguin, who recommended that the "institution's physical plant should be located where future inmates are born and raised" (Talbot 1964 in Scheerenberger 1975, 10). Capital cities, such as Albany, New York, Columbus, Ohio, and Trenton, New Jersey, were favored sites for training schools, since the state legislators could conveniently oversee and show off the institutions they supported. In an article entitled "Historical Notes on Institutions for the Mentally Defective," the unknown author commented:

It is interesting to note that this first institution was located near Albany, the legislative seat of the State. The reason is found in the first report of the Trustees when they write, "As the enterprise was experimental there seemed great propriety in its being conducted so near the Capitol that the members of the Legislature might from time to time examine it and become acquainted with its success." (*Journal of Psycho-Asthenics* 1940, 188)

But what about the children who were not sent to training schools? "The single overwhelming feature of the changes in policy toward retarded people between 1850 and 1875 is that they led to very little change in the daily lives of most of those individuals. Most mentally retarded people, especially those with severe retardation, continued to live in almshouses, with their families, or elsewhere in the community" (Ferguson 1994).

The 1870s–1880s:
Education and Protection in the Asylums

The residential training school was intended to be a temporary situation, and it was for some children who did return home. However, not all children were "cured" of their mental retardation, and superintendents were pressured to keep them, as well as to admit additional children identified as "incurable" or "unteachable" because of their severe disabilities. The training schools acquired a second function when the social policy became that of protective custody; by the 1880s, the popular view of idiocy was dominated by the idea of the "moral idiot," a person who was vulnerable to "criminal exploitation and vice" (Trent 1994, 21). This view was crucial in transforming the schools into custodial institutions (Trent 1994, 20). Operating in the same physical place, the ideologically incompatible policies of education and custody began an administrative and management conflict that plagued state schools for almost a century.

A more than fivefold increase in the number of feeble-minded or idiot people in the general population was reported in the decade from 1870 to 1880 (from 14,485 to 76,895) (Johnson 1898, 31–32), indicating the growing problem. The concept of "institutions" evolved as the original training schools and asylums were forced to grow in order to meet the various needs of the residents and to facilitate the accompanying administrative duties.

Siting institutions in the countryside was the obvious choice to reinforce the trends of isolation, enlargement, and economization that were consequences of the policy of protective custody (Wolfensberger 1972, 29). This resulted in the ubiquitous institutional landscape in North America.

The 1890s–1920s: Protection of Society, Public Education, and Community Supervision

Two different social policies prevailed from the 1890s to the 1920s—custodial care of people with mental retardation for the protection of society and the start of formal community services, most notably special education. Segregation, in different degrees, was used to accomplish these goals, illustrating the variations in scale of distances.

Custodial Care on Behalf of Society

As the nineteenth century drew to a close, the original educational function of the training schools was obscured by the rise in custodial care, and the idea of permanent custody took hold. Those who could earn their keep at the "schools" did so. This arrangement "provided a life-time home and useful employment for the pupil" (Kuhlmann 1940, 11), which was challenged occasionally, but not strongly enough to stop the practice. The shift in functions was marked by the replacement of "schools" by "institutions." By 1900, there were

> twenty-five State schools, almost universally spoken of as institutions. . . . The inmates number something over 15,000. The institution now usually includes an administration building or wing, a school plant with class rooms and training equipment, separate dormitories arranged for inmates, classified according to age, sex, and of mental deficiency, or physical condition. It has shops for industrial training and land for farming and dairying. It has its own power, light, and heating plant kitchen, bakery, and laundry, as well as hospital where at times attendants and nurses receive special training for their duties in the institution. In its major physical aspects the institution has already come of age. Abandonment of the idea of cure was the important factor in the development of the physical plant. (Kuhlmann 1940, 11–12)

During this time, another justification for custodial care emerged as a result of increasing urbanization and immigration. The professional perspective on mental retardation changed radically as class status continued to be an issue in the United States. Histories of the social policies of mental retardation from the 1890s through the 1920s recount the assumed correlation between feeblemindedness and the burgeoning lower classes and, disproportionately, immigrant families. Instead of viewing children as potential victims of their immoral surroundings, the children were labeled "mental defectives" who threatened society by their inherent immorality; society assumed that they would likely reproduce (unlike those with more severe mental retardation) unless they were "controlled." The problem was that

> mental defectives were viewed as a menace to civilization, incorrigible at home, burdens to the school, sexually promiscuous, breeders of feeble-minded offspring, victims and spreaders of poverty, degeneracy, crime and disease. (Kanner 1964, 85)

While children from the lower classes were targeted for institutionalization and the rich could pay for live-in services or private facilities, middle-class families were literally caught in the middle. During the 1920s, both the cost of services and family pride prevented middle-class families from applying to social agencies for help (Smith 1922, 59); institutionalization became the solution for some middle-class families seeking to preserve their respectability and status despite the liability of a child with mental retardation, a condition closely associated with the lower classes.

The protection of society and family overrode the protection of the "moral idiot" and was the argument used to justify superintendents' requests for larger buildings and more space. The first sizable increase in the institutionalized population occurred from the mid-1900s through the early 1920s. Still neatly accomplished by the locating of the institutions in rural areas, segregation was now more than a mere feature of social policy; it became the geographical solution much as sterilization became the physical solution.

Rural locations also offered the equally desirable opportunity for agricultural production, a principal cost-efficiency measure. The decision to build an institution "out among the hills of Venango County, PA," in Polk, Pennsylvania, illustrates the importance of opportunities for farming in the choice of location:

Resolved: That the legislature of Pennsylvania be advised to establish a State Institution for the care of the idiotic and feebleminded children in Western Pennsylvania, to be located on the western slope of the Allegheny mountains; and be it further Resolved: That it is the opinion of this Board that one of the essential features of this institution should be the development of the agricultural industry, for the practical or entire support of a large number of inmates; also the development of such trade industries as shall be within the compass of the inmates' capacities. (*Journal of Psycho-Asthenics,* "The New Institution for Feeble-Minded of Western Pennsylvania," 1898, 129)

Agriculture also played an important part in the "colony" programs, with farm colonies established as early as the 1880s for the purpose of "provid[ing] suitable homes and employment to the boys, and secondly to supply the home institution with fresh food" (*Journal of Psycho-Asthenics,* "From the Institutions," 1896, 69). As satellites of the parent institutions, colonies were associated with a parent institution, and their locations were chosen on the basis of the suitability and cost of available farm land. They were not necessarily physically close to the parent institution.

Charles Bernstein greatly expanded the colony program during World War I until the onset of the Great Depression in 1929. In addition to farm colonies for boys and men, domestic colonies for girls and women and industrial colonies were established for both genders in areas where labor shortages existed. The colonies included housing in the communities where the "boys and girls" worked, which freed up beds for incoming residents at the parent institutions.

In 1914, the first domestic colony for girls was "located in a rented dwelling in a good residential section of the city of Rome, two miles from the institution" (Davies 1930, 263). Its success created a demand for others to be located elsewhere in New York (Davies 1930, 266). An industrial colony for boys opened in 1917 in Kossuth, New York; "occup[ying] a large corner dwelling on one of the main streets, the colony has been favorably received by the townspeople" (Davies 1930, 251). The domestic and industrial colonies, segregated but located in the midst of communities, reveal that townspeople generally accepted the people with mental retardation to some degree (mainly as workers), and institutions continued to exert control over every aspect of their patients' lives. Admissions continued at the parent institutions as well, particularly when informal and formal services were unavailable. Then, as now, the death of parents created a crisis for the retarded person that the community was not always able to resolve, though this was a reason for only a "small minority of new patients" (Vanuxem 1925, 18–19).

Ironically, at the same time that the institutions maintained productive colonies in towns and cities that led to patients' parole, they also admitted women of child-bearing age who had formerly been employed:

> Another type of the adult defective that presents a problem is the woman who has been out in the industrial world. . . . Because of the fact that they have been wholly or partially self supporting, they are restless and dissatisfied since they are under the restraint of an institution and no longer receive remuneration for their work. (Vanuxem 1925, 18–19)

Community Supervision: The Professional Reach of the Institutions

In the 1910s, the practice of "parole," or discharge back to the communities, had begun. Particularly after people had proved their competency and good behavior in the colonies, paroled was recommended. Places for parolees to live were found with families, in boarding houses, or on their own, and social workers and other professionals from the institutions visited them periodically to report on their progress. Once it was established that they were living safely and productively in the community, they were formally paroled and disconnected from the institutions, though some maintained relationships with staff and friends at the institutions.

Not much is known about the daily lives of children and adults with retardation who lived in the community, other than what impassioned and motivated superintendents ironically claimed, usually in order to rationalize the expansion of the institutions. In a speech intended to demonstrate the problem of the unserved, one superintendent claimed that the uninstitutionalized "crowd our schools, walk our streets, and fill alike jails and positions of trust, reproducing their kind and vitiating the moral atmosphere" (Barr 1899, 210). To the dismay of another superintendent (Taylor 1899, 77), many parents were unwilling to admit that their children were different, and they resisted professional intervention. Despite the possible hardships, the parents were more than willing to raise their children themselves.

Public education was the first formal and large-scale community service to be offered to children with mental retardation. To acculturate the immigrants who had been arriving since the 1890s, most of the states passed compulsory education laws by 1900. This had the unintended but powerful consequence of identifying children with mental retardation who otherwise would have not been so labeled (Weiner 1993, 254), alerting the professionals to the extent of mental retardation in the general population. At the annual meetings, presenters from Cleveland, Ohio, New Haven, Connecticut, St. Louis, Missouri, and San Francisco, California were among those who boasted about their city's special education classes in the first quarter of the twentieth century. These reports revealed the persistence of segregation; some students had separate classes in shared school buildings, and others attended totally separate schools:

> The special schools are organized with the idea that not only should the children be segregated from normal children in their class instruction but that they should also be segregated from the regular elementary school environment. Consequently nearly all of the schools have been established in locations set apart from regular elementary schools. (Wiley 1922, 231)

While Wiley occasionally questioned the expense of operating segregated special classes, segregation was not otherwise explicitly justified, except as a mention of the importance of separate schools for these children because they were less crowded (Wiley 1922, 232). At the same time, he did not deny that "the experience" of the three regular elementary schools that contained three special schools for children with mental retardation "had not been unsatisfactory" (Wiley 1922, 232), perhaps suggesting an initial feeling of doubt about segregation. Nonetheless, the preference for segregation, despite its cost, was simply unquestioned.

Reports describing public school classes and school buildings not surprisingly revealed a concentration in lower-income neighborhoods, some of which were heavily populated by foreign-born families. For example, in the neighborhood of Locust Point in the city of Baltimore, Maryland, Public School No. 76 served children whose families "not uncommonly use the German, Polish and Hungarian languages" (Fairbank 1933, 178). In Cleveland, Ohio, several classes were in Little Italy.

The provision of public education for some retarded people did not resolve the predicament of the other unserved children and adults in the community who were assumed to need institutionalization. When, during World War I, it was determined that the rate of mental retardation in the general population in the United States was 3 percent, extrainstitutional services were promoted as an alternative to institutionalization. As early as 1918, at the annual session of the American Association for the Study of the Feeble-minded, Dr. Guy Fernald presented a paper titled "The Problem of the Extra-Institutional Feebleminded in the Community" (1918, 82–91). Significantly, by calling community services "extrainstitutional," he reinforced the role of institutions as the professional location of mental retardation services.

Outpatient diagnostic clinics, called "traveling clinics," were located both on the grounds of state institutions and in cities and were staffed by field workers from the institutions. Generic community agencies such as "Child Placing Agencies, County Agents for State Charities Aid Associations, Detention Homes, [and] School Nurses" (Fuller 1921, 82) referred children and adults to these clinics. The clinics' main function was to evaluate children and young adults for admission to the institutions as part of an attempt to stem the flow of admissions, given the fact that the institutions were already crowded. Field workers began to advise parents on how to take care of their children and sometimes tried to arrange help from a local charitable agency as other means of helping the unserved in the community.

Slowly, there was an increase in the number of reports on formal community services. In 1924, among the eight sessions of the forty-eighth annual meeting of the American Association for the Study of the Feeble-minded, two sessions were organized on community services, one titled "Section on Community Management of the Feeble-Minded," with four presenters, and one called "Section on Special Schools and Education Problems," with three presenters. Of course, there was the traditional section on the administration and construction of institutions, which continued to support the institutional system.

Though not strong enough to dismantle the institutions, the shift toward increasing community services was the result of several factors. First, public special education was able to take over the original reason for the institutionalization of children, who would now likely be labeled with mild mental retardation. Second, there simply was not room for everyone who "needed" institutionalization, so, under institutional supervision, services were extended into the communities to meet the need of those not institutionalized. Third, toward the end of this period, mental retardation was found in families of the "better sort . . . [whose] parents are of average or high intelligence" (Davies 1930, 158). Dr. Fernald, through careful study of many children, determined that "fully half of all cases of mental retardation [were] of non-hereditary type" (Davies 1930, 159). The "new" nonhereditary type of mental retardation, its new association with a "better sort" of family, and Fernald's pronouncement were likely the seeds for the creation of parents' organizations by middle-class families. Indeed, the first parent group was organized in 1933 in Cleveland, Ohio, for children excluded from public school; by the early 1940s, ten other parent groups had been founded, though two groups comprised parents of children in institutions (Farber 1968, 131–132).

There still were the those who were living "harmless lives in the homes and communities" (Hoakley 1922, 118), invisible in the social geography of mental retardation. Doll (1929, 164) acknowledged that many of the unserved

> were at large in the community. No doubt many of these individuals are receiving, or have at some time received, charitable assistance and community supervision of some kind or other. But such assistance is not provided as an organized program of complete control. . . . It follows that many of the feebleminded are getting along somehow or other in the community, "on their own."

He seemed unaware of the irony that satisfactory informal or generic community services were serving the unserved sufficiently.

The 1930s–1950s: Custodial Care and Community Services Expand

The Great Depression and World War II diverted attention and energy from social problems that had received a public hearing in earlier, more peaceful and stable times, and custodial care continued even while communities were expected to do more.

Perpetuation of Custodial Care

The popularity of institutionalization in rural locations was not challenged; in fact, it allowed for the expansion and perpetuation of the institutions (Wolfensberger 1972, 55–56). Rural locations continued to be popular as the ideal sites for new institutions, and service designs were obviously rationalized for this decision. Superintendent Roselle (1941, 465) claimed that

> the traditional large congregate institutional units must give way to an institutional plant that would parallel, as closely as possible a normal community; for it is to house children, and "children have the inalienable right to be reared in conditions approaching as closely as possible those of a normal home and community."

His description of the site makes it clear that the availability of agricultural work dominated the choice of locations. Out of a total of 1,500 acres, "1200 acres of contiguous hilltop farm and grazing land for the large farm enterprise [were] planned from the first as an essential part of the institution" (Roselle 1941, 466). Even in the late 1950s, good farm land was an important reason for choosing a site (Ray 1959, 373).

Shifting the Responsibility for Services to the Communities

Needy but unserved people were a never-ending concern for the professionals in the field of mental retardation. They began to place the responsibility for service on the local communities, and superintendents and other professionals began to look at the communities as services sites.

People were not automatically admitted to residential care, despite the expansion of the institutions. Fuller (1921, 83) reported that

> Institutional care is recommended only as a last resort and, in spite of the fact that a number of cases have been presented to the clinic for diagnosis with institutional commitment in view, only a very few of the cases interviewed have applied for commitment to the institutions for mental defectives and, in most of these cases, the reason for commitment has been the family conditions have been so poor that the patient could not have the proper supervision and care there, and to give the patient a chance to

improve, a change of environment, such as an institution or colony life, was necessary.

In an address at the forty-sixth annual meeting of the American Association on Mental Deficiency, the association's president blamed the development and perpetuation of institutions on the public's great desire for custodial care, despite the protests of superintendents and the existence of laws to prevent the admittance of those who needed such care (Kuhlmann 1940). Another superintendent hoped that

> communities as far as possible [would] meet the problems of the detective in their own midst through better homes, better community recreation, schools better adapted to serve the needs of all the children of all the people; to the end that no child shall be committed to any institution" (Roselle 1941, 471)

The push was on for communities to take responsibility for improving retarded children's lives at a time when the institutions could no longer serve all those who needed help.

The 1950s–1970s: Custodial Care and Parents' Organization of Community Services

The ongoing demand for custodial care and education once again were the dominant elements from the 1950s to the 1970s. In those years, "state authorities built, refurbished, and added to more public facilities than in any other period of their American history" (Trent 1994, 250), driven by the lengthening waiting lists for admission to the state institutions. The Mental Retardation Facilities and Community Mental Health Centers Construction Act of 1963 (P.L. 88-164) authorized federal funds for new construction from 1964 through 1968; consequently, the number of people who were institutionalized rose to an all-time peak of 194,650, in 1967 (Lakin, Prouty, and Bruininks 1996, 24). This law provided only for the construction of new facilities, leaving the states responsible for ongoing operational and other costs. Undoubtedly, state legislatures that failed to provide the funds needed or, in some cases, reduced funding (Trent 1994, 259) contributed to the notorious conditions exposed in the 1970s.

When buildings were added to existing sites, they occupied formerly vacant spaces on both rural and urban institutional grounds. For entirely new institutions, the trend was to decentralize huge state institutions and scatter facilities regionally throughout the state. One of the benefits of decentralization (not, however, a well-defined goal) was that residents would be closer to their families and home communities (Lakin, Bruininks, and Sigford 1981, ix).

Middle-Class Families and Education

Once again, education played a significant role in changing social policy. In the years after World War II, white, middle-class parents of children with moderate and severe mental retardation founded organizations for the express purpose of educating their children who had been excluded from local public-school special education classes. By making the disability of their middle-class children a medical and thereby a charitable and respectable concern, the parents further disengaged it from its historical association with the undesirable lower classes and also distanced it from professional social control (Farber 1968, 147 and 139). Descriptions of such parent-based groups from the 1950s indicate that the members were predominantly white middle-class parents, who would influence the location of services in the community.

This second formal service system for mentally retarded people was created as parent groups grew in numbers. Nursery schools, schools, day activity centers, sheltered workshops, and recreation programs were established in places that did not encroach on residential neighborhoods but that were safe. The community programs served relatively small numbers of children and young adults in otherwise unused and invisible niches in middle-class communities, such as church or school basements. When vacant school buildings were available, they were used, also.

During this time, residential services were not developed in the communities, since the children and young adults with mental retardation were dispersed throughout the neighborhoods, living with their families or sometimes in foster homes. It was not until the 1970s that homes for people with mental retardation (as well as homes for people with other disabilities or socially devalued characteristics or behaviors) became a volatile issue; unlike schools, vocational centers, and recreation programs, homes could be located next door to anyone and were likely to be occupied by people who were unknown in the neighborhood.

The 1970s–1990s: Deinstitutionalization and the Community Services: Convergence

In the 1970s, institutions and community services operated as parallel service systems for people with mental retardation, providing education, recreation, day activities, vocational training, transportation, and residential programs. Both systems competed for state funds, and the parent-based service organizations were supported by charitable donations, as well.

Return to the Community

The profound public and systematic failure of the institutions was the catalyst for other forces that ultimately led to the deinstitutionalization of people with mental retardation. Had reform efforts, which were too late and too little, been at all successful, the institutions might have survived. Deinstitutionalization was the outcome of the failure of the institutions, hastened as well by other forces: parent advocacy, judicial activism, legislative action, the costs of care, and the acceptance of the ideology of normalization (Vitello and Soskin 1985, 26). Popular public figures such as John F. Kennedy and Hubert Humphrey spoke openly about their family members who had mental retardation, somewhat reducing the stigma borne by other American families.

Optimistically, deinstitutionalization was called a "total reorientation of society to the care and treatments of mentally retarded persons" (President's Committee on Mental Retardation 1976, 22–23), with the burden of change placed on society. Except for arguments related to cost, the other forces all represented change in attitudes toward people with mental retardation, mostly among those who were already closely connected to people with mental retardation. People who did not know someone with mental retardation in the community were likely to perceive mental retardation as a condition that necessitated far-away institutionalization.

It took civil rights and legislative actions to bring people with mental retardation under the equal protection of the laws as American citizens. The Federal Court decision in *Wyatt v. Stickney* (1972) resulted in the important ruling that people should be served in the least restrictive environment, specifically including the community. The decision in *Halderman v. Pennhurst State School and Hospital* (1977) established the community as the site of services for people with mental retardation and disallowed that condition as sole justification for institutionalization. Though changes in social policy were hard won and had to be enforced by legal rulings, local communities, rather than institutions, were now the sites for the implementation of official policy. People in institutions began to be moved to places in the community, in the process overburdening the slowly expanding community services.

Locations and Community Services

The locations of the first services organized by the parents were chosen to minimize the need for travel between family homes and the programs, since parents themselves initially had to transport their own children. Certainly the cost of space, as well as safety and centrality, was a consideration, but, generally, locations were chosen that were not unduly far from the homes of the families that would be using the services. Therefore, it was not surprising that, when it came time to select residential locations for group homes, apartments, and other domiciles, parent organizations again chose middle-class or upper-class areas for their aging children (Metzel 1998). As residential services expanded, apartments and homes were located fairly close to other community programs, such as sheltered workshops, maintaining, on a broader scale, strong ties to the earlier community locations of the parent-based community services system.

In one East Coast city where a suburban neighborhood had grown up around a previously rural institution, former patients' ties to the institutional system were evident. Residents who left the institution wanted to be able to get to their jobs there or to visit staff or other friends who remained behind, so proximity to the institution was an important factor in their selection of neighborhood (Metzel 1998).

As the twentieth century drew to a close, the social geography of people with mental retardation was, more than ever, strongly driven by the meaning of community. If we accept the premise that community is defined by social ties, meaningful interpersonal relationships, and belonging, then, for people with mental retardation, there have been two distinct communities. For most formerly institutionalized people, their community was the institution. Many had been removed from their families and institutionalized as children. If they were institutionalized in a rural, out-of-the-way state institution, it is likely that their relationships with their families were severely or totally disrupted and replaced by relationships with staff and other residents. The physical location of the community was, therefore, the physical location of the institution. As services for people with mental retardation began to shift from centralized institutions to the community, the institutional community was itself relocated. However, some people maintained their social community at the institution, especially if they continued to be employed at the institution or if their friends were still there.

For children and adults who never had been institutionalized, their community consisted primarily of their families and, increasingly, the not-for-profit mental retardation agencies, which broadened their roles as service providers to meet growing unserved needs. The physical and social community of these never-institutionalized people has been wherever they, their families, and the mental retardation agencies were located.

Either way, lifelong involvement with mental retardation service systems has meant that other, informal supports have been supplanted by the social relationships that originated in the mental retardation service system. This was not the intention of those who advocated that the retarded remain in the community.

"Where Is the Community?"

Since the 1970s, "community" has been the goal of social policies for people with mental retardation. The rejection of institutions for the care and treatment of people with mental retardation meant that, by default, the community was the only appropriate place for people with mental retardation. But, as people re-entered the physical community, the concept of community was questioned. In an early study of residential services, Baker, Selzer, and Selzer (1977, 215) eloquently summarized the meaning of community, identifying the importance of human relationships as the basis of community:

> The assumption in relocating services in the community was that a more dignified, normalized way of life would be provided for retarded citizens. However, the concept of community was not well defined in this assumption. Where is the community? Who comprises the retarded adult's community? (underlined in the original)

The variations in the meaning of community reflect what did and did not occur in the lives of people with mental retardation that led to changes in service designs, delivery, and, of course, locations. The meaning of community can be examined by changes in mental retardation policy since the 1970s using terms that Agnew, a geographer, has used to conceptualized place: location, locale, and sense of place (1987, 28). His concept of place forms one-half of the framework for understanding the refinement of "community" (see Figure 17.2).

Figure 17.2. Concepts of community and mental retardation policy

Community	Mental Retardation Policy
Location	Normalization and deinstitutionalization
Locale	Community integration
Sense of Place	Inclusion: Membership and belonging

Community as Location

"Community" has been defined as "the geographical area encompassing the settings for social interaction as defined by social and economic processes operating at a wider scale" (Agnew 1987, 28). Community as a location corresponds to the depiction of community as the antithesis of confinement. Knoll's identification of the issue in the mental retardation field of the 1970s and early 1980s as "the institutions versus community" (1990, 246) reinforced the dichotomy between the locations of people with mental retardation and those of their services and supports.

Communities were clearly viewed as sites of goods and services. As the movement toward deinstitutionalization took hold, in 1969, Dybwad described the likely neighborhoods as "upper lower-class neighborhoods of medium density and with a large array of resources (post office, library, churches, playgrounds, movies, stores, etc.)." He also noted that "Thinly populated upper-class suburban areas beyond easy walking distance from community resources would probably be least suited" (1969, 387–389). A service provider that opened several homes in the early 1970s claimed that "The most important consideration in terms of location is what is available outside the house in a particular neighborhood or area" (Gerry 1975, 30–31). The idea of community as a source of goods and services was irrevocably captured when the U.S. District Court of Pennsylvania, in the case of *Halderman v. Pennhurst State School and Hospital* (1977), rejected the lack of community services as justification for the institutionalization of people with mental retardation. At the same time, education, the service that had been used to justify the institutionalization of children (Boggs et al. 1988, 246), was eliminated as a reason by the passage of the Education for All Handicapped Children Act (P.L. 94-142), in 1975.

Although they were now to be educated in the community, for the most part children with mental retardation continued (and continue) to be segregated in separate schools or in separate classrooms within schools. Despite their locations in the community and off institutional grounds, many community locations were so absolutely and relatively physically isolated that they drew criticism, as early as the mid-1970s, for continuing the separation of the retarded from the community. The appearance of "new" or mini-institutions continued into the 1990s and was a critical and persistent concern. Merely having access to goods and services outside the institution constituted a lifeless and incomplete meaning of community when loneliness and social isolation were still unhappy characteristics of people's lives.

Community as Locale

Agnew considered "locale" the "most central element [of community] sociologically" (1987, 28). "Locale" adds to definitions of "community" the dimension of personal interaction, which humanizes an otherwise inanimate space that provides goods and services, thus transforming "location." "Locale" has also been described as a setting for personal interactions, often characterized by a combination of physical and human features (Giddens 1984, 118). The connection between "locale" and "community integration" hinges precisely on the addition of, or the possibility of, the interactive human dimension.

The term "community integration" appeared sometime after the introduction of the principle of normalization, and, since it was based on the concept of "community," it has proved to be just as ambiguous and popular. Its meaning has been construed in a number of ways, from physical integration to social integration based on physical integration (Wolfensberger 1972; Nirje 1980), to the forthright claim that "community integration does not just mean physical placement in the community, but participation in community life (Taylor, Biklen, Knoll 1987, xvi).

Several interpretations of "integration" correspond closely to Agnew's concept of locale because of the integral element of social relationships that can result from the physical setting. Community as a locale was legitimized by the Developmental Disabilities Assistance and Bill of Rights Act of 1984 (P.L. 98-527) when Congress embodied the social element of locale as integration as:

> (A) the use by persons with mental retardation of the same community resources that are used by and available to other citizens, and participation by persons with mental retardation in the same community activities in which nonhandicapped citizens participate, together with regular contact with nonhandicapped citizens, and (B) the residence by persons with mental retardation in homes or home-like settings which are in proximity to community resources, together with regular contact with nonhandicapped citizens in their communities.

"Regular contact" fell short of a deeper meaning of community: social relationships. Several years earlier, Nirje defined the term "social integration" this way:

> Social integration is the interpersonal or impersonal social relationships in neighborhoods, in schools, in work situations, and in the community at large. Manners, attitudes, respect, and esteem are mutually involved here. (1980, 48)

Relationships were clearly identified as the crucial element in community in the now classic statement of Bogdan and Taylor:

> Being in the community is not the same as being of the community. . . . Being in the community points only to physical presence; being part of the community means having the opportunity to interact and form relationships with other community members. (1987, 210)

"Having an opportunity" corresponds to locale as a setting for personal relationships and changes the meaning of community from an absolute physical location to a relative social location. Growing out of this consideration of community was the belief that "where" was intimately related to "who," implying that "other people in the community" were to be found outside the mental retardation services system.

Community as Sense of Place

The next aspect of "community" moves from the opportunities available in a setting to a "sense of place"—a feeling of identification with a particular place and a sense of association with it (Agnew 1987, 26). This is compatible with Dybwad's observation, made almost twenty years earlier:

> Integration implies . . . not just the sense of belonging but the closest possible physical proximity between the mentally retarded and the family . . . the other dimension . . . bears upon his contacts with society, usually in the context of a community . . . he should have a definite ongoing relationship with the community, a relationship that has meaning. (1969, 420)

In the 1990s, that "other dimension" was captured by the phrase "community membership and belonging." Walker defines community as "a sense of membership and belonging whether that be derived based on geographic location, kinship, friendship, common interest, or other connections and bonds" (1996, 18).

By describing residential services for retarded people in the 1990s as "the era of community membership," Knoll (1990, 236) stressed the importance of belonging. Research on the friendships and social lives of retarded citizens has revealed that the majority have social contact primarily with people with mental retardation or other disabilities, with staff associated with service provision, and with family. By the early 1990s, to combat these insular contacts and relationships, as well as the loneliness and social isolation discussed earlier, mental retardation professionals concluded that their concept of community would emphasize social connections, membership, and belonging—implicitly, and significantly, with people outside the mental retardation service systems.

Summary

The historical social geography of people with mental retardation shows a clear association between social policy and locations of services, in institutions and communities. Congregation and containment in rural areas suited the needs of different social policies, not a few of which were connected with the increasing number of lower-class families in the late 1800s and early

1900s. Compulsory public education resulted in the creation of special education classes that were segregated within school buildings or located in separate structures and that themselves excluded children with more than mild mental retardation. "Extrainstitutional" services, while maintaining the professionals' control, reached into the local communities to relieve the demand for institutionalization when the number of people with mental retardation was acknowledged as too large for their total containment after World War I. The professionals decried the lack of organized services and at the same time admitted that many people were living productive, "harmless" lives in the communities, helped by others or by generic community agencies. This awareness, and the realization that mental retardation was not found only in lower-class families, led to the development of parent community services organizations, again directed toward special education. As the children aged, more services were added; service locations were chosen to keep the aging children safe and not too far from their families. When deinstitutionalization occurred, the state service systems and local parent-based systems converged in communities, raising the question of the meaning of "community" and binding the concepts of social policy and spatial location yet again.

REFERENCES

Agnew, John A. 1987. *Place and Politics: The Geographical Mediation of the State and Society.* Boston: Allen and Unwin. pp. ix–267.

Baker, B. L., G. B. Selzer, and M. M. Selzer. 1977. *As Close as Possible: Community Residences for Retarded Adults.* Boston: Little, Brown.

Barr, Martin W. 1899. "Training Feeble-Minded Children." *Journal of Psycho-Asthenics,* 4(1): 204–211.

Bogdan, Robert, and Steven J. Taylor. 1987. "Conclusion: The Next Wave." In *Community Integration for People with Severe Disabilities,* ed. Steven J. Taylor, Douglas Biklen, and James Knoll. New York: Teachers College Press, pp. 209–213.

Boggs, Elizabeth, Cheryl Hanley-Maxwell, K. Charlie Lakin, and Valerie Bradley. 1988. "Federal Policy and Legislation: Factors That Have Constrained and Facilitated Community Integration." In *Integration of Developmentally Disabled Individuals into Community,* ed. Laird W. Heal, Janelle I. Haney, and Angela R. Novak Amado. Baltimore: Paul H. Brookes Publishing Co., pp: 245–271.

Davies, Stanley P. 1930. *Social Control of the Mentally Deficient.* New York: Thomas Y. Crowell.

Deutsch, Albert. 1937. *The Mentally Ill in America.* Garden City, NY: Doubleday.

Doll, Edgar A. 1929. "Community Control of the Feeble-Minded." *Journal of Psycho-Asthenics,* 34: 161–175.

Dybwad, Gunnar. 1969. "Action Implications, U.S.A. Today." In *Changing Patterns in Residential Services for the Mentally Retarded,* ed. Robert Kugel and Wolf Wolfensberger. Washington, DC: President's Committee on Mental Retardation, pp. 385–428.

Fairbank, Ruth E. 1933. "The Subnormal Child—Seventeen Years After." *Mental Hygiene,* 17(2): 177–208.

Farber, Bernard. 1968. *Mental Retardation: Its Social Context and Social Consequences.* Boston: Houghton Mifflin.

Ferguson, Philip M. 1994. *Abandoned to Their Fate.* Philadelphia: Temple University Press.

Fernald, Guy G. 1918. "The Problem of Extra-Institutional Feeble-Minded." *Journal of Pycho-Asthenics,* 23: 82–91.

Fuller, Earl W. 1921. "Extra-Institutional Care of Mental Defectives." *Journal of Psycho-Asthenics,* 26: 82–89.

Gerry, William P. 1975. "Selection of Homes." In *Community Homes for the Mentally Retarded,* ed. Joel S. Bergman. Lexington, MA: Lexington Books, pp. 19–32.

Giddens, Anthony. 1984. *The Constitution of Society.* Berkeley: University of California Press.

Gregory, Derek, and John Urry. 1985. "Introduction." In *Social Relations and Spatial Structures,* ed. Derek Gregory and John Urry. London: Macmillan, pp. 1–8.

Hoakley, Z. Pauline. 1922. "Extra-Institutional Care for the Feeble-Minded." *Journal of Psycho-Asthenics,* 27: 117–137.

Johnson, G. E. 1898. "Psychology and Pedagogy of Feeble-Minded Children." *Journal of Psycho-Asthenics,* 2(1): 26–32.

Journal of Psycho-Asthenics. 1896. "From the Institutions." 1(2): 69–70.

———. 1898. "The New Institution for Feeble-Minded of Western Pennsylvania." 2(4): 128–137.

———. 1940. "Historical Notes on Institutions for the Mentally Defective." 45: 187–189.

———. 1940. "Historical Notes on Institutions for the Mentally Defective." 45: 340–342.

Kanner, Leo. 1964. *A History of the Care and Study of the Mentally Retarded.* Springfield, IL: Charles C. Thomas.

Knoll, James. 1990. "Defining Quality in Residential Services." In *Quality Assurance for Individuals with Developmental Disabilities,* ed. Valerie Bradley and Hank Berani Jr. Baltimore: Paul H. Brookes, pp. 235–261.

Kuhlmann, F. 1940. "One Hundred Years of Special Care and Training." *American Journal of Mental Deficiency,* 45: 8–24.

Lakin, K. Charlie, Robert H. Bruininks, and Barbara B. Sigford. 1981. "Introduction." *In Deinstitutionalization and Community Adjustment of Mentally Retarded People,* ed. Robert H. Bruininks, C. Edward Meyers, Barbara B. Sigford, and K. Charlie Lakin. Monograph no. 4. Washington, DC: American Association on Mental Deficiency, pp. vii–xvi.

———. 1981. "Early Perspectives on the Community Adjustment of Mentally Retarded People." In *Deinstitutionalization and Community Adjustment of Mentally Retarded People,* ed. Robert H. Bruininks, C. Edward Meyers, Barbara B. Sigford, and K. Charlie Lakin. Monograph no. 4. Washington, DC: American Association on Mental Deficiency, pp. 28–50.

Lakin, K. Charlie, Robert W. Prouty, and Robert H. Bruininks. 1996. "Longitudinal Trends in Large State-Operated Residential Facilities, 1950–1995." In *Residential Services for Persons with Developmental Disabilities: Status and Trends through 1995.* Minneapolis: University of Minnesota, Research and Training Center on Community Living, Institute on Community Integration, pp. 23–29.

Metzel, Deborah S. 1998. *Approaching Community: The Residential Location Decision Process for People with Developmental Disabilities.* Unpublished doctoral dissertation, University of Maryland, College Park.

Nirje, Bengt. 1980. "The Normalization Principle." In *Normalization, Social Integration, and Community Services,* ed. Robert J. Flynn and Kathleen E. Nitsche. Baltimore: University Park Press, pp. 31–49.

President's Committee on Mental Retardation. 1976. *Mental Retardation Past and Present.* Washington, DC.

Ray, David B., Jr. 1959. "Wanted—A Site to Build a State Institution for the Mentally Retarded." *American Journal on Mental Deficiency,* 63(6): 1098–1103.

Roselle, Ernest L. 1941. "Connecticut's New Institution for Mental Defectives Dedicated." *American Journal of Mental Deficiency,* 45(4): 465–471.

Rothman, David J. 1971. *The Discovery of the Asylum: Social Order and Disorder in the New Republic.* Boston: Little, Brown.

Scheerenberger, Richard C. 1975. *Managing Residential Facilities for the Developmentally Disabled.* Springfield, IL: Charles C. Thomas.

———. 1977. "Deinstitutionalization in Perspective." In *Deinstitutionalization: Program and Policy Development,* ed. J. L. Paul, D. J. Stedman, and G. R. Neufeld. Syracuse: Syracuse University Press, pp. 3–14.

———. 1983. *A History of Mental Retardation.* Baltimore: Brookes.

Smith, Groves B. 1922. "Practical Considerations of the Problems of Mental Deficiency as Seen in a Neuro-Psychiatric Facility." *Journal of Psycho-Asthenics,* 27: 57–64.

Taylor, J. Madison. 1899. "Hints to the Officers of Institutions for the Feeble-Minded." *Journal of Psycho-Asthenics,* 3: 76–81.

Taylor, Steven, Douglas Biklen, and James Knoll. 1987. *Community Integration for People with Severe Disabilities.* New York: Teachers College Press.

Trent, James W., Jr. 1994. *Inventing the Feeble Mind: A History of Mental Retardation in the United States*. Berkeley: University of California Press.

Vanuxem, Mary. 1925. *Education of Feeble-Minded Women*. New York: Teachers College Press.

Vitello, Stanley J., and Ronald M. Soskins. 1985. *Mental Retardation: Its Social and Legal Context*. Englewood Cliffs, NJ: Prentice-Hall.

Walker, Pamela M. 1996. *The Social Meaning of Place and People with Developmental Disabilities*. Ph.D. diss., Syracuse University.

Weiner, Terry S. 1993. "Prejudice and Discrimination against the Mentally Retarded: A Socio-historical Perspective. *International Journal of Group Tensions*, 23(3): 245–262.

Wiley, Frank L. 1922. "The Organization and Administration of the Education of Subnormal Children in the Public Schools." *Journal of Psycho-Asthenics*, 27: 231–239.

Wolfensberger, Wolf. 1972. *The Principle of Normalization in Human Services*. Toronto: National Institute on Mental Retardation.

18

The Litigator as Reformer

David J. Rothman and Sheila M. Rothman

Introduction

In February 1972, a young television journalist, Geraldo Rivera, raided Willowbrook State School with his cameras rolling. He was brought in by a staff physician, Bill Bronston, who had been desperately but unsuccessfully trying to improve conditions in this New York State school for the developmentally disabled. The Willowbrook administration, tired of Bronston's agitation, fired him. He then called Rivera, told him that kids at Willowbrook were living in their own excrement, and expected that the sense of outrage that would follow from the films would finally bring reforms.

Bronston proved half-right. Two and a half million viewers, the highest rating ever achieved by any local news special in the history of American television, watched the broadcast. Soon, other television stations, along with the print media, picked up the story. First New Yorkers and then the nation learned that Willowbrook (and, by implication, other residential facilities of its kind) resembled concentration camps. Lacking cleanliness, privacy, care, affection, and education, Willowbrook would soon become the nation's touchstone for publicly funded abuse and neglect.

But it was not the cameras or the public outrage that led to systematic change. TV exposures generally come and go, stimulating outrage, to be sure, but generally for too short a period to accomplish lasting results. What made this exposé different was not the cameras or the public but litigators ready to turn for redress to the federal courts.

This chapter traces in some detail how they mounted their case, which proved to be compelling and effective. Led by Bruce Ennis, an attorney at the New York Civil Liberties Union, they had to find the facts and spell out the theory that would make institutional wretchedness the object of court intervention. The odds against their succeeding were high; Willowbrook, after all, was not a prison, and its residents were free to go whenever they wished. But, through inventive legal thinking and the most diligent accumulation of the nasty facts about Willowbrook, the lawyers succeeded. In 1975, they won a consent decree that compelled the state to establish group homes for the Willowbrook residents, in the process helping to establish a system and a bureaucracy that were able and ready to deliver care outside an institution's walls. When *The Willowbrook Wars* appeared in 1984, New York State officials had already announced plans to close the state institution. By 1986, Willowbrook had only 250 residents. State officials soon placed most of them into community settings. On 17 September 1987, Willowbrook closed "officially and forever."

The shift from institutional to community-based services that began with Willowbrook continued at a fast pace through the 1980s and 1990s. During the period, New York closed its largest and once most prominent institutions: Craig, Westchester, Rome, Newark, Letchworth, and Syracuse. Aiding the shift was federal approval in 1991 of a plan that allowed New York to use Medicaid funds for community-based services.

This chapter tells the story of events in 1972 that led to the class action lawsuit against New York State. There were two groups assisting the lawyers: parents of the Willowbrook residents and professionals, of a variety of stripes, interested in developmental disabilities. There were tensions among these groups, and the chapter describes their different concerns, tactics, and goals. It recounts the remarkable retreat in which the groups managed to join together, with the lawyers' perspective winning the day.

Before 1971, Ennis, like most lawyers, knew almost nothing about intellectual disabilities. In that year, he became part of the team of attorneys that argued *Wyatt v. Stickney* before federal judge Frank Johnson, in Alabama. In New York, following on the Rivera raid, Ennis listened to experts, heard the stories of parents, and toured Willowbrook. By 1972, Ennis and others were using the courts to try to transform custodial institutions. But, even more than that, they, with the courts as their allies, cast doubt on the nation's 150-year faith in the asylum.

. . .

The first campaign in Willowbrook's ways was waged in the media. Within twenty-four hours of Rivera's telecast, ABC received 700 telephone calls expressing outrage about Willowbrook, and other networks hastily dispatched reporters to cover the story. The *New York Times* ran an editorial on this "tragedy" and "disgrace," declaring that "the State dishonors itself by its dehumanization of these helpless children." The *Village Voice* provided a poignant account of two young women who had been confined to the facility all their lives, not because they were retarded but because they were the victims of a crippling disease. No one, of course, could predict the long-term impact of the publicity and whether the scandal would generate change. It was not the first time that Willowbrook—or other institutions, for that matter—had been exposed, and it would not be the first time that a spasm of indignation would give way to malevolent neglect.

It quickly became obvious that the presence of the film crews affected the behavior of the protesters. The microphone was like a magic wand—wave it and parents once timid and helpless became radical and aggressive. When a reporter asked one of them, Rosalie Amoroso, whether the institution was really so terrible, she replied that it was horrible and then lashed out: "Why don't you ask the administration . . . why the children are so scratched and why they're full of cuts and bruises and why they're burned? All these things the administration must be accountable for." Bring a TV camera into a peaceable meeting and participants become charged; bring it to Willowbrook and the protesters became agitated—which guaranteed that the camera would return.

Taking their cue from the civil rights movement, the Willowbrook parents quickly learned to stage events for the media. The same techniques that evoked the cruelty of a Birmingham sheriff demonstrated the callousness of a Willowbrook superintendent. So, on a Tuesday morning in January, the demonstrators announced a rally for eight o'clock, but then postponed it for several hours until Rivera could arrive; he first had to "raid" another building for fresh film clips and interview Bernard Carabello, the cerebral palsied resident who had been cross-examined by the assistant directors.

The rally itself was well attended, and the crowd played skillfully to the camera. Gathering outside the entrance to the institution, the parents held up placards that read: WILLOWBROOK IS A SNAKE PIT—LET'S CLEAN IT UP AND REMEMBER DACHAU, REMEMBER BELSEN, REMEMBER WILLOWBROOK. They then marched half a mile (shades of Birmingham) to the administration building. In the lead was Bernard Carabello, arms linked with those of his mother and another parent (shades of Martin Luther King). When they reached the building, three security men blocked the door (shades of Wallace); the parents pushed past them and went up to [Superintendent] Hammond's office, and the encounter became the highlight of the evening news. Malachy McCourt, a popular radio talk show host who was the stepfather of a Willowbrook resident, presided. In a resonant Irish brogue, he asked Hammond "how long it has been since you laid your hands on a child to heal him instead of fiddling your papers up here in this centrally air-conditioned building with carpets and beautiful furniture? There's no shit [beep] here. There's no piss [beep] here. There's no disease." Hammond was silent; on the screen he looked pathetic and tired. The Willowbrook agitators, like those in the civil rights movement, rarely lost a confrontation on camera.

Appearances on TV talk shows followed. Bill Bronston, Bernard Carabello, and a few Willowbrook parents told Dick Cavett their story and ripped apart the feeble efforts of two representatives from the Department of Mental Hygiene (DMH) to defend its record. Bronston and the others also testified at hearings in Albany. "The Pandora's box of our state school system for the retarded has been opened," Bronston told the legislators. "Our citizens have had a true glimpse of the misery, loneliness, and stench that have existed within for so many years."

No matter how exhilarating and personally satisfying these occasions were, the protesters knew better than to trust to the state to improve conditions. Aware that another scandal would eventually replace Willowbrook on the evening news, they were at once impatient to map out a reform campaign and uncertain of how to go about it. To resolve the dilemma, they convened a "Policy and Action" conference for the first weekend in March at Mount Augustine Retreat House, in Staten Island, inviting the most concerned Willowbrook parents, sympathetic professionals in the field of retardation, and several civil liberties attorneys.

At the retreat, fifty participants divided themselves into three separate working groups—parents, professionals, lawyers. Each group conducted its own deliberations and then joined the others in a plenary session to frame decisions. The parents' discussions were more emotional than tactical. One of them would relate the horrors that had befallen his child, another would tell her story, and the tension in the room soon became intolerable. Useful as the confessions were psychologically to individual parents, they were of little help politically to the group. So, at the plenary session, they offered a few proposals ever so modestly, presenting themselves as only "ordinary people."

Their first plank called for bringing Willowbrook up to "humane living standards," which to parents of backward children meant placing "greater emphasis . . . on the care of the severely and profoundly retarded." They also wanted a governing board established for each institution, with parents composing a majority of the members. ("The responsibility for the care of the handicapped person should be exercised jointly by the parents and the state.") But how past policies were to be reversed, how residents' lives were to be enhanced and their guardians empowered, were questions they were unable to address.

The sessions of the professionals were led by members of Syracuse University's Center on Human Policy, whose ranks included the most radical thinkers in the field. Although one could never have known it from Willowbrook's history, the 1960s was a decade of remarkable creativity in mental retardation. Through World War 1, professional and popular opinion alike had focused on the need to curb "the menace of the feebleminded," to ensure that the retarded did not corrupt the eugenic stock of native America, a corruption that already seemed well under way with the rise of immigration. To this end, custodial care in institutions and sterilization procedures won approval on the grounds that three generations of imbeciles were enough. Over the next thirty years, as eugenic nightmares subsided (and eventually were discredited by the Nazi experience), a medical-psychiatric model took hold. Now the retarded were "sick," in need of hospital "treatment" as "patients." The proposition seemed more humane, save for the chilling fact that the severely and profoundly retarded were considered beyond the skills of medicine, falling into the category of incurable. Hence, the shift in terminology from "menace" to "patient" meant little in practice. The retarded were still warehoused in distant institutions.

In reaction against these punitive and despairing judgments, a new generation of experts originated a concept of "normalization." Owing more to sociology than to medicine, it took its departure from labeling theory. In its most imaginative formulation, by Wolf Wolfensberger (who was then teaching at Syracuse), it conceived of a label (delinquent, mentally ill, or retarded) as a stage direction that told the director (the public) how to think about the actor (consider him deviant) and how to respond (segregate him). Thus, to label someone retarded was to evoke a strategy for "managing" or "coping" with him that would inevitably set him apart as an object of either pity (hopelessly ill) or fear (uncontrollably mad) or disdain (subhuman). In turn, the person so labeled took his own self-definition from this negative or hostile attitude and, in self-fulfilling fashion, fit his behavior to it. A child placed in an institution for the retarded would make less progress than his counterpart in the community, both because his instructors would be less inclined to teach him and because he would be less inclined to learn.

To counter the deleterious influence of the label, Wolfensberger (and others, particularly in Scandinavia) advanced the idea of the retarded as "normal," that is, deserving conditions of everyday life that are as close as possible to those of the mainstream of society. By this principle, the retarded child, like every other child, should be living in a family-like setting, attending public school, and receiving medical care in a doctor's neighborhood office. Normalization also answers seemingly tough questions: Should a retarded man and woman be allowed to share a bedroom or get married? The theory says yes; they should enjoy sexual expression like the rest of us. Should retarded people be allowed to travel alone on public transportation and spend their own money? Again the theory says yes; they, too, deserve "the dignity of risk." Normalization, let it be clear, is not intended as a legal regulation or a medical panacea. It does not insist that a retarded person must never be placed in a special class or be supervised on public transportation. Rather, it provides new directions and new goals: Set the stage in accord with what is normal and help the retarded to become insofar as possible like everyone else.

In the United States, normalization theory has had another policy implication: Do not incarcerate the retarded. Proponents have read Erving Goffman's *Asylums* carefully and are persuaded that institutions, whether they hold 100 or 1,000 inmates, are, perforce, total institutions. By necessity these facilities impose abnormal routines on their inmates; the very scale of operations forces residents into rigid schedules (up at six, dinner at four-thirty), into uniformity of dress (the gray shift), and into impersonal relationships (identification not by name but by number). And, inevitably, such a regimen makes it all the more difficult for an inmate to adapt to life outside the institution.

Does this anti-institutional perspective allow for exceptions? The question is highly controversial, for, although most retardation experts subscribe to the principles of normalization, only one wing is consistently and uncompromisingly anti-institutional. A significant segment of professional opinion (especially in Scandinavia) believes that institutions cannot be completely abolished. The severely and profoundly retarded will have to remain confined, and for them normalization should mean making large institutions smaller and more homelike. Other specialists, however, insist that normalization theory never (and they mean never) allows for institutionalization, no matter how handicapped the person or well designed the facility. It was such a group that was present at the retreat and helped to define the goals for Willowbrook's residents.

The professionals opened their workshop with an excess of ambition, attempting to describe the ideal service delivery system. But they soon recognized that the task required more than a weekend's work and narrowed the assignment to composing emergency guidelines for relief at Willowbrook. They reported to the plenary session that the institution should be divided into smaller units under team leaders and that every resident should have a medical and an educational program. But the heart of their recommendations looked beyond the facility to the community: New York should undertake a program to build group homes. Important as it was to reduce Willowbrook's overcrowding immediately, no one should be transferred to another institution. Rather, all the residents should enter ten-bed group homes and begin using community services, schools, and doctors. The goal ought to be "integration into society, not segregation and dehumanization."

However advanced the agenda, the professionals, like the parents, did not have a sure sense of how to implement their demands. They all recognized that an enormous gap separated their rhetoric from Albany's reality, but they were unable to formulate a strategy to bridge it. Where were they to get the power to compel DMH to establish group homes?

The third group at the retreat, the attorneys, had a ready response and a total confidence in its efficacy. The power would come through the federal courts, in a class-action suit on behalf of the Willowbrook residents that would culminate in a judicial decree. The others present had little idea what a class-action suit was or why a federal court would assume jurisdiction over an institution like Willowbrook. But the lawyers, particularly Bruce Ennis, had come fully prepared to explain these matters.

Ennis's route to the retreat was a roundabout one. Trained at the University of Chicago Law School, he came to New York in the 1960s, joined a large Wall Street firm, and litigated on behalf of corporations. One night, after watching a television debate in which Aryeh Neier, then the director of the New York Civil Liberties Union, got the best of William Buckley, whom Ennis admired for his wit, he called Neier and volunteered to do some litigation for NYCLU. (One of his first assignments was to bail Neier out of jail following an anti–Vietnam War demonstration. Neier was embarrassed by the incident, not because of a few hours in a lockup but because he had carefully instructed NYCLU legal observers on how not to get arrested.) In the fall of 1970, Ennis became restless in his Wall Street practice and asked Neier whether NYCLU had an opening for a full-time attorney. Neier had no vacant general staff positions but invited Ennis to apply to direct a new litigation project on behalf of mental patients' rights.

Ennis was not familiar with psychiatry or psychiatrists, and no one in his family had ever been institutionalized. But he started reading, mostly books by Thomas Szasz on the "myth of mental illness," and, finding the "abstract legal and social policy issues" fascinating, decided to apply. His ignorance was little barrier—no one in 1970 knew what mental health law was or what the rights of the mentally ill might be.

NYCLU's eagerness to litigate in mental health testifies to a revolution in the history of American reform that had occurred during the 1960s, a revolution that had altered both the composition of the reformers' ranks and the strategies they pursued. The roots of this transformation lay in the civil rights movement. Until the campaign that culminated in the Supreme Court's *Brown v. Board of Education* decision in 1954, those who agitated on behalf of minorities, especially the poor and the mentally disabled, typically came from the helping professions and argued their cause before legislators. Whether it was Jane Addams advocating more generous support for needy widows with children or Harry Hopkins negotiating for larger relief appropriations for the unemployed, social workers with their allies conducted what were essentially lobbying campaigns. They would marshal their facts, offered testimony, joined together with other constituent groups, and regularly got their bills approved. Later, historians would note the frequency with which reform fell short of its goals, but, at the time, the strategy seemed effective and the innovations significant.

Progressives and New Dealers were wary of the judiciary, and with good reason. State and federal courts, elevating property rights over the general welfare, struck down Progressive legislation regulating workers' hours and wages and early New Deal legislation setting prices. Indeed, reformers distrusted not only courts but lawyers as well; they feared that attorneys who focused on client's rights, who valued procedural protections more than open-ended therapeutic encounters, would disrupt the rehabilitative process by which social workers assisted the delinquent and the poor.

The first movement to break with this tradition was civil rights. No black determined to desegregate Southern schools could conceive of the legislature as anything but the enemy. Imagine mounting an integration effort in the 1930s in Jackson, Mississippi, or in the 1940s in Montgomery, Alabama. Those who would end segregation saw only one option—a move to the courts. Hence, in the 1930s, the National Association for the Advancement of Colored People began a twenty-five-year litigating effort that would culminate in *Brown*, and, for the first time, lawyers like Thurgood Marshall determined the tactics: Take on graduate schools first; make initial inroads in desegregating law schools, where it would be easier to demonstrate that separate was unequal (compare libraries and faculty); and culminate with a plaintiff who is a girl and wants to enter a white public school when the colored school is miles away and in primitive condition.

The civil rights movement encouraged women, prisoners, and, eventually, the disabled to define themselves as oppressed minorities and to search for constitutional, not political, grounds for winning their rights. It taught them to think of themselves not as poor unfortunates who should be the object of paternalism but as competent individuals who had entitlements. This shift marks a major divide in twentieth-century social thought and social action. It moves us from Progressive protective legislation, which prohibited women from working in strenuous occupations, to agitation for equal rights; from involuntary commitment laws, which incarcerated the incompetent, to agitation for mental patients' rights.

Civil rights also engaged a generation of law students in a great crusade. Dozens of graduates of prestigious Eastern law schools, for example, traveled to Mississippi in the early 1960s to assist illiterate blacks in registering to vote; and although they spent only a short time there, the experience stimulated them to use their legal skills on behalf of the disadvantaged. (When Ennis was still a law student, he applied to the Mississippi project and was keenly disappointed to learn that so many law school graduates were volunteering that students were ineligible.) Frequently, one encounter with social injustice led to another. Attorneys like Alvin Bronstein learned from their black clients about Southern jails and prisons where conditions of incarceration were barbaric. Arkansas had the "Tucker Telephone," which guards used to apply electric shocks to inmates' genitals. Texas had the "hole," solitary confinement for months on end in bare, airless, and dimly lit cement boxes. Certain that such conditions violated Eighth Amendment injunctions against cruel and unusual punishment, Bronstein, with Neier's encouragement and support, established the National Prison Project and began litigating on behalf of prisoners' rights.

He and fellow attorneys in the movement were notably successful in persuading federal judges to look behind "administrative expertise" to the practices themselves. Traditionally, when inmates complained (as they regularly did) about inadequate conditions or unfair procedures, judges had steadfastly maintained a hands-off posture. As late as 1951, one court of appeals judge, reviewing a prisoner's claim to a right to receive and send letters, insisted: "We think it is well settled that it is not the function of the courts to superintend the treatment or discipline of persons in penitentiaries." His colleague wrote a concurring opinion just to decry the waste of time involved in even considering such a suit: "I think that a judge of a court as busy as the one below should not be compelled to listen to such nonsense."

By the late 1960s, however, judges were no longer willing to keep "hands off" the prisons and to trust to their administrators' supposed expertise. Not that they were eager to exercise oversight, but when the factual record of horrendous circumstances came into the lower courts in the days when Earl Warren presided over the Supreme Court, it made a powerful case for judicial intervention. Were judges really to look the other way after learning that Arkansas guards cranked up their Tucker Telephone? Or that inmates in Texas solitary cells were forced to live in their own excrement? Surely judges could rule that the Eighth Amendment prohibited such practices without themselves becoming entangled in the day-to-day running of a prison. But no sooner did the doctrine of abstention weaken than other abuses, only somewhat less severe, were on the court dockets. If the Constitution did not stop at the prison walls, was it appropriate to punish a prisoner without giving him a hearing? Was it fair to deprive him of reading material, or law books, or the right to practice his religion as he saw fit? And what were judges to do when states persisted in violating their orders? Was it not necessary to appoint a master to make certain that the orders were enforced? One decision followed another, until it was apparent, in the words of one Tennessee federal judge, in 1969, that, "As to the traditional preference for leaving matters of internal prison management to state officials, an analysis of recent cases indicated that . . . the federal judiciary . . . will not hesitate to intervene in appropriate cases."

No reform group worked harder to expand the roster of clients and causes who might benefit from expanded judicial oversight than the American Civil Liberties Union, which in the process transformed its own character. From its founding in the Progressive period through the 1950s, ACLU had focused its energies on protecting free speech, on ensuring that the First Amendment covered pacifists, Communists, Ku Klux Klan members, and, eventually, neo-Nazis in Skokie, Illinois. Although it certainly supported the early civil rights movement, it did not exercise leadership; desegregation was not a First Amendment issue. But in the aftermath of the civil rights movement, Aryeh Neier (who became its director in 1972), together with Ira Glasser (who succeeded Neier first at NYCLU and then at ACLU), took the organization beyond the First Amendment to litigate on behalf of women, prisoners, students, and children. With this enlarged purpose, an altogether predictable split occurred between ACLU traditionalists (who wished to maintain the centrality of free-speech issues) and the Neier-Glasser camp (which wanted to do battle for other rights), and many of the new projects alienated an old-guard constituency. To sue a principal on behalf of a student's right to dress as he wished was to receive an angry call from the principal demanding to know why ACLU would sue one of its own members; to proceed with the suit was inevitably to offend New York schoolteachers and lose them and their friends as members and donors. But the rights strategy also won support, particularly from those eager to extend the civil rights model to other minorities. Since a significant number of them were foundation directors (e.g., Leslie Dunbar at Field, McGeorge Bundy at Ford, and, later, John Coleman at Clark), Neier had the resources to hire Bruce Ennis to begin litigating on mental health.

From 1970 to 1972, Ennis helped to establish some of the first principles of mental health law, to bring the Constitution behind not only prison but asylum walls. Courts now ruled that a diagnosis of mental illness did not automatically render a defendant incapable of standing trial and thus made it more difficult for prosecutors to use competency hearings as a way of avoiding criminal trial when their evidence for conviction was weak. Courts also determined that patients did not lose all their rights when entering a mental hospital, thus making it more difficult for psychiatrists to impose treatment regimens against a patient's wishes.

Perhaps most notable was the litigation that Ennis was helping to conduct on behalf of patients' right to treatment. The idea that a mental hospital was obliged under the Constitution to provide residents with therapy originated in a 1960 article by a Brooklyn physician and lawyer, Morton Birnbaum; searching for some legal remedy for substandard state institutions, he suggested that anyone involuntarily committed and denied treatment was unfairly deprived of his liberty, imprisoned as though guilty of a criminal act. It was Birnbaum's hope that the courts would find such a constitutional right and compel states to turn their warehouses into genuine hospitals.

The argument was first tried out before the federal court in the District of Columbia, because one of its leading judges, David Bazelon, wanted the judiciary active in cleaning up the snake pits. It received its important test in the case of Kenneth Donaldson, a patient at the Florida State Hospital.

Donaldson had entered the hospital in 1956 when his eighty-year-old parents petitioned the local county court to commit their forty-eight-year-old son because he was suffering from a "persecution complex." Two physicians (not psychiatrists) and a deputy sheriff concurred, and so did a judge (after a few minutes of questioning). For the next fifteen years, Donaldson remained confined, the victim of neglect—for the hospital provided no treatment—and of the animosity of two staff psychiatrists. He kept up a steady barrage of petitions to the courts for release, which the hospital psychiatrists successfully opposed. Then, by accident, his predicament came to the attention of Morton Birnbaum, who wanted to apply his theory on right to treatment to Donaldson's case. For five years, no court would so much as grant him a hearing. Then, in 1971, to everyone's astonishment, the Supreme Court instructed the Florida district court to give Donaldson a hearing.

Knowing of Ennis's involvement in mental health law, Birnbaum invited him to serve as co-counsel, and together they argued that Donaldson's right to treatment had been violated by the Florida State Hospital and that he was entitled both to release and to $100,000 in damages. In an effort to moot the case, the state immediately released Donaldson (after fifteen years he was suddenly pronounced cured), but, since the action for damages stood, the case continued. After Donaldson prevailed in several lower-court decisions, the suit reached the Supreme Court, which in 1975 also found in Donaldson's favor. Nondangerous patients could not simply be kept in custody against their will; something more had to be done for them. In the absence of danger to himself or others and in the absence of treatment (left undefined), a person cannot be committed against his will to a mental hospital. To Ennis, the ruling was a victory that established the first significant limits on the practice of involuntary commitment. Perhaps someday he might win a ruling that hospitals could not hold patients against their will under any circumstances.

Ennis received other requests for assistance from would-be plaintiffs and other attorneys. In the fall of 1970, George Dean, an Alabama lawyer, asked him for help in a case before federal judge Frank Johnson, known for his uncompromising orders in desegregation suits. The Alabama commissioner of mental health, Dr. Stonewall Stickney, had ordered the dismissal of some 100 employees at Bryce, the state mental hospital, and a group of psychologists, social workers, and nurses had retained Dean to argue that the dismissals violated their contracts and jeopardized the well-being of the patients. In a preliminary session, Johnson gave short shrift to the contractual claims—the state courts could adjudicate them—but he asked Dean (this before *Donaldson* was litigated) to brief him on whether the state could enforce involuntary hospitalization without providing suitable and adequate treatment. Dean, who had little familiarity with right-to-treatment principles, was referred to Ennis, who rushed off a packet of cases and articles.

Dean's brief to Johnson contended that "patients confined to any state-operated mental health facility are constitutionally entitled to adequate, competent treatment," and Johnson, intrigued, asked him to pursue the point in a full trial. Dean again contacted Ennis, and he, together with another public-interest lawyer, Charles Halpern, toured Bryce and joined Dean as special amici (which gave the right to examine and cross-examine witnesses). The experience prompted Halpern and Ennis to create the Mental Health Law Project. Halpern headed up the Washington office and Ennis the New York office, as an adjunct to NYCLU.

As George Dean learned more about the dismal conditions at Bryce, he became increasingly concerned about patient care at Alabama's other facilities. He went to visit Partlow, the institution for the retarded, and discovered that, however much a warehouse Bryce was, Partlow was worse, its floors and walls covered with urine and excrement. Dean petitioned Johnson to include Partlow in the complaint against the state, and, in August 1971, Johnson agreed.

Through the fall of 1971 and into the winter of 1972, Dean, Halpern, and Ennis prepared and then conducted a two-day trial before Judge Johnson. Their aim in *Wyatt v. Stickney,* as the case was called, was to make the deficiencies of Bryce and Partlow declared a violation of a right to treatment. In the division of labor, Dean handled most of the local witnesses, and Halpern assembled a supporting coalition of the leading mental health and retardation organizations. The Department of Justice joined plaintiffs, invited in by Judge Johnson, who was accustomed to relying upon its resources in desegregation cases.

Ennis assisted generally but was freed of many of the burdens of preparing a case for trial. He therefore had time to learn about retardation and institutions for the retarded and soon was wondering why he had litigated only for the mentally ill. Hardened to institutional sights and smells, he still gagged upon entering Partlow—even the standard practice of taking short breaths inside the building and gulping air outside did not work. As expert witnesses came to tour and prepare testimony, Ennis met many of the leading practitioners, including James Clements (who directed a highly regarded institution in Atlanta), Linda Glenn (who directed research and planning for an exemplary community placement program in Omaha), and Philip Roos (who headed the largest voluntary association for the retarded in the nation). The experts taught him the most critical lesson about the institutionalized retarded: The gross disabilities and bizarre behavior that the visitor saw, limbs twisted into brambles and residents banging their heads against the wall, were not the reason for incarceration but the result of incarceration.

Tours of Partlow reinforced Ennis's already deep distrust of custodial institutions. As a civil libertarian, he instinctively thought of inmates not in clinical categories but as citizens. A Rockefeller five-year mental hygiene plan might opt to place the mildly retarded in the community and leave the severely retarded in institutions, but Ennis saw little reason to make such a distinction and to parcel out constitutional entitlements by degree of retardation. Indeed, as he began to learn about normalization theory, he found it completely congruent with his own position. Both the professionals and the litigators wanted to avoid stigmatizing labels and to integrate the retarded into the community.

As Ennis was formulating these ideas, Wilkins and Lee were bringing the television camera to Willowbrook. Ennis was in Alabama finishing up the *Wyatt* trial when Rivera broadcast his story, and he immediately knew what his next case would be. Arriving in New York at the start of February, he began drafting a formal court complaint without even visiting Willowbrook. Its hell, he reckoned, could not be significantly different from Partlow's.

In preparing the class action, Ennis's first, and simplest, assignment was to enlist the cooperation of experts whose testimony in *Wyatt* had impressed him. "I will soon be filing a similar lawsuit," he wrote Clements, Glenn, and Roos, among others, "seeking to establish a constitutional right to habilitation for the [Willowbrook) residents." He also met with parents of Willowbrook residents who might be willing to serve as named plaintiffs or testify in the case. In the course of this, he learned that Robert Feldt, from the Staten Island Legal Aid Society, was thinking of bringing his own case. (In fact, litigation was so much in the air that Edward Koch, then congressman from Manhattan's "silk stocking" district, had suggested to Aryeh Neier that ACLU sue New York over Willowbrook, and he volunteered to serve as one of the complainants.) Ennis worried about too many lawyers sitting around the plaintiffs' table, not only because of the possibility of contradictory strategies but also because of the threat of clashes in personality. In Alabama he had spent considerable energy keeping peace among the attorneys, whose swollen egos had kept bumping into each other, and he had no desire to repeat the experience in New York.

For Ennis, going to the Mount Augustine Retreat was an occasion not to decide strategy but to advance strategy. Once the parents and the professionals completed their presentations, he explained the legal principles that had been so successfully presented in *Wyatt*. He reported on Frank Johnson's receptivity to a right to treatment and how he had already issued a preliminary decree ordering the state to hire 300 additional staff, correct fire hazards, improve the diet, and initiate an immunization program. Ennis outlined additional improvements that the attorneys wanted the court to impose and with which he was confident it would concur. A few weeks later, on April 13, 1972, his prediction proved right. Finding conditions at Alabama's institutions so "grossly substandard" as to violate residents' "right to habilitation," Johnson issued a twenty-one-page order which specified the "minimum standards for constitutional care." It included precise definitions of staff-client ratios (1:1 for the severely retarded), adequate living space (ten square feet per resident in the dining room, forty in the dayroom), and the correct building temperatures (no less than 68 degrees, no higher than 83). Johnson also ruled that residents "have a right to the least restrictive conditions necessary to achieve the purposes of habilitation." Hence, the state was to "make every attempt to move residents from (1) more to less structured living; (2) larger to smaller facilities; (3) larger to smaller living units; (4) group to individual residence; (5) segregated from the community to integrated into the community living; (6) dependent to independent living."

Ennis, then, was fully confident of winning a Willowbrook case in New York—and he had no difficulty arousing the enthusiasm of others at the retreat. The principal resolution of the plenary session was to avoid taking "direct legislative action . . . because of the impending federal class action law suits [on the] 'right to treatment.'" Given the federal court's readiness to "encompass so many areas of proposed improvement in the care of the handicapped," the conference decided "not to . . . endorse any action which, in the opinion of the legal group . . . might in any way jeopardize the outcome of the litigation." In short, the lawyers were now in command.

Behind this transfer of leadership was a widespread and well-warranted distrust of going to the New York legislature. Those at the retreat could see little sense in lobbying the body that had neglected Willowbrook for years and, through its recent budget cuts, precipitated the crisis. Moreover, litigation seemed to promise something for everybody. Many of the parents who had no desire other than to see Willowbrook improved were encouraged that Judge Johnson's first order was for more staff and that most of his emergency remedies looked to improve institutional conditions. The professionals, on the other hand, sensed immediately and correctly that Ennis's civil liberties principles were at one with their notions of normalization and that the ultimate aim of the suit was community placement. No one dampened the glow of Ennis's presentation by suggesting that a suit would take years, or that the legislature might someday have to be reckoned with, or that the parents' intention to upgrade institutions did not coincide with the professionals' intention to close them down. What mattered most now was that someone was ready and seemingly able to do something about Willowbrook.

Immediately after the retreat, Ennis and Feldt met to resolve questions of turf. Feldt, with an insider's knowledge of Willowbrook, was afraid that Ennis would be unable to convey to a judge its true misery. He was also concerned, not unwisely as it turned out, that Ennis, NYCLU, and MHLP would receive all the publicity, leaving Feldt and Legal Aid in the cold. For his part, Ennis worried that Feldt would drown the case in atrocity stories, obscuring the relevant constitutional principles. In the end, they compromised. Each would initially file his own suit, and then, after a few months, they would ask the court to consolidate them. In this way, both organizations would take credit for the case and both attorneys would have standing to examine witnesses. The only remaining issue was the order in which the lawyers would file their suits, which of them technically would be first. They decided to flip a coin, and for those who take portents seriously, Ennis won.

The details resolved, Ennis had to identify his named plaintiffs and assemble a group that justified a motion for a class action suit. He needed a broad base, first to make certain that the state did not here, as it had so often in mental health, moot the case by releasing the client. Moreover, so many groups and subgroups made up Willowbrook's population (from different level of retardation to different level of physical disability) that the state might challenge the eligibility of a handful of parents to represent the interest of the entire class. Accordingly, Ennis chose eight individual parents, most of whom he had met at the retreat and almost all of whom had been leaders in the protests. Murray Schneps was ready to join him, and so were Diana McCourt, Rosalie Amoroso, Ida Rios, and Jerry Isaacs. Ennis also enlisted the now radicalized Willowbrook Benevolent Society, whose leaders, Jerry Gavin and Tony Pinto, were eager to cooperate. But he was well aware that Benevolent was an organization with no fixed rules on membership or procedures. It was not inconceivable that a hundred people would show up at a meeting, capture the organization, and immediately dismiss Ennis or redefine the purpose of the lawsuit. He had enough to do in the courtroom without looking over his shoulder to monitor Benevolent's politics.

These considerations left him facing his most delicate decision: Should he bring into the case the New York State Association for Retarded Children (NYARC) as a named plaintiff? More precisely, should he try to cooperate with its director, Joseph Weingold, who had a reputation for being as politically well connected as he was personally irascible?

NYARC was, and is, the state's single largest and most powerful parent organization in retardation. Its origins, although modest, reveal its ongoing aims. In the winter of 1948, two Bronx families whose children were mildly retarded tried to enroll them in public school. When they were refused admission and no other public or private classes were available, the parents created their own program. They advertised in the *New York Post,* seeking other parents of retarded children interested in organizing a day nursery, and, within a month, 200 people attended the association's first meeting. Within a year, the group was large enough to hire from among its parent members a professional executive director, Joseph Weingold.

Over the next two decades, NYARC grew in size to some 30,000 members, with chapters all over the state, and its political influence grew, too. Weingold, an indefatigable lobbyist, was able to win legislative appropriations for several community programs. What he could not do was loosen the hold that psychiatrists (and mental health concerns) had on the Department of Mental Hygiene. Weingold repeatedly urged the creation of a separate department for retardation, but, when his bill finally passed the legislature, Governor Rockefeller vetoed it.

Weingold did persuade the Benevolent Societies at three state institutions, including Willowbrook, to come under the ARC umbrella, but the alliance was always uneasy. ARC periodically protested institutional overcrowding, the lengthy wait for admissions, and substandard physical conditions. But its major purpose was to serve parents who kept their retarded children at home, to obtain for them more workshops and camp programs. The two groups squabbled over their rightful share of state appropriations. Benevolent Society members feared that dollars allotted to community programs meant reduced expenditures for institutions. ARC parents believed that, because dollars were locked into institutional budgets, community services were stunted.

Weingold's own style exacerbated these differences. There is a story, perhaps apocryphal but widely circulated, that when Weingold met with the Willowbrook Benevolent Society in early 1972 and its members asked him to join the agitation, he retorted that those who institutionalized their children deserved what they got. At his most consistent, Weingold probably preferred a triage in services: institutions for the severely and profoundly retarded, community programs for mildly and moderately retarded.

This history had very particular implications for Ennis. To include the most important parent association among the plaintiffs would probably resolve any doubts about his legal standing to represent the Willowbrook class. Ennis also anticipated that the governor might try to negotiate a settlement before trial, in which instance Weingold's Albany connections would prove useful. And if Ennis excluded Weingold, he might find ARC using its political influence to sabotage the case. Equally compelling reasons suggested not including ARC. Not only were the Benevolent parents suspicious of it, but so were many of Ennis's retardation experts. Although the New York chapter had been the moving force in organizing the national ARC, it had subsequently severed ties because of fundamental differences in perspective. A terminological distinction framed one issue: National changed its title from the Association for Retarded Children to the Association for Retarded *Citizens*. The New York group kept the designation *Children*. And the difference between thinking about the retarded as citizens and thinking of them as children was at the heart of Ennis's case.

Yet Ennis did not want to give up on Weingold. Too much was to be gained if an agreement could be reached. To explore the possibility while protecting himself from later embarrassment, Ennis had recourse to a practice that is commonplace in the world of commercial law but unusual in the world of public-interest law. He drew up a three-page retainer agreement defining the aims of the litigation: ARC retained him to challenge "the adequacy and constitutionality of conditions at Willowbrook" and agreed to remain with the case "to its conclusion." Ennis hoped "to secure [institutional] standards of education, care, treatment, training and habilitation which are as good as, or better than, the [*Wyatt v. Stickney*] standards for Partlow." But more:

> The ultimate goal of the lawsuit is to make it necessary for the State of New York to provide community-based alternatives (including halfway houses, hostels, group homes, community education and training programs, etc.), so that Willowbrook (and similar institutions) can be promptly and completely phased out of existence.

The goal in absolute terms was to close institutions for the retarded.

To this end, the retainer explained that "it will be necessary to demonstrate (a) that the conditions at Willowbrook are barbaric . . . (b) that the administrative personnel in the Department of Mental Hygiene and at Willowbrook have long been aware of those conditions and are unable or unwilling to correct them." Ennis intended to ask the court to order that Willowbrook be run in a "humane and constitutional manner" until it was "phased out" in favor of a community-based system and to appoint a master, or a panel of experts, to oversee the effort. Finally, he promised to "regularly consult" with Weingold, although "counsel will exercise final authority with regard to litigation strategy."

Never one to leave a loophole open, Ennis demanded not only that Weingold, as ARC executive director, sign the document but that the president of his board, Robert Hodgson, do so too. Lest anyone claim later that a salaried employee had no authority to commit ARC to a lawsuit, both of them had to sign. And they did. Not to join the suit would create public relations problems and, at worst, provoke the radical parents to try to take over the organization the way they had Benevolent. So the alliance was made, and, for the moment, Ennis had his named plaintiffs in place.

The Willowbrook retainer demonstrates a more formal arrangement between a public-interest lawyer and his client than those who think of such lawyers as runaway horses, litigating at will, normally concede. Nevertheless, it is true that Ennis, and not the clients or their guardians, set the terms of the suit. Further, Ennis treated the document as a private treaty, not circulating it to any of the other parties, not even the parents named as plaintiffs. This fact poses sharply one of the central controversies around reform efforts on behalf of the dependent. Who has the right to speak for disabled persons, especially when, as in the case of Willowbrook, the vast majority are unable to speak for themselves? If not the attorneys, then who? The parents—who, until the exposé, suffered from personal and political constraints that rendered them immobile or who had never gone out to visit Willowbrook or their children? The state—which had let the facility degenerate? The legislature—which made budget cuts with impunity? The professionals—who accredited the institution even at its most inhumane? One point is clear: Ennis did not wrest power from other claimants. Everyone, from parents to professionals, had a long record of failure; insofar as reforming Willowbrook was concerned, power was lying in the streets until Ennis picked it up. Who ought to speak for the retarded? In 1972, there was good reason to select someone with a clean record, someone who, with whatever presumptuousness, defined himself as acting in the public interest.

One last assignment remained: to draw up the formal complaint initiating the lawsuit in federal court. Ennis took his facts from the parent plaintiffs and his theories from Wyatt. The facts were depressingly easy to marshal:

Lara Schneps, age four, profoundly retarded and severely disabled. She "is not engaged in any program"; she is on a ward that is "for substantial periods of time . . . left entirely unattended." She does not receive "minimally adequate medical care," and, because of this, in July 1970, she fell into a coma and almost died.

Nina Galin, age ten, IQ 19, "receives no schooling or training." Her room has no toys, she is given tranquilizers four times a day. On their frequent visits, her parents "almost always discover new physical problems and injuries."

Evelyn Cruz, age thirteen, lives on a ward with 100 other children "which is staffed by approximately four employees." When her parents visit, they find her "almost always . . . severely scratched." "Except for Dr. Bill Bronston, no employee at Willowbrook has ever told Evelyn's parents anything about her."

David Amoroso, age twelve, has suffered frequent injuries and second-degree burns. Drs. Michael Wilkins and Bill Bronston got him enrolled in a school program. But the teacher soon suspended him from class "because he had started to soil himself," and now he is receiving only an hour a day of instruction.

Lowell Isaacs, age seven, is retarded, deaf, and mute. He was assigned to a hearing program but then removed "for being 'too active.'" Lowell's clothing is "deplorable," his ward has no toys. "He is forced to eat only mashed meals, even though he is able to consume solid food."

These widespread abuses, the complaint averred, violated residents' right to habilitation. Willowbrook "is not a therapeutic institution. It more closely resembles a prison," and no one could be confined there unless the facility "provided an adequate habilitation program." Its residents were deprived of "the habilitation necessary to enable them to speak, read, communicate, in violation of the First Amendment; deprived of rights to privacy and dignity, in violation of the Fourth and Fourteenth; deprived of services given to others, in violation of the Fourteenth; and subjected to cruel and unusual punishment, in violation of the Eighth."

Given these denials of rights, the complaint asked the court to hold a hearing to determine standards of adequate habilitation and then to order appropriate relief. The court should also enjoin the defendants from expending funds on any institution for the retarded in the state until it was satisfied that adequate community facilities existed. Finally, the court should appoint a receiver or a master to oversee implementation. In effect, the court should declare the institution bankrupt and assume control.

NOTE

This chapter is excerpted from *The Willowbrook Wars* (New York: Harper & Row, 1983) by permission of David J. Rothman and Sheila M. Rothman.

19

No Profits, Just a Pittance

Work, Compensation, and People Defined as Mentally Disabled in Ontario, 1964–1990

Geoffrey Reaume

In early 1964, the superintendent of the provincial mental hospital in Pene-tanguishene, Ontario, Dr. B. A. Boyd, wrote that he thought that it was "therapeutically valuable" to share "small profits" among patients who made products at industrial therapy and occupational therapy in this psychiatric facility approximately 150 kilometers north of Toronto.[1] Since this material originated with private industry, no objections had been raised to giving some extra "pin money" to those patients who made these products. However, when officials from Ontario's Department of Health found out about a display of items made by patients, they informed the hospital that since there was no law that allowed private industries to profit from the work of patients, this profit-sharing had to stop. The Business Administrator of Penetanguishene concluded that, henceforth, items made by patients with materials bought with provincial funds were to be sold at cost, with "no profit being allowed for the patients."[2]

The same year that this policy was established, a recently admitted patient at the provincial psychiatric hospital in Port Arthur (later Thunder Bay), in northwestern Ontario, found himself on the receiving end of this policy. "Jinx" described how patients were required to "line up and mop floors in the morning."[3] They were routinely required to do ward work and to clean the halls during his inpatient stay at Lakehead Psychiatric Hospital, in 1964. He was eighteen. He was assigned similar jobs during his subsequent admissions, in 1966, 1968, and 1969, when he was a patient for several months at a time. He had about thirty-nine shock treatment over this five-year period. He received no pay for his work, which took about half an hour each day.

This situation began to change only when he was put to work as an outpatient laborer, in 1973. He made picnic tables in the woodwork shop in this mental hospital, where he worked five days a week and was paid a weekly wage of around $5.00 (he cannot remember the exact amount). "Jinx" said he found this work to be good therapy, because he did not have anything else going on at that time.

These anecdotes highlight an issue that would become a major point of contention for people who were legally defined as mentally handicapped in Ontario and who were certified as "unemployable"—a fair wage for people who worked as inpatients or outpatients in mental institutions and in the community. It also brings to light the issue of work as therapy, what people in these facilities actually thought of their jobs, and how public health officials justified wage discrimination on the basis of disability classification. As this essay shows, the supposed therapeutic aims espoused by proponents of work as therapy were unable to mask the exploitative nature of the system, which used people categorized as disabled for cheap labor. It was perhaps most appropriate that this exploitation was first seriously challenged in Canada by Christine Kaszuba. She was one of the people who toiled in a system that cast aside considerations of equitable compensation as if the people involved were damaged assembly-line items. In 1981, she initiated a legal challenge that argued that she should be considered an employee of the Toronto Salvation Army sheltered workshop where she worked and that she was therefore entitled to be paid the minimum wage, a requirement from which all provincial sheltered workshops were exempt. Workers were instead paid well below the minimum wage because they were certified as "unemployable," having been categorized as mentally disabled. Eventually, this legal challenge was dismissed, and sheltered workshop employees, other than management, continued to be paid below the minimum wage in Ontario. However, the struggle was far from over. Indeed, its origins were as old as the practice of segregation for those who found themselves in workshops for the disabled.

Work and Compensation for People Defined as Mentally Disabled in Ontario before 1980

The history of putting people who were defined as disabled or handicapped to work in segregated facilities was not new to the second half of the twentieth century. Workshops for people with disabilities have existed since the late sixteenth century, when St. Vincent de Paul established the first such facility, in France, for people who were physically handicapped.[4] In North America, the first workshop for people with disabilities was set up in Massachusetts in 1837 to serve people who were blind.[5] While workshops for people who were disabled increased by the 1930s, especially under the auspices of Goodwill Industries (which originally was founded in Boston, in 1902, to help the unemployed and poor get free clothing), it was not until after World War II that a large number of workshops began to be established in the community for people who were defined as mentally handicapped.[6] Prior to this, there was a well-established practice of having people who resided in mental institutions work at various jobs within the asylum. In Ontario, during the second half of the nineteenth century and the first half of the twentieth century, it was a matter of policy among hospital administrators to advocate the use of free patient labor, especially among nonpaying public charges. This policy was rooted in the adoption in Canada of Anglo-American therapeutic ideas of work as therapy. It also had a great deal to do with keeping costs down for administrators by having patients do tasks free of charge. Labor done by residents of asylums was divided by gender, with men and women working in areas that were segregated from each other.[7]

Prior to 1950, a very small number of privileged patients were allowed to work out in the community while they remained residents of a mental hospital. These individuals were considered more "trustworthy" as workers because of their reliability in getting work assignments done and because they presented no serious behavioral problems for staff. These privileged workers were sent out on a trial basis to see whether they could be successfully integrated back into the community.[8] However, beginning around 1950, and especially during and after the 1960s, with the increasing emphasis on deinstitutionalization, mental health workers began to organize workshops outside institutions to accommodate people who otherwise would have been confined in mental hospitals.[9] The primary impetus for initiating community-based sheltered workshops in Ontario came from the parents of people who were then called mentally retarded.[10] In 1949–50, two schools funded by the federal government were opened in Toronto for people ages 12–21 who were defined as retarded, and by 1955 a workshop was opened on Beverly Street, in downtown Toronto, with help from municipal and provincial governments.[11] By 1967, there were ninety workshops in Ontario for people with disabilities. Sixty-three of these workshops included people who were defined as mentally handicapped, but the vast majority, fifty-two, were re-served for individuals labeled "mentally retarded."[12] This figure increased to 161 sheltered workshops in Ontario by 1980, with 8,600 employees, including Christine Kaszuba.[13] Eighty percent of the funding for sheltered workshops in Ontario by this time came from Ontario's Ministry of Community and Social Services, while the remaining 20 percent had to be raised by the workshops through their regular business operations.[14]

As these figures indicate, by 1979, when Christine Kaszuba started working at the Toronto Salvation Army facility, sheltered workshops had become a central part of the mental health social service system in Ontario.[15] For many disabled patients, the "stepping stones" on this path of vocational rehabilitation began with occupational therapy (OT) with an emphasis on craft-orientated programs in an environment that was not supposed to be stressful or competitive—no time clock, no assembly-line work.[16] If a person was assessed as suitable by the staff, he or she could then "graduate" to a sheltered workshop, either within the institution, where it was called industrial therapy, or after discharge, into a community site such as Goodwill Industries.[17] A person had to be referred to a work site by a mental health professional and certified as "unemployable" to gain admission to a sheltered workshop, where a "simulated" working environment was created—a time clock, sanctions for being late, assembly-line work, expectation of completing an assigned task even if the person was not supposed to be under a specific deadline, and so on.[18] This too was intended to be a noncompetitive environment, which was why it was called a "sheltered" workshop, though there were higher expectations for workshop participants here than there were at OT. But, as in the OT setting, overseers saw people who worked in a sheltered workshop as being in a rehabilitative training stage. Thus, authorities were able to exempt people who worked in sheltered workshops from minimum-wage laws in Ontario.[19]

People who worked in sheltered workshops were not considered genuine employees under the provincial labor code. This policy was very much a continuation of the idea of work as therapy, which earlier mental health professionals had advanced when putting patients to work in mental institutions. While the earlier practice of not offering any financial compensation to mental patients for their work was no longer publicly justified, the situation could hardly be called a great improvement when it came to offering a reasonable wage to people defined as mentally disabled.[20] In the early 1970s, people who worked in Ontario's sheltered workshops earned between 3 and

11 cents per hour.[21] Any suggestion of raising the wages of sheltered workshop employees was undermined by the fact that a raise would cut into an employees' provincial social assistance support, which in 1980 was $315.00 a month.[22] The most a person who worked at a sheltered workshop could make in 1980 without having his or her benefits cut back was $75.00 a month, plus an additional $10.00 allowance, for a total maximum allowable of $400.00 per month.[23] In reality, most sheltered workshop employees in 1980 Ontario earned no more than $40.00 to $50.00 a month for five-day-a-week jobs, in addition to their monthly pension of $315.00, and indeed some workers were paid nothing at all beyond their social assistance checks.[24] Thus, provincial law militated against increasing wages beyond a mere pittance. Unchallenged by the proprietors of sheltered workshops throughout Ontario, it was left up to a assembly-line laborer to protest the inequities.

Christine Kaszuba and the
Salvation Army Sheltered Workshop

In 1981, Christine Kaszuba, a thirty-seven-year-old former worker at the Salvation Army's Sheltered Workshop in Toronto, and her lawyer, David Baker, of the Advocacy Resource Center for the Handicapped, filed a claim with the Ontario Ministry of Labor asking that she be considered an employee under the provincial Employment Standards Act. This would have allowed Christine to receive the minimum wage and also entitled her to benefits, including paid sick leave.[25] Her lawyer noted that during the eighteen months she worked at the Salvation Army workshop, Christine Kaszuba earned a total of $1,096.50. During her employment, she worked a thirty-hour work week, laboring five days a week from 9 A.M. to 4 P.M. with one hour off for lunch.[26] It was acknowledged that she did not work every single day during her job; she had missed some days due to sickness. Had she been protected under minimum-wage laws and worked every day without exception, Baker noted, she would have been paid "$6,795.00 or $5,698.50 more than she actually received."[27] In other words, her pay would have increased by 84 percent. This situation was not unique; it was in fact the norm in Ontario and elsewhere in North America. In the United States during the early to mid-1980s, one workshop paid its workers 32 cents per hour, even though the minimum wage was $3.85 per hour.[28] As in Canada, these places were well established south of the border, where 3,800 sheltered workshops operated with 200,000 "clients" toiling away for a pittance; some of the workers, such as those at the workshop mentioned earlier, earned "less than one twelfth of a minimum wage."[29] With such a firmly entrenched system of officially sanctioned wage discrimination, in Ontario and beyond, any legal challenge faced enormous odds against succeeding. On the shop floor, the working environment had few financial incentives and no relief from dreary monotony.

During the one and a half years she spent at the Salvation Army workshop, Christine worked primarily on the "Brown line," so called because it consisted of packaging index tabs for the Brown Brothers company.[30] She stated that she had found this work boring and had requested another job but was unable to get one, as there were no other positions available. At the workshop where Christine worked, there were approximately 150 people who were certified as "unemployable" and who were paid 50 cents an hour "for their time at the workshop."[31] This amount was described by the Salvation Army as "an incentive wage payable for good attendance, punctuality and behavior. It has nothing to do with productivity."[32] In addition to this "wage," most of the people who worked at the sheltered workshop received social assistance benefits under the Family Benefits Act.[33] The "clients," as the workers were called, punched a clock and had their work examined by supervisors at the completion of the assigned task.[34] Workshop tasks at Christine's job site included packaging index tabs, greeting cards, sanding blocks, muffler clamps, hangars, and nuts and bolts and putting together clip lights.[35] All of these tasks were done for outside contractors. The manager of the workshop where Christine worked stated that the shop did not accept deadlines for the completion of a contract.[36] This point was used by the Salvation Army to justify its argument that its workers were not employees as defined by Ontario's labor code, an argument with which the provincial adjudicator and the appeals court agreed.[37] Some people had worked at their jobs in Ontario's sheltered workshops for as long as twenty years.[38]

Christine Kaszuba mentioned that "for a good portion of the time" she was at her job, she spent two hours a day at a school program run by the Toronto Board of Education, located at the workshop itself, in which about half (eighty) of the workers were involved.[39] The 50-cent "incentive wage" was not deducted for time spent in class. This fact was also used by Referee Kevin M. Burkett, appointed by the Ontario Ministry of Labor, who decided in favor of the Salvation Army, in 1981.[40] However, if a person was late for work, his or her pay of 50 cents an hour was docked accordingly.[41] Kaszuba's lawyer emphasized this point in an attempt to show that laborers at sheltered workshops had work-related obligations like those encountered by people in nonsheltered workshop jobs. Furthermore, it was argued that there was sufficient "control and direction" of employees at the workshop, through supervision and the possibility of suspension or dismissal, to enable workers to fall under the protection of provincial labor laws.[42] Indeed, after eighteen months at the Salvation Army workshop, Christine Kaszuba was "discontinued," that is, fired, in June 1980.[43] According to her rehabilitation counselor, Roy Dart, she was let go because she was "disruptive" toward her coworkers. She had made "caustic remarks" to two female coworkers and did not stop after being requested to do so. Also, "she continued to burden others with her problems."[44] In contrast to these claims put forward by her former superiors, Christine claimed that she had been told that her job was in danger because her epileptic seizures were considered disruptive.[45]

While the provincial referee, Kevin Burkett, did not explicitly dismiss Christine Kaszuba's views, he did attempt to raise doubts about her reliability. Referring to her lawyer, Burkett wrote, "the complainant relies on the evidence of Ms. Kaszuba that she was a good, productive worker," implying that perhaps she was not a trustworthy source.[46] There are no similar comments in his judgments about the reliability of evidence supplied by people who appeared on behalf of the Salvation Army, including a rehabilitation worker, a psychiatrist, and a manager. Instead, the professional qualifications of one witness were noted, and in another case the university degrees of another Salvation Army witness were recorded.[47] By contrast, Christine Kaszuba's troubled life, including an unsteady work record since 1969, was detailed, as was her medical history. Included in this report were references to her stays in two psychiatric facilities, as well as mention of her antipsychotic medication, said to be used "to treat thinking disorders."[48] The Salvation Army also introduced testimony that a majority of people who worked at this facility were "chronic schizophrenics" who could not function in a "regular job."[49] In his decision, Burkett returned to this point, noting that Christine Kaszuba and her coworkers had been medically certified as "unemployable" and that they were "under constant medication to control their behavior."[50]

The implication of these repeated references are clear: When dealing with compensation, people who have psychiatric diagnoses are less credible than those who supervise them, and people employed at sheltered workshops should be characterized by their medical history, rather than by the work they do. This leads to the argument that people who are defined as mentally disabled are in a state of rehabilitation for an undetermined length of time. Burkett used this claim to demonstrate that people who worked in sheltered workshops were not "real" employees requiring legal protection but were instead in a "therapeutic" relationship with those who oversaw them.[51] An application for a judicial review of Burkett's 1981 decision was dismissed by three provincial court judges in 1983.[52] There would be no back pay for Christine Kaszuba or anyone else in Ontario's sheltered workshops. The dismissal of her claim fit very well within the tradition of denigrating the work of people defined as mentally disabled. Their work was viewed as being part of their ongoing medical treatment, rather than as jobs for which they deserved fair and equitable wages. Christine Kaszuba's efforts to secure minimum-wage protection raise a number of important issues related to disability and wage discrimination.

Mental Disability, Compensation, and First-Person Experiences in Ontario

One of the most consistent issues in the compensation of people classified as having mental disabilities—in addition to the most obvious one, economic exploitation—is the lack of standards for any type of uniform payment for this group of workers. Instead, in Ontario, confusion, inconsistency, and outright neglect are pronounced when it comes to paying this group of people a respectable wage for their work. This is revealed by Christine Kaszuba's claim and by the personal experiences of several contemporary psychiatric inpatient and outpatient workers, as well as by the experiences of people labeled mentally retarded who were interviewed for this study. In 1964, when the Ontario Department of Health asked for the views of various hospital superintendents about what would constitute appropriate financial remuneration to patients from occupational therapy and industrial therapy, J. N. Senn, superintendent of the Ontario Hospital, Hamilton, suggested paying all patients $1.00 a week to get around the problem of paying some patients for employment in workshops while paying nothing to others who toil on the wards. He stated, "We should either pay all working patients regardless of the type of work, or pay none at all."[53] It was not only administrators who were aware of these "wage" differentials among patient laborers within the mental health system. One former psychiatric patient remembered that he was paid for work in one type of hospital, but not in another.

Wayne Lax, born in 1940, experienced "108 admissions, and approximately 80 [electroshock] treatments from 1967 to 1992" along with "up to 17 different pills per day."[54] This history has seriously limited his memory of many past events, though he was able to recall some things and was helped in this by friends and family members, as well as by examination of his medical records. During this twenty-five-year period, he was in the psychiatric facility at Lake of the Woods Hospital, in Kenora, Ontario, and in the Lakehead Psychiatric Hospital, in Thunder Bay, for stays that lasted from three weeks to six months at a time.[55] He also lived in nursing homes in Kenora for several years. The jobs he knows that he worked at included mopping floors, cleaning toilets and windows in "mile-long hallways," and working in the garden at the hospital in Thunder Bay. At times, he did these jobs within two weeks after getting shock treatment.[56] He made $7 a week for working 8 A.M. to 3 P.M. Wayne said he was determined to do this work, not because he liked it but because the work allowed him to get a bit of money, for which he was desperate so that he could buy snacks from the patients' canteen. It was the only thing he had to look forward to inside the mental hospital. Like many other patients in Ontario mental institutions, he had no other access to money, since social assistance payments were cut off after one payment when a person entered the hospital.[57] He also worked at sheltered workshops in Kenora, where he vaguely remembers making fish hooks from 8 A.M. to 4 P.M. He said that, from what he remembers about the different hospitals and nursing homes in which he lived, both in Kenora and in Thunder Bay, during his twenty-five years as a psychiatric patient, staff expected patients to work because if you "didn't get out and work you'd get hassled." This was especially so at Lakehead Psychiatric Hospital, where patients were pressured to get to work, as the staff "were pushing you to do things." At Lake of the Woods Hospital, where he was admitted to the psychiatric ward seventy-five times over a quarter of a century (and from where he was often transferred to Thunder Bay), he was put to work carrying trays to patients, dusting, and helping people who were physically infirm. He was never paid for this work in Kenora, unlike in Thunder Bay, since general hospitals do not have to pay working patients in their psychiatric wards. Thus, monetary compensation, as minuscule as it was for inpatient laborers in provincial public mental hospitals, did not reach to inpatient workers behind the doors of general-hospital psychiatric wards.

Within the sheltered workshop system of wage inequity and the uneven application of compensation, one source of inequity was the type of disability with which a person was classified. As was noted earlier, in 1980, people who worked at the Salvation Army workshop in Toronto and who had perfect attendance were paid 50 cents an hour, which resulted in a paycheck of $15.00 a week. At the same time, people who were employed at a training center for adults defined as "mentally retarded" in the same region were paid as little as 50 cents to $3.00 *per week*, on top of their social assistance checks. This was for working at a five-day-a-week job, 9 A.M. to 4:00 P.M.[58] Isabella Patrick protested the 50-cents-a-week payment at the facility run by the Metropolitan Toronto Association for the Mentally Retarded, where her thirty-year-old daughter, also named Isabella, did contract jobs that included filling bags of confetti and assembling nuts and screws. She noted that this work left her daughter tired at the end of the day and that a "raise" from 50 cents a week to 55 cents a week was "equally insulting."[59] Mrs. Patrick, a widow who received an old-age pension and who lived with her daughter, asked, "My goodness what can you get for 50 cents? You can get maybe two ice cream cones."[60]

The 50-cent-a-week "wage" that Isabella Patrick received and the 50-cent-an-hour "wage" that her contemporary Christine Kaszuba was paid, highlights the wage discrimination that people who were defined as mentally disabled faced, not only in relation to Ontario's workforce but also in relation to one another. This is an important point, for it indicates the confused and uneven application of wages at workshops in Ontario and also the way that classes of disability influenced wage discrimination.[61] The type of mental disability that was diagnosed influenced this wage discrimination; people with psychiatric disorders were paid more than people classified as mentally retarded. The contrast in 1980 between the meager "wages" of people at the Salvation Army workshop, which employed primarily psychiatric patients, and the even lower "wages" paid only a few miles away to people labeled "mentally retarded" indicates the practice of devaluing work done by people simply because of the nature of their disability.

Certainly, the experiences of three people who were classified as mentally retarded but who rejected that label indicate the difficulties common in sheltered workshops. Russell Havill worked, from 1983 to 1985, at a sheltered workshop, in Kenora, Ontario, that was operated by ARC (Association for Retarded Children) Industries.[62] He was employed in the wood room, where he operated several large saws, a drill press, and sanders. The shop made picnic tables and patio tables. He said people did not like getting paid only $15.00 a week at a place where "if you acted up your pay would reflect the same!"[63] He also stated that people became bored with the workshop, "counting screws day after day to get inventory done!" He also mentioned the difficult working conditions. The paint room in which he worked had such poor air circulation that he had to leave his job some days because of the strong smell of paint and varnish. The dust in the wood room was not much better when all the saws were running.

Sharon Myron worked at the same workshop, beginning when she was eighteen, in 1976, and continuing well into the 1980s, though she cannot re-call the exact number of years she worked there.[64] During this time, she did various jobs and helped her brother to silk-screen products such as table place mats for restaurants, posters, and t-shirts, then placing and drying them on racks. She also made flowers, the job she liked the best. She was paid $5.00 or $6.00 a week for working six hours a day between 9 A.M. and 4 P.M., with half an hour off for lunch and two coffee breaks of fifteen minutes each, as well as some time to rest when silk screens were changed. There was one job that was especially memorable and that she liked—plucking ducks that hunters brought in to be cleaned. When Sharon did this job, she had to work inside a steel wire cage, where she would stand and pluck the dead ducks (though in one instance a duck that had been shot was brought in half-alive, which she noticed when she began to pluck its feathers; a coworker took it outside and killed it). The cage was built to keep the feath-ers from the plucked ducks from flying around the room. Sharon was not able to sit down while plucking the ducks but had to stand the whole time she was inside this cage. Otherwise, her fingers would have gotten caught in the machine. "It was safer for me to stand." The length of time she did this job depended on how many ducks had been brought in by the hunters. When she was asked how long it took to pluck one duck, Sharon replied, "When I boogie, I boogie!" Sharon was paid 50 cents for each duck she plucked, while other coworkers cleaned out their insides and washed them. The ducks were then put in a freezer with the name of the hunter on them; the hunter would then pay ARC Industries when he came to pick up the ducks. Sharon said she and the other workers were expected to get all the ducks plucked and cleaned in one day; if they did not do this, they would have their pay docked "a dollar, two dollars, maybe more, can't remember." Sharon said that they were always under pressure from supervisors to get their jobs done within the deadline. The most she made for one day's work was $15.00 for plucking 91 ducks; 91 x .50 = $45.50, so she was grossly un-derpaid, even on the basis of the small amount she was supposed to receive.

On that day her supervisors let her work through her entire work shift without a lunch or coffee break. This was an upsetting job at times, because one of her coworkers would throw clay in at her while she worked in the cage and nothing was ever done about it. She eventually quit her job at ARC because, she said, "I'm not coming back to that jail." As much as she disliked this place, she regrets that it was shut down by People First in 1992, since it has been hard for people with mental disabilities to get a job around Kenora in the years since then.

The disdain that former sheltered workshop employees of ARC in Kenora felt for the shop was expressed by another man, R. J. Gordon, who said, of his relationship to staff, "We're the inmates, they're the wardens."[65] He worked at ARC for five years when he was in his early twenties, in the mid- to late 1980s, and did woodwork, piled lumber, and received a low wage like that earned by his friend Sharon. Again like Sharon, he was involved in cleaning ducks, which he called "messy," "slimy," and "cold." He also mentioned how unpleasant the working environment was; in the summer, "Boy, was it hot. In winter it was freezing." The building was also very poorly lit, a situation that did not improve while it was used by ARC. Since he left this job, R. J. has earned more money working at private-sector jobs, as well as doing cleaning work at the Kenora Association for Community Living, which is housed in the former ARC Industries building—though with a good deal more light now.[66]

ARC Industries was intended as a workshop for people classified as "retarded." One of the few people who was employed there as a psychiatric outpatient revealed how differences in mental disability classification could also lead to differences in treatment within the workshop. "Elizabeth Horn" worked for more than a year, from 1986 to 1987, at ARC Industries, in Kenora, Ontario, when she was in her forties.[67] While there, she did knitting and painting, though she cannot recall all of her work or how much she was paid, other than that it was a "small token." Most of the people who worked at ARC were classified as "retarded" or developmentally disabled, but she and "a few others" were among the psychiatric patients who were sent to work at this workshop. Elizabeth said that she found it "disturbing" that people with developmental disabilities were mistreated at ARC, but she was too intimidated to speak up, except on one occasion, when a man with Down Syndrome was locked in a closet because he was screaming. A few times in the years since then, she has seen this man walking with his parents in Kenora and remains friendly with him. She found many of the staff at the nursing home she lived at in Kenora, as well as at ARC Industries quite in-sensitive; they often made cruel comments and treated people badly, as they did the man with Down Syndrome. Though there were also some good staff, she felt that working as a patient-laborer was "extremely demeaning at times." On her last day of work at ARC Industries, she was asked rather sar-castically by one of the staff, "Do you think you are special?" "Elizabeth" replied, "Well, no. Everyone here is special."

The absence of any mention of gender differences in compensation by people interviewed and in documents examined for this chapter does not mean that men and women were treated equally in regard to job opportuni-ties within the workshop system. Documents make clear the influence that gender had on the types of work that were allotted from the earliest stages of rehabilitation. Beginning in occupational therapy at hospitals like Kingston, in 1968, men were expected to be involved in "masculine activities," such as woodworking, whereas women were involved in "feminine activities," like sewing.[68] This tracking process could also influence the types of jobs men and women were expected to perform in the community. In the mid-1960s, at Ontario Hospital, Woodstock, which housed people with both physical and mental disabilities, women were trained for jobs such as domestic serv-ice or work in the laundry, while men were expected to hold jobs such as gen-eral laborer and gardener once they returned to the community.[69] Dr. M. Barrie, superintendent of the Ontario Hospital, Cobourg, wrote, in 1964: "As practically all our girls are trained for domestic duties, or assisting in hospi-tals or nursing homes, it appears improbable that we will be obtaining con-tact from industrial firms."[70]

Underlying these practices was the assumption that industrial-type work, such as that for which workshops received contracts, was more suitable for training or retraining men than women. As well, having male patients do tra-ditional "masculine" work and female patients do "feminine" work was firmly rooted in long-established work practices promoted by hospital au-thorities, just as it existed nearly everywhere during this period.[71] Although these attitudes of mental health officials are not surprising, it is important to note them because of the impact they may have had on the types of work apportioned to men and women at sheltered workshops.[72] In the early 1980s, at Goodwill Industries, in Windsor, Ontario, both men and women did jobs such as sorting clothes, cutting rags into small pieces, and putting small products, such as vitamins, into packages. However, only men were given the opportunity to work on heavier jobs, such as constructing pallets, assembling automotive parts, driving the forklift, or working in the large moving van to pick up and drop off various household items.[73] Both men and women who worked in Ontario's sheltered workshops at the time of Christine Kaszuba's employment were paid extremely low "wages," with men no better off financially than their female coworkers. However, the available jobs at these facilities may have offered more choice to men than to women, inside and outside mental hospitals. As the following accounts suggest, this choice of jobs could also lead to workplace safety hazards, as well as to emotional attachments among patients who worked togehter.

A thirty-eight-year-old man who wishes to remain anonymous did several jobs during the late 1970s, 1980s, and 1990s, while he was a psychiatric outpatient and inpatient in northwestern Ontario.[74] During this period, he was readmitted thirty-four times over a twenty-year period to Lakehead Psychiatric Hospital, beginning in 1978, when he was seventeen. He said his diagnoses have included schizophrenia and manic depression, and he also suffered brain damage after being in a car accident. While an inpatient in Thunder Bay, this man worked at the hospital garage and cut cloth into cleaning rags for $1.50 to $2.00 an hour; assembled test-tube kits for medical tests; worked at the car wash, where his pay started at $1.50 an hour and went up to $2.00 an hour, from 7:30 A.M. to 3:30 P.M. five days a week; worked in the woodshops making picnic tables; and washed the furniture around the ward. As a rule, patients were never paid for working inside the ward, only for work performed outside the ward.

While an outpatient, he worked for two years, from 8 A.M. to 4 P.M., in a sheltered workshop at ARC Industries in Dryden, Ontario. His jobs included sorting scrap metal, which consisted of taking metal articles apart and placing the pieces in jars for resale; making wooden survey sticks and markers for surveyors; twisting guy-wire cables for Bell Canada telephone poles; cutting large grounded wires; taking apart telephone relay systems and plug-in connections; making cushion pads for people who were undergoing medical treatment for heart problems; putting price stickers on retail items; drilling holes in metal plates for signs; cutting wood with a large circular band-saw; operating a velcro-cutting machine that required precise cutting of material; shoveling snow; grinding the edges of copper pieces, though he could not recall why he had to do this; and doing contract work with a local landscape company, thinning bushes and trimming trees. The man who did all this work was never paid an hourly wage, even though he worked a regular forty-hour week for two years doing these tasks. He was instead paid in the form of a monthly disability pension of between $800 and $900 a month in the early 1990s, or from $9,600 to $10,800 per year. The man said he would have preferred an hourly wage like one would get in the private sector for comparable work. Prior to his confinement at the age of seventeen, he had been learning the metal trade, one of the reasons he was given work in this particular type of job.

He was not required to wear a hard hat while working at the various jobs. He maintained that he was on neuroleptic medications, which can induce drowsiness and blurred vision, while he was operating the band-saw, sanders, drills, and similar tools, even though he was not supposed to be operating machinery while on medication. No staff members ever questioned this. While working at grinding copper, he accidentally put a steel pick into the bone of his hand. Since then, he has had nerve problems with that hand; it is weaker, and he can not open and close it as easily as the other hand. He was brought to the hospital for first aid for the injury but was back on the job the very next day. He said there was pressure from supervisory staff on some people, including himself and a woman who was blind, to get their work done, though others with developmental disabilities who worked at sanding jobs were not pressured as much. Fifteen men and women worked as laborers in this sheltered workshop, including people with developmental, physical, and psychiatric disabilities (this number does not include management or supervisors).

As is evident from this man's testimony, and that of "Elizabeth Horn," from Kenora, workshops set up for people labeled "retarded," like ARC Industries, could also include people with other disabilities, especially in small towns, where there were fewer workshops than in large cities.[75] At the Dryden workshop, men did the heavier and more varied industrial work described earlier, while women were employed in lighter jobs such as making flowers. As will be seen, the work women did inside mental hospitals was also intensive.

"Mabel N." was a patient at Lakehead Psychiatric Hospital for one year (1982-83), when she was in her late forties. The death of her mother and what she called "illusions" about the future were the precipitating causes of her confinement.[76] She said she was required to work on and off all day as an inpatient. Her regular workday included cleaning tables after breakfast, then, with another woman patient, making the beds on her ward and on the geriatric ward, cleaning tables again after both lunch and supper, and doing this job again after the late-night snack before bed. She also had to clean the bathroom and make coffee for staff. While she was an inpatient, "Mabel" said she told the staff "lots of times I didn't want to do this work but they told me I had to," even though she felt she was "too sick to do it." She was given no choice in the matter. "Mabel" does not consider the work she did during this period to have been therapeutic. She said that she was never paid for any of these jobs while an inpatient, and staff pressured her to do this work. While some nurses (one in particular) treated her very poorly, like a prisoner in a jail, she said, others valued her work. There was also one female patient coworker with whom she did not get along while doing her various jobs, but otherwise she got along well with her coworker inmates in the hospital.

She also worked as an outpatient at Lakehead Psychiatric Hospital for about five years in the mid- to late 1980s, while living in a rooming house in Thunder Bay. During this period, her regular work week was Monday to Friday, from 8 A.M. to 4 P.M. (she was sometimes required to work ten hours a day ending at 6 P.M.); for her work, she was paid a total of $16.00 per month. She liked working as an outpatient, because she did not feel as much pressure from staff. The pay, as little as it was, was a monetary acknowledgement that she had never received as an inpatient worker. Her bus fare to and from work was also paid and she was allowed to eat breakfast and lunch at the hospital as part of the compensation for her labor. "Mabel" said her work as an outpatient included two years working as a caregiver to elderly patients, which she liked to do, though it was also upsetting to see how they were treated "so mean" by being restrained in chairs. She helped to feed, clean, and bathe them, as well as to clean their beds with a carbolic solution. She mentioned that she became friends with some of the elderly patients she worked with and that it was upsetting when some of them died, especially one man, Paul. The elderly patients often expressed appreciation to "Mabel" for her help, and Paul's way of doing this was to give her perogies, pickles, and cabbage rolls that he had saved in his bedside cupboard for her.

It was not only patient-laborers who found their working conditions exploitative and distressing. An idea of the repressive working environment for patients within the Lakehead hospital was provided by a former employee, Mr. Primeau, who worked in the laundry department in 1979. Mr. Primeau said that when he was there, patients who tried to talk with staff who brought the laundry in were strongly reprimanded, so most patients were too afraid to be friendly. One patient who wanted to visit with her parents on the ward was not allowed to do this and had to stay at her job. "She bawled her eyes out,"

Mr. Primeau said.[77] After this, she did not come back to her job for a few days; he believes she was put in an isolation room as punishment. He said that both male and female patients had to work for nothing in the laundry and were told by staff what jobs to do, that they were not there as volunteers. The patients' job was to fold the clothes that had been washed (only paid staff did the washing), a job which they did five days a week, six hours a day, from 9 A.M. to 3:30 P.M. with half an hour off at noon for lunch. By contrast, these unpaid patients worked alongside paid staff who received $6.00 an hour.

The stark difference between the compensation paid to people classified as mentally disabled and that paid to those not so classified helps to explain why Christine Kaszuba, a contemporary of these individuals, fought the economic exploitation they all experienced. It also reveals the enormous obstacles faced by anyone who challenged this deeply entrenched system—entrenched in attitudes, laws, and history.

Did Nothing Change? Wage Discrimination and Mental Disability in Ontario, 1964–1990

Twenty years after a hospital official reported that patients would not be allowed a share in the profits for work done at Penetanguishene mental hospital in 1964, as described in the opening paragraph of this essay, a Toronto newspaper reported, in 1984, that "Patients don't share in any profits" made in provincial psychiatric hospital workshops.[78] As far as provincial policy was concerned during this two-decade-long period, when it came to compensating people with mental disabilities for their work, nothing had changed. Their work was barely worth a pittance. Provincial policy was so rigid that if workshop laborers earned more money than a hospital had budgeted, they were penalized. At the Queen Street Mental Health Center, in Toronto, "patients were told they would suffer a pay cut because they had exceeded the budget allocation for their wages."[79] When this episode occurred, in 1984, a year after Christine Kaszuba's claim was dismissed, people in Ontario's psychiatric workshops were being paid from 25 cents to 85 cents an hour, "with special exceptions made to pay a few patients $1 an hour."[80] A few years later, in 1990, the Salvation Army was still paying 50 cents an hour to people who worked in sheltered workshops in Toronto, the same as in 1979–80, when Christine Kaszuba worked there, a policy they continued to justify by claiming that the work was not work but rehabilitation—that is, work as therapy, rather than work to earn a living.[81] Some people in Ontario's sheltered workshops were paid as low as 15 cents an hour in 1990.[82] At this time, there were 166 sheltered workshops in Ontario, where 9,971 people classified as disabled worked. The majority of these workshops, 126, served 7,300 people with developmental disabilities (formerly called mentally retardation), while the remaining forty workshops served 2,671 people classified as having psychiatric and physical disabilities.[83]

One of the contractors who took advantage of the cheap "wages" and of the people who worked in sheltered workshops during this period provided a succinct summary of what motivated companies, like Air Canada, to have products packaged by people who were paid next to nothing: "There's a high percentage of dependability, the work we get is good, and the price is right."[84] Dependability, good work, the "right" price—except that it was not considered "right" by many of those who worked there, as this essay has revealed. The fact that this contractor spoke well of their work indicates that workshop laborers were much more reliable than the image suggested by those who opposed Christine Kaszuba's application to be considered an employee. Yet, it is also important to note that throughout this period, there were people who worked at jobs where they were paid very little but who did not express the view that they were being economically exploited. Isabella Patrick, the thirty-year-old woman who was paid 50 cents a week at a workshop run by the Metropolitan Toronto Association for the Mentally Retarded in 1980, said to her mother that the low pay "does not mean much to her."[85] It was not an issue for Isabella, as it was for her mother. Similar sentiment was expressed by an anonymous psychiatric patient-laborer who worked in woodwork shop at the Lakehead Psychiatric Hospital, in Thunder Bay. Male patients who worked there made picnic tables, small furniture for kindergarten classes, and deacon's chairs and connected lawn chairs and coat racks. This job required workers to labor five days a week, five and a half hours a day, from 9 to 11:30 A.M. and from 1 to 3 P.M., and paid them between $1.00 and $2.00 per hour.[86] The forty-one-year-old man who provided this information has been in and out of the hospital for fifteen years, beginning in the early 1980s, and was diagnosed as having schizophrenia. He says he was upset that the woodwork shop closed down, since he liked this job which he felt was more of a sheltered workshop than regular employment. He felt that this and other jobs he worked at, as both an inpatient and an outpatient (e.g., cutting rags and working on bicycles at the March of Dimes store in Thunder Bay) helped him and were therapeutic.

The views of these two people highlight the contradictions inherent in this story, where some workshop laborers clearly felt exploited, while others did not make any such claim. Understanding the views of those who did not claim to be exploited helps us understand how work done by people defined as mentally disabled in Ontario was situated in the context of their emotional and economic vulnerability as workshop laborers. Many of the people who worked either in sheltered workshops in the community or in provincial mental institutions were especially vulnerable because of the social stigma attached to their disabilities and their isolation from people in mainstream society. They were also particularly vulnerable to unemployment; by 1991, only 48 percent of people defined as mentally or physically disabled in Canada were employed, whereas 73 percent of people who were not disabled had jobs.[87] With this in mind, it is not surprising that some people defined as mentally handicapped did not complain about their very low rate of compensation. People like Isabella Patrick had no other workplace to turn to. Their chances of finding jobs elsewhere were extremely small, if not nonexistent, especially for those who had little or no work experience outside the sheltered workshop system. Some laborers had passed their entire work lives being treated as less worthy than those who oversaw them and had internalized this wearing down of self-esteem. They worked in an environment where people were so desperate for some kind of paid occupation, and the self-worth that goes along with it, that working in sheltered workshops inside or outside the hospital was something they wanted to do, even though the only "jobs" available were the lowest-paid work around. Others had to work in order to get their social assistance checks, or were required to toil for little or nothing by mental health workers. Many of these same people who worked in sheltered workshops or in mental institutions had spent much, if not all, of their work lives in a system where getting paid a pittance for a day's work was the norm. For some people, going to work, even in a highly exploitative system like workshops for the disabled, was better than being kept on a locked ward or in residential housing all day, with little opportunity for socialization outside one's living quarters.

People who operated this work system took advantage of the emotional and social vulnerability of people classified as mentally disabled. This most marginalized group of workers had long been so isolated that their chance of securing minimum-wage protection in Ontario seemed remote indeed. Neither mental health professionals nor contractors had much, if any, desire to improve the extremely low level of compensation that existed into the 1990s in Ontario for workers defined as mentally disabled. Yet, things had slowly started to change, at least in attitude, by the time Christine Kaszuba tried, and failed, to get her rights as a worker recognized in law. A crucial part of this change was the increased awareness of these issues among workshop laborers themselves. Since the 1970s, Pat Worth has been a leading self-advocate with the advocacy organization People First, which has been in the forefront of the struggle for employment equity among people who have in the past been labeled "retarded." He pointed out that many people who worked in these facilities "did not understand the idea of a minimum wage and how they were deprived of earning a salary like anyone else. A lot of us were conned into believing that a disability pension was actually a salary."[88] In 1990, a group of people who had worked at sheltered workshops, in cooperation with advocacy groups, organized conferences and demonstrations where they called for minimum-wage protection in Ontario, an end to economic discrimination, and "the closure of segregated workshops so that people will have a chance to earn living wages in the community."[89] They were encouraged by the case of Bruce Fenton, a psychiatric patient in British Columbia who, in 1989, fought for and received minimum-wage protection and back pay for sixteen years of work.[90]

Efforts to secure equitable wages and employment for people who are classified as mentally disabled continued past 1990.[91] The developments that prior to this point were an important impetus for change, as well as establishing a tradition among supposedly incompetent people, who are increasingly unlikely to accept the patronizing tone of those who have categorized them in this way, of challenging unfair labor practices. The unsuccessful attempt by Christine Kaszuba to get legal protection under Ontario's provincial labor laws was not futile; her efforts revealed to a wider audience that people certified as "unemployable" are not as incapable as this term suggests. Her struggle for a fair wage continues to be built upon as more people come to recognize, despite that hospital administrator in 1964, that "profits" should indeed be allowed for the patients.

NOTES

I would like to thank all of the people interviewed for this study for their insights: Wayne Lax, of Kenora, Ontario, and Lynne Moss-Sharman, of Thunder Bay, Ontario, for their help in arranging interviews in northwestern Ontario; John Playter and the staff of the Advocacy Resource Center for the Handicapped, Toronto, and Don Weitz for their very helpful research assistance; and Steven Noll, for his comments on an earlier draft. Portions of this paper were presented during the conference "Gender, Science, and Health in Post-War North America, Comparative Canadian-American Perspectives, 1940-1980," York University and the University of Toronto, March 6, 1999, and during the annual meeting of the Canadian Society for the History of Medicine, University of Alberta, Edmonton, May 27, 2000. Research for this study was funded as part of a postdoctoral fellowship by Associated Medical Services, Hannah Institute for the History of Medicine, Toronto, at the Institute for the History and Philosophy of Science and Technology, University of Toronto.

1. Archives of Ontario (hereafter referred to as AO), RG 10-20-A-2, Container 3, Psychiatric Hospital Services Subject Files, McNeel: Minutes—Vocational and Recreational Services, 1961-1969. File 3-4: Patients Profits, O.T. and I.T., 1964: Letter to Dr. B. H. McNeel, Chief, Mental Health Branch, from B. A. Boyd, Superintendent, Ontario Hospital, Penetang, January 31, 1964. These products included bird houses that were sold to Eaton's; workers also performed baseball sewing, furniture refinishing, and crafts that were paid for by other companies.

2. AO, RG 10-20-A-2, Container 3, Psychiatric Hospital Services Subject Files, McNeel: Minutes—Vocational and Recreational Services, 1961-1969. File 3-4: Patients Profits, O.T. and I.T., 1964: Letter to Dr. B. A. Boyd, Medical Superintendent, Ontario Hospital, Penetanguishene, from E. M. Hill, Business Administrator, Ontario Hospital, Penetanguishene, January 31, 1964.

3. Interview with "Jinx" (pseudonym), Thunder Bay, Ontario, September 27, 1999.

4. Nathan Nelson, *Workshops for the Handicapped in the United States: An Historical and Developmental Perspective* (Springfield, Ill.: Charles C. Thomas, 1971), p. 24.

5. Ibid. p. 26.

6. Ibid., pp. 36-37.

7. For a discussion of this topic see: Geoffrey Reaume, *Remembrance of Patients Past: Patient Life at the Toronto Hospital for the Insane, 1870-1940* (Toronto: Oxford University Press Canada, 2000), pp. 133-180.

8. Lykke de la Cour and Geoffrey Reaume, "Patient Perspectives in Psychiatric Case Files," in *On the Case: Explorations in Social History,* ed. Wendy Mitchinson and Franca Iacovetta (Toronto: University of Toronto Press, 1998), pp. 258-259.

9. For a discussion of the impact of deinstitutionalization in Ontario see Harvey Simmons, *From Asylum to Welfare* (Downsview, Ontario: National Institute on Mental Retardation, 1982), pp. 179-215; Harvey Simmons, *Unbalanced: Mental Health Policy in Ontario, 1930-1989,* Part II and Part III (Toronto: Wall & Thompson, 1990).

10. People who have in the past been classified as "feeble-minded," then "mentally retarded," and still later people with developmental disabilities will be referred to primarily as "mentally retarded" in this article, as this is the historical term used at that time.

11. Matthew B. Dymond, *A Spectrum of Mental Retardation Services in Ontario,* Report to the Federal Provincial Conference on Mental Retardation, Ottawa, October, 1964, p. 6. Betty Anglin and June Braaten, *Twenty-Five Years of Growing Together: A History of the Ontario Association for the Mentally Retarded* (Toronto: Canadian Association for the Mentally Retarded, 1978), pp. 7, 9–10; *Profile: News Magazine of the Metro Toronto Association for Community Living* (spring/summer 1997), p. 6; Vera C. Pletsch, *Not Wanted in the Classroom: Parent Associations and the Education of Trainable Retarded Children in Ontario: 1947–1969* (London: Althouse Press, 1997), pp. 41–45.

12. Manpower Division, *Directory of Workshops in Canada* (Ottawa: Vocational Rehabilitation Branch, Department of Manpower and Immigration, 1967). This survey (which does not have page numbers) explicitly lists fifty-two workshops in Ontario for people labeled "mentally retarded" but lists only two workshops for people defined as mentally ill. A note on the page headed "Grand Totals for Canada" records the existence of nine "Goodwill-type" shops in Ontario, which are included in the category "Community and General." Since Goodwill Industries by this time was employing people defined as mentally handicapped, this total of nine has been added to the two workshops in Ontario for people defined as mentally ill. These eleven workshops have been added to the fifty-two in the category "Mentally Retarded" to come up with the figure cited in this article of sixty-three workshops for people defined as mentally handicapped. It is important to note that people who were labeled "mentally retarded" as well as people referred to as mentally ill could also work in workshops that were outside either of these two categories, such as at Goodwill (see note 75).

13. Dorothy Lipovenko, "Sheltered Workshop Employees Eligible for Benefits, WCB Rules," *Globe and Mail,* August 29, 1980. This article is about "no-fault" disability coverage provided for workshop employees by the Ontario Workmen's Compensation Board. General statistics are provided for workshops in the province.

14. Advocacy Resource Center for the Handicapped, Toronto (hereafter referred to as ARCH), Sheltered Workshops File: Referee's (Kevin M. Burkett) decision re *Christine Kaszuba and Salvation Army Sheltered Workshop,* Toronto, December 10, 1981 (hereafter referred to as *Kaszuba and SA, 1981*), p. 20.

15. The dates of Christine Kaszuba's employment (January 1979–June 1980) can be found in ARCH, Sheltered Workshops File: undated letter, David Baker, Advocacy Resource Center for the Handicapped, Toronto, to Mr. J. R. Scott, Director, Ministry of Labor, Employment Standards Branch, Toronto, p. 9. It should be noted that this letter has Christine Kaszuba's name whited out, as it was written before the case had become public.

16. J. J. Weber, Superintendent of the Ontario Hospital, Woodstock, noted that occupational therapy for some patients was "a stepping stone to outside work around the hospital, work on the wards, industrial therapy, etc." AO, RG 10-20-A-2, Container 3, Psychiatric Hospital Services Subject Files, McNeel: Minutes—Vocational

and Recreational Services, 1961–1969. File 3-4: Patients Profits, O.T. and I.T., 1964: Letter to Dr. B. H. McNeel, Chief, Mental Health Branch, from J. J. Weber, Superintendent, Ontario Hospital, Woodstock, April 9, 1964.

17. A report on a facility for people labeled "retarded" in Ottawa noted this process when reporting that "clients are first admitted to the Training Centre for assessment after which it is decided if they should be retained for training or transferred to the sheltered workshop. Clients who have completed their training and are ready for employment placement are also transferred to the sheltered workshop." Manpower Division, *Directory of Workshops in Canada*. See section "Ontario C—Programs for the Mentally Retarded (Cont'd)" under "Ottawa—The Adult Training Centre, 221 Donald Street." See also references in AO RG 10-163-0-731-739, No. 34, Printed Materials: Ontario Department of Health, *Rehabilitation in Ontario, 1965* (Toronto: Ontario Department of Health, 1965), pp. 5–6; AO, RG 10-163-0-682, Printed Materials: Barry Swadron, *Report of the Study Project on Mental Health Legislation* (Toronto, September 1966), pp. 103–105.

18. *Kaszuba and SA, 1981,* pp. 4–6. It should be noted that the argument that sheltered workshops did not have deadlines for the completion of a contract, which was used successfully by the Salvation Army in the Christine Kaszuba case, was not universally true. When the author worked at Goodwill Industries, Contract Division, in Windsor, Ontario, in 1980–81, it was not at all unusual to be told to get a particular job done by a deadline because the contractor wanted it that way. At times, some employees were pulled off other, less urgent jobs to do the one that faced a looming deadline.

19. Gail Czukar notes that sheltered workshop employees are "designated as trainees or persons who are being provided with vocational rehabilitation services. Even workers who have been in the same workshop for five or ten years or more, sometimes doing the same basic work for all that time, may be considered to be trainees or in the process of rehabilitation." ARCH, Sheltered Workshops file: Gail Czukar, *Payment of Less Than Minimum Wage in Sheltered Workshops* (Toronto: submitted to Canadian Disability Rights Council, December, 1988), p. 2. See also, ARCH, "Will the Charter Change Sheltered Workshops?" *Phoenix Rising: The Voice of the Psychiatrized* 5: 2, 3 (August 1985): 31A–32A.

20. People with physical disabilities were also paid extremely low wages and in some places worked at the same workshops as people defined as mentally handicapped, such as at Goodwill Industries. Some people at workshops also had a "dual diagnosis," that is, they had both physical and mental disabilities. Since the focus of this essay is people who were labeled mentally handicapped, the discussion is limited to this group of people. However, an obvious subject of future research would be to evaluate whether there were differences in the compensation rates paid out by workshops to people with physical and to those with mental disabilities. Since places like

Goodwill employed people with both physical and mental disabilities, it is likely that there was no difference in workshop "wages" for the two groups.

21. Simmons, *From Asylum to Welfare*, p. 204.

22. Charlotte Montgomery, "50¢ a Week 'Slavery' of Retarded, Mom Says," *Toronto Star*, May 6, 1980. In 1964, people who were "unable to work competitively" (i.e., workshop employees) in Ontario received $75.00 a month, a figure that later rose to $170.00 per month. In 1974, the amount increased to $217.00 per month, and in 1977, social assistance income for workshop employees rose to $270.00 per month. For reference to these figures see Anglin and Braaten, *Twenty-Five Years of Growing Together*, p. 52.

23. Montgomery, "50¢ a Week 'Slavery,'" *Toronto Star*, May 6, 1980.

24. Lipovenko, "Sheltered Workshop Employees Eligible for Benefits." The description of workers who were not getting paid anything beyond a social assistance check is based on the author's experience at Goodwill Industries in Windsor, Ontario, April 1980–June 1981.

25. *Kaszuba and SA, 1981*, p. 1.

26. ARCH, Sheltered Workshops File: undated letter, David Baker, Advocacy Resource Center for the Handicapped, Toronto, to Mr. J. R. Scott, Director, Ministry of Labor, Employment Standards Branch, Toronto, p. 1. In the referee's decision, the working day at the Salvation Army workshop is recorded as being from 9 A.M. to 5 P.M. *Kaszuba and SA, 1981*, p. 9.

27. ARCH, Sheltered Workshops File: undated letter, David Baker, Advocacy Resource Center for the Handicapped, Toronto, to Mr. J. R. Scott, Director, Ministry of Labor, Employment Standards Branch, Toronto, p. 1.

28. "Which Clients Should a Sheltered Workshop Serve?" *Hastings Center Report* (October 1984), p. 52.

29. Stanley S. Herr, "Commentary," *Hastings Center Report* (October 1984), pp. 53–54.

30. *Kaszuba and SA, 1981*, p. 8, 15.

31. Ibid., pp. 6, 9.

32. Ibid., p. 9.

33. Ibid., p. 10.

34. Ibid., p. 9.

35. Ibid., pp. 8–9.

36. Ibid., p. 10.

37. Ibid., p. 41; "Re Kaszuba and Salvation Army Sheltered Workshop et al.," *Ontario Reports, 1983*, second series, vol. 41, pp. 316–318.

38. Montgomery, "50¢ a Week 'Slavery,'" *Toronto Star*, May 6, 1980. Isabella Patrick noted that her daughter, also named Isabella, had worked for almost ten years at a workshop for people defined as retarded, in Richmond Hill, just outside

Toronto, before they moved to Toronto, where she continued working in another fa-cility. A man named Bill R. with whom the author worked at Goodwill Industries, Contract Division, in Windsor, in 1980-1981, had been an employee there since 1965, and there were at least two others who had been working there for a decade or more. Pat Worth stated: "Most of us were put into workshops doing the same thing every day for 20 years, for very little money, for nothing because people thought we were too disabled." Quoted in Bruce Kappel, "A History of People First in Canada," *New Voices: Self-Advocacy by People with Disabilities,* ed. G. Dybwad and H. Bersani Jr. (Cambridge, Mass.: Brookline Books, 1996), p. 117.

39. *Kaszuba and SA, 1981,* p. 16 for quote; p. 11 for description of school.

40. Ibid., p. 41. In Ontario, at the initial investigation stage of a complaint under the Employment Standards Act, a referee is appointed by the province to determine whether a complaint should go to court. In this case, Referee Burkett found for the respondent in June 1981, and the case went to court only after a request by the com-plainant for a judicial review of the referee's decision. Three provincial judges upheld the referee's decision in March 1983.

41. Ibid., p. 27.

42. Ibid.

43. Ibid., p. 16. The dates of Christine Kaszuba's employment (January 1979-June 1980) can be found in ARCH, Sheltered Workshops File: undated letter, David Baker, Advocacy Resource Center for the Handicapped, Toronto, to Mr. J. R. Scott, Director, Ministry of Labor, Employment Standards Branch, Toronto, p. 9.

44. *Kaszuba and SA, 1981,* p. 16.

45. Ibid.

46. Ibid., p. 28.

47. Ibid., pp. 6, 10.

48. Ibid., p. 15.

49. Ibid., pp. 6-7.

50. Ibid., pp. 39-40.

51. Ibid., pp. 39-43. Gail Czukar notes that "a person is a trainee until he or she becomes fit for employment, and if that never occurs, the person is considered to be a trainee forever. This is hardly a reasonable interpretation by any generally accepted definition of 'training', but the government would have to concede that this is the ef-fect of the current wording of the [Vocational Rehabilitation for Disabled Persons] *Act* and that this is, in fact, what occurs in workshops." ARCH, Sheltered Workshops file: Czukar, *Payment of Less Than Minimum Wage in Sheltered Workshops,* pp. 32-33.

52. "Re Kaszuba and Salvation Army Sheltered Workshop et al.," *Ontario Reports, 1983,* pp. 317-318.

53. AO, RG 10-20-A-2, Container 3, Psychiatric Hospital Services Subject Files, McNeel: Minutes—Vocational and Recreational Services, 1961-1969. File 3-4: Pa-

tients Profits, O.T. and I.T., 1964: Letter to B. H. McNeel, Director, Mental Health, from J. N. Senn, Superintendent, Ontario Hospital, Hamilton, April 9, 1964, p. 2.

54. Wayne Lax, "Speak Out against Shock (ECT): A Personal Statement," unpublished statement, January 2000.

55. Interview with Wayne Lax,, Kenora, Ontario, September 20, 1999.

56. In my discussions with Wayne Lax, he mentioned that one of the side effects of shock treatment was a sore back, which would not help someone who was expected to do work requiring the use of back muscles.

57. Dorothy Lipovenko, "Patients in Psychiatric Hospitals Earn Pittance on Assembly Lines," *Globe and Mail*, June 5, 1984.

58. Montgomery, "50¢ a Week 'Slavery.'" Isabella Patrick was protesting the drop in her daughter's income from $2.50 to $3.00 a week at a Richmond Hill workshop (just outside Toronto) to 50 cents a week after the family moved to Toronto.

59. Ibid.

60. Ibid.

61. The confusion within the sheltered workshop system was noted in the 1983 ruling, which dismissed Christine Kaszuba's appeal. Judge Linden pointed out that in order for a sheltered workshop to pay its workers below the minimum wage it had to apply for an exemption from the provincial Employment Standards Act. Only one-third had applied for this exemption, which "indicates, of course, that there are two-thirds of these sheltered workshops which have not done so. Despite our ruling today, it seems as though some confusion may persist." It was made clear in this ruling that proprietors of sheltered workshops should not assume that they were exempt from the Employment Standards Act: "Re Kaszuba and Salvation Army Sheltered Workshop et al.," *Ontario Reports, 1983*,, pp. 317–318.

62. ARC is the acronym for Association for Retarded Children, which was founded in Ontario in 1953. Anglin and Braaten, *Twenty-Five Years of Growing Together*, pp. 11–13.

63. Undated three-page statement written by Russell Havill, which he gave to the author at the time of an interview during a visit to Toronto to attend a People First Conference, November 18, 1999.

64. Interview with Sharon Myron, Kenora, Ontario, September 20, 1999.

65. Interview with R. J. Gordon, Kenora, Ontario, September 20, 1999.

66. The Kenora Association for Community Living is one of numerous ACLs in Canada that are involved in integrating people who have been previously excluded from society in institutions for the "mentally retarded." The interview with both Sharon Myron and R. J. Gordon took place in the building where they had once worked for ARC Industries.

67. Interview with "Elizabeth Horn" (pseudonym), Kenora, Ontario, September 22, 1999.

68. AO, RG 10-20-A-2, Container 3, Psychiatric Hospital Services Subject Files, McNeel: Minutes—Vocational and Recreational Services, 1961–1969. File 3–9: Vocational and Recreational Services, 1967–1969: Occupational Therapy in the Ontario Hospital, Kingston, Westwood Division, January 1968, p. 2, attached to letter to Dr. B. H. McNeel, Director, Professional Services Branch, from J. S. Pratten, Superintendent, Kingston, February 5, 1968.

69. AO, RG 10-20-A-2, Container 3, Psychiatric Hospital Services Subject Files, McNeel: Minutes—Vocational and Recreational Services, 1961–1969. File 3–4: Patients Profits, O.T. and I.T., 1964: Letter to Dr. B. H. McNeel, Chief, Mental Health Branch, from J. J. Weber, Superintendent, Ontario Hospital, Woodstock, April 9, 1964.

70. AO, RG 10-20-A-2, Container 3, Psychiatric Hospital Services Subject Files, McNeel: Minutes—Vocational and Recreational Services, 1961–1969. File 3–4: Patients Profits, O.T. and I.T., 1964: Letter to Dr. B. H. McNeel, Chief Mental Health Branch, Toronto, from Dr. M. O. L. Barrie, Superintendent, Ontario Hospital, Cobourg, March 4, 1964.

71. It should be noted that while many people who were employed in mental hospitals had not worked in the community before, especially people who were classified as mentally retarded, there were psychiatric patients in mental hospitals who had been employed outside prior to hospitalization. See Reaume, *Remembrance of Patients Past,* pp. 133–180.

72. The 1967 Canada Manpower survey (cited in notes 12 and 17) and a survey sent that same year from the Ontario Department of Health to workshop managers provides a good deal of useful information, including the number of workshop participants. However, neither of these surveys provides quantitative data that would allow for a breakdown of sheltered workshop employees by gender, nor have any other documents that have been examined for this essay. The returned questionnaires from the 1967 Ontario Department of Health survey can be found in AO, RG 10-20-A-2, Psychiatric Hospital Services Subject Files, Volume 9, File 6: Industrial Survey, 1967.

73. This is based on the author's experience at Goodwill Industries in Windsor, Ontario, April 1980–June 1981. Women were never employed at the industrial site, Contract Division in the east end, except for one assistant forewoman who was a supervisor for several months. Both men and women worked in stores and in the main building downtown on Dougall Avenue.

74. Interview with Anonymous (1), Thunder Bay, Ontario, September 27, 1999.

75. People with developmental disabilities could also be put to work in workshops that were occupied mainly by psychiatric outpatients or people with physical disabilities. The author worked with a man named Bill R. at Goodwill Industries in Windsor, Ontario, in 1980–81. He was a long-time employee of 15–16 years who had devel-

opmental disabilities. Thus, workshop laborers did not always exclusively consist of people with one kind of disability, even though this is how it appears on paper.

76. Interview with "Mabel N." (pseudonym), Thunder Bay, Ontario, September 25, 1999.

77. Interview with Mr. Primeau, Thunder Bay, Ontario, September 27, 1999.

78. Lipovenko, "Patients in Psychiatric Hospitals Earn Pittance on Assembly Lines."

79. Ibid.

80. Ibid.

81. Glenn Cooly, "Workshop Wage Wrangle," *Now,* March 15–21, 1990.

82. Press Release, People First, "People First of Ontario March against the Wage Policy," March 21, 1990.

83. Cooly, "Workshop Wage Wrangle."

84. Ibid.

85. Montgomery, "50¢ a Week 'Slavery.'"

86. Interview with Anonymous (2), Thunder Bay, Ontario, September 27, 1999.

87. Alfred H. Neufeldt, Alison L. Albright, and Patricia Donovan, "Canada," in *Disability and Self-Directed Employment: Business Development Models,* ed. Alfred H. Neufeldt and Alison L. Albright (North York, Ontario: Captus University Publications, 1998), pp. 186–187.

88. Kappel, "A History of People First in Canada," p. 117. See also Pat Israel and Cathy McPherson, "Introduction," in Gwyneth Ferguson Matthews, *Voices from the Shadows: Women with Disabilities Speak Out* (Toronto: Women's Educational Press, 1983), pp. 18–19.

89. Letter by Patrick Worth, President, People First of Ontario, to Hon. Mr. Charles Beer, Ministry of Community and Social Services, Toronto, undated, but, considering the contents, probably written around March 1990.

90. Cooly, "Workshop Wage Wrangle."

91. Since 1991, the provincial government has funded businesses and organizations operated by people who are current and former psychiatric patients. By 1998, the Consumer/Survivor Development Initiative funded forty-two ventures. The Ontario Council of Alternative Businesses has more recently been set up to work with and to support consumer/survivor businesses. For references to these developments in Ontario see CSDI, *Consumer/Survivor Development Initiative Project Descriptions* (Toronto: CSDI, March 1996); Scott Simmie, "Investing in Pride: Unique Small Businesses Are Giving People with Mental Health Problems Something as Important as Drugs—a Regular Job," *Toronto Star,* October 10, 1998.

20

Family Values

Michael Bérubé

One afternoon I was having a long lunch with a pair of friends who have an adult daughter with a severe disability. That was one of the reasons it was a long lunch: I'd met their daughter the year before, I'd just published *Life As We Know It* about my son James, and we had a lot to talk about. Another reason it was a long lunch is that the girl's mother, a teacher and feminist philosopher, had been taking part in a year-long symposium on the ethics of "selective abortion"—or "preventative" prenatal screening for fetuses with disabilities—and my lunch companions and I had a similar jumble of ambivalent feelings, philosophical positions, hedges, and worries about the subject. But the heart of our conversation, interestingly, had to do with the siblings of our children with disabilities—a young man graduating from college in their case and a precocious, sensitive, eleven-year-old in mine. How did *they* feel about being part of the support system for a child with disabilities, and how did they feel about things like abortion and prenatal testing? Did they feel privileged, burdened, neglected? Were they overcompensating or deflecting or acting out or dealing just beautifully, or all of the above in gradual rotation?

At one point during lunch, I started to mention some advice that had been given to Janet and me by our therapist, a woman we began to consult in September of 1996, as James turned five and just before my book about him was to appear. But I wasn't sure whether I should disclose that Janet and I were "in therapy" to a pair of relative strangers. I was in a fashionable New York City restaurant at the time, and I knew from my twenty years as a New Yorker that in such situations one is more likely to feel conversationally squeamish about the fact that one is *not* seeing a therapist, but still, I paused uncomfortably before saying that my wife and I had started therapy a few

months earlier in order to deal with some of the accumulated stress of raising James—as well as some of our underacknowledged grief about him,
which had begun to warp our otherwise rich and deeply textured marriage.
The moment I mentioned therapy, however, my companions stared at me in
alarm. *Oh, no,* I thought. *They're weirded out. Just what I was afraid of. They think
we can't handle it, we're not strong enough. They think we're traitors to the cause. They
think. . . .*

"Michael," said my philosopher friend, "Jamie is how old now?"

"Five and a half." Her eyes widened still further.

"Five and a half," shaking her head slowly. "*And you and Janet went five years
without therapy?!?*"

Well, I laughed in relief, at the time. But before long, I had begun to wonder yet again: Janet and I always worry about whether we're doing enough for
James, and we always weigh ourselves in the scales and find ourselves wanting. But in all our worries about James, and all our ancillary worries about
Nick, had we forgotten to worry about ourselves?

The point of this anecdote is not to advocate therapy for all couples who
have children with disabilities—though my sense is that in many cases it sure
wouldn't hurt. The point is that the family dynamics of families with such
children are more complicated than most of us can reasonably keep track of,
let alone calibrate and control in an emotionally harmonious and mindful
way. But the irony is that I was unaware of some of the most important of
those dynamics even when, in 1995-96, I thought I was writing about them.
This essay, then, is about some of the stuff I hadn't known to think about
when I thought I was thinking about James and his family. It's also something of an update on James's relation to his brother Nick, and the extent to
which his desire to emulate Nick contributes to his cognitive, motor, and social development. And it's also a reminder—to myself as well as to other parents—that whatever we try to do for ourselves and our families, checking on
the emotional status of our fellow family members is something we can
never do too much of.

I thought that by writing *Life As We Know It,* I was doing what I could for
James. I think of myself as a writer and a teacher, and I'm accordingly torn
between the conviction that my work makes a difference in people's lives
and the fear that I'm utterly useless in the world. My first book sold six hundred copies, almost entirely to university libraries, and is now useful mainly
for killing large crawling insects. But my book on Jamie, I thought, might

actually matter to people—Jamie not least among them. Since his birth, I'd been struck by the relative invisibility of people with developmental disabilities in the general culture, an invisibility that is being remedied only slowly and fitfully. I wrote the book during a scary political time during which antigovernment conservatives were crusading against the Americans with Disabilities Act and even talking about refusing to reauthorize the Individuals with Disabilities Education Act, so I worked with a sense of urgency that's probably pretty clear on every other page of the manuscript. And when, in the fall of 1996, I prepared for a national book tour in the middle of an election season, my hopes were as high as they could be. I worked on crafting my message into media-friendly sound bites like "we don't know what 'normal' is until we try inclusion first"; I chose passages for public readings of the book; I made up interview questions and answers for my "media packet." And whenever I felt that twinge that we weren't doing enough for Jamie—say, when I agonized that he still couldn't put on a pair of socks by himself—I could look at my book and say, "but at least I'm doing *this*. . . ."

How convenient this turned out to be for me: I could displace my personal worries onto my professional work, and my professional work would actually help to assuage my worries. Only too late did it occur to me that Janet didn't have the same mechanism. We'd talked about co-authoring the book, and of course she worked on it with me at every stage, but still, it didn't "solve" things for her the way it was doing for me. In an unexpected way, then, *Life As We Know It* became one more thing we had to figure out. Needless to say, that particular difficulty is specific to my family and my family alone. But what *isn't* specific to us is the emotional dilemma underlying our different reactions to the book: each of us, as it turned out, was silently trying to live up to (what we thought was) the other one's expectations, thinking all the while that we shouldn't confess to our feelings of failure or foreboding lest we damage the other's emotional equilibrium. So Janet wasn't allowing herself to speak freely because she feared, as she put it, taking the wind out of my sails; meanwhile, I was doing all I could just to match her incredible competence and compassion as a parent. Something like an emotional version of the famous O. Henry short story "The Gift of the Magi."

Of course, it could be much, much worse. We were caught in a strange cycle in which each of us admired the other's ability to cope, so much so that we sometimes just weren't coping. But many parents go through more difficult cycles than this; they withdraw, they become depressed or angry, they go into massive denial, they experience the entire range of mental and physical states to which we mortals have access whether we want to or not. There's a recent novel written by a brilliant writer who just happens to be a good friend—*Galatea 2.2,* by Richard Powers—and in it there's a family that looks a lot like mine: two children, the older one based on Nick and the younger one based on Jamie, and a single mother whose resemblance to Janet is remarkable. In *Galatea 2.2,* the father of this family has abandoned his wife and children because he couldn't deal with the disparity between his "gifted" child and his child with Down Syndrome. When I finished thanking Rick for rendering this flattering portrait of me (and informing him that there's no significant increase in the divorce rate for parents with "disabled" children), I decided to take his book as something of a reminder that there are *many* ways in which one can express one's feelings of inadequacy as a parent, and that it's probably best to try to feel inadequate—since one can never fully insulate oneself from feeling inadequate—in the least destructive way possible.

Easier said than done? Yes, but that's my point. As long as Janet and I were talking only to each other about Jamie, there was no way for us to break the cycle we were in. We couldn't work this one out by ourselves, because *we* were actually part of the problem. It was impossible, we've learned, to calibrate our feelings about ourselves and each other as parents of James without the help of a third party—and we strongly suspect that we're not alone in this respect. The third party doesn't have to be a therapist; he or she can be a close friend, a member of the extended family, a minister, or a mentor. More important, the third party doesn't have to be someone "private"—in the sense that he or she is in the family's private circle, or in the social sense that he or she works in the private sector. One of the reasons that public funding for disability services, including respite care, is so important and so necessary is precisely that public services can do so much to address the "private" difficulties of families, some of whose difficulties may indeed be intimately emotional and personal, and some of whose difficulties may more properly be said to be matters of public policy. Janet and I were (in this as in so much else) lucky: we had resources other than those provided by our local and state governments, services other than those provided by public disability services. Most families can't afford the luxury of a therapist—or long lunches in New York restaurants, either. And for most of Jamie's first four years, that was our condition, too: we just didn't have the time or the money to stop and check on ourselves, and so consulting with others, be they therapists or professionals at our local Developmental Services Center, seemed like an indulgence. But when two parents are orbiting each other, as couples usually are, it's hard for either parent to get a good idea of who's doing what or why. Motion is relative, after all, and sometimes, if you want to figure out what's going on, you need the perspective of someone who's not in your orbital path and who can see your world from a relatively stable frame of reference.

In physics, it's fairly easy to predict orbits when you're dealing with only two objects. For low speeds, Newton's laws work just fine. *Three* objects orbiting one another, however, will produce mechanical mayhem: it's called the "n-body problem," and nobody can figure it out. Nobody even wants to try. Fortunately, however, the third body in *our* system—Nick—isn't worried about how well he's doing. He's doing very well, thank you. He has an identity as Jamie's brother, but he also has a life of his own—plenty of playmates; a fondness for computer games; a deep fascination with history, geography, and the configuration of the world; and a very interesting, gradually emerging aesthetic sense that he applies to music, movies, clothes, and buildings. Adolescence, I know, is right around the corner. I can't wait for him to meet other siblings like himself, though, because he's never exchanged notes with another child who has a brother or sister with Down Syndrome. Right now, he's serving James as a guide, a shepherd, and a role model, and he seems pretty comfortable in all three roles—each of which I'll explain briefly.

Nick as role model: this is probably the most predictable identity for an older brother, regardless of whether the younger sibling has Down Syndrome. But because Jamie is Jamie, there's not a lot of competition between Jamie and Nick. Certainly Jamie draws parental attention away from Nick, but that's not always a bad thing; and certainly Jamie sometimes angers or upsets Nick, but it would be odd to expect otherwise. Every once in a while, on the rare occasion when Jamie demolishes one of Nick's elaborate Lego structures or exits Nick's computer game, I have to console Nick; but I always remember to remind him, "Jamie didn't mess up your stuff because he's your little brother with Down Syndrome—he messed up your stuff because he's your little brother. All little brothers are required by law to mess up their big brothers' stuff a certain number of times per year, and Jamie's just abiding by the rules." In partial compensation, James admires Nick completely and emulates him in everything, from basketball to tae kwon do to drawing to climbing trees. Few things motivate Jamie so emphatically as the desire to *be like Nick* (it's our own personal family ad campaign), and Janet and I are not shy about exploiting this to full effect. We've dutifully pointed out that

Nick eats lettuce to get strong and that Nick puts on his own pants; this past spring, as we got Jamie ready to start kindergarten in the fall, we noted that he took real delight in the thought that he would be going to *a big school like Nick.*

Nick as guide and shepherd: we've always been amazed by how watchful, how observant Nick is. Nick cautions Jamie—sometimes gently, sometimes sternly, as circumstances dictate—not to put balloons in his mouth, not to run unescorted through the parking lot, not to growl gutturally when he asks for things. Nick is *solicitous,* and just by being Nick he shows Jamie how to be solicitous too. Best of all, Nick shows other children, by example, how to deal with Jamie: how to listen to him, how to play with him, how to shoot baskets or work the video games, how to include him in the gang. For the most part, Nick does this simply by treating Jamie like a nice little brother, thereby letting all the other kids know that there's nothing "special" they have to do in order to play or talk with James—just listen carefully, and treat him as you would any younger child who needs the basket moved a little lower or the video game set a little easier.

How different our family would be if our *first* child had Down Syndrome and our second did not; how different it would be if Jamie had two, three, four siblings—or none. Every family configuration produces different dynamics, and every family configuration is bewilderingly complex. The more I talk with other parents of children with disabilities, the more I realize how many subtle differences underlie our similarities, and vice versa. Some parents need help with the child who keeps throwing car keys down the toilet; some parents need help with the nondisabled sibling who feels burdened; some parents need help with feelings of failure; some need help with feelings of denial. Sometimes the children are far apart in age, sometimes less than a year apart; sometimes the child with a disability is the oldest, watching his or her siblings grow up more quickly; sometimes the youngest, getting more developmentally remote from siblings each year; sometimes there's more than one child with a disability, or more than one disability. . . . And sometimes I think the only advice that's equally applicable to all of us is the advice that we should seek advice.

But whenever I think this way, I remember something Jamie has taught me over the past year. It was during the spring of 1997, Jamie's last season at First United Methodist day care before he would start kindergarten in 1997-98, and the occasion was a classroom game in which each of the children told the teachers what they wanted to be when they grew up. From every child except James, the list of occupations bore out the Lily Tomlin joke that if we'd all grown up to be what we said we wanted to be at the age of five, we'd live in a world populated by cowboys, firefighters, and ballerinas. When the class got to James, though, the teachers weren't even sure that my little boy would understand the question, let alone come up with an intelligible answer. Still, they politely asked him, last among the preschool kids, "and what would you like to be when *you* grow up, James?"

Later that day, Janet and I were told that James had answered the question immediately, and with just one word.

Big.

To their credit, James's teachers were duly astonished: not only had James understood the question, he'd come up with an answer that changed everyone else's understanding of what the question meant. All of a sudden, in other words, that stock query, *what would you like to be when you grow up,* a question no adult expects a five-year-old to answer seriously, had some real substance to it. For what had Jamie said, by saying "big"? That he wants to grow up. That he wants to be healthy. Perhaps even that he wants people to treat him well. In his odd way, Jamie had readjusted his classmates' and teachers' understanding of the parameters of the question. And that's not just my interpretation; that was *their* interpretation. Janet's interpretation (and, henceforth, mine) is this: precisely because Jamie answered the question so literally, people saw him differently. In saying he wanted to grow up to be big, James was no longer the "special needs" child; on the contrary, he became the *normal* child, the universal generic Child. Think about it for a moment. What Jamie said is something almost *all* children can say or sign or hope, whether they were born in Australia or Algeria or Albania or Alabama. Janet and I have seen such moments before, moments in which Jamie is not only irreducibly and idiosyncratically Jamie but also, somehow, representative of children everywhere. And in such moments we realize how Jamie has helped us to see that all children have fundamental needs that we share in common as humans. Of course, some children have "special" needs, and we wouldn't deny it for an instant; James himself needed a good deal of physical therapy, occupational therapy, and (most obviously) speech therapy just to get to the point at which he could tell adults he wanted to be big when he grows up. But the general lesson, I hope, should be clear—that whatever our differences and whatever our family dynamics, it's our job to help make a world in which all our children can grow up to be "big."

About the Contributors

Michael Bérubé is the Paterno Family Professor in Literature at Penn State University and the author of four books, including *Life As We Know It: A Father, a Family, and an Exceptional Child.*

Janice A. Brockley is Assistant Professor of History at Jackson State University in Mississippi. She is currently writing a book on intellectually disabled children and their parents in the twentieth-century United States.

Katherine Castles is writing a dissertation entitled "'Little Tardies': Intelligence, Social Class, and the Construction of Disability in the U.S., 1945–1975." She is a doctoral candidate in the Department of History at Duke University.

Ellen Dwyer has appointments in criminal justice and history at Indiana University–Bloomington, where she co-directs the Center for the History of Medicine. The author of *Homes for the Mad: Life inside Two Nineteenth-Century Lunatic Asylums,* she also has published several articles on the history of epilepsy and is completing a book-length manuscript, *The Burden of Illness: Families, the State, and Seizure Disorders, 1890–1950.* Her new research project focuses on race and psychiatry in twentieth-century America.

Philip Ferguson is the E. Desmond Lee Professor in Education of Children with Disabilities at the University of Missouri, St. Louis. He is the author of *Abandoned to Their Fate: Social Policy and Practice toward Severely Retarded People in America, 1820–1920.*

William B. Fish, a native of New York State and a graduate of the Albany Medical College, was the Superintendent of the Illinois Asylum for Feeble-Minded Children at Lincoln from 1883 to 1893.

Steven A. Gelb is Program Director and Professor in the Learning and Teaching Program at the University of San Diego. He is interested in the impact of evolutionary thought on persons with intellectual disabilities.

Samuel Gridley Howe (1801–1876) was a surgeon, soldier, and relief worker (1824–1830) in the Greek War of Independence, the superintendent of the Perkins Institution for the Blind (1831–1875) and of the Massachusetts Asylum for Idiotic and Feebleminded Youth (1848–1875), and a noted abolitionist and humanitarian.

Kathleen W. Jones is Associate Professor of History at Virginia Tech and the author of *Taming the Troublesome Child: American Families, Child Guidance, and the Limits of Psychiatric Authority*. She is currently writing a history of youth suicide.

Karen A. Keely is Assistant Professor of English at Mount Saint Mary's College (Emmitsburg, MD). Her recent publications include "Poverty, Sterilization, and Eugenics in Erskine Caldwell's *Tobacco Road*," in the *Journal of American Studies*, and "Eugenics Goes to Hollywood: Sexual Selection on the Silver Screen," in the forthcoming volume *Making It Modern: Popular Culture and Eugenics in the 1930s*. She is currently working on a book about literary depictions of "white slavery."

Daniel Kevles is the Stanley Woodward Professor of History at Yale University. His works include *In the Name of Eugenics: Genetics and the Uses of Human Heredity* and, as a coauthor, most recently, *Inventing America: A History of the United States*.

Molly Ladd-Taylor teaches U.S. history at York University in Toronto. Her publications include *Mother-work: Women, Child Welfare and the State*, *"Bad" Mothers: The Politics of Blame in Twentieth-Century America* (co-edited with Lauri Umansky), and "Saving Babies and Sterilizing Mothers: Eugenics and Welfare Politics in the Interwar United States," *Social Politics* (1997).

Harry H. Laughlin (1880–1943) was the superintendent and director of the Eugenics Record Office of the Department of Genetics of the Carnegie Institute, from 1910 to 1940. He served as the eugenics expert for the Committee on Immigration and Naturalization, U.S. House of Representatvies, from 1921 to 1931. His model sterilization laws were used by several of the thirty states that passed sterilization laws. Nazi Germany's 1933 sterilization laws were also modeled after Laughlin's.

Deborah S. Metzel has a Ph.D. in geography with a primary interest in the social geographies of people with disabilities, especially those with cognitive disabilities. She is presently a research associate at the Institute for Community Inclusion, UMass-Boston. Her influence has been her fifty-four-year-old sister, who has Down Syndrome. Her most recent work has been co-editing, with Michael Dorn, the Fall 2001 *Disability Studies Quarterly: Symposium on Disability Geography: Commonalities in a World of Differences*.

Wendy Nehring is Professor of Nursing at Southern Illinois University Edwardsville. She is the author of *A History of Nursing in the Field of Mental Retardation and Developmental Disabilities.*

Steven Noll is Visiting Associate Professor of History at the University of Florida. He is also an adaptive technology teacher for students with special needs in the Gainesville, Florida, public schools. He has published *Feeble-Minded in Our Midst: Institutions for the Mentally Retarded in the South* and is currently co-editing a volume on disability in the South for the University of Georgia Press.

Nicole Rafter, a professor at Northeastern University, has written on diverse topics including the history of women's prisons, eugenic criminology, and crime films. She is currently preparing new translations of the key criminological works of Cesare Lombroso. She is a Fellow of the American Society of Criminology and in 1999 received the American Association on Mental Retardation's Wilbur's Founder's Award.

Geoffrey Reaume is the author of *Remembrance of Patients Past: Patient Life at the Toronto Hospital for the Insane, 1870–1940.* He teaches an undergraduate course, "Mad People's History," in the School of Disability Studies, Ryerson University, and is also involved in establishing the Psychiatric Survivor Archives, Toronto.

Penny L. Richards is a Research Scholar with UCLA's Center for the Study of Women. She holds a Ph.D. in Education from the University of North Carolina at Chapel Hill and did postdoctoral work in the history of special education at the University of California at Santa Barbara. Her current research interests include the history of developmental disability, nineteenth-century immigration and family caregiving, and antebellum geographic education for girls.

David Rothman is Professor of History at Columbia University and Bernard Schoenberg Professor of Social Medicine and Director of the Center for the Study of Society and Medicine at Columbia University's College of Physicians and Surgeons. He is the author of numerous articles and books on the history of medicine, prisons, and social reform, including *The Discovery of the Asylum* (1971) and, with Sheila Rothman, *Willowbrook Wars.*

Sheila Rothman is Professor of Public Health in the Division of Socio-Medical Sciences at the Joseph L. Mailman School of Public Health and Deputy Director of the Center for the Study of Society and Medicine. She published *Women's Proper Place* and *Living in the Shadow of Death: Tuberculosis and the Social Experience of Illness in American History.*

Gerald Schmidt has recently completed his doctoral dissertation at Clare College, University of Cambridge, on the theme of intellectual disability in the novel from Dickens to Faulkner. His current research focuses on the construction of feeblemindedness in the works of George Gissing and Jack London.

Elizabeth F. Shores, M.A.P.H., is an independent scholar in Little Rock, Arkansas. She has written several monographs on policies that affect children and families and books on assessment and curriculum development in early childhood education. She is a doctoral student in public policy at the University of Arkansas.

Eunice Kennedy Shriver is Executive Vice-President of the Joseph P. Kennedy Jr. Foundation and founder and honorary chairperson of Special Olympics, Inc. She has advocated for the rights of people with mental disabilities since the 1950s and was the driving force behind President John Kennedy's Presidential Panel on Mental Retardation in 1961.

James W. Trent Jr. is Professor of Sociology and Social Work at Gordon College, Wenham, Massachusetts, and the author of *Inventing the Feeble Mind: A History of Mental Retardation in the United States.* He is the recipient of the Hervey B. Wilbur Award of the American Association on Mental Retardation.

David Wright holds the Hannah Chair in the History of Medicine, a joint appointment between the Department of History and the Department of Psychiatry and Behavioural Neurosciences at McMaster University. He is the author of *Outside the Walls of the Asylum: The History of Care in the Community, 1750–2000,* and, with Anne Digby, he edited *From Idiocy to Mental Deficiency: Historical Perspectives on People with Learning Disabilities.*

Leila Zenderland is Professor of American Studies at California State University, Fullerton. Her writings explore the history of American popular culture as well as the history of science and medicine. In addition to several articles, she is the author of *Measuring Minds: Henry Herbert Goddard and the Origins of American Intelligence Testing* (1998) and editor of *Recycling the Past: Popular Uses of American History* (1978). In 2002 she was a Fulbright Professor of American History at the University of Bremen, Germany.

Index